BEHIND THE SCENES

The Life and Work of William Clifford Clark

William Clifford Clark, federal deputy minister of finance from 1932 to 1952, had a profound impact on Canadian history. An important intellectual figure during the first half of the twentieth century, he was leader of 'The Ottawa Men,' a group of federal civil servants who shaped a new liberal vision of the nation. Robert A. Wardhaugh chronicles Clark's contributions to Canada's modern state in *Behind the Scenes*, which reconstructs the public life and ideas of one of Canada's most important bureaucrats.

The Department of Finance sat at the centre of critical federal decisions and debates. From this axis, Clark's wide-ranging contributions to Canadian policy were nothing short of phenomenal: he was the driving force behind the creation of the Bank of Canada, and he spearheaded national housing policy. Clark also managed the economy during the Great Depression and the Second World War, and he was instrumental in forging Canada's international economic role in the post-war era.

ROBERT A. WARDHAUGH is an associate professor in the Department of History at the University of Western Ontario.

The Institute of Public Administration of Canada Series in Public Management and Governance

Editor: Patrice Dutil

This series is sponsored by the Institute of Public Administration of Canada as part of its commitment to encourage research on issues in Canadian public administration, public sector management, and public policy. It also seeks to foster wider knowledge and understanding among practitioners, academics, and the general public.

For a list of books published in the series, see page 471.

BEHIND THE SCENES

The Life and Work of William Clifford Clark

Robert A. Wardhaugh

with Douglas MacEwan and William Johnston

UNIVERSITY OF TORONTO PRESS
Toronto Buffalo London

Toronto Buffalo London
www.utppublishing.com
Printed in Canada

ISBN 978-1-4426-4126-6 (cloth)
ISBN 978-1-4426-1052-1 (paper)

Printed on acid-free, 100% post-consumer recycled paper with vegetable-based inks.

Library and Archives Canada Cataloguing in Publication

Wardhaugh, Robert Alexander, 1967–
Behind the scenes : the life and work of William Clifford Clark / Robert A. Wardhaugh.

(The Institute of Public Administration of Canada series in public management and governance)
Includes bibliographical references and index.
ISBN 978-1-4426-4126-6 (bound). – ISBN 978-1-4426-1052-1 (pbk.)

1. Clark, W. C. (William Clifford), 1889–1952. 2. Canada. Dept. of Finance – Officials and employees – Biography. 3. Government executives – Canada – Biography. 4. Canada – Officials and employees – Biography. 5. Canada – Economic policy – 20th century. I. Title. II. Series: Institute of Public Administration of Canada series in public management and governance

FC581.C53W37 2010 971.063092 C2010-903158-X

Canada School of Public Service École de la fonction publique du Canada

Financial support from the Canada School of Public Service for this book is gratefully acknowledged. The views expressed herein are not necessarily those of the Canada School of Public Service or of the Government of Canada.

University of Toronto Press acknowledges the financial assistance to its publishing program of the Canada Council for the Arts and the Ontario Arts Council.

Canada Council for the Arts Conseil des Arts du Canada

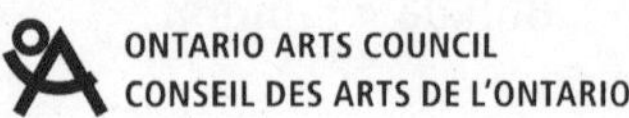

University of Toronto Press acknowledges the financial support of the Government of Canada through the Canada Book Fund for its publishing activities.

Contents

Foreword

The work of government is often portrayed as bloodless and driven by organization charts, economic imperatives, and broad ideological constructs. This book shows that it is also a story about people. Indeed, with this volume, the Institute of Public Administration of Canada (IPAC) renews its acquaintance with its old friend Clifford Clark. Clark knew IPAC very well in its stirring first years of the late 1940s. He saw it brought to life by his counterpart in Ontario, Deputy Treasurer Chester Walters and his able deputy, Philip Clark (no relation to Clifford). Clifford Clark eagerly showed his support by becoming a charter member of the Institute in 1948 and was a member of its governing Council from 1949 until his death in 1952.

When IPAC was finally put on a solid financial footing in the early 1960s following an intergovernmental agreement to support its operations, it launched the 'Clifford Clark Lectures' to memorialize one of its heroes. Starting in 1964, they were organized by regional groups, and guests were invited to give lectures across Canada. Many of the speakers came from abroad, including the Right Honourable Lord Bridges, the president of the Royal Institute of Public Administration, who inaugurated the series by speaking about the relationship between ministers and permanent department heads (deputy ministers, as we would call them in Canada). He was followed by Roger Grégoire, a French mandarin, who visited Canada to speak of the differences between the British and the French public services and to discuss the influence of the École national d'administration and the conseil d'état. Over the years, guest lecturers included visitors from the United Kingdom, Belgium, France, New Zealand, and the United States and included the likes of John Deutsch, Gunnar Myrdal, Carl Friedrich, Duff Roblin, and Jack Pickersgill.

Sadly, the program did not survive the financial crunch of the early 1980s. The series ended with Alexander King's lecture, 'Change and Uncertainty: The Challenge to the Administration.' Like his predecessors, King, a pioneer of the sustainable development movement, incarnated Clark's vision of the dedicated public servant: rigorous, scientific, forward-looking, and dispassionate. Indeed, the list of lectures reflects a consistent interest in the meta-topics that Clifford Clark obsessed about, such as the relationship between the political and the administrative, the role of the public service, and intergovernmental relations. Many of the lectures were published in book form or were reprinted in *Canadian Public Administration*. They are now available on IPAC's website.

To this day, these lectures are a tribute to a fine man. Clark was an engaging colleague who was deeply interested in learning and in tying theory to practice. He was concerned by what made public administration better and more efficient, he was worried about government's capacity to deal with issues, and he was endlessly fascinated by emerging 'problems' of the state. Indeed, his story is more than a personal one. Through the prism of his career readers of this fine study will perceive the evolution of the public sector as it struggles with the Great Depression, helps the mobilization of the nation in the Second World War, and assumes the control of new programs that will define the welfare state. As he served the King, Bennett, and St Laurent governments, Clark's career also offers readers a glimpse of the public service culture in these trying years. Robert Wardhaugh vividly brings to life the issues that tested Clifford Clark and shows that he has earned his place in the pantheon of key architects of the modern state.

Patrice Dutil
Editor, IPAC Series in Public Management and Governance

Preface

> In practice, the politician functions as the centre-stage extrovert embodiment of policies; the bureaucrat is the behind-the-scenes introvert who both conceives policies and puts them into effect.
>
> – Christina McCall-Newman, *Grits*

Who was William Clifford Clark? This is not simply a rhetorical question asked by a biographer about his subject. When I was asked by Clark's family to write a biography of the former federal deputy minister of finance, even though his name and career were generally known to me, I have to admit that my knowledge was not extensive. I knew that he was an influential bureaucrat who played a role in shaping the Canadian civil service and economy during the Great Depression and Second World War. I was aware that despite being a *mere* civil servant, Clark appears often in the literature dealing with the Canadian government during the 1930s and 1940s, and he receives impressive accolades from historians. But, beyond this knowledge, I was unsure of the nature of Clark's contribution to Canadian history. I *was* aware that most Canadians had no idea who Clifford Clark was. Even at the time of his death in 1952, few people knew his name: 'Most Canadians who learned over the weekend of the sudden passing of Dr W.C. Clark,' one newspaper observed at the time, 'probably have little inkling of the influence on their own affairs wielded by a small and extraordinarily talented group of men, of whom the deputy minister of finance was the most distinguished. Members of that group tend to go quietly about their own business, which is helping to guide the economic and financial policies of Canada. They appear rarely in the public eye.'[1] To be honest, I was unsure if Clark was deserving of a full-length biography. My doubts were soon dispelled.

Clifford Clark had a profound impact on Canadian history. Of most significance, he was one of what J.L. Granatstein has dubbed 'The Ottawa Men' – 'an extraordinary group of civil servants who collectively had great influence and power in Ottawa from the Depression through to the late 1950s.'[2] I will go one step further and argue that Clark was *the* most important figure in this group. O.D. Skelton founded the mandarinate and served as Clark's mentor, but he died in 1941. The influence of Norman Robertson is indisputable but he came onto the scene relatively late as Skelton's successor in External Affairs. 'Dr Clark,' as he was widely known, recruited most of the mandarins and served as the leader and inspiration for this highly intelligent and influential group. The clique was dubbed 'Clark's boys.' Clifford Clark was the deputy minister of finance and it was his department that sat at the centre of so many federal decisions and debates, including fiscal and economic matters, banking and currency concerns, federal–provincial arrangements, social policy initiatives, and international trade issues. As Bob Bryce observed, 'Skelton and his men at External Affairs had made it possible for Canada to have a policy of its own; Clark and his works made it possible for the Government to have an economic policy.'[3] This group, working from behind the scenes, was instrumental in building the modern Canadian state.

But Clark was more than the leader of the Ottawa Men. As an individual civil servant, his contribution to Canadian government in policy was nothing short of amazing. 'Clifford Clark was the dominating genius of the department and, in fact, of wartime Ottawa,' Walter Gordon remarked. 'He was always interested in any new idea and generated more of them himself than the rest of us put together. Intellectually speaking, he was the most exciting man I have ever worked with. And his contributions in terms of proposals for social security legislation – family allowances, old age pensions, hospital insurance, and so on – have made a lasting impression on this country.'[4] But these were only a few of Clark's contributions. He was the driving force behind the creation of the Bank of Canada; he introduced the federal government to national housing policy; his management of the economy during the Great Depression led to a fundamental rethinking of dominion–provincial relations and the Canadian federal structure; he was the architect of the Canadian economy during the Second World War; and he was instrumental in forging Canada's international economic role in the 'Brave New World' of the post-war era.

Clark's role as a civil servant justifies a biography. But he was clearly more than a civil servant. As Doug Owram has demonstrated, Clifford Clark was part of 'the Government Generation.'[5] He was an important figure in the intellectual history of Canada during the first half of the twentieth century. Clark was an economics professor at a time when Canadian universities were coming of age. Together at Queen's University, Clark and Skelton helped establish the discipline of political economy and commerce. Barry Ferguson notes that their outlook on life was shaped by a revisionist account of political economy, 'one that reflected American and British scholarly debate about the workings of capitalism and the nature of politics and government.' This 'new political economy,' according to Ferguson, was instrumental in shaping twentieth-century political and economic debate in Canada. But Clark and Skelton also established the critical link between the world of the ivory tower and society, demonstrating that the university-trained social scientist had a practical and influential role to play in society and government. When the universities could not keep pace with their expanding roles (and ambitions), the government emerged as a logical and exciting alternative. From their respective positions in the departments of finance and external affairs, Clark and Skelton set out to recruit other like-minded men who shared their 'new liberal' vision of the nation. As Ferguson notes, 'Their place is found in the discussion of the such key topics as the changing role of the university and especially the emergence of professional social science, the definition of an autonomist or liberal-nationalist interpretation of Canadian history, and the related issues of social reform and the rise of the positive or – as it is commonly known – interventionist state.'[6]

But aside from his impact on Canadian history, what kind of person was Clifford Clark? This is a more difficult question to answer: This book is a political biography, not necessarily by choice but by necessity. While I attempt to bring this man to life, the attempt largely fails. The records left behind, in combination with Clark's modest personality and his particular choice of career, do not lead naturally to an intimate portrait of the man. A biographer's task is made much easier if the subject is colourful, eccentric, or controversial. But Clark was none of these; instead he was the consummate civil servant and he prided himself on this identity. His personal life was stable and routine. His life and work were performed behind the scenes. Indeed, his work was his life. As one magazine commented in 1942, 'It is hard to make a colourful figure out of a man who works so hard at his job. If he were a bit of a card with the boys, if perchance he danced well, or played a devastating game of bridge, or had a golf score in the 80's, or had crossed Africa on a bicycle, we might have something to chronicle … His life is dull, his routine is slavish. Instead of dining sumptuously up the street with the politicians and patricians at the club, he'll send out for a sandwich, then go at it again till midnight. He is in real life that perfect example of the biographer's phrase, the indefatigable worker.'[7]

Clark enjoyed the high-powered world of executive decision-making. He thrived on the pressure to perform and the atmosphere of top-level negotiations. But he was not comfortable with publicity. Officially, he took this stance because as a civil servant he was not supposed to be in the limelight. His primary task was to serve and advise his minister to the best of his ability. But in truth, Clark was modest and relatively shy. He did not have the thick skin required of a politician. When he was subject to criticism in Parliament or the press, the jibes genuinely hurt him. In 1946 one magazine commented on Clark's canny ability to wield so much influence in Ottawa and yet remain out of the spotlight when it came to public scrutiny: 'It just happens that nobody seems sufficiently concerned about what he says or does to go and get it down on paper. Never a man more under-estimated, never a man of so much activity so little chronicled.'[8]

Clifford Clark was the model civil servant. J.L. Granatstein's description of Norman Robertson also rings true about Clark: 'He wanted influence and sought constantly to exercise it, but he had no craving for power and none for the limelight. His role was to advise, and he performed that task superbly, offering his political masters the benefits of his well-stocked brain and his deep learning.'[9] Clark was the ideal adviser, the ideal deputy minister. He was a rock, an anchor of stability, and a workhorse, not only for his minister but for the prime minister, the civil service, and the government at large. He was dependable, reliable, and extremely hard-working and knowledgeable. Those around him with much more power and influence came to rely upon Clark, and they knew it. Clifford Clark believed in his role, he was proud of it, and he practised it better than anyone. Yet, despite such an impressive list of attributes, history rarely remembers those who work behind the scenes. Indeed, according to Mitchell Sharp, 'The contribution of this man to the Canadian nation will never be fully appreciated, because the story can never be fully told of his influence upon the course of events. Being a civil servant, he worked anonymously, in the background, his views and his actions finding their expression in official utterances of Ministers and in the statutes approved by Parliament. Nor would he have wished it otherwise.'[10] Sharp may be correct, but it is my hope that this book goes to some length in highlighting this contribution.

Acknowledgments

My debts are primarily to the two family members of Clifford Clark – Douglas MacEwan (nephew) and Bill Johnston (grandson) – who worked on the biography long before I came onto the scene and whose vision and determination would not allow the project to die. Bill put together a massive document, based on secondary sources and primary family sources, that set out Clark's life in impressive detail. This document proved invaluable to my work and became the foundation of the biography. Doug came to me with the project, provided financial support, and became the most energetic and effective archival researcher I have ever worked alongside. This work would not exist had it not been for these two individuals.

I would like to thank two archivists in particular: Glenn Wright of Library and Archives Canada, and George Henderson of the Queen's University Archives. Glenn's consistent interest, knowledge, and advice always went beyond the call of duty. George's impressive knowledge of the Mackenzie King era combined with his gentle, caring, and charming personality proved invaluable. More generally, I would like to acknowledge the staff of Library and Archives Canada, Queen's University Archives, University of Chicago Archives, and the Library of Congress.

Len Husband at University of Toronto Press is the best in the business. He has made what can often be a frustrating process enjoyable. He has single-handedly restored my faith in the Canadian academic publishing industry.

Special thanks go to research assistants Bryan Rosati, Craig Greenham, and Teresa Iacobelli.

I would like to acknowledge financial support from the Faculty of Social Science at the University of Western Ontario.

BEHIND THE SCENES

The Life and Work of William Clifford Clark

1

An Academic Mind, 1889–1922

A man approachable at all times, he had gained the loyal admiration of all who had the good fortune to come in contact with him, and with such a background of personal contact with his students he was able to establish for himself an unusually high distinction as a lecturer. Prof. Clark had the rare gift of imparting his own knowledge to others in a way that his words were not easily forgotten; and his keen insight and deep appreciation of the intricacies of economics, both in theory and practice, made his periods amongst the most enjoyable, and richest that we may number with the classroom hours.

– *Queen's Journal*, 1923

William Clifford Clark was born on 18 April 1889, at Glen Falloch, Glengarry County, Ontario. The Scottish influence on Clark's birthplace was unmistakable and it existed in more than name. According to a local history, *Glen Falloch* is Gaelic for 'The Hidden Glen' and is 'symbolic of all Glengarry. It is buried in quiet shade, beautiful, bewitching; and its heart is entirely Highland.'[1] The Clark family descended from Highland Scottish immigrants and this identity was very much part of young Clifford's childhood: 'When I was a very young lad I remember that when my grandmother was "blue" she used to hum the refrain of "Lochaber No More" and I have very hazy recollections of her telling about the horrible experiences suffered by her parents when they came to Canada in a sailing boat which took several months to arrive.'[2]

The village nearest Clark's birthplace, Martintown, was founded by Scots from Invernesshire – the centre of support for the Stuart line and 'Bonnie Prince Charlie' in the Jacobite Rebellions of 1745. The repercussions for those who supported the uprising were severe. Many highlanders were uprooted in an attempt to crush their culture. High rents prompted an exodus to the New World.[3] After initially basing themselves in New York, some of the settlers fled north to British North America because of their support for the Crown during the American Revolution. After 1784 these settlers were granted land in Glengarry, the oldest and most easterly county of what became the province of Ontario. Malcolm McMartin Jr founded the village of Martintown, at the centre of a farm community where he constructed a series of mills.[4] The farm upon which Clark was raised was just three kilometres to the south.

Throughout his life, Clifford Clark maintained an abiding fascination with the rich history of his home county, as well as his own genealogy. As an amateur historian, he was able to trace his father's line to his great-great-great grandfather, one James Clark of the King's Royal Regiment of New York. On his mother's side, Clark traced his line to his great-grandfather, John Urquhart, the first settler in Glen Falloch, who obtained a Crown patent to a property on Indian Lands in 1852. This land would eventually become the dairy farm where Clifford was raised.

Clifford's father, George Ellis Clark, was born 12 June 1864, the illegitimate son of Catherine Martha Clark and Thomas Dow. George, and his younger brother William, were raised on a nearby farm by their uncle, Benjamin Clark. George attended public school but not high school, and became a farmer. On 20 October 1886, he married Clifford's mother, Katherine Urquhart, who was born 5 November 1864. When Katherine's father, Kenneth, died in 1880, the farm passed to his wife and children. Katherine and George took over the farm in 1890, a year after Clifford was born.

Clifford Clark was born and raised in an agricultural community. Until the 1880s the lumber from farm woodlots provided Glengarry with its main source of revenue – from the wood that was burned for fuel or used for buildings, railway ties, and telegraph poles, as well as from the wood ashes, which were turned into potash and the lye used in making soap.[5] But by the 1890s, farms were being consolidated for serious (which usually meant dairy) operations.[6] The ideal farm consisted of 100–160 acres and from twelve to twenty cows. The milk produced in the Martintown district was taken to cheese factories and the product was then shipped mainly to Britain.[7] The Clark farm consisted of 163 acres and forty head of cattle.

By the turn of the century, George and Katherine Clark had five children. Kenneth was born in 1887, Clifford in 1889, Muriel in 1891,

Linden in 1894, and Winnifred in 1899. The family home was a substantial two-storey log farmhouse with four upstairs bedrooms. Dairy farming involved work for the entire family, and young Clifford was expected to help carry out the morning milking while also performing a variety of other chores such as rock-picking with a team of horses to make ploughing easier.[8]

Martintown was the geographic centre of the local farming community but the railways bypassed the village and it never became as large as other Glengarry communities. Despite the boom in the cheese-making industry and the appearance of factories 'at nearly every crossroad,' Martintown remained small with a population of 500 by 1931.[9] As a result, many of the innovations transforming life in rural Ontario came to Martintown relatively late. Most homes did not have running water until the turn of the century, there were no refrigerators, and the telegraph linking Hamilton and Toronto by 1846 did not reach Martintown until the 1870s. The telephone, which began commercial service for the first time in Hamilton in 1877, reached the village in 1901, with full service arriving in 1913. Electricity, which was lighting up Ottawa by 1885 and Cornwall by 1887, reached Martintown only in 1921.[10] Regardless, in 1900 Martintown was a flourishing community. It was home to five general stores, two cheese factories, a hotel, a livery stable, a boarding house, two Presbyterian churches, a Roman Catholic church, a Masonic Lodge, a Royal Templar Lodge, and a Sons of Scotland Lodge. Many trades operated in the town, including five blacksmiths, three carriage-makers and wheelwrights, two shoemakers, one baker, two barbers, two tailors, one cabinetmaker and undertaker, one miller, one tanner, five dressmakers, one butcher and drover, one doctor, one telegraph operator, and one veterinarian.

Clifford started school in the fall of 1895[11] at the one-room Glen Falloch Public School, a kilometre walk west of the family farm. He later recorded that this first day at school along with the federal election of 1896 (which saw the defeat of the Conservatives and the victory of Wilfrid Laurier's Liberals) were his earliest recollections. By all accounts, Clifford was a small and quiet lad. He was naturally drawn to academics but could also hold his own at sports. At the age of ten he missed several months of school after injuring his leg in a wrestling match. While the exact nature of the injury is not known, it was serious enough that Clifford missed the examination for passing into what was then known as Fourth Book. Young Clifford, however, had obviously demonstrated enough aptitude and he was advanced regardless.[12] It would be the first of many health problems to plague Clark throughout his life.

In June 1900, after only a few months in Fourth Book, Clark travelled to the larger neighbouring town of Williamstown to write the entrance exam for high school. Williamstown was the nearer of Glengarry's two high schools. On 18 July the eleven-year-old was informed he had secured a pass. But Clifford's education was put on hold. Either due to difficulty with financing or because he was regarded as too young, Clifford did not immediately go to high school. Instead, he was kept back on the farm for the 1900–1 year.[13] School attendance in rural Ontario at this time was irregular and not highly valued, particularly by the rural population. Few students actually went on to high school. Around the turn of the century there were approximately four thousand students (which was 80 per cent of the potential school population) enrolled in public and separate schools in Glengarry. Attendance averaged only 45 per cent. On average 225 students attempted the entrance examination for high school each year, with 150 passing but only 90 actually entering the program.[14]

Katherine Clark, Clifford's mother, died suddenly on 28 April 1901 at the age of only thirty-six. The cause of death is unknown and it is unclear what the impact of this event was on Clifford and the rest of the family. Tragedies of this sort were not uncommon and families (including children) came to accept them as part of the harshness of life. Grief in the Anglo-Celtic tradition was generally internalized and those left behind were expected to soon move on. With five children to raise and a farm to look after, George Clark remarried two years later to Christy McMartin. Once better settled and more secure, George took an increasingly active interest in education. He became trustee of the local public school and was appointed trustee of the area high school in Williamstown from 1906 to 1911. This role commenced a career in local politics in which George served as deputy reeve of the Township of Charlottenburgh in 1914 and reeve in 1915. In 1916 he was selected as warden of the United Counties of Glengarry, Stormont, and Dundas. Although years later Clifford would claim he voted nothing but Liberal, 'his father had been a solid Conservative.'[15]

Clifford entered Fifth Form at Martintown Public School in 1901–2. Finally, in the fall of 1902, he received his opportunity to go to high school at Williamstown. According to one story, it was only through the urgings of an enthusiastic school teacher (and the fact that the boy was too small to be of much value on the farm) that his father was persuaded to send Clifford on to high school.[16] It was a twelve-kilometre journey from the Clark farm to Williamstown and because of the distance, he boarded there. The packed-earth roads were often in rough shape. 'In summer, [I] usually bicycled to Williamstown with Gordon McIntosh,' Clark later remembered, 'and in winter usually drove by sleigh or cutter early Monday morning and came back Friday night. When roads were bad, we skied.'[17] Clifford boarded with Mrs D.D. McCrimmon, who cooked the week's provisions he brought from home and put food on the table. 'For this service,' Clark noted, 'and for a room, the monthly charge was very low – $2 or $2.50.'[18] The keen mind of the economist was already forming.

By his teenage years, Clark was demonstrating an impressive academic mind. In July 1905 he passed the Part II Junior Teachers' examination for the Ontario Education Department with honours. The following year he passed junior matriculation, winning the gold medal. Clark was also the 1906 recipient of the McLennan Glengarry Foundation Scholarship of $320, which was awarded annually and allowed one Glengarry student to attend Queen's University.[19] The principal of the Williamstown school noted in a letter of recommendation, 'I do not think that in my twelve years experience I have ever had a more satisfactory student. With ability very much above the average, he also possesses the enthusiasm and painstaking industry, without which natural ability goes for very little.'[20]

The scholarship provided Clark the opportunity to enter Queen's College at Kingston in the autumn of 1906. Until this time Clifford had never set eyes on a town larger than neighbouring Cornwall, so Kingston, with a population of approximately eighteen thousand, seemed impressive indeed.[21] Clifford's world was rapidly expanding and he joined what had by this time become a significant migration from rural Glengarry. As ready sources of timber declined, lumbermen went north and west looking for fresh supplies or other sources of resource work. Many children of large families had no option to remain on the family farm and instead moved into the burgeoning cities in search of employment. In this sense, the Clark family was typical. Only Clifford's younger brother, Linden, remained in the local area where he would eventually take over the dairy farm.

For 'a freshman newly arrived from the country,' Clark wrote, the reception in Grant Hall at Queen's College was a moment of high excitement.[22] The college's most popular principal, George Munro Grant, had died only four years before and his spirit and vision were still very much alive at Queen's. The college, at the time Clark arrived in 1906, was a compact campus, consisting of a small rectangle on the east side of University Avenue with just eight limestone buildings. But Clark's arrival coincided with a period of rapid expansion. Enrolment in arts and theology doubled in the first decade of the century and new buildings appeared at a rapid rate. The excitement of expansion and growth, however, was overshadowed by the bitter process of turning the religious college into a secular university and formally separating Queen's from the Presbyterian Church, a transition that would not be complete until 1912.[23]

Clark planned to pursue a degree in mining engineering. But he registered for the combined arts and science course because the mining school was affiliated but not yet part of Queen's and he wanted to take advantage of his scholarship.[24] The young student entered straight arts in Latin and French, and produced a very impressive record. By the end of his first year, Clark was first in junior Latin and French, and second in French and astronomy. In his second year, he was first in senior French, and by his third year he was first in preliminary honours French and Latin. Clifford capped his triumphs in his fourth year, standing first in final honours Latin and French.[25] At the time Queen's awarded a master's of arts 'on the Scottish model' for achieving final honours with first class in two subjects. In 1910 Clark graduated with an MA in Latin and French.[26]

Clark had not just done well at college; his record was exceptional. His list of academic prizes was daunting and he certainly caught the attention of his professors.[27] Over the next two years, Clifford applied himself to the honours courses in English, history, and political and economic science, which he had completed by 1912. 'It is doubtful,' W.A. Mackintosh later reminisced, 'if any other student in the history of the University has completed the full honours courses in five subjects.[28] Beyond academics, however, it is difficult to ascertain what type of student Clifford was. 'When I was in college,' he later recollected, 'it was distinctly "against the fashion" to study. The man who made even an attempt at serious study was called a "crammer." We boasted of the small amount of reading which it had been necessary for us to do to "get off a class." Not a little "surreptitious study" was done by the man who wanted to stand well up in the examination lists.'[29] This statement seems to indicate that because Clifford was a more diligent student than most, he received his share of scorn for being too bookish.

Clark became involved in debating at the intercollegiate level and this seemed to stimulate his interest in politics and economics. Surprisingly, perhaps, Clark also wrestled on the college team and according to later reports 'was a competitor to be reckoned with at one hundred and twelve pounds.'[30] He participated in a Queen's match on 28 February 1908 in which he was beat in the final of the light wrestling category.[31] This excursion into competitive sports was, however, unusual. Throughout his life, he indicated little interest in sports, other than recreational fishing.

There was no respite from academics for Clark even during the long summers. Instead, he spent his summers teaching public school in western Canada, pursuing a common vocation for college students at the time and an important source of funding for the upcoming academic year. The school system in the West was only just being developed and there was a stark lack of teachers willing to move into the pioneering areas being settled. As a result of travel difficulties in wintertime, the majority of western rural schools held sessions during the summer. Clark taught public school for three summers, teaching in three different Prairie districts. For a time he organized and operated the teachers' employment exchange, charged with finding placements for Queen's students.[32]

The experience in the rural Prairie West during the first decades of the twentieth century came as a shock to young Clifford Clark. On the one hand, emerging from a rural farming background himself, Clark was more prepared than most for life on the Prairie frontier. That said, the rural communities around Glen Falloch were worlds ahead of the pioneering West. This experience affected Clark's view of his rapidly expanding nation. He witnessed the West in the early years of the new century, during its golden era. He came to appreciate the important economic role played by the agricultural region but he also sensed that the West was at the intellectual vanguard of the nation. As with other members of the emerging Canadian intelligentsia, Clark observed in the region the seeds of a new and reforming liberalism. Yet, at the same time, sectional grievances were emerging that would define the West's relationship with central Canada. Along with many other academics of the day, such as Harold Innis who also taught in the West, Clark 'learned something of the West's peculiar problems. The anxieties and vexations of high interest-rates and transport problems had become familiar to him through very real examples. He brought back with him some understanding of the West's conception of its own nature, and of its attitude to the nation as a whole.'[33] In the summer of 1912 Clark also taught at Haileybury High School north of North Bay, Ontario.

But all was not well back home on the dairy farm in Glen Falloch. Clifford's eldest brother, Kenneth, was still there helping his father. According to family lore, Ken was frustrated by the attentions being heaped upon his younger brother over his growing academic acclaim and he felt Clifford flaunted his education.[34] Ken Clark left home in either 1908 or 1909 and never returned or contacted the family again. He went west, to Fernie, British Columbia, where he settled and worked as a logger, eventually becoming a shareholder in the Fernie Brewery and later running Fernie Cartage. Ken married and had a daughter but he died of tuberculosis in April 1915 at the age of twenty-seven. It is not known for certain what transpired in the Clark household that led to the sudden and final break between Ken and his parents, or what role, if any, Clifford played in the severing of relations.[35] As so often happened, the unfortunate incident became a matter that was rarely discussed, even behind closed doors.[36]

In the meantime, Clark's academic achievements brought high praise from his professors at Queen's. W.L. Grant, professor of colonial history, commented on Clark's ability to combine 'clearness and even subtlety of thought with a lucid style.'[37] The praise that undoubtedly meant the most to Clark, however, came from O.D. Skelton, the John A. Macdonald chair in political science. Skelton had earned his PhD in political science and economics at the University of Chicago and returned to Queen's in 1907 as a lecturer under Adam Shortt. When Shortt went to Ottawa as chairman of the Civil Service Commission a year later, Skelton (then only thirty years old) succeeded him as head of the department. The young scholar brought from his training at Chicago 'a keen appreciation of the possibilities of empirical investigation into the problems of an industrial society.' But, like Shortt, Skelton was 'sceptical of abstract formulation' and instead focused on practical applications of political and economic theories. He was committed to the political economy of liberal capitalism but he distrusted concentrations of power. Instead, Skelton favoured selective state intervention. He believed that public policy required impartial experts who would stand above the clash of private interests and safeguard the public welfare. Such expertise could come only from those who had studied economic and political problems with the detachment of the scientist. Skelton looked to the developing university system, and Queen's in particular, to educate a new generation of social scientists who would also shape the new state.[38]

O.D. Skelton was honorary vice-president and then honorary president of the Inter-University Debating League during Clark's two years with the club. The professor quickly stepped into the role as Clark's mentor. As later commentators noted, 'There had never been before and there was never thereafter a man for whose judgment, integrity and intellectual capacity' Clark felt such respect. As a teacher he found Skelton to be exceedingly knowledgeable, but it was his thirst for the truth, ability to balance evidence objectively, and openness of mind to new evidence and ideas that were particularly alluring. Of most impact, however, was Skelton's ability to demonstrate how learning gained in university could be applied to the problems facing modern society. 'No one could better expound the positions of any of the great economists of the past,' Clark wrote, 'revealing its strength and exposing its limitations, but such exposition was not his usual method. His classes which had most influence on his students were those on current national and imperial problems in which he used no text-books but intrigued the student by engaging with him in a joint exploration for the truth. The stimulus of such teaching, the mental discipline it provided, the new horizons which it opened, led all his advanced students to bless the name of Skelton.'[39]

The professor, however, was also impressed with the student. In March of 1912 Skelton noted that Clark 'has in him, I believe, the making of a brilliant scholar and teacher. He has a quick and wide grasp of facts, power to analyse and correlate them in a systematic fashion, and ability to make what he reads his own. His vital interest in social and political problems and his habit of persistent wrestling with difficulties give promise of successful original work and his powers of clear exposition mark him out for success in teaching. Throughout his course he has taken a prominent part in student affairs.'[40] The two had become friends by the time of Clark's graduation,[41] although according to Terry Crowley, Skelton 'did not have friends, only colleagues and associates.'[42] Regardless, Skelton would have more influence on the career of Clifford Clark than any other individual.

It was Oscar Skelton who first taught Clark economics, although he had taken only two such courses by the time he left Queen's in 1912. Much of the reason for Clark's modest training in economics was due to the condition of the discipline in Canadian universities at the time. Adam Shortt, 'the founder of Canadian economics,' was one of the first appointments made in the field and that had occurred only two decades previous.[43] Indeed, there was no discipline called economics; instead, it was termed political economy. Until the early 1920s, the University of Toronto and Queen's University were the principal centres of economic study in the nation and the latter was the only centre for Canadian economic studies.[44] Those students wishing to pursue graduate studies in economics had to leave Canada, mainly for the United States, and universities such as Harvard, Chicago, and Oxford. There were only approximately forty-five economists teaching in Canadian universities by 1930 and it was not until 1936 that a doctorate in economics was earned in Canada.[45]

Skelton directed Clark toward graduate work in economics at Harvard, where Frank W. Taussig, one of the best-known economists of the day and 'the acknowledged centre of the economics constellation,' was firmly ensconced.[46] Clark entered Harvard in the fall of 1912 on a $300 Thayer scholarship for postgraduate work in history and government. According to later reports, 'with his unusual background of undergraduate work and his quick and now mature mind,' Clifford immediately made his place and was 'a great favourite of Taussig who always spoke of him with almost parental pride and affection.'[47] Taussig wrote volumes on the field of international trade and was very interested in tariff and commercial policy, but he was better known as a 'systematizer and clarifier of economic thought rather than as an original theorist.' His major contribution came in the impact he had on students. Fundamentally conservative, Taussig offered his students a neoclassical economic view: 'The world he described was one of many firms competing in each and every market, the flawing exception of monopoly aside. Production provided the income to buy what was produced. There were cyclical rhythms that brought occasional bad times, but these were self-corrective. Trade was best when free, although measures to arrest the exploitation of consumers or workers commended themselves to men of good will.'[48] Taussig believed that the issuing of currency should be left to the banks, to be exercised with a minimum of government restraint. He was interested in applying economics to public policy and supported academics entering the government service.[49] According to Owram, 'Classical economic theory, modified by the marginal utility theorists of the late nineteenth century, had become strongly entrenched in western economic thought,' and it would be this viewpoint that dominated the field until it was shattered by the Great Depression.[50]

Clark wanted to go to Harvard but had alternative plans. In the winter of 1911–12, he wrote to his uncle (his father's half-brother), William Clark, expressing some interest in going west. William lived in Stockton, California, where he was co-owner of a construction company as well as full owner of a hotel.[51] William's son, Arthur, who was in charge of the Oregon branch of the construction business, responded to Clifford's query with a job offer as 'cashier, material man, or timekeeper.'[52]

Clark went to Harvard. For the 1912–13 academic year there were 344 full-work students in postgraduate studies of arts sciences at Harvard, 105 of whom were in history and political science. Twenty-four graduate students were Canadian. In the following year, twenty-seven Canadians were part of this group, six of whom were from Queen's University.[53] For the 1914–15 academic year, twenty-eight full or half courses were offered in economics with fourteen aimed primarily at graduate students. In addition, eight courses on research in economics were offered.[54] Clark paid for board at Foxcroft Hall and he excelled in his studies. In the spring of 1913, he was awarded the leading fellowship for resident graduate students in economics, the Henry Lee Memorial Fellowship worth $525.[55] Skelton acknowledged the award with congratulations and enclosed a list of possible 'Canadian' thesis topic ideas. Skelton's strong sense of nationalism was tweaked; he was justifiably concerned that Clark's star would rise in academe and the young man would then be tempted away with full-time employment in an American university: 'Keep steadily in mind the possibility of a Canadian College opening and by preference let your thesis subject be a Canadian one. We can't afford to let you stay permanently in the United States.'[56] The correspondence was written on letterhead belonging to the Canadian Political Science Association, recently founded by O.D. Skelton and Adam Shortt. Clark, on Skelton's invitation, joined the organization in April.[57] By July 1913, Clark was planning on a doctoral thesis dealing with the western Canadian grain trade. Skelton discussed every job opportunity in Canada with Clark during these years. On 5 January 1913, Clark received a letter from his former history professor, J.L. Morison, suggesting he apply for a job in British constitutional history at Queen's.[58] In June, Skelton wrote Clark seeking recommendations for any Harvard men who might qualify for a new chair in economics at the University of Saskatchewan. If the department could wait for two years, 'you would be the best man in sight,' Skelton noted.[59]

In April 1914 Clark won the Ricardo Prize Scholarship, worth $350, open to all Harvard graduate students but designed for studies under the supervision of the Department of Economics. In the same year, he was offered assistantships in economics or government and chose to serve as assistant to Professor Taussig. By May, Clark sat and passed the general examination for the PhD in economics, with Taussig heading the examination board. He spent the summer of 1915 conducting research for his thesis on the Prairie grain trade, including a trip through western Canada.[60] In Edmonton, a group of lawyers who had gone to Queen's hosted a lunch for him. Clark had an annual income for each of his years at Harvard in excess of his costs. He would later remark that his university education ended up costing neither him nor his family.

In the middle of his third year, Clark was asked to postpone the completion of his doctoral thesis and instead accept an additional appointment as tutor (or preceptor) in history, government, and economics at Harvard. Not long after, he suddenly received an offer from Skelton of a teaching appointment at Queen's: 'Under ordinary circumstances, I should certainly advise you to accept the new tutorship offered for next year even if it involved postponing the taking of your degree for another year. We have decided, however, in view of the increased demands made by the work in Banking, to enlarge our department this year, without waiting for the return of more prosperous times, as might otherwise have been decided. If then you are attracted by the offer of a lectureship at Queen's, I am authorized to make the proposal to you.'[61] If he accepted, Clark could to return to Harvard at the end of the following year to finish the PhD. The salary at Queen's would be $1,000.

But the decision weighed heavily on Clark's mind. Taussig advised him to refuse the Queen's offer and remain at Harvard with the tutorial and assistantship positions. At the end of the year, he could accept a travelling fellowship to go to Europe and complete his thesis. Skelton understood the lure of remaining at Harvard so he countered with nationalistic arguments:

> The chief question to decide, and it is one that only yourself can decide, is whether you wish to do your life work in Canada or in the United States. There is much to be said in favor of staying permanently on the other side, particularly the possibility of doing more specialized work than is possible in the two or three man departments of Economics in Canada. The scale of salaries, again, is higher in the United States, so far as the bigger Universities go, though averaging all the college departments of economics in

> both countries it would be lower. At the top of the profession, it is and will likely be somewhat higher, though here salaries are slowly on the up grade.
>
> On the other side is the attraction of being in one's native country, with its crowding new problems and wealth of opportunities. To different men that will appeal with varying force. Another point to bear in mind in making a comparison is our shorter term. You know the difference in the case of all the eastern and to a lesser extent the western Canadian colleges as compared with the U.S., and what a difference that makes for plans for travel or research.[62]

In April Clark decided to accept the Queen's offer. Taussig was 'greatly disappointed and somewhat hurt' when he learned of the decision.[63] According to later accounts, Clark informed Taussig that his reasoning was based on the fact that Skelton had served as a kind of 'father' to him, to which Taussig responded, 'Haven't I been a father to you? Clark had no words and he could only look down at the ground and wish it would open and swallow him.'[64] Clifford Clark would never complete his PhD dissertation. All that was published from what W.A. Macintosh later called 'a vast accumulation of material' on the grain trade was a single article in 1916 in *Queen's Quarterly*, 'The Country Elevator in the Canadian West.'[65] In 1918 Clark received a master's degree in arts (economics) from Harvard.

When he returned to Queen's in September 1915, Clark was described as 'a very young man with the face of a cherub and an academic record at Queen's and Harvard so distinguished that the world, so to speak, lay at his feet.'[66] The young man had changed, but so also had Queen's. Now in its second year, the Great War cast a shadow over university life and its influence was felt everywhere. By the spring of 1915, 300 undergraduates, as well as many graduates and faculty members, had volunteered for military service.[67] By spring 1917, 980 'Queen's men' were in service. The impact of such a large number of student volunteers on the small university community was immediate. Enrolment plunged to 600 full-time students in the 1916–17 academic year.[68] In late 1916 the university transferred control of Grant Hall and Kingston Hall to the federal government, and the buildings were turned into a hospital to house 600 servicemen, invalided home from war. In the following year Nicol Hall and the Old Arts Building were used by the government for rehabilitation.[69] But the impact of the war on the university's financial position was 'little short of disastrous.' Falling enrolments combined with the necessity of carrying the half-salaries for overseas professors produced sharp deficits. These financial problems followed in the wake of a long and bitter dispute, and finally a break, with the Presbyterian Church in 1912.[70] The university had to wait for the end of the conflict to receive any grant monies from the provincial government.[71] The funding difficulties meant salaries at Queen's remained low, especially compared with the rival University of Toronto.

Unlike many of the students and young professors at Queen's, Clark did not volunteer for military service, but there is no record of why he made that decision. He was twenty-five years old when war broke out in 1914, so while Clifford was not of prime age for enlistment, he was not too old. He was in the United States at Harvard at the time, and this distance likely diminished the pressures to enlist that were so strongly felt throughout English Canada. While there is no indication that what were to become nagging back problems were already plaguing Clark, it is possible that health reasons affected or even prevented his enlistment. It is most likely, however, that the influence of Skelton – whose criticism of and opposition to imperialism, as well as his general position in favour of Canadian autonomy in British affairs – played a role in convincing the young professor not to enlist.[72] Regardless, Clifford Clark did not serve in the First World War. Whatever his reasons, they seem to have been sound enough to hold up under scrutiny because there is no indication that he was ever embarrassed by his war record, as was often the case with other public figures of the day, Prime Minister Mackenzie King being the most notable.

The department of political economy at Queen's was small in 1915, consisting of only four members: O.D. Skelton (department head), W.W. Swanson, Humfrey Mitchell, and W.C. Clark.[73] In his first year teaching, Clark was responsible for one advanced course in international trade and he also assisted in the courses on banking, which Skelton had established in cooperation with the Canadian Bankers' Association in 1914. Among his first students was W.A. (Bill) Mackintosh, who would become one of Clark's closest friends and colleagues.[74] In his first year, Clark lived at the home of W.L. Grant, where he roomed with Humfrey Mitchell and George Kirkpatrick.

The banking courses were the first of a number of 'Skelton projects' in which Clark became first an active participant and later a partner. This particular project originated from banking programs being designed at the universities of Chicago and Wisconsin; Queen's was the first university in Canada to experiment with the idea, which was to provide university extension work by fulfilling the demand for training bank clerks.[75] Despite the war, the new course of study was launched in 1914 with a registration of 1,055 students. Skelton wrote the bulk of the texts.[76]

Early in 1916 Clark published his first academic piece when the *Queen's University Economics Bulletin* published three articles under the collective title 'Economic Aspects of the War.' Included in the three was a lengthy piece by Clark, titled 'Financing the War.' It was a fitting first subject for a man whose reputation would be built largely upon financing the next world war. Clark opened the article, ironically, by challenging claims that financial strength was the decisive factor in winning wars: 'The other great wars of modern times seem to show that seldom, if ever, has actual want of money or financial distress brought war to an end.' Wars were fought, not for financial reasons, but because of the failings of humanity. He dismissed arguments that fell back upon economic determinism as the root cause of human conflict. Economics, however, did play a critical role in the process by which war was carried out: 'To deny the all-importance of finance is not to belittle the really great part that an effective financial mobilization may play in assisting the armies in the field, not to forget the difficulties and the chaos which unsound financial arrangements may cause both during the struggle and in the subsequent period of readjustment.' Clark discussed the specific financial methods of nations involved in the Great War and made the point that their costs and debts were rising dramatically. The war was already projected to cost $39 billion in 1916 and these numbers were increasing by $32 billion annually. Debts were also skyrocketing, from $25 billion to $60 billion. On average, 70 per cent of the national income of participating nations was being spent on the war.[77]

In the summer of 1916 Clark's second academic publication appeared in the *Bulletin of the Departments of History and Political and Economic Science in Queen's University* and was titled 'The Country Elevator in the Canadian West.' The article emerged from Clark's graduate work but also reflected his broad interests outside economics. Clark believed that the western grain trade could serve as an important and successful example of government regulation: 'The Western grain trade is more subject to Government regulation than any other Canadian trade, and more subject to regulation than the grain trade of any other country in the world ... Certainly the fact does not seem to have discouraged the free flow of capital towards the trade ... Government regulation has not made them [western farmers] less able or willing to stand on their own feet.' The farmers' organization of the grain trade, and in particular their development of the country elevator system, was responsible for what Clark boldly described as 'the strongest force making for real democracy in present-day Canadian life.' Both farmers and governments responded effectively to the 'evils' that developed through the emergence of the private elevator monopoly. Improvements over a decade and a half, based on protective legislation, education, marketing alternatives, and active participation by farmers in their own organizations led to a correction of abuses. Clark placed great importance on education that allowed the farmers to understand the political process and the legislation necessary to regulate their industry effectively. He was also impressed with the cooperation between the government and the farmers. Government was serving as referee for the industry and the farmer was learning 'to be alert, ready to stand up for his own interests, ready to call upon the referee to enforce the rules of the game.'[78]

In the summer of 1916 Clark first worked for the Canadian government. The work related to the Natural Resources Commission, headed by Conservative Senator James Lougheed. The commission (despite its rather specific title) was set up by Conservative Prime Minister Robert Borden in 1915 to investigate an array of economic conditions in Canada related to natural resource production. Its mandate was broad and included the improved production of agricultural goods; interprovincial trade; the manufacture and transport of products to national ports and then to markets abroad; immigration, settlement, and land policy; the return and employment of Canadian troops; and the capital production necessary for expanding agricultural and manufacturing industries.[79] The commission, however, was an example to Skelton and Clark of Ottawa's ineffective attempts at regulation during the war. Skelton, in particular, did not take the Lougheed Commission seriously: 'Hope you get along satisfactorily in your task of trying to make Sir James' half-baked, tired-statesman's ideas look fairly plausible,' he wrote Clark in July 1916.[80] 'From all I hear in Ottawa,' Skelton commented, 'the proceedings of the Commission are typical of the government's drifting planless policies, but as I'm staying with Sir Wilfrid [Laurier], perhaps my surroundings at present are not quite unbiased.'[81] By the end of the summer, Skelton could not contain his sarcasm: 'I think it will be necessary for the Government to appoint a commission in the fall to investigate the whereabouts of Lougheed's commission.'[82]

In July Clark was informed that his colleague W.W. Swanson had accepted the position of chair in the economics department at the University of Saskatchewan. As a result, Clark was appointed assistant professor of political science and his pay was increased to $1,500.[83] Skelton spent much of that summer trying to find a new lecturer for the department. Contacts at Harvard suggested the young and impressive Jewish-Canadian Jacob Viner for the position but, as Skelton explained to Clark, 'I am afraid our Gentile prejudices would be too strong.'[84] Viner would go on to become one of the top economists Canada ever produced. Skelton's department, in the end, had to get along without an economist and instead hired a sessional lecturer in history. As a result, Clark ended up teaching additional courses in general, agricultural, and theoretical economics, as well as currency and banking.[85]

On 13 September 1916, Clark married Margaret Hilda Smith from Martintown. Little is known about the courtship but it seems likely that it was Clifford's first and only serious romance. Margaret was one of two daughters of John Smith and Mary Margaret McPhadden, and she was a descendent of Martintown's founder. Their father perished while on a trip to seek lumber, and after their mother's death the two girls were raised by their aunts, Eleanor and Annie McPhadden, who owned and ran McPhadden's General Store in town. Margaret, like Clifford, had graduated from Williamstown High School and gone on to Queen's University. She graduated in the spring of 1914 with a BA and passed the general course in the Faculty of Education the following year. Aside from being academic and athletic, by all accounts Margaret had a kind and gentle personality. The wedding between Clifford and Margaret was held at the big stone house known as 'Grant's Folly' beside the Aux Raisin River in Martintown.

For the first year of married life, Clifford and Margaret subleased a house on Frontenac Street in Kingston from Professor G.B. Reed. In the summer of 1917 they moved into a home on Centre Street, near the campus, from which Clark would often bicycle to work.[86] But it did not take long for the Clark family to expand. Later that summer, Margaret gave birth to their first child, George Clifford, and by November 1918 a second child was born, Eleanor Urquhart. The Clarks' third child, Catherine Ruth, was born in November 1919.

In 1918 Clark published two essays dealing with wartime finance and in particular the federal government's response to the increasing problem of rising inflation. Despite his developing views on the role of the interventionist state, Clark was opposed to the establishment of price ceilings in wartime as an impractical control measure: 'The overwhelming weight of evidence is against a policy of fixing maximum prices ... for arbitrary prices determined with no reference to competition must be supplemented by arbitrary regulation of production and consumption.' Clark concluded that the most effective remedy to deal with the serious problem of profiteering during wartime was heavy taxation of excess profits, 'taxation far more drastic and pervasive than we have yet determined.' But he refused to accept the argument that a different policy of war finance, based on taxation measures instead of loans, was 'politically possible for Canada.' The man who would later become known as 'the architect of the Canadian economy in the Second World War – with its panoply of controls,' according to J.L. Granatstein, began as an 'orthodox economist.'[87] Yet within Clark's early thinking could be discerned the seeds of a new approach to economics, and financing a major war in particular. He was prepared to admit the possibility of such economic controls, although the obstacles seemed insurmountable. In order to fix prices, Clark argued, the state would have to understand thoroughly the nature of the economic system. 'Whether a single authority could be set up with wisdom enough to exercise the power with any certainty of beneficial results,' he observed, 'is doubtful.' History was full of unsuccessful attempts. 'But,' Clark went on, 'an age of supermen, of super-organizers, may defy the teaching of history. Success is still conceivable.'[88]

Clark's work at Queen's reflected Skelton's focus on applied economics. The lofty world of the ivory tower had to offer solutions to everyday problems; academe had to demonstrate practical relevance. It was a matter of 'bringing clear thought and good scholarship to bear upon the problems of the day.'[89] Clark found an outlet for applied economics when, in 1918, he was offered contract work with the federal government, this time within the census and statistics office of the Department of Trade and Commerce under Dominion Statistician R.H. Coats. The office was being reorganized and enlarged, and Coats was seeking to use collected data to enter 'into the economic discussion of the country. In other words, it is desired to constitute the Office an "economic laboratory" for the intensive investigation of Canadian social and economic problems.' To this end, Coats was seeking to build a bridge between his office and the university departments of economics, 'so that the latter may teach from Canadian texts, while the former may have the benefit of advice and assistance of the most expert character.' This objective would be achieved through the office employing professors during the summer months. Clark undertook such work in the summer of 1918.[90]

The experience with government work led to additional opportunities. By the end of October, Clark was negotiating with fellow Queen's graduate Bryce Stewart, of the Department of Labour. Clark took leave from teaching to act as special adviser to Stewart in planning and organizing a national employment service. But controversy immediately erupted among the civil servants over whether Clark would be working for the department directly or through a special committee. 'I am afraid that you will think that the Government service is a rather subterranean place,' Coats wrote apologetically to Clark, 'that "works in a mysterious way its wonders to perform."'[91] Once he was hired, Clark's role was to work primarily on the statistics to be published, including the internal working figures and indexes of employment. The Employment Service of Canada was created when the Employment Offices Co-ordination Act became law on 18 May 1918 in response to a farm labour shortage, but its focus quickly shifted to finding work for returning soldiers. Although employment was viewed as a provincial responsibility, Ottawa was prepared to aid and encourage the organization of employment offices through subsidies and matching grants to provincial governments during post-war reconstruction. According to James Struthers, the measure indicated a new federal commitment to tackling unemployment, not only as a reconstruction problem, but as a general industrial problem. By June 1919, there were eighty-eight government employment offices across Canada, compared to twelve only six months earlier. In the first year, almost four hundred thousand job placements were made, mostly among unskilled seasonal workers.[92]

The work highlighted the importance of compiling and making effective use of statistical data. Together, Clark and Stewart developed the first national statistical survey of employment trends in North America, which was published biweekly in a newsletter sent free to employers and provincial governments. The data allowed the employment service to track seasonal fluctuations and to transfer workers from industries in seasonal decline to those in need of labour. It provided information the government could then use to decide where to direct contracts and immigration.[93] In 1923 an article in the *Journal of the American Statistical Association* described the National Employment Service as 'the most complete informing statistical record of employment changes ... available in any country.'[94]

The Employment Service Council of Canada was created in 1919 to guide the work of the employment service and recommend ways to prevent unemployment. Its first conference was held in Ottawa on

12–14 May and brought together twenty-six representatives of employers' associations, labour organizations, Great War veterans, the Soldiers' Civil Re-establishment Department, provincial employment services, and the Employment Service of Canada. Clark addressed the conference on 'The Regularization of Employment,' dealing with the technical issues of countering seasonal and cyclical unemployment. In the speech Clark did not shy away from the serious situation developing in Winnipeg with the General Strike, what he called 'the Western Labour Outbreak.'[95] Clark noted the negative personal effects of unemployment on the average worker but he also laid out his own political philosophy by drawing a direct connection to the development of social unrest: 'Perhaps more important at the present time than the hardships due to loss of wages and the demoralization due to idleness and worry is the inevitable tendency of unemployment, present or prospective, to make men question the foundations of the present social system.' While Clark referred to himself, and his audience, as 'individualists' seeking to develop initiative, he refused to rule out state involvement: 'We would prefer to solve our problem without calling in the aid of the State. We believe too that much can be done by private individuals, especially by employers – though it will take a long time before substantial results are achieved. But that does not mean that we will refuse to recommend state action if such action is needed to meet an immediate situation. Too long have we been blinded by mere catchwords; too long have we feared to take action through co-operative groups such as the state, the municipality, the trade association, the trade union, when action through individuals was shown to be hopelessly inadequate and destructive of the very ends we sought to achieve.'

Despite the gloomy atmosphere of recessionary post-war Canada, Clark refused to be pessimistic. He was confident that ultimately the value of cooperation would prevail and social harmony would be restored. Ten years previous, nothing had been done across the world to deal with such issues as unemployment. By 1919, Clark noted, the forces of labour had pushed the issue onto the political agenda and it was being wrestled with as never before; it would be solved, no matter what agencies it was necessary to call into action. 'Call it a quickened social conscience,' Clark observed, 'or call it simply enlightened selfishness, the world is coming to regard as intolerable the concept of workmen as simply parts of a machine which are to be laid on the shelf when the machine is not working.' Labour forces were demonstrating what was already being highlighted by scientific study: 'Unemployment is due, not so much to personal causes, as to social maladjustments, to imperfect industrial organization.' The primary cause of unemployment was, Clark argued, 'the irregularity of modern industry.' The industrial machine was far from perfect and at times it was close to breaking down. By 1919 it was in desperate need of repair and unemployment was a symptom of this malaise. 'While the industrial machine is being adjusted,' Clark claimed, 'good men as well as poor men are out of work. It is folly to blame such unemployment on the individual. The cause is social; the responsibility is social; the remedy must be social.' And Clark's social remedy called for state planning. Public improvements and expenditures should be planned on a ten-year program with a certain variable percentage of such expenditure deferred in each normal business year of the decade. The accumulated deferred improvements would constitute an employment reserve, which could be utilized to compensate for decreased private employment, due to lessening demands of private employers in the lean years of the decade.[96] In June, Clark planned to attend a meeting of the American Federation of Labour (AFL) in Ottawa – 'the A.F. of L. or as my Western friends say the A.F. of Hell!'[97]

The employment service ran into difficulties and ultimately failed. Provincial governments staffed offices with poorly paid and poorly qualified patronage appointees. Ontario, Quebec, and British Columbia refused to abolish private employment agencies as agreed in 1918, thus keeping the employment service to a minor role for unskilled railway, mining, and logging workers, and crippling any assault on seasonal employment. In addition, the provincial and federal governments refused to provide the advertising budget seen as essential to producing an employment service for all workers, not just those on relief.[98] Still, Clark viewed the creation of a government body with permanent interest in employment as reason for optimism. That optimism was further dashed, however, by the election results of 1921. The Liberals under Mackenzie King defeated the Union government that had created the employment service. The Progressive Party burst onto the electoral scene, breaking the two-party system and forcing the creation of the first minority government in Canadian history. The King Liberals courted the Progressives to maintain power and the largely western- (and rural-) based party opposed the role of the employment service as a means of increasing the salaries of workers rather than dealing with the difficulties of farmers in placing workers. In addition, Prime Minister King did not favour conditional grants to the provinces, because they left Ottawa with the blame for taxing people for activities the federal government could not control. Bryce Stewart resigned in 1922 and the semi-monthly statistical bulletin ceased distribution. Instead, responsibility for gathering data from employers was transferred to the Dominion Bureau of Statistics. By 1924 the conditional grants were reduced from 50 to 34 per cent. Not long after, the budget of the service itself was slashed. Unemployment research was abandoned, two of four regional offices closed, and federal inspection of provincial offices ended. The employment service, Struthers notes, 'was little more than a patronage-ridden clearing-house for casual help.'[99] According to Michael Stevenson, it 'floundered on the shoals of federal–provincial jurisdictional disputes and starved on a meagre diet of public funding.'[100]

Clark's work with the employment service ended in August 1919 and he left Ottawa to undertake an investigation for Queen's University of the One Big Union movement in western Canada that had been so active in the Winnipeg General Strike. Skelton, meanwhile, lamented the fact that Queen's, once a pioneer through its banking courses, had since fallen behind other universities in the new fields of social work, commerce, finance, and accounting. He advanced ambitious plans for academic development that entailed universities encouraging their scholars to pursue practical research that could then produce results helpful in dealing with present conditions. Canada was facing the problems of an advanced industrial system, Skelton argued, such as sectional and class conflict, land settlement, and the rehabilitation of returned soldiers, social reconstruction, taxation, foreign trade, and international organization. He won board approval for some research provisions, and it is likely that Clark was among the first to apply and receive assistance for specific research projects.[101]

Skelton also proposed a new degree course in commerce or business administration at Queen's as part of the Faculty of Arts. The program had been discussed between Skelton and Clark for several years, and in the academic session of 1918–19 it was placed before the Board of Trustees, the Senate, and the Faculty of Arts, and given formal approval. There was opposition from the Arts Faculty, however. James Cappon, dean of arts and professor of English literature, was opposed to technical training and education for 'merely a vocational purpose.'[102] Despite claims that the commerce course at Queen's was the first in a Canadian university, the University of Toronto had actually already pioneered the field with a two-year diploma course in commerce in 1901. By 1909 Toronto had a four-year course leading to a bachelor of arts called Commerce and Finance. In 1920 a second four-year course leading to a bachelor of commerce was established. The two courses were combined in 1923. In addition, two-year diploma courses had been established at Manitoba in 1904, McGill in 1914, and Alberta in 1916. The McGill course became a three-year program in 1917 and in 1910 L'École des hautes études commerciales opened in Montreal with a three-year diploma program.[103] Upon his return to Queen's in the fall of 1919, Clark took over direction of the courses in commerce and administration. Skelton, meanwhile, became dean of arts.

But the Department of Economics at Queen's was small in 1919, and with Skelton moving into administration, the staff was meagre to handle the responsibilities and energy necessary for the success of the new commerce program. In the fall of 1920 Skelton brought back another Queen's graduate to teach in the department. Bill Mackintosh had been a student of Clark's in his last year at Queen's before moving on to Harvard for doctoral studies. While still finishing his PhD, Mackintosh had moved to Brandon College in Manitoba to take up a teaching post, and he now joined the faculty at Queen's.

As with Skelton, Clark's academic work focused increasingly on the application of scientific methods to business. In 1920 he made a tour of the universities and schools of commerce in the larger centres of the eastern and midwestern United States. He observed in an article published in 1920 that business administration was traditionally approached as a 'trade learned in the school of experience and following a traditional rule-of-thumb routine.' In contrast Clark lauded the movement that aimed to professionalize the practice of business. This movement had been started by F.W. Taylor, the father of time studies of work and scientific management, whose ideas Clark heard in 1914. But Clark's main objective was to describe in general terms the advances being made in the United States in developing business statistics, especially those indicating the trend of the market that might allow predictions of economic activity. The *Harvard Review of Economic Studies* was leading the way in this field and one of its innovations was a monthly review that included an index of business conditions providing accurate forecasts.[104] In Canada, Clark noted, there were not yet any elaborate statistical organizations specializing in the field of business forecasting, but beginnings were being made. In particular, he pointed to the Dominion Bureau of Statistics, which had begun issuing a quarterly publication providing statistics 'with some attempt at interpretation.'[105]

By the fall of 1920 Clark was promoted to associate professor with an annual salary of $2,700. He became director of the banking courses and increasingly focused his time on the commerce program. According to Fred Gibson, the program was scarcely launched before Clark, 'a born initiator of plans and organizer of projects, began to modify it.'[106] In 1921, on Clark's recommendation, Queen's launched a program under his direction whereby the university provided instruction by correspondence to all students registered with the Institute of Chartered Accountants of Ontario. In the first year 271 students were enrolled and the courses were later adopted by the institutes of other provinces.[107] Among those first hired to teach accounting were J.W. Ballard and E.H. Morrow, and by the autumn of 1922 Skelton had recruited four accountants: R.G.H. Smails, C.E. Walker, C.A. Ashley, and A.H. Carr.[108] The Department of Economics and Political Science was the largest department of the Arts Faculty at Queen's in the 1920s.[109] Still, Clark found it necessary in April 1922 to ask for a telephone to be added to the budget and placed in the banking and accounting office of the New Arts Building.[110]

Clark's scholarly work continued to highlight the need for experts in helping formulate government policy. When Conservative Prime Minister Arthur Meighen established the Tariff Commission in 1921, however, Clark was critical. While the Tariff Commission was claiming to offer a 'scientific investigation of Canada's tariff needs,' Clark did not believe it was given the necessary 'free hand' to carry out its work. Instead, it was a political tool created to advance the interests of protectionism. The tariff was the central issue in Canadian politics and according to Clark it was beyond mere scientific formulation: 'There is no easy automatic scientific solution of the tariff problem which can be left to a small board of experts.' Clark argued that it was up to Parliament to set tariff policy, and 'when the majority has once declared for a particular policy, the expert can step in and use thorough research and scientific method to determine the best means of accomplishing the results desired. In this detailed application of fiscal principles there is urgent need for the expert.' In other words, the parliamentarians were capable of making the larger political decisions that would set policy but they required the aid of experts to apply that policy. Despite the fact that the present government bureaucracy did not offer the standard of expert Clark was advocating, he did not 'regard as hopeless the possibility of getting efficiency out of the present Civil Service.' Clark went so far as to call for 'the establishment of a permanent board or commission or department holding a watching brief over the whole industrial field.' This board, it was hoped, would be able to take appropriate action in 'proved cases of extortion or misconduct, without imposing unnecessary shackles upon legitimate trade.'[111]

In a rare instance Clark also commented on current political affairs in Canada. The situation he claimed in early 1921 was 'chaotic.' The generation of such statesmen as Robert Borden and Wilfrid Laurier was gone, to be replaced by the new generation of more pragmatic politicians led by Arthur Meighen, William Lyon Mackenzie King, and T.A. Crerar. The traditional two-party system was being recast with the rise of the western Progressives. Regardless, from all potential leaders and parties, Clark was most impressed by Crerar and his Progressives. Crerar, 'quietly and apparently as a result simply of his transparent honesty and his high ideals of public service,' had 'built up a large personal following in every part of Canada.' Prime Minister Meighen won points from Clark for 'his ability, his untiring industry, his courage,' while the Liberal leader, Mackenzie King, 'seems not yet to have developed the political wisdom which is expected of the leader of a great party – much less the genius which is required of the leader of the traditional Liberal Party in any country at the present time when Liberalism threatens to be crushed between the upper and nether millstones of extreme doctrine.'[112] It would be one of the few times Clark publicly expressed his political views.

Clark was concerned with the political situation but his attentions were focused mainly on the deepening economic recession. He studied the causes of business cycles: the fluctuations between periods of weak economic activity and high unemployment, and periods of rapid growth and high demand for workers. Business in Canada was experiencing a low point and recovery would be 'very gradual and halting,' leading Clark to describe the general tone as one of 'enthusiastic pessimism.' Despite the pessimism, Clark was fundamentally an optimist and he usually sought the bright side of most situations. There was, he claimed, 'reason for confidence and courage. Indeed now almost for the first time, those who face facts squarely find solid ground for optimism.'[113] That optimism emerged out of an understanding of economic cycles. The lessons of the recent recession were clear. Economic hardship had followed the war but at the first sign of recovery, governments threw patience to the wind and adopted reckless policies: 'As the wheels of industry began to turn faster and faster, the business world once again made the mistake that has been made in every period of boom. Men thought that they had at last surmounted economic laws and that this time an artificial boom would not have the usual results. The brakes therefore were thrown off and the machine was driven full steam ahead, regardless of possible consequences.' Prices increased, and more money was printed and put into circulation, thereby driving up inflationary pressures and depreciating currencies: 'More importantly, it encouraged the spirit of speculation which still further raised prices by creating artificial shortages and by raising exaggerated hopes of future price increases ... The present depression is, therefore, the result not so much of an industrial reaction as of a price collapse following a period of unprecedented credit inflation.' But while lessons were to be learned, Clark urged, the worst was now over: 'The optimist is the one who sees how serious the depression has already been. It would be madness to imagine that we can escape paying a high price for our follies of the last few years. If much has already been paid on the account, less remains to be paid. A dark picture of the past or immediate present is the only real ground for optimism.'[114] As Owram points out, 'Having described the state as machine, the social scientific community sought to become its mechanics.'[115]

Clifford Clark was also having a positive impact in the classroom. Although he was highly critical of his own speaking ability, his skills were impressive enough that when combined with his knowledge and passion, they made him a good teacher. His main teaching interests were currency, banking, and international trade.[116] Clark was popular. One of his most impressive traits was his ability to inspire those under him, gain their respect, and transfer his own passion and excitement to them. He was warm and personable and this made him approachable to students. The *Queen's Journal* of 1923 described Professor Clark as 'a man approachable at all times [who] had gained the loyal admiration of all who had the good fortune to come in contact with him, and with such a background of personal contact with his students he was able to establish for himself an unusually high distinction as a lecturer. Prof. Clark had the rare gift of imparting his own knowledge to others in a way that his words were not easily forgotten; and his keen insight and deep appreciation of the intricacies of economics, both in theory and practice, made his periods amongst the most enjoyable, and richest that we may number with the classroom hours.'[117]

Clark's career was going well when disaster struck at home. On 5 April 1921 the Clarks' third child, Catherine, died of pneumonia. It is difficult to determine the full impact of this tragedy on the family because it was rarely discussed afterward. The eldest child, George, remembered that while he did not understand at the time what had happened, he did recall a heavy sadness that fell over the household and kept him awake at nights.[118] Six months later, on 14 November, another child was born, Margaret (Peggy) Catherine. On 17 March 1922 misfortune struck again when Clark's father, just fifty-seven years old, died. George Clark had been ill for about seven weeks and his death was reported as caused by 'a complication of diseases.'[119] Skelton came with Clark from Kingston to attend the funeral. With George Clark's death, the family house and farm passed to the fourth Clark child and second son, Linden.

Clark responded to these personal tragedies by immersing himself in his work. The commerce program at Queen's was now well established, but opposition to the idea of vocational education at the university continued. J.M. Macdonnell, Queen's first Rhodes scholar, a member and later chair of the Board of Trustees, and a senior officer with National Trust, published an article lambasting this form of practical education. Macdonnell argued that a traditional humanities education that produced 'a well-trained mind capable of rapid sustained and intense intellectual effort on any problem' was the best preparation for business or any other field. Vocational education, on the other hand, emphasized immediate aims and results, and was a sign of the deterioration in education. Macdonnell argued that vocational studies would render the classical subjects useless and impractical: 'It is so easy for the aggressively practical student to make the student who is pursuing purely intellectual things feel that he is a dreamer, impractical, almost unmanly to spend his time at Latin or Greek or Philosophy!'[120]

Clark offered a rebuttal in an article in the same issue of *Queen's Quarterly*. He refuted Macdonnell's claims that vocational education led to a decline in the development of the enquiring mind. According to Clark, standards for class, essay, and examination work were rising. Indeed, there was now an increase in seminar and class discussion, based on the Socratic method, which was an improvement over the traditional use of lectures: 'The best lecturer may incite the admiration of his students by the range and profundity of his thought or the beauty of his language or the masterly arrangement of his ideas, but in actual practice the lecture system fails because while the professor's mind is, or may be, active, it is the student's arm, not his mind, which is active. The moving finger writes, yes, writes with such nervous speed, lest a word be missed, that the chief result of the professor's lecture is not intellectual activity but a more or less violent form of gymnastics in the college corridors.'

Clark emphasized that the program at Queen's was not solely based on highly technical courses but was blended with liberal arts courses so that students learned the principles of business administration while at the same time receiving the training necessary for a career. Macdonnell, Clark claimed, was railing against a narrow technical program that did not exist. Clark's arguments ended up defending commerce as a 'noble' profession. Those in the ivory tower maintained a traditional condescension towards the business world; they turned their noses up at the thought of commerce courses running alongside those on ancient philosophy or the literary classics. But commerce was changing and that positive transformation could continue if the scientific methods now being applied to other subjects could also be applied to business.[121] Clifford Clark revelled in the academic debate and he was positioned comfortably as a professor at Queen's. He was enjoying his work. His career path, however, was about to change dramatically.

2

American Financier, 1922–1932

> I believe, also, that the work of the economist should be related very much more closely than in the past to actual business. This closer relation is necessary not only in the interests of the business but in those of the economist himself. As a class, economists have failed in their analysis of current business activity, and in their function of interpreting to the public the function and working of our various economic institutions.
>
> – Clifford Clark to H.N. Gottlieb, 1 November 1922

Clifford Clark was about a month into the 1922–3 academic year when he received a letter that would dramatically change his future plans. It was from S.W. Straus and Company, one of the largest real estate firms in the United States. Clark was being offered a new career.

The Straus company, founded by F.W. Straus, since 1898 had been under the control of his son, S.W. Straus. In 1909 the company originated the idea of real estate bonds used to finance building projects. The company sold industrial bonds while also initiating the underwriting of bond issues on high-grade apartments, office buildings, hotels, and industrial properties. Straus was a pioneer in the development of some of America's most impressive skyscrapers, including the Chrysler Building. The company expanded by founding banks and trust companies, including the Franklin Trust and Savings Bank of Chicago in 1911.[1] Straus had principal offices in Chicago, New York, and San Francisco, and branch offices in fifteen other American cities.

The letter to Clark boasted that the company was contributing 'to the upbuilding of all the principal cities and industrial localities of the country.'[2] Straus was looking 'for a man equipped with a thorough knowledge of the sound scientific principles of economic theory and practice.' Clark was referred to the company by L.C. Marshall, dean of Commerce and Administration and chair of the Department of Political Economy at the University of Chicago.[3] The position being offered involved analyzing the company's business relations to the economic development of the United States. Responsibilities would include recruiting, training, and educating the sales and underwriting organizations in economic principles, particularly those applicable to the real estate business. Clark would also be expected to represent the company at public occasions and to help prepare sales and public literature.[4]

The offer to enter the world of high finance appealed to Clifford Clark. The Straus company was known to him, and the opportunity fitted into his crusade to apply academic economics to the world of practical commerce. Clark was hesitant, however, both to leave academe for the business world and to leave Canada again for the United States.[5] He felt the pull of nationalism. 'I am a Canadian and have a great deal of faith and pride in Canada,' he informed Straus company officials. 'It is a young man's country and young Canadians find here great fields of service and much joy at assisting in the up-building of a new nation.'[6] But Skelton, Mackintosh, and Clark were becoming increasingly discontented with the 'penny-pinching' administration at Queen's and the limited scope of its vision for the university. They were also frustrated by some of the hiring decisions. The commerce courses were not proceeding as Clark had hoped and were 'only loosely related to the general arts curriculum and the wider areas of public policy.' The new programs 'comprised exactly the narrow and technical courses the political economists disdained and the university's limited adoption of reform represented a rejection of the essence of Skelton's aims.'[7] Robert Bryce would later note that 'while Clark as a teacher is said to have found great interest both in his subjects and his students, and must certainly have found the company of Skelton and W.A. Mackintosh wholly congenial, it seems that his enterprising spirit could not find scope at any university.' When an opportunity arose to become one of the first business economists in the United States, he jumped at it.[8]

Clark travelled to Chicago in early November to meet with President S.W. Straus and other company officials. The meeting proved decisive. 'I may say frankly,' Clark wrote, 'that I went to Chicago with my mind pretty well made up that I would not be interested in your proposition. However, the personnel of the organization, and the obvious opportunity that exists for good work in your Company, has turned the tables.'

He requested time to reach a final decision but his mind was made up.[9] A month later Clark wrote the company to negotiate his final contract. He asked to be allowed to finish the semester at Queen's and remain in Kingston until the beginning of February. In addition, Clark explained that his salary as a professor was just under $5,000 per annum but the five summer months were used by academics to add to this amount through research contracts. He indicated that it was possible to earn an additional 50 per cent of his salary during the summer months. As a result, Clark expected a yearly salary in private business of at least $10,000.[10] Straus claimed that the requested salary was more than the company expected to pay at the outset but the terms were agreed to nevertheless.[11] Still, Clark had misgivings, particularly about leaving Skelton. 'I would like you to know how much my association with you and your constant help and example has [*sic*] meant to me,' he wrote. 'I can honestly say that daily association with you as a colleague for 7 or 8 years has not decreased but rather immeasurably increased the affection and admiration you aroused in me as a student, as in all other students. My greatest regret in accepting the Straus offer was not in leaving Canada or Queen's, but in leaving you. My best friends express something of my regard for you when they prophesied that I would not leave Queen's because I could not leave Skelton. Perhaps the statement was so true that I accepted it as a challenge.'[12]

In early February 1923 Clark moved his family to Chicago and he joined the Straus company. The city had a population of 2.9 million, equal to that of the entire province of Ontario at the time. Clark stayed in a north-side residential hotel while looking for a house. Over the next three years, however, the family never really settled in Chicago. Instead, houses were rented in Evanston, Wilmette, and then Evanston again, two of the most upscale neighbourhoods in Chicago. The Clarks spent only part of their first summer in Evanston, returning to Martintown for the wedding of Margaret's sister, Eleanor, at the McPhadden home (Grant's Folly) on 18 July.[13] It became a tradition for the family to try to return for a holiday on the farm every summer.

Clark settled in quickly to his new job, but his work allowed him to keep one foot planted in academe. By late December 1923 he was in Washington to attend the annual meeting of the American Statistical Association to present a paper on the problem of forecasting business activity using statistics. This topic became one that fascinated and perplexed Clark for the rest of his career. By summarizing the information available in a particular market, including population and number of families, population growth, average family size, number of residential units, units demolished or destroyed by fire, vacancy rates, and building permits, it was possible to calculate an apparent deficit or need for housing units as well as the time necessary to complete the required units. The national building industry could then react to these figures. Clark went so far as to argue that if the information was available for a large number of cities, the industry could be predicted and fit into a business cycle. The industry was rebounding in the 1920s after the slump during and immediately following the war. Clark made observations about the way in which it fit into larger economic patterns and noted that building activity generally commenced a decline two to six months before a decline in overall economic activity.[14] The Straus company 'provided Clark with many chances to grapple with specific problems and exercise his talent for balancing a promoter's zeal for what appears to be a constructive, imaginative project against a careful economic and financial analysis.'[15] In the meantime, he also taught some courses at the University of Chicago on money and banking.

Even though Clifford Clark was working in private business in the United States, his university connections kept him informed on Canadian affairs. By the early 1920s, for example, he had become a vocal proponent of a central bank for Canada. When the issue began to be discussed in government circles, Clark took notice. The idea of a central lending institution was discussed by the Canadian government as early as the end of the war. It was rejected by the Union government, however, as inconvenient and dangerous at such an unstable time. After the federal election of 1921, some Labour and Progressive members of Parliament began calling for its creation. By 1923 many farmers faced a drastic fall in prices for their produce. At the same time, they had invested heavily in expanding their operations and were now facing mounting debts. The banks were usually blamed for the restriction of credit and even for the collapsing prices.

During the fall of 1923 Ontario Progressive W.C. Good embarked on a tour through western Canada and the United States in order to interview banking experts. Clark provided Good with a memorandum on the need for a central bank in Canada. When a motion was put forward in Parliament on 2 July 1924 by a group of Progressive MPs seeking permission for the Banking and Commerce Committee to study the issue, Good referred directly to Clark's memorandum: 'Only through a central bank and a central reserve board would it be possible to exert that control over the expansion of credit and over price levels.' Good went on to argue that Canada already possessed the necessary elements to establish a central bank, including rediscounting facilities under the Finance Act, the central gold reserve, the Bankers' Association, an inspection system, the government savings bank, and a 'centralization of financial power in this country.'[16] All that was needed was government notes and a coordinated scheme under the supervision of a board of experts.[17] Good introduced Clark's memorandum anonymously, describing its author as 'a gentleman who is now in the United States. He is connected with one of the large investment banking houses, and is a lecturer at one of the universities in the States. Before leaving Canada, he was professor of banking at one of our universities.'[18]

The motion was defeated with votes coming in opposition from both the Liberal and Conservative parties. In truth, the Canadian government at the time had little interest in a central bank: 'Prime Minister King was not particularly at home in financial matters, and his Ministers of Finance were strongly conservative and unlikely to favour as major an innovation as a central bank.'[19] The banking community in Canada was also opposed to such an innovation. As Owram points out, prior to 1914 it was the banking community that acted 'as the arbiter of economic wisdom and financial planning.' In 1914 the government passed the Finance Act, thereby tying bank deposits either to gold or Dominion notes and easing pressure on the gold standard by effectively suspending it: 'The result was a contradiction in Dominion monetary structures. The system no longer operated automatically, because it was not based purely on gold, yet the government had neither the power nor the expertise properly to manage the monetary system. Over the next few years various amendments only patched up a rather cumbersome and inefficient structure of monetary management.'[20] The debate on a central bank sat moribund for the next decade. When the issue was picked up again, Clifford Clark would play an even more influential role.

On 8 May 1925, the Clark's last child, Kenneth, was born in Evanston. The household was now filled with children, but Clark's penchant for work, indeed his addiction to work, put him in a position where he had little time for relaxing with his family. Such may have been the norm at the time, but Clark's devotion to his work was exceptional. As a result, however, he failed to develop a close bond with his children. The eldest child, George, was particularly affected by this lack of attention. He viewed his father as detached from the household, and most of his childhood memories involve Clark making seemingly unfair decisions that interfered with his happiness, such as thwarting his musical and other creative aspirations because they were impractical. Clark appeared as the distant father figure who entered the domestic scene only as the dominating patriarch.[21] The family's second-youngest child, Peggy, remembered things differently. She was much less harsh on her father for his hectic work schedule: 'Dad was a kid at heart when he had a chance to be. I can remember as a child we would be sitting on the porch ... in Scarsdale, there was a big verandah, Dad would be sitting there, particular with Ken I remember, he would always be pulling nickels and dimes from behind your ears. He enjoyed us when he had the chance. Because when we were older, teenagers, he was too busy. He liked to play tricks and have some fun.'[22]

Clark did develop some new interests while working for the Straus company. The company's work in financing the construction of skyscrapers – the new symbols of modernity – led him to develop an abiding fascination with the topic. Along with a leading member of the management profession, Leo J. Sheridan, Clark wrote an article for *Architectural Forum* on the Straus construction of a new grandiose office building at the corner of Michigan Avenue and Jackson Boulevard.[23] This would be the first but not the last foray he would make into this field.

By 1926 the usually optimistic Clark was worried about the state of the building industry. Much of the problem lay in the fact that the 'abnormal features of the war and early post-war years' made it difficult to forecast economic trends. 'In no other case, however,' Clark argued, 'has this difficulty been so great as in the statistics of the building industry.' He perceived a tremendous increase in speculative building in some sectors, based on the stimulus of easy money, which could prove risky if the cost of borrowing increased. Clark was concerned with what he viewed as 'unsound' building projects that were poorly conceived and constructed, or with poorly chosen locations. In addition, he commented on trends he perceived in housing in general, such as the increasing expectations of the rising middle class in North American society: 'In spite of the progress which has already been made, it is probably safe to say that less than half of the American people are housed today according to standards which they believe they have a right to expect.' At the same time, 'the movement from the rural districts to the cities is a continuing movement, the influence of which cannot be overlooked.' People were moving into the cities but were also flooding into suburban areas: 'Much of the residential building in the larger cities in the last few years is a result of this movement from the congested centers of our cities to the suburbs where the advantages of living in the country can now be secured without sacrifice of many of the conveniences and pleasures of the city.'[24]

Clark's views on the health of the industry, meanwhile, were becoming increasingly out of step with those of the other experts at Straus. Indeed, he felt that this difference of opinion was sufficiently strong that he might not be able to represent the company at the annual Harvard meeting in the fall. 'I am expressing my own personal views,' Clark wrote Professor Charles Bullock of Harvard, 'and they are not fully shared by certain other members of the organization whose judgment of trends in the building industry and in real estate fields I have learned increasingly to respect. It may be that I am altogether too conservative.'[25]

But Clark was doing an impressive job with the company and his stock was rising. By that summer he was requested to move to the head office in New York to advise company President S.W. Straus directly. He accepted the promotion and the family moved and settled in a house in Bronxville. Clark joined the vast flood of commuters pouring into the city every day. One million people lived in Manhattan, south of 59th Street in the mid-1920s, and two million more arrived each day, more than half a million of them by train.[26] Margaret drove Clifford to the train station each morning and returned to retrieve him each evening. While he would eventually learn to drive himself, Clark was never comfortable behind the wheel of an automobile. Family stories recall how he would be constantly turning around while driving in order to speak to someone in the back seat of the car. On other occasions, he would actually request that passengers not speak to him while he was driving, so he could concentrate on the road.[27]

Clark's star continued to rise with Straus. Company executives, most notably S.W. Straus himself, were aware of Clark's astute business sense but also his sound judgment and reliability. Just before Christmas in 1926 Clark received a bonus of $1,000 and he was informed that his salary was being increased from $13,500 to $15,500 per year.[28] The bonuses were offered despite a downturn in the real-estate industry because the company felt that 'the troubles which our industry, as a whole, has experienced are about over, and that after certain readjustments are made, which should come early in 1927, we can all look forward to a prosperous and happy New Year.'[29]

But the portents of danger continued to appear. On 3 September 1926, a competitor of the Straus company, G.L. Miller & Co., went into receivership. The smaller company had failed to meet a deadline to pay one of its investment-banking clients. Miller had little cash but considerable sums of its own real-estate bonds which it hoped to sell to the public but had failed to do so. In fact, the mortgage bonds it had sold were often construction bonds, with no collateral behind them other than the construction site itself. When projects failed, the company did not inform bondholders but rather paid them their interest and principal from the company's own funds. Thus, according to this Ponzi scheme, each new wave of investors paid the preceding group.[30] Straus Vice-President Herbert Martin dismissed any lessons to be learned from the Miller case and argued that the 'more responsible houses,' such as the Straus company, were beyond dispute.[31] Yet Straus was following methods similar to those employed by Miller to fulfil its boastful advertising claim, 'Forty-Three Years without a Loss.' In 1927 the company was prohibited from making such claims after a New York state investigation of the mortgage bond business. The investigation found that defaults on mortgage bonds were in fact common; Straus had at least forty issues, totalling $54 million in default. Yet no one holding Straus bonds was aware of this fact. The company continued to pay the interest to support its advertising claims – a practice it would continue as long as the public kept investing in real estate bonds.[32]

And for the short term at least the public was willing to keep investing. The volume of new real estate bonds issued in 1926 reached almost $1 billion, three times the 1925 total.[33] The Straus headquarters was in the heart of a booming area in a booming city. Along the 1.6 kilometre stretch from 41st to 61st street, ten new office buildings went up during the 1920s, totalling 352 stories and housing 30,000 office workers.[34] The pace of development was frantic: 'Investors large and small jumped on the real estate bandwagon, with developers who were putting up twenty-, thirty-, even forty-storey buildings becoming a dime a dozen.'[35] By 1927, however, there was a surplus of rental space on the market. Experts in the field advised a halt to new construction for six months to a year.[36]

Office-building construction declined by 13 per cent in 1927, but there were still plenty of optimists. The section of 50th Avenue that included the Straus office had two new buildings open in 1926, one in 1927, two in 1928, and three in 1930. In June 1928, when the Chrysler Building was still on the drawing boards, experts advised that there would be no problem renting out the huge building, even with millions of square feet of office space then vacant in other buildings. The Chrysler Building went ahead with Straus financing, and for a time became the tallest building in the world and the first building that was higher than the Eiffel Tower. Other builders also refused to hold back. In the first nine months of 1929, plans were filed for 709 buildings worth $472 million in New York City alone, compared to 760 worth $258 for the same period in 1928. By July 1929 1.5 million square feet of office space was vacant between 34th and 59th streets, totalling 13.3 per cent of all office space. Completion of buildings then under construction would add another 6 million square feet.[37]

It was difficult for Clark to remain cautious amidst the building frenzy. With his new level of pay, he was able to purchase a large, expensive house in the upscale neighbourhood of Scarsdale, at 13 Harcourt Road, even though he found his personal income 'always a little behind expenses.'[38] In August of 1928 S.W. Straus offered shares in the company to employees at $40 each. Clark purchased 300 shares. By January 1929 fifteen new company directors, including Clark, were elected to the board. He became a vice-president of the company in October 1930, as well as a director and treasurer of S.W. Straus Investing Corporation, a newly formed investment trust. The year-end balance sheet for Straus and subsidiary corporations for 1928 showed assets of $78 billion. A statement of earnings listed both sales and profits for the past six years. Sales had peaked in 1925 at $142 million and declined year by year since to $126 million. Profits also peaked in 1925 at $4.4 million but had risen from the two previous years to $3.9 million in 1928.[39]

In March 1927 Clark published an article on the Federal Reserve System in the United States. He lauded the system 'in contrast to the chaos which preceded it,' which had consisted of 'an impossible heterogeneity of banking laws and banking practices with several uncoordinated groups of independent banks offering neither a uniform nor safe nor flexible currency.' But the article allowed Clark to return to one of his most passionate causes: the need for a central banking system. Although he was discussing the situation in the United States, Clark's line of argument would soon be applied to Canada: 'Before 1913 we had not a banking system at all but rather a congeries of thirty thousand banks under thirty thousand managements, independent of each other, uncoordinated by any central agency, with no effective leadership and no effective cooperation with each bank in time of trouble trying "to save its own skin" and therefore making disaster almost inevitable. The result was abnormal credit strain with every seasonal expansion of industry, utter absence of effective control or restraint of credit abuses during periods of boom, and the ushering in of every period of economic depression by a financial panic more or less serious.' The Federal Reserve Act, however, brought coordination of control to the chaotic system. Calls for one central bank based on the European model 'had split on the rock of "un-American centralization of power" in the hands of financial interests.' The United States was unique, Clark argued, and needed more than one central bank.[40]

Despite being out of the country, Clark maintained his contacts at Queen's University, mainly through his friendship with Bill Mackintosh. O.D. Skelton left Queen's for Ottawa in 1925 to become undersecretary of state for external affairs. But Skelton also maintained his ties with Queen's, becoming a member of the board of trustees in 1926.[41] He refused to be considered for principal of Queen's, however, pleading poor health and a desire to build up the Department of External Affairs. Clark wrote the new university chancellor, James Richardson, late in 1929 to urge a renewed effort to convince Skelton to accept the appointment as principal. Skelton's refusal was made more emphatic as a result of Prime Minister Mackenzie King's desire to keep Skelton in the government post.[42]

Clifford Clark might have expressed caution about economic forecasts for Straus and the real-estate industry in general, but he could never have foreseen the full implications of the looming financial disaster. In October 1929 the over-inflated stock market balloon suddenly burst and on 29 October the market crashed. A former Queen's student happened to be in New York on 'Black Tuesday' and visited Clark on that exact day. He found the economist 'on this black day busy checking collateral in his Fifth Avenue office with the Strauss [*sic*] firm. The depression had begun and grim days were ahead.'[43] Yet, in February 1930, Clark's analysis of the construction industry that was published in the *Review of Economic Statistics* was cautiously optimistic. He believed that the 1929 downturn in construction activity might allow the industry to correct excesses that had developed over the previous six or seven years and might leave the industry in a position to 'save us from business collapse.' Easy money and President Hoover's efforts to use public works to encourage private construction, Clark believed, were critical factors: 'For the first time in history we have seen at the very inception of a business recession the prompt mobilization of the business forces of the country in an aggressive campaign designed to minimize incipient unemployment and accelerate the slowing wheels of industry before recession reaches serious proportions. For the first time in history we are seeing a deliberate endeavor made on a far-reaching scale to use the construction industry as the balance wheel of general business.' He argued that a 'complete reversal in business psychology' was already at work, a 'change from the deep gloom so universal during the stock market crash to the general attitude of constructive courage and cautious optimism which prevails at present.'[44]

Clark's prediction proved far too optimistic. It was uncertain whether planned construction would actually take place. Clark hoped that total construction in 1930 would approximate 1929 levels, with an increase as the year progressed to offset a general decline in business activity in other sectors of the economy. Construction in 1930, however, turned out to be 21 per cent lower than in 1929 (and this was already 13 per cent below comparative 1928 levels). It would drop another 31 per cent in 1931, with disastrous effects for the Straus company.[45]

In March 1930 the American Institute of Steel Construction published a book co-authored by Clifford Clark and architect J.L. Kingston titled, *The Skyscraper: A Study in the Economic Height of Modern Office Buildings.* The book was a study of the skyscraper, 'a new and powerful economic idea or force with which is being recreated the framework of the cities which our grandfathers fashioned in an age of horse-drawn vehicles and of small things in population and in commerce.' According to Clark and Kingston, 'With each passing decade it has become more and more a part of the fibre of American civilization, contributing to its efficiency, reflecting its economic conditions, typifying its passion for achievement, furnishing it with an outlet for creative genius in the aesthetic field.' Not surprisingly, the Straus vice-president argued for the benefits of continued skyscraper construction: 'The factors making for diminishing returns of the intensive development of such plots are more than offset by the factors making for increasing returns until a great height is reached, thus establishing the point of maximum economic return or true economic height for such sites at an unexpectedly high level.'[46]

The book was also an exercise in applied economics that analyzed eight alternative architectural designs and engineering plans as well as the influence of size and height upon the details of capital, operating costs, and rentals. This analysis was then reconciled with considerations of municipal problems and public policy.[47] Clark was well aware that his assertions would meet opposition from the traditionalists who viewed the modern office building as an eyesore and an affront to architectural beauty; he knew that his views would be perceived as a defence of big business and the construction industry in particular, with little regard for city planning or the needs of the less affluent. 'We have no quarrel with the idealist, or with the visionary,' the authors claimed, 'but only with the idealist whose ideas are half-baked and with the visionary whose vision is too limited.' Typical of Clark, he supported his arguments on the basis of sound economics rather than ideology. 'This does not mean that city planning and zoning have no place,' he asserted. 'Quite the contrary! It means merely that deliberate planning of city development should be intelligent and based upon sound economic analysis, and it should be flexible rather than arbitrary, that it should regulate rather than block the natural working of economic forces, that it should prevent parasitic development by making each economic activity bear its own fair costs rather than by attempts at arbitrary prohibition.'[48]

It was clear, however, that the purpose of the book was to defend and promote the building industry and the Straus company in particular. According to John Bacher, the book argues that the best indicator of optimal height of a building is maximization of its profitability to its owner. Clark viewed the skyscraper as not only the ultimate symbol of modernity and progress, but also as the most economical form of urban development. Even greater benefits would accrue as large developments covered entire city blocks. He predicted that 'as large development becomes typical, ownership will be in more responsible hands and, therefore, a more scientific determination of development is begun.' Clark, according to Bacher, was advocating the 'self-contained city, accommodating many thousand people, carrying out practically all their activities in a single structure … the most profoundly efficient and adequate conception of gigantic size ever created by man.' He was envisioning 'large-scale corporate ownership of urban land, giant skyscrapers linked to city arterials by special express runways and joined together by elevated sidewalk arcades.' While Bacher is largely correct, he does exaggerate his conclusions that Clark's view was a 'technocratic vision that almost parodies the most lurid nightmares of a dehumanized, mechanistic megapolis.'[49]

Late in 1930 S.W. Straus died. Around the same time Clark was named to U.S. President Herbert Hoover's Advisory Committee on Unemployment. Hoover's committee reported on state efforts to deal with relief costs and worked to prevent the federal government from becoming directly involved.[50] Exactly how long Clark remained a member is unclear, but when an expanded committee was named on 21 August 1931, he was not among them. His work for the U.S. government, however, was not yet complete. In 1931 Clark became a member of a committee of the National Conference on Construction established under the auspices of President Hoover and the secretary of commerce to consider certain problems of the building industry in the United States. He was also one of the cooperating experts in a study of the current business depression by the National Bureau of Economic Research of New York City.[51]

Clark was aware of the devastating effects of the Depression but, as with most of the experts, he could not foresee how long the crisis would last. When asked for investment advice by his brother-in-law, Clark advised against any investment at the present time. He expected corporate earnings to show further declines by 30 June, and stock values would therefore likely decline further as well. Any recovery, he told J.U. MacEwan, would be postponed until the autumn.[52] A month later his pessimism was increasing and he predicted a third winter of unemployment. Regardless, Clark was confident that the capitalist system could be repaired and made efficient enough to meet the twin challenges posed by the Depression and the 'social and economic laboratory' of Russian communism. Even the most conservative businessmen, Clark asserted, were recognizing the need for coordination and control in industry, but this would not lead to socialism, at least not in the near future. The effects of the uncertain atmosphere and the very real questioning of the capitalist system were apparent, however. 'If these measures of control and co-ordination lead to socialism,' Clark noted, 'it is so very far off that it doesn't really matter. Even if eventually we evolve toward socialism, the change will be so gradual that we won't realize it, and we will find that socialism fits us like a glove.' In order to deal with the Depression Clark called for greater coordination and control of the economy, especially when it came to banking. He also suggested such remedial measures as a national employment exchange service, intensive statistical research, unemployment insurance, and a review of the European reparation repayment situation.[53]

Clark's health began to reflect the pressures he was under. He suffered from an osteoarthritis attack that left him with chronic back pain for the remainder of his life.[54] On 30 March 1931, Clark underwent a back operation and he spent the next six months recovering. Unfortunately, the operation did not help the situation and seems to have only increased his pain. Clark's health forced a prolonged absence from work and, in the tense and stressful economic setting, his ability to maintain his position came into question.[55] The Straus company had voluntarily placed its New York operation under the supervision of the New York Building Department, and as a result its books were scrutinized by bank examiners, just as if it were a bank. But the company's troubles were only just beginning. In March some of Straus's bond issues went into default and, without a recovery in construction activity, the company could not rebound. Another Straus vice-president informed Clark that 'the defaults have not stopped, and if business does not pick up they are not likely to stop for some time to come.'[56]

Years later Clark argued that he often warned the company about the dangerous trends toward overbuilding in the leading American cities, particularly when it came to large apartment houses, apartment hotels, and office buildings. The industry witnessed recurrent cycles of boom and bust. According to Clark, he recommended that the company diversify its highly specialized business in order to be in a position to meet an inevitable recession. But S.W. Straus was a highly dynamic and forceful individualist who had built up his business to world prominence on the basis of his own initiative and judgment. He possessed a profound faith in the soundness of real estate and the seemingly unending expansion of the American city. He had weathered all previous depressions purportedly without allowing a single investor to lose a dollar and he was confident that he could bring his business safely through any difficult period. The result was that when the most severe of depressions hit, and the real estate values in New York and other leading cities declined 'with catastrophic violence,' the company did not react sufficiently to ensure or even enable its own survival. The New York operation went into liquidation in December 1932.[57]

By April 1931 Clark recognized that there was no future with Straus and he began talking with Bill Mackintosh (who was now head of the department at Queen's) about returning to academe. Mackintosh moved quickly to ensure that if Clark was indeed returning to academic life, it would be to Kingston and Queen's. Within a week he was offered his old position as chair of the commerce department at the maximum salary possible, $5,000 per annum. It would be a very significant drop in salary from Straus but it was still a good wage.[58] If Clark accepted, Mackintosh agreed to relinquish his position as head of the commerce courses but he would remain head of the Department of Political and Economic Science. Mackintosh was excited by the prospect of Clark's return. ‘It would raise us,’ he crowed, ‘without any question to the first position in Canada.’ Mackintosh also believed that with Clark on faculty, commerce would likely become a faculty or separate school on its own.[59] By 29 April Mackintosh had discussed arrangements to fit Clark into the commerce staff, including specific courses he would teach. There would be no shortage of opportunities for Clark to supplement his university income with external work; the challenge would be in getting academic work done. Mackintosh was a bit worried that after Clark’s stint as an American financier, his ambition would be difficult to check: ‘I suppose the greatest danger is that you should feel that things you are dealing with here were small and less important than the matters you are handling in New York.’[60]

But Clark’s reputation now preceded itself and Queen’s was not the only university interested. Faculty at both Harvard and the University of Pennsylvania showed interest in obtaining Clark for their economics departments, but full positions could not be opened.[61] From the Department of External Affairs in Ottawa, Skelton was also monitoring Clark’s employment opportunities. He provided Conservative Prime Minister R.B. Bennett with a memo outlining Clark’s career and suggested that he be hired, either to fill the vacant post of deputy minister of finance or into one of three positions on the Tariff Advisory Board. However, Bennett made no offers.[62] Skelton had always believed that Clark’s future lay in Canada and that it would likely be in a position other than university professor. Clark’s old Harvard mentor, Frank Taussig, was wisely prophetic: ‘It seems to me more than likely that a post having wider possibilities will be open to you at no distant date.’[63]

In late July Clark accepted the offer put forward by Queen’s and he returned the family to Kingston. But he could not escape the state of his personal finances, which collapsed along with those of Straus. His 300 shares in the company that were once valued at $12,000 were now virtually worthless. The upscale Scarsdale house proved impossible to sell in the Depression conditions and soon became an albatross around Clark’s neck that plagued him for the rest of his life. He would never fully recover financially from this loss. In May the Clarks took out a second mortgage on the property for $10,000, in addition to the first mortgage of $26,000. Payments of $150 per month were to be made on the second mortgage until 16 October 1933, when the balance was to be repaid in full. Margaret and Clifford also signed a bond to back the second mortgage. By mid-August, the house was leased for $350 a month for thirteen months. This rent, however, did not even cover the mortgage payments, let alone the taxes. The Clark family settled into rental premises at 148 University Avenue in Kingston.[64]

Queen's university welcomed Clark back and by September 1931 he had returned to the classroom. He was still on crutches as a result of what was proving to be a slow recovery from his back operation. 'For the last six or seven months, following an operation,' he wrote, 'I have had to keep away from work of any kind, and it was with some trepidation that I approached my university work this fall.' A few days later he was feeling more optimistic: 'I have shown steady improvement in recent weeks and I hope that it will not be long before I shall be restored to complete health.'[65] The prediction proved too optimistic. Despite a light teaching load to allow Clark time to get 're-acclimatized,'[66] he pressed ahead with his work and travel, and this set back his recovery. During the ensuing months, Clark often complained of serious bouts of pain and he was forced to cancel several speaking engagements.[67]

Clark found the most significant change since he had last taught at Queen's in the quality of his colleagues. He was part of an impressive group of academics who were more than willing to discuss public affairs, including the likes of Bill Mackintosh, Norman Rogers, Frank Knox, Clifford Curtis, and R.G.H. Smails. While Mackintosh and Smails were on staff when Clark left Queen's, Knox was hired in 1924, Curtis in 1927, and Rogers in 1929. Even though Skelton was in Ottawa, he was accessible, and contact was regular.[68] The course structure at Queen's had not changed much, meanwhile, although degree standards were more rigorous. Overall enrolment at Queen's had actually declined from 2,100 in 1922 to 1,700 in 1930. Despite considerable building additions to the campus, grants from the provincial government and income from endowments were both falling and the university was operating under increasingly tight financial restrictions.[69]

With the world wracked by the Depression, it was an interesting and busy time to be an economist. When pondering what textbook to use for his finance courses, one friend of Clark's observed that 'certainly there is enough happening these days to give you an opportunity to give a course in economics with the daily newspaper as a source book.'[70] According to Mackintosh, Clark recovered his vigour and 'was soon engaged in discussions which were going on concerning the shattering events that were falling upon the world of that day.' That world was 'patently out of joint,' Bryce claimed. 'Here was something to baffle any economist and for which neither his pre-war teachings nor his intensive work with Straus had prepared him. Yet he plunged into with zest and soon had ideas as to what should be done.'[71]

When Clark and his colleagues looked at the economic situation in 1931, there was little reason for optimism. 'I get occasional letters from my economist friends in New York and also some in London,' Clark wrote. 'They are all exceedingly bearish. Personally I have for months been unable to see anything at all that would warrant optimism, and I am still in this unfortunate position.'[72] His gloom deepened with the British decision on 21 September to take the pound off the gold standard – a decision that 'marked the end of an epoch in the financial history of the world.'[73] While many nations, including Canada, abandoned the gold standard during the First World War, Britain had resumed the system in 1925. Proponents claimed that the gold standard had two main virtues. First, it made changes in the money supply automatic because it would expand or contract, depending on the growth of gold reserves. This fact prevented authorities from arbitrarily printing money and causing inflation. Second, it provided for stability of exchange rates, thus encouraging trade, because exporters did not have to worry about profits from sales abroad being wiped out by decreases in the value of the currency in which they were paid.

In an article published that fall in *Queen's Quarterly*, Clark examined the causes and destabilizing effects of the British decision to resurrect the gold standard. Britain surrendered its central role in the gold standard system, Clark argued, only under extreme pressure. The value of the pound was fixed at its pre-war level when Britain restored the system in 1925, but this level was too high. France, on the other hand, restored the franc at one-fifth the pre-war value. Refusing to devalue and face the advantage given to French producers in world markets, Britain found that its pound came under increasing pressure. To keep attracting money, the Bank of England maintained a very high interest rate that further injured exporters and damaged the domestic economy. It did encourage a large volume of short-term investment that could be and was suddenly withdrawn in the summer of 1931. In May, there was a run on the leading bank in Austria that, as Clark argued, 'set off a powder-train which in turn created explosions in one important country after another, precipitating a breakdown in international confidence and a run on most of the leading money markets of the world.'[74] British assets were frozen in foreign banks, and concern with the stability of British banks led to a rush to withdraw funds. By 21 September, after a billion dollars had been withdrawn from London in two months, Britain suspended its commitment to sell gold at a fixed price, and the value of the pound fell quickly.

The most serious impact of Britain's decision to abandon the gold standard, Clark claimed, was 'the tremendous shock to confidence caused by the event not only in the pound and in England's financial stability but also in the soundness financially of all institutions and countries throughout the world.'[75] Most of the world's exchanges were closed, and prices tumbled to new lows. With private and central bank funds tied up in London, there was an immediate tightening of credit in other domestic markets, further depressing economies. More than $721 million in gold was withdrawn from or tied up in American banks in the month after Britain's decision. Worried Americans began withdrawing their funds from U.S. banks and hoarding the currency, making the situation even worse.

Canada reacted to these events on 21 October by announcing that exports of gold were prohibited except under licence from the finance minister or a chartered bank. According to Clark, this move was 'tantamount to suspension of the gold standard.' The dollar was then at a discount of between 8 and 15 per cent in New York – a situation that Clark claimed was unwarranted on the basis of the country's balance of payments. The dollar was further depressed, he argued, by speculation, pressure on American branch plants to remit funds, and doubts as to the ability of Canadian authorities to manage the situation:

> In view of all the circumstances, the decision to prohibit gold exports is probably a sound one. The depreciation of the Canadian dollar will aid our export industries in their attempt to climb the tariff walls of the United States and other gold standard countries, though our prompt application of the dumping duties against countries with a depreciated paper currency looks too much like an attempt to keep our cake and eat it. We would be in a sounder position, however, if we had central banking machinery properly equipped and definitely responsible for the exercise of credit control in an emergency of this character instead of the present anomalous condition of divided responsibility as between the banks and the government and lack of special equipment or traditions in the Department of Finance.[76]

In a private letter Clark was more critical of the government's handling of the situation, referring to 'the comic opera management of our currency situation.'[77]

Clark's public declaration in support of a central bank coincided with a similar decision reached near the same time by Prime Minister Bennett. When the value of the Canadian dollar fell, Bennett sent a representative of the Bank of Montreal to the United States to sound out the prospects of a loan, first from private sources, and when that proved unlikely, from the Federal Reserve. The Federal Reserve, however, would only lend to foreign central banks.[78] Bennett later claimed that it was this experience in the fall of 1931 that convinced him of the need for a Canadian central bank. The British bankers, meanwhile, were pushing Canada in this direction and the prime minister also felt that pressure.[79] He suggested the creation of a central lending institution to the Canadian Bankers Association on 24 October while discussing government debt issues. The bankers, however, were less than encouraging.[80] They supported the Finance Act because it left decisions on monetary and credit matters to themselves. A central bank would serve as competition when it came to their long-standing privilege of note issue. Most importantly, however, they feared that a central bank would become a political organ of the government.[81]

Prime Minister Bennett received two memoranda offering advice on handling the situation. One came from Watson Sellar, assistant deputy minister of finance, and the other came from Skelton. Both urged the creation of a central bank to deal with the international crisis.[82] Advice to the prime minister also came from outside the civil service, notably from Professor T.E. Gregory of the London School of Economics and S.R. Noble, assistant general manager of the Royal Bank of Canada. Both advised legislative restrictions on gold exports, centralizing all gold reserves under government control, and deliberate exchange management at a devaluation of up to 20 per cent. Sellar and Skelton rejected this advice, as did Bennett.[83]

But the situation did convince the prime minister that the finance department did not have the necessary expertise to advise government adequately. Indeed, Bennett was coming to the conclusion that the bureaucrats in the department had long been lacking the necessary expertise.[84] And this liability was noticed in the House of Commons. 'What has impressed me very much since I have been here,' W.C. Good told the House as early as 1925, 'is the conspicuous difference between the organization in the Department of Finance and the organization of some of the other departments. Take, for instance, the Department of Agriculture, where those in charge of the different branches are specialists in the respective fields. We admit the need of securing the services of experts in these several departments. But in the Department of Finance we have, so far as I can find out, no man who has any general knowledge of economics, who has given any special study to the questions that ought to be well known and thoroughly considered in that department.'

Good was particularly critical of former deputy minister J.C. Saunders, who served in the position from 1920 until 1930. From appearances before parliamentary committees, as well as through private conversations, Good concluded that Saunders was 'totally unqualified to advise in regard to the many matters which must come before that department.'[85] Yet the situation only worsened. In 1929 the assistant deputy minister, G.W. Hyndman, was convicted of stealing bonds and defrauding the department, and was sentenced to seven years in prison. In April 1930 Saunders died and the position remained vacant for two and a half years. The department was run by a five-man committee during the crucial time of dealing with the full impact of the Depression. To make matters worse, instability in the finance department went beyond the civil service. Liberal Finance Minister J.A. Robb had died in November 1929 and was replaced by Charles Dunning. An election in 1930 brought the Conservatives to power and Bennett was his own finance minister until February 1932, when he appointed Edgar Rhodes. The Department of Finance was in 'disarray.'[86]

Because the prime minister also served as the finance minister, he felt the lack of adequate guidance acutely. Months earlier, Bennett updated government accounting procedures and the government's ability to monitor spending, but the work convinced him that he needed a deputy minister with experience in banking and exchange.[87] Minister of Trade and Commerce H.H. Stevens had suggested appointing an economic advisory council under the chairmanship of Skelton, who would then cooperate with representatives from labour, industry, and the universities in studying problems such as unemployment. Apparently, Bennett's reply at the time was notably dismissive: 'Why talk such nonsense? Do you think I want a lot of long-haired professors telling me what to do? If I can't run this country, I will get out.'[88]

Although he was convinced that Canada needed a central bank, Clifford Clark believed that only an international solution would provide a way out of the current crisis. He was critical of the trend toward protectionism. The events of the previous five months provided 'a convincing demonstration of the absolute economic interdependence of the Western world.' Clark called for an international conference of central bank governors, prominent businessmen, and finance ministers of the leading nations. Immediate action was required to better distribute the world's gold stock, to stabilize the pound, and to achieve international price stability:

> Either the gold standard must be saved and modified to meet present world conditions or a suitable substitute must be devised. The policy of separate national gold reserves and independent gold policies has broken down under the terrific task of post-war readjustment. This does not necessarily mean that the gold standard is impracticable. It may mean merely that the world has been trying to operate it under an impossible set of conditions – reparations, war debts, high tariffs, rigid wage and production costs, political discord and national jealousies. It may mean that these conditions, chiefly the political results of a stubborn nationalism, cannot be reconciled with the economic forces which tend to make the world one, and that they must be radically changed if we are to retain the benefits of economic specialization, mutual exchange of products, and a common monetary standard.[89]

Despite returning to Canada and Queen's, Clark still had a significant backlog of work from the United States to clear up. He was asked in June by the Trades and Industry Section of the Social Science Research Council in New York to submit his ideas for possible research work on the economics of the construction industry. In October he was informed that the newly organized Falk Foundation in Pittsburgh had been impressed by the research program the council put together and had decided to support economic research. Clark was asked to develop some of the ideas he had presented, including specific recommendations on how some of them might be scientifically researched.[90] While Clark turned down other projects, he did accept invitations to speak at Harvard to the Economic Society's annual convention in November and in Washington to the American Statistical Association at the end of December.[91] He also remained in close contact with financial events in the United States through people at Straus as well as academic colleagues. In particular, he maintained contact with Harry Herwitz of Paine Webber and Co. in New York. Clark contributed $1,200 toward a margin trading account in June, which Herwitz invested and actively traded. Whether this project made money is unknown, but his frequent reports on the progress of the account were used by Clark to gain news about Wall Street.[92]

Clark also carried out responsibilities he had undertaken on behalf of the National Bureau of Economic Research Inc. in New York. The bureau was founded in 1920 with a mandate to prepare reports on topics of national importance, in the hope that public debate would be increasingly based on knowledge rather than opinion. Its research directors were Edwin Gay, who as a Harvard economics professor had been a member of Clark's doctoral examination board, and Wesley C. Mitchell, whose work on business cycles had formed the basis for Clark's paper on the Canadian recession of 1920–1. The bureau produced a report, *Recent Economic Changes in the United States*, commissioned in January 1928 by a committee headed by Herbert Hoover. Clark was one of a number of collaborating experts on a major bureau follow-up study to be published in early 1932.[93] He travelled to New York on 10–11 October to meet with those involved in the new National Bureau report and discuss draft chapters.[94]

Clark's back, however, was acting up, causing him considerable pain and discomfort: 'They kept us in sessions all day Saturday and Sunday and ... during the evenings I had to retire to the couch.'[95] The severity of the medical problem was enough to keep Clark from carrying out his responsibilities: 'Apparently my New York trip was too much for me,' he informed his colleagues several weeks later, 'either because of that or some unfortunate juncture of Canadian weather and my sacro-iliac joints has made it impossible for me to carry out until to-day the promise to drop back to you a report on the initial draft of "Economic Changes, 1929–1931" ... I regret more keenly than words can express the fact that I have not been able to give any real help to your Committee on this work.'[96]

In the seven pages of comments on the bureau's draft texts, Clark urged greater emphasis upon what he viewed as the role of two key industries: automobile manufacturing and building construction. He argued that overproduction was a critical factor in the general economic decline. Clark also argued for more emphasis to be placed upon what he termed 'the psychological factor': 'I miss the proper weighing of the psychological factor, and an analysis of the cumulative aspect of the forces at work in the depression. I think the last two years can be broken up into a series of rather definite phases, each one leading to the following one, with the forces at work acquiring cumulative momentum as a time elapses. Certainly, in the latest phase of the depression the psychological factor has been tremendously important – we have been living since May in a world of panic of proportions unprecedented, and to some extent of unprecedented character.'[97] Nothing Clark was reading or hearing lifted his sense of gloom about the economy. 'I had some fear that I might be thrown out of the Department, or even the country,' he noted sarcastically, 'for unmitigated bearishness. I am wondering how the race between confidence and catastrophe is coming along.'[98]

If news on the Depression was gloomy, reports coming from Clark's old employer were even more pessimistic. Straus Vice-President Roy Amott informed Clark that general business conditions were showing no signs of improvement while the company continued to grapple with its 'default experience.' He now agreed with Clark that 'a complete revamping of our business was going to be necessary.'[99] In November 1931, Amott suggested the company hire Clark from time to time to provide advice on investments and reorganization plans. Regardless, company officials were already writing Clark to ask for advice on a variety of issues and they indicated a preference to pay for the advice. Amott did note, however, that he was 'afraid that Cliff's health is still so bad that he won't want to assume any such responsibilities for the present.' Clark rejected a fee, indicating that he was uncomfortable determining a suitable compensation and that he did not want to feel compelled to take on additional work. It is also likely that he did not wish any further official association with the floundering company. He was willing, however, to offer informal advice. On the day of Clark's reply, a general plan for reorganization of real estate properties financed by Straus, upon which bonds were in default, was announced by bondholder committees organized by the bankers.[100] In February, Clark journeyed to New York and spent a day with Straus officers going over a proposed portfolio of investments, which he followed up with further advice in early March.[101]

The real-estate and construction industries were in severe difficulty and the troubles were just reaching their lowest point. Clark again emphasized the importance of the public mood on the state of the economy. Only when employment and incomes ceased to decline, he claimed, would consumers once again be inclined to spend and make long-term commitments. 'Only when the processes of deflation have been reversed,' he wrote, 'when at least a proportion of frozen credits have been liquefied, and when confidence has been restored in the general soundness of the country's financial structure, will the financial institutions be able and willing to finance such long-term commitments.' There was clearly a credit crisis. The volume of construction activity in the United States had fallen every year since 1928 and the figures for 1931 had fallen 53 per cent in a span of three years. The monthly indexes were the lowest since 1919. Even the government stimulus to public works and utilities was largely spent. Urban municipalities were staggering under the pressure of increasing debt and taxation burdens. Clark pointed out that only the federal and state governments were now in a position to make ready use of further borrowing or higher taxation in order to raise funds for public works designed to relieve the burden of unemployment. Yet even these governments now had to face the difficulties of unbalanced budgets and abnormal conditions in the financial markets: 'It is apparent, therefore, that from now on stimulation of the construction industry through the public works respirator will meet almost insuperable obstacles, and that for some time this branch of construction is likely to show a decline. Probably a sharp decline, for if there is one thing clearer than any other in civic finance today, it is that all governmental bodies must now "cut their coat according to their cloth" – must adjust expenditure to a revenue which a much harassed citizenry is able and willing to pay.'[102]

One of the few notes of optimism was that construction costs for materials and labour had also declined. Clark described the general situation facing real-estate finance but it was clear that his analysis and lessons for the industry were taken directly from his experience with Straus: 'Partly as a result of unsound lending practices, and partly as a result of the drastic deflation in real estate values – which in turn is due to over-building, the general business depression and the serious decline in the general level of commodity prices – a condition has recently prevailed in the real estate securities market, the importance of which can scarcely be exaggerated.'

Rents were falling, new buildings were not filling up, vacancies in old and new buildings were increasing, tenants were failing to pay rent, and builders were left with new homes unoccupied. As a result, building owners were unable to pay all or part of their fixed charges on mortgages outstanding. Banking institutions, mortgage companies, insurance companies, and building and loan institutions had vast amounts tied up in frozen mortgage credits. This led to numerous bank and building, and loan association failures. It also led to defaults in institutional portfolio mortgages as well as real-estate bond issues held by the public. Foreclosures were numerous and equities of huge amounts in the aggregate were wiped out. New real-estate bond issues, as with most other corporate securities, had become impossible to market. 'These conditions of distress and chaos in the real estate securities market,' Clark noted, 'have had a powerful effect, of course, in deterring new commitments by builders or prospective home-owners and the lending of available funds even on sound new projects or the extension of old loans by institutions or individuals in a position to lend. They have also served to intensify the current crisis of confidence and consequently to aggravate the business depression. This intensification of business depression serves to increase the amount of unemployment, the fear of future unemployment and consequent unwillingness to make future commitments, the continuous deflation of real estate values, and the resulting financial embarrassments. In such a vicious circle, events have run their round in the last year or so.' While it seemed to Clark that the crisis had reached 'rock bottom' in 1932, 'the psychological and political hazards inherent in the domestic situation or arising out of possible repercussions from untoward developments in Europe are still too important to enable one to speak of the future with anything but great caution.'[103]

Clark broadened his analysis of the Depression on 23 November 1931, when he addressed the annual luncheon of the Professional Institute of the Civil Service of Canada at the Chateau Laurier in Ottawa. The address attracted a crowd of over four hundred people. The speech titled 'What's Wrong with Us?' was broadcast over radio and reprinted in the institute bulletin. It offered a diagnosis of the world economic state with suggestions for remedy.[104] The situation was bad but there was certainly no crisis in capitalism, as far as Clifford Clark was concerned. The economic 'machine' was in trouble but not beyond repair: 'The engine needs to be overhauled, the battery recharged, the tires renewed, nuts tightened and moving parts relubricated. The brakes need relining and a more powerful system of headlights needs to be installed if we are to drive again at the pace of 1929.' But the problems lay as much with the driver as with the machine. Clark was critical of those in government as well as in the civil service: 'Back seat driving must be eliminated and more responsible, more intelligent direction at the wheel is required. With such a thorough overhauling and such improvement in control, it will probably be found that the "old bus" is still without an equal, still superior to the old competitive model which has yet appeared, and still capable of carrying us at record speed on to new peaks of prosperity. This, of course, is a diagnosis for long term recovery and not a forecast of what may happen immediately.'[105]

Clark noted four critical aspects to what he called 'a depression unparalleled in its severity.' First, it was more of an international crisis than any previously experienced and it could, therefore, be solved only through international efforts. Second, much of the cause was a persistent and calamitous decline in the general level of wholesale prices. Clark returned to the gold standard issue to place much of the blame for the serious dislocation in business relationships. If prices were going to remain at approximately two-thirds their previous levels, then wages, salaries, and taxes would have to come down to the same levels before an 'increase in efficiency' could occur.[106] The third serious feature of the Depression was the declining activity and prices in agriculture, brought on largely by the growth in food supply through increases in the amount of arable land and application of scientific methods and new technologies to farming. The extensive barriers to international trade then in place affected agricultural products more than manufactured goods because the former were likely to be traded abroad. The fourth critical aspect was the crisis in banking and credit, caused by 'the reparations and allied debt agreements which were the heritage of the war; to the stupendous totals of debt, private and public, which were built up in the years prior to 1929 when rising trends seemed to be immutable laws of nature; to the replacement of England by the United States as the world's lending nation with all the evils of inefficiency, inconsistency and timidity which are inevitable in amateurish lending; to the weaknesses of the gold exchange standard and the other modifications introduced in the normal working of the international monetary standard; and to the sins of economic nationalism committed chiefly by the great new creditor nations of the world which failed to realize that one cannot eat one's cake and have it too.'[107]

Clark called for international 'statesmanship of a higher order.' France had to recognize that Germany had been brought close to the economic breaking point through heavy war reparations: 'Both France and the world have everything to lose and nothing to gain by forcing Germany once more into financial and political chaos.' Again, he urged joint action in the form of an international conference of the world's central bankers, finance ministers, and prominent business leaders to stabilize currencies, especially the British pound, and to break 'the vicious circle of deflation.'[108]

In a speech to the Empire Club of Canada in Toronto on 10 December, Clark offered much of the same analysis. This time, however, he developed in more detail his prescription for Canada's problems.

Beyond agriculture, he noted, the country's most serious problems lay in the burden of debt accumulated by municipalities and provinces. Many of these debts were financed abroad and, with the Canadian dollar depreciated, 'these commitments will in many cases prove burdensome, if not intolerable to many taxpayers already beset with numerous other ills.' He called for thrift and praised the federal government's timely conversion of war loans. Clark also recognized the importance of solving the railway problem, which dated back to the war and pre-war years, 'but which has been aggravated by a decade of wasteful competition between our two great transportation systems, resulting in needless duplication of facilities and ridiculously lavish standards of service.'[109]

If Clark was looking for international responses to the Depression, he was pleased with the situation in Britain. In July 1931 the *Macmillian Report* was released. The Committee on Finance and Industry, chaired by Lord Macmillian, was established in 1929. Its report recommended that Britain's exchange rate be maintained. The report also drew attention to the fact that Britain's balance of payments with the rest of the world was kept in balance, not by export of manufactured goods, but by 'invisible' items such as banking, shipping, and the interest on foreign investments, all hit hard by the Depression. In a minority report, committee members John Maynard Keynes and Reginald McKenna added tariffs and import restrictions to the main recommendations.[110] Clark analyzed the report in December, calling it 'an exceedingly able piece of work.' He was hopeful that international experts would get together to solve the problems that 'threatened to wreck a storm-ridden world.' He also voiced his belief in free trade, referring to 'those of us who believe that geographical specialization is a necessary condition of optimum world prosperity.'[111]

By the end of 1931 it was apparent that W.C. Clark was viewed as a prominent, if not the most prominent, economist in Canada. His reputation also extended into the highest circles within the United States. One investment banker told Clark that his analyses of the Depression were being quoted so widely by financial executives that he ought to exact a fee. Clark responded, partially with tongue in cheek, that he could certainly use the money.[112] Yet while his public speaking engagements were building an impressive profile, Clark was always aware of his limitations when it came to playing the role of orator or politician. 'I give most of my talks under compulsion,' he wrote, 'not from any love of talking. I am also a terrible speaker, regardless of anything that you may have heard. On some of these current business topics I do feel very strongly, and an evangelical fervour may get me by sometimes, but that is all.'[113]

Clark's reputation was also reaching government circles. In early February 1932 the economics professor met J.C. Macfarlane in Toronto, an old friend as well as a solicitor for General Electric. While there, he chatted with W.S. Campbell, manager of General Electric's transportation and customs department. Campbell was sufficiently impressed with Clark and felt he should be hired by the federal government. Campbell wrote the manager of the Canadian Manufacturers' Association, 'It appears to me that Prof. Clark's experience is exactly what the Government is looking for at the present time, and there need be no hesitation in recommending him ... to the right party in Ottawa who is interested in obtaining men of experience to help prepare the necessary data for use at the forth-coming Conference.' The conference being alluded to was the Imperial Conference planned for Ottawa that summer.[114] And it was in this context that Clifford Clark had his first contact with Prime Minister R.B. Bennett at the end of March. The economist sent the prime minister a memo dealing with currency problems. Clark noted, 'It is obvious that it would be somewhat easier to work if we had a central bank' and explained the negative impact of tying the Canadian dollar to the British pound.[115]

Meanwhile, Clark continued to speak publicly about the Depression. He was now calling the crisis 'unprecedented' in that it was a global phenomenon 'from which no industry and no community, even in the remotest corner of the globe, has escaped.' The reasons for its massive scope were due 'to the simple fact that the world to-day, as never before, is economically one world. All the nations are inescapably interlocked, interwoven with each other.' Clark placed increasing importance on the 'crisis of confidence' that he viewed as an important development, particularly in the past year. 'This spread of paralysing fear,' he noted, 'this loss of confidence in all financial institutions, was a world-wide phenomenon but it reached its most extreme manifestation in the United States during the past winter.' But Clark's characteristic optimism was returning. He was convinced that governmental budgets could and should be balanced. The past two months in the United States had seen 'a co-ordinated program of emergency legislation, perhaps the most spectacular ever adopted by any nation in peace time.' This program included the Reconstruction Finance Corporation, which could use federal government credit to save collapsing financial institutions, as well as the Glass-Steagall Bill, which allowed the credit facilities of the

Federal Reserve System to be made available to failing banks while also releasing about $1 billion in gold previously held by the reserve as collateral against Federal Reserve notes. In addition the Federal Reserve had adopted a controlled expansion of credit. Clark was critical of Congress's failure to balance the budget by passing a suitable tax bill. Progress also seemed to be occurring in Britain. Clark applauded British efforts to cut governmental expenditures while tolerating heavier tax burdens in order to balance the budget. The result was a renewed belief in Britain's ability to provide international financial leadership, which Clark believed was essential.

When it came to Canada's handling of the Depression, Clark was surprisingly generous with his praise. 'Governments – Dominion, provincial, and municipal – ,' he claimed, 'are undertaking to balance their budgets and some, particularly the Western provinces, deserve to be congratulated upon the heroic efforts they have made under the most difficult conditions.' There was still a need to eliminate waste and to reduce expenses, rather than simply increase taxation. The burdens of reduced wages and purchasing power, Clark indicated, were being borne without the panic shown in the United States: 'For this we have to thank the financial strength and general soundness of our great financial institutions.' There was good reason to praise the chartered banks in the first few years of the Depression. Canadian dollar depreciation in both the U.S. dollar and pound sterling, for example, had been negligible until the autumn of 1931. In comparison with the situations facing the banks in other countries, Canada was in an exemplary position.[116] Only when it came to the prospects for solutions to the European crisis was Clark glum. He hoped the upcoming Lausanne Conference would agree on a substantial reduction of German reparation payments and then, after the American elections, a proportionate reduction in allied debt payments to the United States: 'Certainly this much at least would seem to be necessary if a sound basis is to be laid for the return of permanent prosperity.'[117]

Although his arguments were tainted with nationalism, Clark explained that by 1932 there was more reason for optimism in Canada than in the United States: 'We have our little problems up here such for instance as a railway system far in excess of our needs, operated in recent years with the lavish tastes of a Sir Henry Thornton, and absorbing funds at a rate of a million dollars a day or more; a heavy national, provincial and municipal debt, multiplied many times since 1913 and much of it payable in your confounded dollar; and an agricultural problem which is not unlike that of other agricultural countries.' But Canada's financial structure was 'still substantially impaired by the ravages of the last few years.' While the nation's industrial structure was more 'artificial' than the American in some respects, Canada had functioned 'much more normally' than its 'crippled financial partner.' As a result of this healthier financial structure, 'business and public sentiment has been immeasurably sounder, more poised, more objective.' Clark went so far as to suggest that 'we have up here a little better understanding of world problems and the way they impinge on our own situation.' He was also critical of the American political system, even if his analysis of the Canadian system was damning in its praise: 'Still another thing is to be counted in our favour: We have a political system that works – even though at the present time it is run by a Mussolini – but one with great courage, tremendous industry, and much ability – also of considerable capacity to make mistakes because of snap judgments but to correct the mistakes shortly afterwards. I am inclined to place more importance on this political factor than I used to, because I visited your Capital City during the Christmas week and I came home completely disillusioned.'[118]

Two days later, on 15 April 1932, Clark was hired to work for that 'Mussolini,' in preparation for the upcoming Imperial Economic Conference.

3

Civil Servant, 1932–1935

> I well remember Mr Bennett phoning me early one morning, asking, 'What can you tell me about this Queen's man of yours, this Dr Clark? I know he's a Grit but I want him here.' 'Cliff' Clark did not go under any discount in my reply. Mr Bennett added – it was just after the Imperial Economic Conference – 'I want him. He stood out head and shoulders above any but the tops of the U.K. delegation here. He's one of the few men in the country who think and talk their language.'
>
> – Charlotte Whitton, October 1959

In the summer of 1932 O.D. Skelton, as undersecretary of state for external affairs, was assigned the task of organizing the work of the Imperial Economic Conference in Ottawa. Since the inception of the imperial conferences in the aftermath of the Great War, there had never been a full-scale gathering held outside London. Nine delegations were now set to arrive from Britain, and the dominions and colonies of Canada, Australia, New Zealand, South Africa, Ireland, India, Southern Rhodesia, and Newfoundland. The delegations numbered 280 people, including advisers and support staff, to which were added some two hundred representatives of business and industry, and 190 journalists. The Canadian government had to both prepare the agenda and develop its own position on the issues to be discussed.[1]

Skelton compiled a list of fifty-two briefs to be prepared. Most dealt with trade issues and were drafted by government officials, but the monetary questions, including the stabilization of currency values, were of pressing importance to the Canadian prime minister. On 25 February Parliament passed a resolution that monetary issues be placed on the conference agenda.[2] There was no one in the public service competent to brief ministers on such issues, so Skelton again recommended Clark to Bennett. The prime minister approved the recommendation and on 15 April Clark was commissioned to prepare a memorandum on monetary reconstruction.[3] The professor was pleased with the opportunity and excited by the challenge of the work: 'For me the last month has been absolutely wasted in the reading of student essays and the correction of examination papers.'[4]

Clark was not content unless he was working. While he enjoyed a few leisurely pursuits and spending time with his family, he was always more comfortable at his desk: 'We have joined the Golf Club and I intend to try it out anyway. Margaret has been playing ten shots to a hole, nine holes to a round about fourteen times a day and already has recovered most of the money which the family paid out in annual dues, initiation fee, etc. I shall, of course, be much more temperate, and confine myself to a round or two a week if, indeed, my sacro iliacs do not interfere altogether too much with my well-known swing.' Despite his obvious lack of skill, a week later Clark was pleased that he was able to spend a bit more time on the Cataraqui Golf Course (within a mile and a half of his house in Kingston). He noted that he was spending part of every second day 'cutting grass and killing snakes upon it. This will sort of relieve the tension involved in the heavy responsibility of saving the Empire next July.'[5]

In May, British economist John Maynard Keynes published an article in the *Atlantic Monthly* that described in popular terms his prescription for combating the Depression. It was an argument that would be expanded upon in his *General Theory* three years later. Competition, retrenchment, and strict economy, Keynes argued, would not lead out of the Depression, and those who believed such were 'fools and madmen.' Instead, Keynes advocated increased public investments, regardless of budgetary deficits. Otherwise the world would have to 'wait for a war to terminate a major depression.'[6] Clark was aware of Keynes's article and its arguments, and while cautious, he generally supported them. Clark had been using Keynes's *A Treatise on Money* for his course on business cycles and monetary theory at Queen's for years.

In typical style, Clark threw himself into his work on the memorandum for the imperial conference. 'I did not realize how far behind in monetary theory I actually was,' he admitted to Skelton.[7] But scholars have since described Clark's memorandum on monetary reconstruction as 'pivotal' and 'crucial,' even referring to it as his 'master-work.'[8] The economist supported maintaining stable exchange rates with the money supply, while allowing the rates to vary as the balancer of payments varied, as opposed to allowing exchange rates to vary while controlling the money supply at home: 'The soundest general policy for most countries is to aim at external stability by accepting an international standard such as gold and then to secure international co-operation to stabilize the value of gold.'[9] International cooperation could coordinate expansionary measures that would help overcome the instability in the general price level, which Clark viewed as responsible for fluctuations in unemployment and production.[10] When it came to Canada, he argued, 'our monetary policy should aim primarily to secure stable exchange rates with other countries because of the important role which both foreign trade and foreign borrowing play in our national economy.'[11] The exchange rate difficulties of 1928–9 demonstrated the 'vital weakness' of the Canadian monetary system under the Finance Act: 'There could be no question that the existence of a central bank would greatly facilitate the task of achieving the objectives we have set up as the goal of monetary policy.' Clark recommended that Canada continue to allow its exchange rate to be set by the market (a 'floating' rate) while implementing controls over foreign borrowing.[12] According to Owram, 'The drive for the bank among Canadian economists thus indicated a growing belief that, given the right tools, society could indeed manipulate business cycles. Macro-economic management, so long submerged by the rhetoric of self-correction and inevitability, was beginning to surface in Canadian economic writing.'[13]

But Clifford Clark had yet to win the trust of the sceptical prime minister. Bennett sent out copies of the draft memorandum on 2 July to thirteen Canadian economists for peer review. While the responses pointed to a few fundamental disagreements within the academic community, the reaction was positive and ended up endorsing Clark's positions.[14] Clark, meanwhile, took it upon himself to also get reaction from his colleagues. Humfrey Mitchell, who had worked with Clark at Queen's before moving to McMaster, had connections with the Canadian Bankers' Association. He passed on the bankers' 'unofficial viewpoint': 'I think you would like me to tell you the real situation, which is this. They are quite perturbed and have got it firmly fixed in their minds that you are unfriendly to the banks ... like Queen Victoria, they are not amused ... What they want now is for the whole thing at Ottawa to be discussed amicably without any definite decision being arrived at, and then to thrash it out afterwards at length. They rather resent it having been fired at them at such short notice and would have liked to have had the report in their hands a couple of months ago when they say they could have got to work on it and evolved something really definite and acceptable to everyone.'[15] On 16 July Clark was informed that he had been appointed adviser to the Canadian delegation for the imperial conference to commence in five days.[16] He was also to serve as financial advisor to Watson Sellar, who as assistant deputy minister of finance was the senior employee in the finance department since the death in April 1930 of J.C. Saunders.[17]

For several weeks in the summer of 1932 Ottawa became the focus of world attention. There were high hopes for the imperial conference. 'We believe we can set an example to the whole world in breaking down obstacles to commerce,' British Prime Minister Stanley Baldwin announced, '... and so bring people safely through the tragic depression of recent times.' C.A. Curtis commented to Clark sarcastically, 'I get quite a kick reading the paper and seeing about all the things the Imperial Conference is going to do. As far as I can see the only thing which has not been recommended to its attention is the problem of ingrown toenails.'[18] Pierre Berton's description of the conference atmosphere provides some interesting colour: 'In the crowded lobby of the Chateau Laurier in Ottawa that week, two hundred newspapermen from the British and world press joined the jostling, cosmopolitan throng – turbaned Hindus carrying briefcases; hard-eyed businessmen in eighty-dollar suits; stylish women on the arms of florid politicians; statesmen or would-be statesmen in striped pants and pearl grey vests to match their pearl grey hair. The air crackled with talk about Danish ham, Australian wool, Canadian wheat. As one observer noted, "more economics, statistics and monetary theory are being talked about in Ottawa at this time than in all the other capitals of the world combined."'[19]

The conference, however, was a failure. It made little headway with the monetary issue, mainly because Britain's chancellor of the exchequer, Neville Chamberlain, was adamant that Britain would not return to the gold standard until there were assurances that the maladjustments that had led Britain to abandon it in the first place were remedied.[20] Regardless, there were serious obstacles to the success of the conference. 'The harsh fact,' Blair Neatby claims, 'was that Imperial solidarity was a myth.' Trade agreements and preferential tariffs held little impact if any dominion could then subsequently alter the value of its currency unilaterally. A stable exchange rate was necessary. The importance of the monetary question was not lost on the delegates but the interests of the various parts of the empire were too divergent. South Africa with its gold mines, for example, favoured the restoration of the gold standard while Britain stood opposed. Australia and New Zealand's currency was at a discount to the pound sterling. The Canadian dollar was at a premium to the British pound because Canada had to borrow money in the United States. Clark argued that Canada's commercial and credit relations with the United States were more important than the corresponding ties with the empire. His conclusion was that Canada must retain control over the exchange level of the Canadian dollar and so should reject any proposals that would bind it to the British pound. In the meeting of his subcommittee, Clark asked the British delegation for a clear-cut statement on British monetary policy and he called for more cooperation between the United Kingdom and the United States.[21] There was no resolution to these very real impediments prior to the commencement of the conference, and failure, therefore, was inevitable: 'None of the Dominions was prepared to sacrifice its control over its currency in the interests of Imperial unity.'[22]

In the end, the conference accepted the British view supporting the restoration of a satisfactory international monetary standard and concluded that although the dominions could take certain steps toward these goals, the problem was international and its resolution had to await an international conference being organized the following year by the League of Nations.[23] Positive results emerging from the gathering dealt with issues Clark had no role in, most notably a trade agreement that gave Canada the preferred access it was seeking to the British market for such products as wheat, butter, cheese, apples, and other food items. Britain gained preferred access to the Canadian market for iron and steel products, textiles, chemicals and drugs, glass, and other manufactured products.[24]

A history of monetary policy later produced by the Department of Finance (and overseen by Clark) searched for a silver lining in the conference results. The report argued that the deliberations were 'significant because they marked an important change in the monetary opinion of the Dominion Government.' Conference discussion made it clear that it was neither possible nor desirable to stabilize exchange rates under any and all circumstances. Opinion was also against deliberate currency depreciation as a solution. As a result, no options were left other than to approve an attempt to raise prices through government action. In assenting to the conference report, the Canadian government concurred in the view that intra-imperial exchange rate stability was not then possible. 'This position,' the document argued, 'is in contrast with the view hitherto professed by the Prime Minister, and, by its assent to the conclusions of the Conference on monetary policy ... the Dominion Government also gave the first hint of any departure in its thinking from the strictest canons of monetary orthodoxy.' This departure became evident in November 1932, as the worldwide depression reached its climax. There was a steady decline of chartered bank cash, and the federal government intervened by increasing the issue of Dominion notes under the Finance Act by $35 million. The increase came through compulsory discount by the banks of that amount in dominion two-year Treasury bills that they had been forced to buy from the government: 'Financial circles in Canada had expected no significant change in the policy of the Government as a result of the Conference and their surprise is indicated in the reaction to the Government's action of increasing the monetary base. Both the Government bond market and the exchange market reacted adversely, apparently under the impression that the Government had succumbed to the pressure of those within Canada who urged inflation, despite assurances from Ottawa that no change in monetary policy was contemplated. Indeed, the Minister of Finance, during the 1932–3 session, made it quite clear that the Government still adhered to a "sound money" policy.'[25]

On 20 August the imperial conference came to an end, as did Clark's contract with the federal government. He was paid $2068.35 for the four months' work.[26] Before the conference ended, however, some of the Canadian delegates and officials did have the opportunity to discuss the idea of a central bank with R.N. Kershaw of the Bank of England.[27] Despite the failures, Clark came away from the experience pleased. He enjoyed rubbing elbows with financial experts from around the world. He was also not as quick to denounce the conference as a complete failure: 'People must read between the lines; disappointed and all as some of us were at the extent to which we fell short of our objective, we managed to work up a little pride when we realized how far we had pushed an irresistible force.'[28]

That summer Clark received bad news about his old employer. A Brooklyn Supreme Court judge signed an order on 23 August requiring S.W. Straus and Co. to show cause why a receiver should not be appointed. The judge also issued a temporary injunction restraining the company from selling securities. The injunction was sought not only against the company but also against its senior officials, including Chairman S.J.T. Straus, President Nicholas Roberts, Treasurer William R. Gillespie, directors Harry R. Amott and John L. Laun, and former sales manager John S. Reitenbaugh. New York Deputy Attorney General Lazarus Joseph alleged fraud and misrepresentation in the sale of securities to the public, estimating that Straus had sold more than $1 billion in bonds over fifty years and that $300 million of them were in default. In an affidavit the deputy attorney general noted several practices that led to the action. After 1924 the Straus company began to sell bonds against general mortgages, which Joseph called a deceptive term because these securities were actually third and fourth mortgages. There were also instances of bonds sold against leaseholds. In buying these, Joseph argued, the public believed it was getting first mortgages. Joseph claimed that Straus had also sold bonds against properties in which taxes were in default and interest had not been paid. Customers were not informed of these situations unless they specifically requested the information. The deputy attorney general also included in his affidavit samples of Straus literature from 1926 to 1929 that characterized the Straus bonds as safe. S.J.T. Straus rejected the material allegations as 'not true,' claiming that in its half century of operations the company had 'conducted its business upon the highest ethical lines' and that after a fair day in court, the company's course of business would deserve 'credit rather than censure.'[29]

Within a month the news out of New York was even worse. Before the Supreme Court in Brooklyn on 20 September, Joseph argued the motion for an injunction, describing Straus's methods as 'vicious.' Until 1927, he noted, Straus pamphlets carried the slogan that no loss had ever accrued to an investor. The company backed new buildings, Joseph claimed, and if the borrower defaulted on interest and amortization charges when due, Straus paid up its investors out of the earnings on other investments, including other buildings. Then the company concealed the default from its bondholders and proceeded to issue new bonds at full value to unwary buyers on the defaulted building. The deputy attorney general focused on particular cases, such as when S.W. Straus owned a hotel in Florida that failed financially. To recoup his losses, Straus sold the hotel to his own business interests. Joseph also pointed out that for ten years, Straus occupied, free of charge, the entire twelfth floor of the Hotel Ambassador on Park Avenue, depriving the hotel of an estimated $500,000 in revenue, and then gave away all the furnishings to his wife, costing an additional $250,000, even though he had not paid for them. The lawyer for Straus, along with former Supreme Court justice Joseph M. Proskauer, argued that the prosecution presented only half truths. The defence claimed that the charges relating to the pamphlet material were valid, but only until the time that the slogan claiming no losses was dropped in 1927. The slogan was dropped, Proskauer argued, not out of concern for the safety of investments but because Straus broadened its list of securities. He also insisted that Straus literature did not unconditionally guarantee all securities.[30]

A separate court action before another supreme court was heard the same day. Bondholders sought to have receivers appointed for five Straus properties in default. They also wanted the removal of present trustees of rents from the properties. Specifically, the applicants wanted Straus officers, directors, and employees removed from the reorganization committees. The court held that two of the reorganization plans were unfair to certificate holders but noted that both plans had been abandoned and new plans were being prepared that would have to be approved by the court. No action was taken on two other cases because a full trial had been scheduled and the case would be heard then.

On 6 October 1932, S.W. Straus and Company was ordered into receivership by a justice of the New York Supreme Court. Among other findings, the justice cited the fraudulent sale of junior bonds to customers who were under the impression that they were purchasing first mortgages, and the selling of bonds not in good standing because the properties behind them had previously defaulted on taxes.[31] Straus planned to appeal the decision. 'I am sorry to say that things look VERY dark in this immediate neighbourhood,' Roy Amott wrote Clark.[32] On 11 December 1933, S.J.T. Straus decided to close down what was left of the family business. In March, the company accepted receivership, and a petition of bankruptcy was filed.[33] Former president Nicholas Roberts was arrested on 29 August on suspicion of grand larceny, connected to the sale of Straus bonds,[34] but the charges were thrown out of court in October for lack of evidence.[35] The following January, Roberts wrote Clark, 'I wish I had a chance to sit down and tell you just what happened. Briefly, S.J.T. decided to fold up and notified me on November 13th that we would be out business on December 1st. I had to move and move fast.' Roberts was now working as an investment consultant on

Wall Street. 'There isn't a dollar's worth of Straus money in the picture,' he informed Clark. 'We are entirely separated and divorced.' Roberts did suggest to Clark that if he could 'think of any way we can make any money or any bonds that we can handle, I would certainly like to hear from you.'[36] The Straus company remained in the courts, and the news, for the next several years as bondholders continued to allege misrepresentations in sales and to pursue compensation. Despite Clark's concern for his former employer and the friends he had made in the company, he realized that he got out just in time. In the years to come, Clark rarely spoke about his work with Straus.

The imperial conference might not have been a great success but Prime Minister Bennett was impressed by Clifford Clark. Bennett contacted Charlotte Whitton, prominent social worker but also a Queen's graduate and member of the university's board of trustees, for her view of Clark. Whitton later recalled the conversation: 'I well remember Mr Bennett phoning me early one morning, asking, "What can you tell me about this Queen's man of yours, this Dr Clark? I know he's a Grit but I want him here." "Cliff" Clark did not go under any discount in my reply. Mr Bennett added – it was just after the Imperial Economic Conference – "I want him. He stood out head and shoulders above any but the tops of the U.K. delegation here. He's one of the few men in the country who think and talk their language."'[37] Even though Clark was not partisan, Bennett was aware of the crowds in which he moved. Bill Mackintosh speculated that the prime minister's concerns about Clark's politics could have been eased somewhat when he learned, 'and not fortuitously, that while Clark's political leanings might appear murky, his father had been a solid Conservative.'[38]

It is not clear when the prime minister first approached Clark about becoming Canada's fifth deputy minister of finance. It is likely that informal discussions about the position were held during the imperial conference. By early October Clark consulted his doctor about the advisability of taking on added responsibilities.[39] He also began turning down and withdrawing from academic projects.[40] On 15 October Clark wrote Bennett to say that after careful consideration, he would accept the position. Because the appointment came just over a month into the new academic year, Clark asked that he be listed as 'acting' deputy minister of finance for the time being, until he could arrange things at Queen's.[41] The prime minister responded a week later that the appointment had been arranged at a salary of $12,000 per year, minus the 10 per cent salary reduction approved earlier in the year as a result of the Depression: 'In recommending your appointment, I did so with great confidence, believing that your fine academic training and very considerable practical experience will enable you to bring to the discharge of your new duties an understanding of Canadian problems that has not been possessed by any Deputy Minister since the days of Mr Courtenay [*sic*], and in many respects you are better equipped than he.'

Bennett wanted Clark in Ottawa as soon as possible so he could prepare for the upcoming World Economic Conference.[42] Clark was also named secretary of the treasury board. In the official announcement of the appointment, Bennett noted, 'Mr Clark rendered very great service in connection with the Imperial conference. He was held in high esteem by all those with whom he came in contact. The university has been good enough to grant him leave of absence so that we might immediately secure the benefit of his services in dealing with monetary problems, on which he is an admitted authority.'[43] The announcement offered a brief biography of Clark, indicating that he had worked for an investment banking firm in Chicago and New York but not mentioning it by name. Whether Edgar Rhodes, who had succeeded Bennett as finance minister, was consulted is unclear. According to rumour, Rhodes was summoned to the Prime Minister's Office and told to meet his new deputy.[44]

Bob Bryce later claimed that Clark agreed to become deputy minister of finance 'only when he had found out that the prime minister was prepared to accept in principle the establishment of a central bank for Canada and the introduction of unemployment insurance.'[45] There was no such discussion, however, in the correspondence between the two men, nor is there any indication in correspondence to others that Clark had any conditions. Discussions on the possibility of such policy initiatives likely occurred but it is doubtful that any promises were made. Discussions did commence immediately after Clark went to Ottawa, and he was soon advancing them with vigour.

Likely prodded by Skelton, Queen's University grudgingly agreed to let one of its highest profile faculty members leave. J.M. Macdonnell, chairman of the Board of Trustees, informed Clark that Principal Fyfe was 'desolated.' A year later the university was still holding the door open in the event that Clark wanted to return. His replacement, J.L. McDougall, was reappointed in economics on a one-year probationary term, just in case. 'This is a gesture in your direction,' Fyfe wrote Clark. 'I have given up all hope really of getting you back, because I realise that you are well into your saddle and making a fine ride of it. But, if during the coming year you should feel the struggle intolerable and yearn for the peace of Queen's, our arms would be open for you in the following session.'[46] The larger academic community, and in particular the economists, were very pleased with the appointment of the new deputy minister of finance. 'It is a great pleasure to all of us economists,' S.A. Cudmore wrote, 'to feel that henceforth there will be an economist in the Department of Finance.'[47] For his part, Clark was saddened to leave Queen's and academe again. 'I leave Queen's with very great regret,' he wrote. 'I would very much prefer to stay here, and did not know until this past year how much I really enjoy university work.'[48]

Clifford Clark was aware of the heavy workload he was taking on. He was becoming deputy minister of finance in the middle of the worst economic disaster the nation, and indeed the western world, had witnessed. As a trained economist he would be expected to offer solutions to seemingly unsolvable problems. In answering the more than 125 letters of congratulations, Clark repeatedly acknowledged the weight of his new responsibilities and noted that this fact caused him to accept the position only with great reluctance.[49] He was, however, prepared to rise to the challenge: 'It was only because I too have been so much impressed with the seriousness of the present situation that the opportunity to serve in my present capacity came to me as a challenge which I found it finally impossible to resist. I still have confidence, however, that if we can secure a modicum of intelligent co-operation on the part of the leading countries of the world it will still be possible to avoid the danger of collapse which you envision ... Hope for international action should not be allowed to constitute an alibi for failure to act at home. Such domestic action is, of course, beset with many difficulties, and it is hard to see clearly what can be done effectively and without the danger of doing more harm than good.'[50]

Clark's friends worried about the impact of the workload on his often fragile health: 'This position will require you to burn the candle at both ends, unless you make a Golden Rule that all business transacted in your Department and all consultations are made between the hours of 9 A.M. and 5 P.M. Mindful of your health and your family, I am taking the liberty of putting forward this suggestion.'[51] These concerns proved justified but there would be no such golden rule for Clifford Clark. Mac MacEwan, Clark's brother-in-law, saw irony in the appointment. 'I remember when O.D., Doug Findlay and I were at

Lake Clear just after the last election,' he wrote, 'and [you] three people could not understand how Bennett won the election, and now both you and O.D. are the holders of the two highest positions in Bennett's Government.'[52]

At the age of forty-three Clifford Clark became the federal deputy minister of finance. He was named to the position on 24 October 1932, and took up his new duties on 4 November in an office at the Wellington Street end of the East Block of the Parliament buildings. Clark was entering a position that had, up until this time, held little weight or importance for the Canadian government. This was all about to change. According to Derek Chisholm, Clark's acceptance of the position marked 'the beginning of a new era in policy formulation.'[53]

At the end of October the Clark family moved into a rental house at 295 Manor Road in Ottawa's upper-class Rockcliffe neighbourhood.[54] The family's financial situation, and the continuing problems selling the Scarsdale house, prevented the new deputy from immediately purchasing a house in Ottawa. Clifford and Margaret were plagued by financial worries and it was the major source of strain at home. The realities of the Depression also altered the affluent lifestyle to which the Clarks had become accustomed. The family had a live-in maid while in the United States, and the maid moved to Kingston with the family but returned after a few years. From this point onward the Clarks employed no hired help. The children, however, did attend private school.[55]

With Clark's arrival, the Department of Finance for the first time was under the guidance of an economist – a startling fact, given the department's functions. But even though Bennett complained about the civil servants in finance, he was partly responsible for the poor state of the bureaucracy. 'One of Bennett's failings,' Larry Glassford notes, 'was the long delay he incurred before deciding upon the appointments that were within his prerogative.' Cabinet ministers had to remind the prime minister repeatedly of the need to appoint deputies for their departments.[56] But the lack of trained economists in finance did not mean that there were no talented individuals in the department. After Saunders's death, the department was run by a five-member executive committee that included Watson Sellar (assistant deputy minister), B.J. McIntyre (comptroller general), Bennett Roberts (comptroller of government guarantees), W.C. Ronson (director of estimates), and R.B. Viets (solicitor of the treasury).[57]

On Bennett's direction this executive committee undertook a study of the public accounts, concluding that the existing system was inadequate to prevent expenditures from exceeding the amounts authorized by Parliament. Along with justice officials, this committee drafted what became the first major revision in the federal government's financial controls in fifty years. These sweeping amendments to the Consolidated Revenue and Audit Act of 1878 created a powerful new post, comptroller of the treasury, to centralize and control the accounting, pre-auditing, and cheque-issuing functions of government. Sellar was appointed to the post in February 1932. Although inside the department, Sellar reported directly to the finance minister and consulted with the Treasury Board. McIntyre became his chief assistant.[58] With Ronson focused on Treasury Board work, Roberts handling debt issues of the Canadian National Railway, and Sellar and McIntyre in their new posts, there was no one left to focus on financial issues when Clark arrived in the fall of 1932.

The department had one other key employee. Hector McKinnon had been commissioner of tariffs since March 1930 and secretary to the Advisory Board on Tariff and Taxation since 1926. McKinnon, along with Norman Robertson of external affairs and Dana Wilgress of trade and commerce, played a major role in developing the Canadian trade proposal that was accepted by Britain at the Imperial Conference the previous summer.[59] It was the Dominion Bureau of Statistics, meanwhile, that had emerged as 'the centre of professional economic expertise in Ottawa.'[60] R.H. Coats had been dominion statistician since 1915 and was developing a reputation for quality work. He had at least one economist working under him, C.A. Cudmore. Other bureaucrats with whom Clark would come to work closely included Fraser Elliot, commissioner of income tax, Hugh Scully, commissioner of customs, and David Sim, commissioner of excise. Clark moved into the position of deputy minister and he quickly became a one-man show. An assistant deputy minister was not appointed until April 1935, when Bennett Roberts was given the position. Yet by all accounts Clark was not an able organizer. Instead, he was always viewed as more of a thinker, a recruiter, and a generator of ideas and policies.[61]

The situation in Canada when Clark became deputy minister of finance allowed ample opportunity for the economist to put his expertise into practice. The seriousness of the economic crisis was daunting: 'The economy of the Western world was in the depths of an unparalleled depression that everyone explained but no one understood. Trade, the life-blood of Canada, was spiralling downward because of the depression itself and a host of barriers created in defence against it. The growth and confidence of North American society seemed to have been shattered. Canadian public finances, like all else, were in the grip of the depression, and though the banking system was strong, it was going through the throes of deflation and no machinery existed for arresting this movement and promoting recovery.'[62] These were 'desperate days.' One financial crisis followed upon another. Prices were falling, the Prairie region was in the grip of drought and deflation, unemployment was increasing, and the federal government had abandoned its works policy in favour of direct relief. 'It was indeed a forbidding time,' Mackintosh noted, 'in which to assume the administrative responsibility for the federal treasury.'[63]

Before coming to Ottawa, Clark was more critical of Bennett's leadership than his economic policies. Clark believed that Bennett's approach to tackling the Depression lacked the sophistication and forethought present in those of American President Herbert Hoover. What the two leaders did have in common, however, was a belief in high tariffs. The Bennett Conservatives campaigned in 1930 primarily on the unemployment issue, pledging that 'the Conservative Party is going to find work for all who are willing to work, or perish in the attempt.' Although he promised a national old age pension plan and improvement in the transportation system, Bennett's main means for dealing with unemployment was through trade and tariffs – a policy of protection and a plan for greater imperial trade based on mutual advantage. Canadian farmers were promised that tariffs would be used to protect the domestic market and to assist them in regaining their position in the world market.[64] By the fall of 1932 the Conservative government had most of its tariff policies in place. Canadian tariffs were at their highest levels ever and tough 'anti-dumping' measures were in place to block the selling of goods in Canada at prices below those in the country of origin. At the Imperial Conference in Ottawa, preferential entrance to the British market for Canadian wheat, lumber, apples, bacon, fish, and minerals had been obtained in return for preferential access of certain British metal and textile products. Indeed, despite the general malaise of the Depression, Bennett and Rhodes were able to boast that Canada's trade balance was positive again.[65] While Clark was all in favour of increased trade during the Depression, he was opposed to protectionism. As a civil servant just entering a new position, however, he was not inclined to tackle Bennett on the issue.

The Bennett government had largely fulfilled its campaign pledges but with unanticipated results. The trade policy failed to reverse

Canada's slide into depression. In the fall of 1930 Ottawa provided $16 million to share the costs of provincial and municipal public works and $4 million to share the costs of relief. That same autumn, the prime minister reluctantly guaranteed the financial obligations of the three Prairie wheat pools, in exchange for imposing his appointee, John McFarland, as general manager of the pools' Central Selling Agency. In early 1931 the federal government instituted a wheat bonus of five cents a bushel for the 1931 crop when the price of wheat fell below an unprecedented forty cents. Ottawa increased the transportation subsidy on Canadian coal by twenty-five cents per ton to help Maritime and western coal producers compete in central Canada with American coal. The federal share of old age pension costs was raised to 75 per cent. The 1931 Relief Act provided federal assistance to provincial road-building programs and the government agreed to provide half the costs of municipal relief projects in the four hard-pressed western provinces, as well as to lend money needed to make up any shortfall in the provincial or municipal share.[66]

Bennett and Rhodes remained adamant that the budget could still be balanced. Deficits proved unavoidable, however, despite fears that they would erode international confidence in Canada's ability to pay its debts to foreign lenders. The prime minister and finance minister resisted calls to lower interest rates on outstanding government bonds or to expand (inflate) the currency to stimulate the economy. The fear of shaking investor confidence was also the main reason for the aid extended to the Prairie provinces to prevent them from defaulting on bonds and further injuring the nation's credit rating. Bennett, then Rhodes, imposed rigid economy on all government departments, including cuts to the salaries of civil servants. The government even abandoned public works because it was cheaper to pay relief, which did not involve the cost of materials and administration.[67]

The prime minister remained convinced that some of the money spent on relief was being wasted at the provincial level through inefficient administration. Charlotte Whitton agreed, arguing that relief was being administered by amateurs. She convinced the prime minister to send her on a fact-finding mission to the West, where she concluded that waste was indeed prevalent. Partly as a result, 'relief camps' were established by Ottawa in which single, unemployed men were housed and put to work on such projects as clearing landing fields, building roads, and constructing parks, all for twenty cents a day. The first camps, administered by the Department of National Defence, were established in the fall of 1932. Clark shared Bennett's concern that the provincial treasuries were not being careful enough with their finances. He agreed that the federal government had no choice but to offer increased aid through relief, but this process had to be carefully monitored and only done when absolutely necessary.

When Clark became deputy minister of finance, he was effectively in charge of debt management. One of the first problems he had to confront was the issue of Treasury bills. He was concerned that the issue was being touted as an expansionary measure, which he did not support. Instead Clark was convinced that international action, not unilateral action by individual nations, was the only way to get economies moving again.[68] The new deputy minister drafted an explanation for the 1 November issue of Treasury bills and the prime minister read a statement in the House on 8 November. Bennett explained that a $35 million loan was in two-year Dominion notes, bearing interest at 4 per cent, and that the banks would use the notes as security in obtaining an advance of an equivalent amount under the Finance Act, thereby increasing their cash reserves and substantially increasing their loan capacity: 'After having proved our ability to ride out the storm, I feel that we are justified – to the very limited degree necessary in our case – in joining other countries in the adoption of monetary measures designed to encourage recovery.' Bennett also noted, however, that 'this country will not depart from the established principles of sound money.'[69]

Clark's primary objective was the creation of a central bank. Already by the end of November, before he had even fully settled into his new position, he wrote a memorandum for Rhodes outlining the steps needed to create a royal commission to undertake an 'authoritative examination of the pros and cons of the argument for a central bank and the working out of the details of organization for such a central institution.' The idea of a royal commission had first been suggested the previous summer by Clark's colleague Bill Mackintosh. Clark suggested to the finance minister that Sir Josiah Stamp, an economic advisor to the Bank of England, be appointed chairman of the commission, because 'if Sir Josiah told our Canadian bankers, as he probably would, that a central bank was desirable in this country his arguments would likely be accepted.' Clark went so far as to recommend possible commissioners: Walter W. Stewart, formerly of the Federal Reserve Board in the United States, Sir Thomas White, Canada's finance minister in the Borden Cabinet during the First World War, and a few bankers and industrialists.[70] But there was stiff opposition to a central bank. 'All the bankers are making a dead set against a central bank,' Clark wrote. 'It seems to me to be a fearfully short-sighted policy.'[71]

Clark had to focus his immediate energies on an upcoming dominion-provincial conference, scheduled for 17 January 1933. The prime minister originally wanted three issues on the agenda: unemployment, security frauds prevention, and allocation of taxation powers. In a speech to Parliament on 29 April 1931, Bennett promised an unemployment insurance scheme at the earliest possible opportunity. Ottawa and the provinces were locked in a battle over who was responsible for providing relief to the unemployed. The federal government loaned more than $4 million to the four western provinces to cover their relief costs. By the fall of 1932, however, it looked as if more money would be needed. Bennett resisted calls from certain provinces for Ottawa to create an unemployment commission, arguing instead that the responsibility lay with the provinces. But in the face of increasing opposition, the prime minister told Parliament on 22 November that he would call a dominion-provincial conference for January and ask the provinces if they would be willing to give the federal government responsibility for creating a contributory system of unemployment insurance.[72]

Clark believed that the agenda was too ambitious and too hastily prepared. 'It is certain that the agenda will amount to a considerable "mouthful,"' he wrote his friend Bryce Stewart. 'In fact, I regard it as much too big a "mouthful," and regret that there is not a much longer time for thorough preparation.'[73] Stewart was opposed to government intervention and urged 'the desirability of keeping government out of the financing of unemployment insurance, and, further, keeping the administration of unemployment insurance as far away from government departments as possible.' Clark considered Stewart one of the nation's experts on unemployment and valued his opinion: 'I think you are correct in stating that the State should throw the burden upon employers and employees, assuming at the most the cost of administration. However, in Canada the habit of depending on Ottawa has become so fixed that I am afraid the pressure upon us will be heavy.'[74] Clark advised Bennett to this end.[75] But the deputy minister was receiving baptism by fire. He would soon learn that federal–provincial relations were a frustrating and complex quagmire and there was no easy or quick solution to the unemployment issue. 'There was no settled pattern for dealing with the provinces nor for dealing with unemployment relief,' Mackintosh later recalled. 'It was a matter for guessing and bargaining and no process of government is so wearisome and exacting.'[76] Regardless of his personal views on the issue of state intervention or the needs of the provinces, Clark was in the position of having to safeguard the credit and treasury of the federal government.

Before the end of December, Prime Minister Bennett departed on a trip to England, leaving his private secretary, Rod Finlayson, to draw up an agenda for the conference along with O.D. Skelton.[77] Finlayson, after consulting Clark, Skelton, and Coats, recommended that a royal commission be appointed to make a thorough statistical and actuarial survey before Ottawa made any proposal on unemployment insurance to the provinces. He also suggested that employees and employers bear the costs of premiums, with Ottawa covering only the cost of administration.[78] If the federal government took over responsibility for single unemployed men, as it had by establishing the relief camps, and moved to bring in unemployment insurance, it would deflect criticism that Ottawa was doing nothing, and the provinces could be made to assume all the responsibility for those still requiring direct relief.[79]

In early January the four western provinces demanded that Ottawa accept the cost of financing both the municipal and provincial shares of relief costs, since both the banks and federal finance minister had denied them credit for further loans. Clark recognized the seriousness of the provinces' financial crisis but he argued that continuing indefinitely to finance relief would result in 'abominable ... waste and inefficiency.' Instead, he argued, the banks should force the provinces to take 'a more realistic attitude in regard to their present financial position.' Clark recommended that the provinces 'commit themselves to some definite programme for putting their financial houses in order in the very near future.' In a memorandum to Finlayson, Clark suggested the provinces take the initiative in working out a scheme with Canadian bond houses for long-term financing rather than pressing ahead with an unemployment insurance scheme.[80]

It was unlikely, based on the attitudes of federal officials, that the conference would produce a solution to the relief crisis. To make matters worse, the federal government lacked even the basic information it needed to contemplate introducing an unemployment insurance scheme. Material from the 1931 census on the extent of the unemployment problem was not available until 10 January, a week before the conference opened.[81] Backed by his officials in Ottawa, the prime minister's stance on the issue only hardened. Ottawa had spent over $131 million on relief payments, Bennett told a Vancouver audience on 9 January, without the provinces being forced to surrender any autonomy.[82]

The Dominion-Provincial Conference of 1933 opened in Ottawa on 17 January. The issue of relief was immediately brought forward by Prime Minister Bennett, who asked whether the provincial premiers were prepared to agree to transfer jurisdiction over an unemployment insurance scheme to the federal government and, if so, how much they would be willing to contribute. Bennett asserted that there would be no cost-sharing as in the case of old age pensions. Only after an agreement in principle had reached would the details be worked out. Not surprisingly, the premiers rejected the request.[83] The prime minister complained that the provinces could hardly expect his government to do more in the way of providing relief when they refused to grant him authority over unemployment insurance. According to James Struthers, Bennett wanted the conference to fail so that he could blame the provinces for inaction.[84]

But federal officials continued to work on a draft plan.[85] The following day Clark sent Bennett a memorandum urging the prime minister to 'segregate these cases of unemployment relief from the insurance scheme.' This would make it easier, Clark hoped, for the provinces to surrender any new constitutional powers. He realized that Bennett's aggressive stance with the premiers would not pay dividends: 'To-day they are naturally hesitant about accepting a share in the cost of unemployment relief when the size of that burden is entirely uncertain. If you merely say to them that you will take care of the unemployment insurance programme, but that they must not expect such an insurance programme to do everything, particularly in the initial stages and in times of unprecedented depression, they will, I think, be prepared to accept the major responsibility which they now have for unemployment relief.'[86] The deputy minister believed that unemployment insurance was not an immediate solution to the problems of relief and that, following advice he had received from Bryce Stewart, the two should probably remain distinct from one another: 'The insurance scheme can be allowed to continue to stand on its own feet, doing what it was actuarially calculated that it could do and not being asked or expected to do more.' In Clark's view, this approach had the advantage of allowing a clear division of responsibilities between the provinces and the federal government.[87] The conference did at least resolve that Ottawa would continue to provide matching grants for a third of the cost of relief.[88]

The prime minister had asked that the division of taxing powers be placed on the agenda but because of his trip to Britain, it was left to Clark to take the initiative. The deputy minister discussed the issue with Rod Finlayson, and, along with Fraser Elliot, background papers were prepared. Clark noted that the chief problems facing the federal government included the duplication and overlapping of taxation powers. Many Canadians were, for example, subject not only to federal and provincial income taxes but to municipal income tax as well. Clark suggested either a new allocation of tax fields or intergovernmental agreements for cooperation in tax collecting. He was also concerned with the inability of the provinces to raise revenue to meet their growing demands due to constitutional restrictions on their ability to tax directly. He was opposed to the 'easy solution' of increasing federal subsidies. Such subsidies, Clark claimed, 'involve a vicious principle; where one government raises the revenue for another government to spend' and 'there is no effective brake upon expenditures by the latter.' The solution for Clark was for the dominion to take over certain provincial responsibilities. He was prepared to contemplate the provinces having sole access to personal income tax revenue in order to simplify the process and provide them with the much needed revenue, but only with a 'substantial quid pro quo' for the federal government. One possibility would be the provinces surrendering succession duties to Ottawa.[89] Fraser Elliot thought it highly unlikely that the provinces would surrender any source of taxation. He believed the best that could be expected was administrative improvements.[90]

Prime Minister Bennett discussed these proposals at the conference. Both Ontario Premier George Henry and British Columbia Finance Minister James Jones argued that the federal government should leave income taxes entirely to the provinces. Bennett responded by insisting that Ottawa could not consider reducing its revenues while spending $30 million a year on relief and another $70 million on railway deficits.[91] The premiers referred the issue for further study to a committee on taxation, chaired by Clark and consisting of the provincial treasurers. This committee provided Clark the opportunity to put forward his ideas while receiving an understanding of the provincial positions. Further meetings were planned but they never took place.[92]

The conference adjourned on 19 January and Clark refocused his efforts on the establishment of a central bank. The idea may have been 'bruited about for at least twenty years,' and pressure both within Parliament and academe was building, but as Granatstein points out, 'still, the new Deputy Minister was the key man.' According to Floyd Chalmers of the *Financial Post,* Clark told him in January 1933 that 'Canada is going to have a Central Bank anyway. The public wants it and if the government does not set one up the radicals will set one up some day. It would then be a dangerous institution.' Under present circumstances, 'there is no one to initiate any policy of credit control; no one to say how the Finance Act is to be used. The government has handed over control of the country's monetary policy to the banks and the banks have not assumed that control with the result that it drops between two stools and often very menacing and dangerous things happen.'[93]

While the exact wording does not sound like Clark, the analysis does. The key players were coming onside – the government, the opposition, the academics[94] – and only the banks were still putting up resistance. Clark envisaged a central lending institution controlled jointly by government and the chartered banks. The Liberal Party was largely onside by early 1933. Mackenzie King noted that he was reconciling views on banking and currency issues in caucus, but opinions were becoming more moderate, and 'the Central Bank idea seemed to furnish the point of convergence of many views. There was, in fact, unanimity for a central bank.'[95]

R.B. Bennett's hard line in dealing with the provinces continued in the aftermath of the Dominion-Provincial Conference and this stance was fully supported by Clark. On 9 March the prime minister announced a new policy on federal financial assistance that echoed Clark's advice. Bennett indicated that future requests for federal assistance would be considered only if the provinces pledged to present balanced budgets in the upcoming fiscal year, or at least deficits no larger than $1 million. Otherwise, to receive a federal loan, the province would have to place all future spending under the supervision of a financial controller acceptable to Ottawa.[96] Watson Sellar, the comptroller of the treasury, undertook a two-week tour of the four western provinces in April and reported that their provincial budgets were 'balanced on hope.' Any savings were offset by rising debt interest costs. Sellar argued against new federal loans in an attempt to preserve the federal government's ability to meet its own obligations.[97]

On 21 March 1933, the Conservative government brought down its budget; for Clark, it was to be the first of many. According to Bryce, it was too early to expect Clark's influence to be evidenced by the budget, but his participation did lead to some improvement in the style of the speech and more particularly the expert review of economic conditions. Rhodes called for serious cutbacks, but Clark urged patience and moderation. The deficit for the fiscal year ending in 1933 reached a Depression peak of $220 million, equal to about two-thirds of the revenue of that year. Revenue had fallen off dramatically, especially from customs duties, which had been reduced from $180 million in 1929–30 to $70 million in 1932–3.[98] Demands were increasing for relief assistance to the provinces and municipalities, for direct relief works, for government price support and marketing of western wheat, and for something to be done about the increasing Canadian National Railway deficits.[99] Relief costs had risen from nothing in 1929–30 to $37 million in 1932–3; the railway deficit had risen from $7 million to $62 million in the same period.[100]

The federal government searched for alternate sources of revenue to battle the Depression. Taxation was increasingly employed as one of the few viable options. Dominion corporation income taxes, charged at a rate of 8 per cent in 1929, were already up to 11 per cent by 1932. In addition, most provinces were now levying corporate income taxes. Personal income taxes had also increased sharply, despite the fact that in 1929 they were expected to be eliminated altogether. The dominion sales tax was increased from 1 per cent in 1930 to 6 per cent in 1932.[101] The budget of 1933 offered little reason for optimism, but one positive note, in Clark's view, was the finance minister's announcement that a royal commission would be appointed to study the organization of the banking system and the possibility of a central bank.[102]

By the spring of 1933 Manitoba, in particular, was reeling under the economic weight of the Depression. The unemployment relief problem forced the province into requesting further aid from Ottawa. The provincial budget showed 'a considerable deficit,' and Manitoba found it impossible to sell provincial government bonds. Any further relief work by the province was in jeopardy and the government feared 'complete disorganization of constituted authority.'[103] Rhodes responded that nearly a year ago Ottawa had advised Manitoba that it could not 'indefinitely find all the money for all the relief granted' and that 'under these circumstances the Province of Manitoba must accept its responsibilities as other Provinces have done.'[104] The insinuation that the province was not accepting its responsibilities and was mishandling its finances rankled Premier John Bracken: 'The economic situation now facing us is not one of our own making. You are aware of the difficulties with which all the Provinces had to contend in financing since England went off the gold standard. Following that event and the Conversion Loan of 1931, and with the continued low prices of farm products, there has been no reasonable market for provincial securities of the four Western Provinces. The gross income of all our primary industries is but one-third of what it was a few years ago, and the price of our chief staple commodity in the last few months has reached the lowest point in history.' If aid was not forthcoming, Bracken warned, the province would be unable to meet its financial debt obligations, thereby damaging the credit of the country.[105] Ottawa responded that the province had already been advanced monies for costs clearly outside federal jurisdiction. 'This was done,' Bennett wrote, 'against the protests of a great many people in Eastern Canada, but in accordance with my declared policy of assisting provinces in cases where necessity for such action arose.'[106]

In June 1933 the World Monetary and Economic Conference was held in London under the auspices of the League of Nations. The Canadian delegation, consisting of R.B. Bennett, Edgar Rhodes, Clifford Clark, Norman Robertson, Dana Wilgress, Rod Finlayson, Howard Ferguson, and Georges Vanier, sailed from Montreal aboard the *Duchess of Bedford*. The six-week gathering held in the Geological Museum at South Kensington was chaired by British Prime Minister Ramsay MacDonald and split into two commissions, one dealing with monetary issues and the other dealing with economic questions. Bennett attended the monetary meetings with Clark as his advisor while Rhodes attended the economic commission.[107] As with the Imperial Conference, however, the meeting would result in few accomplishments and would go down in history as a failure. According to British historian A.J.P. Taylor, 'All the representatives deplored tariffs, exchange restrictions, and unstable currencies. All of them clung to one or other of these devices. The principles of Free Trade had become fossils, suitably preserved in the Geological Museum. On 5 July President Roosevelt killed the conference by refusing to stabilize the dollar, which he had previously taken off gold and devalued as part of the New Deal. After some lamentations, the conference adjourned forever.'[108] After Roosevelt's intervention, the monetary commission shifted to other issues, all much less pressing. Among its final resolutions, it called for a return to monetary stability, with gold as the standard, and for the establishment of independent central banks. The conference did at least produce two trade agreements of importance to Canada, one on wheat and one on silver.[109]

Upon return from the conference, Clark continued to press for a central bank. His experience at two ineffective world conferences had only further convinced him that Canada desperately needed expert and impartial advice on fiscal matters. The British model of a central lending institution was instructive for Canada, and Clark's work paid off. Prime Minister Bennett finally agreed to the establishment of a royal commission headed by Lord Macmillan. It is likely, however, that Bennett had already reached the same conclusion. According to Mackintosh, the prime minister was now prepared to proceed with a central bank and simply 'wished expert confirmation.' The appointment of Lord Macmillan was certainly a move in this direction because it was clear that the British commissioner would come down in favour of a central bank and 'give weight to the verdict.'[110] The question in Canada, Craig McIvor argues, was not whether some change should be made in the existing arrangements but rather the direction and the form that the change should take.[111]

Clark's influence can be seen in more than the selection of the royal commission's chair. B.J. Roberts of the finance department was named secretary, and, on Clark's direct recommendation, A.F.W. Plumptre became assistant secretary. When Roberts was forced to deal with the illness and resulting death of his wife, the role of Plumptre increased.[112] By early August 1933, the Banking Commission was already meeting and holding hearings. The majority of bankers remained opposed and the commission hearings became the final battleground. The bankers argued that the existing system had proven strong yet flexible enough to survive the Depression and it would be dangerous to experiment or disturb the existing system at such a tenuous time. Clark appeared on the second day to support the creation of a central bank but he was not the only economist to appear.[113] Led by the Queen's group (Mackintosh, Curtis, and Knox), thirteen of seventeen economists supported a central bank.

By the end of September the commission's report was in the hands of the government. Not surprisingly, it was favourable, despite opposition from most of the Canadian banks. According to Owram, 'The economists won out over the bankers.' Still, the commission's verdict was not unanimous. Two of the five commissioners, Sir Thomas White and Beaudry Leman, dissented. 'Given such a narrow victory for the principle of a central bank,' Owram notes, 'the role of the professional economic community, both inside and outside the commission, may well have been decisive.'[114] Regardless, Bennett was now determined to move. Legislation was brought into Parliament, drafted by Clark but under the prime minister's direction. 'In a very real sense,' Clark observed, 'it may be said to signal Canada's "coming of age" financially.'[115] The deputy minister persuaded Bennett to add a preamble to the bill that placed additional emphasis on the bank's domestic functions.[116] On 20 November, only a week after the royal commission report was made public, Bennett announced that a central bank would be established.[117]

On 22 February 1934, legislation to create the Bank of Canada was introduced into Parliament. When the chartered banks objected to the government bill, Clark viewed the reaction as a knee-jerk response to their loss of control. 'I am afraid our bankers have been spoiled by the Finance Act, which operated without requirement and without the possibility of control,' he told Bennett. The bankers were not objecting to provisions that failed to give the central bank adequate control; they were objecting to the fact that 'the Central Bank will have control for the first time in this country.'[118] Interestingly, during debate on the Bank of Canada, J.L. Ralston, while sitting as a Liberal opposition member, moved an amendment that would have given the deputy minister of finance the right to a suspensive veto of actions taken by the bank's governor. The intent was to give the deputy minister the power to assert the state's interests in bank decisions. The motion, however, was defeated.[119] The government's bill, which Clark drafted, made no provision for the deputy minister of finance to even sit as a member of the board of directors. A parliamentary amendment to have the deputy minister a non-voting member was, however, accepted by the government.[120]

The Canadian Bankers' Association submitted a brief to the Select Standing Committee on Banking and Commerce, which was studying the bill to create the Bank of Canada. The brief was critical of the proposed requirement that the chartered banks surrender their gold to the new central bank at the old price of $20.67 an ounce at a time when the price the government paid for newly minted gold had increased to $35. They also argued that the gold owned by the banks was held solely against the liabilities outside of Canada.[121] The government's reply was made by Clifford Clark. The deputy minister of finance reminded the chartered banks that the gold presently held against their domestic liabilities was acquired by them as a counterpart to the essentially national function of issuing currency. He pointed out that the right to issue notes to circulate as currency was usually regarded as a prerogative of the state alone. In addition, it was widely recognized that the exercise of these privileges involved the obligations of maintaining cash reserves (in the form of gold and other legal tender) against the liabilities assumed. In most countries, the banking laws stipulated a definite minimum percentage of gold that must be held against either notes or deposits outstanding, or against both note and deposit liabilities. In Canada, Clark wrote, 'Parliament has seen fit to leave the exact proportion of cash reserves to be carried to the good judgement of the banks themselves and in doing so has accepted an argument which has been strongly pressed by our bankers throughout our entire banking history.' The banks should not, he asserted, be allowed to treat the gold as an ordinary investment with speculative profit.[122]

The prime minister felt it was iniquitous that the chartered banks should reap a huge gain at the expense of Canadian taxpayers and he was determined to see the banks receive only what they had paid for their gold. When asked if he could fight all the banks, Bennett responded, 'We are going to get that gold and it is just about time for us to find out whether the banks or this government is running the country.'[123] A motion to pay the banks the market value of the gold was defeated in the House and the original sections of the bill carried.[124] The issue was settled by Order in Council in April 1935. By this time, the question of the price to be paid for gold was no longer an issue; the banks failed to have the price raised from the old value.[125]

Clifford Clark was making his presence felt in Ottawa. In January, W.D. Herridge, Canadian ambassador to the United States and Bennett's brother-in-law, advised the prime minister to set up a committee of experts, consisting of Skelton, Clark, Wilgress, McNaughton, and a few others, to formulate the 'Bennett Recovery Programme.' It is unlikely that the prime minister seriously entertained the proposal of having a group of bureaucrats set his agenda but it was testament to their growing influence. Regardless, Clark was focusing on problems of economic recovery. In particular, he was in charge of debt management and he introduced the sale of three-month Treasury bills in Canada by auction. These sales were continued later in 1934 and became a regular practice.[126] They were designed to provide the government more flexibility in financing its debt.

The Prairie West was the region hardest hit by the Depression and the agriculture industry, in particular, was devastated. As Ferguson notes, 'The problems of Canadian farming had interested Queen's political economy professors at least since the last years of George M. Grant's principalship.'[127] Clark was certainly no exception, as his doctoral studies indicated. Skelton had also long argued that the grievances of the farmers were central to the more general problems of Canadian society; the nation had not properly apprehended the importance of agriculture to its overall well-being. Since this time Canadian farmers had organized to increase their economic and political power. This fact was evident in the increase in their organization after the 1911 election and the defeat of reciprocity. By the end of the war the agrarian revolt had become an influential force in the nation.

Clark argued as early as 1916 that the Prairie farmers' response to the grain marketing system was leading to fundamental changes in Canadian economic and political life. Clark shared Skelton's judgment that the organized farmers were in the midst of contributing to the democratization of the nation. Indeed, the dynamic change affecting Prairie farmers was the result of their place as international producers. Their response to the complexities of pricing and marketing in this global system led them to examine their own practices as well as those of the middlemen – those involved in storage, shipment, and sales. In both these areas, and especially the latter, the farmers found considerable need for economic reform. But this improvement was aimed at increasing market efficiency, not at overturning market structures. As a result of their inquiry, the farmers demanded and obtained state supervision over the inspection, storage, and transportation of grain. Furthermore, they themselves created grain storage and selling cooperatives. The effect of these developments was remarkable. The resulting availability of capital and profits testified to the commercial success of the reformed, regulated, and competitive system. The reformed grain trade, according to Clark, was 'the strongest force making for real democracy in present-day Canada' because it contributed to economic well-being and active participation in commerce of all involved in the trade.[128]

Clark's influence on agriculture can be seen as early as 1934 with the introduction of the Farmers' Creditors Arrangements Act, which provided a process of liquidation for farmers where none had existed before. Along with F.P. Varcoe, Clark revised the act. In January he produced a memorandum for the prime minister on an agricultural program. While the suggestions, he admitted, were tentative, Bennett's sponsorship of the program would indicate 'your desire to grapple realistically and sympathetically with what is a very real problem – a serious "sore point" in our national economy.' The program dealt with farm indebtedness, debt relief legislation, and farm credit institutions in Canada. When it came to making recommendations, the Macmillan Commission had complained of insufficient material for agricultural credit and suggested that Ottawa investigate the problem of provision of short and intermediate rural credits.[129] P.B. Waite argues that this piece of legislation was 'the best example of R.B. as an authentic radical ... R.B. knew prairie life too well to stick at such points when dealing with the hardships of Saskatchewan and Alberta in the early thirties ... The act was designed to allow families to stay on the farms rather than lose them to foreclosure.'[130] In July the scope of the operations of the Canadian Farm Loan Board was widened through amendments that authorized the minister of finance to purchase and hold bonds of the board for up to $40 million, compared to the previous maximum of $15 million. The government was also authorized to guarantee the principal and interest of bonds issued by the CFLB for up to $30 million. The amendments enabled the board to make additional loans to applicants.[131] Clark became a member of the board in 1935 and would remain so until his death.

When Clark began preparations for the 1934 budget, he was at least pleased to see some signs of economic recovery. Preparing the budget was the centrepiece of his work at finance and he was determined to give it all his focus and expertise. These lengthy and involved preparations became legendary among those who worked under Clifford Clark. The preparations in 1934 were aided by the appointment of Kenneth Eaton, a specialist in tax policy. According to Bryce, 'Eaton relieved the burden on Clark in a field with which he was not very familiar and provided the foundation on which an expert tax staff would later be built.'[132] Still, the budget introduced no changes to corporation or personal income taxes. Taxes on sugar were reduced to one cent per pound while a tax was introduced on bullion to share in the windfall profits resulting from the American decision to revalue gold from $20.67 an ounce to $35.00. The budget also proposed a 10 per cent tax on gold, which the finance minister, after representations from the mining industry, changed to 25 per cent on the change in price.[133]

By late June the long parliamentary and committee debates on the Bank of Canada were complete and Clark rejoiced that the central bank's creation would at last 'repair this major defect in our financial set-up.'[134] On 3 July the act received royal assent. But the debate now shifted to the choice of governor for the new institution and whether that choice should be a Canadian. On 21 June Bennett told the House that no Canadian had the necessary knowledge or experience. Later the same day, however, he added, 'It does not follow from that that a Canadian will not be appointed and will so acquire knowledge to carry on the functions of this office ... I endeavoured to make it clear to the committee it well might be that a Canadian might be appointed if he had sufficient time to acquire the necessary knowledge and information to discharge the duties of governor of this bank, but in any event he would have to be assisted by someone who had knowledge.'[135]

Clark tried to convince Bennett that restricting the search to Canada was too limiting, 'having in mind the very limited number of Canadian bankers who have, for instance, university training and a theoretical grasp of economic and monetary principles.' One Canadian who might be qualified, Clark observed, was Sir Thomas White, the finance minister in the Borden government during the war and a member of the Macmillan Commission.[136] But Clark had been counselling Bennett on the governor appointment for months. The main qualification for the position was not banking, he claimed, but rather economics. Despite Clark's prejudices against the banking community, he was also reiterating his belief that the government, and its institutions, required university-trained experts. 'The major problem of central banking,' he told Bennett, 'is not one of routine administration but rather of economic interpretation and monetary principles.'[137]

Once it was decided that a Canadian would indeed be appointed, the pool of candidates narrowed quickly and came to focus on one individual – Graham Towers of the Royal Bank.[138] The young Towers had come to the prime minister's attention in April 1932 through a memo he had written on the banking crisis.[139] According to Bryce, it was Clark who proposed Towers directly.[140] The two men certainly knew each other. Clark had Towers in to speak to his classes at Queen's, both were members of the Canadian Political Science Association board in 1933, and they had corresponded several times during the central bank debate. According to Towers, he was consulted on drafting parts of the bill resulting in the bank's creation because he was one of the few bankers who supported the institution.[141] On 6 September 1934 the federal government announced that Graham Towers would be the first governor of the Bank of Canada. He assumed the post four days later.[142] Within a week, the Bank of Canada was established with shares held by the general public, and within two days, the stock was oversubscribed with some 12,200 Canadians holding shares. Until the board of directors could be elected by the shareholders in 1935, the bank operated under a provisional directorate of civil servants under the chairmanship of the deputy minister of finance.[143] The bank took over the note-issuing activities of the finance department and later received provision for the issues of the chartered banks to be reduced over a period of ten years to approximately one-quarter of their existing amount.[144]

On 7 September Clark delivered a speech on the Bank of Canada to the Dominion Association of Chartered Accountants at their annual banquet in Montreal. The majority of the text later appeared in the *Financial Post,* under the headline 'Godfather of Bank of Canada Explains How It Should Work: Deputy Minister of Finance Sees Bank of Canada Act as Most Important Statute since Confederation.' In the speech Clark pressed the point that the new institution had to be accountable to the Canadian people. 'Central banks, like government,' he claimed, 'can never be much in advance of public opinion.' He also tied it directly to avoiding, or at least better managing, economic crises like the Depression: 'If by individual and co-operative action central banks can develop controls and policies that will do something to foster a greater measure of stability in production, trade, prices and employment, then the world has a right to expect such action from them.'[145]

It was accurate to describe Clifford Clark as the bank's godfather. He was instrumental in its creation and he played a critical role in recruiting its very able personnel. Indeed, he would maintain an intimate interest in the affairs of the bank throughout the remainder of his life. Even though at times the officials in finance were pitted against those at the bank, more often than not the two groups worked closely together. After Towers was selected as the first governor, the two men worked to recruit the most able and impressive minds onto the bank's staff, including Alex 'Sandy' Skelton (O.D. Skelton's son), who was a Rhodes scholar from Ontario and became chief of research early in

1935. Robert Beattie, a Rhodes scholar from Manitoba and an actuary at Manufacturers Life, joined the research department soon after the bank opened. The research department was further strengthened in 1936 when John Deutsch, a Queen's commerce graduate from Saskatchewan, and James Coyne, a Rhodes scholar from Manitoba, joined the staff. Another critical addition was Donald Gordon, who was hired away from the Bank of Nova Scotia to become bank secretary early in 1935.[146]

But for the next eighteen years it would be the two powerful personalities of Clark and Towers that would dominate the financial scene in Ottawa. 'It is sometimes said,' one commentator observed, 'that our national economic and financial affairs are somehow settled at a long table, with W.C. Clark, Deputy Minister of Finance, at one end, and Graham Towers, Governor of the Bank of Canada, at the other.'[147] According to Sandy Skelton, when Clark and Towers would disagree, it was 'ideological differences' that usually explained their differences on policy: 'Towers was an "Anglophile" and this sentiment was expressed as an "anti-American prejudice."' Clark, on the other hand, was a strong nationalist who, like his mentor O.D. Skelton, was at times suspicious of British control: 'Clark lacked Towers's gifts as an "expositor" and his "faculty of detachment," and instead often thinks as an improviser: creatively and imaginatively, but he sometimes has to correct tomorrow what he said today.'[148] But disagreements were uncommon and the two men shared most economic views. They could not, however, have possessed more contrasting personalities. Clark was the quiet and modest introvert; Towers was the outgoing and social extrovert. They were an odd couple indeed:

> Clark and Towers were a most impressive team which had great influence on successive governments. They were opposites in almost everything except that they shared a progressive view of things. Clark was hopeless at organization, planning ahead, and the delegation of authority. In the department, he often asked two or three men, all of whom were overworked, to take on some new assignment, each one thinking it was his sole responsibility. Towers, as I have mentioned, was not only a very able central banker but also one of the best organizers I have ever come across. Clark was highly imaginative and continually bursting forth with new ideas. It was Towers' job to persuade him to discard those that were quite preposterous. Clark had a deep and abiding respect for the position of elected representatives of the people, especially ministers of the Crown to whom he was

responsible. Towers always managed to keep under tight control any private adulation he may have felt for politicians. The personal interests and social habits of these two men were very different. Towers was always punctual; Clark, just the opposite. Often they seemed to irritate one another almost beyond endurance. But their deep respect for each other's abilities and talents never seriously wavered. As a team, there was no one who could touch them.[149]

4

A New Boss, 1935–1939

> I asked him what he thought of Clark as a deputy. He said: I brought him in, and I must say that he has practically been the Department of Finance. He said something about Rhodes not being too well qualified, and stressed that the deputy had been the whole department. He also spoke about Rhodes not being well. I said that I personally had gathered a very favourable opinion of Clark. Bennett added that the bankers did not like him, because he was too exacting. I told him that I thought that was no fault.
>
> – Mackenzie King speaking to R.B. Bennett, 22 October 1935

Political events in Canada were moving quickly. The Depression had not only devastated the Prairie west and the Canadian economy in general; it had destroyed the Conservative government of R.B. Bennett. Even though an election was not held until October 1935, Liberal leader Mackenzie King was already preparing to enter office. In particular, he was scanning the horizon (and the federal civil service) for potential people to remain in their positions. On 2 August King met with O.D. Skelton for breakfast. Skelton had proven his worth far beyond partisan politics and had set a precedent by surviving the transition in government from Liberal to Conservative in 1930; there was no doubt he would remain in external affairs when King returned to power in 1935. The Liberal leader told Skelton that he would be looked upon for advice on whom to keep in the federal bureaucracy and whom to drop. Skelton immediately urged King to keep Clifford Clark as deputy minister of finance.[1]

Prime Minister Bennett, meanwhile, was well aware of the political situation facing his government. Early in 1935 the 'New Deal' radio broadcasts were delivered, indicating a 'crisis in capitalism' and promising a whole spate of radical reform measures, including 'the end of laissez faire.'[2] Clark, as with the rest of the Bennett government, was not consulted on the strategy and did not know the New Deal broadcasts were coming until the last minute. In the days immediately prior to the broadcasts, Clark was asked by Herridge to do some work on the speeches but his role was minor. On 3 January, between the first and second broadcasts, the deputy minister wrote a memo to Rod Finlayson, reiterating a proposal already made to Bennett and Rhodes on aid to the western provinces. Clark proposed that the four provinces sell three- to five-year notes, guaranteed by the federal government, to fund more than $100 million in floating debt to the dominion and the banks. The objective was to reduce the interest burden on the provinces while providing the dominion a large amount of cash. As long as the guaranteed loans were outstanding, Clark believed there had to be some amount of federal supervision of the provinces' finances. This would include the provinces agreeing not to issue any new loans without the approval of the governor of the Bank of Canada as well as agreeing to submit their budgets to Ottawa for general approval. While the proposal went nowhere under Bennett, it would be resurrected when the Liberals came into office at the end of the year.[3] Clark was worried that the Depression was severely damaging dominion–provincial relations. On 5 January he wrote a memorandum on the inability of the provinces to meet their increasing expenditures for unemployment relief and social services. To meet the crisis, Clark suggested administrative cooperation when it came to collecting taxes, reduction of overlapping services in fields of concurrent jurisdiction (particularly in the fields of agriculture and public health), and provincial acquiescence to federal invasion into areas of social security.[4] Canada's federal structure was strained to the point of breaking.

Late in January 1935 two Conservative backbenchers, T.L. Church and James Arthurs, urged the federal government to inaugurate a national housing policy. The housing issue had not been dealt with in Bennett's New Deal package and the prime minister suggested instead that the issue be referred to a parliamentary committee to make recommendations.[5] At the end of the Great War the federal government identified the existence of a housing problem in Canada but no action was taken and the period of economic expansion in the late 1920s pushed the problem into the background. There was a general assumption that the market had regained its equilibrium. The boom in housing, however, obscured the presence and growth of slum areas in many parts of urban Canada.[6] Pressure from housing reformers to develop a national housing policy increased as the Depression deepened. By 1933 housing construction had fallen to 31 per cent of the 1929 level. Vacancy rates increased as families were forced to double up. Real estate values declined and countless people defaulted on mortgages; both situations made lenders reluctant to provide money for mortgages.[7] Between 1932 and 1935 local studies of housing problems emerged in Halifax, Montreal, Toronto, Hamilton, Ottawa, and Winnipeg. Reformers argued that it was impossible to build housing of reasonable quality that was affordable to low-income earners. Public housing subsidies therefore were necessary. Such subsidies, they claimed, would cost less than the social costs of inadequate housing. With the collapse of the construction industry during the Depression, reformers were joined by builders, architects, and union leaders, all of whom saw in the reformers' program a chance to revitalize their industry. Pressure was also coming from local municipalities for federal intervention into housing. Industry groups created the National Construction Council in 1933, which commenced a campaign for public housing.[8] The *Bruce Report*, chaired by Ontario's Lieutenant-Governor H.A. Bruce, produced a study of the housing problem in Toronto. The report urged slum clearance and public housing, and called for Ottawa to provide the necessary financial assistance.

Prime Minister Bennett was already feeling overwhelmed by financial demands from both the municipal and provincial levels. 'Please do not project a provincial or even civic problem into the realm of federal politics,' he told Bruce in 1934.[9] In replying to the backbencher motion on 24 January 1935, Bennett indicated that he was 'appalled' at the suggestion of the *Bruce Report* that Ottawa spend $12 million on the slum situation. The prime minister was careful to distinguish between government aid in the form of a loan and government aid suggested by the *Bruce Report*. A federal loan to be distributed by the provinces could be arranged, Bennett noted, but direct aid from Ottawa would set a dangerous precedent: 'It does not seem to me that it was ever intended to be the function of a national government to deal with matters of that kind in the community.' But the issue was serious and unlikely to go away. Bennett decided to refer the matter to a parliamentary committee.[10] On 2 February the prime minister wrote Bruce, 'I am interested in the housing problem. The only difficulty is the financial one. Unfortunately, everyone is now turning to Governments for help. If we assist agriculture with low-priced money, I am afraid we will have to leave the cities to the private lenders. However, the matter is to be studied by a Committee and we will see what develops as a result of the investigations.'[11] On 21 February the Parliamentary Committee on Housing met. Headed by Arthur Ganong, a member of the Canadian Manufacturers Association and the Maritime Board of Trade, its job was to 'consider and report upon the inauguration of a national policy of house building to include the construction, reconstruction and repair of urban and rural dwelling houses in order to provide employment throughout Canada.' This mandate inferred that housing policy was a means to create employment rather than a way to deal with the social costs of inadequate housing to the poor.[12] As John Bacher points out, 'That housing became a subject of political interest in the Depression was more a consequence of the collapse of the construction industry than the condition of the ill-housed.'[13]

The pace of reform in the early months of 1935 proved too much for Bennett. By 24 February a heavy cold turned into an acute respiratory infection. Then, on 7 March, the prime minister suffered a fainting spell and possibly a mild heart attack. He was ordered to rest and soon after left the country for the Silver Jubilee in London. Bennett was effectively out of action from late February until mid-May. The government had to scramble since, as Rhodes put it, the prime minister 'had kept both the contents of the Bills and the material to be used with them entirely to himself.'[14]

With Bennett ill, Rhodes was required to pick up the slack, which included bringing in an early budget. This placed considerable pressure on Clark. 'The last paragraph of the first draft was only completed at twenty minutes to six the day before the Budget was delivered,' Rhodes told a journalist.[15] The budget of 1935 called for tax hikes, including increases to the dominion corporation tax, a graduated tax on all unearned income in excess of $5,000 as well as earned income above $14,000, and a tax on gifts. Faced with a major decline in revenue from the tax on liquor, the budget cut the liquor duty, based on the assumption that the government had priced itself out of the market, thereby encouraging black market sales.[16] On 1 April the Department of Finance took control of the administration of old age pensions from the Department of Labour in order to control its rising costs.[17]

Also in April the Parliamentary Committee on Housing conducted its study. The committee interviewed some twenty witnesses and the conclusions drawn were heavily influenced by the findings of local reports produced in Montreal and Toronto, urging federal aid for the poorest members of the community. The committee heard, and summarized in its report, extensive testimony about slum conditions and the resulting costs. The report also dealt with the huge backlog in housing construction and the ensuing portion of the population who were forced into crowded conditions but could not be evicted because there was no place for them to go. The committee studied programs in other countries that provided low-income housing. The report echoed the view that 'the very essence of the Housing Problem' sat at 'the point at which private enterprise working on ordinary commercial lines cannot provide for certain groups of the community.'[18]

But on 4 April two key witnesses appeared: Clifford Clark, deputy minister of finance, and D'Arcy Leonard, solicitor of the Dominion Mortgage and Investment Association. Their views largely shaped the legislation that followed the committee's report. Both men shared the opinion that government intervention should be limited to mortgage assistance for prospective owners and builders. Once it became clear that their views coincided, Clark and Leonard joined forces and 'negotiated for two months behind the scenes.'[19] Leonard represented the residential mortgage industry, consisting of loan, trust, and insurance companies.[20] Mortgages were restricted by law to a maximum of 60 per cent of the appraised value of a property and, although his members had money to lend, Leonard told the committee that 'there are not so many people who can put up the difference between 60 per cent and 100 per cent.' When asked if there would be substantially more construction if the government put up another 20 per cent, Leonard replied, 'It undoubtedly would; I am quite satisfied of that.' He warned, however, that mortgage lenders had to be careful in putting up money for new housing: 'We would always have to be satisfied that the erection of a certain number of new houses in any particular district was not going to intensify the trouble that we are in the present time with respect to the surplus of houses, low rental values or selling values.' Moreover, if low-rent housing was introduced, it would tend to depress the rents of the next several classes of rental housing. This was a central dilemma for the committee.[21]

Clark had considerable expertise in the building industry but he admitted to the committee that he was not a housing expert. His interests were threefold: he was interested in housing 'as a social and economic problem, looking at it from the long point of view'; he had an interest 'in the short run problem of providing some stimulant to business recovery, and to seek to absorb unemployment'; and as deputy minister of finance he was concerned with 'safeguarding the public treasury.' When it came to the issue of slum clearance, Clark advised caution and more study. The issue would inevitably come with considerable cost to municipal, provincial, and federal governments, and would carry complicated legal implications. In the meantime, Clark advised immediate action on the 'emergency problem of using housing as a stimulant to business recovery and as an absorber of unemployment.'[22]

Clark made several proposals. He suggested creation of a 'central housing corporation' whose role would be to supervise and assist in financing local housing corporations that applied for federal assistance. The central agency would be responsible for formulating sound construction standards, approving specific projects, and financing the corporations through the purchase of their preferred stock, 'thus providing on a low-cost basis the junior money which it is so difficult and so expensive to obtain for housing purposes.' Clark suggested that the government assist the profitability of private mortgage lending companies in the housing market but strive to keep its role to a minimum. It should assist the recovery of the housing market but not deal with the low-rent issue. This approach was desirable, according to the deputy minister, because it avoided competition with private lenders. There would be no need for a federal department or even a major federal role, and the focus would be on home ownership rather than on rentals. Where subsidized rental was necessary, this approach favoured private limited dividend corporations over public housing authorities.[23] As an alternative to limited dividend corporations, Clark proposed that the federal government set up an insurance corporation to guarantee the last 20 per cent of an 80 per cent mortgage.[24]

Clark's limited dividend proposal was criticized as unworkable in a letter from consulting architect F.W. Nicolls, whom, ironically, Clark would soon hire to run the National Housing Administration created in the Department of Finance. Nicolls argued that the rate of return was too low to attract investors at the same time as interest rates on mortgages of 5.0 to 5.5 per cent were too high to permit quality low-rental housing to be profitably built. Clark replied that a more ambitious low-rental scheme was too much of a financial burden on Ottawa: 'In view of the very high financial burdens upon the Dominion exchequer I tried to develop a plan which would make the federal dollar or federal guarantee do as much as possible. It might be desirable from many points of view to develop some grandiose projects for the use of very large amounts of Dominion funds or credit, but a practical appreciation of the financial burdens we already bear make one pause in considering such schemes.'[25]

The Housing Committee issued its report on 16 April 1935, and its recommendations went much further than either Bennett or Clark was prepared to go. After indicating that a national emergency would soon develop unless the construction of homes was greatly increased, the report called for the 'formulation, institution, and pursuit of a policy of adequate housing as a social responsibility.' There was no apparent prospect of the low rental housing need being met through unaided private enterprise, so the report called for the provision of 25,000 dwelling units to be built throughout Canada immediately. The committee recommended provision for long-term mortgages and the establishment of a national housing authority to initiate, direct, approve, and control projects and policies supported by the federal government.[26]

But Clark was already drafting legislation on the housing issue, even prior to his appearance before the committee. He used the committee to prepare the public, the housing specialists, and in particular the mortgage lenders for the government's program. A draft bill was worked out between Clark and Leonard. Several weeks later Leonard wrote Clark to inform him that the Dominion Mortgage and Investment Association 'had been working steadily in the past three weeks endeavouring to work out a plan whereby the lending institutions might cooperate with the government in a housing scheme.'[27]

The housing debate was interrupted for Clark by a pleasant interlude on 8 May when he received an honorary doctor of laws degree from his alma mater, Queen's University. The deputy minister finally earned the doctorate he had never completed, thus allowing him to be officially called 'Dr Clark.' As a result of his academic reputation and mannerisms, he was already widely known by this title, regardless. Clark was chosen to speak (much to his chagrin) for the honorary degree candidates but, despite his nervousness and claims to be a poor orator, he ended up offering a speech that demonstrated his personal blend of humility and wit. The speech also carried an ominous message about the current state of affairs in Canada and the world:

> In my day it was the custom of speakers, on such occasions as this, to give a heartening and encouraging message to the new graduates … I would not be candid or truthful if I brought to you such a message today … It is, of course, true that you are the heirs of all the ages. But what is this heritage you are to receive? ... By and large, my generation has made a sorry mess of its trusteeship. Of course we blame our failure on the Great War and on the Great Depression, on world wide factors beyond our control … We may try to avoid responsibility but I am afraid we cannot cast it off altogether. In any case we are now turning over to you the results of our stewardship, a world ripe for reorganization – a world which is indeed already in process of reorganization. But what form is that reorganization to take? ... To this question we have no certain answers … We are confused and befuddled – confused by a Babel of conflicting counsel, a multitude of panaceas, a caravanserai of catch phrases and emblems, of symbols and labels, Green Shirts, Brown Shirts, Black Shirts, Swastikas, Communism, Fascism, Reform, Capitalism and what not.[28]

After his visit to Queen's, Clark returned to the work of developing housing policy. For much of May the deputy minister was on his own. Rhodes, also suffering from ill health, was now bedridden.[29] Clark and Leonard went to work putting together the legislation. Leonard played a pivotal role and in a letter dated 2 June he laid out the basis for the eventual bill: 'We believe that the soundest housing scheme would be one that would enable the existing mortgage lending institutions to lend up to eighty per cent on approved new houses, in approved locations, to be built for home owners … If approved, a loan up to an amount of eighty per cent of the value of the property would be made by a lending institution, of which sixty per cent would be supplied by the institution and twenty per cent by the government. The government contribution would be in the form of a cheque handled by the lending institution so that the borrower would have only the one organization to deal with himself.'[30] By mid-June Parliament discussed possible government action. Wilfrid Hanbury, a member of the Special Committee on Housing, indicated that his own views could best be summed up by quoting from Clark's testimony. 'We had many proposals placed before us,' Hanbury observed, 'but I believe the function of any government, as outlined by Doctor Clark's evidence, is in the first place to avoid the socialization suggested by many of the witnesses.' The fact that most workers could not afford housing was related, Hanbury argued, to general economic conditions and when they improved, housing would not be such a serious matter. Despite the apparently 'socialistic' tone of the committee's report, Clark helped shift the recommendations back into the realm of free-market capitalism.[31] According to Bryce, the principles of the legislation 'reflected Clark's philosophy and the circumstances of the budget. According to the legislation the Government accepted a large share of the economic risks and offered relatively low cost credit, but did not become involved in outright construction or ownership of housing, rental subsidies, or direct expenditure of any kind.'[32]

The Dominion Housing Act came before Parliament on 24 June. The bill itself was brief, with just eight sections consisting of about nine hundred words. As Clark suggested in his testimony, the issue of slums was not dealt with at the time but was referred for study to the Economic Council of Canada, whose creation had been authorized on 17 April. The Economic Council was also to study the adequacy of existing housing conditions and the best means of improving them, in addition to methods of increasing the efficiency of housing construction.[33] The heart of the legislation – following Leonard's lead – authorized the minister of finance to enter into contract with an approved lending institution or local authority to assist in making loans for the construction of new housing units. The act authorized such institutions to lend up to 80 per cent of the cost of construction or appraised value of a new house, whichever was lower. Up until this time, as Leonard later explained, life insurance and loan companies that provided most of the first mortgage money for building houses were prevented by law from lending more than 60 per cent of the value of a property. The legislation was designed to protect the policyholders and investors in the mortgage and loan companies. It was customary to provide part of the remaining cost through a second mortgage. Because of the higher risk involved, interest rates on second mortgages were generally 10 per cent or higher. Second mortgage investors were so devastated by the Depression, and by legislation passed for the relief of mortgagors, that there was no second mortgage money available. There was a surplus of funds seeking safe first mortgages, but the balance of the financing was 'missing.'[34]

The Dominion Housing Act failed to provide low-income housing for the large segment of the Canadian population suffering under the Depression. This critical fact was not missed by Parliament. On 24 and 25 June the act ran into vehement opposition from the Labourites and the United Farmers. The major parties, however, were also divided. One of the most scathing reactions came from the Conservative chairman of the Housing Committee, Arthur Ganong, who felt the committee's work had been appropriated and then ignored in the eventual policy: 'I met a good many persons who might be called town planning and housing cranks. I worked with them for two months and at the end of that time was converted. I think rather than cranks they are torch bearers to something that is coming. This housing problem must be faced. We cannot continue to allow thousands of families in this country to live in one room under unsanitary conditions as they are and have been for the last few years. It is a tremendous problem ... With all due respect to the minister who has introduced this bill, I must say that it makes no provision for housing the low paid worker.'[35]

Only those who could afford the down payment and possessed a decent-paying job would benefit, but such people could already arrange to secure a house without government assistance.[36] The opposition claimed that the government bill was so different from the committee report that it was not worth pursuing. Liberal MP R.W. Gray suggested that 'when one takes the evidence from the beginning to end, one can almost feel that this bill was based upon the fears of the lending institutions.'[37] Mackenzie King, however, did not criticize the bill. Like Clark, he approved of its objective to stimulate employment in a way that would also help some people in need of housing and in his response, he focused mainly on effective coordination of employment measures.[38]

Despite considerable opposition, Clark remained convinced that the Dominion Housing Act offered revolutionary innovations to the mortgage market. In particular, he noted, borrowers with small cash resources were allowed to build their own homes without resort to financing by means of second and third mortgages. This form of financing had virtually disappeared during the Depression. 'Much of the building financed under the Housing Act,' he noted several years later, 'would therefore not have been possible, let alone probable, without the Act.' Clark also praised the fact that in contrast to traditional three- to five-year terms, loans under the act were made for ten years and were renewable for a second period of ten years. Renewal costs, therefore, were avoided and the risk of having to pay off or reduce the mortgage at inconvenient times was largely eliminated. In addition, the rate of interest on the mortgage could not exceed an effective rate of 5 per cent.[39] Clark used the lending provisions of the Housing Act to insist on certain standards of design, specification, and inspection of houses being built. The deputy minister later pursued this objective through the formation of the National Building Code in 1941.[40] Faced with the charge that the act did nothing to alleviate conditions for low-income earners, Clark responded, 'If a municipality desires to encourage low cost housing, it will be possible for the municipality to contribute a portion, or all, of this 20 per cent equity.' He concluded, 'It is, of course, incorrect to say that the Bill makes no provision for low cost housing or slum clearance.'[41] According to Clark, 'Most of the alleged solutions of this problem which I have seen involve financial burdens of such magnitude that I do not see how anyone with a realistic conception of the financial problems of government in this country can contemplate them.'[42] But the criticism was ideological and would not go away. There is truth in Bacher's frank observation that 'Canada's initial housing legislation was almost a caricature of the inequities of Canadian society, its benefits going mainly to the rich and middle class even when supported by public funds and wrapped in the rhetoric of concern for the underprivileged.' The act was passed on 25 June and became law on 5 July.[43]

For the rest of his career Clifford Clark viewed the Dominion Housing Act, including future additions, as his own personal project. He took the administration of the legislation under 'his own wing' in the Department of Finance and devoted what Bryce calls 'a surprising amount of his time and energy to it.'[44] The first requirement to bring the act into operation was to develop a contract to be used by mortgage lenders. Since the act depended on the cooperation of the lenders, the government was in an awkward position. By mid-July Clark prepared a draft contract and submitted it to the Dominion Mortgage and Investment Association. With Leonard's revisions, the contract was approved by the Privy Council.[45] With the Conservative government facing an election (and almost certain defeat), Clark was forced to wait and see how the Liberals would deal with the housing issue. During the election campaign, renegade Tory H.H. Stevens, now leading his Reconstruction Party, dismissed the legislation as 'a bill for the relief and protection of trust, loan, mortgage and insurance companies' and argued that sections of the country would be 'black-balled' by the lenders who would refuse to service certain regions and communities.[46]

While Parliament was debating his housing legislation, Clark was at St Lawrence University in Canton, New York, where he took part in the first of four biennial conferences on Canadian–American relations. The proceedings were designed to bring experts from the two nations together to consider common problems. The relationship was becoming increasingly important for Canada. In his conference presentation Clark noted that there was $4 billion in U.S. investments in Canada and $1 billion of Canadian investment in the United States. 'These are striking figures,' he observed. 'They represent the most extraordinary example in world history of the financial interrelationship of two countries.' This 'cash nexus,' he noted, is really '"the tie that binds"' and would certainly contribute to a better mutual understanding and a closer fellowship between the two nations. American investment in Canada, Clark went on, 'has transformed our whole economy – opened up many of our waste places, reshaped much of our industrial fabric, conditioned our standard of living, and affected to an important degree the whole tempo of our national life. It has brought obligations, dangers and difficulties, as well as advantages.'[47] As with Mackenzie King, Clifford Clark viewed close relations with the United States as Canada's inevitable, logical, and beneficial road into the future.

On 23 June King George V bestowed honours and a list of Canadians, including Clifford Clark, received titular distinction. Such British honours were a rarity for Canadians after the First World War. A resolution passed by the House of Commons in 1919 requested that the King not confer titles on residents of Canada. The practice was halted until 1933 when Prime Minister Bennett restored it.[48] Clark was made a Companion of St Michael and St George for his contribution to commerce. The titles were eliminated again at the end of 1935 when the Liberals came back into office under Mackenzie King. Despite Clark's liberal philosophy, he always spoke of his companionship with a particular sense of pride.

With an election not held until October, Clark managed to find time to get in some fishing in northern Quebec with some friends, including Oscar Skelton, Bill Mackintosh, Donald Gordon, Loring Christie, Bryce Stewart, and Dana Wilgress.[49] According to Wilgress, Clark had an ulterior motive for the trip. He wanted to establish a fishing club for his civil service colleagues and he was scouting possible locations. Fishing was Clark's most beloved past-time. According to Mackintosh, he was not a fisherman 'of great skill but of immense enthusiasm,' and it was certainly more of a social vocation than a sporting one. Clark's eldest son, George, remembered his father going fishing straight from work while still wearing his suit, but the deputy minister was not the only one to do so.[50] Clark was searching for an atmosphere where he could combine fishing and socializing with his closest friends, all of whom, not surprisingly, were work colleagues.[51] Observers also felt that Clark was settling nicely into his position at finance. The hiring of experts, particularly during the crisis of the Depression, was reaping dividends. In September Clark was praised by the *Financial Times* for the department's handling of government debt issues.[52]

On 14 October 1935, Clark witnessed his first federal election since becoming a bureaucrat. Because he prided himself on his professionalism and non-partisanship, it is impossible to know for certain how he voted; it is also unclear how he felt about the inevitable result. He was closer to the Liberal party philosophically, and his closest colleagues (including Skelton) were even more predisposed to the Grits, but Clark's role as 'protector of the purse' also made him an easy fit with the Conservative party. In his three years working under Bennett and Rhodes, there was no sign of ideological incompatibility. Indeed, Clark had come to share many of Bennett's hard-line, fiscally orthodox views when it came to handling the Depression (and the provinces) and there were few disagreements. During the debate over the Dominion Housing Act, or in negotiations with the provincial premiers, Clark's critics viewed him as a fiscal conservative and clearly in Bennett's camp. And Clark's opinion of Bennett had improved since entering the civil service. The prime minister may have had 'erratic emotions' but he generally built positive relationships with those working under him. That is, as long as they did not 'cross swords.'[53] Clark never crossed swords with the prime minister but he also never found the need.

Regardless of the fact that Clark had come to respect R.B. Bennett, in the federal election of 1935 the Conservatives were swept from power. Mackenzie King and the Liberals were returned with an overwhelming majority: the Liberals won 171 seats to 39 for the Conservatives, 17 for Social Credit, and 7 for the Co-operative Commonwealth Federation (CCF). Despite the change in government, Clark found little difference in the economic policies advocated by the Liberals. Bennett was vilified by having the misfortune of leading the nation during the Depression, but in truth there was little difference between the Conservative and Liberal response. 'Five years of depression had challenged many of the traditional assumptions about politics as well as economics,' Blair Neatby notes, but King's own views 'had undergone little change.' Economic recovery depended ultimately on private enterprise; governments would play a secondary role. As far as King was concerned, he already possessed experience in dealing with economic crisis, having faced the post-war recession. His government had come through that crisis successfully by adhering to a policy of rigid economy. The same recipe should produce the same result: 'Economic recovery might be slow but it would be sure, and King had four years to prove that he was right.'[54]

On 23 October Prime Minister King announced his Cabinet and Charles Dunning was named minister of finance. Dunning had served in the post briefly in 1930, before the Liberals were defeated. The selection of Dunning, according to Bryce, assured the consistency of a 'conservative economic strategy.' King wanted Dunning, Neatby claims, because he represented fiscal conservatism. He had shown administrative ability and he would bring Prairie support as the former premier of Saskatchewan, but his presence in government and orthodox views would also reassure the manufacturing sector. The Depression, according to Dunning, had been caused by 'reckless and irresponsible business practices.' Society was doing penance for its infractions against the laws of sound economics. Recovery would not come through miracles but rather through returning harmony to natural economic law. Recovery would have to precede reform. As minister of finance, Dunning intended to 'stand for stability, non-interference with legitimate business, sanctity of governmental contracts and prevention of provincial raids upon the Federal Treasury.'[55] Clifford Clark had a new boss and he would have no problems working under Mackenzie King or Charles Dunning.

King met Bennett on several occasions to discuss the transfer of power. On 22 October, the day before the new Cabinet was announced, Bennett spoke of the problems to be confronted immediately by the new government. The four western provinces were facing bankruptcy. In addition, a loan of the Canadian National Securities was falling due and had to be dealt with immediately. Bennett suggested that the new finance minister should meet with Clark as soon as possible. King then asked Bennett directly if he recommended that Clark remain in his post: 'I asked him what he thought of Clark as a deputy. He said: I brought him in, and I must say that he has practically been the Department of Finance. He said something about Rhodes not being too well qualified, and stressed that the deputy had been the whole department. He also spoke about Rhodes not being well. I said that I personally had gathered a very favourable opinion of Clark. Bennett added that the bankers did not like him, because he was too exacting. I told him that I thought that was no fault.'[56] Clifford Clark was invited to remain as deputy minister of finance.

One of the first major economic issues that the new government tackled was a free trade deal with the United States. Mackenzie King was intent on concluding an agreement within a year of taking office. In mid-November Canada and the United States signed the first reciprocity agreement between the two nations in almost seventy years. The intermediate tariff schedule was granted and the deal did not have to be sweetened with additional reductions. In addition Canada managed to negotiate 'most-favoured nation' status with the United States. The deal was put together quickly with little obstruction and it was expedited by King personally visiting President Roosevelt.[57] As a result, Clark was not heavily involved in the process. He did participate, however, in a cooperative agreement reached at the beginning of December at a conference on Trans-Atlantic Air Services, which took place in Ottawa. Representatives were present from the United Kingdom, the Irish Free State, Newfoundland, and Canada. Because the conference delegates wanted the cooperation of the United States, at the close of the meeting the representatives accepted an invitation to travel to Washington. An agreement was reached with American officials that led to the institution of a regular transatlantic air mail, passenger, and express service.[58] Clark's involvement is ironic because the deputy minister was terrified of flying and would never in his life cross the Atlantic by air.

A dominion-provincial conference was also held at the beginning of December. The delegates spent the week in committees on finance, relief, constitutional reform, mining taxation, and agriculture.[59] Finance Minister Dunning put forward the idea of amending the British North America (BNA) Act to enable the dominion government to guarantee provincial debts and allow the provinces to pledge certain specific revenues as security for borrowing. Most of the provinces expressed difficulty in bearing the burden of debt charges and instead urged the dominion to come up with increased aid. Dunning hinted that he might be prepared to transfer certain tax fields to the provinces and to back provincial bond issues by a federal guarantee, which would make it easier for provinces to borrow money and reduce their interest rates. The finance minister did not go into details but he did link this to a refunding operation that would involve federal supervision of provincial finances. The proposed 'Loan Council' would also seek agreement for joint security from the provinces on a fifty-fifty basis. Federal officials, including Clark and Towers, perceived the discussions as indicating general provincial consent to at least consider the proposal and discuss it in the future. 'Representatives of all the provinces,' Clark argued, 'agreed that the Dominion should take immediate steps to secure the necessary constitutional authority to make such an arrangement effective.'[60] According to Towers, 'no Province stated definitely that it would participate in the plan, although no Province objected to the creation of the necessary machinery.'[61] The conference, in general, did express interest in the idea and decided that the provincial treasurers would meet with the minister of finance to continue the discussion. The National Finance Committee was created as a result. According to Robin Fisher, however, such unanimity was not so obvious. Premier Duff Pattullo of British Columbia 'made it clear from the start' that he would 'have nothing to do with the proposed Loan Council if it meant any reduction in provincial autonomy.'[62]

Clark supported the creation of the Loan Council (he had previously suggested such federal supervision of provincial finances) and he provided Dunning with background papers. The deputy minister served as expert advisor to the financial sub-conference and urged Dunning to deal with issues of duplication of taxes between the two levels of government. In particular, Clark recommended that corporation taxes be collected federally and he was instructed to gather information on this proposed policy. He also urged the creation of a National Employment Commission, which the Liberals had already endorsed and Norman Rogers put forward at the conference.[63] In January, Dunning met his provincial counterparts to discuss the Loan Council but federal officers met immediate opposition.[64] Premier Mitchell Hepburn of Ontario wanted no part of 'piecemeal' refunding operations.[65] The representatives from British Columbia and Alberta also had serious misgivings about the federally controlled council.

At the same time, much to Clark's frustration, the operation of his housing legislation ran into obstacles. 'Considerable difficulty has been experienced in the initial stages,' Clark admitted in January 1936, 'in getting the lending institutions to sign the contract with the Minister of Finance, and to co-operate enthusiastically in the operations of the Act.' For months, Clark worked to iron out problems with the legislation. Frank Nicolls was hired as the first director of the Housing Branch in the finance department. Although he had been hired as Ken Eaton's assistant, Harvey Perry was assigned to work with Nicolls for a time to implement the act. Clark found an empty office for the two in the East Block of Parliament and provided specific instructions that he wanted to see the first applications that came in.[66] Clark was confident that the act was working smoothly in Ontario and Quebec,[67] but lending institutions in western and maritime Canada were proving more obstinate, mainly as a result of the state of the real estate market in these regions.[68]

Any prospect of the act even stimulating study of low-cost housing was eliminated when Liberal backbencher Jean-Francois Pouliot introduced a bill to abolish the Economic Council of Canada. Three days later the bill was given final approval with almost no debate. The indirect result was to render void the one clause of the Dominion Housing Act that specifically addressed low-income housing by referring study of the issue to the Economic Council. With the council gone, the finance department was strengthened in its handling of housing, which might have been challenged by external housing experts. Prime Minister King argued that the Economic Council was redundant since the government had access to the economic advice and expertise of the entire federal civil service. Neither the government nor the opposition mentioned the impact of the decision on housing, nor did editorials in Canadian labour journals.[69]

Regardless, Clark's intentions for the Dominion Housing Act were aimed primarily at the middle and not the lower classes. In September new regulations came into effect to encourage lending institutions to make loans to prospective house owners of moderate means. 'So now it can be said without fear of contradiction,' Clark claimed proudly, 'that the Dominion Housing Act is accomplishing one of the primary purposes for which it was intended, that of assisting the small house owner, particularly the man of moderate means, to own his own home.' The act was also accomplishing many things, Clark added, 'which cannot be shown in figures.' He lauded the legislation for providing minimum standards of construction to avoid excessive maintenance, rapid depreciation, and shoddy construction. In particular, it was making the Canadian populace 'house conscious' by demonstrating to people of low income that it was indeed possible 'for them to have a well-built, convenient, modern home, structurally sound and of pleasing appearance at a minimum of cost.' These sentiments, of course, were of little comfort to those in most need. Clark admitted that 'the possibilities contained in the Dominion Housing Act for solving the low-cost housing problem have not, as yet, to any great extent been touched.' The problem of saving the required equity often proved insurmountable. In his defence of the legislation, Clark's own ideological position inevitably emerged: 'It may entail great sacrifices by the family, but the family which is not willing to make sacrifices for a home of its own might, perhaps, be better off not to own its own home. Having a home of your own usually is, and always should be, the reward of saving and sacrifice and not a gift from a benevolent government.'[70] Publicly, Clark argued that the act was not a suitable vehicle for ambitious slum clearing projects and it was not intended to serve such a purpose: 'If it is considered desirable that such projects should be undertaken in this country and that the Dominion Government should participate in them, new legislation will probably have to be passed. Whether or not such legislation is desirable and, if so, what form it should take, it is not appropriate for me to discuss.'[71]

The spring of 1936 was a dark time for the federal Department of Finance. The impact of the Depression made a mess of Canada's federal system. In mid-March Dunning warned of a $125 million deficit. Relief payments to the provinces were cut.[72] The Alberta Social Credit government led by Premier 'Bible' Bill Aberhart balked at participating in the proposed Loan Council on the basis that it was little more than an attempt by Ottawa to usurp control of provincial finances. Clark moved quickly to counter these charges. 'As I have assured you on several occasions,' he told Charles Cockroft, Alberta's provincial treasurer, 'there is no desire here to infringe upon provincial "autonomy" – in fact, that is the last thing we would want to do.' Clark reminded Cockroft that the purpose of the council was to enable the provinces to refund their existing debt at substantially lower rates of interest without affecting adversely their credit or that of the dominion. The vital feature of the arrangement was that the dominion would undertake to give its guarantee to any securities issued to refund the outstanding debt of the province and to any future borrowing by the province: 'Neither Parliament nor the country, I am sure,' Clark argued, 'would support this Government in sponsoring such a program unless appropriate steps were taken to safeguard the Dominion against loss under the guarantee either immediately or in the long-run future.' Clark was shocked that Alberta would consider facing default rather than accept the Loan Council: 'I cannot believe that your province will be so misled by a false and unreal issue that for this reason alone it will throw overboard an opportunity for lowering its debt charges in a way consistent with honourable treatment of its creditors and accept instead an alternative which will probably mean the destruction of its own credit for a great many years and serious damage to the credit of its neighbouring provinces, if not of the Dominion itself.'[73]

On 16 March Premier Aberhart announced that his province was going forward with the refunding of the province's outstanding debt, apparently without reference to the Loan Council. Aberhart criticized the federal government for taking no action, even when faced with Alberta's requests for aid in refunding its debt. The following day Dunning informed Aberhart that if Alberta ignored the Loan Council, he could not justify to Parliament the federal government helping the province meet its upcoming maturity with further loans.[74] Clark remained hopeful that Aberhart would come to his senses. Graham Towers at the Bank of Canada, meanwhile, was already prepared to let the province default. 'My own feeling, however,' Clark told Dunning, 'is that Aberhart will not risk a break with Cockroft and a break with the Dominion Government ... and that before the end of the week he will come through with an acceptance of the Loan Council perhaps with some conditions.' The optimistic Clark was prepared to offer a compromise by which the Loan Council would not disapprove of borrowing unless a province reached a certain percentage of ordinary revenues. He also suggested that if any proposed new borrowing for capital purposes was disapproved by the Loan Council, the provincial government would have the right to submit the question to a plebiscite of the people.[75] But Clark misjudged Aberhart.

On 1 April the province of Alberta defaulted, and the move sent panic through the Bank of Canada as well as the Department of Finance, who both feared the stability of Canada's lending rates. 'I believe that the comparatively slight effect which the Alberta default has had on the high-grade market and the fact that its effects on Western Provinces have not been fully seen as yet,' Clark told Dunning on 4 April, 'are likely to lull the public generally, and ourselves also, into a false sense of optimism.' But if BC and Saskatchewan defaulted as well, 'the effect on the whole Dominion credit structure would be serious.'[76] Premier Duff Pattullo of BC also refused to cooperate with the proposed Loan Council because he felt it was 'too rigid and inelastic,' and would curtail the provinces' ability to control their own finances.[77] Pattullo realized that his platform of large-scale capital expenditures would likely not get past the Loan Council.[78] Saskatchewan, on the other hand, agreed to come under the terms of the council. Towers noted that the Alberta default did not cause any serious disturbance in the national market for bonds or of the eastern provinces. It did, however, hurt the western market.[79]

Premier Aberhart came to Ottawa on 19 May to discuss financial relations between Ottawa and Alberta. Clark spent considerable time and effort seeking solutions to deal with the renegade province. But he found Aberhart's logic baffling. The premier was making considerable political capital in the west by vilifying the federal government for interfering with the province's autonomy and attempts to implement a 'social credit' program. As a result, Clark suggested to Dunning that Aberhart be informed that the dominion in fact had no objections to Social Credit: 'We believe it will not work but we do not oppose it.' On the contrary, Aberhart should be encouraged to implement Social Credit immediately: 'Uncertainty as to what he is going to do is a definite deterrent to business recovery. If it is going to be done at all, it had better be done quickly.' Clark hoped that by allaying Aberhart's fears, the premier could then be convinced to accept the Loan Council. It had, after all, already been modified according to Aberhart's wishes to meet the request for the right to create internal debt without being subject to Loan Council veto.[80]

Aberhart proposed that Alberta issue 'consols' (consolidated annuities) to cover the entire provincial debt. These consols would have no fixed date of maturity and the dominion would provide their guarantee. Because the consols had no maturity date, the guarantee would be merely 'nominal or psychological' and would thus simply involve the guarantee of the interest payments. In order to cover the dominion's liability, Aberhart wished to 'ear mark' certain funds for that purpose, thereby assuring all interest payments.[81] Clark, however, was already prepared for Aberhart's consol scheme and countered that 'it is quite impossible for us to consider giving our guarantee to his perpetual consols which he wishes to give to the holders of his existing securities. If his argument were correct that we would incur no liability because of the perpetual nature of these securities, then it would seem to be possible to wipe out our public debt liability by changing it from the terminable to the perpetual form.'[82] As Dunning pointed out to Aberhart, far from the guarantee being merely nominal or psychological, the credit of the dominion would be pledged forever to protect the payment by the province of interest on some $180 million of provincial debt. Aberhart pledged to earmark certain revenues to cover interest payments, yet admitted to being unable to bind future governments to the same commitment. 'It was obvious,' Dunning argued, 'that the commitment of the province should be commensurate in term with the liability of the Dominion.' The finance minister again pointed to the Loan

Council as a means of gaining dominion guarantee. He knew Aberhart would continue to refuse, so he suggested that the Social Credit government hold a meeting with its bondholders to attempt a solution. He hoped the bondholders could push Aberhart and his government toward a 'realistic' solution.[83] Regardless, in late June the Senate refused to proceed with the proposed constitutional amendment to clarify and widen the taxation powers of the provinces. With no amendment, the proposal to pass legislation to create the Loan Council also died.[84]

On 1 May Charles Dunning brought down the federal budget. The pessimistic tone was a marked difference from the confidence expressed by Dunning in his first budget as finance minister back in 1930. Recovery was underway, but barely: 'I do not wish to exaggerate the extent of that recovery, for to those who are charged with the responsibilities of government in these hard times the distance yet to go and the problems still to be solved are the features of our economic record which are most impressive – and at the same time most distressing.'[85] In the previous year, the government's deficit was $160 million. Dunning sought to employ an aggressive strategy to balance the budget. The federal government raised the corporation tax to 15 per cent and 17 per cent on consolidated returns in 1935.[86] The sales tax was increased from 6 to 8 per cent, and a three-year exemption from tax on new mines was introduced.[87] The provinces were also moving into new taxation fields, but only under the aegis of the federal government. Ontario withdrew its municipal income taxes and imposed a provincial income tax to be collected by Ottawa. Over the next four years, Manitoba, Prince Edward Island, Quebec, and the Yukon reached similar agreements, all under the jurisdiction of the deputy minister of finance.[88] Duties on gasoline and farm implements were reduced, and the most popular item in the budget was the exemption from duty three times a year of $100 worth of personal purchases by tourists. This incentive was part of the free trade deal signed with the United States.[89]

In November Clark provided Dunning with the departmental revenue estimates. He estimated a deficit of $101 million for the fiscal year. But the deputy minister believed that both the revenue and expenditure estimates were low. Account was not being properly taken of the appropriations, the grants-in-aid to the provinces, the writing down of Saskatchewan's indebtedness to the dominion, and concessions that would likely have to be made to Manitoba and Alberta.[90]

The prime minister seemed pleased with his new finance minister but, as was typical for Mackenzie King, he was much more critical in his diary. Dunning did not 'like being over-ruled,' King commented. 'He has beneath all a nature that is "hostile," aggressive, & which causes antagonism. He also has a way of taking things in his own hands, and "telling" others what to do.'[91] It is difficult to ascertain how exactly the guarded Clark viewed Dunning. The deputy minister seemed to hold Dunning in high regard but there was no closeness between the two men. It is perhaps more revealing to analyse what Clark did not say, rather than what he did. Clark offered little in the way of comment regarding Dunning; on the other hand, he later remarked on how impressed he was with some of the other ministers under whom he served.

In early December the only meeting of the National Finance Committee took place. The agenda for the meeting called for a fundamental restructuring of the dominion-provincial tax system.[92] In particular Clark made a pitch for federal collection of corporation taxes, but Ontario, Quebec, and British Columbia had reservations, and nothing further ensued.[93] Further action was made redundant by Prime Minister King's announcement in February that a royal commission was to be established to study the state of dominion–provincial relations. The idea of establishing such a broad and ambitious royal commission, according to Bryce, first emerged officially in the form of a memorandum from Sandy Skelton. The idea, however, had been bandied around, particularly in the Department of Finance, for some time.[94] The desperate financial plight, especially of the Prairie provinces, made the situation acute and Graham Towers of the Bank of Canada was very alarmed.[95]

On 7 December Clark wrote a memo on a proposed commission, similar to that penned by Skelton. The confidential memorandum was titled 'Royal Commission on Economic Basis of Confederation.' Clark suggested Newton Rowell as chair and such individuals as Louis St Laurent, J.L. Ralston, H.F. Angus, and Jacob Viner as possible members. He emphasized the need for a particularly able secretariat and research staff, for the sheer breadth of what was being proposed. When it came to the terms of reference, Clark argued that the commission should offer a comprehensive scope, examining 'the economic and financial basis of Confederation with special reference to the allocation of governmental burdens on the one hand and revenue sources on the other hand to Dominion, provincial and municipal governments; to examine such allocation of responsibilities and powers in the light of the developments over the last seventy years.' These terms were very similar to those eventually adopted by the prime minister. Clark went further, even hinting at some 'inevitable' conclusions that such a report would reach. Social expenditures, including relief, were growing at a rate never contemplated at Confederation; the taxation powers given to the provinces by the BNA Act were inadequate to meet present and future burdens; the dominion would have to assume some of the provincial financial burdens; and the provinces would have to be compensated for fields of taxation taken on by the dominion. Clark's memo also listed the obstacles to such a commission, the main one being provincial obstructionism: 'It is certainly true that the difficulties at present surrounding a Constitutional amendment and arising out of narrow "provincial rights" attitudes on the part of one, two or three provinces, form a serious obstacle to any major constructive change. Nevertheless, sooner or later these difficulties must be faced and, as the present situation is intolerable, the sooner the better.' The inability of the federal system to deal with the expansion of new governmental functions, expenditures, and revenues had 'seriously disturbed the financial balance' of the nation, but the Depression had now aggravated the situation to the point that drastic action was necessary. In particular, the 'hazardous' situation facing the Prairie region had recently led to the 'extremes' of Social Credit in Alberta: 'In the West particularly we have a steady deterioration of public morale, the immediate and ultimate consequences of which are difficult to contemplate.'[96]

The failed attempts to proceed with the constitutional amendment and the ensuing death of the Loan Council also played a significant role in demonstrating that substantial change in the Canadian federal system was necessary. Clark and Dunning recognized this need and were already attempting to organize another National Finance Committee in the face of the Loan Council failure. They hoped that dominion and provincial officials could meet twice a year to discuss such issues as tax collection, administration, and duplication, and the raising of public funds through borrowing.[97] These issues would become central to the proposed royal commission. Indeed, when Aberhart aggressively opposed the creation of the commission, his objections to its terms of reference revolved mainly around the belief that the dominion was merely seeking an end-run method to establish the Loan Council.[98] But the prime minister was also wary of the idea of such a royal commission. When Towers and Dunning suggested the idea on 21 January, King indicated 'that there was no chance of a Commission.'[99] On 16 February 1937, however, he announced the intention to create it. After reviewing the Bank of Canada's reports on the financial position of Manitoba and Saskatchewan, the prime minister expanded its terms of reference.[100]

The members of the Royal Commission on Dominion–Provincial Relations were appointed on 14 August. Newton Rowell and John Dafoe came to Ottawa for discussions with the prime minister, and O.D. Skelton had them to dinner along with Clark, Towers, and Sandy Skelton. Clark recommended Sandy Skelton as commission secretary.[101] Clark was also influential in shaping the role of academic experts, and the commission ended up hiring numerous academics to conduct studies, including professors from Queen's, such as Bill Mackintosh, Frank Knox, and J.A. Corry.

The 1937 budget, meanwhile, was delivered on 25 February. The previous year witnessed a modest recovery, despite a disastrous drought and the worst wheat crop since 1919. The recovery was brought on through increased exports to Britain and the United States, as well as increased income from gold mining and the American tourist trade.[102] The budget introduced increased defence expenditures and resulted in considerable debate on general spending.[103] Mackenzie King was impressed with the general economic situation but not with the budget document overall. 'Much of it was a course on economics and finance,' he commented in his diary. 'It was well prepared but had all the earmarks of academic preparation.'[104] The comment was a direct criticism of Clark and his staff, a criticism that was gradually coming to colour the prime minister's view of his deputy minister of finance. For now, however, it was directed mainly at Dunning. 'No man in the govt. leans more on his deputy,' King commented, '& takes suggestions from a few sources & does less in the way of acknowledging these sources or help from anywhere than Dunning. What is worse, he presents in the most childish way that the ideas are his own, next the phrases, & finally even the words, when all the time it is Clark or Skelton or Towers or some one else who has worked out the idea, drafted the document & determined its words.'[105] Salary reduction for the civil service, an issue introduced by the Bennett government, came to nothing in the budget and was dropped completely. As a result, Clark's salary reached $12,000 a year.[106]

Supplementary estimates to provide temporary grants to Saskatchewan and Manitoba to prevent loan defaults were introduced on 9 April. Clark had strongly supported such estimates as early as January 1935.[107] Five days later, a government Order in Council approved a fundamental reorganization of spending estimates, the first since Confederation. Dunning, who was given credit for the change, argued that the old system not only lacked in essentials, but was actually misleading. The new system required much more work and doubled the size of the estimates, but offered Parliament much more detailed information with which to exercise control of the public purse.[108]

Despite the Depression and the insular approach to international trade displayed by many nations, including Canada, Clifford Clark remained optimistic that a new attitude of multilateralism would prevail. But he was frustrated by the slow progress. In September he travelled to Geneva to accept appointment as a member of the Financial Committee of the League of Nations. This was one of two committees that made up the Economic and Financial Organization of the League. The members of the Financial Committee were appointed by the Council of the League, not as governmental representatives, but as individual experts. They could, it was assumed, speak with a certain degree of autonomy. The committees were expected to offer disinterested advice and, working through expert subcommittees or individual specialists, carry out special investigations on commercial policy, tariffs, raw materials, exchange control, clearing agreements, agricultural production, double taxation, and many other problems connected with the economic aspects of international relations.

The committees, however, as with so many aspects of the league, did not have the impact many hoped. Clark was aware of these limitations as early as April. He commented on the 'present extremely low ebb of the League's prestige, lack of interest in its activities and the general state of unsettlement.' The committees would have to 'avoid the political aspects of the existing set-up and gradually attract an increasing number of countries.' In addition, they would have to be set up as separate bodies independent of the assembly.[109] As F.P. Walters points out, the committees were unsuccessful at 'breaking down the intense nationalism of the Treasuries and the Ministries of Commerce.' In later years, the economic work of the league was turned increasingly in the direction of immediate practical questions, such as housing and food. Clark's concerns were further justified when it was realized that the economic and social services of the league had to be separated from the control of the council.[110]

Clark's work with the league, however, did provide the basis for an idea that was rejected at the time but would be applied in Canada by 1944. The assembly asked the committees to study methods of providing medium-term credit to industry. The Financial Committee reported the next year and rejected the assumption that there was such a need. Five years later, Clark reached a different conclusion during preparations for the post-war period and he was instrumental with Graham Towers in setting up Canada's Industrial Development Bank to provide just such financing.[111]

In January 1938 the final report of the National Employment Commission (or Purvis Commission) was presented to the government. Mackenzie King was not pleased with its recommendation that the dominion take full responsibility for relief of the 'unemployed employables.' The commission also recommended unemployment insurance but the federal government was already committed to this policy. Regardless, in June the government announced that any further policy initiatives would have to await the Royal Commission on Dominion–Provincial Relations.[112] King's reaction to the Purvis Commission highlighted more than his desire to avoid further expenses to the federal treasury; it demonstrated his disagreement with the civil service over the increasing power and centralization of the federal government. This rift would widen as the 'Rowell' Commission took its course. Members of the increasingly influential mandarin class in Ottawa, including the Skeltons, Mackintosh, Towers, and Clark, were advancing a more centralist form of federalism against King's wishes and designs. The prime minister was not impressed:

> Skelton, in conversation with me, told me that he thought differently of Purvis and Mackintosh than I did … these men, all of whom are Queen's University, Department of Economics, have come together, and have been working jointly to seek to bring about a change in constitutional relations which will lead to a centralization of powers and away from the present order of things.
>
> The Rowell Commission will be doing the same thing; with Skelton's son as Secretary, and with Clark, will be working toward the same end. I told Council, quite frankly, this was my sizing up of the whole situation, and that these University men who had this inside opportunity, thought they had more in the way of wisdom than the rest of us put together … doubtless, from the best of intentions and the belief that the Department of Eco-

nomics, at Queen's, knows more about these matters than any corresponding group in Canada.[113]

By the spring of 1938 Clark's attention returned to housing issues and he spent considerable time formulating revised legislation. At the same time, ironically, he was losing the battle to keep his house in Scarsdale. The house had a $26,000 first mortgage and a $10,000 second mortgage, as well as a personal bond to repay the $10,000. By April $6,441.94 was still owing on the second mortgage, as well as interest from November 1937, but the Clarks had reached their limit in keeping up the payments. 'I have used all savings and all I could borrow,' Clark scribbled in the margins of a letter from the second mortgage holder. As a result on 21 April the first mortgage holder took possession of the house. The lawyer for the Clarks advised on 11 May, 'I am extremely doubtful whether it is possible at the present time to find a purchaser for this property who would be willing to pay the amount of the two mortgages not to mention anything in excess of them.' Houses in Scarsdale had lost at least one-third and often half of their value. The depreciation of large houses (like the Clark home) was often even greater. The two mortgage holders did not believe that the property was now worth more than $25,000. The lawyer advised that the first mortgage holder would give up all claims if the family did not oppose foreclosure, which duly proceeded. By mid-June appropriate wording to that effect had been approved, although it took until 9 December before the lawyer reported that all claims against the Clarks from the first mortgage had been released and that the house would be put up for sale on 17 December, with the only bid likely to come from the mortgage holder. Settling with the second mortgage holder proved even more costly. 'Your loss has been so substantial on this property that it seems a shame to have to pay out any more,' the lawyer wrote on 28 May, 'but unfortunately as far as making an advantageous settlement is concerned you are regarded as a person of considerable financial responsibility.' By 17 June an agreement was reached with the second holder that involved the Clarks paying $3,317.60, a bit less than half the amount outstanding.[114]

The irony was complete when on 8 June Finance Minister Dunning introduced the National Housing Act in Parliament. This new act was drafted by Clark and replaced the Dominion Housing Act. It was designed to sort out some of the problems that had arisen in lending provisions, especially for lower-priced housing and for loans in areas not served by lending institutions. Clark found that even with the housing issue, Premier Aberhart was a thorn in his side. Loans under the old act were not being negotiated in the Prairie provinces. No loans were being made in Alberta, Clark argued, because of existing or feared Social Credit legislation. Only a few loans had been made in Saskatchewan and Manitoba 'because of the fear that the type of legislation which has been passed in Alberta would spread' to these provinces.[115]

The National Housing Act was also designed to allow the federal government for the first time to make provision to local authorities for low-income housing through federal loans. According to Neatby, this initiative came from Clark 'who had a special interest in both the economic and social benefits of subsidized housing for low-income families.' Neatby goes on to note, however, that 'this clause was a dead letter because no applications for low-rental projects were ever submitted.'[116] The requirements for enabling provincial legislation took the initiative out of federal hands, and the stipulation that municipalities waive almost all taxes on projects was opposed. The result was that no low-rental projects were actually built. The onset of war a few years later further interfered with effective implementation of the act. Regardless, Clark was confident that his new legislation was accomplishing its objectives. He argued that a period of high construction had not yet been experienced under the act. In addition he argued that the number of new loans was increasing and more remote communities now had access to the plan: 'Furthermore, the number of loans made on low-cost houses is steadily increasing and the average size of loan per family housing unit is steadily decreasing.'[117]

Overall the economy continued to show signs of recovery throughout 1937, but it was still uneven growth. The western crop failed again as a result of drought, but gold production and the tourist industry were reasons for optimism. Prices of exports increased, but so did imports. As the budget of 1938 approached, Clark urged Dunning to hold the line and work towards a balanced budget. The economist had not fallen completely under the influence of 'Keynesian' ideas of deficit financing, although he did optimistically revise his projections of revenue by budget time, despite the recommendations of the National Employment Commission. But Dunning's budget speech did reveal some Keynesian influences. 'We are, of course, well aware of the arguments for pump priming in times of depression,' Dunning claimed, 'and we have had to increase Government expenditures substantially as a partial offset to the gap in private investment. But we have never believed that public spending could be a substitute for private enterprise ... Nevertheless, a government cannot stand idly by and allow the ravages of depression to take their toll because of the too slow revival of private investment.'[118] It was also possible to discern the influences of Keynesian ideas in the budget document, particularly when it came to taxation policy. A sales tax exemption for building materials was described as a 'radical proposal' designed 'as further powerful stimulus to the construction industry.'[119]

After prolonged Cabinet debate the budget came in with a $23 million deficit. It provided for a $50 million national recovery program (mainly for road building but also youth training projects in forest conservation) and low-interest loans to municipalities for public works. Clark's position on the shift toward deficit financing in the budget is not clear. Only several months previous he had been urging fiscal restraint. It is possible that he accepted the increased spending because of the influence of Bill Mackintosh, who was a member of the National Employment Commission. The development of Clark's thinking was likely following a route similar to that of Graham Towers: 'The weight of events since 1930 has been such to force the government of most countries to take some degree of action along the lines of deficit spending, regardless of the theories of fiscal policy which they happened to hold.'[120] If Keynesian influences were making their way into the budget, it was under Clark's cautious guidance. The prime minister certainly felt this way: 'It had been carefully prepared by the officers of the Department,' King observed, and 'Clarke [*sic*] in particular.'[121]

The development of the Bank of Canada continued into 1938 and Clifford Clark maintained his influential role. On 20 June Dunning introduced a bill to amend the Bank of Canada Act to make the institution completely nationalized. Clark was a vocal proponent of this move.[122] By September Donald Gordon was appointed deputy governor. Two days after introducing this bill, Dunning complained of heart pains and then collapsed in the House. His health seemed exhausted and it was apparent that the prime minister would have to surrender to Dunning's frequent requests and accept his resignation. King asked J.L. Ilsley to handle the budget resolutions and Norman Rogers to deal with the housing legislation.[123] In the following days, however, King concluded that Dunning's condition was likely more 'a sort of self pity and neurasthenia' and that it was difficult to discern 'how much of his condition is mental and how much is physical.'[124] By November Dunning's health was slowly returning and his exit from government was uncertain.

But Clark was also showing the strain of work. In the summer of 1938 a trip to Europe involved work but also gave him an opportunity for rest and relaxation. He was hosted by Louis Rasminsky (the League of Nations economist Clark had tried to recruit in 1933)[125] in Geneva, including a stay on the shores of Lake Leman. Clark also spent three weeks in Paris. 'During the latter,' he wrote Rasminsky, 'I was able to get two or three long week-ends out in the country, and these week-ends together with the pleasant boat trip home succeeded in making a completely new man out of me. I am afraid that when I landed at Geneva I was exhausted physically and mentally.'[126]

One of Clark's most impressive skills was his ability to recruit talented individuals. No hiring by Clark was more influential than that of Robert Bryce on 1 October 1938. The story of this recruitment also reveals much about the process. According to Bryce, he came to Ottawa from Harvard in the spring of 1937 to ask Clark for a job. The deputy minister of finance had apparently heard of the young and talented Bryce, who had been a student of John Maynard Keynes at Cambridge before moving on to Harvard. Clark's first suggestion was that Bryce join the staff of the Royal Commission on Dominion–Provincial Relations but Bryce indicated that he was interested in a permanent job in finance. Clark told him to send in some of his written work. The interview ended at this point and Bryce heard nothing for the next two months. By the time Clark phoned to offer a position in the finance department, Bryce had accepted an offer from the Sun Life Assurance Company in Montreal. Clark indicated that he would phone the president of Sun Life to obtain Bryce's release but the youth responded that he wanted to fulfil his commitment.[127]

About ten months later Clark ran into Bryce and told him that a position in finance was still possible.[128] Bryce wrote an intense examination paper on Canadian monetary questions, which Clark himself set. He was then interviewed by a committee that included Clark and Towers. Bryce passed the test, left Sun Life, and joined the department.[129] By the time he arrived in early October, Clark already had work lined up for him.[130] Bryce's first impressions of the finance department under Clark are also revealing: 'I found the department in 1938 a congenial and often exciting place to work. Eaton, Johnson, Perry, Lowe, and I all reported directly to Clark and could be, and often were, summoned at any time by an old-fashioned buzzer. We were expected to be versatile, to be capable of studying emerging problems, and to provide background papers and even advice. We had no junior assistants or library in the department, but we had a very stimulating boss. He never held regular staff meetings, and there was no indoctrination.'[131]

Another rookie civil servant at the time, James Gibson, had similar memories of working for 'Dr Clark.' Gibson remembered that those working under Clark were constantly amazed at his ability to remember their personal details: 'One didn't have to be there very long before discovering that he had an uncanny knack of working with people. It was partly because he knew them, partly because he took the trouble to find out what their interests were. And in this sense he was a very human figure.'[132]

In October Jack Pickersgill sent Clark a memo arguing that the federal government should take over responsibility for relief before the Rowell Commission reported. Pickersgill had been hired by external affairs the year before and seconded to the Prime Minister's Office two months later. In the memo Pickersgill argued that unemployment was not primarily the result of local conditions but of national policy. Provincial resources were not equal, and only by making Ottawa responsible for relief could the burden of unemployment be shared equally throughout Canada. Pickersgill urged the federal government to act immediately. With all the provinces in worse shape than the federal government, the release of the Rowell report would lead to a conference on financial and constitutional responsibilities and likely calls by the wealthier provinces for an expansion of their revenue sources at the expense of the federal government. If, however, Ottawa moved now to assume the whole cost of unemployment relief, it 'could instead make a prima facie case for the enlargement of its sources of revenue and the further curtailment of Provincial revenues.' The premiers of Ontario, Quebec, and British Columbia had already advocated Ottawa's assumption of the full cost of relief, so they could hardly complain about an invasion of provincial rights if the federal government followed their advice.[133]

The arguments, Clark wrote in a response to Pickersgill, were 'admirable' but the deputy minister could not support them. The reasons were based more on 'method and timing' than on principles. Clark supported the federal government taking over the whole cost of unemployment relief but he viewed the issue as simply one among many in the overall struggle for jurisdictional control. At present, the likelihood of Ottawa taking over these burdensome costs was a critical 'bargaining lever' in the negotiations to obtain constitutional amendments in this and other areas as well. If the federal government moved at present, 'without any quid pro quo whatsoever,' it would be in a much weaker position when a financial settlement with the provinces was reached: 'In other words, we would have no bargaining power left.' Clark viewed the issue of unemployment as a significant piece in the much larger puzzle that had become dominion–provincial relations. Regardless, he wished to await the report of the Rowell Commission. As Struthers points out, despite their disagreement on timing and tactics, the debate indicated that Prime Minister King, who still opposed the federal assumption of these responsibilities and powers, was increasingly surrounded by officials who accepted the inevitability of a new centralist federalism.[134]

By 1939 the international situation with Germany dominated the headlines. Whereas Canada was negotiating tariff deals with nations such as Great Britain, France, and the United States, Ottawa was forced to consider controls on the movement of foreign exchange out of Canada in the event that hostilities broke out. Graham Towers presented Dunning and Clark with a detailed proposal for such controls. As events in Europe grew more ominous, money was fleeing to safer havens. If Canada went to war, money would move again, likely to the United States, particularly if the nation remained neutral. But Canada would need foreign currency, especially American dollars, in order to purchase materials and equipment for itself and Britain.[135] Towers had known since 1937 that the British were already drawing up such plans and shortly after the Munich Crisis in September 1938, he commenced work with several members of the Bank of Canada staff to develop plans for a foreign exchange control board. Dunning and Clark approved of the proposal and began the necessary preparations.[136]

In general, however, the federal government conducted little planning for wartime finance prior to late August 1939.[137] 'Despite the obvious and ominous signs of approaching war,' Bryce noted, 'we were devoting most of our efforts to domestic issues of the day and were under no pressure to develop contingency plans for war.' In this respect, the department of finance was in no way different from the government in general. 'Eaton and I,' Bryce wrote, 'in that last prewar summer, were able to find an afternoon each week to play golf and to take vacations before late August brought the crisis to a head and plunged us into frenzied activity.'[138] In retrospect, Bryce was critical of Canada's lack of preparation of controls and the failure to strengthen the gold and foreign exchange reserves in anticipation of war: 'During 1937 and 1938, when the dangers of war were apparent, and Canada understood that the US Neutrality Act would prevent belligerent borrowing in the US in wartime, the Canadian balance of payments and Canadian credit standing were strong; surely it would have been prudent to accumulate more reserves at the cost of some medium-term borrowing.'[139]

Clifford Clark, meanwhile, continued to wrestle with housing issues. He was scheduled to speak to the National Conference on Housing in Toronto in February. The conference was organized by the leading advocate of social housing of the day, Humphrey Carver, together with similar reform-minded experts, such as Percy Nobbs, S.H. Prince, and George Mooney.[140] The gathering was particularly important because it was the first of its kind. Delegations attended from Toronto, Halifax, Winnipeg, and Hamilton. Clark's housing policies, despite the changes and amendments in the new act, were still viewed as fiscally conservative and favourable to the construction industry. Not surprisingly, it was an unsympathetic crowd of over two hundred people who heard Clark's message. In the conference brochure Carver noted that even if full advantage were taken of the new legislation, the problem of adequate housing for the great mass of low-wage families would remain unsolved.

Clark knew what he was in for and he talked with Dunning about the need to tread warily. While he wanted to give a broad speech that outlined the housing problem and how the act would address it, he realized that he should instead stick closely to the details of the legislation. 'I thoroughly agree that I should not go to make the type of address I had in mind,' he informed Dunning. Nicolls was going to be present but Clark was adamant that he also should 'not make any speech unless it were limited solely to a description of Part II of our Act.' His speech should be 'carefully gone over here' beforehand, but as it turned out, Nicolls was not back in Ottawa before the conference. Clark also tried to withdraw from the event: 'I certainly prefer very much to refuse that invitation but I wonder whether I should. If your second thoughts are the same as on Saturday, I will be happy about it; but I did not, without full consideration, want to allow something to get started which we might regret later.'[141] In the end, Dunning had already committed his deputy, and Clark had to go and give his talk. He explained to Carver that it was 'difficult for a civil servant to speak publicly in regard to these matters, nevertheless my Minister had consented to my accepting your invitation. I shall therefore plan to be present at the Conference and speak to you factually about Part II of the National Housing Act.'[142]

On 20 February Clark attended the conference at the Royal York Hotel in Toronto. His role was to explain the terms of the new act. In conclusion, he asserted, 'Neither I nor anybody else at Ottawa is trying to force something on you. The Dominion has been persuaded to initiate an experiment in low rental housing by providing a vehicle and offering what it believes to be generous assistance. It is up to you in the municipalities to decide whether you wish to accept this assistance on the terms on which it is offered.'[143] Throughout the conference Carver argued that in 1938 housing subsidies for low-income families should have been provided by the federal government rather than the municipalities because it was a matter of public health.[144] He concluded that 'authoritative speakers at the conference all alluded to the fact that no Housing Act can be expected to reach low income families without direct government contribution to a rent-reduction fund or without a capital grant.'[145] Another speaker was Arthur Purvis, the recent chair of the National Unemployment Commission. Purvis gave a speech in which he 'castigated the federal government for introducing the concept of a high-minded philanthropic limited-dividend housing corporation, without offering any kind of instrument, agency, or financial support for community organizations of this kind.'[146] Regardless of the criticism, Clark remained convinced that his housing policies were effective.

Upon returning home from the conference, Clark had to prepare the budget. April was always the busiest time of the year. Dunning was operating under poor health but it was understood that this budget was of particular importance. Hitler's Germany had marched troops into Prague on 15 March and Britain joined France in offering guarantees of protection to Poland, Romania, Greece, and Turkey. Prime Minister King informed Parliament on 20 March that 'if there were a prospect of an aggressor launching an attack on Britain, with bombers raining death on London, I have no doubt what the decision of the Canadian people and parliament would be. We would regard it as an act of aggression, menacing freedom in all parts of the British Commonwealth.' Prewar jitters, meanwhile, were slowing economic activity.[147]

Clark and Towers were also in the midst of helping save Saskatchewan from defaulting on its most recent loan. The Bank of Canada could not advance the necessary amount of money to the province to handle a maturity coming due on 1 May. Since 1936, when Saskatchewan had found it impossible to sell its bonds in the market, the province had been propped up on four separate occasions to deal with maturities and thereby avoid defaulting. Graham Towers urged Dunning to again assist Saskatchewan to avoid the province defaulting. 'In any event,' he wrote, 'it is clear that the major arguments for avoiding default are not related to the effects on the Province of Saskatchewan, but to the effect on Dominion credit.'[148]

On 25 April what has been called 'Canada's first Keynesian budget' was brought down. The budget speech contained a very cautious balancing act between not undermining the nation's financial position on the one hand and the idea that 'in these days, if the people as a whole, and business in particular, will not spend, government must,' on the other. The budget anticipated a deficit more than twice that of 1938 yet provided a tax credit of 10 per cent of business capital expenditures incurred in the next twelve months as an incentive to such investment. The finance minister noted that 'in order to expand production, employment and incomes, we must have substantially more capital creation, a more rapid rate of private investment.'[149]According to Bryce, this tax credit was 'one of the first clearly Keynesian measures in Canada.' While Bryce was clearly sold on Keynesian economics, other members of the finance department, including Clark, were more cautious. By 1939, Bryce observes, 'Clark was quite prepared to listen to Keynesian arguments, indeed he asked for them. He remained, however, very careful in their application to the Canadian economy because it was such an open one and its financial community did not yet understand the essence of Keynes's analysis.'[150] Simon Reisman later claimed that Clark was too practical to be considered a 'Keynesian': 'At the heart of it was good economics. If it was a good proposition, it should be able to pay for itself ... He was a sound money man. I don't think he was ever won over by the Keynesian philosophy ... Not that Clifford Clark ever said "I am not a Keynesian, I believe something else," but the way he went about doing things indicated he never believed you could spend your way out of problems.'[151]

But if the budget was innovative, the fact was lost on the prime minister. Mackenzie King was more intent on noticing Dunning's appearance: 'Dunning gave his budget speech. Lapointe and I were highly amused at his little vanities, dressed up with spats on, wearing morning suit with a flower in his button-hole, but what was most amusing was the presence on his desk of two separate glasses – one with water, the other, a dark coloured glass, which when he came to speak, we all came to see was whisky and soda. A little bottle of pills or pellets also laid out. All these taken at intervals during the time of speaking.'[152] King did notice again, however, just how much influence Clark and his staff had on the budget: 'It was evident that he was reading a Professor's statement and not speaking his own mind from conviction. Our party is beginning to resent too great reliance upon University minds and insufficient original and direct thinking and expression on the part of the Ministers of the Crown.'[153] The budget of 1939 implemented part of the trade agreement reached the previous year with the United States, by which Canada agreed to surrender the 3 per cent excise tax on all U.S. imports that had been imposed in the early 1930s.[154] It also provided for a sharp increase in defence expenditures from approximately $36 million to more than $64 million.[155]

In early May a bill was introduced into the House by Dunning to create the Central Mortgage Bank. Plans for the bank were devised by Clark early in 1939. He wanted to involve the government in sharing the costs of writing off excess debt as an inducement to creditors. The objective was to provide a system of long-term mortgage credit on a more flexible, economical, and equitable basis. Under the act, insurance, loan, and trust companies that became members of the new Central Mortgage Bank would be required to adjust all their existing mortgages of certain amounts on farm and non-farm homes. Interest rates would be reduced to 5.0 and 5.5 per cent respectively and all arrears of interest in excess of two years would be written off. The new institution would be a 'guiding and to some extent a supervisory organization, a bank of last resort, and a bank which will provide a source of funds at economical rates and for a term of years appropriate to the mortgage lending business.' It would be designed to serve purposes and perform functions in the mortgage field 'somewhat analogous to those which are served and performed by the Bank of Canada in the field of commercial credit.'[156]

The governor of the Bank of Canada, however, had problems with the proposal. Towers agreed that mortgage lending practices in Canada could be improved, notably in the provision of long-term funds as well as methods of repayment for both urban and farm debts. He was hesitant, however, to see the dominion government take on a substantial contribution to the writing down of mortgage loans held by lending companies. Amidst the 'dangerously unsettled state of international affairs,' Towers was worried that the Mortgage Bank would eventually hold so many lending company debentures that 'the Bank – and therefore the Government – would then be the main creditor of the companies, and would, in effect, have a tremendous stake in their mortgage loans.' Towers was also concerned that the provinces would not cooperate and the result might force Ottawa into the position of disallowing provincial legislation designed to interfere with the position of adjusted mortgages: 'On the face of it, any Government would find such a position particularly uncomfortable, having in mind that the Dominion itself would be vitally interested, in its position of mortgage creditor, in preventing the provinces from exercising their statutory powers in regard to property and civil rights.' Towers was worried that 'the proposed arrangement would only shift the battle to the Dominion-Provincial field.' He suggested that action be postponed until the mortgage situation was discussed at an upcoming dominion-provincial conference to consider the Rowell-Sirois Commission. 'Dominion action,' Towers warned, 'minus provincial co-operation, is extremely dangerous.'[157]

Despite Towers's concerns, the act creating the Central Mortgage Bank was passed and the first meeting of the CMB was held on 14 July. David Mansur resigned from Sun Life and became general superintendent of the new organization. It was public knowledge that Clark was the author of Canada's housing legislation, including the CMB, but the attention embarrassed the deputy minister. As a civil servant he found it inappropriate. 'The bouquets thrown at me are amusing,' Clark informed the editor of the *Monetary Times*, but they were 'highly unfair to my Minister.' Clark noted that Dunning had been a student of mortgage lending over the last twenty-five years and he certainly deserved credit for the legislation. He then went on to lecture the newspaper: 'I would also expect a responsible financial paper to realize and respect the constitutional proprieties in respect of legislation in this country. No Bill introduced by a responsible government can be attributed to a civil servant.' Clark could not avoid the temptation, however, of advising the editor to come and speak to him concerning any questions related to the legislation.[158]

As it turned out, the outbreak of war several months later led the government to postpone the operations of the CMB. The organization had not yet made any agreements with member companies. In addition the war made a fair appraisal of real estate values throughout the country virtually impossible, particularly across the Prairies.[159] By war's end the CMB was no longer needed, although some of its functions were absorbed by the Central Mortgage and Housing Corporation.[160] 'In retrospect,' Bryce claimed, 'the Central Mortgage Bank Act is a vivid illustration of Clark's abilities and the influence he had upon Finance Minister Dunning.'[161]

During the debate on the Central Mortgage Bank, Clark was singled out for vicious criticism by Jean-Francois Pouliot, the Liberal member of Parliament for Temiscouata, Quebec. Pouliot was a veteran back-bencher who was already infamous for both the volume and the sharpness of his criticisms. He was dubbed 'the wordiest MP in Ottawa,' 'a vocalamity,' and the 'clown prince of Parliament.'[162] Still, the public criticisms were among the first levelled at Clark who, as a civil servant, was normally safe from such barbs (particularly from the government benches). The incident caused the rather sensitive deputy minister considerable discomfort. Traditionally, civil servants were immune to personal criticism in the House because, among other reasons, they did not have an opportunity to answer their critics. The increasing influence of the 'Ottawa Men,' however, challenged this tradition.

Pouliot styled himself a 'rogue' politician, both within the House and within the Liberal Party. He considered himself a defender of the democratic system against the 'big interests,' 'brass hats,' 'so-called intellectuals,' 'bureaucrats,' and 'the self-styled intelligentsia,' all of whom, according to Pouliot, were wielding undue influence without ever facing public scrutiny.[163] As chairman of a parliamentary committee enquiring into the administration of the Civil Service Act in 1938, Pouliot argued that MPs had the right to question or criticize bureaucrats because Parliament voted the money to pay their salaries.[164] As a result of his antics, however, he was removed as chairman of the committee.[165]

Pouliot's assault on the civil service continued into 1939, only this time his sights were set directly on Clifford Clark. The deputy minister was singled out because Pouliot was convinced that the bureaucracy was littered with leftovers from the Bennett term in office, or in Pouliot's words, 'the pets of the Tory government.' These 'pets' were mainly financial experts. They were 'supergeniuses' and therefore 'dangerous men' if left unattended to work behind the scenes. In addition, they had grown too influential. 'Nobody can touch them,' Pouliot informed the House.[166]

The attacks on Clark began on 14 March during a debate on a proposal to create a defence purchasing board under the Department of Finance. Pouliot began by noting that the proposal came from an interdepartmental committee headed by O.D. Skelton. He then moved the criticism directly onto both Skelton and Clark: 'I want to say something about the progressive and nefarious influence of some high-posted civil servants, who probably do not mean badly but who are intriguers of the worst kind and who try to serve their own interests or the interests of those who are close to them rather than the interests of the state.' Pouliot then hit a sensitive spot for Clark. He began to question the deputy's role in the Straus company, and the financial and legal mess that ensued: 'I have in my hand a most interesting book, the Canadian Parliamentary Guide for 1939, which contains some autobiographies. In one of these, it is interesting to note, there is a gap covering seven or eight years; that is, the autobiography of Doctor Clark.'

The Speaker of the House intervened at this point to inform Pouliot that he was out of order by not dealing with the motion on the defence purchasing board. Prime Minister King also came to Clark's defence, suggesting that personal attacks on members of the civil service who could not defend themselves were inappropriate, as well as irrelevant to the matter before the House. Pouliot answered that while he had no 'personal grievance' against Clark or any other civil servant, he was 'very much concerned' with the manner in which 'high officials of the civil service are acquiring greater importance at the expense of the government.' This was a matter of grave concern, Pouliot noted, because these men were 'responsible to no one.' King again came to the defence of Skelton and Clark, indicating that they were 'wholly deferential to all hon. Members of the house.' Pouliot repeated that he had 'no vengeance to satisfy.' He went on, however: 'Of course according to parliamentary practice a minister is responsible for everything that is done by those under his control; but with the new system of things – and this defence board is part of that system – I feel that the ministers will have less and less authority over the civil service.' Pouliot proceeded to criticize the organization of the civil service and its general lack of accountability:

> What I notice … is the easy way in which several high officials try to evade all authority and all responsibility. That may not always be noticed, of course, but it is a very dangerous practice. My right hon. leader knows that if there is communism in Russia to-day it is due entirely to the extravagance of bureaucracy; and in Germany and Italy the members of their bureaucracy were so powerful as to cause the destruction of democracy in those countries. Their influence was not always apparent. They were like termites, which were undermining the pillars of state. Today there is no more democracy in Russia, there is no more democracy in Italy, there is no more democracy in Germany; and here in Canada we are on the eve of having a dictatorship of bureaucracy … If order is not restored in the civil

service we shall run the risk of falling down as other countries have done where bureaucracy was not checked.[167]

Late in May Pouliot returned to his attacks on Clark during the debate on the Central Mortgage Bank, a proposal known to have been initiated and developed by the deputy minister. The rogue MP delivered a long assault on the closed nature of the finance department and its lack of accountability: 'We have no responsible government in this country now, especially in the Department of Finance, because members of Parliament cannot get the information they ask for about the expenditure of public money.' Pouliot attacked the Bank of Canada as well and insinuated that it was under the control of the finance department. Now the CMB would join this cabal. It would have the same governor and deputy as the Bank of Canada; the deputy minister of finance and three other directors would make up its board of directors; its executive committee would consist of the same individuals. Pouliot then proceeded to highlight the salaries of the officials both in the Department of Finance and the Bank of Canada.[168] Then, quite suddenly, Pouliot turned his attention back to Clark: 'It is time for me to tell you something I feel very strongly in my heart. I do not wish to be offensive to anyone; I do not wish to go to great trouble to kill a fly, but when it is in the public interest I have to inform hon. members of what I know. I am going to ask them to look at the Parliamentary Guide and read the history of the deputy minister of finance. They will find a gap of seven years between 1923 and 1930.' Dunning immediately leapt to his feet, asserting, 'It has long been a tradition of this House, that personal attacks on civil servants cannot be made in this manner.' The Speaker agreed. Pouliot then alluded to matters in Clark's past that were 'conspicuously hidden.' The intention, Pouliot claimed, was to 'tell the House about the record of experience of a man who is mainly responsible for the blind and bold dictatorship of the Finance Department in the Dominion government.'[169]

And Pouliot was still not finished. On 2 June, as the debate on the CMB continued, he condemned the legislation as 'both state socialism and Toryism.' Farmers had been handicapped in obtaining loans when they were made subject to the Bankruptcy Act at the end of the Great War, and further by the Farmers' Creditors Arrangement Act, passed by the Bennett government. Both increased the risk to lenders, who were thus less inclined to lend farmers money. He claimed that the legislation 'does not help the farmers who have borrowed money on mortgage from their neighbours or someone in the community; it helps only the insurance and loan companies.' In making this claim, Pouliot returned to his criticism of Clark: 'When the Minister of Finance was sworn in there was a letter for him ... it was from the member for Temiscouata, who was congratulating him and warning him against his deputy, who was called in that letter a crank ... I feel greatly humiliated to think that the very same crank is more listened to by the Minister of Finance than the whole House of Commons together.'

Pouliot was ruled out of order and instructed to keep to the matter before the House. 'In the first place,' he responded, 'I cannot understand why freedom of speech should be curtailed to any degree. In the second place I cannot understand how it is that the big boss of dominion finance should be the very one who has wrecked an old reputable concern by unsound investments. That is all I have to say.' The latter comment was clearly an assertion that Clark had single-handedly destroyed the Straus financial empire through bad investments. By this time, Dunning had had enough:

> Mr Chairman, on behalf of a civil servant who cannot speak for himself I must object to a statement which, if made outside this house, would be distinctly libellous and which to my personal knowledge and the knowledge of every member of this government is wholly untrue. I can only say that this bill is introduced by this government on its cabinet responsibility. The government is unanimously behind it, and I speak as the cabinet officer responsible for these matters and acting for the whole government. This is not my personal measure; it is the measure of the government, and with respect to the deputy minister who has just been so vilely slandered by the hon. member for Temiscouata, I can say furthermore that the deputy minister of finance, in the discharge of his important duties, has the confidence of every member of the government from the Prime Minister down. We have full knowledge of his record and complete confidence in him.

Although Pouliot's attacks on Clark were winding down, on 3 June he did request a copy of the statement made by Bennett dealing with Clark's appointment.[170]

Clark was deeply hurt by the criticisms. In the privacy of his home, he complained bitterly about Pouliot's attacks, and it was clear to those closest to him that the matter was a cause of considerable stress and anxiety. Clark's children never forgot the stir that the incident caused at home.[171] The deputy minister did not possess the thick skin of a politician and he was by no means acclimatized to such focused scrutiny. He always claimed that he did not have the constitution for a politician and was much better suited to advise the government from behind the scenes. To be thrust into the limelight made Clifford Clark uncomfortable.

As a result of the Pouliot incident, on 29 May Clark responded to a request by Dunning to supply additional information on his career. The information was to be used as potential ammunition in defending against Pouliot. Clark claimed humility in not 'tooting his own horn' but in the circumstances he felt it necessary to detail his entire academic, professional, and business career. 'There is nothing in my career,' Clark noted, 'that I think I should be ashamed of. It is an open book for anyone who wishes to check it up.' When it came to his career with the Straus Company, he claimed, 'It was my misfortune that the firm for which I worked did not survive the depression, like many other investment banking houses, but, strange as it may seem, I think it is no exaggeration to say that this was in considerable part because they did not follow, at least not with sufficient promptness and thoroughness, the advice which I gave. I believe Mr S.W. Straus, if he were still alive, would be the first to admit this.' Clark could not, however, explain why no reference was made in the Parliamentary Guide to this part of his career. He claimed that he had no part in putting together the biographical information in 1932 and that it was probably prepared by his secretary on the basis of information contained in the newspapers at the time.[172]

Clark then provided a step-by-step defence to Pouliot's charges. He claimed to have been deeply insulted by the insinuation that his 'greed for remuneration' was 'never satisfied.' That charge, Clark asserted, 'is so much out of character for me that I hope no Member of Parliament or of the general public will place any credence in it.' When Prime Minister Bennett appointed him deputy minister, Clark argued, there was never any reference to salary: 'Never in my life have I had to haggle with an employer, never in my life have I asked an employer for a promotion or an increase in pay. In all my previous connections, the promotions and increases have come in most generous abundance without my having to raise a finger.' But the most offensive charge, Clark went on, was whether he was doing his job satisfactorily:

> If anyone of substance has any real doubt on that score, I will make my decision very quickly. Life at the pace I have been working in the last few

years can only be expected to be for a very short one at best. The only thing that makes it tolerable is the belief that one is doing something for the good of his country and not merely to increase his employer's profits. If once I begin to suspect that I am not obtaining this intangible reward, you will have my resignation forthwith. Fortunately, I do not think I need to be worried about inability to find a meal ticket. I have always had alternative opportunities and even since I came to Ottawa I have turned aside several approaches. Certainly I would never be worried by fear of inability to earn what I am receiving from the Government, although the strange mentality of Mr Pouliot appears to think that a $12,000 salary is a plum which no civil servant would voluntarily give up!

It was the only time Clark would ever discuss his resignation. He did go on to make a rather interesting remark about his own political views and Pouliot's charges that he was a 'Tory Pet': 'I may have been appointed by a "Tory Prime Minister" but at the time he was aware that I was, and took occasion to call me, "one of those damn Queen's Grits." It should not be a matter of concern to anyone else, but it is a fact that I have never voted anything but Liberal in my life. Nevertheless, I shall always be loyal to whoever may happen to be my boss for the time being.' Pouliot's attacks ended not long after. The deputy minister, however, never changed his Parliamentary Guide entry.[173]

At the end of April 1939 Premier Duff Pattullo of BC wrote a letter to Mackenzie King. He claimed to be having difficulty with 'Eastern' financial interests in dealing with BC's short-term debentures falling due. The province had to meet a maturity of $3 million to be paid partially out of revenue and partially out of sinking funds. As a consequence BC borrowed approximately $3.6 million for unemployment relief. According to Pattullo, because the federal government 'refused to grant the loan and also because we could not secure funds in Canada on a satisfactory basis,' the province was forced to go to the United States and sell an issue of $3 million. The premier accused the federal finance department of forcing any provincial surplus on revenue accounts to be applied to unemployment relief rather than to pay off maturing obligations, even though the market would not accept renewals, nor would the finance department consider replacement of sinking funds: 'This policy places the Province in a position that unless we are able to dispose of bonds to meet maturing obligations, we might be compelled to default.'[174]

Clark penned a lengthy response to Dunning, regarding Pattullo's complaints. The deputy minister admitted that much of what Pattullo complained was, indeed, government policy. When the Liberal government came to power in 1935, it made clear that the previous policy under which dominion loans were obtained, in order to retire maturing obligations or to pay for ordinary operating expenditures of a provincial government, was unsound and could not be continued without jeopardizing the credit of the federal government, as well as 'producing an impossible situation in the relations between the Dominion and the provinces.' Therefore, under the Relief Acts, the dominion limited itself to loans for the provincial share of relief expenditures pursuant to an agreement between Ottawa and the province. Such loans would be made only where the province was able to demonstrate that it could not otherwise raise the funds for its own share of relief expenditures. To demonstrate this necessity, each province desiring to borrow from Ottawa was required to submit certified statements about its financial position. Manitoba and Saskatchewan followed this directive; Alberta and BC submitted only occasional statements. Clark emphasized that there was no new policy adopted by the federal government and so the previous policy still applied. He dismissed Pattullo's claim that the dominion had invaded the provincial income tax field, thereby forcing BC to borrow from the federal government. Clark pointed out that under the BNA Act, the dominion 'has the power to raise money by any mode of taxation whatsoever.' He hoped that the Royal Commission on Dominion–Provincial Relations would ultimately solve the problem.[175]

The months of May and June 1939 were more busy than usual for Clifford Clark. He was elected a Fellow of the Royal Society of Canada and vice-president of the Canadian Economic and Political Science Association. On 1 June the *Report of the Standing Committee on Banking and Commerce* was tabled, featuring extensive testimony from Clark and Towers, who took the opportunity to explain various monetary terms as well as the operation of the Bank of Canada. The deputy minister focused on such terms as money, legal tender, credit, currency, bank deposits, bank reserves, the gold standard, and inflation, but the analytical thrust was not how the Bank of Canada was controlling its currency but rather how the supply of money was regulated in accordance with scientific principles of monetary management. The committee deemed the evidence to be so informative that it recommended the testimony be printed in a separate document. The 'Blue Book' was widely circulated and became the standard text on the Bank of Canada's operations.[176]

In the historical imagination, the summer of 1939 prior to the outbreak of war was reminiscent of the 'Golden Summer' of 1914. People remember a sleepy, lazy atmosphere of calm and tranquillity before the approaching storm. But this memory is a romanticized construction based on the stark contrast between war and peace. There was an essential difference between the summers of 1914 and 1939: the memories of the Great War were still very fresh in people's minds. And the government was already preparing for the coming storm.

During that summer Clifford Clark was immersed in preparations for war. The work of the Defence Purchasing Board took up considerable time. The board was created on 14 July to provide contracts for purchases of defence supplies and construction of defence works. The contracts were then submitted to the minister of finance for his recommendation. Yet despite his increasing workload, Clark pressed ahead with his plan to create a fishing club to provide an escape from work, and as it turned out, this escape was to prove even more critical in the years to follow.[177] 'For those of us who must continually burn the midnight oil,' Clark observed, 'the chance of getting out in the country for an occasional Sunday would be a godsend.'[178] But the search for a suitable site for the club had been ongoing for almost five years. The 'window-shopping,' as Margaret Clark called it, proved just as enjoyable as actually selecting the site for the club. Other than Clark, Mackintosh was the most frequent participant in these 'shopping' trips: 'For several years, I shared with him and others a series of expenditures to view (and of course fish) possible properties. Some were poor, some far beyond any practicable finance, some required tramping through the bush too arduous for sedentary civil servants, all yielded an enjoyable weekend with good companions.'[179]

In May 1939 Clark believed he had found the ideal site in the Five Lakes Fishing Club in the Gatineau Hills. The John Gilmour estate in Wakefield Township included four lakes – Trout, Long, Dunning's, and Round. A corner of Forked Lake was also on the property and provided a fifth lake in which to fish. Clark and a group of his closest friends made a trip to fish in Trout Lake. While it was early in the fishing season, fourteen red trout were caught, with some of them weighing as much as two and a half pounds.[180] On 3 August Clark put forward an offer of $8,500 for the property. He organized a group of twenty of his friends to put forward $200 each for the down payment. It was agreed that annual membership fees would run from $75 to $100 until the mortgage was paid off. The Gilmour trustees claimed the offer was too low, however, and broke off negotiations.[181] By mid-August it appeared that no property would soon be purchased so Clark shifted his focus to at least getting in a week or two of fishing with his Queen's friends, Bill Mackintosh, R.G.H. Smails, and C.A. Curtis, as well as Bryce Stewart from New York. 'I am almost completely fagged out,' Clark told Mackintosh on 14 August, 'and must get away soon or bust.'[182]

Government officials were aware that serious trouble was on the horizon and that it was unlikely to be avoided. Timing, therefore, was critical and Clark hoped that he would be able to fit in one last fishing trip before all hell broke loose. On 17 August he wrote Stewart, 'As Mr Hitler appears to be acting up again I am afraid that I must get away soon or run a grave risk of missing a holiday altogether.'[183] By 23 August the Russo-German pact went into effect and the following day the Cabinet agreed that Canada would participate in the war if Poland was attacked. Years later the *Ottawa Journal* reported that 'associates of the late Mr King remembered the lights burning late in Dr Clark's office as the Germans and Russians signed their non-aggression pact.'[184]

The Cabinet approved a plan for what amounted to a limited war, with the emphasis on the defence of Canada. If any overseas participation were to be undertaken, priority would be given to air service and a training program. In addition, the Cabinet authorized emergency expenditures of $9 million and the following day approved the calling out, on a voluntary basis, of militia units to man coastal defences and other vulnerable points.[185] But the Canadian military was ill equipped in 1939[186] and the nation's industrial complex was in little better shape, particularly for a country intent on being a supplier of munitions and supplies rather than manpower. 'There was not much equipment capable of producing war supplies or machinery,' economist A.F.W. Plumptre observed. At least 'the country was fairly well situated in regard to production of raw materials.'[187]

Canada may not have had the military or economic infrastructure ready to fight a war but it did at least have a remarkable group of officials in government capable of setting the nation on a war footing quickly and effectively. The recruiting talents of Clifford Clark had much to do with the impressive group ready to shoulder the burden to come:

> It was one of the great achievements of Clifford Clark that when the war finally came he was able with the assistance of Towers and the Bank of

> Canada to field a team that was keen, competent and young. Kenneth Eaton with the help of Harvey Perry had taken over taxation; R.B. Bryce had recently come in and was already showing his versatility and enormous industry; David Johnston was solicitor of the treasury, and George Lowe was a miracle of information and administrative know-how. All of these men were of Clark's selection. From the older staff W.E. Hunter, B.G. McIntyre and W.C. Ronson each ably carried heavy loads of responsibility. Of course there were wartime recruits but they were additions to the team which existed. But even this capable staff could not have carried even the early wartime load of work had it not been that functions had been transferred to the Bank of Canada and that the equally able staff of the Bank was available for much government work.[188]

According to Bruce Hutchison, 'Canada's first real brain trust' had quietly been forming for years without much public notice: 'In the pinch Canada discovered that it already possessed an upper echelon of civil servants as able as any in the world ... technically equipped as no other Canadian government had ever been to manage the economic side of war.'[189]

In late August many in this 'brain trust' were preparing for one last fishing trip. The lights may have been burning late in Clark's office on the night of 23 August, but according to the deputy minister, he was 'trying to clean up my desk ... and get rid of the burden of office by the end of today' so he could head out the following morning. Mackintosh, Smails, and Curtis were already on their way to Ottawa, and the next morning they all planned on leaving for White Deer Lodge, sixty miles from Ottawa on the Lievre River. 'I hope I can stay away for at least two or three days before Mr Hitler calls me back,' Clark wrote. 'I am completely fagged out and at noon today I did not think I could last through the afternoon. Somehow or other I must peg through it.'[190]

It was 5:40 on the morning of 1 September 1939 – shortly before midnight on 31 August in Ottawa – when the German military invaded Poland and the Second World War began. Just over twenty years separated the two most devastating global conflicts. Clifford Clark was at White Deer fishing lodge with Stewart, Smails, Curtis, and Mackintosh when the news arrived. 'I well remember the evening of that day in August,' Stewart later wrote to Clark. 'In the morning we bundled up our stuff and hastily drove back to Ottawa. During that drive I thought most about the weight of the burden you would have to carry.'[191] Despite being exhausted, the mandarins were up to the challenge.

'Prostrate with fatigue when we arrived,' Mackintosh recorded, 'his [Clark's] amazing recuperative powers brought him to his feet again, and after a couple of days of fishing, he cut his promised week short, eager to get on with the preparations.'[192] If Clark and the boys figured they were already under strain and worn out, they hadn't seen anything yet.

5

Preparing for War, 1939–1940

> My own opinion, however, is that we should try to avoid imposing at the start tax increases that would tend to retard the recovery of our economy to full activity and employment. During the first few months we should try to engineer the fiscal policy in such a way as to stimulate maximum production and maximum national income at the earliest possible date.
>
> – W.C. Clark to J.L. Ilsley, 5 September 1939

War had come again. Twenty years after 'the war to end all wars,' it was difficult to believe, but it was happening all over again. In Ottawa the Cabinet ministers and their chief advisors were summoned for a 9:00 a.m. meeting on 1 September 1939. It was agreed that Parliament would be called at the earliest opportunity, which in the days before regular air travel was 7 September.[1] Britain was certain to declare war and there was no doubt as to what Canada would do. As Prime Minister Mackenzie King made clear in a press statement, his government would seek Parliament's authority for 'effective co-operation at the side of Britain.' Proclaiming a situation of apprehended war under the War Measures Act, the Cabinet placed the armed forces on active service. By early Sunday afternoon, 3 September, Britain declared war on Germany; France followed later the same day. Although Canada was not yet officially at war, the Cabinet authorized the commanders of coastal military districts to 'take all necessary defence measures which would be required in a state of war.'[2] Mackenzie King and several members of the Cabinet went on radio that afternoon, repeating the statement to the press that the government would recommend to Parliament that Canada go to war at Britain's side.[3]

The government also announced over the radio the creation of the Wartime Prices and Trade Board by Order in Council under the War Measures Act to prevent profiteering and hoarding. The severe inflation of the Great War was not forgotten and already there were signs of hoarding.[4] The board's objective was to 'provide safeguards under war conditions against any undue enhancement in the prices of food, fuel and other necessaries of life, and to ensure an adequate supply and equitable distribution of such commodities.' It was responsible to the minister of labour and consisted of five senior civil servants.[5] Although provided with wide powers of investigation and control, they were not immediately used, as Clark later observed: 'Except in the case of rents (in certain areas), butter, and for very short periods, one or two other commodities, the Board has not attempted to fix prices or embark upon any widespread schemes of price control, but rather has sought to achieve its objective by anticipating shortages and making provision for an adequate and regular flow of supplies to the Canadian market. To assist in carrying out these functions, it has secured the appointment of six Administrators or Controllers – for wool, coal, hides and leather, sugar, animal and vegetable oils, and residential rentals.'[6] Clark was critical of the rigid price controls employed in the Great War. It was not the symptoms of inflation (in the form of prices) that needed to be targeted but rather the shortages themselves: 'Where labour, materials, capital, etc., are painfully limited,' Clark argued, 'every possible care should be taken to direct them solely to the production of essentials.'[7]

Canada's relations with the United States had become increasingly important as Clark's career in Ottawa from 1932 to 1939 demonstrated. This relationship took on a critical importance with the outbreak of war. President F.D. Roosevelt confirmed American neutrality on 3 September; two days later he proclaimed an embargo on the sale of arms to belligerents.[8] Canadian officials knew that the neutrality legislation would, in Clark's words, 'almost certainly close the United States investment markets to all borrowing by belligerent countries.' Shortly afterwards, Roosevelt issued an exemption for ordinary commercial transactions on the prohibition of loans and credits. The result, according to Clark, was that most trade between Canada and the United States 'continued very much as in peace-time, but at an accelerating rate.'[9]

Canada's most pressing and immediate financial problem was preserving foreign exchange, especially American dollars. The problem involved two distinct parts: Canada's trade with Britain and Canada's trade with the United States. In his 1919 article, 'The International

Exchange Situation,' Clark discussed the 'peculiar triangular nature of Canada's trade' in which the nation carried a trade surplus with Britain and a trade deficit with the United States. During the Great War, Britain was unable to keep paying cash for its Canadian purchases and instead bought on credit. Canada was 'in the position of selling largely to a buyer who cannot pay cash and of buying largely from a seller who demands cash terms.' The result in 1919 was to drive down the value of the Canadian dollar relative to the U.S. dollar.[10] With the value of the Canadian dollar fixed in 1939 relative to the American and British currencies, the feared result was that Britain would run out of Canadian dollars and have to either curtail buying from Canada or to again buy on credit. Canada, meanwhile, would run out of U.S. dollars, needed not just for normal purchases of American goods, but for growing purchases of materials needed for Canada's own war effort, as well as to produce munitions and equipment for Britain. Indeed, Britain was planning to both curtail its purchases from Canada and buy essentials only on credit. A telegram from British Prime Minister Neville Chamberlain to Mackenzie King made clear that the British believed the best financial aid Canada could provide in the early stages of the war was to help Britain buy Canadian goods. There would be a demand for Canadian dollars and Canada's trade surplus with Britain would increase. The British were looking for approximately $300 million in additional credit. King's Cabinet was surprised by the expectations, to say the least. To conserve its purchasing power for essential imports, Britain halted imports of luxury items and goods that could be produced in Britain. This eliminated approximately 5.25 million pounds of annual Canadian trade.[11]

But preparations to meet this exact situation had been going on for months. Britain imposed foreign exchange controls when war broke out and Canada was urged to do the same. A meeting of Bank of Canada officials and general managers for the chartered banks was held on 27 August. Another meeting with foreign exchange experts was held on 4 September. At the latter meeting, Bank of Canada officials suggested that more than the usual care should be taken in handling foreign exchange transactions, especially those involving funds to be transferred abroad. While no hint was given of the bank's plans for full foreign exchange controls, it was largely inevitable.[12]

Before foreign exchange controls could be implemented, a wartime budget had to be prepared. This complex and intense process had to be undertaken without a finance minister. Charles Dunning had been complaining of ill health for months and had submitted his resignation in July. Mackenzie King was planning an election for the fall of 1939 and he convinced Dunning to delay, but election plans were now put on hold with the outbreak of hostilities.[13] Dunning agreed to postpone his resignation but he was absent from his duties for months. The finance minister was not even in the country when war was declared. J.L. Ilsley, the Nova Scotian minister of national revenue, also served as acting finance minister. For the past several months the prime minister had been thinking of a replacement for Dunning. King 'does not think much of Ilsley for the job,' Winnipeg *Free Press* reporter Grant Dexter commented, 'but it may well work out that way.'[14] King felt that Ilsley was 'far too impulsive and absolute in his views and often too narrow, though thoroughly honest. He reminds me of a high spirited horse travelling with blinders, ready to go straight ahead but not willing to see the bearing of what lies upon the larger horizon.'[15] Instead, the prime minister had his sights set on J.L. Ralston for the finance portfolio.

In the fall of 1939 Ilsley worked with Clark and his team (Eaton, Towers, Bryce, and Fraser Elliot) to prepare the budget.[16] A Cabinet meeting on 24 August set the priorities and King told Ilsley a few weeks later that all requests for expenditures other than defence should be refused.[17] Clark sent Ilsley a memorandum on 5 September outlining his strategy for meeting the war situation. Clark estimated revenue yields for the present fiscal year to be $495 million, some $5 million in excess of the budget estimate. He warned that this figure was likely optimistic but it was based on the assumption that after some hesitation, business would increase in response to extensive war orders from within Canada and the United Kingdom, as well as the large wheat crop and rising wheat prices. Accurate numbers for expenditures were impossible to calculate, Clark noted, but he estimated a possible deficit of some $308 million. 'It is clear that the deficit which we must anticipate will be of staggering proportions,' he informed Ilsley: 'Consequently, it is equally clear that we must provide for a substantial increase in tax revenues by the raising of existing rates of tax or the imposition of new tax devices. In my opinion, the Government must show that it is making the most serious effort to reorient its tax structure to the new burdens if it is to retain confidence and enable the huge borrowing operations which we will be compelled to proceed with to be carried out at reasonable interest rates ... We will have to keep effective control of our capital markets, but to maintain such control many devices will be necessary.' Clark wished to avoid imposing tax increases 'that would tend to retard the recovery of our economy to full activity and employment.' Instead, 'during the first few months we should try to engineer the fiscal policy in such a way as to stimulate maximum production and maximum national income at the earliest possible date.'[18]

J.L. Ralston was sworn in as finance minister on 6 September. Colonel Ralston had been minister of national defence before 1930 and a prominent member of the Liberal opposition during the Bennett years before retiring in 1935. King was looking to strengthen the wartime Cabinet in 1939 and Ralston was offered either Dunning's post in finance or Ian Mackenzie's portfolio of national defence. Ralston chose finance and Clifford Clark had a new boss. 'Jim Ilsley feels dished in the matter of the successorship to Dunning,' Dexter observed.[19] King admitted that Ilsley seemed 'a little disappointed' but noted that he 'accepted the situation very nicely.'[20] Ralston plunged into the preparations for the war budget while the prime minister arranged for a by-election to win him a seat in the House of Commons. According to Pickersgill, King 'had great confidence in Ralston and in Ralston's advisers, particularly W.C. Clark, the Deputy Minister of Finance.'[21] It is difficult to discern exactly what Clark thought of Ralston but Bryce later commented that while Ralston provided strong leadership, he was 'too fussy about detail, to an extent that prevented him from getting as much as possible out of himself and those who worked for him.'[22]

Parliament opened on 7 September and three days later, without a vote, the House approved a declaration of war. But as Granatstein notes, 'This was to be a war in which Canada's primary assistance to England would be in the form of economic aid – a war of limited liability.'[23] As deputy minister of finance, Clifford Clark was instantly moved to the forefront of Canada's war effort. Only two days later, with Ralston not yet holding a seat in Parliament, Ilsley presented the first war budget. The document had been put together, as one newspaper put it, 'in efficient haste by Dr Clark and the staff he had gathered about him.'[24]

The budget speech was more important for its explanation of the government's plans for financing the war while managing the economy than for the measures and spending plan it introduced: 'In the situation today, when we are entering upon a war of whose nature and duration we can guess only a little, it is difficult even to foresee the order of magnitude of the cost we shall eventually have to incur, and to pay.' The speech attempted to provide a sense of economic stability that had been so lacking when the Great War broke out in 1914:

> What a contrast with the cataclysmic events of the first two weeks of August 1914! What has happened is, of course, a strong tribute to the vastly improved position which we enjoy today. True, we start with a much higher

> public debt, but in most other respects our economy is infinitely stronger. We are no longer dependent on vast imports of foreign capital on which the old pre-war boom was based. During and since the war, Canadian savings have increased enormously and we have built up a vast and efficient mechanism for the mobilization of these savings. The strength of our banking system has always been recognized, but the changes which we have made in monetary and banking legislation during the last few years have greatly improved its efficiency and flexibility and its ability to promote the public welfare in wartime as well as in peacetime. In recent years we have increased enormously the diversification of our industries and in particular the remarkable expansion of our mining and metal industries will be of unique importance in a modern war. In every way we are far better able to undertake immediately the great economic tasks which war has thrust upon us.[25]

Much of this credit went to the 'tribunes of Canadian economic development – Clifford Clark and Graham Towers.'[26] The speech was also the first in a series intended to educate the public. Three years later Clark wrote, 'One of the good things about a war is that it leads to a process of general economic education.'[27] According to Harvey Perry, success in meeting the government's war finance goals depended on the extent to which they were 'understood and accepted' by the population: 'No opportunity for an exposition of the basic problem of wartime finance was overlooked, and the constant repetition of the theme in the annual budget speech and elsewhere undoubtedly gave the general public a grasp of the essentials that in large measure was responsible for the success achieved.'[28]

The budget speech indicated that much of the economic calamity of the last war occurred because the nations involved lacked the courage to finance the crisis 'solely by resort to taxation and borrowings out of savings.'[29] In wartime the state had to divert economic resources from private use to war production and to distribute them accordingly. During the last war, however, inflationary means were employed to finance the struggle. Clark had been lecturing on these lessons for years: 'Canada like other countries followed inflationary methods of financing the war (borrowing from the banks and selling bonds based to a large extent on bank borrowing, etc.) and there started the inflationary spiral of rising prices and rising wages … In my humble opinion most of the troubles of the last twenty years find their origin in the inflationary financing (by practically all countries) of the last war, and in this series of troubles I include the ultimate rise of Hitler and the refractory depression of the 1930s.'[30] This strategy, according to Clark, was disastrous. Inflation, which took the form of borrowing through the banks as well as the printing of money, was the easiest (for the government, but not the people) of all methods to finance a war. The temptation to use it again would be strong:

> What happens is that the Government simply expands bank credit – gets an ever-increasing volume of bank credit in its own name and throws this extra purchasing power into the market to compete with the public for available goods and services. As the Government must get what it needs and as it is easy to expand bank credit, the process goes on apace, driving up prices in an ascending spiral, and thus diverting economic resources from civilian use to Government use, because the incomes of civilians will not purchase nearly as much as previously. It is not only a most devilishly unfair method of distributing the cost of war, throwing an undue share of the burden on people with small and fixed incomes, but it also sets up vast distortions in the economy and gives rise to other evils, the ultimate end of which is economic collapse and ruin for nearly everyone, perhaps even for the State itself.[31]

Taxation and controlled borrowing would be the preferred methods for financing this war. Clark had also been studying the use of taxes as anti-inflation measures since the Great War. Greater revenue from taxation would mean that the government would not need to raise as much through credit loans. Less inflation would result and one of the chief reasons for high prices would be avoided: 'A policy of war finance based, not on inflation but on drastic taxation, chiefly of incomes, is long overdue in all countries.'[32] This sentiment was echoed in the 1939 budget speech: 'The record of some countries was much better than that of others but all suffered from a world-wide inflationary rise in prices of enormous magnitude. For the last twenty years the world has been paying the price – a colossal one. Indeed it is perhaps not too much to say that some of the roots of the present war are to be found in the world-wide unsound financing of the last war and the great economic dislocations and continuing burdens of which it was in part the cause.'[33] But if the burdens of taxation became too heavy, the average citizen would feel that there was no use working for additional income. Efficiency and production would decrease. What could not be raised by taxation therefore would be financed by borrowing from the Canadian public at rates as low as possible.[34]

The government was preparing the public for what lay ahead if the war dragged on for any length of time. But the major sacrifices were still months away. In September 1939 the economy, still recovering from the Depression, needed a boost not controls. According to Clark,

> We began the war in September 1939 with a very substantial slack in our economy – with a substantial volume of unemployment and with factories, transportation facilities and other capital facilities being utilized at something substantially less than full capacity. The first task was to stimulate the economy, to draw unutilized labour power and other economic resources into production, to get the economy rolling as rapidly as possible. In the early stages, therefore, financial policy was definitely stimulating and expansionist in character. We refrained from imposing high taxes. We deliberately decided to make our first borrowing operation a large short-term loan obtained from the bank in order to expand bank deposits. We postponed borrowing from the public, which would have had a somewhat deflationary effect, and avoided immediate slashing of public works construction and other Government expenditures. What we were trying to do was to get the machine rolling.[35]

The budget appropriated $100 million for the war effort to 31 March 1940, including more than $16 million of emergency expenditures already authorized by governor-general's warrants. Less than $13 million of the pre-war $60 million for defence had been spent by the end of August, so that amount was also available. The total appropriation for the fiscal year was $144.5 million.[36] Total spending was forecast to be $651 million with a deficit of at least $156 million resulting, based on previous estimates of revenue. Because the government was already heavily indebted, the budget speech announced that additional taxes would be necessary.[37] The budget imposed a 20 per cent increase on existing personal income tax rates.[38] Levies were increased on articles regarded as luxuries. Excise duties and tariffs were raised sharply on spirits, beer, tobacco, tea, and coffee. The 8 per cent sales tax was applied to domestic electricity and gas, as well as salted, smoked, and canned meats and fish, which had previously been exempt. Corporation income taxes were raised from 15 to 18 per cent.[39]

But the most controversial move was the introduction of an excess profits tax. The objective, according to Perry, was to 'recapture' for the government 'the profits derived by business from a level of activity regarded as directly attributable to the war.' The excess profits tax was aimed mainly at industries indirectly stimulated by defence buying. The government provided an option for defence supply contracts to be renegotiated upon completion, in an attempt to avoid profiteering.[40] Clifford Clark had long favoured an excess profits tax. In a 1918 article he wrote that to handle profiteering, 'the most effective remedy is drastic taxation of excess profits, taxation far more drastic and pervasive than we have yet attempted.'[41] In total, the new taxes were designed to reduce the expected deficit by approximately $21 million.[42] Bob Bryce claimed to have written most of the budget speech because 'everyone else then around was busy on other things.' As a result he described it as 'the initial extended application of Keynes' method of analysis': 'The fact that we got into Keynesian analysis under wartime conditions, when justifying more public expenditures and government deficits didn't look like reckless spending for economic policy purposes, made it much easier to get acceptance. It really hit Ottawa, hit the country, hit the politicians, the business community and Canadian economists at a time when it seemed like a fairly responsible attitude.'[43]

In addition to working on the budget, finance officials drew up the War Appropriation Act. Under this legislation $100 million was allocated for war purposes and authority was granted for raising loans up to a total of $100 million, in addition to the unused borrowing power existing at the time. The department also took part in drafting the Canadian Patriotic Fund Act. A similar fund had served well in the last war as a means by which voluntary contributions were collected and used to assist wives, children, and other dependents of men in the fighting forces.[44]

The ambitious schemes of economic planning proposed by the federal government required considerable coordination. A number of special committees were created to aid in this endeavour: the Cabinet Sub-Committee on Defence, which became the Defence Committee of Cabinet on 5 September; the Emergency Council ten days later; and the Cabinet War Committee on 5 December. The last was the most important and consisted of the prime minister, the ministers of finance, national defence, justice, and mines and resources, and the Senate leader. The ministers of munitions and supply and national defence for air and naval services were added later.[45]

The same day as the budget was approved by Cabinet, the Economic Advisory Committee (EAC) was also created. This committee proved to be immensely influential. Clark had suggested its formation even before war broke out and had discussed it with O.D. Skelton and Norman Robertson. When war appeared imminent at the end of the summer of

1939, the case was made for a body of senior government advisers to coordinate the activities of the numerous departments and agencies of the government in the fields of economic policy, supply, and finance. The committee would investigate and report on a vast range of issues but would also deal with specific questions in areas where policy had not even yet been established. It was Skelton who passed the idea on to the prime minister on 9 September in a brief memorandum along with a draft Order in Council. Skelton noted that as a result of 'the important and close inter-relation of financial and economic measures,' the EAC could be of 'material help for primary surveys to make sure that all necessary points are being examined and measures co-ordinated.' The draft added that the EAC would facilitate the work of Cabinet committees working on supply and war finance, help avoid duplication of effort, and ensure effective coordination of economic and financial policy.[46]

At the Cabinet meeting it became apparent that Ralston had not even heard of the proposed committee, despite the fact that his new deputy had originated the idea and played a critical role in its drafting. In addition, the Order in Council claimed that the finance minister concurred with the idea. This revelation annoyed the prime minister. 'That is one of the mistakes our bureaucracy continually makes,' King complained, 'taking for granted Ministers will simply follow what they suggest.' As the role and influence of the new civil service increased, particularly during wartime, so did their presumptions about wielding that influence. The politicians, while conceding their importance, also came to criticize this influence. Mackenzie King felt that there were already too many committees.[47]

Despite these grumblings, the prime minister and the Cabinet agreed to the formation of the EAC, although there was a slight change in membership. The EAC would consist of W.C. Clark, Graham Towers, Norman Robertson, H.D. Scully (commissioner of customs), Hector McKinnon (chairman of the Tariff Board and recently named chairman of the Wartime Prices and Trade Board), Dana Wilgress (deputy minister of trade and commerce), R. H. Coats (dominion statistician), G.S.H. Barton (deputy minister of agriculture), Charles Camsell (deputy minister of mines and resources), R.A.C. Henry (economic advisor to munitions and supply), and Lt Col H. DesRosiers (associate deputy minister of national defence). Robertson was included because his knowledge of economic and financial issues was respected by both Clark and Towers; DesRosiers was included because it was belatedly realized that this powerful committee had no francophone members.[48] In addition, Bill Mackintosh, as special assistant to Clark, attended meetings, serving as assistant to the chairman while Robert Bryce served as committee secretary. Later, Bryce Stewart, as deputy minister of labour, was also added.[49] It was desirable that the membership represent as many government departments as possible while not becoming unwieldy: 'This essential condition of workability had to take precedence over the representation of individual Departments.'[50] According to Bryce, the EAC was 'the first general-purpose interdepartmental committee of top-level officials established in Ottawa.'[51]

The EAC lost no time getting organized. The first meeting was held on 18 September, and it became immediately clear that the committee had a wide mandate, 'one that permitted it to examine questions on its own or at the behest of the cabinet of any Minister.'[52] On 20 September, for example, the Cabinet was beset with the problem of orders going through the War Supply Board. Agriculture Minister Jimmy Gardiner wanted a separate commission appointed to regulate the prices of butter and cheese. Instead, King followed the advice of Ralston and handed the issue to the Economic Advisory Committee for review. King was pleased with the quick and efficient review performed by the EAC: 'Dr Clark came in and explained the situation in a very clear and direct way, making an alternative suggestion which we accepted to appear in the press tomorrow.' The breadth of the EAC's mandate was confirmed just over a week later when Gardiner complained about its role and more generally about the increasing role of this select group of bureaucrats. 'Had first another discussion with Gardiner abt [*sic*] the right of the Economic Advisory Committee to review any economic question or matter of policy,' King recorded, 'and got all the Cabinet on my side in opposition to his desire to prevent any review of Departmental policy by a committee of public servants.'[53]

As a result of the hectic schedules of members, many meetings of the EAC were held in the evenings (each Tuesday from 8:15 until 11:00 p.m.). The committee faced a constant barrage of general questions, but the workload was particularly heavy during the first fifteen months of the war when the main lines of organization and policy were formulated.[54] It met an astounding forty times between September 1939 and May 1940,[55] with topics ranging widely 'from housing assistance to the problems of apple growers and of pork and bacon producers, from coal policy, cost-of-living bonuses, and rentals to a host of import and export problems.'[56] For Clark, the EAC represented his desire to knit together 'all the various strands of economic and financial measures.' The economist was in his element, although, as Bryce notes, Clark found it difficult at times to reconcile his role as chairman of the committee with his desire to present a full range of proposals and opinions.[57] As an interim report of the EAC noted, 'While most of the matters dealt with by the Committee are referred to it either by Council or by the Minister or Ministers concerned, there have been in recent months a number of matters considered by the Committee on its own initiative.'[58] The EAC also widened its representative character and strengthened its technical competence when necessary by bringing in experts from a particular field. On a few occasions, joint sessions were held with other boards or agencies. Subcommittees were also employed in order to lessen the load.[59]

On 13 September Parliament prorogued but not before legislation was passed to create a new department – munitions and supply. Clark's experience with the Defence Purchasing Board (a peacetime organization) demonstrated the need for such a department and he began urging its creation as soon as war was declared. The legislation was not proclaimed until 9 April so in the meantime other provisions were made for defence procurement. At Clark's suggestion, the Defence Purchasing Board, which had taken over military procurement from the Department of National Defence in the spring of 1939 and was responsible to the minister of finance, was replaced on 1 November by a War Supply Board.[60] Despite its broad powers to purchase or contract for all the requirements of the defence services, the board handled most of its purchases through competitive tenders.[61]

On the afternoon that the brief parliamentary session ended, Louis Rasminsky was home on leave and in Clark's office. 'The telephone rang,' Rasminsky later recorded, 'and I knew it was Graham Towers telling how much foreign exchange we had lost that day. "Well, this is it," said Clark, and hung up.' In the week or so since Canada had declared war, the rate of flow of foreign exchange out of the country had dramatically increased. The Canadian dollar had slipped to ninety cents in relation to the American dollar, and the slide was not over. The time for action was at hand.[62]

On the morning of 15 September chartered bank executives assembled for a meeting with Bank of Canada officials. It was clear that a serious situation had arisen and Graham Towers wasted no time. He announced that a complete and compulsory system of foreign exchange controls would be imposed within a few hours, under the authority of the War Measures Act. Towers then headed for his office to await word that Cabinet had approved the plan while the bank's deputy minister, Donald Gordon, provided details to the gathered officials. He locked the door and announced, 'Nobody leaves and nobody uses the phone till the Order-in-Council's passed.' It turned out to be a long day. Not until approximately 6:00 p.m. did Towers finally call with Cabinet approval for the first official restrictions ever placed on foreign exchange transactions in Canada.[63]

At of the opening of the business day the following morning, no dollar could leave or any goods enter the country without official permission. The exchange rate was fixed at $1.10 to buy an American dollar and $4.43 to buy a British pound. These rates prevailed until mid-1946. 'The elimination of the wide and erratic fluctuations which would otherwise have been probable under war-time conditions has removed the factor of uncertainty which is one of the greatest deterrents to international trading operations,' Clark observed nearly two years later.[64] A devalued Canadian dollar also encouraged trade with the United States.

Prime Minister King was briefed by Ralston on 13 September about the plans: 'I approved all he had brought forward which had come from Clarke [*sic*] and Tower [*sic*] – very carefully thought out.'[65] The entire operation was under the direction of the Foreign Exchange Control Board (FECB) with Towers as chairman. Members of the board came to include Clifford Clark, Donald Gordon, Norman Robertson, Lester Pearson, Escott Reid, Arnold Heeney, Hugh Scully, Fred Bull, Maxwell Mackenzie, David Sim, Dana Wilgress, John Deutsch, Wynne Plumptre, and Louis Rasminsky. Only Clark and Towers served on the board for its entire existence. On 16 September the FECB met for the first time and held another five meetings that month. It met regularly throughout the war and into the post-war period.[66] David Mansur was put to work on foreign exchange control, as was Jimmy Coyne, both of whom had been slated to work with the Mortgage Bank.[67] When Graham Towers called the Toronto accounting firm of Clarkson Gordon in mid-September for help in setting up the board, Walter Gordon took on the task for the next four months.[68] Rasminsky was encouraged to join the Bank of Canada on 1 April 1940, and he became head of the exchange board's research and statistical section.[69] Even Clark's daughter, Peggy, was eventually employed by the board. Peggy graduated from Queen's in 1942 and her new job involved research into Canada's stocks of gold.[70] Clark summarized the work of the Foreign Exchange Board during the first nine months of the war:

Exchange control was used solely to prevent, or at least to reduce to small proportions, any export of capital from Canada. While exports and imports were subject to licensing, this was not for the purpose of restricting trade but merely to assure that Canada would receive from her export trade the amount and type of foreign exchange she should receive and that she would not lose as a result of her import trade any unnecessary foreign exchange due to fictitious transactions. No restrictions were placed on the sale of foreign exchange for travel purposes. The board also provided United States dollars for fulfilling lawful contracts stipulating payment in United States currency, for payment for normal and necessary services rendered to residents by non-residents, for small benevolent remittances abroad, and also for the full amount of net income accruing to non-residents from Canadian sources even though that income might be lawfully payable solely in Canadian dollars.[71]

By mid-September Poland was occupied by Nazi Germany. On 18 September the Cabinet met to discuss the program prepared by the military chiefs of staff. It recommended a budget of $491.7 million to finance the first year of the war. A Cabinet subcommittee had already concluded that this was 'an expenditure the country could not begin to afford.' Clark and Towers were brought in to advise. They argued that Canada might be able to afford half of what the chiefs of staff were proposing.[72] King recorded the meeting in his diary: 'Towers made an excellent statement ... making clear that what was being asked for by the Defence forces would take about a third of the national income, representing a point today which Germany has only geared up to after 7 years' intensive effort. He doubted if without materially affecting the credit of the country, we could contemplate an expenditure of over 250 millions of dollars. We might possibly go to 300 millions.'[73] The reaction of his financial tribunes pleased the prime minister. It was 'an immense relief,' he noted, 'getting back to sound economics.'[74] The Cabinet agreed that the military would have to work out the best possible program on a budget of $250 million. In the end, the budget for the first year of war was $314 million, but subsequently 10 per cent of this was set aside as a reserve for unforeseen contingencies.[75]

Clifford Clark had spent considerable time and effort on Canada's housing problem during the Depression. With the outbreak of war, however, the housing programs received low priority on the government's agenda. According to John Bacher, even Clark gave the problem low priority. Bacher goes so far as to claim that 'Clark initially regarded the war as an opportunity to eliminate all government-assisted housing programs and so to return the field to private enterprise,' and that his 'plan' was to 'create a housing shortage to provide post-war employment,' but there is no support for such exaggerated and conspiratorial claims.[76] Plans for the Central Mortgage Bank were put on hold, and in mid-October Clark informed Ralston that the federal government could avoid paying the taxes on newly built low-priced housing. The general uncertainty about price, wage, and interest levels, and therefore property and rental values, could lead to large contributions by the dominion government and mortgage companies.[77] In early December Clark again wrote Ralston, this time supporting a decision to end National Housing Act loans for homes costing more than $4,000 as of the end of the year: 'Persons wishing to finance higher cost houses, should under normal circumstances, have comparatively little difficulty in arranging their financing directly with an insurance, loan or trust company.'[78] Clark did not feel that the issue of funding low-rental housing projects could be so easily ignored, however. He informed the finance minister that while no projects had yet been financed, considerable work was being done on projects in both Winnipeg and Montreal. Clark admitted the government was 'stalling' but he suggested that both projects receive the 'go ahead.' After this, however, Clark recommended that Ottawa refuse new projects.[79]

Mackenzie King was intent on avoiding casualties in the early period of the war but he was just as intent on avoiding expenses. It would be difficult, indeed impossible, to avoid both. On 26 September, British Prime Minister Neville Chamberlain proposed to Ottawa what became known as the British Commonwealth Air Training Plan (BCATP).[80] King cautiously welcomed the proposal, which he publicly announced on 10 October. But problems soon emerged over the shared financing of the plan. The British wanted an equitable cost-sharing that would have the least impact on Britain's already limited pool of foreign exchange.

At the first meeting in Ottawa, the British negotiator, Lord Riverdale, stressed the seriousness of Britain's dollar shortage and indicated that his nation might have to purchase more Canadian wheat in order to get a deal done.[81] Canadian officials were already irritated going into the discussions because of Britain's recent decision to impose controls on Canadian imports of tobacco, as well as canned and fresh fruit, at a time when Britain had undertaken to accept all of Australia's wool supply and surplus agricultural products. To add insult to injury, a similar deal had been worked out with New Zealand. In response to Canada's official reply, Dominions Secretary Anthony Eden sent a memorandum to the British Cabinet, noting, 'The Canadians will obviously feel that it is wrong that we should be pressing them to supply and even finance purchases in Canada essential to *our* interests while we are taking unilateral action which must damage *their* essential interests.'[82] The British expected a trade deficit with Canada of some $445 million in the first year of the war and hoped, indeed expected, that Canada would finance most, if not all, of it. Yet Canada had received few orders from Britain.[83] C.D. Howe informed the Cabinet on 8 December that orders at present totalled only $5 million.[84]

Canada proposed to supply food, some equipment and munitions, and a small expeditionary force. Britain and France would be charged for supplies used by the force and Britain would ship it overseas. The Canadian government, however, would assist Britain (and possibly France) in financing purchases in Canada; in return, the British would repatriate Canadian securities held in the United Kingdom. The Canadian officials were determined that the contribution had to be considered as a whole, not piecemeal, as had happened with other imports such as apples. The financial assistance would come as a package, and fair treatment would have to be offered Canadian producers. Under no circumstances would Canada tie the dollar to the pound sterling. In addition, Ottawa wished to use Canadian credit balances in London to reduce both public and private indebtedness to Britain.[85]

Clark agreed with King's desire for a large but limited Canadian war effort. In hindsight the government's desire to avoid expenses may seem petty, particularly when placed in the context of the dire situation facing Britain in the first two years of the war. The experience of the Great War loomed large, however, and Clark was intent on serving responsibly in his role as one of the financial gatekeepers. He argued that the nation could not be expected to devote as large a proportion of its national income to the war as Britain, for a number of reasons. First, the war was a European conflict in which Britain's vital interests were at stake in a manner in which Canada's were not. Three thousand miles from the fighting, Canada also enjoyed the protection of the United States. Second, Canada faced the issue of national unity, and the war was a particularly sensitive topic for French–English relations. Third, the nation was less accustomed than Britain to the controls and regimentation that might make possible a large diversion of national income to war. Canada's governmental structure was less efficient than that of the United Kingdom, a reference to the existence of both federal and provincial jurisdictions with, among other complications, their own rights to taxation. Finally, Canada was 'relatively and absolutely ... the greatest *debtor* country in the world.'[86]

J.A.C. Osborne, the British treasury representative in Ottawa who had been the first deputy governor of the Bank of Canada, met in October with Clark, Towers, and Robertson to discuss the financing of British spending in Canada. Faced with the costs of Canada's own war effort, financing British purchases in Canada, and the negotiations over the costs of the air training plan, the discussions led to the ultimate question of what Canada could actually afford and what percentage of the nation's income could realistically be devoted to war.[87] No national accounts existed at the time, so Clark, Towers, and their staffs had to come up with calculations. Statistics on Canadian national income were published in British economic studies prior to the First World War but they were based on inadequate information. Demands for more accurate estimates followed, but the statistics produced were tentative.[88] Clark's team estimated that Canada's national income for 1938 was $3.575 billion, and this figure might rise by 15 per cent during the first year of the war as a result of new orders. The maximum that the Canadian government could take from this was assumed to be 42 per cent. While these numbers were admittedly rough estimates,[89] after allowing for the military budgets already approved, approximately $237 million was left for financial assistance for British purchases in Canada as well as the nation's share of the air training plan.[90] These numbers were shared with the British.

The negotiations over the British Commonwealth Air Training Plan were prickly from the beginning. When Lord Riverdale arrived in Ottawa on 15 October, he was met at the Chateau Laurier by Clark and Arnold Heeney, secretary to the Canadian Cabinet. Heeney was not impressed by Riverdale and his large party of senior civil officials and staff officers from the Air Ministry: 'After assuring ourselves that all was in order for their comfort and convenience, and before we had had a chance to mention arrangements for the following day, Lord Riverdale drew Clark and I aside and asked us to go with him into the next room. There he proceeded to fish in the drawer of his bureau and select two small tissue-wrapped packages which he solemnly presented to us. They turned out to be pen knives clearly marked with his firm's name. Poised as we were for immediate exchanges on urgent issues, Clark and I found it incongruous that the first move by the noble Lord, however kindly intended, should have the colour of sales promotion rather than serious negotiation between governments.'[91]

King met Riverdale on 17 October, and the prime minister was also immediately annoyed. Apparently Riverdale referred to the air training plan as 'your scheme' and gave King the distinct impression that he took it for granted that the Canadians would accept whatever the British proposed. King informed the British official that it would not be easy to reach an agreement, partly as a result of the physical difficulties but mainly because of the costs. Riverdale had no estimates of the costs of the proposed plan and he spent the next two weeks working to come up with the numbers in conjunction with the Royal Canadian Air Force, and likely officials of the Department of Finance and the War Supply Board.[92] But Riverdale was surprised at how little the Canadian government wished to offer up for the project. He learned from W.D. Euler, minister of trade and commerce, that Canada contemplated an eventual defence expenditure of $300 million a year. In a letter to British Secretary of State for Air Kingsley Wood, Riverdale observed, 'It is doubtful whether even if they doubled their taxation the Canadian Government would be able to find the money for our training scheme as well as the help which they are giving to the Navy and the Army.'[93]

The first meeting of the British delegation with the Canadian Cabinet Committee and Emergency Council occurred on 31 October. According to C.P. Stacey, 'The negotiations immediately ran aground on the rocks of finance.' Riverdale indicated that the total cost for the program to the end of March 1943 would be approximately $888.5 million. Britain would make a contribution of $140 million for aircraft and $51.5 million in maintenance equipment. He proposed that Canada, Australia, and New Zealand divide up the remaining costs, adding that Britain would bear the cost of supporting the force turned out by the training schools, at an estimated cost of $1.5 billion a year.[94] The Canadian officials were surprised by the costs involved. 'Chubby' Power recalled King saying that he did not want Canada's spirit of cooperation crushed at the beginning of the war by excessive demands from Britain, while Ralston emphasized that Canada was already making other important contributions and 'must not be bled so white as to become an ineffective partner in the war effort of the Commonwealth.' Canada had to plan for a long war.[95] King noted that by the end of the meeting Riverdale was backtracking, realizing that 'he had gone a little too far in his attempted railroading,' and was instead complimenting the Canadian government on what the nation had already achieved in a short period of time.[96]

The British and Canadian officials had different approaches to war finance, based on their particular situations. The British were not worrying about where the money would come from because for them limited liability had been abandoned in the spring of 1939. The Canadians, on the other hand, were working within the calculations made by the finance department on Canada's capacity to spend on the war.[97] The British wanted as much financial commitment from Canada as possible, while Canada was doing everything possible to limit, or at least tightly control, that expenditure. By 1939 it was an old story that been repeated numerous times since the turn of the century in Anglo-Canadian relations on defence policy and military contributions. Regardless, the extent of the differences came as a shock to both sides. The British were left 'blue and depressed' that the Canadians could not come 'within shooting distance' of the figures quoted. To make matters worse, King and Riverdale became involved in misunderstandings over poorly chosen words, and frustration mounted.[98]

On 3 November King cabled a memo to Chamberlain, which indicated that the proposed Canadian share of the BCATP costs was beyond Canada's capacity. It also noted that while the British were pressing Canada on the air training proposals, for many weeks Canada had been pressing for a British decision on purchases of wheat, 'which is the biggest single item in our whole economic program and the most far-reaching in its public consequences.' Until a decision was made on wheat, King claimed, 'I frankly cannot see how a decision can be arrived at in regard to the proposals for the special air training program.'[99]

To further the wheat and other purchasing negotiations, T.A. Crerar, minister of mines and resources, was sent to London.[100] Aside from negotiating a price for wheat, Crerar discussed Canada's financing of British purchases, during which he produced the calculations of Canada's maximum possible contribution to the war effort. Since no one on Crerar's staff or in the London High Commission was knowledgeable about the calculations, the minister asked that Clark or Towers be sent to London by the end of November.[101] Towers ended up making the trip.

While Towers was travelling to London, Grant Dexter of the Winnipeg *Free Press* spoke with Clark about the negotiations. The discussion demonstrated the depths of concern expressed by Canadian officials regarding a repeat of the financing debacle of the Great War. It also helps explain why Canada was so intent on remaining firm with the British when it came to wartime financing: 'I gathered from a talk with

W.C. Clark last night that the British would like to keep their investments in Canada as a kind of reserve war fund and to have us begin at once providing them with credits. Clark intimated very clearly that everybody here is opposed to this course. We want our bonds back first and after we have repatriated all our own stuff we will deal with credits. He said one thing that surprised me – that the second stage of the operations might well be the repatriation of Canadian debt in the U.S. Clark is very keen to come out of this war without foreign debt.'[102]

While these discussions were taking place, the U.S. Congress was embroiled in a bitter debate over President Roosevelt's proposal to repeal the arms embargo. On 3 November the embargo was lifted and the United States was in a position to sell arms on a cash-and-carry basis, a move that primarily benefited Britain and France because they controlled the relevant sea-lanes.[103] But as a result, Britain was even less willing to lose any of its limited American dollars. The cash-and-carry provisions did include special exemptions, Clark later noted, under which 'trade with certain areas presumed to be relatively safe might continue in American vessels and without prior transfer of title except for munitions. American vessels were allowed to carry passengers and goods still owned by Americans "on or over lakes, rivers, and inland waters bordering on the United States." Thus, normal trade relations, except in respect of traffic in munitions, remained in most respects unchanged between the United States and Canadian citizens.'[104]

Negotiations continued on the air training plan when delegations from Australia and New Zealand arrived in Canada in early November. Both nations wished to do as much training of their pilots and crews at home as possible, thus forcing new cost estimates to be calculated. One set of figures was worked out on 9 November and further refinements that shifted more costs onto Britain resulted in an arrangement acceptable to the Canadian War Committee on 14 November. Canada would bear costs estimated at $313 million.[105] This, King believed, 'was going much further than we intended,' but was acceptable 'so that the British Government might feel that we had acted generously.' Towers agreed. He informed Cabinet that British purchasing officials 'would likely go much further with us if we were not niggardly with them.' The War Committee did, however, lay down two conditions: the plan would have to take priority over all other forms of Canadian contribution to the war effort, and there would have to be a satisfactory agreement on the wheat discussions presently underway in London.[106]

By December the cost figures had changed again as a result of Australia's intention to do even more of its own training and thus contribute less to the joint plan. The final estimate called for Canada to pay $353.4 million, Britain $185.0 million, Australia $39.9 million, and New Zealand $28.6 million.[107] O.D. Skelton was not impressed by the deal and expressed his typical concern that Canada had surrendered too much to British pressure. He wished to see the Canadian pilots organized into Canadian squadrons, but knew that it would be difficult to insist on this organization and then have the British pay the maintenance costs. 'I do feel,' he informed King, 'that there is some danger of sliding into a position where we would have no answer either to the British Government or to some vociferous elements in the Canadian public if it were suggested that if we call the tune we should pay the Piper.' The cost, he estimated, might be as much as $750 million a year, which the government, guided by the estimates of the finance department, was clearly not prepared to contemplate.[108] Early on the morning of 17 December – the same day the first Canadian Division landed in the United Kingdom – the British Commonwealth Air Training Plan was signed. It was a huge undertaking, even in its initial stages. Sixty-seven schools were required and about twenty airfields had to be enlarged with an additional sixty new ones created. Nearly forty thousand officers and men were needed to run the program.[109]

Clifford Clark worked behind the scenes in the BCATP negotiations, but his role was significant. James Gibson, who had been seconded from external affairs before the war to work in the Prime Minister's Office, claimed that a substantial share of the credit should go to Clark: 'In practical terms, Clifford Clark was the great solvent in the negotiations leading up to the British Commonwealth Air Training Plan in December 1939 … I fancy it was Clark who kept the fiscal part of the negotiations on the rails … Now Clark wasn't concerned with the operational part of it but the financial underpinning owed an enormous amount to his know how, his ability to work with people and the general sense that the concerns of the finance department were in good hands.'[110]

In London, meanwhile, British officials were frustrated with the Canadian calculations of the maximum possible contribution to the war effort put forward by Crerar and Towers. The British dismissed the Canadian estimates as 'mildly preposterous.' From the British perspective, Canada was underestimating its national income and the calculations were based on 'theoretical reasonings and rough estimates which make it a ridiculous method to choose.' Towers, who shortly after his arrival met with Sir Frederick Phillips, undersecretary of the treasury, held firm, arguing that the total amount Canada could lend was $237 million, minus the Canadian costs for the first year of the air training plan then estimated at $46 million. Canada, Towers insisted, would not offer an impossible sum. If the estimates were indeed low, the nation would do more, he assured Phillips, but it must be understood that even the present estimates would involve 'considerable sacrifice by the Canadian people.' Phillips concluded that the assurances were 'reasonably satisfactory' and it was doubtful the stubborn Canadians would yield more at present.[111]

But Crerar and Towers were unable to secure a deal on wheat, despite Canada's commitment to the air training plan. The price being demanded by Canada was too high for the British. When contacted by Towers from London on 12 December, Clark concluded that there was no point in trying to convince the British otherwise and attempting to negotiate a long-term contract.[112] As a result, the British continued to buy wheat on the open market until May 1940 when the British contracted to buy 50 million bushels at 82.5 cents.[113]

In order to provide the British with dollars to purchase Canadian foodstuffs, raw materials, and war supplies, the Canadian government borrowed $200 million from commercial banks in November at 2 per cent interest for two years and used $92 million of it to repatriate Canadian securities held in London. The Bank of Canada's assets grew in November by $107 million as a result of the purchase of securities and an increase in the value of gold and foreign exchange reserves. This growth provided cash to meet enlarged public demand for money in circulation and to increase the cash reserves of the chartered banks, thereby enabling the banks' total deposits to increase by slightly more than $300 million and their loans to grow by $147 million, mainly to finance the large wheat crop.[114] According to Fullerton, 'The slack in resources of manpower and plant capacity was much greater than anyone had thought; war production grew rapidly; and a bumper wheat crop added to the need for more bank credit.'[115]

As a result of the rapidly increasing workload, Ralston went in search of reinforcement for his deputy. At the end of November, Ralston appealed to Queen's University Principal R.C. Wallace to release W.A. Mackintosh for full-time work in the Department of Finance as special assistant to Clifford Clark. Mackintosh by this time was a known quantity in Ottawa circles. He had served as a member of the National Employment Commission, and that work was followed almost immediately by Mackintosh's role with the Royal Commission on Dominion–Provincial Relations. He directed its principal economic research and wrote an influential report on Canadian economic history.

Mackintosh, Ralston informed Wallace, was 'the best man, and indeed probably the only man, who could be brought into the Department and immediately ease the burden on my Deputy.'[116] Wallace agreed and Mackintosh returned to Ottawa and joined the Department of Finance on 12 December, where he would remain until the summer of 1946.

Aside from being a colleague, Bill Mackintosh was also one of Clark's closest friends. Their vision of Canada was similar and they both believed in the need for a stronger role for the federal government. Clark was more suited to the bureaucracy and played the role of the consummate civil servant; Mackintosh, on the other hand, was more the university professor who, while enjoying the fast-paced work in Ottawa, always looked ahead to a time when he could return to the relatively quiet world of academe. Mackintosh did enjoy the atmosphere of the developing mandarinate in Ottawa and, as Granatstein notes, it was the attraction of working with the likes of Clark, Bryce, Towers, Skelton, Robertson, and Wrong that made going to Ottawa so exhilarating. When Mackintosh moved to Ottawa in 1939, he lived in Clark's Rockcliffe neighbourhood. The two men often saw each other socially (in each other's homes and for fishing trips) and 'their relationship became especially close.' Mackintosh worked alongside Clark and was immediately taken into the inner circles of wartime finance. He attended the meetings of the Economic Advisory Committee and chaired the sessions when Clark was absent. When Mackintosh came onto the scene in December, the EAC was dealing with wage policy and unemployment, areas in which he had developed expertise with the Purvis Commission.[117]

Aside from fishing, bridge was Clark's main source of recreation, particularly during the long winter months. Indeed, it became one of his few diversions from his extremely long days at the office. 'Certainly,' Mackintosh noted, 'he could always rouse himself from weariness if bridge was a possibility.'[118] Clark's eldest son, George, remembered that his father often talked about doing a wide variety of social things but work always came first. George did not remember his father ever 'coming home and sitting down and having a good time. Bridge, as a result, was his only social outlet at home.'[119] When time allowed, Clifford would ask Margaret to make some phone calls in order to round up some bridge partners. As with fishing, what he lacked in skill was made up for with enthusiasm. The Gordons, Mackintoshes, and Mansurs became the most frequent guests in the Clark home during the war years.[120]

One surprising aspect of government policy during the war was how quickly attention turned to post-war planning. Almost before the war had even begun, officials in Ottawa were anticipating plans for post-war reconstruction. This anticipation and preparation did not emerge from the belief that the conflict would be over quickly. On the contrary, the government had learned its lessons from the Great War. On 8 December, only months into the war, the Cabinet Committee on Demobilization and Re-establishment was created. Ian Mackenzie was appointed chairman. The aim of the committee was to reintegrate members of the armed forces into civilian life after war's end.[121]

While the federal government might already have been thinking about war's end, the war effort was developing slowly. According to Stacey, the effort on the industrial front was disappointing because 'the spirit of limited liability, and the small appropriations for the armed forces ... were not favourable to rapid growth.'[122] The Department of Finance was responsible for these 'small appropriations' and maintaining the authorized estimates, but it was Clark who monitored the public purse most closely. General Andrew McNaughton, for example, blamed Clark rather than Ralston for the fact that manufacturers, while geared up for war production, were not receiving orders. 'I asked if Ralston was at fault,' King wrote after a conversation with McNaughton. 'He said he had found Ralston most agreeable in first conversations, but thought he had come lately under the influence of Finance officials. He spoke rather strongly against Clark as being too much of a bureaucrat; thinking only of the fiscal year, not understanding war conditions.'[123] The next afternoon, King raised McNaughton's concerns with some of the members of the War Committee, including Rogers, Howe, Ralston, and Mackenzie. Without directly naming McNaughton as his source, the prime minister indicated that there was an impression that the Department of Finance was reluctant to allow the War Supply Board to place orders for future requirements and that Clark was being blamed for the obstacles. These allegations, according to David Slater, caught Ralston off guard and both he and Howe were left wondering why Clark was subject to criticism. They responded that the deputy had been 'entirely agreeable' during the air training plan negotiations, and they asked for specific examples of orders being stalled. Rogers also defended Clark, agreeing that finance had approved spending commitments beyond the fiscal year. King then asked Rogers whether the Department of National Defence felt it was able to obtain the necessary equipment and supplies. Rogers replied that there were difficulties but that in some cases his own department was responsible for the delays in requisitions. Ralston 'wished to make it quite clear that his deputy minister had never had anything to do with the War Supply Board, and that he was not responsible for any delays or for any of the matters apparently complained of by the chairman.'[124] The explanations were sufficient for King: 'I satisfied my own mind from what the Ministers said that the fault is in no way ours. Simply that the British have not placed orders in Canada that were anticipated by the manufacturers.'[125]

On 15 January 1940, the government launched the first public loan campaign of the war, seeking to raise $200 million. When the war began, it was decided not to issue a public loan until economic activity and national income had increased substantially. At the end of 1939 preparations were commenced. Clark held discussions with officials of the Bank of Canada and a working committee representing investment dealers and chartered banks. The discussions lasted several weeks and a publicity campaign was launched to inform the populace.[126] The stimulus to business activity that followed the previous fall's credit expansion had been reflected in indices of retail and wholesale turnover, as well as industrial production and prices. These factors, however, showed a considerable sag in the early months of 1940. After the government floated the public loan and increased its own spending, there was a renewal of business expansion. But selling the first war loan did present some problems. Individual Canadians had not been significant loan buyers since the last war and most new Canadian bond issues were sold to financial institutions, of which insurance companies in Canada, Britain, and the United States represented the largest markets. Investment dealers, cut off by the war from their normal markets, pressed Clark and Towers for a role in the bond issue. A committee of bankers and dealers presented their views on the form and selling approach for the first issue, which would be sold cooperatively rather than competitively. This approach was adopted and a temporary war loan committee was formed.[127]

Despite the pressures of preparing for war, as well as planning for an election in 1940, Prime Minister King had two other projects that he wanted Cabinet approval for early in the year. One was the St Lawrence Waterway. Negotiations had been impossible as long as Premier Hepburn in Ontario and Premier Duplessis in Quebec continued to object. But Duplessis' Union Nationale had been defeated by the Ottawa-friendly Liberals and Hepburn had withdrawn his objection in November 1939. In the Cabinet meeting on 18 January, King had a long and difficult discussion on the project with Ralston, who objected to diverting funds for this purpose in wartime, although he finally admitted to the need to retain the goodwill of the United States. The government decided to go ahead.

The other issue was unemployment insurance. The defeat of Duplessis also removed the main obstacle to provincial consent on a constitutional amendment to bring UI under federal jurisdiction. As early as 1938, all provinces except Quebec, Alberta, and New Brunswick had agreed to an amendment. On 8 January, King was informed that Adelard Godbout, the new Liberal premier of Quebec, was favourable. The prime minister was confident that he could get approval from Alberta and New Brunswick, which he did that spring. 'The public will appreciate the necessity of having Unemployment Insurance to help to meet the post-war conditions,' he observed.[128] It would also be a boost to the government's record before facing the electorate. That same day the prime minister sent a four-page letter to his labour minister, Norman McLarty, outlining the reasons for moving ahead and directing him to give the measure 'precedence over all other matters.'[129] But King ended up having more difficulty obtaining approval from members of his own Cabinet than from the provinces. Most of them approved, but Ralston, Howe, and Ilsley were opposed: 'Ralston, on the score that we needed the money for the prosecution of the war, that we had spent enough on socialistic legislation in what we had done for unemployment relief, housing, etc.' The finance minister also argued that it would appear too much as a pre-election bribe. King claimed that 'Ralston has set his whole mentality in the direction of keeping down expenditures ... He has been closely associated with large corporations and is out of touch with the social trend.'[130] The prime minister's strong insistence on the measure apparently silenced the opposition.

Unemployment insurance was strongly supported by Mackintosh but for different reasons, which he outlined in a 20 January memo to Clark. 'During the expected brisk activity of the war period, the plan would act as a scheme of compulsory saving,' which would provide workers with money if the expected post-war depression in fact occurred. This large pool of savings would then be 'available for Government use, just as if individual workers bought savings certificates.' UI contributions would have the same effect as taxes in helping 'hold down consumption and make labour, equipment and resources available for the war effort.' Most important to Mackintosh was that unemployment insurance was another step toward centralization and would require an efficient and well-staffed national employment service, in place of the scattered and often patronage-dominated provincial services. The employment service would become the 'informed field staff at the service of the Dominion' providing expert knowledge on the 'changes and conditions of employment.' Such an organization was 'immediately necessary if we are to make use of the available idle labour. On that will depend the possibility of meeting the next year's war effort out of increased production rather than out of decreased consumption and capital maintenance.' The value of having an operating employment service made unemployment insurance worthwhile, even for those opposed to the principle.[131]

In February 1940 Clark renewed negotiations with the Gilmour trustees on the Five Lakes Fishing Club. The wartime workload was increasing and Clark had not given up hope of creating a reprieve from Ottawa: 'On one or more occasions recently, when the sun has been shining and the snow melting, my mind has run back to our negotiations over the Gilmour property which were sadly interrupted by the outbreak of war. Under present conditions, a fishing club is, of course, a luxury and it will become more and more so as the war goes on. On the other hand, for those of us who must continually burn the midnight oil, the chance of getting out in the country for an occasional Sunday would be a godsend.'[132] The negotiations proved fruitful and concluded with a sale at $12,500. On 20 February Clark wrote to Montreal architect Percy Nobbs (with whom he had clashed over housing policy). Nobbs happened to be an expert on fishing and had written several books on the topic. Clark sought the names of possible caretakers for the property who also knew something about fishing. The deputy minister was convinced the five lakes on the Wakefield property would need restocking. Over the next two months Nobbs sent along several suggestions.[133]

Despite the participation of a few others, Clark was the club's founder. According to Granatstein, Clark established it 'much as he had largely shaped the mandarinate.' He put together a list of potential members and began contacting them, aided by Stewart, Stone, Eaton, and Bryce. On 16 June the Five Lakes Fishing Club came into being. At a meeting at Stone's house in Rockcliffe, fourteen of the prospective members met and agreed to the purchase of the property. The initial membership fee was set at $200 and the regular annual dues, to begin the following year, were set at $75. Thirty memberships were to be offered. Ralston was the only politician on the list and Gratton O'Leary the only journalist. The list of mandarins and other officials was long: Bob Bryce, Donald Gordon, Bill Mackintosh, Norman Robertson, Jack

Pickersgill, O.D. Skelton, Dana Wilgress, A.K. Eaton, J.R. Beattie, David Sim, T.A. Stone, D.B. Mansur, Jimmy Coyne, W.R. Hadley, Ross Tolmie, Gordon Maclaren, R.H. Coats, Fraser Elliot, F.E. Bronson, D.G. Marble, A.W. Rogers, Russel Smart, Bryce Stewart, and B.J. Roberts.[134] The group approved bylaws for the club as well as an executive committee. Clark was named honorary president. Located only thirty-one miles from Ottawa, Five Lakes was, according to Macintosh, able to bring 'the friendly bureaucrats face to face with the myth of the wilderness.'[135] 'The club was rustic, a large cottage with rough sleeping accommodations for eighteen to twenty, no electricity, a communal kitchen where each fended for himself (although washing-up was provided by the resident caretaker and his wife), and for many years with sometimes good angling a collection of rowboats and canoes (no powerboats were permitted), and some splendid treed country for walking. The Club was a safety valve, a refuge. And always the talk was of policy.' As Granatstein notes, 'The club offered little luxury' but it did provide 'a relief valve, a place away from the East Block to let off pressure, to wear rough clothes, to eat and drink and sing, even to fish.' But the club also added to the criticism that the mandarins were an exclusive and elitist clique.[136]

By the spring of 1940 the Economic Advisory Committee was at the peak of its activity. Clark used the meeting of 12 March 'as a sort of clinic for appraising the work the Committee has done, and to see what could be done to improve its normal functioning.' The deputy minister admitted that the role of the EAC had changed since its inception. While its original purpose was to coordinate activity and organization in wartime economic fields, it had tended to become more of an interdepartmental committee called to deal with specific subjects. Clark noted that the committee was designed to consider broad questions of policy and he wished its activities to be directed more closely to this original purpose. Norman Robertson noted that no representative of the War Supply Board was serving on the EAC. This omission was important because the board was 'in a sense the dynamic department of the Government at present being the one which is spending the most money and presumably having the most direct economic effects. Unless the Committee has some contact with their plans it is apt to neglect, or at least be ignorant of the biggest single factor in the whole economy.' Clark responded that he had requested a representative but had received no response. Mackintosh produced a memorandum for the EAC meeting, suggesting that the committee initiate a periodic survey of economic conditions, which could then be used as a basis on which to consider questions of organization and policy.[137]

But the major problem was that the EAC was overwhelmed with work. Such a diverse range of issues were being brought forward for discussion that the committee was bogged down in detail, thereby preventing them from being handled 'quickly and intelligently.' At a meeting on 1 May it was suggested that more preliminary discussion be given to problems by subcommittees, prior to the EAC having to deal with them directly. Towers also requested that the committee be informed about what action was being taken by government on matters already dealt with by the EAC: 'The Committee is to some degree responsible for what it recommends, and it is only reasonable that it should have some chance to know how its recommendations are being carried out.'[138]

In mid-February the *Rowell-Sirois Commission Report* was received by the government. It was withheld, however, until after the anticipated election. The breadth of the report was sweeping. According to Harvey Perry, the Royal Commission on Dominion–Provincial Relations was 'a landmark in Canadian history comparable to Lord Durham's Report of a century before. Seldom anywhere has a similar attempt been made to weigh up at one stroke the economic, political, and financial progress of an organized system of government from its inception, and to chart its future course.'[139] Bryce called it 'a radical prescription, persuasively set forth against a background of history and analysis the likes of which Canadians had never seen.' The document was recognized even by its critics, such as economist and historian Harold Innis, as one that 'should be read by all students of government in Canada.'[140] The report recommended that the dominion assume the full burden of relief of unemployed employables; provincial debts be assumed by the dominion with adjustment for revenue-producing assets; the provinces retire from the fields of personal and corporation income taxation, specific corporation taxation, and succession duties; the provinces surrender all existing subsides; the dominion recognize an obligation to respect the revenue resources remaining to the provinces and in addition to pay over to each province an amount equal to a tax of 10 per cent of the net income derived from mining, smelting, and refining of ores and oils produced in the province; the dominion pay the provinces annual adjustment grants, determined by a proposed finance commission, to provide adequate social, educational, and developmental services; and the provinces retain control of their expenditures.[141]

The anticipated general election was held on 26 March 1940. The King Liberals again won office, this time with the largest majority to date. The Liberals took 181 seats, compared to 40 for the Conservatives, 8 for the Co-operative Commonwealth Federation, 10 for the Social Credit, and 6 independents and others.[142] Mackenzie King had reason for confidence but personally he was plagued by insecurities. The bachelor prime minister had few close friends and he was constantly suspicious of others. Despite his ability to shape successful working dynamics and to build impressive cabinets, King was distant in his personal relationships. He became infamous for being a difficult man to work under, and stories abound of the prime minister's pettiness. King was close to very few ministers, even among the most powerful. The same was true of the civil service. It was not until after 1939, when Clark's role and influence increased dramatically, that King became increasingly impressed with the deputy minister.[143] To an extent, it was impossible for the prime minister not to be impressed by Clark. The complexities and pressures of wartime finance were so overwhelming that Clark's steady and calming presence served as a crutch for the beleaguered King. Clark became a highly dependable fixture in Ottawa during these years. Yet King remained suspicious of the increasingly influential mandarins and their centralizing agenda. As Pickersgill points out, Mackenzie King 'regarded Clark as someone who really knew everything that he didn't know. He had a great respect and regard for Clark and a profound suspicion of him at the same time.'[144] Both sentiments would grow as the war progressed.

6

Dark Days, 1940–1941

> The news is terrible these days, almost incredible. Naturally, the pace here is very rapid. Tonight I should be writing the Budget Speech but the pile of unanswered correspondence is so large that I could not get a place on my desk to write unless I cleared some of it up.
>
> – W.C. Clark to Bryce Stewart, 15 June 1940

On 9 April 1940 the 'phoney war' came to an abrupt end. Germany delivered an ultimatum for surrender to Denmark and Norway; Denmark capitulated immediately, while Norway resisted but was soon overrun. Britain landed two brigades on 20 April but barely managed to evacuate them by 2 May. The conflict entered a new phase and the artificial period of calm, which had provided Canada crucial time to prepare for war, was over. Dark days lay ahead.

The bad news reached Canadians over breakfast on 9 April. Mackenzie King had spoken with C.D. Howe and J.L. Ralston four days previous about proclaiming the Munitions and Supply Act and naming Howe as minister 'to underline the government's determination to do something with Canada's chaotic munitions industry.' Howe was reluctant to leave the transport department but indicated that he would organize the new department as acting minister. With the new crisis in Europe, however, the prime minister decided to establish the department immediately with Howe as full minister.[1]

As the battle for Norway intensified, Canada took further measures to shore up its foreign exchange position. On 30 April the Foreign Exchange Order required all Canadian residents to sell their foreign exchange holdings (banknotes, cheques, bank deposits, etc.) to the

Foreign Exchange Control Board. Companies could, under certain circumstances, retain foreign exchange for particular short-term commitments. At the same time, the Exchange Fund Order authorized the board to purchase all gold and foreign exchange held by the Bank of Canada. On 1 May the Bank sold the board $253.5 million worth of gold and foreign exchange.[2] On the morning of 10 May Germany invaded the Netherlands, Luxembourg, and Belgium. The same day, British Prime Minister Neville Chamberlain, who barely survived a vote of confidence the day before, resigned and was replaced by Winston Churchill. By 15 May the Netherlands surrendered, Belgium was overrun, and France prepared for the inevitable invasion around the Maginot Line.

When Parliament returned on 16 May, according to Jack Pickersgill, 'the country was in shock, and government itself had been severely shaken by the speed of the Nazi advance.'[3] The atmosphere was sombre and the pace of activity increased dramatically. The Cabinet War Committee met eight times between 10 May and the end of the month. The dispatch of a second division of troops to Britain was accelerated, a Canadian corps was formed, and the creation of a third division was approved.[4] The schedule for the air training plan was also bumped up. Training establishments originally planned for construction in two years were now to be completed during 1940.[5] But the expanded war plans could not be financed under the existing budget. On 21 May Ralston introduced the War Appropriation Bill in order to gain the authority to spend up to $700 million for war-related purposes for the year ending 31 March 1941. This amount was approximately $200 million more than the finance department estimated in late January. Ralston noted that actual spending on defence for the first nine months of the war was $112 million and actual commitments were $267 million. The estimates would remain uncertain and in constant need of re-evaluation during wartime.

By 20 May the situation in Europe had worsened again for the Allies. The German army reached the mouth of the Somme River, splitting the Allied forces and trapping the Belgians, the British Expeditionary Force, and three French armies. Britain now called on Canada for all possible aid. The British could not supply Canada with planes for the air training program as originally planned. Instead, Britain needed its aircraft to defend the homeland, in addition to whatever Canada could supply. According to Grant Dexter, the government faced 'the complete breakdown of the war program.'[6] King was annoyed at what he perceived as the lack of British foresight: 'They had assured us they would be in a position to help us ... Did not wish us to start a factory of our own for later production. Told us of great surplus they had, etc. Now they are in danger of having their own plants bombed ... They are behind in everything. It is an appalling day for Britain when she has to seek from one of her Dominions ships, ammunition, aircraft, additional land forces, etc.'[7]

The Canadian government responded that it was in no position to help. The prime minister told caucus on 23 May that he feared having to announce publicly that the cost of war would exceed $1 billion a year, 'that we had to consider whether that would not occasion a run on the banks. The Governor of the Bank of Canada and officials there were fearful of just something of the kind which might create a very serious internal situation.' King took Ralston aside and informed him of the seriousness of the situation so the finance department could prepare for the increased spending.[8]

By 24 May the only hope for the trapped British and French forces was to escape by sea. Surprisingly, the German advance hesitated long enough for the French to establish a defence that allowed the motley armada to cross the Channel and begin, on 27 May, the evacuation from Dunkirk. A day later Belgium surrendered but the evacuation continued until 4 June, by which time 338,000 British and French soldiers had been saved. Hundreds of tanks and thousands of trucks and guns were abandoned to the enemy.

On the day the Dunkirk evacuation began, the Canadian government launched a new fundraising program – the sale of twenty-five-cent War Saving Stamps and five-dollar, ten-dollar, and twenty-five-dollar War Saving Certificates. The stamps could only be converted into War Savings Certificates, which paid no interest but did pay a 25 per cent tax-free premium on maturity in 7.5 years. The purpose of the campaign (which would raise $370 million by the end of 1945) was to stem inflation by curtailing current spending, to encourage people to save now so that their post-war spending would be increased, to stimulate war consciousness through self-denial, and to augment the federal war chest.[9] While Ralston indicated in Parliament that even the small amounts enabled all citizens to partake in Canada's war work, he also explained that the program provided a continual stream of funds.[10] 'Night after night Dr Clark would be in the office of the Finance Minister, explaining item after item preparatory to final acceptance,' Wellington Jeffers, financial editor for the *Globe and Mail*, later commented. 'Important delegations were calling on both and at noon Dr Clark either continued work with only a glass of milk and a biscuit or he had lunch with members of the Treasury Board or others with whom it was desirable to have a meeting. His method was to encourage the expression of every opinion and if adverse, to meet it on the spot but never in irritation. It might have been a method derived from the classroom and, I think, on the whole on such important matters, it was a very good one. Peremptory decisions, leaving large numbers of unconvinced opponents without explanations they could at least partially accept would have been a mistake.'[11] The second war loan campaign was conducted in September. Although it met its target, there were difficulties. Clark and Towers discussed the problems, resulting in a complete reorganization and the creation of the National Victory Loan Committee.[12]

On 29 May, Ralston's War Appropriation Bill was passed. But despite receiving support from the prime minister, Ralston was coming under increasing scrutiny from within Liberal ranks. Senator Norman Lambert complained to Grant Dexter that 'Ralston is impossible because he is unable to delegate work and has already become the bottleneck of the government where he is.' Lambert was known for his factional nature and vociferous criticisms of fellow Liberals, including a deep dislike of Mackenzie King, but on this issue even the more reflective Dexter was in agreement: 'This is perfectly true as the ministers testify whenever or wherever they get together. Treasury Board has been going on almost daily and until midnight and after, because Ralston cannot pass even an order for superannuation without putting in an hour or more arguing whether it is too much.'[13]

The bad news from Europe, meanwhile, was getting only worse. On 5 June, Germany launched a massive assault across the Somme against the badly outnumbered French. The shock of this blow forced the Canadian government to reformulate its entire wartime financial program. King spoke to the Liberal caucus that day, warning about 'the possibility of France being unable to withstand the terrific onslaught' and urging MPs to think 'only in terms of the utmost war effort that our country could put forward.'[14] In a letter to Towers, Ralston agreed to accumulate sterling above the agreed upon limits in an effort to absorb Britain's trade deficit with Canada. According to Granatstein, 'The war of limited liability in the financial sphere had ended.'[15]

The Canadian government began preparing for the worst. Towers drafted a memorandum for Clifford Clark, Donald Gordon, and Norman Robertson on 'emergency measures of an extreme character,' to prepare the financial framework in Canada in the event that Britain also fell. The memo discussed the interruption of trade and communication with Britain that would result, as well as an end to dealing in pounds sterling. Either the U.S. or the Canadian dollar would necessarily become the currency of the commonwealth.[16] But Clark was ever the optimist. By September he claimed to be confident that Britain would 'probably not be taken' and that Germany would 'crack,' although not for several years, and only if 'during which time we can manage to establish definite air superiority.'[17]

On the morning of 10 June, Italy declared war on Britain and France. Then, just as Prime Minister King was about to enter the House to move a declaration of war on Italy, he received word that the plane in which Norman Rogers was flying to Toronto for a speech had crashed. All on board were killed.[18] 'Chubby' Power was named acting minister of national defence. It was a temporary measure, however, because King wanted Ralston in the post and it was announced that he had accepted. Ralston would not leave the finance department, however, until he had delivered the budget.

On Friday, 14 June, Paris fell to the advancing German army. The news stunned Canada. Overnight, the dominion became Britain's ranking ally in what seemed an increasingly hopeless struggle of epic proportions. 'The news is terrible these days, almost incredible,' Clark wrote to Bryce Stewart on the Saturday night. 'Naturally, the pace here is very rapid.' The deputy minister was working through a backlog of correspondence. 'Tonight I should be writing the Budget Speech,' he confessed, 'but the pile of unanswered correspondence is so large that I could not get a place on my desk to write unless I cleared some of it up.'[19] On 25 June, France capitulated. The fall of France marked the darkest day of the war for the Allied cause, and the outcome looked grim. With the collapse of France and the loss of so much British equipment at Dunkirk, Clark observed, 'the allied strategical plan had now to be completely revised in the light of a Britain without a major European ally, almost without military equipment, and now subject to invasion by an enemy which controlled most of continental Europe.'[20]

In light of the new situation, the Economic Advisory Committee was concerned that serious constraints and bottlenecks would inevitably occur if there was not more efficient coordination, planning, and control of the economy.[21] The EAC considered the problem and recommended improved liaison between the departments of national defence and munitions and supply, so that war requirements could be worked out in advance of physical terms. The committee also concluded that the Department of Munitions and Supply, and the Wartime Prices and Trade Board, were failing to effectively handle prices and supply, and as a result there was conflict between the two agencies. It was recommended that either their powers be extended and they be brought under one minister, or their powers be rearranged and expanded with the personnel of each instructed to work out the necessary coordination informally.[22] The National Resources Mobilization Act was introduced in Parliament on 18 June, providing the federal government with full power to mobilize all human and material resources for the defence of Canada. While the act added little to the powers already possessed by the government under the War Measures Act, according to Pickersgill 'it had symbolic value as a fresh expression by Parliament of its intention to support prosecution of the war wholeheartedly.'[23]

The fall of France led Graham Towers to request the return of Walter Gordon to Ottawa. Gordon had gone back to his company in Toronto. He was asked to work secretly with Alex Skelton and Dean Marble on the implications of what would happen if Britain fell.[24] Gordon was gloomy that summer as he summarized his small committee's work: 'We had access to all available information about the state of the war in Europe, shipping losses, the troops in Britain equipped to repel a possible invasion (or, more accurately, the lack of them), the aircraft and air crews available to take part in what was to become the Battle of Britain and so on. It was a most unpleasant summer. Knowing what we did, it seemed incredible that Britain would be able to survive.'[25]

The declaration of war in 1939 had forced Canada's economy into high gear; the fall of France in 1940 forced it to seek the next level. According to Clark, the situation 'called for the accomplishment in a very short period of what has not inappropriately been termed an industrial revolution.'[26] The nation not only had to expand its existing production, but also create whole new industries, and in doing so, develop designs and specifications, find locations and build plants, recruit management, and train workers. Supplies had to be secured to produce munitions, and the power and fuel to run the plants obtained. On 24 June the War Industries Control Board was established to regulate sectors of the economy and guarantee supplies.[27]

For Clark the increasing demands spelled trouble on the foreign exchange front. Canada had large and immediate needs for machinery and tools, component parts such as airplane engines, and industrial materials that could be acquired only in the United States. This demand placed immediate pressure on Canada's limited supply of American dollars. 'Each month of war brought increasing confirmation of the accuracy of the forecast that led to the establishment of foreign exchange control,' Clark observed, 'increasing confirmation of the fact that the most fundamental bottleneck in Canada's war economy was the short supply of United States dollars.' With virtually all foreign exchange now under the Foreign Exchange Control Board, it was possible week by week to measure the drain on that vital resource.[28] The budget speech (that Clark had been preparing the weekend France fell) indicated the government's intention to further preserve its supply of American dollars. Towers and Robertson travelled to Washington to explain Canada's problem directly to the Americans and warn of the drastic action that would have to be taken, including a 10 per cent War Exchange Tax on all imports from outside the sterling area. The Americans accepted the explanation but warned of difficulties such actions would create in Congress.[29]

Even though the majority of the 1940 budget was written prior to the disaster at Dunkirk, the situation was used to highlight the need for extra expenditures. 'We know only too well that we are paying the price of long years of wishful thinking,' Ralston announced on 24 June. 'There is no doubt that all of us in the democratic countries, governments and people alike, have been blinded to the stark potentialities of force and evil.'[30] The objective of the budget was to use the 'wisest financial methods of paying for the maximum effort which is physically possible.' This would not simply mean extracting additional money from the economy but rather 'producing soundly the maximum possible increase in our national income in the shortest possible time' and ensuring that the increase went directly to war purposes. The budget called for major tax increases. 'I come to you,' Ralston announced, 'to collect part of the price to which I have referred.' In order to avoid slowing economic growth, most of the increases would not be implemented in the present fiscal year.[31]

On the positive side, the economy had grown more than expected. The large wheat crop, combined with war orders and American imports, stimulated business activity. More than 100,000 idle wage earners were drawn into employment in the twelve months prior to April 1940 and national income grew from $3.8 billion in 1939 to $4.5 billion for the fiscal year 1940–1. The government's revenue was higher than expected and reached $562 million for the year ending 31 March 1940. With higher-than-expected revenues and lower-than-expected spending, the deficit was $70 million less than predicted, but $118 million nonetheless. Ralston estimated that non-war spending would be

$448 million, $77 million less than the previous year. Improvements in railway operations, reductions in relief spending, and a tightening of internal governmental spending reduced costs. War expenditures, as already provided for in the War Appropriations Act, was estimated at $700 million. That figure, however, was not firm.[32]

An economic survey of the first year of the war also indicated that the Canadian economy was performing well. Prior to the outbreak of war, capital expenditures were relatively low and business had only just begun to recover from the recession of 1938 and 1939. After the outbreak of war, Canadian business hesitated only briefly, and then production and employment advanced rapidly until January 1940. Wholesale prices adjusted themselves to the premium on the American dollar. In the first half of 1940 there was 'a pause in the advance.' War expenditures and supply contracts increased, but exports to the United States slowed, as did construction during the winter. After May, however, employment, production, trade, and incomes again increased rapidly.[33]

The budget of 1940 included two significant proposals to conserve foreign exchange. A tax of 10 per cent on all imports not eligible for the British preferential duties was announced. In addition, the existing excise tax on automobiles was increased. Ralston argued that these two measures would ensure that the maximum possible amount of foreign exchange was available. The automobile tax would also reduce demand at a time when the war was forcing a reduction in supply, thereby reducing the tendency for prices to rise.[34] Ralston also encouraged gold production and American tourism to increase the supply of foreign exchange. The finance minister highlighted government efforts to increase spending on tourism promotion, and the need to counter misinformation and rumours about the nature of restrictions and regulations that Americans faced when visiting a country at war. It was hoped that these measures aimed at conserving American dollars would also provide the government with some $51 million revenue in the present fiscal year.[35] Early in July the government announced that it would no longer sell U.S. currency to Canadians for pleasure travel abroad.[36] Clark observed that 'this step was taken with even more regret than any concerning imports, since it would inevitably mean a reduction in the personal contacts between Canadians and Americans which have done so much in the past to establish a mutual understanding.' Nevertheless, he argued, the amount of exchange saved in this way was substantial – probably as much as $80 million in a full year – and 'long-term considerations, however important, had to give way to immediate necessities.'[37]

But the government still needed more revenue, so a new Excess Profits Tax was introduced. Average Canadians, however, would not escape. The budget opted for increases in income taxes rather than sales taxes because the former 'approximates ability to pay.' Ralston noted that 'we realize that increases in indirect taxes disguise the burdens imposed by war but they are much more likely to distribute these burdens harshly and unfairly.' The concept of fairness would be referred to constantly in the war budgets to follow. The budget of 1940 also introduced the National Defence Tax, which would be collected through deductions by employers 'as far as it is administratively possible.' The finance minister urged taxpayers to voluntarily pay their income taxes through an instalment plan.[38]

Ralston left finance and was sworn in as minister of defence on 5 July. Three days later James Ilsley was sworn in as finance minister. Ilsley, however, was not the first choice for the job. Ralston had suggested him for the post in mid-June but King was considering George Spinney of the Bank of Montreal. Spinney declined the offer.[39] Whereas Ralston had the respect of the prime minister, Ilsley and King never got along. According to Pickersgill, 'The prime minister never found him congenial, did not appreciate his capacity, and appointed him reluctantly.'[40] Overall, King found Ilsley temperamental, weak, and often on the edge of emotional breakdown. The Nova Scotian was by all accounts an intense and serious character. C.D. Howe's biographers describe him as 'honest, upright, and seething with integrity.'[41] Clifford Clark, however, had more respect and admiration for J.L. Ilsley than any minister under whom he worked.

In mid-July the bill to create unemployment insurance was introduced, just four days after the amendment to the BNA Act was approved to transfer jurisdiction to the federal government. Clark and Mackintosh wanted the bill passed as quickly as possible because it would have a significant and immediate wartime benefit. Premiums would be paid to the federal government at a time when low unemployment meant few benefits would be paid out. The funds could then be redirected toward war production. The act was given royal assent on 7 August.[42]

Pressure, meanwhile, was mounting amongst the provinces for government action on the *Rowell-Sirois Report.* Graham Towers had numerous meetings in early 1940 with provincial representatives, bankers, and investment dealers concerned with debt refinancing.[43] Ilsley met with representatives of Canadian banks and insurance and investment companies that had put up substantial sums of money to avoid provincial defaults while the Rowell-Sirois study was underway.[44] On 24 July, Sandy Skelton sent a memo to Towers urging federal action, especially on the report's proposals for dominion control of personal and corporate income taxes and succession duties (which in 1939 had produced only $30 million in revenue for the provinces).[45] The same day Towers sent a memo to Ilsley urging the report's adoption as a war measure: 'The need for developing an efficient taxation system which will yield the maximum of revenue with the least possible burden on the national income was never more urgent.'[46] An unsigned finance department memorandum of the same date echoed Towers's concern: 'In addition to being a necessary step to make the maximum war effort, it has constructive and lasting value for post-war difficulties. It need not be presented as war legislation, but it should have a very wide appeal to the many Canadians who are eager to see Canada brush aside petty sectional differences and selfish local interests which weaken her in the present emergency.'[47]

A month later, Towers was still pressing for adoption of Rowell-Sirois. In a memo to King, he noted that Alberta had defaulted on its debts, and the other three western provinces faced great difficulty meeting interest payments. Saskatchewan and New Brunswick could face default, which would damage dominion credit and war financing.[48] Towers agreed with finance officials that the federal unemployment insurance scheme was not enough. Only one-quarter of the unemployed would be covered by UI in the expected unemployment surge of the post-war period, and if Ottawa tried to insist that responsibility lay with the provinces or municipalities, as it had in the past, workers would demonstrate even deeper resentment than displayed during the Depression: 'In the interests of peace, order and good government the Dominion may well have to assume full responsibility. But if it does so without having made other arrangements along the lines contemplated in the Sirois Report, the financial situation will be chaotic.' Towers concluded that 'if this were understood by the public, might not an effort to deal with the Report receive popular support; and, so far as the provinces are concerned, might action not be represented as the first constructive piece of work which the provinces could do on the home front?'[49]

The timing of the report's release came up again in mid-September. Clark and his boys pressured Ilsley and, according to Granatstein, this pressure 'seems finally to have forced the issue.' There were three possible courses of action: call an immediate dominion-provincial conference, postpone action until after the war, or implement the report's essential recommendations as war measures, subject to a promise to hold a dominion-provincial conference after the war to modify details.[50] The prime minister responded by creating a special Cabinet committee, headed by Ilsley, to handle the issue. On 19 September the committee held an all-day meeting with officials of the finance department and Bank of Canada.[51] It was decided that Ilsley would approach each of the provinces to see how willing they were to implement the report. The finance minister was authorized to be firm with the reluctant provinces, warning them that succession duties and corporation taxes would increase as would liquor and gasoline rationing.[52]

As far as Clark was concerned, the Cabinet was painfully slow in recognizing the need to take over provincial tax areas. After a conversation with Sandy Skelton, Dexter recorded that the 'Cabinet, as a whole, are very complacent about war finance and general prospects economically – for reasons which nobody who is aware of the situation can understand. But the odd minister is becoming a little alarmed and Ilsley, under the constant prodding of Clark, Towers and the other experts, is beginning to see that if sound financial measures are to be taken, the Dominion must greatly enlarge its field of taxation and impose new taxation upon a scale which might well embarrass the provincial governments. That, of course, is putting it mildly.' [53] By mid-October the finance department had worked out a 'temporary' way of adopting the report. If the dominion invaded provincial tax fields, it 'should shoulder the full burden of provincial debt.' The provinces could then turn over the taxes as outlined in the report after the war was over, and the dominion could look at the problem more closely and deal with the issue of provincial debt. 'Meantime it could be taken care of, temporarily, by larger grants than those outlined in the report of the commission.'[54]

Despite relatively optimistic reports on the economy, the EAC was concerned. Cost estimates were rising rapidly. The departments involved in military spending issued their estimates to the Treasury Board. 'The total money they would require was $1,250,000,000,' Dexter commented, 'which knocked the wind out of the rest of the cabinet.'[55] The EAC was very worried about the exchange situation, and the atmosphere at the 15 August meeting was tense. Ilsley and Towers had met with Sir Frederick Phillips of the British Treasury at the end of July to discuss Britain's financial problems. As a result of the fall of France, the British wanted French gold held in Canada released, but three days later King angrily told Phillips that this was impossible because the gold was held in trust. Less than a week later Ilsley announced in Parliament that Canada's financial commitments to date exceeded $1 billion. Of that total, $96 million was recoverable from Britain, but Canada was on the hook for $940 million.[56] A week later, British estimates indicated that the nation would need some $3.2 billion worth of goods from North America in the coming year.[57]

Labour Minister Norman McLarty wrote Clark, requesting that the EAC consider whether the federal government should control rents. McLarty indicated agreement with the assessment of the Wartime Prices and Trade Board that, as a result of the localized nature of the problem of rising rents, it might make sense for provinces or affected municipalities to be invited to deal with the issue.[58] The EAC concluded in July that, given the reasons for rent increases, the federal government should accept responsibility for controlling these spiralling costs. This control would, however, be extended only to municipalities where the need was shown to be acute. Controls were needed because nothing could 'be used so quickly as the basis for increases in wages as the rise in rents, for house rents constitute the biggest single expenditure of the wage earner.'[59]

At the meeting of the EAC on 15 October a recommendation was approved to end National Housing Act loans.[60] Towers argued that 'in the first place the Housing Act had the stimulation of employment as its principal purpose and that other things were secondary. This stimulation of employment was now unnecessary and even undesirable or would be within a reasonable period.' Nicolls and Mansur, meanwhile, argued for continuing NHA loans. Terminating them, they claimed, would lead to a return to usurious second mortgages, while the end of NHA inspections would result in shoddy construction. Clark was aware of the hardships the proposal would cause. He examined a report from Nicolls, indicating that 42 of 155 Canadian municipalities had residential vacancy rates of zero, and another 61 had vacancy rates of less than 1 per cent. Nicolls advised Clark that 'if half the number of families who are now "doubled up" were to be properly housed in individual dwelling units, there would not be a vacant dwelling in Canada.' Vacancies had disappeared in many municipalities and a large proportion of the remaining municipalities were reporting serious shortages and acute increase in rentals.[61]

Clark wrote up the report for Cabinet, expressing the EAC's position on housing policy. It was delivered on 13 November. He pointed out that if war demands for labour and materials were such important considerations that they overrode the normal expansion of house-building in most communities, then it followed that during the war 'Canada must accept an increasing amount of "doubling up" and overcrowding in existing housing units with all the social disadvantages which are thereby involved. These lowering housing standards are part of the reduction of the standard of living which we must accept as a price of the war. The outlook in this connection is not bright and we should not gloss over the evils that will result and the unrest, and public criticism that will follow.'[62]

On 28 November the Cabinet approved the EAC's recommendation to end NHA loans but made no further decisions on a general housing program. The Department of Munitions and Supply was given the task of providing appropriate temporary accommodation for workers in war production. This facet of the decision concerned Clark. He informed Angus L. Macdonald, acting minister of munitions and supply (while C.D. Howe was overseas), that he had learned 'of two housing projects already undertaken where I consider that the present national war interest has suffered by too much architectural refinement, too expensive a type of construction, and by paying too much for the housing accommodation secured.' If Canadians were to be expected to contribute one dollar and two dollars weekly to war-savings bonds, Clark felt that it was necessary 'to impress the local population that an economical job is done.' The government, therefore, should not 'build a more fancy or more costly house than local workmen occupy' and should resist 'the tendency of architects to plan garden villages, introduce special trim, special doors, special roofs, special porches, all of which increases expense.' Instead, according to Clark, the government should examine 'the possibility of using bunk houses ... as in mining, paper and other industrial towns. The families might easily remain in their home localities, as do soldiers' families, and thus decrease the dislocation of those towns, and thus facilitate the post-war return of population to its pre-war domicile.'[63]

Clark also proposed the creation of a wartime Crown corporation to build temporary housing. He felt, however, that much of the additional war-related housing needs could be met 'by filling up existing vacancies, such as they are, by encouraging the taking in of lodgers and by conversion of older houses to give more dwelling units.' A subsidized transportation system could also move war workers to areas of higher residential vacancy rates, which would prove 'much more economical than government housing on the one hand, or higher wages to cover fares, on the other.'[64] Supporters of the NHA lobbied for its continuation, and through the Appropriation Act of 1942, $1 million was provided for the government's share of NHA loans, although the ceiling for loans was lowered from $4,000 to $3,200.[65] Despite approval of the EAC recommendation, NHA loans continued throughout the war and amounted to more than $3.5 million in 1941 and $2.0 million in 1942, before falling below $1.0 million in subsequent years. Loans for 1,093 dwellings were approved in 1942, 1,721 in 1943, and 1,393 in 1944 – a total of 4,207, which was less than the annual figures for the three previous years – 5,973 in 1939, 5,621 in 1940, and 4,323 in 1941.[66]

By late autumn 1940 Mackenzie King was worried whether the nation could 'maintain the burden she is assuming.' In the War Committee the prime minister argued 'that we must be careful to view the war as one likely to last three or four years and not get the country in a position where there will be a financial panic or collapse before the war is over.' The Cabinet agreed to an expenditure of $30 million for manufacturing aircraft engines and accepted a previously approved outlay on tanks. On 24 October Clark was invited to a meeting of the committee to discuss war financing. He attempted to reassure those present about Canada's financial capacity to handle the increasing burden. The finance department was studying the country's productive capacity, Clark noted, and while the conclusions were still incomplete, Canada's probable national income for the coming year in round figures would be $5 billion. The known commitments by the national, provincial, and municipal governments for war and ordinary purposes amounted to some $3 billion, or 60 per cent of the national income. Under existing conditions, Clark claimed, Canada could *not* spend such a proportion; 45 per cent would be the likely maximum. What was possible *physically* in the way of production, he emphasized, was possible *financially*. Clark concluded, however, that there was no need to worry about the financial problem, provided the problems of men and material were solved.[67] Prime Minister King was satisfied with Clark's assurances. He interpreted the deputy minister's message to mean that 'national income will be expanding and enable, in Clark's opinion, further commitments to be met in so far as industrial capacity will permit, without occasioning any financial panic or collapse.'[68]

Ilsley gave a speech in the House on 21 November that dealt with wartime finances. King was impressed with the contents of the speech, which he described as 'a treatise on war finance ... all carefully prepared by the men in his Department.' The prime minister noted 'how important study of economics had become in these times, and what it means to have scientifically trained minds in the public service. Queen's University has made a great contribution to government in Canada.' He was impressed and even surprised by what the country was able to achieve. 'The whole war effort,' he wrote, 'has been a magnificent example of constructive coordinated effective achievement.'[69] Several days later Douglas Abbott, a Liberal MP from Montreal, gave a speech that also dealt with war finances. 'As clear an exposition as I have heard in Parliament of a very difficult subject,' King commented. 'I said to Lapointe, that man would make a good Minister of Finance.'[70]

But the need to develop a strategy to deal with the *Rowell-Sirois Report* would not go away. At the beginning of November the Cabinet decided to arrange the much anticipated dominion-provincial conference. Clark, Towers, and Ilsley were convinced that such a gathering was essential before any further action could be taken. Even if the provinces resisted, the conference could still achieve the desired effect.[71] Clark headed a committee to prepare for the conference, including O.D. Skelton, Towers, Mackintosh, and F.P. Varcoe (deputy minister of justice).[72] Joseph Sirois was invited to be part of the committee but declined because of ill health. This committee, Clark told Sirois, would be 'very informal' and would carry out its work 'primarily behind the scenes.'[73]

In the meantime, Clark's efforts to control spending and the outflow of foreign exchange brought him increasingly into conflict with the Department of War Supply. Under the industrious but stubborn minister C.D. Howe, the work of the department had expanded enormously. Since the fall of France, Dexter observed, about $500 million in contracts had been awarded and a vast armament and explosive industry was being built: 'Some $235 millions are being spent on new plants alone which is a greater investment in new plants than is ordinarily made in Canada in a decade.'[74] But the government was being criticized for its handling of the exchange situation. In November the American minister in Ottawa, Pierrepont Moffat, met with Robertson and Skelton to discuss possible measures Canada might take to curb its loss of American dollars. Clark and Towers joined them for the discussions in Washington. On 28 November, Clark and Robertson reported the outcome to the Cabinet War Committee, and the following day they reported to the entire Cabinet.[75] 'It was the first time that Members of the Cabinet, other than the War Committee, had any intimation of what was proposed re conserving exchange,' King commented. 'They accepted it remarkably well. As a matter of fact, the explanations were so obvious that little room was left for discussion.'[76]

But there were other problems. Now minister of defence, Ralston was dissatisfied with the state of the army's supplies and equipment, and he blamed Howe. There were also suggestions from the British that Canada was producing the wrong equipment.[77] Clark was concerned about the inadequacy of Howe's financial controls and, as it turned out, these concerns were justified. Under the guidance of Clark, Ilsley raised the issue of Howe's spending in Cabinet and asked whether some system could not be devised to regulate and systematize the department's purchasing and production priorities. Apparently Howe's answers were indefinite. He was confident that his department was doing well but he did not have up-to-date figures. According to his biographers, 'In the rush to control the economy and set up production, the statisticians had been left behind.' The Cabinet agreed with Ilsley that 'Howe's accounting left something to be desired.'[78]

As was often the case, the EAC was one step ahead of the government. The committee had already been discussing the problem and came up with the idea for a separate committee or board to analyse the economic requirements of the defence program and its changes, to determine what limits they would imply for civilian use of materials and labour, and to recommend means for adjusting civilian requirements to those of war. The EAC claimed that the plans and estimates of the defence department were seldom practicable and failed to consider 'Canada's capacity to supply equipment at home, or obtain it abroad, within any given time.' The chief of the General Staff considered 'his function to be to recommend the things which it was desirable to do, and not to assume the responsibility of saying whether these things were practicable from the point of view of labour and material resources.' As a result, the EAC concluded that 'the weakness of the present organization ... is so appallingly evident that no one at the meeting last night questioned the necessity for a Committee or some group which could do the necessary work.' That committee, the Wartime Requirements Board, was created on 20 November with H.R. MacMillan in charge. Clark was put on the board, an indication that 'it would become a powerful, if not decisive, factor in Canadian war planning.'[79] The board was granted the power to secure from any source information on war-related production and to use this information to formulate plans to ensure that wartime needs took priority over all others. The board reported to the Cabinet War Committee through the minister of munitions and supply.[80]

To be fair to Howe, the minister was receiving conflicting directions from Britain that made it difficult to plan production. He sailed to

Britain in early December and was nearly lost at sea when his ship was torpedoed.[81] During Howe's absence, Clark and Towers persuaded Ilsley to 'try and straighten out the financial side of the Munitions and Supply department.' Attempts were made to determine the costs of contracts so that Ilsley could prepare his next budget.[82] While Howe was gone, and without the minister's knowledge, the Cabinet requested that MacMillan prepare a report on the state of war production. When Howe returned to Ottawa in late January, he discovered that MacMillan had gone beyond his mandate. MacMillan was a critic of King and it was known that he favoured creating a coalition government. According to Howe's biographers, MacMillan was intelligent and industrious but he possessed an 'imperious temper.' Apparently he had 'only reluctantly come to Ottawa, believing that the King government was a mediocre collection of second-rate hacks and time-servers with an infirm and temporary grasp on power.' But MacMillan was even less impressed with Howe's department, which he viewed as 'positively hopeless' with an organization that was 'deplorable.' MacMillan went so far as to recommend some of Howe's appointees be fired and to add insult to injury he leaked most of his conclusions to the press.[83] Among those unhappy with MacMillan was Clark. The deputy minister of finance wanted to bring expenditure under control but he was not willing 'to meddle in politics above the waterline separating the bureaucracy from the politicians.' He even began to absent himself from meetings of the Wartime Requirements Board.[84]

By the time Howe returned home, the press was filled with stories about MacMillan and how there was an attempt by the King government to control Howe. The minister rejected most of MacMillan's suggestions and proposed scrapping the Wartime Requirements Board.[85] Yet Howe also refused to fire MacMillan, who in subsequent days considered resigning but was talked out of it by Clark and Towers. According to Dexter, both men, while critical of MacMillan, also recognized the truth in his report. It would be 'impossible to budget,' unless the 'position' of munitions and supply was clearly known: 'All efforts to get Howe to straighten out his accounts and find out where he is at have failed. MacM is the only man in sight who can do the job. If we lose MacM the position will be well-nigh hopeless.'[86]

The issue of exchange was back in the spotlight by year's end. On 2 December, in a desperate bid to stem the flow of American dollars, the War Exchange Conservation Act was passed, prohibiting the importation of a wide range of goods from countries outside the sterling area, except under licence from the minister of national revenue. Some 250 tariff items were covered. Some goods (mainly luxury items) were prohibited completely, while for others the intention, according to Rasminsky, was to 'effect a gradual reduction in imports while giving Canadian industry time to adapt itself to domestic sources of supply or materials from sterling area sources.' The same act also provided assistance for Britain to increase its exports to Canada. Import duties were remitted on all cotton items, all artificial silk items, bituminous coal, and a number of other commodities, and were reduced on others.[87]

The seemingly unending workload for finance led inevitably to an increase in the size of the staff working under Clifford Clark. By December Walter Gordon had returned to Ottawa, this time to the Department of Finance, thus providing practical business experience. During a luncheon Gordon told Clark that he had 'some reservations about serving under him because in the business circles I worked in he was considered to be extremely left-wing and socialistic in his thinking.' Clark assured Gordon that he was not a socialist. Gordon did claim to be 'impressed, however, with the progressiveness of his thinking and with his conviction that after the war a great deal should be done to alleviate the plight of the less fortunate in our society.'[88]

But Clark had his critics. His old nemesis Pouliot returned to the attack in Parliament on 2 December. Pouliot charged the 'brain trust' with having too much influence and becoming 'a curse to the country.' Ilsley came to Clark's defence and the Speaker pointed out again that attacks on civil servants were unfair because they were not in a position to defend themselves. Criticism should come only if accompanied by specific charges.[89] By the following June, Pouliot was back on the attack. 'I want the war to be conducted upon an effective basis,' he told the House. 'I want my people to suffer the least possible during the war, and I want this government to keep power, but I want also to get rid of once and for all the asses that have been put in high places by R.B. Bennett.'[90] A year later, Pouliot was at it again. This time Ilsley not only came to Clark's defence but he launched into a full vindication of his deputy minister by lauding his many achievements: 'In respect of ability, in respect of character and in respect of devotion to duty I have never met anyone who ranked higher, and I have met very few who ranked as high.'[91] Clark was becoming accustomed to Pouliot's attacks and, while they always bothered him, he was now able to chalk them up to the erratic behaviour of the Quebec MP.

In December 1940 Clark returned to Washington for more talks with American officials. Towers also urged Clark to speak with Phillips regarding British approaches to U.S. credit. Clark had to tread warily because the Americans were already feeling that the British were not disclosing information necessary to appraise their position accurately. Henry Morgenthau, secretary of the treasury, was particularly concerned about British purchasing operations in the United States. But despite Clark's urgings, the efforts failed to 'assuage American suspicions.' As Bryce points out, 'Clark had his own problem of disclosure.' When asked by American officials for a detailed report on Canada's balance of international payments, Clark provided the information, but he handled 'the delicate question of French gold by excluding it from Canada's assets.' The gold, Clark indicated, was a French asset and not for Canadian use. Regardless, Clark won the respect and confidence of Morgenthau.[92] In a phone conversation with King, Morgenthau offered a favourable impression of Clark and indicated that he could work effectively with him.[93] According to Bryce, 'It was fortunate that Clark gained Morgenthau's confidence at this relatively early stage, for it was to bear fruit later.'[94]

Walter Gordon's first task with the department was to prepare information for Clark while he was in Washington, including details on the state of Canada's exchange reserves, balance of payments, external trade, wheat production, industrial capacity, and liquid assets held by Canadians abroad. According to Gordon, Clark gave him twenty-four hours to get the information:

> I decided the only thing to do was to call on the Bank of Canada for assistance and proceeded to discuss the matter with Graham Towers and Donald Gordon. After expostulating about Clark's way of doing things and saying it would be quite impossible to get the information asked for in a week, let alone twenty-four hours, we all got down to business. Towers and Gordon supplied me with an office, telephone, secretary, and for practical purposes all the resources of the Bank of Canada. Twenty-four hours later, practically all the information had been collected, and I was about to telephone Clark in Washington when Donald Gordon burst into the room. He said I must remind Clark of our oaths of secrecy and that the conversation would be monitored.
>
> When I got Clark on the line, his only interest was whether I had all the information he had asked for. I replied that, while I had it, I was doubtful of the accuracy of many of the statistics. This did not seem to trouble him any more than my warning that the call would be listened in on. Clark's reply to this intelligence was to instruct me to disguise my voice and to hurry up and give him the information. It took about half an hour to do

> this, and the job was not made easier by the fact that both Clark and I were talking out of the sides of our mouths like a couple of Chicago gangsters, presumably to confuse anyone who was listening to our conversation. Whoever was doing so must have gained a peculiar impression of the behaviour of two officials of His Majesty's Government in Canada.[95]

Clark returned from Washington on 19 December and immediately briefed the prime minister. Morgenthau wanted the Canadian prime minister informed of an idea that would have the United States cease charging Britain for its war purchases. The British were complaining about being bled by the Americans. The idea was to have the United States provide Britain with supplies without payment. Material would be 'lent,' to be repaid after the war. President Roosevelt announced the Lend-Lease program on 6 January 1941.[96]

Preparations for the upcoming dominion-provincial conference continued throughout December and January. The prime minister was given a draft of his opening speech prepared by Clark, O.D. Skelton, and Sandy Skelton. It outlined the arguments for using taxation rather than inflation or borrowing to pay for the war. It rejected forcing the provinces to accept the *Rowell-Sirois Report* but indicated hope that the provinces would acquiesce during such a national emergency. The alternative, regrettably, would be for the dominion to take the required taxes regardless. Mackenzie King was appalled by the strong-arm tactics proposed in the speech, so much that he took the draft to Cabinet and asked for comments. He was alarmed by the influence of the mandarins. The new civil service was functioning as a powerful machine, filled with intelligent men who were not simply prepared to follow the directives of the politicians but who were instead taking the lead in directing policy. They shared a philosophy as well as a vision of the nation, and they were determined to work towards making that vision a reality. The prime minister was concerned about the aggressiveness of the mandarins. 'It was interesting how the point of view of the intelligentsia by whom I am surrounded,' he recorded in his diary '... was attacked from the entire cabinet.' King was determined to keep 'my own point of view very strongly to the fore.' The influence of Queen's University, he noted, with its 'orthodox money theories,' would have to be 'handled with circumspection.'[97] The prime minister would use the speech but only after a more conciliatory tone was added.[98] Regardless, the prime minister and Cabinet fully expected the conference to fail. Ilsley hoped to see each provincial position put forward and then 'the whole break up without friction.' According to King, 'We would have to construct a mattress that would make it easy for the trapeze performers as they dropped to the ground one by one. I have never believed that the conference could succeed at this time of war. Were the government not to make the attempt, it would be blamed for whatever financial disasters will follow, as it certainly will, in the course of the next year or two.'[99]

Amidst this sceptical atmosphere, the Dominion-Provincial Conference of 1941 opened on 14 January. The major objective was to offer a response to the Royal Commission on Dominion–Provincial Relations received by the government in February 1940. Premier Mitch Hepburn of Ontario flatly rejected the report and he was supported in his opposition by premiers Duff Pattullo of BC and Bill Aberhart of Alberta. The following day the federal government responded with an equally tough and frank statement. Ilsley gave a speech that he had drafted with Clark. The financing of the war made it necessary to adopt either Plan One of the *Rowell-Sirois Report* or some alternative. The war burden could not be distributed fairly so long as the provinces occupied the progressive fields of taxation and used them inefficiently. The result was a tax system with varying rates of burden and incidence in different provinces, and with inevitable conflicts, overlapping, duplication, and needless expense and waste. The dominion, Ilsley claimed, was left in a position of having to add its own levies to this existing jumble of taxes. The war had produced vast distortions of the Canadian economy, creating fortuitous gains in some areas and for some classes, and fortuitous losses in others. Under the present system of taxation it was impossible to tap these gains or alleviate the losses. If Plan One, or some alternative, was not introduced, certain provinces would be driven into such financial difficulty by measures forced upon the dominion that national credit would be adversely affected. There was a need to maintain minimum national standards of decency and justice, and it was necessary to prepare for the problems that would emerge in the post-war era.

Ilsley realized he was treading on thin ice by issuing the provinces an ultimatum but he outlined the steps that Ottawa would possibly take to prosecute the war effectively. The dominion would if necessary invade provincial tax fields, such as succession duties, and would increase its rates in such fields as the income tax. These steps would mean a curtailment of provincial revenues. On the other hand, the dominion would not be able to go on providing the provincial governments with 40 per cent of the costs of unemployment relief, nor could the federal government undertake to meet maturities or otherwise assist the provinces in any difficulties that might arise. Ottawa might also ration gasoline and so reduce revenues from gasoline sales and automobile licences. Ilsley argued that there was no question of the federal government's power to take on these measures under the BNA Act. The taxing authority of the national government was not limited under the constitution. Regardless, the dominion could act under the authority of the War Measures Act. But, Ilsely noted, softening his tone, 'we preferred to call this conference and to try to reach by agreement a satisfactory solution of the problems that Canada faces. We tried to do it in the democratic way. It is wholly unfair to accuse us of lukewarmness in our support of this Report because we went about the matter decently instead of with the big stick. We are not lukewarm in support of the Report nor of its recommendations. We believe it is the best solution yet devised for the solution of our problems, which are problems of staggering magnitude. If the Conference has any other suggestions for the solution they should, I respectfully submit, certainly be made and made now.'[100]

But, as expected, agreement could not be reached and the conference failed. The position of the dominion was far too interventionist and centralizing for the provinces, despite its emphasis on the dire wartime situation. As BC Premier Duff Pattullo later pointed out, the provinces could not be expected to surrender in perpetuity their rights to impose income tax. And despite Ottawa's apparent desire to implement the recommendations of Rowell-Sirois, in reality the dominion was focusing only on select aspects of the agreement that entailed the provinces' surrendering fields of taxation. Not surprisingly then, the provinces viewed the report as highly centralizing, although that was not the commissioners' intent.[101]

The federal government had issued an ultimatum and it intended to carry it through. The failure of the conference prevented the implementation of Rowell-Sirois but that failure could now be blamed on provincial obstruction, narrow thinking, and sectional selfishness. As far as Ottawa was concerned, premiers such as Pattullo, Hepburn, and Aberhart were enemies of national unity. Mackenzie King viewed the conference as a success because the antagonistic provinces would end up allowing for a greater federal invasion into provincial taxation than Rowell-Sirois ever contemplated: 'While, to appearances it has been a failure, in reality it has served the purpose we had had in view, of avoiding attack for not having called the conference, and particularly for what would certainly have followed, invasion of provincial sources of revenue.' He noted that the dissenting premiers had been caught in their own trap: 'We have now got the pledge of the provinces to let us take their revenues if we need them – a tremendous achievement.'[102] While King was not in favour of increased federal powers, the wartime conditions necessitated action and the *Rowell-Sirois Report* justified the method. Either way, it was not an appropriate time to discuss the permanent resolution of longstanding dominion–provincial disputes.

Walter Gordon later claimed to have come up with the eventual 'solution' to the dilemma. On the second day of the conference, Hepburn made it clear he would have nothing to do with the federal government's proposals based on Rowell-Sirois, and the meeting broke up. Two or three days later Gordon went to see Clark: 'I thought there might be a solution to the problem; not one that would accomplish the social objectives of the Rowell-Sirois Commission, but it was at least a method of financing the wartime budgets.' Gordon argued that the tax proposals should be confined to financing the war effort and not mixed up with social policy objectives. He suggested to Clark that the federal government announce the taxes that it intended to impose while at the same time offering to enter into an agreement with any province that would surrender its rights to levy taxes for the duration of the war. These provinces would be paid a fixed amount each year based roughly on the amounts of their present tax revenues and augmented somewhat in the case of the poorer provinces. The federal government would make it clear that no province was being forced to enter an agreement but remained free to continue levying its own taxes. In this case, however, the provinces would not qualify for the fixed amounts to be paid by Ottawa: 'Moreover, the taxpayers in any province that failed to enter an agreement would be required to pay a total level of taxation that would not be bearable; the full tax rates to be levied by the federal government, plus the taxes imposed by a province that was unwilling to enter an agreement, would exceed one hundred per cent of taxable income in many cases.' Gordon believed that all provinces would come on board if such a proposal was put forward. These wartime taxation agreements were accepted, but it took a year before all the provinces agreed. Ontario was the last province to acquiesce.[103]

Gordon's account is plausible, but likely an exaggeration. According to Dexter, Ilsley had been contemplating a plan for invading provincial tax areas prior to the conference, and forethought was certainly evident in the ultimatum delivered to the provinces on the opening day.[104] In September 1940 Mackintosh had recommended Ottawa invade the main taxation fields as a temporary wartime measure, with compensating money transfers and expenditure relief for the provinces. Clark had been working on the problem both before and after the conference and, according to Bryce, he deserved the credit.[105] Alex Skelton circulated a paper on the subject on 11 February 1941 titled 'The Aftermath of the Sirois Conference,' in which options were suggested. Therefore, as David Slater points out, Gordon's account 'appears to be oversimplified, and compressed in time.' While he played a significant role, 'fortunately, in wartime Ottawa, Finance and the government more generally were able to pick up useful ideas on any problem from several quarters and put them together into a solution.'[106]

Regardless of who deserved credit, the 1941 budget proposals on tax arrangements with the provinces were built on these ideas: 'The dominion announced personal income and business taxes as if the provinces had vacated the fields for the duration of the war.' Two alternative transfer programs were offered by Ottawa to those provinces agreeing to vacate the personal and corporate income tax fields. The federal government also introduced a succession duties tax without requesting that the provinces vacate their estate, inheritance, or succession duties.[107]

Mackenzie King's trap worked to perfection. Within a year Pattullo's stand against national unity cost him the premiership. He remained bitter against the centralizing financial managers in Ottawa, and Clifford Clark was signalled out for particular criticism. According to Pattullo, Clark meant well enough but even 'the self seeking financial interests have led themselves to believe that they are actuated and acting solely for the good of everybody concerned and that the poor boobs running political affairs are the real stumbling block to progress, to which deterrent, it seems, our so-called democratic system peculiarly lends itself.'[108] Despite King's delight at having the provinces at his mercy, he also agreed with much of Pattullo's criticisms.[109]

The federal government would look back at the failed Dominion-Provincial Conference with some satisfaction, but in January 1941 the ability of Canada to finance the war remained worrisome. At the War Committee meeting on 27 January, Ilsley presented the results of a study, prepared by his staff and the Wartime Requirements Board, on national productive capacity. The conclusion was that $1.3 billion was likely the maximum production available for war purposes in 1941–2 and $5.3 billion was the estimated national income.[110] Ilsley reported that the government was spending about $1 billion a year; that amount could be raised to $1.3 billion, but only by great strain and widespread sacrifice. The next day, it was agreed that the maximum war spending for 1941 should be kept to $1.3 billion, even though the estimates for the three services and munitions and supply totalled $1.5 billion. As it turned out, the final appropriation for defence for 1941–2 was $1.0335 billion and expenditures were in fact $1.0115 billion.[111]

On 28 January, Clifford Clark received the shocking news that O.D. Skelton was dead. Frank Taussig had died only three months previous. Within a brief time Clark lost the two greatest influences on his career. But the death of Skelton hit Clark particularly hard. On his way back to work after lunch, while driving his car, Skelton suffered a severe heart attack, resulting in his automobile colliding with a streetcar in downtown Ottawa.[112] As far as Clark was concerned, Skelton was a victim of the intense workload the mandarins were suffering under as a result of the war. 'The immediate cause of his death was a heart attack,' Clark wrote. 'In fact, however, he was a casualty of the war': 'Four years ago the strain of the life he led, the unremitting devotion to the varied duties of his great office, had brought on the first attack. For a few weeks he was confined to his bed and for a few months thereafter he paid perfunctory respect to the warnings of his doctor by trying to get away from his office before 6 P.M. But even then he would take his unfinished work to his home and soon he was wholly back in the old routine. After the outbreak of war, the regimen became almost intolerable even for one in the prime of health. It was futile to argue with him. He died, as he willed to die, "in harness" – giving his life for his country just as truly as any member of the armed forces.'[113] Clark's comments highlight not only the difficulties of working under the stresses of wartime, but also the stresses of working under Mackenzie King. According to Mackintosh, the prime minister was 'an exacting and to a degree unpredictable taskmaster. His heart bled for those who sewed mail-bags, but he was only rarely perceptive about those who worked for him. There are few certainties about the life of Mackenzie King, but this is certain: he could never have been elected by the wives of those who worked for him!'[114]

The loss of Skelton was not only a loss for Clark; it was a major blow to the Canadian government. In his eulogy, Clark called his mentor 'one of the truly great men of our time.' It was difficult to exaggerate Skelton's impact on the nation. Every facet of his career, whether as an educator or political economist, was enough to stand on its own and had served as a model for Clark's own life. But it was Skelton's career as a civil servant that was most impressive and that Clark sought to emulate: 'As a government official, he was the ideal public servant, working unselfishly for the honour and advancement of Canada as a nation, serving successive Prime Ministers with equal loyalty and competence, winning the esteem and affection of all who came in contact with him, helping greatly by his wisdom and his genius to shape the course of public affairs. If such a statement can truly be made in respect of any public official, Oscar Skelton was, all would agree, the one irreplaceable civil servant. In these troubled times his loss is a disaster.' Clark went so far as to describe Skelton as 'the Deputy Prime Minister of Canada.' He was the trusted adviser of prime ministers and Cabinets in nearly all matters of public policy: 'As a result, he was aware of, and had some influence upon, nearly everything that went on in government circles.'[115] But if the deputy minister of finance saw portents of danger for himself in Skelton's fate, he did not admit it. The pace of work that killed Skelton was now unrelenting for Clifford Clark.

Clark did not have long to mourn Skelton's passing. By February he had to turn his attention to the import and exchange situation between Canada and the United States that was rapidly becoming an issue of grave concern. Howe warned the War Committee that Lend-Lease could mean a diversion of British orders to the United States, and there was talk that Clark could be sent to Washington to protect Canada's interests.[116] But the problems in Howe's department would not go away and they complicated the situation for Clark. According to Dexter, there was talk of having the Wartime Requirements Board answerable directly to the War Committee of Cabinet rather than to Howe.[117]

The Lend-Lease Act was passed in the United States on 11 March 1941. The bill had several aims. It was intended to speed up munitions production, eliminate the need for cash payments on Allied orders, and increase the American president's freedom in foreign affairs.[118] The following day the federal government considered the effects of the agreement on Canada. Clark, for one, was worried about its ramifications. He believed that Lend-Lease provided the United States with too much leverage and that Canada was already in a relatively weaker position than Britain due to its proximity to the United States:

> There seems to be in Washington a very strong desire to get Canada under Lend-Lease, and I think it is because there is no fundamental understanding of Canada's position. It seems difficult for them to believe that Canada is sincere in wishing to stand upon its own feet (at least as long as possible) and not become a burden to the United States taxpayer. I think they would

> appreciate our point of view if they gave a few minutes' thought to the danger of jeopardizing in the future the good relations which have prevailed for so long between the two countries. If Canada should be content to throw part of her war burden on the shoulders of the United States taxpayer, geographical proximity and the constant social and business interrelationships of the two peoples would, in my mind, greatly aggravate this danger.[119]

But Clark realized that Lend-Lease entailed a new financing structure for Canada and the United States. There had to be assurances, for example, that Britain would not simply shift its procurement of supplies away from Canada and to the United States.

On 13 March Clark met with the War Committee and offered what King called 'an exceedingly able and lucid account of the largest problem Canada has ever faced.'[120] Clark opposed accepting Lend-Lease because he feared the Americans would later drive a hard bargain on tariffs if Canada was indebted through the legislation.[121] Clark also suggested that Canada finance the British deficit if the British would agree not to divert orders to the United States.[122] King summarized the arguments in his diary:

> As matters stand, to do what is expected of us we may have to take something like 65% of the national income to meet war obligations. I believe that it is a greater burden than the people of Canada can be led to bear … The Lend-Lease Bill will be used exclusively for Britain. We do not intend to avail ourselves of the Lend-Lease Bill but to allow its advances wholly to Britain … I have no doubt the U.S. will wipe off a good part of the obligation especially if Britain loses heavily meanwhile. If, however, she were not brought very close to her knees, the U.S. would undoubtedly keep the obligations arising under the Lend-Lease Bill hanging pretty much over her head to be used to compel open markets or return of materials, etc. It is a terrible position for Britain to be in, bankrupt, insolvent, under obligation to those who were formerly of her own household. Indeed without Canada and the U.S., she would have no chance to exist.[123]

Howe indicated his opposition on the grounds that Britain would purchase all its supplies from the United States, which would be a disaster for the Canadian industrial program.[124] Lend-Lease solved the British problem but it made the issue of Canada's shortage of American dollars even more acute. Clark returned to Washington on 16 March. Over the next five days Canadian, British, and American officials met to discuss the issue. Jimmy Coyne was dispatched to serve as financial attaché with the Canadian legation. He 'essentially became Clark's agent in Washington.'[125]

By the end of March discussions in Cabinet regarding the upcoming budget revolved around the issue of the wartime tax rental agreements with the provinces. The Cabinet agreed that the majority of wartime taxation would come from income and corporate taxes and succession duties, while the provinces would be given the equivalent to what they had raised that year. The strong-arm measure would be announced in the 1941 budget.[126] 'What is now being done,' King noted in his diary, 'will last until the year after the war which may mean that, at that time, the provinces will have come to see that the Sirois Report is, after all, what is best for them as well as for us. It is a bold and far-reaching policy but will, I believe, succeed.' In reality the tax rental agreements flew in the face and spirit of the *Rowell-Sirois Report* but they were viewed as temporary measures until the actual recommendations of the commission could be implemented after the war. Regardless, King was impressed with Clark. After the Cabinet meeting, the prime minister recorded that 'Clark, the Deputy Minister of Finance, is doing exceedingly good work. His mind is very clear and far-seeing in financial affairs. Ilsley is a lucky man to have so able a group of advisers at his back.'[127]

Also in March the Committee on Reconstruction was established. Headed by Cyril James, principal of McGill University, all the members of the committee were notably from outside the civil service. They included R.C. Wallace, principal of Queen's University, Edouard Montpetit, director of the School of Social, Economic, and Political Sciences of the Université de Montreal, D.G. McKenzie, chairman of the Board of Grain Commissioners, J.S. McLean, president of Canada Packers, and Tom Moore, president of the Trades and Labour Congress. Such a move was almost bound to cause conflict with the 'Ottawa Men' who had become accustomed to directing the war effort.[128]

7

Mobilizing the Nation, 1941–1942

> Here we find the characteristics of a war economy – the mobilization of the nation's productive resources for the abnormal emergency objective of winning the war, the Government taking an ever-increasing share of the national income and becoming more and more the virtual dictator of the country's economic life, and an ever-widening network of regulations governing production, distribution and consumption. The degree to which these tendencies are carried will depend, of course, upon the importance and magnitude of the war itself, the stage which it has reached, the character of the people concerned, the intensity of their support of the war, and the nature of their economic and political institutions.
>
> – Clifford Clark, 24 May 1941

The Hyde Park Agreement was signed between Prime Minister Mackenzie King and President Franklin D. Roosevelt on 20 April 1941, to solve a serious trade dilemma. Canada was purchasing vast amounts of American defence materials destined for Britain and was facing a shortage of American dollars as a result. The problem was exacerbated by the U.S. Lend-Lease policy, which threatened to divert war orders from Britain to the United States. The Hyde Park Agreement moved towards integrating the economic structures of Canada and the United States for the duration of the war. It sought to employ the most prompt and effective utilization of the productive facilities of North America for defence. In order to mobilize the resources of the continent, each country would provide the other with the defence articles it was best able to produce. By the terms of the agreement, the United States undertook to lease-lend to Britain component parts and goods manufactured in Canada for Britain. The United States also undertook to purchase materials and equipment from Canada. The Hyde Park Agreement reflected an emerging spirit of continental defence at a very dark time for the Allies. If Britain was going to fall to Germany, as so much of Europe had already done, Canada and the United States had to prepare to stand together. As a result, the agreement marked a new height in Canadian–American relations. It would become one of the greatest achievements of Mackenzie King's long career and was viewed as a product of the prime minister's close relationship with President Roosevelt.

But King did not accomplish the deal alone. Clifford Clark deserves significant credit, as the *Ottawa Journal* noted: 'Dr Clark was the inspiration of the Hyde Park Declaration ... He advised Mr King of the need and the solution. Mr King advised President Roosevelt. And it was done.'[1] Jack Pickersgill expressed the same view: 'I think it can fairly be said that the only question of international finance that Mackenzie King ever understood was embodied in the Hyde Park Declaration. He did realize that, and Clark convinced him that we had to get something done by the Americans or we were going to be bust.'[2] It was not this simple, but Clark's role was important.

The issue of increased Canadian–American economic cooperation was discussed as early as the autumn of 1940. At that time the channels of communication between Ottawa and Washington were unable to provide a satisfactory degree of coordination and integration of the two nations' war industries. In an effort to meet this situation, the Permanent Joint Board on Defence recommended that supply members be appointed by each government to its respective sections. This recommendation was rejected. A series of informal meetings and discussions took place in the Department of External Affairs, led by Skelton and Clark, which emphasized the importance of providing some sort of machinery of cooperation. In February 1941 negotiations began with American officials to set up the Joint Economic Committees. While discussions were still underway, the Hyde Park Agreement was signed.[3]

On 13 March Clark told the Canadian War Committee that he had met with American Treasury Secretary Henry Morgenthau and suggested to him that raw materials and components required by Canada to manufacture munitions for Britain should be eligible for Lend-Lease on the British account. Morgenthau was not receptive and responded that Canada should liquidate her securities if she had an exchange problem. Clark felt that Morgenthau seemed to be the main obstacle to a solution and told journalist Grant Dexter that 'a good deal of education was needed in the U.S. to prove to them that it was not in their own interest to put Canada through the wringer.'[4] On 16 March Clark returned to Washington. He took Jimmy Coyne along so he could begin his five-month stint as financial attaché to the Canadian legation.[5] Clark, meanwhile, also met with Sir Frederick Phillips and other representatives of the British Treasury. He then met with representatives of both the British and U.S. treasuries to discuss Canada's balance of payments. Clark's information indicated that over the next year Britain would have a deficit in its balance of payments with Canada of approximately $1,152 million and that Canada would have a deficit in its balance of payments with the United States of $478 million. The deputy minister was instructed by the War Committee to attempt to get Morgenthau to agree to have the British transfer a large amount of gold to Canada to meet part of their deficit, which would in essence 'divert' the British gold from the United States to Canada. But after feeling out the situation, Clark concluded that it would be a mistake to press Morgenthau. The timing was bad because the Lend-Lease Appropriation Bill was going through Congress: 'It seemed to me from a psychological point of view the moment was particularly inopportune for us to attempt to secure a favourable decision in regard to what the United States would allow the British to do towards meeting our deficit during the next twelve months.'[6]

Finance Minister Ilsley told the War Committee on 21 March that Clark felt only direct representations to President Roosevelt could resolve the matter. According to Clark, King 'should raise ... the question of securing a solution or at least an easing of our exchange problem with the United States, basing his arguments on the larger considerations and the more intangible factors in the long term relations between our two countries.' The prime minister was planning to go south in April and would tackle the issue then.[7] Clark and Howe were sent to Washington to prepare the groundwork for King's visit. Howe prepared a summary of materials that Canada could produce for the United States. The Americans needed arms while Canada needed dollars.[8] On 9 April, Clark prepared three memoranda for the prime minister. The first contained a forecast of Canada's balance of payments with Britain; the second provided an estimate of Canada's balance of payments with the United States; the third argued that Canada should not liquidate its holdings of American securities. Clark concluded that it was desirable for the United States to allow Britain to 'lend-lease the United States' component of British purchases in Canada.' He was now leaning towards Howe's idea of the United States deliberately purchasing war supplies that Canada was 'geared up' to produce and paying with American dollars.[9]

On 16 April, King met Roosevelt in Washington. The president was fatigued and the two leaders refrained from discussing finances. The following day King met Morgenthau. The prime minister explained Canada's problem and attempted to convince Morgenthau that the problem was immediate and not one that could be handled at the end of the year. King wanted an agreement reached to exchange a variety of war materials; Morgenthau urged Canada to have its own industries manufacture everything. The prime minister argued that this was already being done but it would be jeopardized if the Americans began manufacturing the same products. According to King, Morgenthau indicated that since the Americans were slow in developing their manufacturing, the United States would pay in dollars for items that Canada manufactured: 'I can do a lot on that line if we can now work out the list of articles that you could manufacture for us. We can place large orders.' King responded that those dollars would go to purchasing American war material. The only specific manufacturing the two men discussed was aluminium and the prime minister argued that Howe would have to handle the details. Morgenthau responded that he would work it out with Clark because 'he could work with Clark, but he found others difficult.' It was becoming clear that Morgenthau liked Clark and was comfortable working with him on such potentially divisive issues.[10]

King had lunch with Clark and informed him of the conversation. The objective was to reach an agreement that King and Morgenthau would then take to the American president. Clark met Morgenthau on 18 April to discuss the details of the Canadian proposal. Morgenthau again suggested that the exchange situation could be alleviated by the United States purchasing munitions in Canada and he indicated that the president supported the idea: 'Morgenthau said the United States could give Canada very sizeable orders if there was any available capacity ... Morgenthau said he wanted to find some way to give additional dollars to Canada, so that Canada could pay for its orders in the United States.' Clark was confident that Canada could meet this demand. The details could be worked out later but Morgenthau pointed out that 'with the Prime Minister in the United States, they could do as much in three days as might otherwise take three months.' When Clark asked if there was an agreement in principle that the United States was willing to use Canada's surplus capacity, Morgenthau responded that 'they would take every dollar's worth that could be provided, and that it would be the height of stupidity if they didn't.' He added that the orders would fill American requirements as well as those for lend-leasing to Britain.[11]

Prime Minister King had travelled to Virginia Beach for some rest but he was having difficulty relaxing. He arranged to move his meeting with President Roosevelt up one day to the Sunday. By that morning Clark had produced the draft statement as requested. It is unclear exactly who worked on the crucial statement that would serve as the basis for the Hyde Park Agreement. Hume Wrong, counsellor at the Canadian legation in Washington, indicated that he, along with Clark and Coyne, drafted the statement that 'was in fact issued on April 20th by the President and the Prime Minister with scarcely any alterations.'[12] On the other hand, E.P. Taylor of the Department of Munitions and Supply recalled that he also worked on the draft agreement 'with two other men, Clifford Clark, the Deputy Minister of Finance, and John H. Carswell, who was the purchasing representative of the Canadian government in Washington. The three men met in Carswell's New York hotel suite and worked late into the night on Friday, all day Saturday, and again late into Saturday night. They produced a finished aide memoire which, through special secretarial arrangements, was typed and ready on schedule for King as the basis for his proposal to Roosevelt.'[13] It is unlikely that both stories are correct, although Clark could have worked with Wrong and Coyne in Washington on Thursday, and Taylor and Caswell in New York on Friday and Saturday. Regardless, Clifford Clark was heavily involved. It also seems clear that the draft document was not altered by the prime minister or president. Indeed, when the agreement was printed in the *New York Times*, even the Canadian spellings were used.[14]

Mackenzie King met Clark and Taylor on Sunday morning at the Harvard Club in New York. Taylor recalled the meeting: 'We went to the billiard room on the top floor. There was no air-conditioning in the club and, believe it or not, New York was ninety-three degrees fahrenheit that day. We all took off our coats, even the Prime Minister. He was certainly a great statesman, and a great politician, but he hadn't much knowledge of practical things. He approved of our document. He didn't change it at all. We coached him so that if he was asked questions beyond what was set forth in the documents, he would know what it was that we could probably supply. He didn't have to use that information, he told me subsequently. A special train was waiting to take him up to Hyde Park, which was only about an hour's run from New York City.'[15]

Upon arriving, King and Roosevelt went for a drive in Hyde Park, the president's home on the Hudson River. The two leaders discussed a number of matters and finally King raised the issue of his talk with Morgenthau: 'The President told me that Morgenthau had seen him, after talking with me and had explained the situation to him.' Roosevelt thought 'perhaps it might be going a little too far to have something manufactured in Canada for the U.S. to Lease-Lend to England.' Harry Hopkins, who had joined Roosevelt and King for the drive, indicated that he had talked with Howe. They discussed the variety of items that could be manufactured in Canada for the United States, including aluminium, ships, gun barrels, explosives, small ammunition, and clothing. King then told Roosevelt that he had drafted a statement which would 'cover the ground pretty well.'[16]

After dinner Roosevelt asked for the draft. He seemed pleased and accepted it with only a few changes. All references to American purchases from Canada for Lend-Lease were deleted and a reference to American purchases of aluminium from Canada was added.[17] The prime minister apparently then suggested that Morgenthau be consulted. Roosevelt phoned him, King read the statement, and Morgenthau was in full agreement. Copies of the statement were then prepared for the press and Roosevelt suggested King himself could give them out. The following day Clark provided Morgenthau with the memorandum and schedules showing the tentative estimates of Canada's available surplus for the production of munitions and other supplies. Morgenthau wanted Clark to remain for the following week to work out the details but the deputy indicated that he had to go back to Ottawa to get ready to bring down the budget.[18]

Even though the two leaders played no role in drafting the substance of the agreement, they were both pleased at being able to agree to it by themselves: 'I really think,' King recorded, '... that he [Roosevelt] got a great kick out of our having worked out this Agreement together without any Ministers or advisers or secretaries around, but as something on our own. He feels very strongly, as I do, about this perpetual circumventing of effort by others and the assumption that only those in specialized positions have any brains or judgment. To my mind, there never was stronger evidence of Divine guidance and answer to prayer on that score, more completely evidenced than in this transaction.'[19] The prime minister was willing to give credit to those involved in putting the agreement together but they were lumped into one large 'coming together' of divinely inspired circumstances, leading to 'the Lord's work on the Lord's day.'[20] The following day King told Dexter that it was Roosevelt and he who were instrumental in getting the deal done:

> In dealing with Roosevelt on the balance of payments he [King] had gone about it his own way. He had ignored Towers and Cliff Clark – who had been unable to get anywhere with Morgenthau. He evidenced a mite of vanity here. People were inclined to forget, he remarked, that he is an economist and a much better one, so far as studies, degrees etc. go, than any of the Finance department or Bank of Canada men. He recalled that he had the highest degree in economics that Harvard can give and had, in fact, taught economics at Harvard. He had asked Clark to tell him the kind of arrangement he would most like to get. Clark had written out a formula, far and away beyond his fondest hopes. This was that we should get all the U.S. dollars we need without going through the wringer or incurring debt ... Roosevelt had said to King that he didn't know much about the exchange situation: that he would like King to tell him about it and outline the policy which Roosevelt should follow. King hadn't bothered with the economics of it. He told Roosevelt that if he were in his place, he would have regard only for the neighbourly phase of it. What the U.S. and Britain had done was one thing. Canada as the neighbor on this continent, the only one that really mattered, was another proposition entirely. If the U.S. insisted upon taking from Canada what few possessions she had in the U.S. it would only give voice to anti-U.S. sentiment in this country. If we got a loan, the same sort of thing would happen. Why not buy from Canada as much as Canada is buying from the U.S. – just balance the accounts. Roosevelt thought this a swell idea.[21]

King's version of the story inflates his own role while downplaying the influence of his advisors. Prior to the meeting, Clark had been urging King to base 'his arguments upon the larger considerations and the more intangible factors in the long term relations between our two countries.'[22] But was Clark in fact the 'inspiration' behind the Hyde Park Agreement? He did recommend at least half the idea on 12 March with his proposal that materials purchased by Canada in the United States be used to manufacture war goods for Britain and be counted as part of Britain's Lend-Lease account. But Norman Robertson made the same suggestion that day. The other aspect of the agreement – that the Americans buy needed war goods from Canada – seems to have come from Howe. Yet both ideas were recorded on 1 February by *Financial Post* reporter Kenneth Wilson. And the idea put forward by Howe was actually the same one that brought Canada out of a similar crisis in 1917, although there is no evidence that any of the participants in the 1940–1 discussions realized the parallel.[23]

Regardless, the modest Clark had his own opinions on the creative force behind the Hyde Park Agreement. Morgenthau, Clark recorded in a letter to Howe, was 'the real originator of the program.'[24] Clark congratulated him 'on the speed with which he had put through the agreement of policy announced by the President and the Prime Minister.'[25] It is also likely that Clark's relationship with Morgenthau eased the controversial negotiations. The talks in Washington emphasized 'how much Mr Morgenthau likes to discuss things with you,' Coyne told Clark, 'and likes the way in which you present your views.'[26] And if Clark's health was any barometer of his efforts, he had indeed played a major role. The finance official had worked himself to the point of exhaustion. Clark contracted a bad cold while in Washington, which effectively took him out of commission for over a week after he returned to Ottawa. It also prevented him from returning to Washington to meet with Morgenthau to work out some leftover details.[27]

The Hyde Park Agreement solved the balance of payments problem but it took months for all the difficulties and details to be ironed out. It was a simplistic solution to a complex dilemma and it could not solve all the problems overnight.[28] Hyde Park was a godsend for Canada's U.S. dollar position but even with the agreement in place, it was estimated that a gap would remain 'of some $210 million.'[29] In the first months the atmosphere in Washington vis-à-vis the agreement actually looked quite gloomy. In November 1941 a ruling by the Office of Lease Lend Administration (known as the Young Ruling) indicated that the United States could not buy 'completed articles' in Canada to be lease-lent to Britain or any other part of the British Empire. To make matters worse, Clark realized that Canada had experienced a bad fourth quarter of the year and reserves were falling more than expected. At the end of December, Clark was able to travel to Washington where he raised the question of the Young Ruling with Morgenthau, who promised to do what he could to have it changed because it abrogated the spirit of Hyde Park.[30] In January 1942 Morgenthau informed Clark that he would raise the issue if Canada's exchange situation worsened substantially.[31]

Coyne's letters to Clark also reveal misunderstanding and frustration as the Hyde Park Agreement was put into place. Howe, in particular, was often furious over delays in moving through requisitions and orders. 'I was greatly disappointed,' Clark wrote Coyne, 'to learn of all the difficulties which are being experienced in connection with the lease-lending of U.S. components of British orders in Canada, and particularly the lease-lending of articles to be transferred to Canada for our own use. I cannot believe that part of the difficulty is due to the fact that our liaison officers are not fully seized with the importance of this aspect of the Hyde Park deal from Canada's point of view and are too easily discouraged by alleged delays and difficulties involved in dealing with over-worked U.S. officials. It may be that this part of the Hyde Park deal should be placed in charge of some one who would be solely responsible for its administration and for nothing else.' But Clark was also critical of the Canadian Department of Munitions and Supply. He was annoyed when Carswell wrote a memorandum to Howe, attacking Canada's lack of a definite economic policy when it came to Lend-Lease. There was a policy, Clark responded, but it was not being carried out by officials in munitions and supply. The problems were being aggravated by 'insufficient forecasting' in Howe's department. Orders were being placed 'only when the need is upon them, which is too late for the time-consuming procedures involved in U.S. purchasing.'[32]

The Hyde Park Agreement effectively removed the need for the Joint Economic Committees. For the remainder of the year, and into 1942, the committees met with reasonable regularity to deal with the problems emerging from the agreement and they did make a number of recommendations to the governments. But there was little willingness in the Canadian Department of External Affairs or the American State Department to make use of the committees. Only a few minor matters were ever referred to them and 'in a number of cases, the intervention of the Committees was not welcomed.' Agencies on both sides of the border preferred to deal directly with their counterparts rather than through the Joint Committees.[33] By 1942 the Hyde Park Agreement was circumventing their work. They were now directed towards post-war problems but, as Mackintosh pointed out, their influence here was also minor: 'International collaboration in the field of economics must depend very directly upon national policies, and so far neither Canada nor the United States has reached any solid conclusion as to the character of its own post-war economy. This in turn has been, in part at least, due to the inability of either Washington or Ottawa to forecast with assurance the general terms of international economy in the post-war world.'[34]

By 1943 Mackintosh was chairman of the Canadian committee and even he was advising that the Joint Economic Committee be disbanded.[35] Alex Skelton blamed the Americans: 'The United States, in the throes of mobilizing her economy for total war, tends to ignore Canadian interests.' He did not, however, shy away from also criticizing Canadian officials and the agencies involved: 'While paying lip-service to the ideal of continental integration ... we are in fact daily doing things that make it impossible to achieve this ideal ... It is positively dangerous to have such glib expression and ready acceptance of vaguely worded utopian generalities on continental integration; they merely create an atmosphere, or rather a smokescreen, which conceals the real divergencies, inconsistencies, and embryonic conflicts which are developing.'[36]

With Hyde Park complete, the Canadian budget was brought down on 29 April 1941. It introduced what Clark admitted to be 'very heavy' tax increases: 'We were approaching the zone of full employment, and it was seen that the task to be accomplished would increasingly be that of diverting resources from civilian use to war production.'[37] The budget did not change the rate schedules for business, but the minimum rates for combined corporation and excess profits taxes increased substantially, reaching levels of 40 per cent of all income plus 75 per cent above the pre-war base.[38] Dividends were also subjected to higher personal income taxes. The rates for single taxpayers earning just above the average industrial wage of about $1,500 more than doubled; a married person in the same income bracket, with two dependants, faced a 150 per cent increase. And much higher rates were applied to investment incomes, starting at $1,500 instead of the previous $5,000.[39] A federal inheritance tax was added to the succession duties already imposed by the provinces, but the rate was low. It was intended to be a permanent addition to federal taxes. Although it did not bring in a large amount of money, the introduction of inheritance taxes helped Ottawa in its income tax collection.[40] The budget also announced the dominion-provincial taxation plan approved by Cabinet on 26 March. 'These tax increases,' Ilsley announced, 'if taken together with the existing provincial rates, would result in too heavy a burden and it is proposed therefore as a temporary expedient for the duration of the war only, to ask the provinces to vacate these two tax fields [personal and corporate income taxes].'[41]

Clifford Clark supported the heavy taxation. He was convinced that it was the only effective way to pay for and distribute the costs of war.

When a nation reached the stage of full employment during a major war, heavy taxation allowed debts to be handled and the nation to enter the post-war period with a low debt load: 'A high internal debt may involve no added burden to the economy as a whole, but it makes the task of the financial authorities somewhat more difficult, it may lead to public controversy in regard to fiscal and financial policy, and it may create psychological or real deterrents to business activity unless financial policy is wisely handled and widely accepted.' But aside from the practical reasons, Clark perceived a 'theoretical' argument in dealing with the debts through taxation, even while the war was still being fought: 'The theoretical argument is based on the fundamental fact that the *real* costs of war must be borne by the generation which fights it. Apart from the loss of life and the human suffering, the real costs of war are the real things which are used up by the war machine during the course of the war ... We, and not the post-war generation ... must make those sacrifices today. By no financial sleight-of-hand can the burden be passed on to the oncoming generations. They will have their own price to pay but it will be of a different kind.'[42]

Mackenzie King agreed. The budget, according to the prime minister, was 'the largest single transaction ever introduced in the Parliament of Canada. It places a burden that would have been beyond belief on the shoulders of the Canadian people, a year and a half ago. There seems to be an immediate acceptance of the situation, people realizing that the choice is between present sacrifice or loss of freedom.'[43]

Clark was scheduled to give the presidential address to the Canadian Political Science Association in Kingston on 24 May. A lengthy and detailed speech explaining Canada's war effort was prepared. But the speech was never given and the session was cancelled. Clark was unable to attend because of the burdens of work in Ottawa. In a draft of the speech, the deputy minister argued that it was effective economic mobilization and not just raw economic power or potential that would win the war: '[The Great War] proved, and the present war to date has confirmed, that victory *should* go to the side with the greatest *economic* potential, but that such may not be the issue of the conflict unless that potential is fully and quickly realized by an effective mobilization of economic resources, before the completely mobilized striking power of the economically weaker antagonist proves decisive.' The 'peace-loving state' was at a marked disadvantage over the use of 'totalitarian warfare' because it had to transform a highly complicated economic system designed for peacetime into a system that could turn out the minimum requirements of the civilian population while also producing a colossal quantity of war material. Clark's main point was that such an objective could not be achieved without 'drastic changes in the peacetime structure of private enterprise.' Modern war required 'too drastic an economic readjustment, too sudden a break with the past, and too great a revolution in social values to enable the vast reallocation of resources to be made speedily, smoothly and economically by the free pricing system.'[44]

Just over a month later, Clark travelled to Kingston, where at the Queen's–St Lawrence College Conference on Canadian–American Affairs, he provided an account of Canada's economic relations with the United States during the first two years of the war. His closing remarks highlighted the nature of the relationship at the time, as well as his own role in building this rapport: 'I cannot pay too high a tribute to the competence, the understanding, the goodwill, and the co-operative attitude of these friends of ours from the United States. I think I scarcely exaggerate when I say that Canadian officials who nowadays sit around a common table to discuss a mutual problem with their opposite numbers from south of the line usually find it difficult to distinguish, at least from the arguments advanced, who are the representatives of a United States point of view and who are the representatives of a Canadian point of view. All the cards are face up on the table and the playing appears to be not for partisan advantages but for the general interest.'[45]

Clark may have been pleased with the Canadian–American relationship and the overall handling of the war effort, but concern was growing over inflation. The cost-of-living-index between April and June increased from 104.6 to 107.8 and these numbers 'seriously frightened the government.'[46] In May the Wartime Prices and Trade Board requested stiffer controls, and even the Canadian Manufacturers Association (which traditionally opposed regulations and controls) offered its support.[47] For several months the main concern of senior finance officials was that existing organizations were inadequate to deal with prices and supplies.[48] According to Dexter, 'The proposition to freeze the economy dates from late June when the Bank of Canada made representations along this line to Mr Ilsley.'[49] But early in June, Mackintosh sent a memo to Clark, arguing for a department of economic control with its own minister, an idea he had proposed to the EAC a year earlier. Jimmy Gardiner was calling for controls on agricultural prices as well as supplies. Hector McKinnon, as head of the WPTB, responded that such action would diminish the influence of the board, but he supported some form of controls. These views were passed on to Cabinet Secretary Arnold Heeney. The position was supported by Robertson and Clark, and their views went to the Cabinet War Committee on 26 June. The committee asked the EAC to 'make a general review of existing machinery for the carrying out of the government's economic policies.'[50]

On 30 July the EAC submitted a report on the machinery of economic control, offering various alternatives, most of which supported a new department. The report indicated that 'we have entered a period in which there will be acute shortage of a considerable range of materials, a strong upward pressure on prices and growing scarcity of labour ... The present organization cannot grapple with these problems.'[51] Towers followed up with a letter to Ilsely on 12 August. He did not believe a new department would be enough: 'Under existing conditions, no monetary policy could, by itself, prevent inflation. While policy in respect to taxation and borrowing can accomplish a great deal, it, too, has very definite practical limitations. In these circumstances, the final developments leading to the reduction of consumption, which is required by an all-out war effort, will be either a substantial rise in prices, or effectively planned and operated direct controls.'[52]

The Cabinet rejected the idea of a new department with its own minister and instead enlarged the responsibilities of the WPTB to cover control of all prices and supplies for civilian purposes. The Cabinet approved transferring responsibility for the board from the minister of labour to the minister of finance, placing what became an onerous responsibility on Ilsley's shoulders.[53] But Ilsley was convinced of the need for a full freeze and asked the WPTB for its views. The members favoured action but not a complete freeze. According to Dexter, by the end of August Ilsley had made up his mind and phoned McKinnon to tell him to make plans to freeze the economy. The finance minister then went to Cabinet to seek approval. He was forced to delay, however, because of absences in Cabinet of such influential ministers as King, Howe, Ralston, Crerar, Gardiner, and McLarty.[54]

Although it was generally agreed that stronger action was needed to control rising prices, there were sharp differences as to how to achieve that goal. The issue was discussed in a long memorandum from the WPTB on 29 September. Most members of the board supported efforts to slow price increases. Selective controls could be extended until they covered virtually all goods and services. Controlled retail prices could be permitted to reflect the necessary markups on authorized wholesale prices and imports, as well as other costs. On the other side of the argument was, as Bryce put it, 'the powerful combination of Towers of the Bank and Clark of Finance, supported apparently by Donald Gordon, Alex Skelton, James Coyne and R.B. Beattie from the Bank, with Mackintosh from Finance as their writer.' This group wanted an immediate ceiling on all retail prices with only minor exceptions. The required adjustments in price and cost relationships at the wholesale, manufacturing, or importing level would be achieved by rolling back prices to earlier levels, not by increasing the retail price ceiling. But there was no precedent for such comprehensive controls. Even the German price stop of 1936 was not as comprehensive or rigid. Few in the United States argued for such a ceiling and those that did were not taken seriously. Clark and Towers were now convinced, however, that fiscal (taxation and spending) and monetary (interest rates, money supply) policies were insufficient to prevent inflation unless they were reinforced by rigorous controls. Canada's open economy exposed the nation to occasional inflationary shocks, no matter how restrictive the fiscal and monetary policy. The cost of living was at approximately the same stage it reached in the First World War before it began to rise rapidly. Thus, it was argued, the time was at hand for strict controls.[55]

Another major advantage of price controls was the stabilization of wages. Provision had been made in December 1940 for wage rates at levels generally prevailing in the period of 1926–9 or any higher level established before 16 December 1940. Bonuses were allowed for increases in the Dominion Bureau of Statistics cost-of-living index above a specified minimum. Thus, if prices were kept stable, wages would be stabilized and the pressure on prices would be reduced. Strict controls on inflation also supported the program of public borrowing by overcoming fears that the value of Victory Bonds would be undermined by inflation.[56]

The Cabinet wrestled with the issue of price controls on 3 October. Clark, Towers, McKinnon, and Robertson were invited by the prime minister to explain the proposal, but Towers led the debate.[57] Mackenzie King did not like the idea and took 'strong issue with the attempt to do everything at once, which is the view that Towers and Clark so strongly hold.' He found the position 'ridiculous in the end trying to do by Order-in-Council something that the economic forces of the world would defy with impunity.' King complained that 'it is not safe to trust bankers ... with human nature and human force.'[58] Despite the opposition, a week later the same officials again met with Cabinet, and the basic plan was approved.[59] Gardiner, who had been absent from the previous meeting, was in agreement as long as wheat was not included in the price ceiling. The prime minister, clearly outnumbered in the discussion, spent much of the meeting discussing how to prepare the public statement announcing the freeze.[60]

Clark did escape briefly from Ottawa during the debate on controls in order to take a holiday at the farm in Martintown. 'I spent a day looking over the records at Alexandria and studying the tombstones in Williamstown and St Andrews,' he wrote. For much of his adult life Clark traced his roots in a genealogical effort that involved countless letters and hours recording information in graveyards and church and government registries. This hobby was already well underway while Clark was teaching at Queen's. The search for information provided a diversion even during wartime: 'The pressure here has been so terrific that I am nearly all in, physically and mentally.'[61]

Wage and price controls were announced by Prime Minister Mackenzie King on 18 October 1941 in a radio broadcast to the nation.[62] It was the most severe freeze in the world. Ilsley defended the policy in Parliament on 6 November.[63] In his diary, however, King remained critical and he blamed Clark and Towers for pushing it through. Ilsley, he claimed, was 'run by the Bank and his staff who are economists but not good judges of public opinion.'[64] In a letter to Clark, the prime minister recalled dealing with the issue of wage and price controls in Parliament some thirty-one years previous: 'However much I may have forgotten in the interval ... there was a time when I did have a certain knowledge – orthodox or unorthodox I would hesitate to say which – of current economic problems.'[65]

Donald Gordon was put in charge of the wage and price ceiling. According to Pickersgill, it was Clark who persuaded Ilsley and King that Gordon, the deputy governor of the Bank of Canada, was the only man who combined intelligence and toughness in the right proportions to do the job.[66] Dexter claimed that it was McKinnon who suggested Gordon to Ilsley.[67] Regardless, when approached on the issue, Towers turned Ilsley down, saying that it was the bank's job to offer advice, not to run things. Towers was swamped with work and he wanted his deputy back. Clark also tried to exert pressure, but Towers turned him down as well.[68] David Mansur recalled Ilsley saying he would resign if King did not get Gordon.[69] In the end, it took the intervention of the prime minister to convince Towers to release Gordon. King realized that Towers had been one of the main forces pushing the ceiling in the first place. On 7 November he met with the bank governor: 'We let Towers know that we felt the Bank and the Finance Department were mainly responsible for the policy, and that they owed it to the Government to help to see that it did not suffer through inadequate administration from the start.'[70] Three days later it was announced that Gordon would join McKinnon as associate chair of the WPTB. Just over a week later, McKinnon resigned and Gordon became sole chair while McKinnon became chairman of the new Commodity Price Stabilization Corporation. Regardless of who deserves credit for selecting Gordon, it was widely felt to be 'an inspired choice.' Gordon was particularly adept at persuading 'business leaders to co-operate in sharing the unpleasant squeeze on profits necessary to make the ceiling fit.'[71]

But selecting the head of the board was easy compared with the task of implementing the freeze. The task was massive and there was little time to put it into effect. No previous planning had occurred. Consequently, there was 'fearful confusion in the public mind, in government and in the personnel trying to enforce the ceiling.'[72] On 20 November, meetings commenced for the administration of the price ceiling. Clark kept in touch with the WPTB through Mackintosh.[73] Clark's thinking on controls had changed over time, primarily as a result of wartime conditions. In the early part of the war he believed that financial measures must bear the main burden, and controls should be implemented only under exceptional circumstances. As the degree of mobilization increased, however, he came to the conclusion that 'in a full-scale war the control measures must constitute the effective first line of defence against inflation and the use of resources for civilian purposes, and that finance must somehow mop up the excessive buying power so as to enable the controls to stand the strain, and to be removable when demobilization came.'[74]

The debate over wage and price controls soon took the form of a larger debate over social security. Immediately after the policy was announced, Ian Mackenzie wrote Ilsley suggesting a way of easing the pain of the controls as well as the burdens of heavy taxation. Mackenzie wanted the stringent finance policies coordinated with reconstruction proposals, in particular a national scheme of health insurance and a more generous system of old age pensions. He estimated the cost to the dominion at $20 million. 'This may sound to you like a bribe,' Mackenzie noted, 'and may have Machiavellian features on first glance, but I am convinced that these suggestions are sound.' Ilsley referred the matter to Mackintosh and then replied to Mackenzie: 'Personally, I would be inclined to give contributory old age pensions priority over health insurance (if we could get the constitutional problem solved). The post-war need will be as great and there will be more chance of accumulating a fund in war-time ... I believe in an integrated program of social security and thought that it was the general understanding that as the unemployment insurance scheme was brought into smooth working operation it was to be a function of the [Unemployment Insurance] Commission to consider and report upon the various other measures of social security that might gradually be developed to supplement our unemployment insurance scheme.'[75]

The finance department was divided on the merits of increasing pensions. Bryce argued that 'consideration for a minimum standard of health and decency for these people would fit in well with a general policy of more progressive attitudes in respect to post-war times.' But Clark felt there was a 'fundamental distinction' between indexing wages and salaries to the cost of living in order to 'induce persons to perform services' and doing the same for old age pensions. The pensions, in Clark's view, were 'really a compassionate payment made ... to assist aged persons who have not made provision for their later life to take care of themselves.' He was sympathetic to their plight but claimed that 'we must have some realism in these matters.'[76] Debate over how to proceed with a social security package dominated finance department discussions for the next four years.

On 7 December 1941 the Japanese attacked Pearl Harbor and the United States entered the war. This event re-forged Canadian–American economic relations. Canada's lynchpin role between the United States and Britain came to an abrupt end. Clark was planning a trip to Washington that December to discuss balance of payments issues but was delayed by meetings with the provinces. The attack on Pearl Harbour led Clark to postpone the trip: 'I am now inclined to think that it would be a bad time to go to Washington. The sudden declaration of war and the troubles in the Pacific would mean that all persons with whom I would have to deal would be extremely busy, and I expect also a little "jittery."'[77]

Meanwhile, back at home, Clark's children were now adults. They were caught up in their own lives, loves, and careers, all of which were inevitably shaped by the war. George was granted his commission in the Navy in December of 1941. The relationship between the eldest son and his father remained strained as a result of Clark's lack of attention, a situation that had only worsened during the war. According to George, his father even discouraged him from becoming romantically involved with

French-Canadian girls or even having friends who were French.[78] On 20 January George married Azelie de Lendrecie Campell in Ottawa and by May he entered active service. Eleanor, who had left Queen's to work for the Victorian Order of Nurses in Ottawa, married Flight Lieutenant David McGinnis, a Queen's graduate in engineering, on 21 May at Rockcliffe. Eleanor spent most of the war in Victoria and Edmonton, returning to Ottawa when David went overseas. Ken was hoping to join the RCAF when he finished university. Clark's youngest child, Peggy, graduated from Queen's with a BA in May. She went to work in Ottawa with the Foreign Exchange Control Board.

With the press of wartime work, Clark needed additional staff and he continued to demonstrate his keen eye when it came to recruiting. His selections rarely proved disappointing. In May 1941, for example, Clark was seeking someone to do work in the Dominion Bureau of Statistics. He claimed to be having 'a hard time getting enough economists.' He wrote Lorie Tarshis of the National Bureau of Economic Research to see if he was going to be in Kingston for the meeting of the Political Science Association: 'As you are probably aware, our national income statistics are pretty poor, and many of the related statistics are not all they should be. With the increasing importance of information on this field in wartime, and the growing chaos in our estimates, there may possibly be a demand arising for a thorough going change in the whole set-up on the thing and a fresh approach along modern lines.'[79]

Mitchell Sharp was recruited by Clark in the winter of 1942. At the time Sharp was working in Winnipeg as an economist with James Richardson's grain company. He received a call from Clark, requesting that he come to Ottawa to discuss a wartime job in finance. 'I was startled,' Sharp later recalled. 'I didn't know that Clark even knew of my existence.' Clark had been a judge in a Royal Bank scholarship competition in which Sharp placed third in his graduating year for an essay on international capital movements. Clark was looking for a specialist on the Prairie West and on the grain trade in particular: 'During the interview with him,' Sharp claimed, 'I challenged the government's wheat policy, admittedly not a very diplomatic thing to do. But, as I was to find, Clark liked people with strong views so long as they were well-informed ... I arrived to take a wartime job in the Department of Finance at the beginning of 1942.' Sharp reported directly to Bill Mackintosh. The core policy group around Clark at the time consisted of Bryce, Eaton (whose principal assistant was Harvey Perry), and Tolmie (who succeeded David Johnson in the fall of 1941). Closely associated were Towers, Gordon, Coyne, Beattie, and Rasminsky from the Bank of Canada. Shortly after his arrival, Sharp was asked by Clark to serve as the liaison between the minister of finance and the chairman of the Wartime Prices and Trade Board. He was to discuss the agenda for meetings, first with Gordon and then with Ilsley, in order to prepare the minister. There were many such discussions and meetings that sometimes went on until midnight, especially when decisions had to be made about agriculture, which inevitably involved a contest with the 'Little Napoleon' Jimmy Gardiner.[80]

Sharp's impressions of the finance department in 1942 are revealing. The department held the dominant position in the Ottawa hierarchy. 'By present-day standards,' he recalled, 'there were few ministers and few public servants.' Until the end of the war, the relatively small and old-fashioned East Block of the Parliament buildings housed the Department of Finance, the Treasury Board, the Department of External Affairs, the Privy Council Office, and the Prime Minister's Office. Sharp quickly learned that Clark held a powerful position within the hierarchy, serving as the 'key figure in the formulation of economic policy.' The main issues of 'macro' economic policy, Sharp noted, 'were very much the concern of Clark and Towers. They met regularly, all the time. It was a very close relationship to which we were not part. In other words, that was something separate.'[81] Sharp found Clark to be 'the inspiration and the model for those around him.' In particular, he was impressed by Clark's profound belief 'in the principles of political neutrality and public anonymity for civil servants.' The deputy minister, however, never hesitated to urge his views on his minister and the prime minister when the opportunity arose.[82]

Sharp was also very impressed by J.L. Ilsley. It was the combination of Ilsley and Clark as minister and deputy that gave the department its 'special character and its enormous influence.' Clark's approach was pragmatic, not ideological, and he held a deep respect for the workings of government. He was very much aware, for example, 'that ministers had to be persuaded and Parliament had to approve before anything happened.' Ilsley was 'conscientious to a fault' and worried incessantly about decisions, even 'before he made them, as he made them, and after he had made them.' And his advisers 'suffered along with him.' The finance minister's approach to decision-making was 'orderly and thorough,' and he would not accept the advice offered to him by his advisers until he had heard both sides of the issue.[83]

In April 1942 Clark arranged and chaired a meeting of the subcommittee of the Economic Advisory Committee to discuss what was being viewed as the desperate need for national income statistics. Bryce and Deutsch were converts to Keynesian methods of calculating such statistics that included a much broader application of government spending. 'While I am not prepared to comment on the details at all,' Bryce told Clark, 'my general opinion seems to be crystallizing around the idea that the state of the national income statistics is really symptomatic of a more fundamental weakness in our statistical and economic information. Broadly speaking, our statistical system is based on Dr Coats' work in the 1920's, when the main purposes were to inform businessmen and the public what was happening in particular fields, to provide certain standard statistics of population, agriculture and business – not very much interrelated or integrated ... I think the time has come, or is rapidly approaching when the whole system should be overhauled to fit in for the far different world of the 1940's – both war and aftermath.'[84]

The national income was viewed as the most comprehensive measure of economic activity and the overall economic welfare of a nation. As a result, it was seen as essential 'in enabling the economist, the statesman, the business man and the citizen to understand and appraise the economic situation.' Indeed, pressure was increasing to have such statistics revealed. Clark described the situation to Ilsley as 'embarrassing.'[85] Both Britain and the United States were paying serious attention to compiling such statistics to be used in developing policy. Graham Towers was in full agreement: 'In determining policy during the war, and in the difficult times which will undoubtedly follow the war, the Minister of Finance is bound to have to rely to a major extent on the information which he receives in respect to national income. I do not see how the Minister or the Government can afford to use estimates which are likely to be very wide of the mark.'[86] Towers ran headlong into the dilemma in January when his staff attempted to produce the estimates of national income in relation to war expenditure for the finance department. He found that the estimates were extremely unreliable and based on old and faulty research: 'In many cases, the basis for such projection is slender, or is simply non-existent, and this has now become increasingly the case as our war economy develops.' The estimates could not be used as a 'satisfactory yardstick either in the analysis of our fiscal problems or as the basis for a comparison of our war effort with that of other countries.' Towers was frustrated: 'I am firmly of the opinion that this is the last time that any such ad hoc estimate should be made.'[87]

The situation was so 'ad hoc' that there were in fact three different estimates of Canada's national income in use – those of the Bank of Nova Scotia, the *Rowell-Sirois Report,* and the Bureau of Statistics. John Deutsch noted that 'none of the three estimates that have been used is really adequate or satisfactory, and it is desirable to improve them substantially, and to secure one official estimate on which we can all agree and in which we can have full confidence.' In the meantime, the Rowell-Sirois figures were most commonly used by the government.[88] Clark wanted to push the Treasury Board to authorize additional expenditures required for the compilation and preparation of national income statistics if a satisfactory arrangement could be worked out for producing improved estimates.[89] Both Clark and Towers agreed that Deutsch would be the best person for the job, and they immediately set to work having him transferred from the Bank of Canada Research Staff to the Dominion Bureau of Statistics.[90] 'It is most necessary to realize that the Dominion Government has now become one of the most important dominant influences on the economic life of Canada,' Deutsch claimed, 'and it must act, and its action must be judged in the light of such facts as national income statistics.'[91] Deutsch was indispensable, however, and the search to get someone for the position went on for the next year.

The British were aware of the issue's importance. At the Post-war Economic Talks held in London between 23 October and 9 November 1942, a full session was devoted to the question of national income statistics. The goal was to explain the methods and purposes of a British White Paper on the Sources of War Finance. The Canadian delegation consisted of Wrong, Rasminsky, and Mackintosh. When notified of the agenda, Clark was surprised to see the issue on the table for discussion but he was mainly embarrassed to have the present Canadian estimates put forward. 'I cannot see how a group of this sort could be expected to carry the discussion very far,' he told Robertson, 'unless they happened to be statisticians with considerable experience in the computation of national income.'[92] Regardless, the two British experts, John Keynes and Richard Stone, spoke to the issue. Keynes argued that national income statistics were having a significant impact on budgetary policy in the United Kingdom, and he urged the dominion governments to follow suit. The statistics, it was argued, 'enabled an intelligent layman to understand the realities of the economic situation and produced widespread acceptance of budgetary proposals.' According to a report from the meeting, Richard Stone outlined the purposes of the various estimates, 'but none of the Dominions representatives present knew enough about the subject to ask anything but superficial questions.'[93] In the absence of a government official to deal with such statistics, George Luxton of the Bank of Canada developed a series of estimates, which the Department of Finance and the bank employed in wartime budgets and financial planning.[94]

The Hyde Park Agreement might have solved Canada's unbalanced trade situation with the United States, but in 1942 it was the British situation that required immediate attention. The sterling area faced a serious deficiency of Canadian dollars and the problem was only going to continue. Clark believed the solution to be quite simple: Canada could give Britain a 'gift.'[95] Towers made the same argument, particularly to deal with the future accumulation of sterling balances. If no action was taken, 'the existence of tremendous unsecured sterling balances at the close of the war would be likely to inspire serious criticism of the Government.' The post-war period would witness difficulties in trade with a war-tattered Britain, Towers argued, and Canada would not want to balance accounts by selling less or on the contrary by continuing to 'pile up' a British debt. War debts would prove difficult to collect through purchasing British goods. A gift, on the other hand, would not increase the immediate burden on the Canadian economy.[96]

On 22 January 1942 it was announced that Canada would give Britain $1 billion in supplies.[97] Prime Minister King indicated that the sterling accumulated in Britain, due to Canada's agreement the year before to finance British purchases, would be converted into an interest-free loan of up to $700 million for the duration of the war. As of December 1941, all war supplies, including food produced in Canada for Britain, would constitute an outright gift of up to $1 billion. Keynes was hopeful that if Canada, the United States, and Britain could agree 'on common lines of development, there will be a good chance of making the post-war world very much better than the pre-war world.'[98]

Clark may have been generally pleased with the state of Canadian–American trade relations but he became alarmed in mid-March over construction of the Alaska Highway. The highway was being built on Canadian soil by the United States, and the project had the acquiescence of the Canadian government, but it was being advanced at such a pace that proper economic arrangements were not being observed. Graham Towers asked American officials whether they would be purchasing their Canadian dollar requirements through official channels rather than through the open market. While Towers assumed the Americans would adopt the former procedure, he realized that with the rush to advance the project, 'they might be taking their present requirements in the unofficial market in New York.' Towers's concerns proved justified.[99]

With the budget preparations approaching, Clark told A.F.W. Plumptre, the new Canadian financial attaché in Washington, that the Alaska Highway remained an unknown quantity when it came to determining the estimates of Canada's exchange situation for the current year. Various estimates had been provided by American military authorities but it was proving difficult to obtain precise information. It was even difficult, Clark noted, to 'guess' at the amount of U.S. dollars that would come into Canada as a result of the project. A considerable movement of American officers and supplies was already crossing the border but Clark was in the dark about much of what was going on. As with Towers, his main concern was that the U.S. authorities employ the official channels rather than the open market to purchase their Canadian dollar requirements. Because there had been no discussion of the matter in the official negotiations for the project, Clark told Plumptre to raise it with the U.S. War Department.[100] A week later Bryce was ordered to contact his American counterparts to determine what effect the project might have on Canada's supply of U.S. dollars. He was informed that it was difficult to make any estimates because the costs of the highway were being only guessed at and the final division of these costs remained uncertain. Bryce was told that the project might cost something in the range of $80 million to be completed by the end of 1943. Canada's share of this amount, however, would be small, perhaps as little as $10 million. The early stages of the project were being undertaken by the U.S. Army and it was difficult to estimate how much the men would spend in Canada, particularly when much of the work was to be done 'in the wilderness.' Bryce could only conclude that the project would not seriously alter the estimates of the exchange situation over the next two years. Clifford Clark was not impressed.[101]

The dollar positions of both the United States and Britain were uppermost in Clark's mind throughout 1942. The deputy met with Sir Frederick Phillips and Gordon Munro of the U.K. High Commission in Ottawa on 24 March to discuss both situations. The British 'painted a rather gloomy picture of the position of the United Kingdom, indicating that they were likely to face an acute shortage of dollars in two or three months' time, unless some radical development occurred in U.S.

policy or in the supply of dollars accruing to the United Kingdom.' Clark informed Phillips of the benefits Canada was receiving from the Hyde Park arrangements but indicated disappointment 'with the relatively small achievements under the Lend-Lease portion.' But Clark also indicated that the outlook regarding Canada's U.S. dollar position was 'fairly black' and suggested that there might well be 'difficulties' by the following autumn. Over the next several weeks, Bryce produced several memoranda in an attempt to determine Canada's actual U.S. dollar position.[102]

In early May, Ilsley, Howe, and Clark met with American officials – Morgenthau, Bell, and White – to discuss a proposal for pooling Canada's total war production through the Joint Munitions Assignment Board in Washington. The Canadians feared that such an arrangement could threaten American orders and thus exacerbate the dollar situation.[103] By autumn, Frank Knox of Queen's University was given the task of preparing exchange estimates so they could then be provided to the U.S. Treasury through Plumptre. He produced a memorandum in November, titled 'The Worsening of Canada's U.S. Dollar Position.' It was given to American officials but the sentiment in Washington was that Canada's position was 'better than ever.' Clark claimed to be 'shocked' at the overall development and the U.S. attitude toward the situation.[104]

Amidst these discussions, the finance department worked on the 1942 budget.[105] The rookie in the department, Mitchell Sharp, was awed by the complexity of the process. He noted that the major issues of wartime finance that would affect the budget were first discussed among the civil servants in finance and the Bank of Canada, all under Clark's leadership. Taxation officials from the Department of National Revenue were also involved. These recommendations were then taken to Ilsley, where more debate occurred between the minister and his most senior officials. In this way, Ilsley was able to use his skill of sitting back and observing the debate from all angles before settling on a position. These debates would often rise far above the realm of economics: 'Ilsley had sat silent, rocking himself in his office chair. Suddenly, he stopped, leaned on his desk, put his head in his hands and said: "Gentlemen, the trouble with the Department of Finance is that we have no civil servants, only statesmen."'[106] Sharp may have been awed by the process but, as Slater points out, preparations for this particular budget were intense. Clark's group commenced work on taxation measures on 27 March and concluded on 16 June, a week before the budget was presented.[107]

The budget of 1942 again introduced significant tax increases. The defence and income taxes were combined and the full pay-as-you-earn scheme was implemented. This provided a major benefit to the government in the form of a regular flow of income at low administrative cost.[108] Tax credits were allowed for married couples and dependents, an idea that would not be used again until the 1980s. Compulsory savings were introduced to make the high tax rates palatable.[109] The federal government also introduced its first estate tax, although Ilsley made clear that he felt constrained in doing so by the existence of provincial estate taxes: 'Some of the provincial legislatures have exploited this field to a greater degree than others, but on the whole ... they have not fully occupied it ... there is room for an additional and independent dominion tax at moderate rates ... the provinces have ... left relatively more room for us in the lower and middle ranges than at the top. Consequently our tax cannot be quite as progressive on the very large estates as I would otherwise suggest.'[110] Coupon rationing was introduced in 1942 for sugar, butter, tea, and coffee.[111] According to Clark, the budget 'was a really stiff one, a budget appropriate to an advanced stage of total war effort, and to the enormous financial job to be done, a task far greater than anything ever contemplated anywhere in the world before by a country of this size.'[112] The prime minister felt that Ilsley had 'gone much too far in his budget – that his taxes are unnecessarily heavy. They are putting a burden on the people greater than they can bear, and only helping to force the whole country into the hands of the C.C.F.'[113] In July the government had to borrow from the banks, thus posing a risk of inflation, but the fall loan campaign was a huge success.[114]

The finance department was struggling to keep the Canadian economy afloat in the face of wartime challenges. Dollar shortages, exchange issues, wage and price controls, and heavy taxation dominated the day-to-day activities of Clark and his boys. Yet, despite the immediate challenges, the department managed to lay out highly developed plans for post-war Canada. Clark recognized that financial requirements in the next several years were likely to be so large as to require unorthodox methods. The Victory Loans were 'skimming off a lot of the cream,' but the major challenge was not simply obtaining money but rather 'to obtain the money in such a way as to create the least undesirable effects immediately and after the war.' The objective involved relieving pressure on direct controls over prices, production, and trade while preventing expenditures being forced into channels where they might cause harm and disruption. The post-war situation had to be safeguarded by ensuring that debt that was built up to finance the war was distributed as widely as possible. Most importantly, inflation had to be avoided.[115]

Despite his critical and often high-profile role in managing the Canadian economy, Clifford Clark was enjoying a career of relative anonymity. He revelled in the role of civil servant because it allowed him influence at the highest levels of decision-making without forcing him to face the wrath of public opinion. Unlike some of the mandarins, Clark never considered entering politics. In truth, his skin was not thick enough to withstand public scrutiny and he did not revel in the public spotlight. But despite Clark's best efforts to remain behind the scenes, the nature of his work, particularly during wartime, along with his growing influence, placed him increasingly in the public eye. The business community, in particular, was often critical of the deputy minister, whom they found too much the ivory-tower professor who expounded economic theory without understanding the practical aspects of business. 'I came away again,' one financial reporter observed in April 1941, 'with the impression that Clark is moving very much in an academic circle and is not in contact with business men.'[116] In March 1942 *Canadian Business* magazine presented a cover story on Clark, 'Canada's No. 1 Economist.' The article noted that the business community was 'of many minds about Dr Clark,' with opinions ranging from 'enthusiastic commendation' to 'the die-hards who want no part of this economist or his ways.' One chief criticism was that although he had 'striven hard to get away from the college campus,' he remained an 'economic theorist.' The business community was critical, and even hostile, to Clark's influential brain trust developing within the civil service: 'They say that the Finance Deputy can dodge the allegation if he likes, but it still holds. They claim he sits in Ottawa, surrounded by professors, consults no practical business men, and dreams up a policy that no business man can make work, no commercial country, even in wartime, can swallow.'[117]

In May, discussions began in Quebec on nationalization of the province's power resources. Clark wrote a long memorandum stridently opposing the proposals. The issue, which would decades later become a bellwether for the Quiet Revolution in Quebec, reflected Clark's lack of sympathy for French-Canadian nationalism. Much of his opposition was justified by the war. Any attempts to implement nationalization, Clark claimed, would result in 'bitter controversy' and 'keen resentment' from the private business interests affected: 'The English-speaking interests which have risked large amounts of capital in the power utilities of Quebec would be all the more resentful at having the fruits of their foresight in risking capital investment, their enterprise and their industry taken away from them, not merely because of sound considerations of public or Governmental policy but also because it was desired to shift jobs and control from English-speaking to French-speaking people.' Clark noted that the friction would be aggravated 'because the controversy would take on the aspects of a racial struggle.' The conscription issue was already straining national unity, and Clark was concerned that nationalization would aggravate the situation at a critical point. The proposal could 'retard' the war effort by 'seriously undermining the morale of the management, dampening further enterprise and initiative, and retarding the production of war materials,' particularly of companies such as Shawinigan, an important producer of essential war materials. In addition, Clark pointed to the impact nationalization would have on the New York market, because a considerable proportion of the bonds and other securities of Quebec utility companies were held in the United States. A final objection related to the loss of corporate income and excess profits tax revenue to the dominion: 'It would be unfortunate, if at a time when the Dominion urgently needs every possible dollar of revenue, for any Province to adopt a policy which is intended to switch revenues of this magnitude from the Dominion to its own coffers.'[118]

The entry of the United States into the war concerned Canadian officials lest Canada would be left out of Allied war planning. By July 1942 these concerns were justified. The creation of the Combined Production and Resources Board and the Combined Food Board were announced in early June with no Canadian consultation. Clark met with British Treasury official Sir Frederick Leith-Ross, to raise the issue. Leith-Ross was in Ottawa that summer, primarily to discuss a post-war relief body that eventually became the United Nations Relief and Rehabilitation Administration (UNRRA), an organization to be managed by a policy committee of the United States, United Kingdom, Russia, and China. Mackenzie King told Leith-Ross that as a major contributor Canada should have a voice in deliberations and not just be called into meetings when Canadian interests were directly affected. Clark threatened the British official that if Canada's position was not recognized, there may well be 'great difficulties' in renewing the 'billion dollar gift.'[119]

The threat did not fall on deaf ears. Britain needed aid beyond the billion-dollar gift and time was of the essence. The British claimed that the gift would be spent by mid-October, rather than lasting into 1943 as planned. Several options were suggested. One way to 'eke out' the gift was for Canada to pay all the costs of RCAF squadrons in the United Kingdom. The costs, approximating $150 to $250 million, would extend the gift by six to ten weeks. 'Chubby' Power supported the proposal because paying these costs would strengthen the case he was making at the time for 'Canadianizing' the RCAF. Another option was for Canada to take over British investments in munitions plants inside Canada. Neither of these proposals appealed to Clark but other suggestions were even less appealing, as a memo from Clark to Ilsley made clear, including reducing British imports from Canada, or Britain purchasing more from the United States under Lend-Lease.[120] The patriation of more Canadian government bonds was no longer an option because, as Clark noted, Canada had 'wiped out its debt to British investors.' The deputy did note that about $1 billion in stocks and bonds for private companies and municipal and provincial governments was still outstanding.[121] The best solution from Britain's point of view would be a kind of reciprocal aid through which the British would cease making claims for equipping and maintaining Canadian forces and the Canadians would provide munitions, raw materials, and food without any monetary charge. British officials did admit that it was 'unfortunate that we have been making so much difficulty about Canadian representation' on the allied combined boards.[122]

The Canadian protests, combined with the British dire straits, produced results. According to C.P. Stacey, 'There is little doubt that the apprehension of financial consequences influenced the subsequent British decision to make concessions to Canada.' The Dominions Office noted that 'the Canadian Government's feeling in the matter has now become so strong that it is beginning to colour their attitude in regard to other aspects of their relations with us, and especially in regard to financial assistance.' On 14 September a meeting of eight British government departments recommended Canadian representation on the Combined Production and Resources Board. Canada became a member in November. The following year Canada also became a member of the food board, the only country other than Britain and the

United States to sit on any of the four combined civilian boards. In practice, however, the two boards had little influence.[123]

But Clark was worried that the situation was helping to cause a 'low ebb' in the morale of the nation. At a time when the populace was facing a reduced standard of living, and yet was being called on for 'an ever-increasing measure of sacrifice,' Canada was being provided only a subordinate role in decisions. 'Over the last few months,' Clark observed, 'there has been developing in my mind an ever deepening sense of alarm, not only at the military course of the war, but also at the organizational developments, the ever-growing development of an Anglo-American monopoly of the direction of all war activities (except those on the Russian front) and the ever-increasing evidences that Washington and London look to a future world authority based on the two, three or four great masses of power.' This alarm, Clark contended, was not based on 'mere emotional resentment nor on mere considerations of national status and prestige.' Indeed, the deputy minister claimed to be less caught up with sentiments of defensive nationalism than most of his colleagues. Instead, his concern rested with prosecuting an efficient war effort and laying the basis for a post-war world that would provide some chance of safeguarding international peace and prosperity. Clark feared a world dominated by a select group of superpowers: 'There is nothing in past experience to indicate that the few large powers possess all the intelligence and the foresight or that in running a world they will be solely guided by unselfish devotion to the general, rather than the national, good. There is much in experience to demonstrate that without the full and equal partnership in vital decisions of all interested nations, one cannot stir the mass of the people to the depths of effort and of sacrifice behind any cause however noble.'[124] In retrospect, Bryce claims that Clark's response was conditioned by pessimism, fatigue, and back troubles. Clark and other officials, Bryce argues, were 'getting too worked up,' and Canada was getting 'the most that we could justify.'[125]

Most of the government's senior officials, Clark included, addressed the Canadian Chamber of Commerce's annual meeting, held at the Seigniory Club in Montebello, Quebec on 30 September and 1 October. Clark was given the task of handling one of the most difficult questions and causes of public criticism facing the government: Were the current high taxes too high? The deputy minister admitted that it was 'a legitimate and important question,' but in typical Clark style, he turned the question (and inherent criticism) on its head by noting that it was 'just as legitimate and just as important to ask: are the present high taxes too low?' The quick answer was that taxes were being pushed as high as possible to finance the real costs of the war and to control inflation. Sacrifice was a necessary part of war: 'Most Canadians have sons or brothers or other relatives in the Armed Forces. When they think of these boys who cross the beaches at Dieppe or man the vessels which brave the submarine nests in the North Atlantic or soar into the clouds to meet Hitler's warplanes, most of them put to themselves the challenge of whether they, on the home front, in their attitude to work and sacrifice, are worthy of these lads. We cannot face that challenge if we let the economic motive alone determine how long we work, how efficiently we produce, how much we save … The capacity of the Canadian people to bear without slacking and in the most direct and obvious form the sacrifices they must make, has not been over-estimated.'[126]

Clark then examined the question of whether the taxes imposed were fair and in the process noted how radically the tax system had been overhauled: 'The higher the tax structure, obviously the more obligation there is upon the taxing authorities to see that it is fair. My opinion is that Canada has now one of the fairest, most modern and most scientific tax systems in the world.' During this process of 'steadily increasing taxes,' Clark argued, the tax structure had been 'revolutionized.' It had been converted from a system that relied mainly on indirect taxes (business costs and consumption) to one in which the main emphasis was placed on taxes 'levied on the principle of ability-to-pay and taxes on luxuries and non-essentials.' Before the war, about two-thirds of the tax revenues were obtained from indirect taxes and only one-third from direct taxes. According to Clark, not only were indirect taxes usually regressive (bearing more heavily on low incomes), but they also tended to increase business costs and make it more difficult for industry to fight world competition. 'Today those proportions are almost exactly reversed,' he noted. 'This year, about two-thirds of the tax revenues will come from direct progressive taxation.' But the backbone of the tax system was now the income tax: 'Many advantages come about through having several millions of taxpayers paying directly their share in the cost of Government and interested therefore in making the Government efficient and keeping its costs down, and also from the adoption of the principle of deducting taxes at the source. All the income tax rates are stiff, but when the need and all the circumstances are considered they are not, I think, too stiff. The various allowances for marital and dependent status, the program of compulsory saving and the offsets which are allowed to the person who is already making contractual savings, the allowances for abnormal medical expenses and all the other special provisions, make for a fair tax structure.'[127]

Clark then tackled another crucial question: Would the high taxes come down after the war? His answer was not quite as succinct or unqualified as a *Vancouver Sun* editorial headline 'Taxes Will Come Down in Canada' made it appear.[128] According to Clark, the same philosophy that led to these very high taxes in wartime would likely dictate a reversal of that policy in the post-war years. At present, both demand and consumer purchasing power were in excess of supply. The taxing authorities, therefore, had to employ high taxes to 'siphon off' as much of that surplus purchasing power as possible if 'the evils of inflation' were to be avoided. On the other hand, Clark noted, the post-war period would pose an entirely different set of conditions. After a temporary period of dislocation and hesitation, followed by a consumer goods purchasing boom, there would likely be a period during which potential supply would be in excess of effective demand. The government would then have to safeguard against deflation rather than prevent inflation: 'If a long depression and mass unemployment is to be prevented, the policy required will be one of stimulation of the economy, one that will create expansionist tendencies, one that will provide incentives to expansion of production, one that will encourage the consumer to spend and expand his purchasing power, in short, one which will keep the national income from falling to abnormally low levels.' Clark was optimistic that if the total national income was maintained at present levels, it would be possible to carry the war debt, 'to do the things that are socially necessary,' and still reduce taxes. Even if the government spent on projects to avoid mass unemployment, there would be room for reduction of government expenditures and taxes: 'A Government which was following a work-creating program to expand the national income with one hand, would not, with the other hand, deliberately defeat that expansionist policy by a deflationist taxation policy. These things,' Clark claimed, 'seem obvious.'

But the question still remained as to whether these objectives could be accomplished in the post-war world. Could national income, for example, be maintained with a lower burden of taxation? Could post-war Canada do as effective a job as wartime Canada? Clark believed that the task would be difficult but it was possible, subject to one condition: 'provided the Canadian people generally believe in a peacetime objective which they think is worth fighting for.' The deputy minister conceded the critical question raised by leftist critics: How was the nation able to raise billions of dollars to finance a war when it was thought impossible to raise hundreds of millions to solve unemployment during the Depression? 'In this war,' Clark responded, 'Canadians as a whole have found a supreme cause, a cause which they have thought worthwhile fighting for, paying taxes for, incurring debt for, and, if need be, dying for. During the depression there was no such unanimity of thought or of ideal, and the expenditure of colossal sums of money to cure unemployment might readily have defeated its own ends by discouraging expansion of enterprise on the part of business men and making consumers even more timid in the purchase of houses, automobiles and other durable goods.'[129] Clark's speech revealed the depths of his thinking about wartime financing and post-war planning. It also demonstrated the national status held by the deputy minister of finance. The war elevated Clark's position and influence to the point that he had become the main architect of the Canadian economy.[130]

8

Building a Brave New World, 1942–1943

> I am sure that the Government cannot solve all economic and social problems acting alone, and I suspect that the problems which the world will face for some years after the war are going to be so serious and so refractory that private business will also be unable to solve them acting alone, even if the Government kept its hands off. I hope that this working partnership can be achieved.
>
> – W.C. Clark to J.E. Rogers, 13 April 1944

Clifford Clark was at the peak of his career. The rather modest economist and civil servant had become indispensable to the Canadian government. But this growing influence had not gone unnoticed by politicians and businessmen, and it did make some people uneasy. The prime minister, himself, was likely the best example. Any unease felt by Mackenzie King, however, was overridden by the value and weight Clark lent to the government. As Arnold Heeney observed, Clark 'stood high in King's confidence and no major economic measures were adopted without his advice. More than anyone else it was Clark, indefatigable and imaginative, who provided the leadership in the formulation and direction of critical wartime financial policies.'[1]

The influence wielded by Clark and the 'Ottawa Men' increasingly made others in government jealous and defensive when their empires were threatened. Likewise, the mandarins moved quickly to defend their own terrain when that influence was threatened. In October 1942, for example, the James Committee on Reconstruction presented an interim report that suggested the appointment of a minister of economic planning or possibly even a coordinating minister without portfolio. It also called for a construction reserve commission to assemble public work projects in order to counteract the expected post-war depression. These suggestions would result in a heightened role for the Reconstruction Committee and its leadership.[2] On 22 October, Arnold Heeney went to see Bob Bryce. Heeney indicated that the suggestions would have to be considered by Cabinet and he asked for the matters to be referred as soon as possible to the EAC. As Robert Young points out, 'This operation, pre-arranged by the dominant officials, illustrates their influence in making minor alterations of procedure which have cumulative effect on policy.'[3] Clark's committee responded immediately, rejecting the report outright, on the surface because its ideas were viewed as impractical but also because it threatened the terrain of the EAC. A non-governmental body outside the scope and influence of the mandarins was putting ideas forward.[4] The minutes of the EAC meeting, held on 10 November, record Clark's reaction. He argued that the main work in preparation for post-war reconstruction would have to be done *within* the various departments, 'and could only be properly done there by those familiar with the problems and with the views of the Government, and able to advise the various Ministers concerned.' Clark suggested that the EAC or a subcommittee of the EAC should be the main agency responsible for the development of post-war plans. He was prepared to allow the Committee on Reconstruction to 'fit into such an organization' but admitted that 'there would be difficulties.'[5]

Graham Towers was doubtful that either the EAC or the Committee on Reconstruction could assume the burdens of post-war planning. The dominion government would likely have to spend an additional $1 billion each year to maintain employment before private employers were prepared to provide enough jobs to absorb those released from war activities. As a result, it was not simply a matter of determining policy but also of devising projects that would put a large number of people to work. Towers worried that 'it might give a false sense of reassurance to the Cabinet, letting them believe that the job was being done when in fact it was not.' According to Bryce, 'There was some discussion on this matter as to whether a committee of Civil Servants was a logical or feasible agency for initiating plans as well as for considering them.'[6]

The EAC again discussed the role of the James Committee on 25 November. Clark suggested that the Committee on Reconstruction report to the prime minister as well as the EAC in order to 'improve coordination between the two Committees ... it would enable the Prime Minister himself to make whatever decisions were necessary in regard to the fields of the responsibility of the two groups.' The EAC discussed the enormity of post-war planning and agreed that the James Committee was not up to the job, although it 'had done useful work on a smaller scale in several fields and had presented many of the problems in general terms in a way that was useful.' Towers again pointed to the danger 'that the work going ahead now under the aegis of the Committee on Reconstruction might give a false sense of security – a belief that things were being looked after in detail as well as in general, which would be most misleading and might eventually lead to a grave lack of detailed preparation.' Regardless, the EAC was adamant that it had a major role to play in directing post-war reconstruction.[7]

On 26 December the Cabinet War Committee approved a recommendation that the EAC be responsible for post-war planning. It would 'allocate responsibility for studying specific problems to the various departments and agencies in order to assure that the field will be adequately covered, to follow up the work being done, to receive reports and discuss them with a view to assuring co-ordination of the various programs and policies proposed, and to prepare the necessary documentary material for consideration of the Cabinet.' The War Committee also requested that the EAC undertake the interdepartmental responsibilities for organizing study of post-war problems and suggest the necessary modification in its own powers, as well as those of the James Committee.[8] The work would be handled by a subcommittee under Mackintosh, and the James Committee would be renamed the Advisory Committee on Reconstruction, reporting to the prime minister (or Arnold Heeney in reality).

Senator Norman Lambert had lunch with Clark at the Rideau Club on 2 January. Clark explained that the prime minister was 'taking matters out of Ian McK's hands' and that the EAC would 'deal with it.' Two days later, according to Lambert, Ian Mackenzie, the minister in charge of the James Committee, claimed not to be bothered about losing reconstruction to King, whom Mackenzie believed had orchestrated the move. According to Granatstein, the influence of the EAC in the matter had been successfully hidden.[9]

In a letter to Mackintosh, Cyril James claimed to be in favour of the 'whole scheme.' He was 'somewhat vague as to the precise division of work between the new committee and my present committee – as well as by the need for a close and continuous liaison between the two if they are to work effectively in harness.' He noted that 'these problems cannot ... be defined in any cut and dried fashion at this stage.'[10] Mackintosh suggested that preparatory studies should be carried on in cooperation with the Committee on Reconstruction. But James and his committee were 'effectively corralled.' The arrangement, James concluded privately, 'made the Committee on Reconstruction look like a fifth wheel.'[11]

The problems with obtaining qualified French-Canadian civil servants, meanwhile, continued. DesRosiers did not usually attend the meetings of the EAC, further demonstrating that his inclusion was a token gesture. 'I have not been able to think of any other French-Canadian official who would be at all suitable,' Bryce told Clark. 'I asked Pickersgill, but he too could not suggest anyone, despite his ardent desire to see more French-Canadian appointees.'[12] A report on employees in the finance department noted in January 1940 that there were no French Canadians in Clark's office.[13]

Despite his mountain of work, Clark kept his hand in housing policy. In this matter as well, the deputy minister guarded what he viewed as his terrain. In early November a dispute erupted between Clark and J.M. Pigott, president of Wartime Housing Ltd. The basis of the feud rested on Clark's opposition in February and again in June to wartime housing projects. Pigott was under pressure from municipalities facing severe housing problems due to the arrival of war workers. He began to plan a substantial program of subsidized rental housing. An arrangement was worked out with the city of Halifax for a 199-unit development in February 1942 and then for 300 permanent homes in Hamilton. Clark and other officials were warned by WPTB Rental Administrator Cyril De Mara that Pigott was 'of the opinion that now and in the future, permanent housing for workers will have to be subsidized by the government, in order to provide homes for workers, at rentals within their earning capacity.' This assumption amounted to 'the New Zealand plan of wide scale state-owned housing for low income groups with capital provided by Government at low interest rates.' De Mara predicted that if Pigott's plans were permitted to become national in scale, the capital values of all existing housing offered for rent would be 'forced down radically.' The result would be the 'socialization of all our housing' and 'the most dangerous and far-reaching programme that has ever been suggested in any of our present wartime endeavours to meet emergencies.' De Mara feared that such ideas would 'inevitably carry through into peace-time conditions with probable disastrous results to our present economic policy of private home ownership.'[14]

Clark was ideologically opposed to Pigott's plans and he had the backing of his minister. Ilsley was afraid that the type of program proposed by Pigott would make it impossible for private companies to compete, even with NHA loans. The construction industry was also up in arms. The controversy led to a meeting on 5 November, attended by Ilsley, Howe, Clark, Gordon, Pigott, and Wartime Housing Vice-President and General Manager Victor Goggin. It was decided that Wartime Housing was 'to leave the field of Permanent Housing to others unless they are required by the Government to take over construction and management of projects that cannot be handled by other means. Further, a new position under the Wartime Prices and Trade Board, the real property controller, would ensure that the most efficient use was made of existing housing stock through surveys and a campaign to bring out voluntary offers of rooms or houses.'[15] Even before the meeting, Howe assured Ilsley that any housing not directly related to manning war industries would be turned over to the real property controller. If the controller found a municipality that needed housing in quantity, the plans would have to go through several stages and finally to a newly created Housing Co-ordinating Committee.[16]

The final decision on Pigott's housing plans came on 7 December when Howe informed Ilsley that he had rejected the Halifax proposals. Howe felt that the expansion of wartime industry had ended and most plants were fully staffed, so 'it is my opinion that exceptional reason must be given to justify further wartime housing.' According to Bacher, 'Clark had clearly triumphed over Pigott and Wartime Housing' in his 'desire to delay the construction of "permanent" housing until after the war.'[17]

On 11 December 1942, a British negotiating team (led by Phillips) met with Clifford Clark to commence Anglo-Canadian financial negotiations on further aid to Britain (which came to be called Mutual Aid).[18] Clark believed the billion-dollar gift would last until the end of the year and that the government would assume ownership of the British munitions plants in Canada and pay for the RCAF overseas. The Canadians hoped the British would pay in gold for supplies to mid-February 1943. Another monetary gift to the United Kingdom did not seem practicable, Clark argued, although a gift through the United Nations[19] might be possible if it were not expressed in currency.[20] Three days later, Clark met British negotiators again and confirmed that view, suggesting that aid might have to come in the form of food and munitions.[21]

Further aid to Britain was discussed in Cabinet on 23 December. The proposal was presented with a long memorandum from the finance department, explaining Britain's difficulties and possible solutions, along with the benefits and liabilities of each. The options of Canada taking over British munitions plants and paying for all RCAF squadrons (at $322 million a year) or all RCAF personnel overseas (adding another $58 million a year) were considered. But allowing a sterling debt to accumulate was not seen to be in Canada's long-term interests, nor was repatriating the remaining Canadian securities held in the United Kingdom. The arguments against this plan, as outlined in the memo, are revealing, because the issue would come up again in negotiations for a loan in 1946:

> A good many people would argue that we should take back all or most of these securities and investments ... They contend that it is only straight commonsense for us to pay off our debts to Britain ... They say that the U.K. would do this if she were in the same position. Some of them allege that it is important to eliminate the power and influence of British business interests in Canadian business circles ... Against this course of action it is argued that the provision of our war supplies, foodstuffs, etc., to the U.K. is part of our fair and reasonable contribution to the joint Allied war effort and that for us to charge our Allies for them – and particularly for us to charge them what the traffic will bear – is to exploit our position unreasonably ... It is maintained that if we build up a reputation for hard bargaining during the war, it may cause other countries to bargain sharply with us.

Moreover, trade followed investment, and to repatriate the securities might damage post-war Anglo-Canadian commerce.[22] Another billion-dollar gift was also possible (the estimated British trade deficit with Canada in 1943–4 was $1.17 billion) but 'it would appear that a gift of this type would be politically less popular today than it was a year ago, particularly as Britain is no longer the centre of the military stage.'[23] The best method, the memo asserted, would be for Canada to donate her surplus production – everything above the needs of her own forces – to the Allies generally, which would place Canada 'on a plane of generosity, statesmanship and leadership indubitably as high as that which the U.S. reached as a result of Lend-Lease legislation.' The Cabinet War Committee struck a subcommittee to consider the recommendations.[24]

As the new year began, Clark was aware that, as a result of the war, his family was 'becoming more and more scattered.' George was now a commando in the Navy and was presently somewhere in Scotland. His location was kept secret for intelligence purposes. 'The work makes me shudder,' Clark wrote in a rare expression of emotion, 'but he likes it very much indeed.' Eleanor was married to 'an Air Force man' and was living in Victoria, 'apparently having a great time if I may judge from the long letter received from her this morning.' Peggy and Ken were both still at home, 'Peg employed in the Foreign Exchange Control Board and Ken at Collegiate.'[25]

Clifford and Margaret claimed to be feeling the financial pinch of the wartime situation at home and particularly the heavy taxes. 'With high taxes and war restrictions Margaret has to get along without a maid, and we all live a very austere life and hope that this war will soon be over,' Clark wrote. For such an affluent family with a high income and living in the upper-class neighbourhood of Rockcliffe in Ottawa, the Clark family deserved little sympathy for its economic plight. 'Getting along without a maid,' is not a sign of 'a very austere life,' but it is interesting to note that even the affluent were feeling the burdens of war, albeit relatively speaking. Still, Clark was paying taxes of about $5,890 on his $12,000 annual income.[26]

But Clark's financial problems were superseded by his health problems. Pain was now a constant factor in his life. He was usually in some state of discomfort and often found himself feeling poorly for long stretches of time. The deputy's workload only made matters worse. When he would actually lift his head up from his desk, and the pile of work that surrounded him, he admitted to feeling rather lost: 'So heavy has been the pressure that when I broke away from my desk I seemed to be living in somewhat of a daze.' Such breaks, however, made Clark realize 'the physical condition I have got myself into and I now realize I will have to get away from this job for two or three weeks.'[27] In October 1942 his doctors told Clark that he was suffering from arthritis, on top of his other ailments. 'This is certainly not very pleasant,' Clark observed wryly, 'but there is hope that when certain of my joints solidify I may be released from pain.'[28]

The Canadian government had been preparing for post-war reconstruction since the war began, but early in 1943, when confidence began to grow of an eventual Allied victory, the emphasis shifted from wartime planning to reconstruction, decontrol, and demobilization. Decontrol of supplies, prices, and wages was to be part of the more general policies for demobilization and reconstruction.[29] The Advisory Committee on Economic Policy to study post-war problems had Mackintosh as chairman and Bryce as secretary, and its membership included J.J. Deutsch, Alex Skelton, and Louis Rasminsky of the Bank of Canada, Arnold Heeney, clerk of the Privy Council, and Leonard Marsh of the James Committee.[30] According to David Bercuson, the subcommittee was 'dominated' by Bryce, Deutsch, Rasminsky, and Skelton. As a result, 'it advocated a co-ordinated approach, with economic and social planning going hand-in-hand.'[31]

In preparing for the war's end, Clark later wrote, the task of public policy was to assist in smoothing the transition from war to peace, restoring and maintaining a dynamic and flexible free-enterprise economy, promoting a high and rising level of employment and income, and containing the inflationary potential latent in huge war-deferred demand and high consumer liquidity: 'In keeping with our North American tradition of freedom, these general aims were to be sought, not by control and regimentation, but rather by fostering the right climate, by offering appropriate incentives, by guiding, steering, or coaxing the economy in the desired direction.'[32]

But Clark also shared the widely held assumption among economists that a post-war depression was still likely. Economists generally feared post-war inflation, as pent-up demand and the end of forced savings exceeded the ability of the economy to adjust to producing consumer goods. After a short period of inflation they feared high unemployment if the economy could not absorb all the returning military and all the laid-off war production workers. Experience with the First World War and the Depression underlay both expectations.[33] Confidence among economists dealing with the wartime situation had risen, however, as they had been called upon to deal directly with the crises of the present war. Perhaps a return to the calamity after the First World War was not inevitable. Debates continued to rage on how best to deal with the situation, as publications such as the *Canadian Journal of Economics and Political Science* demonstrated (listing more than forty publications on reconstruction in 1943 alone). The economists did generally agree, however, that the key strategies had to focus on the provision of jobs and enhanced social security.[34] According to Mitchell Sharp, 'Clark was concerned – and this concern was, I believe, shared by all the principal policy advisers and the leading ministers of those days – to do everything possible to avoid another economic depression, to establish a system of social security that would minimize the poverty and hardship that had been all too prevalent in the pre-war years, and to underpin and improve the ability of the poorer provinces to carry out their constitutional responsibilities. Those were the guiding principles that inspired us and that led over time – and a considerable time it turned out to be – to the emergence of a new kind of country that had little resemblance to the one that had entered the war at the end of the 1930s.' Sharp, as with many of the mandarins, would later become resentful when commentators gave the Co-operative Commonwealth Federation credit for improvements in social security after the war: 'Looked at from an insider's point of view,' Sharp noted, 'the CCF was pushing against an open door.'[35]

But if the post-war era was to be prosperous for Canadians, the economists held to the belief that a stable international economy was essential. Canada's export markets had to be secured. 'We have a greater per capita stake than any other country in an active and healthily functioning world trade,' Clark asserted. 'Although our population is less than 12 million, we are today the third or fourth most important trading country in the world and even in normal times about a third of our national income is derived from the sale of goods or services abroad.'[36]

Canadian officials took an active interest in proposals being developed in both Britain and the United States to provide for stability in international currency relations. Canada had a special interest, Clark claimed, due to the 'peculiar' structure of its international balance of payments. What Clark was alluding to was Canada's shifting economic position vis-à-vis Britain and the United States. Traditionally, Britain was 'Canada's best customer,' Clark observed, but Canada was now the 'best customer – and also the largest debtor – of the United States.' As he told an American audience, trade relations had reached the point where, while both relationships had to be constantly considered, Canada's interests were now 'equally divided' between the United States and Britain: 'When, therefore, the American dollar–pound sterling exchange ratio is unstable, Canada gets "whipsawed" between these two key currencies. When pounds sterling cease to be freely convertible into United States dollars, as from the beginning of this war, our lot may be hard indeed. In order that Canadians may be able to go on being America's best customer and pay you in your own currency, which is what your exporters want, some means must be found of converting our surplus sterling into American dollars. That, after all, is the main purpose of an international monetary organization – to ensure that the proceeds of a country's exports to another country can be spent freely for the purchase of goods in any part of the world.'[37]

Clark had been involved in preparations the previous fall for meetings with British officials on a plan, devised by Keynes, for an improved system of settling international balance of payments issues, or a 'Clearing Union.' The aim was to ensure that money earned by selling goods to one country could be spent on purchasing the products of any other country. It called for a system of multilateral clearing or, in other words, a universal currency valid for trade transactions internationally. Its object was to facilitate the progress of multilateral trade and to eliminate import restrictions, clearing agreements, and other devices that during the interwar period had obstructed trade. Clark, however, was unable to attend the meetings in London. 'With all due respect to Mackintosh,' Sir Frederick Phillips told Clark, 'I feel that a discussion with Dominion financial representatives without yourself would be rather like Hamlet with the Prince left out.'[38] Regardless, Louis Rasminsky, Hume Wrong, and Bill Mackintosh formed the Canadian delegation that went to London for the discussions from 23 October to 9 November 1942. The British plan (which became known as the Keynes Plan) was formulated and then forwarded to Harry White of the U.S. Treasury. The plan was to remain secret but it ended up being released and disseminated among American officials.

Clark met with White on 8 January 1943 to discuss Canada's proposed program of financial arrangements, and the two financial officials had 'a very pleasant and helpful discussion.' Clark explained that Canada's billion-dollar gift appropriation was exhausted and it was necessary for Britain to pay cash and turn over $150 million in gold and U.S. balances until another scheme could be ironed out. Canada's general program of financing Britain would now probably take the form of something like the American Lend-Lease program: 'In other words, our idea would be to pool our surplus war production and make contributions out of it directly to each of the United Nations in accordance with the strategic requirements of the war.' Clark then raised the question of an appropriate American dollar exchange reserve to be maintained by Canada. The program he had in mind could not be adopted without assurances of being able to meet the U.S. exchange problem. Clark sought minimum and maximum figures ($400 to $430 million) for the reserves of gold and U.S. dollar balances and an understanding that if Canada's reserves fell below the agreed minimum, the United States would be willing to increase purchases of war supplies in Canada, in accordance with the Hyde Park Agreement. Conversely, if Canada's reserves increased above the agreed maximum, Canada would accept reductions in U.S. orders for war supplies and also contribute free finished war supplies.[39] White seemed interested and 'impressed by the arguments.' Clark believed that the proposal was generally acceptable but it would first have to be discussed within White's own committee and then taken it up with Morgenthau. The response would be given to Plumptre, the financial attaché at the Canadian legation in Washington.[40]

But after further discussions, White informed Plumptre that Clark's suggested maximum and minimum figures were higher than they could support and were out of proportion with what was accorded other countries, including Britain. White suggested a range from $300 to 350 million.[41] The Maximum-Minimum Balances arrangement was agreed to by both parties in March. An issue arose at the end of the month, however, when the U.S. Treasury proposed to have the Joint War Production Committee implement policy regarding the Maximum-Minimum Balances. The treasury suggested that steps be taken to reduce Canada's U.S. dollar balances by $70 million during the next quarter. Clark and his officials realized that it was desirable to have all arrangements discussed directly between the two treasuries and that any outside interference could result in a decrease in American orders in Canada. The deputy minister went to Washington in early April to meet with White. He explained that the Canadian dollar balances were not as excessive as they appeared because there were large arrears to be paid on Canpay[42] requisitions, there was a large rebate to be repaid by War Supplies Ltd[43] to the U.S. government, and a substantial portion of the apparent excess Canadian dollar reserves had arisen from security movements earmarked for redemptions later in the year. Clark was successful in ironing out the misunderstanding. In early June he returned to Washington to provide the U.S. Treasury with an update on the exchange position. Clark suggested that $50 million in U.S. orders be cancelled with War Supplies Ltd.[44]

On 16 January Plumptre sent a memo to Clark, providing the first early drafts of White's plan for an international system for balance of payments or what he called a United Nations Stabilization Fund. But the result was that there were now two alternative plans – the British plan for a Clearing Union put forward by Keynes and the American plan put forward by White. Plumptre claimed to be 'troubled' by White's plan. Like Clark, he felt that it was too early to be discussing such a detailed proposal. 'It seems essential to reach broad agreement amongst the more important countries concerned regarding the general approach to postwar currency stabilization,' Plumptre argued, before deciding between a highly developed and centralized international organization or a less-centralized international clearing agreement. Plumptre suggested avoiding discussing the issue with U.S. officials in order to avoid being forced to choose between the American and British plans. Meanwhile, a Canadian alternative proposal could be developed. Having three plans might shift debate from details to broad principles. 'I would expect, of course,' Plumptre noted, 'that our plan would resemble the British rather than the American.'[45] By 24 March, Louis Rasminsky developed such a plan.[46]

Keynes explained his proposal to Hume Wrong. He indicated a hope that the two plans could be synthesized and that the Canadian officials 'might use your good offices to put forward something on these lines at the right time.'[47] Clark was also concerned by the two alternate plans being put forward simultaneously: 'I did not like to see the U.S. and the U.K. each submitting a draft of its own to each of the other United Nations, that this put the two drafts into competition with each other and would embarrass a good many Governments which might prefer the British draft but would be very reluctant to state their views frankly lest they offend the United States Government whose cooperation was essential if we were going to have any kind of international monetary co-operation.' Clark believed that the British should allow the Americans to circulate their document because the underlying fundamentals were similar. When a conference was held to discuss the issue, the American proposal could be put forward and the British could then request amendments. While Clark was critical of the Americans for releasing their own proposal without first responding to the British plan, he was, above all else, 'anxious that the approach should be such as not to bring differences between the U.K. and U.S. out into bold relief.'[48]

Clark met with Harry White on 6 April. The Americans argued that they had been forced to publish their plan, 'much to their irritation,' and that they were reluctant to have the United States and Britain coordinate a plan because 'all the brains were not concentrated in two great powers and that many of the smaller countries might have an important contribution to a discussion of this type.' Clark also met with Phillips and discussed the features of the American plan that the British found unacceptable, including the American veto, the unduly limited size of the fund, and the provisions for dealing with scarce currencies.[49] 'Our officials believe it is possible,' Ilsley wrote Morgenthau on Clark's suggestion, 'to arrive at suggestions which would incorporate the best features of the two plans.' The finance minister suggested informal meetings in Washington with officials of all three nations in attendance.[50]

While the international talks continued, the Cabinet worked on its post-war plan for social security. At the beginning of 1943, Ian Mackenzie brought forward a proposal for health insurance based on the Heagerty report, in addition to two pieces of draft legislation (one for Parliament and the other a model bill for the provinces). J.J. Heagerty, the director of Public Health Services in the Department of Pensions and National Health, had led the development of the plan, aided by A.D. Watson of the Department of Insurance and the Advisory Committee on Health Insurance, set up on 5 February 1942. The issue was referred by Cabinet to the EAC for an examination of its financial implications.[51]

At a 16 January meeting of the EAC, Ian Mackenzie and his officials pitched their proposal for health insurance. The plan was to be run by a dominion council on health insurance, with a similar council in each province. Doctors would be paid on a fee-for-service basis, according to schedules adopted by provincial medical associations and approved by the government. Coverage was not to be universal. The dominion government would pay $3.60 per year per registered insured wage earner if a province had a satisfactory insurance plan. At this point, the plan still lacked cost estimates, but Mackenzie suggested that the total would be approximately $240 million a year, of which some $100 million would fall to the provincial governments.[52]

Clark expressed concern at the magnitude of the cost to be borne by provincial governments, particularly Saskatchewan and New Brunswick. Towers was in full agreement. In general, however, Clark was opposed to the health insurance measure being put forward as a separate proposal. Instead, he argued that if Ottawa could be given the constitutional and financial powers to carry it into effect, the dominion should propose a comprehensive scheme of social security that would include the health scheme. He believed that both Parliament and the public would support giving the federal government the necessary powers to this end.[53] According to the EAC minutes, 'Dr Clark stated that he belonged to the other school of thought that Mr Mackenzie had mentioned – those who favoured a comprehensive Dominion scheme and a constitutional revision to make clear the Dominion's responsibility for such measures and to enable the Dominion to have the necessary freedom in its tax fields to finance it.'[54] Clark had been heavily involved in discussions over conditional grants-in-aid, particularly regarding old age pensions, and the process had proved 'very difficult to get efficient results.'

That conclusion was reflected in the EAC's report to the Cabinet War Committee, which was signed by Clark:[55] 'Whatever may ultimately prove to be the wise decision in the field of health services, the Committee is strongly of the opinion that it would be unwise to introduce this proposed measure until the whole constitutional field of social security has been examined and some re-arrangement of powers and revenue sources achieved. If social security is to be established on a sound basis, it is undesirable to set up so important a part of it as health insurance on a pattern which is objectionable if applied to other phases of a comprehensive plan.'

Clark did not believe that the approximate costs put forward by Mackenzie could be 'carried by any of the provinces.' Even if the provinces were able and willing to accept the financial burden, the plan would then scuttle any attempt at further financial rearrangements emerging out of the *Rowell-Sirois Report.* Even 'more dangerous,' Clark went on, the proposal called for the contributing population to be divided into the employed and assessed (working proprietors). In the case of the employed, the deficiency below the set contribution of any deduction from pay would be made up by the employer. In the case of the assessed, it would be made up by the province. In certain provinces, such as Saskatchewan, there would be a high proportion of assessed contributors as compared to employed contributors. As a result, the burden on the provincial treasury would be much higher relative to provinces such as Ontario, with a high proportion of wage and salary earners: 'If in these circumstances, such a province as Saskatchewan met this financial difficulty by exacting a larger contribution from its assessed contributors, it would merely lay the basis for requesting larger fiscal-need subsidies from the Dominion.' The EAC recommended that the bill not be introduced but rather deferred for further study.[56]

When Ian Mackenzie read the report, he was furious. He told the prime minister that 'this is just stalling, by a financial group, of two years' work in the Health Department.'[57] The health minister did acknowledge that the provinces might find the proposal too expensive but he argued that this opposition could be overcome by raising the dominion contribution to 50 per cent.[58] He also suggested that if the bill could not be included in the Throne Speech, it could be referred to a special parliamentary committee. Mackenzie went further in his arguments, pointing out that the Cabinet only the day before had approved $229 million in war contracts and last year had provided $1 billion to Britain: 'Now, when it is sought to help the health of the Canadian people, financial arguments are brought forward to retard the legislation.' He threatened resignation if the bill was not introduced in the present session.[59]

Mackenzie, Heagerty, and Watson presented their health insurance plan directly to Cabinet on 22 January. According to Mackenzie King, they made an 'excellent presentation' while 'Clark gave arguments against.' The debate convinced the prime minister of 'what I had previously said to Cabinet, namely, that the matter could only be considered by reference to a Committee of the House of Commons in the first instance.'[60] The Speech from the Throne six days later announced that a scheme for social insurance would be worked out and that a Commons Special Committee on Social Security would consider establishing a national health insurance plan.[61]

The debate and the outcome, according to Granatstein, was another victory for the EAC: 'The struggle had been with a weak department and a lacklustre politician, of course, but for a committee of bureaucrats to take on a minister in a straight-out fight was still unusual; even more unusual was the speed of the victory.' Clark opposed 'piecemeal solutions where co-ordinated treatment was required.' The bottom line, however, was that the influence of the EAC now extended far beyond its original mandate and did, indeed, include both reconstruction and social security planning. The committee of bureaucrats rivalled even the Cabinet War Committee in its influence.[62] According to Bryce, it was not 'extraordinary' at the time for a minister to come before a group of bureaucrats to explain a policy initiative, before it could be pitched to Cabinet. Mackenzie was 'sufficiently realistic to know that this committee had a very great influence on the Cabinet.'[63]

The Cabinet also discussed the Mutual Aid proposals at the 22 January meeting. Clark made a presentation, similar to what had been given previously to the War Committee, in which he argued for munitions plants to be purchased in order to locate additional funds for Britain. Provision for the following year had already been planned in a draft bill prepared by Heeney, Robertson, and Clark. According to King, 'All members of the Cabinet approved this measure as a very important one. Neither Ilsley nor Ralston were present but both had advocated it before. Indeed it was Ilsley's measure. I was surprised at the unanimity, and doubly so at the favourable attitude of the Quebec Members in the light of the opposition there was last year.'[64]

But Mutual Aid was not simply a gift. To the end of March 1943 Britain's debt, estimated at $385 million, was being met by a cash payment to Canada as well as by Canada purchasing the British interest in munitions plants at $205 million. Beyond March the adverse balance, estimated at $1,115 million, would be met by Canada assuming responsibility for thirty-five RCAF squadrons and by a further gift. For political reasons, however, the money was directed to the Allies and the result was another $723 in 1943–4 going to Britain in addition to another $887 million for the following year.[65] There was considerable grumbling inside the Cabinet that the gift was too generous and that it came at the expense of Canada's own armed forces. An official of the Dominions Office noted the generosity of the Canadian position: 'Per head of population the Canadian gifts will cost Canada about five times what Lend-Lease costs the United States. Canada's income tax is already as high as ours; it may have to go higher. To sum up, Canada is devoting as large a proportion of her national income to defence expenditure as any other country; in no country is the proportion of defence expenditure which is given away in the form of free supplies anywhere near so high as in Canada.'[66]

The aid to Britain, when combined with the anticipated costs for social security measures, put immense pressure on the finance department. On 4 February Ilsley reported to the War Committee that the total draft estimates for all departments was $6.359 billion. This number had been reduced, in consultation with the departments, to $6.068 billion. During the 1942–3 fiscal year, actual expenditures would be about $4.5 billion. The finance department, however, was of the opinion that $5.5 billion represented the maximum amount that should be estimated for the coming year and this would mean a further reduction of $570 million. Through cuts to the military budgets, plus $25 million from finance, the total was brought down to $5.498 billion. Clark explained to the War Committee that the figure included the War Appropriation, $1 billion for Mutual Aid, as well as non-war estimates. And the government would still, he said, have to borrow $3 billion in the coming year, a portion of it from the banks. The result would be pressure on the price and wage ceiling, which could be troublesome. But if the gross national income reached $9 billion as expected, and if the public continued to support the war effort financially, it was possible to achieve a budget of $5.5 billion. The War Committee approved this amount and left it to the finance department to work out the necessary adjustments with the other departments.[67] Regardless, it did not ease external pressures. On 11 February a letter from Walter Gordon (who had returned to private business) suggested the wage and price ceiling be modified. The letter, signed only as by 'a friend,' illustrated the pressures in holding firm to the ceiling. Clark, Mackintosh, and Towers, however, convinced Ilsley that he had to stay the course.[68]

The EAC responded to the pressure in late March by preparing a study on how the wage and price ceiling was affecting facets of government. Clark wrote to the heads of the departments and agencies involved, requesting reports. He was not so much interested in a review of all the relevant details but rather an appraisal of the success and efficiency of the controls and the outlook for the future.[69] But the study soon created trouble for the EAC. 'Before we got very far along with this survey,' Clark told A. MacNamara, deputy minister of labour, 'it was realized that there were grave dangers at work in connection with the price ceiling and the economic stabilization program and that these dangers arose chiefly from the labour and wages side.' There was considerable disagreement within the EAC with 'sharp and basic cleavages.' MacNamara requested consideration be given to the *Report of the National War Labour Board* to avoid embarrassment. 'My own view,' Clark responded, 'is that this would be impossible because the value of the Economic Advisory Committee rests on the confidential relationship between senior Civil Servants and the Government. If their reports cease to have this confidential character I think the Committee might as well close up shop.' Clark did admit concern over whether the EAC should express any opinion on the wages question prior to the Labour Board's report, thereby upstaging the organization.[70]

The EAC also dealt with the suggestion that a minimum rate of forty or fifty cents an hour might be exempted from the provisions of the Wartime Wages Control Order. Donald Gordon was vehemently opposed on the basis that such a move would 'wreck both wage control and the price ceiling.' By this time, however, Clark was backing away from making any proposals on the issue of wages.[71] The Labour Board would report early in 1944 with proposals for general wage rate increases. Clark, Towers, Gordon, and Bryce discussed the proposed amendments to the Wages Order and concluded that the amendments 'involved grave uncertainties and risks to the whole price control policy ... if the result of these amendments to wage control was to produce a flood of wage increases, the whole price control policy would have to be recognized as a failure and some other policy would have to be followed.' But the mandarins also realized that the war would likely soon end. Labour activism had quieted and if the government could hold the line and delay, the pressure on the situation might be averted.[72]

By 1943 James Ilsley was showing the strains of office as well as the mounting pressures. Mackenzie King did not get along with his finance minister, and his diary comments must be kept within this context, but Ilsley was bending under the pressure. On 5 February the two men had a private conversation in which King told Ilsley that he was 'showing the signs of great weariness.' Apparently Ilsley admitted that in the last few weeks he had begun taking sedatives to get to sleep at night, he was 'highly nervous,' and he was worried about his heart and his overall health. According to King, Ilsley even admitted to being on the verge of 'crying at any moment.' The prime minister concluded that 'Ilsley might easily have a complete collapse if he does not get rested at once.'[73]

The budget of 1943 was delivered on 2 March and taxation levels reached their wartime peak. 'The economic and financial requirements of war become greater and more exacting as the scope and thoroughness of our plans grow,' Ilsley noted. 'This fifth wartime Budget will exceed all previous standards and make provision for expenditures on a scale which I confess it is sometimes difficult for any of us to appreciate.'[74] Taken together, David Slater concludes, the budgets of 1942 and 1943 'amounted to a virtual revolution' in taxation policies: 'Canada moved from a regressive to a progressive system, from one in which only the minority paid income taxes to one in which the majority paid them, and from one in which the provinces and local governments collected the majority of tax revenue to one in which the federal government collected the most.' These two budgets produced 'truly gigantic increases' in taxation and would 'change Canada's tax system indefinitely into the future.' For a family with before-tax income of $10,000 in 1941, personal taxation was $1,970, and after-tax income was $8,030, for an average rate of 19.7 per cent; by 1943 personal taxation was $4,762, and after-tax income was $5,238, for an average rate of 47.6 per cent.[75] The budget introduced full pay-as-you-earn taxation, a scheme that had commenced the previous autumn, but Clark, Eaton, and Ilsley had worked on the idea as early as February 1942.[76]

But pressure was also mounting for spending to be diverted into social programs as well as for defence. The *Marsh Report* was received by the federal government on 17 February and recommended a comprehensive program of social security that included family allowances, unemployment insurance, national health insurance, and universal contributory old age pensions. A week later the War Committee endured one of its most bitter meetings with the finance department resisting pressures for increased military spending.[77] Despite the pressure, Ilsley held firm to a $5.5 billion total spending figure.[78]

Two days after the budget was delivered, the Canadian government responded to the American compromise on the United Nations Relief and Rehabilitation Administration. The Americans proposed that a Canadian be named to chair the important supply committee and that this chairman would also participate in the meetings of the policy committee, whenever the issue of supplies emerged. Canada would therefore participate in UNRRA without having full representation. Clark produced a memorandum that, according to Lester Pearson, reflected the prevailing view in Ottawa. Clark claimed to be 'appalled' by the 'lack of foresight and of realism' demonstrated by the world's leaders. 'It seems to me there is only one answer to be given by us,' he noted, 'and that answer should be given now, "Thank you, boys, but count us out." We are still trying to run a democracy and there is some historical evidence to support the thesis that democracies cannot be taxed without representation. We have tried to lead our people in a full-out effort for the war, and we had hoped that we could continue to lead them in such a way as to get their support behind the provision of relief and maintenance for battle-scarred Europe in the postwar years. We will not be able to secure their support for such a program if it, as well as the economic affairs of the world generally, are to be run as a monopoly by the Four Great Powers.' Clark argued that no compromise should be accepted, such as occurred in the 'Combined Food Board fiasco,' because this situation was 'far more dangerous.' The result would 'set the pattern for postwar economic organizations as well as for postwar political organization ... Any Canadian Government that accepts such a compromise would soon be brought to realities by the public – and would deserve what they would get.'[79]

When Pearson went to Ottawa in late March to urge acceptance of the compromise, he found that the 'most violent opposition' came from Clark, 'a very real power in Ottawa.' Clark was 'emphatic' that they should have nothing to do with 'any relief convention which did not put Canada in an equal position in every way with the Big Four.' According to Pearson, Clark had 'little or no appreciation of the obstacles in the way of achieving this.' On 8 April the Canadian government accepted the American compromise. The Americans were far more worried about the Russians, and the Russians opposed the Canadian position, viewing it as a second British vote. The British were worried that UNRRA itself might be jeopardized, and external affairs officials in Ottawa accepted the compromise.[80] On 9 November, representatives of forty-four countries signed an agreement to create the United Nations Relief and Rehabilitation Administration, the first international agency launched in the name of the UN. The signing was followed by a conference in Atlantic City, where a constitution for the organization was approved.[81] The Great Powers agreed that when the Central Committee discussed policies affecting the provision of supplies, the chairman of the Committee on Supplies should be present; the chairman was a Canadian, Lester Pearson. In 1945, when France was admitted to the Central Committee, so was Canada.[82]

On 16 March, Ian Mackenzie appeared before the first meeting of the Special Committee on Social Security to discuss the health insurance plan. The financial requirements of the plan were to be paid through contributions by individuals. Employers as well as the provincial and federal governments were expected to share the expenses, and the overall cost to Ottawa was to range from $40 million to $107 million.[83] Mackenzie vigorously defended his plan, so much so that Ilsley complained to the prime minister that he misled the committee into thinking the bill was sponsored by the entire Cabinet. King forced his health minister to clarify this point on 23 March.[84]

Controversy erupted, however, when the *Marsh Report* was released, at the same time as Mackenzie's health insurance bill. But according to Dexter, 'Marsh's report, however, stole the show. The health bill, which is the only real thing in the lot, was completely ignored in the newspapers, and Ian's heart is broken.' To make matters worse, the *Marsh Report* flew in the face of Mackenzie's plan. Whereas Marsh called for a federal health insurance scheme, Mackenzie was calling for a grants-in-aid program. Mackenzie was bitter and claimed that the agenda had been 'hijacked by the bloody brain trust of the East Block; that the plan of Clark and the others is to make a laughing stock of the whole business.' Dexter could not be certain but he assumed Mackenzie's anger was justified. 'I am not clear as to whether all this just happened naturally,' he surmised, 'or whether there has been a bit of U-boat activity around the Hill.'[85]

Clark's position was that the health proposals were admirable but lacked responsible financial planning. By the end of the year, in response to these criticisms, the Committee on Health Insurance Finance was formed. Bryce represented the finance department. The committee produced an interim report, which suggested numerous changes. The personal contribution to be collected by the provinces would be $12 rather than $26. An income tax levy would be imposed and the federal government would contribute grants to each province, based in part on fiscal need, while the provinces would pay for administration.[86] The committee expressed doubts about the total costs but based on a $250 million estimate, it calculated that Ottawa's share would be $100 million, in addition to the $50 million the federal government would collect through income tax.[87] The committee also raised the objections already put forward by the finance department that health insurance should not stand on its own: 'We believe it would be better if this task could be undertaken as part of a larger whole, that is, of financing an integrated social security program as one side of the whole post-war public finance program.' Despite the suggested modifications, the position marked a major concession from the finance department and the volte-face took even the prime minister by surprise. Prime Minister King's interest in the question had diminished, however, and the prospect of committing the government to both family allowances and health insurance in one session was now considered too much.[88]

Clark's focus by late April returned to post-war reconstruction. The EAC was particularly concerned with constitutional barriers that would interfere with reconstruction efforts and wanted the Department of Justice to confirm whether the dominion had the constitutional power to continue emergency war measures, such as controls, during the transitional period to peace. The Pacific War with Japan would likely continue, thereby possibly allowing the continuation of war measures.[89] The EAC argued that certain economic conditions would confront the nation at the end of the war, including a continuing shortage of consumer goods (particularly foodstuffs and finished manufactured products), uncertain international trade conditions, a surplus of labour, and a public demand for economic security: 'Quite apart from any ideological theorizing on what would be desirable government policy, these conditions in themselves determine what the Government must be prepared to do.'[90] To meet these conditions the government would be expected to assist private industry and agriculture to expand output, launch a broad but flexible public investment program, make adequate provision for unemployed and low-income groups, and promote international trade arrangements. Many of the powers required by Ottawa to carry out this program were still in provincial control. They had been assumed by the federal government during wartime, but they would revert back to the provinces. In particular, the taxation agreements were set for termination at the end of the fiscal year following the cessation of hostilities. The EAC claimed that it was 'of vital importance that the Dominion continue after the war to have the exclusive use of income and corporation taxes which has been secured for the duration of the war, and also that it obtain exclusive jurisdiction to impose succession duties.' Constitutional amendments were to be avoided if possible, therefore the EAC urged the federal government to be prepared to 'spend money' so that the provinces would have difficulty resisting. Regardless, if Ottawa was going to maintain jurisdiction of these taxes, the provinces would have to be compensated. They would not accept a fixed annual settlement in lieu of progressive tax fields because it would be akin to a financial straitjacket. The EAC suggested 'a formula for a fixed minimum settlement and a sliding scale of accretions.'

This argument took the EAC back to the grants-in-aid alternative. Such a system would cause no apparent infringement of provincial autonomy and would 'postpone the necessity of experimenting with new techniques of decentralization.' On any grounds other than expediency, however, the disadvantages seemed overwhelming. The plan would lead to a lack of effective control, coordination, and direction, the committee argued, but more importantly, the grants would become the major portion of provincial revenues: 'This is an obvious danger both to provincial autonomy and national unity. It is possible some of the weaker provinces would become rotten boroughs of the Dominion; it is likely that the Dominion would become the puppet of the stronger provincial organizations built up with Dominion funds. At the same time the desire to qualify for the full amounts of matching Dominion grants would dictate the terms of every provincial budget and result in the most undesirable distortions, and the absence of direct responsibility and provincial autonomy.' The EAC went on to note that this alternative was even more dangerous because 'it can be adopted almost unconsciously, step by step, in an ad hoc piece-meal way. In each individual case it may seem the simplest and most expedient solution to a pressing problem, but the cumulative results would be disastrous.'[91]

By June the Committee had 'not undertaken any work toward the formulation of concrete measures.' It did recommend that a dominion-provincial conference be called in the very near future with the *Rowell-Sirois Report* again on the agenda. 'Action has become much more urgent,' Clark argued.[92] The fact that the EAC was resorting back to the grants-in-aid alternative, however, was a clear indication that the recommendations of the Rowell-Sirois Commission were gradually slipping into the background. As Commissioner J.W. Dafoe had concluded, attempts by the provinces to cope with their financial burdens through dominion grants-in-aid 'are held to be "a mockery of responsibility in public finance."'[93]

By early June memos were passed around the civil service dealing with family (or children's) allowances. Both Robertson and Clark supported the idea. Clark believed that family allowances could kill two birds with one stone: the policy would aid low-income families while maintaining the wage freeze. A balanced policy that combined family allowances with a new labour charter defining the rights and status of workers, and would also allow the dominion government comprehensive jurisdiction in this field, could have important long-term results: 'It would bring home to organized labour the direct stake it has in the ultimate amendment of the British North America Act, which would make possible the establishment of national minimum standard of working conditions in Canada.'[94] Towers also supported the scheme as a means of maintaining the government's wage stabilization policy.[95] Nancy Christie argues that the government's move toward such social security schemes as family allowances was based more on a desire to foster self-sufficient and independent families in which the male was the breadwinner rather than some radical desire to recreate the role of the state.[96] Clark asked Bryce to study the issue and the Cabinet War Committee discussed it on 23 June.[97] On 16 July the EAC proposed family allowances in a memo drafted by Bryce.[98]

A week later the Special Committee on Social Security reported, after hearing from 117 witnesses, including Sir William Beveridge.[99] The report supported the principle of health insurance, recommended dominion officials discuss the proposals with the provinces, and proposed that the health insurance bill continue to be studied by the advisory committee.[100] The following day, Ilsley raised the old age pension to $25 a month. Federal officials grumbled that the cost should really be borne by the provincial governments, since Ottawa was coping with a $3 billion deficit while most provinces were running budgetary surpluses. In announcing the increase Ilsley also indicated for the first time that federal thinking had moved away from the existing plan: 'I, myself, am in favour of old age pensions being within the jurisdiction of the dominion parliament and I look forward to the day when there will be in force in Canada a system of contributory old age pensions, along the lines recommended by the Beveridge report, or something of that kind, and administered on a nation-wide scale by this Parliament.'[101]

In order to help deal with the post-war employment situation in Canada, Clark urged establishment of a national development board. The aim was to have an interim organization that could aid the need for emergency employment that might arise upon the cessation of hostilities. Clark hoped that because the full measure of the board's usefulness could not be attained until financial and administrative arrangements were worked out with the provinces, its powers and scope would be expanded later and it would possibly become a permanent organization. He also wanted the board to report to the Department of Finance.[102] The board was established in June.

In late August Clark found himself in another battle to maintain the wage and price controls. C.P. McTague, chairman of the National War Labour Board, produced a report that recommended an end to wage controls or alternatively the implementation of family allowances. In a minority report J.L. Cohen, organized labour's representative on the NWLB, rejected family allowances as an alternative to wage increases but favoured them as part of a social security program. The reports went to Cabinet on 1 September and to the EAC the next day.[103] McTague was critical of the labour department and claimed that the wage ceiling had never been respected: 'It has been administered in each province by provincial boards and there is a complete lack of uniformity. In the result, a completely chaotic wage structure has grown up. There are all kinds of inequalities and the task of ironing them out by a return to the ceiling is quite impossible.' McTague 'disagreed flatly' with Clark, Towers, and Gordon that higher wages necessarily meant higher prices. Instead, he argued that higher wages would bring about greater production and even lower costs. Clark was 'immovably opposed to any retreat from the ceiling policies,' and this led to a showdown. 'I believe this situation is quite serious,' Dexter recorded. 'If McTague's recommendations are accepted, the price ceiling must go. If they are not accepted McTague will resign and that would be a very serious blow to the government.'[104] A few days later, Dexter noted, 'A real crisis has blown up over the wage ceiling.' McTague's report was the only subject Clark, Gordon, Towers, and Ilsley were discussing: 'The brain trust and Ilsley are in revolt.' Dexter predicted that most Cabinet ministers would be opposed to the McTague report but King would be in favour and would insist on action.[105]

Clark fought the battle through the EAC. The committee was opposed to using family allowances as an alternative to wage policy and argued that tying them together would end up damaging both policies. It rejected decontrolling wages under fifty cents, but did accept more flexibility in wage policy generally to deal with injustices or to compensate for hazardous work. The EAC also accepted folding cost-of-living bonuses into base rates.[106] The Cabinet accepted the EAC recommendations. On 30 September both Clark and McTague attended a Cabinet meeting to discuss modifications of wage controls. According to the prime minister, after considerable discussion 'there was really very little difference between Clark and McTague.'[107] The following day, Clark was again at Cabinet with McTague to discuss labour policy. This time, however, Mackenzie King perceived considerable difference in their positions and he was clearly sympathetic to McTague: 'I doubt if we would ever have got matters satisfactorily settled without having Judge McTague in Council. I am glad I insisted on that. He understands the psychological side of the labour problem. Recognizes he is dealing with human life rather than piles of wood and tons of iron. The economist's mind is very rigid, all for rules, regulations, etc. ... I felt McTague and I think Council generally, had quite the better of the argument. Also McTague was most emphatic about not allowing any discussion of family allowances to become a part of the labour policy as such. Rather they were to be considered in connection with a social security programme. That whole aspect of things will also have to be very carefully considered.'[108]

The issue, however, would not go away. A week later King lamented, 'No one can be at all sure that we can hold the ceiling much longer.' He blamed the Department of Finance, and Clark in particular. 'The mistake that was made was not seeking to remove injustices at the outset. The Finance Department were [*sic*] responsible and they should never have frozen an increasing injustice.'[109] By the end of October Clark remained steadfast in pushing family allowances instead of wage increases, but he was out of step with most of the Cabinet.[110] The Cabinet finally decided to give the Regional and National War Labour Boards authority to adjust wages that were grossly unjust, without the boards being tied to a specific formula.

By the late spring of 1943 the international monetary situation was back on the agenda. Discussions on the White Plan had already taken place in May with representatives of forty-six countries in attendance.

On 15–17 June, eighteen countries, including Canada and the United Kingdom, held informal discussions. Canada's position was on the table so Ottawa had no option but to release it, a decision both Clark and Robertson urged upon the prime minister. 'The Canadian proposal' suggested 'a fund substantially greater than that originally proposed by the United States Treasury experts but not so large as that proposed by the British.'[111] Mackenzie King was not pleased with having an alternative plan directly associated with Canada. He was particularly annoyed at having 'the plan of some of the financial experts: Clark, Towers and Robertson' labelled as 'a Canadian plan.' He wanted it made clear that the submission was that 'of some financial experts' put forward for discussion and not the final decision of the government. 'There is a great danger of members of the permanent service,' King recorded, 'trying to frame policies and make members of the govt their mouthpiece instead of members of govt shaping policy and members of the service carrying it out. While we are fortunate in having a few good men in the public service, it would be a great misfortune if they ever came to be a controlling bureaucracy as some times they threaten to become.'[112] Canada's proposal did influence the amendments eventually made to the White Plan, but Clark was unimpressed.[113] He was increasingly worried about financial arrangements made only between Britain and the United States, which were then to be thrust upon other nations such as Canada: 'For broader international discussions, I think we should object to their undertaking bilateral discussions with a view to reaching an agreement, to which they would then ask other countries to adhere. We should insist on having a share, at least in the formulation of any international agreement on these economic matters which are of such high importance to Canada.'[114]

Despite his concern, Clark continued to play financial umpire between the British and Americans throughout the summer.[115] Keynes was worried that the White Plan did not provide an adequate measure of flexibility in exchange rates. While stability was desirable, he argued, countries ought to have the discretion to vary their rates under certain circumstances. Britain, for example, would have 'political difficulty' in not being able to vary its rates and thus have limitations placed upon domestic policy aimed at securing full employment.[116] By mid-September Morgenthau indicated that after some amendments, the United States was proceeding with its plan for an International Stabilization Fund.[117]

Clark was in Buffalo on 20 October to address a conference on 'The Canadian Plan for Post-war International Monetary Stabilization.' The speech compared the proposals of Keynes, White, and Canadian officials at some length. But the onus of Clark's message was to warn his American audience not to expect such a fund to solve all the world's economic problems. The Canadian experts did not regard the proposed international monetary cooperation as a 'panacea for all the postwar ills of the world' and it would be neither 'omniscient nor omnipotent.' It would be a desirable and necessary weapon, but it would be subject to 'many limitations and weaknesses.' It would be 'international and not super-national – merely a club or association which can be joined upon payment of an entrance fee and subject to certain other conditions, and which will enable its members to realize certain common purposes and advantages which could not otherwise be achieved.' Clark also used the opportunity to criticize the bilateral spirit he perceived within the negotiations: 'No international monetary organization, however perfect in form, could long survive economic distortion resulting from bilateralist trade practices.' That said, the fund was a step in the right direction and, despite the challenges ahead, Clark supported the initiative: 'The fact that there are many complex problems to be faced should not be used as an excuse for facing none. The vicious circle must be broken. We must make a start somewhere, and for the reasons already discussed, the problem of an international monetary organization is a logical and fruitful starting place.'[118]

Clark again addressed the issue of monetary stabilization in a speech given in New York on 10 November. 'It is of the greatest importance that we start off at the end of the war in the right direction and with sufficient speed on the re-shaping of international affairs,' he told his audience. 'It will be a time of great opportunity and heavy responsibility ... The people of all nations will be prepared for substantial change – indeed they will be expecting and hoping for great improvements over pre-war conditions. Those who determine the policies and mould the institutions of this post-war world will leave their mark, we may expect, upon the history of many generations.' The two major objectives in the economic field, Clark went on, would be full and effective employment. By the latter he meant 'the best obtainable division of labour and organization of production, both domestically and internationally.' To achieve both objectives, international conditions and action were required, and both depended on achieving satisfactory monetary and exchange relationships. Full employment depended upon high levels of imports and exports, which then depended upon a nation securing supplies of foreign exchange. Effective employment depended upon effective trade, which then depended upon the optimal environment for international commerce. Clark was convinced that if foreign exchange reserves were adequate, nations could pursue far-sighted policies intended to protect their positions. If these reserves fell short, however, a return to the situation of the 1930s would follow, in which narrow, short-sighted positions would be taken, including high tariffs, bilateral deals, and exchange blocs, thereby thwarting the flow of trade.[119]

While the Liberal government was generally united on issues dealing with international finance and monetary questions, there was at times friction. In September what the prime minister described as a 'singularly remarkable debate' occurred in caucus. Several Liberal members indicated that the government's financial policies 'were being shaped by the Bank of Canada, representative of the orthodox finance and private banking interests.' They went so far as to argue that Clark, Towers, and Donald Gordon were 'all not only Bennett appointees but Tories of the old school of finance.' While King increasingly found himself criticizing the influence of the mandarins himself, he did not agree that they were ideologically out of step with the Liberal party. 'As a matter of fact,' he recorded in his diary, 'all three are, I think, Liberal.'[120]

By the end of 1943 Grant Dexter concluded that the 'brain trust' was 'discouraged' with the direction of post-war planning, and social reconstruction in particular. Whereas the health insurance plan and housing policy were 'worked out,' Clark was adamant that family allowances were the 'only effective way to deal with slum clearance. You have to give the boys the money to buy the houses that you intend to build for them. That is a little crude, but it has the idea.' According to Dexter, 'The brain trust can't get the cabinet to act, to come to grips with post war problems.' Underlying much of the post-war anxiety were dominion-provincial taxation issues. Ottawa had exclusive jurisdiction of income and corporation and succession duties, but the tax rental agreements would expire one year after the war's end. Unless the Rowell-Sirois recommendations could be implemented and the BNA Act amended to give the federal government permanent jurisdiction, 'the brain trusters see nothing ahead but frustration and impotence ... The Dominion will be hamstrung on its whole postwar policy – since it will not be able to impose the taxation required to finance postwar reconstruction.'[121]

But Dexter's account also pointed to a general sense of pessimism pervading the government and civil service. The government seemed to have reached 'the end of an era' and now seemed 'powerless to influence events or to function in a constructive way.' It comprised 'burnt out men.' In particular there was a fear that the CCF was ascendant and the Liberal government seemed unable to rise up and 'contest the field.' Dexter was also alarmed by the 'internal dissensions' within Cabinet: 'Personal feuds and antipathies seem to be reaching the point where in carrying the fight to the other chap, the ministers are likely to lose sight of the policy proper.' Mackintosh apparently was of the same mind, claiming that 'over the past year the cabinet has lost its constructive power.' Ilsley's condition was 'very bad'; he was exhausted and was holding onto a 'sense of persecution, he is convinced that all his colleagues are against him. He can't sleep. He can't detach himself from worries. Unlike Old Walpole he can't put off his cares when he puts off his clothes.' According to Mackintosh, Gardiner was the 'chief architect of Ilsley's ruin.' Gardiner was relentless in pursuit of his goals, and the agriculture minister never backed down from a fight. Mackintosh claimed that his cantankerous personality had already ruined Dunning, and now he was taking Ilsley down. Dexter claimed that it was mainly the 'brain trust' that was resisting the rising tide of the CCF.[122]

There was one positive note at the end of 1943: Canada's exchange position with the United States was surprisingly good. In September a list of contracts supplied by Canadian authorities was cancelled by the Americans, amounting to an estimated value of $116 million. Howe was working to avoid having further contracts cancelled and urged Clark to meet with his American counterparts to come up with a new arrangement.[123] Clark was already thinking along the same lines. He wanted to approach the U.S. Treasury and suggest an end to the Maximum-Minimum Balances arrangement. In mid-November White wrote to Clark complaining about the rising gold and U.S. dollar reserve, despite the contract cancellations. 'It is now $200 million higher than the maximum agreed upon last Spring,' White argued. He suggested the cancellation of more contracts 'in order to bring Canada's cash reserves more nearly into line with the maximum-minimum balance agreement.' Clark claimed to be 'greatly surprised' by the recent exchange trend and argued that Canadian reserves were not actually as high as they first appeared. Further cancellations, therefore, were unnecessary.[124]

Clark went to Washington to meet with White on 7–8 December.[125] The deputy minister explained that large grain shipments to the United

States were mainly responsible for the high numbers, in combination with a variety of other factors. The dollar balance could be brought down somewhat through immediate payment on the Canpay account, payment of the rebate on War Supplies Ltd contract, cancellation of other contracts, and payment to the United States for expenditure on air bases in Canada. The conclusion, however, was that 'the Canadian exchange position vis-à-vis the United States is now sufficiently stable that there is no need for special action to be taken by the United States Government to ensure that Canada has adequate supplies of American dollars.' Canada no longer expected the United States to place contracts in Canada or to maintain existing contracts for exchange reasons alone.[126] As with so many wartime financial issues, Clifford Clark deserved credit for solving the exchange problem.

9

Getting the Job Done, 1944–1945

We could not, in truth, have arrived at a more unsuitable and inconvenient date. Ottawa is in a hectic last fortnight of a parliamentary session which may, conceivably, be the last before the General Election. The spate of measures which they are trying to force through, though some of them have been under debate for months, is almost entirely financial, with the result that Ilsley and Clark are occupied in the House ... all and every day ... Well! You can imagine that the Canadian Treasury have not much spare time over to give serious consideration to our problems. Add that both Ilsley and Clark are tired and indeed ill to the point of physical collapse, and that the temperature is frequently over 90 and in the neighbourhood of 100; and you have a picture of the scene where all we can do half the time, as I have indicated above, is to lie heavy on their conscience, whilst they, on their side, are as kind and considerate and hospitable as they have the strength left to be.

–John Maynard Keynes, summer of 1944

Clifford Clark made his most significant contribution to the handling of the Canadian economy in 1944. As Bill Mackintosh later observed, 'In many ways the culminating year of the war for the Finance Department was 1944. Some day some historian will discover what an impressive docket of financial legislation was passed by the House of Commons in that year.'[1] Bob Bryce came to the same conclusion: 'The decision of the Government to introduce a programme of post-war legislation in 1944 gave Clark an opportunity to turn from the negative operations of war, which he always disliked, to constructive ideas for making the future better than the past. He threw himself into this project with enormous zest, undeterred by the mountains of detail to be worked out or the grave responsibilities in preparing boldly for a most uncertain future.'[2]

Early in the new year, Ilsley submitted his ideas for reconstruction to be included in the Speech from the Throne. Among its proposals was an acceptance of health insurance and family allowances, additional assistance for those whose unemployment insurance had ended, as well as extended and contributory pension plans.[3] Mackenzie King knew where the document originated: 'I then took up Ilsley's communication which clearly had been prepared by Clark and others in his department and read it through paragraph by paragraph and in some cases clause by clause a couple of times ... Though the memo was from Ilsley, he said he was not at all sure of any part of it, and was even more critical of some of the recommendations he had made than he was favourable to them.'[4] Aside from the social policy recommendations, the prime minister decided to proceed with revisions to the Bank Act, despite an earlier decision by Cabinet. 'Clark was hesitant,' King noted, 'feeling no doubt the extra strain it would put on the Finance Department and Ilsley seemed quite struck down when I mentioned it, having in mind what it would involve of his time being taken up by attending meetings.'[5]

But it was the issue of family allowances that came to the forefront of Cabinet deliberations by mid-January and Clark played a pivotal role in the resulting policy decisions. The deputy was convinced that family allowances should be instituted immediately as part of the social security program. While they could be implemented as a war measure under federal authority, he believed it was preferable to pass a special bill, making them 'a permanent part of our social security structure.' Clark was also prepared to deal with criticism coming from the provinces. Premier Godbout of Quebec indicated that family allowances were essentially a matter of provincial jurisdiction and Clark moved immediately to counter the charge. The federal government, he argued, certainly could employ this constitutional argument to justify failure to do anything in the field 'in keeping with attitudes that have been adopted at certain times in the past.' But the argument could also be used to the opposite effect: 'I believe no constitutional argument can be raised against the Dominion's power to do what it wishes in this field. Furthermore, I can see no way in which Dominion payment of children's allowances would infringe on provincial autonomy.'[6]

On 13 January, Clark was invited to the 'decisive cabinet meeting' on the issue.[7] King called it 'one of the most impressive and significant of any I have attended.' According to the prime minister's account, Ilsley was asked to speak to the issue but it became clear that Clark was the main advocate. The deputy minister was brought into the meeting and asked to explain why his department supported family allowances. Clark 'made a very fine presentation,' stressing the difficulties of handling unemployment and housing problems unless family allowances were introduced, and pointing out that the measure would be necessary if wage stabilization and the price ceiling were to be maintained. He estimated the cost at $200 million, but the health insurance scheme would lessen the amount. 'That was a pretty big item for Ministers to face,' King observed, 'let alone swallow.' Before the ministers could respond, however, Clark brought up objections to the proposal and then provided solutions. He argued that without family allowances the federal government would have to pay enormous sums 'to make possible municipally constructed and municipally managed low-rental housing projects.'[8] The fundamental basis for the allowances was that the wage system took no account of the family status of the earner. According to Clark, the family income had to be supplemented. Allowances paid for all children represented the simplest, wisest, and cheapest solution.[9]

The prime minister was impressed. 'I think most of the Ministers who have been opposing the idea,' he recorded, 'did not feel equal to debating matters with Clark.'[10] King went around the Cabinet table to hear the ministers' views. Only Howe was opposed, arguing that 'it meant taxing people of medium incomes to support others who were in many cases not deserving of support.' Ralston surprised the prime minister by voting in favour, largely on the argument that Canada needed a large population which he believed the scheme might help achieve. Angus Macdonald had been opposed, but 'the emphasis that was placed on the maintenance of family, etc. helped to influence his judgment.' McLarty, who also had been opposed, apparently took the position that 'if the Finance Dept favoured the proposal, he would favour it.' Gardiner was now in agreement 'in the light of the discussion that had taken place.' Mackenzie King expected the Cabinet to favour the scheme by a vote of nine to five; after Clark's presentation, the vote ended up thirteen in favour and only one opposed. King was delighted and even phoned the deputy minister at home: 'Tonight before going to sleep I rang up Clark and congratulated him on his presentation. I let him see how happy I felt about it ... He said he was glad Cabinet was so nearly unanimous and had been surprised that it was so. He added that he felt in dealing with this measure we had given real evidence of our zeal for social security and there could be no questioning of motives or sincerity of the Government in its endeavour to do something practical in this way.'[11]

Clark's critics have argued that the hard-nosed economist came to support family allowances primarily on fiscal grounds. Ken Eaton, for example, argued that the measure came about as a result of the efforts of King and Clark, but 'not even their greatest admirers would claim, I think, that either of these two gentlemen was a really great humanitarian.'[12] According to Eaton, 'the hungry, desperate '30s had left a deep and enduring impression on Dr Clark. He wanted to ensure that this could never happen again in Canada ... there would not be multitudes of unemployed, destitute families with no inflow of cash income to feed and clothe the youngsters. This legislation was to be insurance against such tragic happenings.' As an economist, Clark viewed the expenditure as a way of transferring purchasing power into the hands of consumers and ensuring it could never again fall as low as it did during the Depression. 'The Family Allowances Act, in addition to being humanitarian,' Eaton claimed, 'was regarded by Dr Clark as a sort of built-in stabilizer of the economy.'[13] Bob Bryce, however, disagreed. Clark's support, he argued, was not based on an expectation of the need for more spending to support employment. Clark's philosophy transcended mere pragmatic and practical economics and contained elements of the visionary: 'He saw in it the most constructive element in a social security or welfare programme, promoting the better health and education of the future citizen and worker, simplifying the approach to social insurance and housing, extending to the poor that consideration for family responsibilities the income tax allows to others, and rectifying a fault inherent in the wage system.'[14]

The truth lies somewhere in between. There is no doubt that Clifford Clark was an advocate of the capitalist system and he sought to formulate policies to maintain that system. As Nancy Christie correctly points out, social security and increased state intervention were not viewed as radical or as necessarily associated with socialist collectivism. The state was representing a new liberalism that emphasized democracy and individualism. Clark viewed family allowances as a humanitarian social policy, but that did not necessarily make them such. 'Family allowances,'

Christie argues, 'were conceived and introduced by the King government primarily as a means to foster postwar consumption, which in turn would ensure full employment, economic equilibrium, and social stability.'[15] Clark would have agreed with this statement, adding to it that such objectives led *also* to improved social conditions. Regardless, Clark must be given considerable credit for the establishment of family allowances in Canada, and the achievement points to the deputy minister's influence in government. As John Porter concludes, 'An important social security measure was "sold" to the cabinet more by the persuasiveness of a civil servant than by that of a political leader.'[16] According to Bryce, 'Clark had certainly gone far beyond what any civil servant would normally dream of doing.'[17]

At the end of January the Cabinet had further discussions on the government's program for the upcoming session and the Speech from the Throne. But the Cabinet found Clark's plans too ambitious and complex. As King remembered, 'In the morning, a number of specific suggestions came from Clark, of the Finance Dept which I had embodied. In the afternoon, Ilsley had more material – at greater length – given him by Clark, and with some of it he was not too familiar. It all was much too long. We had considerable discussion on some of the paragraphs. I finally suggested that they be left to me to take up with Clark in the morning myself. Everyone seemed pleased to have the matter so arranged.'[18] One of the issues raised was health insurance, a matter upon which Cabinet had yet to make a definite decision. The plan would go forward 'as a separate measure if the provinces were satisfied.' But King was proceeding cautiously. The provinces would have to agree and there was no point in making promises if the taxes involved would be more than the populace would tolerate. 'Again I pointed out,' King wrote, 'that nothing was to be gained by promising something that we could not implement without taxation the people would not agree to bear, and insisted on agreements being reached with the provinces first of all. This, too, was left for me to go over with Clark again in the morning.'[19]

The next day, King met with Clark and Pickersgill. Clark indicated that finance officials were prepared to accept the health insurance plan, although it was against their better judgments. The trepidation expressed by the finance department was enough to convince the prime minister that the scheme was too expensive: 'Frankly I did not think the Treasury could stand it. That we had to hold consistently that whatever was done for health was a part of a nation-wide scheme. Something that would integrate both provincial and federal services along lines of social security. I pointed out that having secured Family Allowances, I did not think we could take on the other until the agreements had been reached in conference between the provinces and the Dominion on the various social service obligations and sources of revenue. Clark seemed relieved and said Ilsley would be, if that was the view.'[20] That afternoon in Cabinet, King explained the situation to Mackenzie. It was impossible, the prime minister argued, to take a piecemeal approach to implementing a social policy agenda.[21] Family allowances would go forward while the health insurance scheme would not. Clifford Clark had his way.

On 27 January the Speech from the Throne was delivered. According to Slater, 'Never before had a dominion government throne speech set out such revolutionary goals or such an extensive set of measures.' The speech promised employment guarantees, family allowances, and a new department of social welfare. Mackenzie King wanted it all done by the end of summer, because a fall election was possible.[22] On health insurance the speech indicated that further consultation with the provinces was necessary.[23] Mackenzie's plan, meanwhile, did go to further hearings of the Special Committee on Social Security between 24 February and 28 July. Plans were developed for a dominion-provincial conference expected later in 1944.[24] The prime minister wrote to the premiers about a possible conference, asking them to suggest a date after the parliamentary session was over. King requested they cooperate with the preparation of the necessary financial materials, and provincial officials were asked to come to Ottawa at federal expense.[25]

As if Clark did not have enough on his plate, the deputy minister was given another appointment in January 1944. In order to match similar organizations being created by the British, the Advisory Committee on Post-Hostilities Problems was created by the War Committee, the membership of which included the undersecretary of state for external affairs, the chiefs of staff, the clerk of the privy council, the vice-chairman of the National Harbours Board, and the deputy minister of finance. The Advisory Committee met five times in the year and dealt mainly with the repatriation of Canadian military personnel.[26] It handled the critical issue of establishing, or rather re-establishing, a 'world security organization'[27] and also examined the security of Newfoundland and Labrador, as well as the U.S. military presence in the region.[28]

The workload of the finance department had increased and, according to the prime minister, Ilsley was at the breaking point. The finance minister spoke of his need to get away for a holiday. In late February, after a Cabinet meeting, King spoke to him: 'He began to nearly collapse, saying the strain had become too great for him ... I felt very sorry for him. It was clear that another day would break him down completely. I talked with him about getting off to the seaside or to Williamsburg, or elsewhere. He did not know where he was going to go or what he was going to do.' But despite his criticisms and general antagonism, King realized that the government relied heavily on Clark and Ilsley: 'He is absolutely indispensable, not only to Canada but to the war effort of the United Nations. Clark is in much the same position. These men have far too much on their shoulders.'[29] Ilsley took a holiday but, even after returning, King saw no improvement: 'He was just about where he was when he left. I felt a real handicap in proceedings of Council because of his condition. It becomes next to impossible to oppose him without producing a reaction which is most unpleasant.'[30] Ilsley took another holiday in mid-March, this time for five weeks. King believed he looked 'quite well and strong again,' when he returned, but within a week the prime minister was complaining 'that the discussion of old questions brings back his highly nervous condition.'[31]

Legislation was introduced at the end of February to create the Industrial Development Bank (IDB). Sponsored by Towers and Clark, the IDB was to establish a subsidiary of the Bank of Canada (with the same board of directors) with the power to make advances or loans, guarantee advances, buy and hold securities temporarily, and underwrite the issue of securities. The intention was to limit the operations of the bank to assisting enterprises in the industrial field by providing loans to small businesses often ignored by commercial banks. Clark later explained that the goal was 'to make sure that no sound industrial enterprise should lack the ability to raise sufficient funds to get started or to finance rapid growth merely because it was small or new or unknown to investors.'[32] While the commercial banks did not feel the creation of the IDB was necessary, and even Towers was unsure of the actual need, the British had already established an industrial development corporation in which the Bank of England participated and the United States had provided certain powers to the Federal Reserve Banks to make loans to industry. Both Clark and Towers supported the idea in the EAC and defended it before the House Standing Committee on Banking and Commerce at the end of March.[33]

Clark spent much of the spring and summer of 1944 attending the monotonous meetings of the Banking Committee. As a result of the detailed arguments from monetary reformers, the committee's hearings dragged on through May, June, and July, exhausting both Ilsley and Clark. In fifty-two days of hearings beginning on 16 May, Clark was absent only twice. The hearings were particularly difficult for Ilsley, whose constitution was wearing down.[34] Indeed, so many matters were being handled by the finance department that the budget was delayed. 'The truth of the matter,' King recorded, 'is that the Finance Department is so far behind in the measures it is bringing forth that the Budget will not be ready until the middle of May.'[35]

Despite the apparent emphasis on multilateralism for the post-war world, Clark remained concerned about the nature of Anglo-Canadian and Anglo-American financial arrangements. Clark was joined by Robertson in being sceptical that the spirit of multilateralism would ultimately triumph. In March, Britain and the United States demonstrated differences in their approach to tariffs and preferential policy. The problem was that their differences were widening rather than narrowing. 'It seems to me that, as the multilateral programme becomes more modest and more remote,' Robertson told Clark, 'we shall have to look more seriously and more quickly at the specific problem of Canadian–American trade relations. I had envisaged a bilateral agreement with the United States, supplementing a general multilateral tariff reduction, but if effective multilateral action is to be indefinitely deferred and, when achieved, prove modest, then I think we may have to look at the question again from the continental viewpoint.'[36] Clark agreed. He had been 'growing increasingly sceptical' for some time about the possibilities of 'real achievement' under the multilateral program and 'therefore increasingly concerned with the advisability, from our point of view, of a radical continental approach coupled with a radical Canadian-British program.'[37] If the multilateral vision was 'fading,' Canada would have to be prepared to deal with nations through bilateral efforts and this would have to be done sooner rather than later.[38]

On 21 April, Ilsley announced the termination of the financial aspects of the Hyde Park Agreement. At the same time, he announced the purchase of important U.S. military installations that had been built in Canada. The reasoning was based on the supply of American dollars.

By late 1942 Canada had moved from a serious shortage of American dollars to a very healthy reserve, so healthy in fact that U.S. officials feared congressional reaction. Canadian and American authorities agreed that the rate of American purchases in Canada should be regulated to keep Canadian reserves within a range of $300 to $350 million, or just slightly above pre-war levels. In early January 1944 the U.S. War Department ordered that no contracts be placed in Canada. Finally, the United States suggested that Canada use up some of its excess reserves by purchasing airfields and other installations. The government agreed and the plan was set in motion.[39] But Canadian finance officials were not so confident that the positive situation would necessarily continue. 'It indicates too great an optimism in regard to the present level of our U.S. balances,' Plumptre told Clark, 'and their probable level next year … and also, as you point out, a failure to appreciate the relative extent of the assistance which we have rendered to Allied countries as compared with U.S. Lend-Lease assistance.'[40]

By early May the British were expressing their own concerns regarding Mutual Aid. A British memo claimed that Canada's decision to provide $887 million in 1944–5 was not enough to cover British purchases. The suggestion that Canada hold a large amount of sterling was viewed as merely postponing the problem. The obvious solution was a loan, but the British did not want to borrow for war purposes and they expected that the Canadians would insist on using British investments in Canada as collateral. One solution was to have Canada pay all the costs of her troops in Britain. Keynes took up the issue with Clark at Bretton Woods in early July.[41]

The Cabinet held its final discussions on family allowances on 15 June, and a week later the Family Allowance Act was introduced in the House by the prime minister. The bill, which did not take effect until 1 July 1945, provided for five dollars per month for children up to five years, six dollars for those six to nine years, seven dollars for those ten to twelve years, and eight dollars for those thirteen to fifteen years. The rates were reduced by one dollar per month for the fifth child, by two dollars per month for the sixth and seventh, and by three dollars per month for the eighth and any more children. The assumption was that expenses for child-rearing decreased after a certain point. The scheme raised the share of federal revenue spent on health and welfare from 2.2 per cent in 1943–4 to 10.3 per cent in 1945–6. On 13 October, Brooke Claxton entered King's Cabinet as the first minister of national health and welfare. His task included setting up machinery to distribute family allowances and publicize their virtues.[42] Ilsley had never been completely in favour of the legislation and in the end he opposed it.[43]

By late spring, pressure on the price ceiling subsided. On 13 June the Cabinet approved the release of part of the compulsory savings collected since 1942. King, after talking to Clark and listening to Cabinet discussion, concluded that this would be more beneficial than increasing exemptions to the price ceiling.[44] A discussion took place at the Cabinet meeting of 22 June to decide how best to describe the release of the compulsory savings in the upcoming budget speech. King, who was worried about the increasing popularity of the CCF, wanted to emphasize that people of low income who had experienced real hardship in the war would get immediate relief. Ilsley did not want to create the impression that the government could afford taxation relief at this stage of the war or that the direction of financial policy was changing. He threatened to resign if he had to 'base his budget on yielding up taxation, heightening exemptions.' King urged the need for flexibility.[45] The following day, Clark was brought into the Cabinet meeting. He resisted King's desire for tax reductions and argued that Towers was also opposed. According to the prime minister, Clark simply did not realize that the real worry was the CCF winning the election. Once again King was frustrated at how the increasingly vocal and influential 'brain trust' had the luxury of taking all their stances based on practicalities rather than politics.[46]

In June the CCF under Tommy Douglas swept forty-seven of the fifty-two provincial seats in Saskatchewan, becoming the first socialist government in North America. Almost immediately Clark found himself involved in an issue that pitted the province against Ottawa. The origins went back to 1937 – the worst year of the Depression for Saskatchewan. The provincial government had been forced to turn repeatedly to the federal government for credit through loan guarantees. By the spring of 1938, after an almost total crop failure, farmers had no money for seed, and their loans from municipalities had to be backed by guarantees from both the provincial and federal governments. Douglas, then a federal MP, argued that some of the stored grain be held back in 1937 for seed, but the federal government failed to act and all the wheat was shipped out.[47] Farmers were paid fifty cents a bushel for wheat they shipped in 1937, then they paid $1.43 or $1.47 a bushel to buy it back for seed the next spring. The money for the seed grain was advanced by the banks and by 1944, with interest added, the grain cost more than $2 a bushel.[48] The 1938 crop failed completely, so the farmers could not repay the loans, and the province was left with a large debt to the federal government. Premier Douglas claimed that this was a natural disaster equivalent to a flood or tornado and that the federal government should have put up all the money.[49] The CCF campaigned in the 1944 provincial election, promising that they would seek to have the federal government reduce its claim.[50]

The banks asked Ottawa to implement its guarantee and pay them. The question arose, however, as to who would cover the cost of forgiveness. Because the farmers were unlikely to repay the advances, Clark believed that Ottawa should bear the cost. Ilsley, however, was less convinced. During the election campaign, the Liberal premier of Saskatchewan, W.J. Patterson, asked the federal government for permission to match the CCF promise of forgiveness. The request was refused. Mitchell Sharp was sent to Regina to discuss the situation with Patterson, Gardiner, and Gordon Taggart, Saskatchewan minister of agriculture. They were adamant that the incoming CCF government should be held to its guarantee and Ilsley agreed.[51]

The new government of Saskatchewan responded by offering a demand note for some $14 million in payment of the amount owing under the guarantee. In reality, however, the offer was little more than a gesture that had become commonplace as security for Depression debts owed to Ottawa. Payment of these demand notes had never been enforced. This time, however, the federal government interpreted the note literally and sent a treasury official to the Royal Bank in Regina to demand $14 million. The startled manager had no such sum available and could not meet the demand. The federal government declared Saskatchewan to be in default. In February 1945 Ilsley informed the provincial government that he would withhold payment due to the province under the wartime tax rental agreements to cover what he felt was owed to Ottawa. Douglas believed the federal government had no right to suspend these payments and sought arbitration on the issue, but lost. The province's position was that the two financial agreements were separate and distinct.[52]

The federal government had legally won the right to take the money but under Clark's influence, Ilsley reconsidered. A compromise was worked out under which Saskatchewan was given eleven years to pay off its debt.[53] Tommy Douglas gave Clark much of the credit for that arrangement, even assuming mistakenly that the deputy was from Saskatchewan: 'I can remember him [Ilsley] pacing up and down his office and saying to Dr Clark, his deputy, "Is there any other way we could solve this? These debts are old, the provincial government will never collect from the farmers, and we have some responsibility. What do you think?" Dr Clark was a former Saskatchewan man, tough when it came to dealing with finances, but he finally said, "I would go along with it if you think you can persuade your colleagues.'"[54] The incident to Mitchell Sharp demonstrated that 'Clark was by no means the hard-fisted Treasury stereotype. He sympathized with those who had suffered during the calamitous thirties, as he had suffered personally ... He wanted to improve the position of debt-ridden governments like Saskatchewan, so that they could better discharge their responsibilities in the future.'[55]

Clifford Clark travelled with Ilsley to Atlantic City in late June for the preliminary meetings of the Bretton Woods Conference on the International Monetary Fund and the International Development Bank. Dexter commented wryly that he was not sure if Ilsley was taking Clark or vice versa.[56] Keynes was also in Atlantic City and he met with the Canadian financial officials to discuss further aid to Britain. Keynes reported 'that the prospects were fairly good and that Clark was seriously considering the expediency of taking over certain military expenses which we have lately suggested to him.'[57] Keynes also used the opportunity to impress upon the Canadian finance officials the seriousness of the economic situation facing Britain. It was agreed that Keynes and Sir Wilfrid Eady would travel to Ottawa for further discussions once the conference was over.

On 1 July delegates from forty-four countries met at the Mount Washington Hotel in Bretton Woods, New Hampshire, for the United and Associated Nations Monetary and Financial Conference. The Canadian delegation was led by Ilsley (who was in attendance for only a portion of the time) and included St Laurent and four Liberal MPs, as well as their experts: Clark, Towers, Mackintosh, Rasminsky, Plumptre, and Deutsch.[58] The work of the conference was divided among three commissions: one worked on the establishment of the International Monetary Fund, chaired by White; another worked on the creation of the International Development Bank, chaired by Keynes; and a third worked on developing other means of international financial cooperation.[59] Clark was involved in detailed work on so many issues back in Ottawa that according to Bryce, 'it is no surprise that he was able to put in only a nominal appearance at the Bretton Woods conference that summer.'[60]

But Clark did have time to meet again with Keynes to discuss the British proposal that Canada pay for military expenses borne by Britain on behalf of Canada throughout the war. Clark had been briefed on the proposal by Robertson, who favoured it.[61] Keynes informed the Bank of England governor, 'We had a very important conversation with Ilsley, Clark and Towers. I have no idea what the way out is, or how Canada can help us on an adequate scale. But at any rate we did our duty in creating a very considerable impression on them and sent them away wiser and sadder men. I think we must give them a breathing spell to think over the situation in light of what we told them. Nothing could have been more friendly and understanding than the way they received what it was our duty to tell.'[62] The Canadians agreed to pay the military costs when Keynes met with them later in August.[63] It was, according to King, 'simply as a means of enabling the British Govt to keep its head above water ... They are now in a very embarrassing position and if we are to get the markets in Britain which we shall wish to have and need to have later on, we shall have to assist ... It is a generous agreement but it leaves Canada in the position that we have paid for everything that relates to any contribution made to the war.'[64]

Even though Clark was not present for the entire Bretton Woods Conference, he did play a role. He spent considerable time prior to the conference preparing Plumptre, who would deal with White and the American delegation.[65] Upon returning to Ottawa, he continued to deal with significant questions raised by the Canadian delegation. On 6 July, for example, Rasminsky phoned to discuss the exchange rate formula, the executive committee and management of the IMF, and the statements of principle regarding countries maintaining convertibility of their currencies.

But Clark returned to Ottawa to deal with the delivery of the delayed budget, which included another $887 million in Mutual Aid for 1944–5.[66] The main provision of the 1944 budget was the termination of the refundable portion of the personal income tax.[67] Another provision allowed C.D. Howe to grant accelerated depreciation to companies converting their facilities to peacetime production. This action permitted a quick write-off of extra expenses against current taxation. At the same time, if the economy turned downward, businesses would already have paid off their gamble on the future. If economic conditions were favourable after the war, they would be paying full taxes on their new productive plants. The objective was to have funds for capital expansion readily available.[68]

Amidst Clark's hectic schedule, there was even less time for his family. The previous summer the Clarks had moved houses in Ottawa, from Manor Road to 14 Belvedere Crescent, Rockcliffe, next to the property of the governor general. In the summer of 1944, Clark's youngest child, Peggy, married Donald Johnston in Ottawa, on a sweltering day. The reception was held at the Clark home. While Clark was proud, as usual he found it difficult to take time from his busy work schedule, even for the marriage of his daughter. In April 1945, he became a grandfather when Peggy gave birth to a son, Donald Robert Johnston.

As if the Bretton Woods Conference, the Standing Committee on Banking, the budget, and the wedding of his daughter were not enough to keep Clark busy over the summer of 1944, a large amount of legislation was passed through the House. The deputy minister found himself involved with almost every policy decision. The Cabinet met through much of July and Clark was often present. After one meeting King commented that there were nearly a dozen measures for the present session being put forward by the finance department: 'Had both Ilsley and Clark present. Was deeply sorry for both, especially Clark. They have kept far too much in their own hands and have a staff only about one-tenth of what they should have.'[69]

On 21 July, the EAC reported to Cabinet on a proposal from Agriculture Minister Jimmy Gardiner. Back in December 1943 the government accepted guaranteed floor prices for key agricultural products for three years to maintain Canada's current level of production. Gardiner now wanted support for prices on all farm products. The EAC suggested that support should apply only to staple products and should be in the form of deficiency payments equal to the difference between the farmers' average selling price and a defined floor price.[70] On 24 July, Gardiner introduced the Agricultural Prices Support Act, one of a number of new and important acts in which Clark 'took a large share' in developing.[71] Three days later, J.A. MacKinnon, the minister of trade and commerce, introduced the Export Credits Insurance Act, another piece of legislation whose origins and development owed much to Clark.[72] Back in May, Ilsley had introduced the Farm Improvement Loans Act in order to, as Clark later put it, 'provide, through the device of a limited pool guarantee of intermediate term loans made by the commercial banks, ample funds to enable farmers to re-equip their farms and to construct or modernize farm homes and buildings.'[73] Mackintosh called the act 'the only successful legislation on intermediate credits,' and indicated that Clark put it all together 'in the early and sleepless hours of the morning.'[74]

Busy or not, Clark always seemed to find time to work on the housing issue. In the early spring of 1944 the *Curtis Report* was released. The report supported the need for large integrated housing companies to be provided by a major government investment in public housing. It recommended a target of 606,000 housing units to be built within the decade.[75] In June, Clark met with Frank Nicolls, director of the housing branch. Nicolls suggested loans to convert existing housing into more units; loans to reconstruction agencies established jointly by local, provincial, and dominion governments to acquire land for development or redevelopment; and loans to municipalities, if guaranteed by the province, for building low-income housing. Clark rejected the suggestions. He was opposed to making loans to municipalities for subsidized rental projects.

Unhappy with the developing housing situation and the resulting policy discussions, Clark undertook a complete overhaul and expansion of the National Housing Act, which Ilsley introduced in the House on 31 July. According to Mackintosh, it was completed 'on a mad Sunday.'[76] The act extended the ideas of the 1938 legislation, making more generous provisions for joint federal-private mortgages and further provision for low-income housing. Provision for home improvement and extension loans were included but not proclaimed for a decade. As he did in 1935, Clark rejected more active federal intervention in housing. There was no provision for federally subsidized rental housing.[77] Ilsley explained that municipalities could not at that time be trusted to independently build or manage subsidized rental projects financed by the dominion. The act did, however, provide for outright grants to municipalities of half the cost of slum clearance if the land was sold to a limited dividend company or insurance company to build rental housing of low or moderate cost. Still, this section proved ineffective. Clark was never able to get a limited dividend project built.[78] He had more success with a provision for insurance companies. In 1945 a group of insurance companies set up a limited dividend company, which in 1946 began work on thirty-two projects comprising 3,299 housing units.[79] According to Bacher, Clark 'had written the most conservative housing legislation of any of the English-speaking nations.'[80] Bacher's criticism of Clark's adherence to the private market is well placed and there is little doubt that the finance department's housing policies did 'promote the appearance of change while blocking the substance of what reformers were urging.'[81]

Another issue on Clark's mind in 1944 dealt with the program for post-war rehabilitation of veterans, particularly the re-establishment credits plan. He viewed these credits as preferable to extended gratuities.[82] Both Clark and Ilsley became increasingly active and vocal in arguing with defence officials over the appropriate measures for returning servicemen. According to Sharp, 'Clark felt that this program should be comprehensive and generous and he did not wait for proposals to be made by the Department of Veterans Affairs, as might have been expected of the deputy minister of finance.' He took the initiative and commenced interdepartmental discussions: 'The returning veterans were to be given not just money but education and training and a stake in the modern Canada that was emerging from the war.'[83] The debate over the amount of war service gratuity to be paid to servicemen lasted from February until July. Clark and Ilsley wanted equal gratuities, regardless of rank, and substantially higher gratuities for overseas service. They eventually won their case.[84] The two finance officials also supported rehabilitation grants, including assistance for university or vocational training and benefits under the Veterans Land Act. Clark recognized, however, that not all veterans would be able to use these grants and might feel a sense of discrimination. He therefore insisted that all veterans receive re-establishment credits.[85] Prime Minister King estimated that if the war lasted until the end of March, the gratuities would cost about $400 million and the re-establishment credits about $350 million.[86]

On 10 August the prime minister introduced the War Services Gratuities (or Grants) Act. This bill provided a basic cash gratuity of $7.50 for each thirty-day period of military service plus twenty-five cents for each day served outside the western hemisphere. In addition it offered a supplemental gratuity of seven days' pay and allowances (varied according to rank) for each six months of service outside. There was also a re-establishment credit equal to the basic gratuity for discharged veterans who did not choose the education or vocational training benefits or those under the Veterans' Lands Act. The credit was not payable in cash but could be used for acquiring, repairing, or modernizing a home, buying furniture and household equipment, providing working capital for a business, assisting in the purchase of a business, and similar purposes.[87] Incapacitated veterans received full medical care, and invalids were pensioned to the full extent of their individual disability. Veterans wishing to take up farming or to buy land for small businesses were assisted under the act. Those who wished to return to their pre-war jobs were given their old jobs back, with seniority as if they had never been away to war. Unemployed veterans received out-of-work allowances.[88]

Officials in defence were surprised to have such generosity coming from finance. The two departments had clashed constantly throughout the war. The minister of national defence for air, 'Chubby' Power, was amazed that Clark was advancing grants twice the size of those proposed by his department: 'He said that we were likely to have a great depression right after the war and money must be distributed widely among the people of Canada ... He must have thought we were penny wise and pound foolish. In any case, there have been no problems about the veterans of the Second World War to compare with those of the First.'[89]

But the issue of demobilization was not without disagreement. At the Cabinet meeting of 22 September, a debate ensued over how demobilization would actually occur once the fighting ended. Ralston wanted to ensure that no jobs went to conscripted men before volunteers were placed. King claimed that this argument was based on the false premise that there would be a shortage of work. 'I pointed out and was supported in this view by both Clark and Robertson ... that we have got work and that we should state frankly that our policies had been to create work, to have a large national economy and that we would have work for all.'[90]

The hectic atmosphere of that busy summer in 1944 was described by John Maynard Keynes, who was in Ottawa in August on a holiday but also to negotiate on behalf of the British government. Keynes was shocked by the workload and pace of the Canadian finance department: 'We could not, in truth, have arrived at a more unsuitable and inconvenient date. Ottawa is in a hectic last fortnight of a parliamentary session which may, conceivably, be the last before the General Election. The spate of measures which they are trying to force through, though some of them have been under debate for months, is almost entirely financial, with the result that Ilsley and Clark are occupied in the House (particularly with the Canadian convention that the Minister in charge *never* leaves the Bench) all and every day.' Keynes was impressed by the docket of legislation, noting that while the social reform measures were similar to the British program, it was 'proportionately two or three times as lavish in terms of money ... Well! You can imagine that the Canadian Treasury have not much spare time over to give serious consideration to our problems. Add that both Ilsley and Clark are tired and indeed ill to the point of physical collapse, and that the temperature is frequently over 90 and in the neighbourhood of 100; and you have a picture of the scene where all we can do half the time, as I have indicated above, is to lie heavy on their conscience, whilst they, on their side, are as kind and considerate and hospitable as they have the strength left to be.'[91]

Keynes's objective in the Mutual Aid talks was to bridge a gap between Canada and Britain, somewhere in the range of $600 million. In addition, there was a sum of $200 million 'held in suspense' for the first air training scheme up to the end of June 1942. The British had never regarded it as an agreed-upon war debt, but Keynes's team discovered that 'Ilsley was quite confidently regarding this $200 million as a war debt due to Canada.' To make matters more difficult for the British, the Canadian officials felt another $200 million was owed them for air training from the end of June 1942 to the end of March 1945. As a result, the British negotiators found themselves looking to make up $1 billion to clear up all war debts in addition to the $700 million secured loan.[92]

The first task for the British was to convince the Canadians that it was 'neither reasonable nor to the mutual interest' to overload Britain with war debts. If Britain was to exhaust its capacity to repay by borrowing before the end of the war, the nation could not afford to buy Canadian produce after the end of the Pacific War, even on credit. The Canadians, however, took the line that 'it was up to them to meet the full charges which we have incurred on behalf of their overseas forces, and that any unpaid charges on their behalf, which we could substantiate, would be properly chargeable on their Defence Appropriation.' The British felt they could substantiate claims of about $800 million. Beyond that, they were due tax refunds of about $200 million. Canada had included taxes on munitions sold through Mutual Aid, which would normally have been refunded on exports. On food, the taxes were remitted.

Canada had also charged Britain $250 million for the capital cost of ships that did not pass into British possession. Keynes was confident the British would get the tax refund but not the ship refund. It was, he wrote, 'a bit of a swindle.' The Canadians recognized 'the justice' of the British complaint, but 'it would create great difficulties for Ilsley and Clark if they had to attempt to undo what, rather naughtily and unnecessarily, they have done somewhat irrevocably in the terms of their mutual aid legislation.' The claims for the refund of costs incurred for the overseas forces were 'admitted in principle,' Keynes went on, but he noted that when it came to the amounts, 'we have to admit that some of our claims are based on highly conjectural and unsubstantiated estimates, certain of which we have had to invent for ourselves here on the spot.' In private Keynes told Clark that if he could get Ilsley to agree 'to the tax refund and to the principle of our not being left out of pocket in respect of the costs we incur on behalf of the Canadian forces ... I will cease to hang about, as we all are doing now, heavy on his conscience, and will not commit suicide on his doorstep but will go home quietly.'[93]

But negotiations were moving slowly because Clark and Ilsley were so busy. To make matters worse, the King government was concerned about the difficulties posed by the recent Quebec provincial election, resulting in the return of Maurice Duplessis and the Union Nationale. Regardless, on 14 August the Cabinet approved the expenses as Keynes had proposed, up to $655 million.[94] On 27 October Keynes wrote to Clark to prepare for another visit and more negotiations for assistance. The British economist returned to Ottawa at the end of November. 'There is no question, in my mind,' he wrote, 'that Ilsley and Howe, and also Dr Clark, mean to do their utmost to meet our requirements in full by hook or by crook.'[95]

But problems with the provinces were by not confined to Quebec. By the middle of August, Premier George Drew of Ontario was criticizing the federal government to the point that Mackenzie King claimed a dominion-provincial conference was no longer feasible.[96] Ontario, however, was not about to accept blame for Ottawa cancelling the conference. Provincial Treasurer Leslie Frost wrote to King arguing that during the war Ontario 'gave to the Dominion certain of its taxing and other powers. This was done patriotically and in good faith.' It was not, however, done permanently. There had to be a federal-provincial conference to arrange for the return of the taxing powers to their rightful owners. It was now apparent that the fundamental recommendations of the *Rowell-Sirois Report* were not to be implemented.[97] According to Bryce, many in Ottawa, including Clark, 'had come to the conclusion that the Sirois proposals involved too great a transfer of constitutional power to be acceptable to provincial governments, and that a continuing solution to the problem of the use of taxing powers should be sought without constitutional change by applying the principles of the wartime agreements.'[98] This might have been the case for Ottawa, but it was not the general assumption of the provinces. Some of the provinces, most notably Manitoba, remained fixed on having the Rowell-Sirois recommendations implemented. The affluent provinces might have opposed and obstructed Rowell-Sirois, but they were certainly just as opposed to continuing the wartime agreements that had resulted in a complete surrender of provincial taxation powers to Ottawa. Clark, along with most of the mandarins, now hoped that in the post-war setting they would be able to maintain many of the taxation powers without having to implement the unconditional grants proposed by Rowell-Sirois.

As the war approached its end, the question arose as to whether the EAC had outlived its usefulness, particularly when the Department of Reconstruction was now doing so much of the relevant work. Clifford Clark told Donald Gordon, however, that while the reconstruction department was to serve as the general coordinating agency, delays were slowing its progress. Clark believed that the department required an advisory body representing the departments and agencies primarily involved: 'Sometimes I wonder whether the Economic Advisory Committee should be that body or whether the new Department would seek to establish its own agency.' Gordon responded by criticizing Clark's beloved committee. He indicated that for some time the EAC (of which he was a member) had failed to carry out its functions: 'I have always had a personal disinclination to sit on any Committee which did not actively discharge the responsibilities which appeared to be entrusted to it.' Gordon concluded that the EAC should be 'wound up and the new Minister left free to decide whether or not he wishes to have an Advisory Committee attached to his Department.' Clark responded with an impassioned defence, claiming that while the EAC seemed an unwieldy committee composed of very busy men, and while it might not have performed the same function in the past year as it had in previous years, Gordon was being unnecessarily harsh in his judgment. The past year had been remarkably busy and it should not be surprising that the EAC had sat largely moribund.[99]

As the year wound down, Walter Gordon urged the government to turn its attention to tax reductions in the post-war period. The finance department, however, was already examining the issue and had dealt with it, to an extent, in the budget. Taxes on corporations had increased from 16 per cent before the war to a minimum of 40 per cent plus a 100 per cent tax on excess profits. Personal income taxes had increased sharply and were much higher than comparable taxes in the United States. Clark's thinking was that the emphasis after the war should be on a reduction in corporation income taxes. Others, including Walter Gordon, pushed for a major reduction in the rates of personal income tax as well as the immediate discontinuance of the maximum rates under the Corporations Excess Profits Tax Act. Gordon wanted a public debate on the subject and asked Clark for his opinion: 'Clark, who was always a dedicated democrat and a firm believer in debate, replied that he thought this might be useful.' Gordon published his views in an article, entitled 'Post-War Taxation,' in the December 1944 issue of the *Canadian Chartered Accountant*.[100]

At the beginning of 1945, Clark's attention again turned toward Anglo-Canadian financial arrangements. In mid-January, Keynes wrote Clark, urging him to come to Britain with an informal party for discussions in the next three or four months.[101] Two days later, on 18 January, 'a decisive meeting' took place in the finance minister's office to discuss the immediate post-war commercial policy outlook as well as a long background paper prepared by Towers titled 'A Proposal for Averting a Breakdown in International Trade Relationships.' Clark opened the discussion by pointing to proposals, which he supported, for having a single appropriation to cover all war requirements, including Mutual Aid and reconstruction. He was worried about the prospects for Canadian trade in the period immediately following the end of hostilities, particularly those concerning trade with Britain, and he was having 'difficulty' recommending to the government a substantial measure of Mutual Aid 'without drawing to their attention the trade difficulties which Canada might face vis-à-vis the U.K.'

According to Towers, Britain was likely to establish a 'cordon sanitaire' around the sterling area and would endeavour to develop, expand, and restrict trade within that area while seeking to bring Western European countries into this sterling bloc. Towers believed that 'ultimately the ambition might be to bring in most of the world outside of Canada and the U.S,' which would lead to Britain discriminating against imports from North America. For Clark and Towers, 'all of this, of course, would be contrary to the desires of Canada and the U.S. to achieve greater freedom of international trade, a greater use of multilateral trade than existed before the war, and ultimately the convertibility of one currency into another.' Correspondence with Keynes indicated that Towers's fears were substantiated. 'This type of opinion' had indeed gained the upper hand in Britain and would 'win out unless some good alternative were put forward.' British agricultural and manufacturing interests did not want to compete with goods coming from North America: 'There is a widespread tendency in Britain to regard Canada and the United States as a stiff competitor and poor customers.' Towers argued that Britain could join a multilateral trading world only with substantial aid and he suggested a $1.2 billion credit at 2 per cent interest. This loan would be expected to cover the period of transition immediately after the war while Britain was re-establishing its own export trade. 'As far as Canada was concerned,' Towers claimed, 'the importance of getting a satisfactory trade situation after the war was simply tremendous ... The alternative is a very grim and forbidding one. It would mean that the end of hostilities would see only a shift from military warfare to economic warfare.' Towers did not want to seem gloomy but he had felt pessimistic prior to the Depression, and as it turned out, 'no pessimistic appreciation of the situation in advance had gone within miles of being too pessimistic.'

Clark asked whether Canada should seek to 'smoke out true British opinions' while still serving 'the more constructive purpose of helping to influence the British policy toward multilateral trade.' Informal talks, meanwhile, could be initiated with the representatives of the U.S. State Department. Ilsley took the practical line of asking how these issues and considerations would affect government policy for 1945–6. The consensus was that once hostilities ended, the onus would shift away from Mutual Aid as a strategic solution of offering war supplies with the ability to pay as secondary. Ilsley then asked if Canada should attach conditions to the provision of Mutual Aid. Clark responded that this was desirable and that he 'could not conscientiously recommend Mutual Aid on the scale required if he believed that the U.K. was going to follow the type of policies that had been discussed.' Both Robertson and Mackintosh opposed attaching conditions during wartime in order to deal with post-war problems.[102]

On 14 February the Cabinet War Committee approved a new Mutual Aid appropriation, which reached $670 million by September. The British had been suggesting they would have to reduce their purchases from Canada and other non-sterling countries as a result of their financial difficulties, which King felt 'might easily bring about a severe depression in this country.' Under these circumstances, the prime minister supported more aid to Britain.[103] Just over a week later, three telegrams were sent to Britain concerning an aid package. The telegrams were drafted by Clark, Towers, and Mackintosh.[104] Keynes's reaction was mixed. 'Beyond question it is generous,' he noted, but he had qualms about many of the proposals, particularly the position that Britain should free up the sterling area to Canada.[105] Clark believed the United States was moving swiftly into the realm of international collaboration, and trade was 'just a matter of timing.' He did not believe there

Clark family (left to right): Muriel May, William Clifford, George Ellis, Kenneth Benjamin, Linden Roderick, Catherine Urquhart. (Peggy Johnston)

Margaret Smith, about 1914.
(Peggy Johnston)

Clark farmhouse. (Woodcut, Dorothy Dumbrille, *Up and Down the Glens.* Toronto: Ryerson Press, 1954)

Clifford as a student at Queen's University, Kingston, 1907–1908. (Peggy Johnston)

The Department of Political Economy, Queen's University, Kingston, autumn 1915. Clifford Clark *second from right*, and O.D. Skelton, *middle*. (Peggy Johnston)

Clark with his youngest children, Peggy and Ken, Scarsdale, New York, 1927. (Peggy Johnston)

Clark while working with the Straus Company in Chicago. (Chambers, Chicago)

The Scarsdale house. This house became a financial disaster for the Clark family when the Depression began. (Copy of sale advertisement)

Clark as deputy minister of finance in 1933. (Photographer unknown)

Clark in East Block office on Parliament Hill. (William Johnston)

Clark portrait. (Blank & Stoller Ltd, Montreal, Quebec)

T & W Club near Roberval, Quebec, August 1935. Clark, *centre.*
(Peggy Johnston)

Clark reading in Rockcliffe living room, 1937–1938. (Peggy Johnston)

Clark fishing on Gilmour Estate, 19 or 20 May 1939. (Peggy Johnston)

Clark portrait (Shelbourne Studios, 450 Madison Avenue, New York)

Five Lakes Club (Peggy Johnston)

Clifford Clark and Graham Towers with fishing guide.
(J.L. O'Brien photographer)

Clark in front of Centre Block, entrance to Parliament.
(*Fortune* magazine)

Clark portrait, 20 February 1943. (Yousuf Karsh, PA-213971, Library and Archives Canada)

Oscar D. Skelton. (C-000079, Library and Archives Canada)

Prime Minister Richard B. Bennett at his desk in 1932.
(Underwood & Underwood, C-007733, Library and Archives Canada)

Charles A. Dunning, minister of finance, 1935–1939.
(Rossie, C-026218, Library and Archives Canada)

Prime Minister William Lyon Mackenzie King in 1941.
(Yousuf Karsh, C-027647, Library and Archives Canada)

Edgar N. Rhodes, minister of finance, 1932–1935. (National Film Board of Canada. Photothèque, C-045314, Library and Archives Canada)

Col. James L. Ralston, minister of finance, 1939–1940. (Canada. Department of National Defence, PA-062515, Library and Archives Canada)

Douglas Abbott, minister of finance, 1946–1954.
(Duncan Cameron, PA-121696, Library and Archives Canada)

Signing the United Kingdom Loan agreement, February 1946. *Left to right*: W.C. Clark, R.B. Bryce, Norman Robinson, Wilfrid Rady, Malcolm Macdonald, Gordon Munro, W.L.M. King, and J.L. Ilsley. (F. Royal / F. Warrander, National Film Board of Canada, PA-150450, Photothèque, Library and Archives Canada)

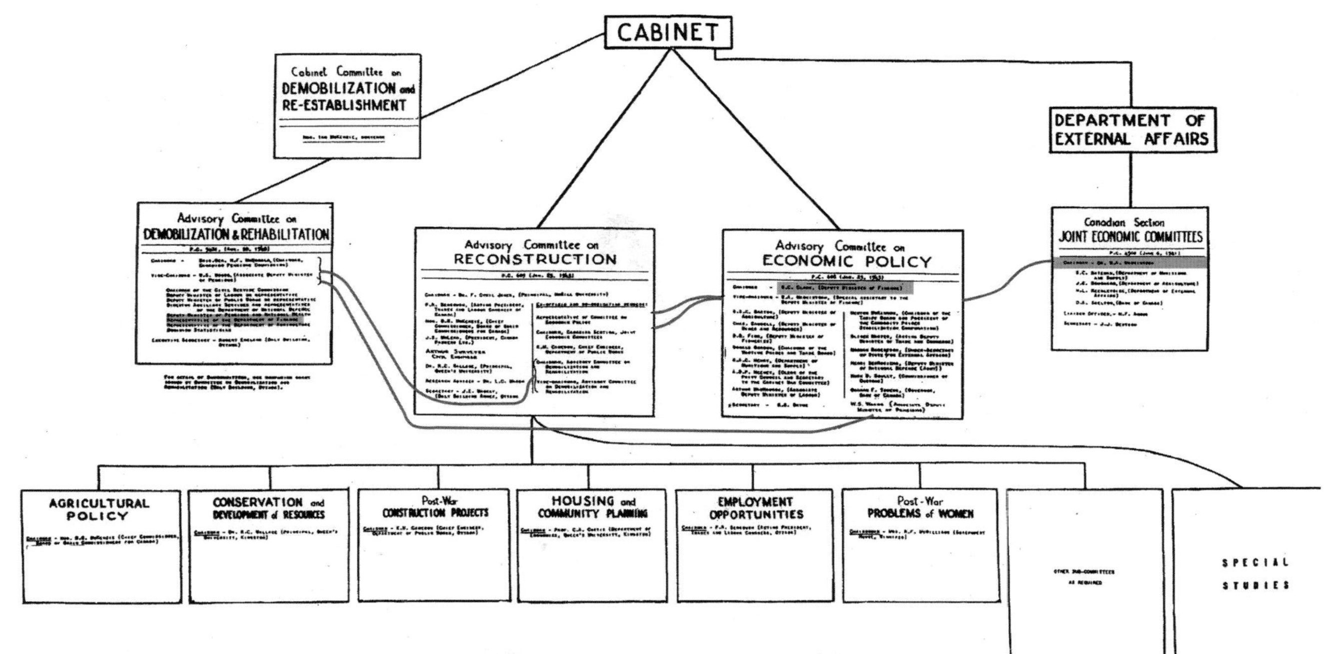

A chart outlining the complex array of government committees during wartime.

Prime Minister Louis St Laurent.
(C-000120, Library and Archives of Canada)

James Ilsley, minister of finance, 1940–1946.
(C-029366, Library and Archives Canada)

The War Committee of the Canadian Cabinet. (PA-187758, Library and Archives Canada)

would be any major developments until late summer or fall and felt that the United States had a clear appreciation of Britain's position. This being so, Clark was opposed to bilateral action and believed that it was 'wisest to gamble on multilateralism later on.'[106]

By the end of April 1945 preparations were underway for the inaugural meeting of the United Nations. But both Clark and Rasminsky were disillusioned and felt that much of the planning throughout the war was now being watered down in tone. 'No stone should be left unturned now,' Clark argued, 'in order to achieve a multilateral convention. I am far more interested in results than in institutions and if we miss the present opportunity for getting results I fear that we may be setting a problem of so refractory a nature that even the best of international machinery will prove futile for a generation or more.' There was some urgency for a multilateral agreement and this could occur only if the situation was sparked by an agreement between the United Kingdom and United States. In particular the Americans had to 'break the log jam.'[107] When the meeting was finished, Rasminsky had other, more far-reaching concerns. He was displeased because, unlike the League of Nations covenant, the San Francisco charter was based on 'the concept that the great powers are above the law and will remain so in perpetuity.' He was having difficulty 'pretending that this is an international organization where in reality it is an alliance among the great powers which operates in the presence of some smaller ones.' Regardless, it would have to be accepted as the only pretence for 'getting American participation in world affairs.'[108]

Preparations were also underway for a pivotal dominion-provincial conference to be arranged prior to an election call. The plans were being handled by two committees, one of Cabinet headed by St Laurent and the other of civil servants headed by Clark. But Clark's health was breaking down and his condition was becoming obvious to those around him. On 1 March Dexter commented, 'Cliff Clark appears to be shrivelling a bit. Getting to look all head and no body. I should think a darn sight more tired and frayed than anyone I've seen. Tiredness makes him seem untidy and unkempt. Expectorates copiously into the waste paper basket which, I must insist is uncivilized ... Desk littered. Odd small table and chairs about his office dust-coated. Just one centre of activity – the chair he sits in and the papers before him.'

Dexter noted that, despite being overburdened and now showing the strain, Clark was intent on using the conference to knock the provinces into line. 'Cliff Clark impresses you because he has guts,' Dexter observed. 'He may be fagged out but he will not yield an inch on points he thinks vital. To hell with the provinces. The government must fight the election on this issue. Put up the proposal at the general election and ask for a mandate. It would be a dirty fight but he thinks this is the only way our William can succeed. When I suggested that W.L.M.K. would no more do this than publicly assault the Cardinal, he simply reiterated his position. With him it is tax agreements or chaos.'[109] Aside from a general desire for increased federal powers, Clark's position was that immediate post-war expenditures were going to be exceedingly heavy, at least three or four times the pre-war levels. They would include debt charges, defence expenditures, war service gratuities, re-establishment credits, pensions and hospitalization, social security costs, employment measures, and other public projects.[110]

James Ilsley was also at the end of his rope. Dexter noted that the finance minister was 'in appalling physical condition.' He had difficulty discussing anything other than his health problems. 'Felt something like I used to with Dunning before he retired,' Dexter commented. Apparently Ilsely claimed that the doctors were describing his nervous trouble as 'compulsive thinking.' He longed to be free from the political pressures, indicating that he 'hated public life – hated it. And then he had reached the point where each morning he had found himself longing to be dead by night. As he shaved he would be thinking, 'I wish I would die today.' Ilsley was now convinced that the state of dominion–provincial relations was 'hopeless.'

Bill Mackintosh was also ready to get out of government. He was 'fed up' and had 'no temperament for the rough and bruising career of a civil servant. Prefers educating young men with open minds to trying to split open the solid craniums of cabinet ministers in order to get ideas in. Is convinced that there is no such thing as an open-minded minister. All hopeless.' When it came to dominion–provincial relations, Mackintosh claimed that the issue was not increased centralization and more powers for the federal government. He was opposed to any significant transfer of jurisdiction, but the situation could not revert back to prewar conditions and demanded a solution. 'It should be presented this way,' he noted, 'not centralization but rationalization of taxation.'[111] The provinces, however, were unlikely to view the situation as simple 'rationalization.'

An article on Clifford Clark appeared in *Maclean's Magazine* on 1 May 1945, to explain Clark's contribution to the nation. Gratton O'Leary began by pointing out that the deputy minister was not without his detractors. 'Money reformers' and 'frightened reactionaries' took a 'dark view' of Clark. But O'Leary, who had known Clark before he came to Ottawa, claimed that he was 'simply a university professor who put off a cap and gown to become a permanent civil servant, going on to do his job so well that he has become a legend. There are those who insist that next to Mackenzie King himself, "Cliff" Clark is the most powerful figure on the Ottawa landscape. Clark is a member of so many boards, committees and other agencies that there is a quip about him going to one committee meeting and running into himself coming from another.' O'Leary was aware that such influence for a civil servant was reason in itself for criticism: 'This adds up to power. It adds up to so much power there are those who fear that Clark's influence in Ottawa is altogether too great; that his authority is more than should be vested with any single non-elected official in a democratic State.' Political commentators had become 'a bit touchy these days' about the size and influence of the 'bureaucracy.' The civil service numbered 46,000 in 1939; it reached 116,000 in 1945.[112]

The article tackled the criticism that Clark was so influential that he, in essence, *was* the Department of Finance and that Ilsley had become his puppet. Ilsley was no mere mouthpiece for Clark, O'Leary argued, but it was true nonetheless that a great deal of what Ilsley brought to Parliament or Cabinet was 'the brain child of Clark.' The deputy minister was undoubtedly 'far more than an able civil servant faithfully executing orders and regulations which his political chiefs have made ministerial policies – clearly he is the author as well as the executor of many of those policies, inspiring and also directing them.' O'Leary was aware, however, that Clark was not comfortable with such acclaim. He was a 'Parliament man to the core' believing in democratic checks and balances, and he would 'hold vehemently that he is nothing more than a servant of Parliament and the Government, that all he represents, or should want to represent, is responsible bureaucracy under democratic control.'

When it came to Clark's political philosophy (often the subject of jibes against him), O'Leary argued that the deputy minister was not a classical economist nor a believer in the 'old laissez faire,' but equally, he was not 'completely a planner or believer in regimentation.' Nor was Clark a full convert to Keynesianism. He was 'no believer in sustained deficit financing.' No government could go on borrowing indefinitely: 'Deficits incur interest charges that must be met if a country is to maintain its credit – and that these inescapable interest payments added to other heavy expenditures under continued deficit financing would, in the course of time, bring crisis.'

When it came to Clark's personality, O'Leary noted that the deputy minister was 'the most lovable of Ottawa's top-flight officials.' He was not pompous and was incapable of pettiness. He was good natured, optimistic, easy to get along with, and on good terms with almost all members of the House. He had a tremendous appetite for work and rarely took vacations. When it came to leisure activities, Clark would occasionally go out for dinner, where 'he becomes a delightful companion,' and sometimes he would sit for a hand of bridge, 'which he plays badly,' but mostly his relaxation was at lunch hour in the Rideau Club, 'which he attends regularly and where he is extremely popular.' Clark belonged to the Royal Ottawa Golf Club but seldom played. Somehow, he found time to read: 'Mention a new book to him, a biography, or some work on economics, and you will promptly discover that he either knows about it or has read it or at least has read a review of it. He has an extraordinarily curious and versatile mind, his interests ranging over all sorts of subjects.' Because Clark was not a socialite like Graham Towers, O'Leary described him as 'more of a home man than a club man.' Margaret Clark, the article noted, 'for her part, takes an active part in war work, stealing time out to take reasonable care of a husband who has no timetable and whose comings and goings are as unpredictable as a deck of cards.'[113]

In the spring of 1945 the housing issue again emerged. The urgency of the crisis could no longer be denied, driven home by the pressure of returning veterans. Despite the signs of strain, Clark took a leading role in shaping policy. J.G. Godsoe, coordinator of controls, told Howe that he and Clark had reached agreement on the terms of reference and membership of an Interdepartmental Housing Co-ordination Committee, with Clark as chairman.[114] At the first meeting of the committee, Clark argued that Canada faced 'a grave national emergency,' arising out of the 'congestion and the housing needs of members of the Armed Forces.' Of the approximately twenty-two thousand veterans returning home every month, 20 per cent would likely 'be urgently in need of additional housing accommodation.' The morale of the returning veterans had already been shaken by 'the prospect of being without adequate housing on return,' and Clark believed that the rehabilitation programs had been jeopardized by the housing shortage.[115] There were severe problems, however, in increasing the supply of housing. One was a shortage of qualified labour, a shortage so severe that Clark suggested 'having members of the Armed Forces build their own homes, however radical this might appear to be.' Another problem was that housing construction did not receive top priority for the limited supplies available. As a result, subcommittees to study both problems were established at the first meeting of the Interdepartmental Housing Committee.[116]

Clark also recognized that measures he had consistently opposed in the past were now necessary. Wartime housing should be 'employed for a considerable extent during the next few months building houses for veterans,' he argued. This would 'eliminate at least some of the speculative profit now occurring to speculative builders.' Wartime housing also had the necessary priority for materials and the organization to make things happen.[117] But Clark still opposed the provision of subsidized rental housing. It would 'complicate the housing problem' by 'raising demands for other groups for similar assistance,' and placing 'further difficulties in the way of private building.' Clark would not oppose such construction, however, due to the 'urgency of getting rental housing built as quickly as possible for veterans' families.'[118] He unveiled his own plans for integrated housing: large-scale housing projects using private developers and government guarantees.[119]

But in late May Clark's health finally collapsed. One week after VE Day he became suddenly ill while at his beloved Fishing Club and he was rushed to hospital.[120] For the next three months, Room 552 of the Ottawa Civic Hospital was Clark's home. It was several days before he could take any nourishment. Towers wrote Keynes to inform him of the illness and to indicate that Clark would not be back for some time: 'To say that his absence leaves a gap is a masterpiece of understatement.'[121] Dexter was more resigned: 'Great concern over Cliff Clark who is in hospital with an infection of one kidney and the prostate gland. Being fed through the veins and his doctors regard the outcome as very doubtful. If he does recover he will be out for at least four months and maybe a year. By the way they spoke I think we should be prepared to do an obit[uary] piece.'[122] Mackintosh wrote, 'After much examining, exploring and operating, the final medical verdict seemed to be complete physical and mental exhaustion.'[123]

Clark was in the operating room twice, on 12 and 15 June; he was X-rayed three times and had two blood transfusions. Four days after the federal election that saw the Liberals again victorious, Mackenzie King noted in his diary, 'Clark, Deputy Minister of Finance, had an operation today. Fortunately it has been successful but I am afraid he will never be too strong. The Government and the country owe almost more to him than to any other man for the war effort, as he has had so much to do with many of its financial and economic aspects.'[124] The operation provided sufficient relief that Clark was able to sit up and read a bit.[125] According to Dexter, 'The emergency operation showed no cancer but an enlargement of a muscle in the bladder somewhere which was blocking the urinal channel.'[126] Ralston told Margaret that 'the break had to come.' The last five years would have been strenuous for anyone, but for Clark they were even more exacting because he 'put the last ounce of himself – both mind and body – into his work for Canada.'[127]

Like numerous other well-wishers, Bryce Stewart insisted Clark take it easy from now on. But Stewart was quite specific: 'Please make a firm resolution to take life more easily when you get back to your job. In your first session with your Minister you should dictate your terms. The Prime Minister, Mr Ilsley and his colleagues value you too highly not to accept any proposal you may submit. Canada cannot repay its debt to you, but the government can make life a bit easier for you. I fear that the cares of the world will press in and that it will not be done unless you insist. Self sacrifice is not all. As a method it is only half-way effective.'[128]

Ilsley was aware of Clark's value, particularly during the war: 'Of Dr Clark, I need only say that to him I owe a debt – and this nation owes a debt – so great and so varied that we must wait for history to recognize it when confidences can be revealed.'[129]

It was seven long months before Clark was able to resume work. In the end, 'the great resilience of his constitution won out and he was back at his desk to carry the load at the end of the war.'[130] By the time he was out of the hospital Clark had lost thirty pounds,[131] although by late August he had apparently regained much of it and was feeling well enough to attend one or two of the meetings of the dominion-provincial conference.[132] By mid-September, Clark was able to go fishing and he hauled in a forty-five-inch twenty-pound maskinonge, caught in the St Lawrence near Cornwall.[133] As late as November, however, his secretary, Ellen Purkiss, noted that his strength was returning only slowly.[134] He did attend the windup meeting of the National War Finance Committee at the Seigniory Club in December,[135] and in January he was able to return to the office.

The work of the department carried on in Clark's absence. In May the Canadians finally took up the British request to send a delegation to discuss post-war finances. 'The Canadians are arriving at the end of next week,' Keynes observed, 'though, unfortunately, without Clifford

Clark.'[136] Mackintosh was acting deputy minister of finance and headed the delegation, which included Towers and MacKinnon.[137]

Mitchell Sharp took over as acting chairman of the Interdepartmental Housing Committee. By 23 July the housing shortage reached a critical stage. Some 8,391 eviction notices had been filed in Canada's twelve largest cities and estimates were that 15,000 to 20,000 families faced eviction. Worse still, 60 per cent involved families of men in the Armed Forces, many still overseas. Emergency Shelter Co-ordinator Eric Gold warned that soldiers who had volunteered to fight against Japan indicated they would not serve without assurances that their families were properly and permanently housed. There were reports of landlords physically forcing people out in the middle of the night and of tenants' leagues forming pickets to prevent evictions. Gordon convened a meeting of the Wartime Prices and Trade Board to approve an order banning all evictions.[138] Howe decided that the target of wartime housing should be 10,000 units rather than 3,000, and that this goal should be pursued immediately.[139] On 24 July, at a meeting in the finance minister's office, Ilsley, Mackintosh, Donald Gordon, W.M. Anderson (national housing administrator), Sharp, and Mansur agreed that the Central Mortgage Bank should be revived, under the title Central Mortgage and Housing Corporation (CMHC). Its purpose, as Mansur described it to Mackintosh, would be 'the development of private investment in real property and marshalling our rather meagre facilities to that end.' The primary duty of the new Crown corporation would be 'one of finding ways and means for private enterprise to look after needs in the economic field.' Mansur prepared a draft bill, based on the CMB legislation Clark had drafted in 1939. The new CMHC would have the power to discount mortgages. Its capital assets were fixed at $25 million, which would be used for the government's share of NHA joint loans. It would be able to loan directly in areas poorly served by lending institutions and it would help establish housing corporations.[140] According to Sharp, Mansur had persuaded Clark, prior to his falling ill, that new comprehensive housing legislation was desirable and that responsibility should be assigned to a new government corporation. Clark had already completed the first draft of the legislation.[141]

Emergency shelter regulations that applied in major cities as of December 1944 were extended by September 1945 to the whole country. 'In effect all Canada became a congested area.' By 3 October the Interdepartmental Housing Committee concluded that 'genuinely low rental housing cannot be constructed at the present time without subsidy of some kind.' Only one in five Canadians had the annual income of $2,150 or more required to buy a five-room NHA standard house.[142] Veterans' Land Act Administrator G. Murchison told the committee on 17 October that NHA loans were not attractive to veterans. In fact some were taking advantage of the act, intended to help veterans establish themselves as farmers, to get housing because the terms were more favourable. The impact on urban sprawl, transportation, education, and taxes would be serious, he warned. It was essential that the government provide subsidies for low-rental housing because such housing would not be built by corporate finance. Sharp referred the issue of subsidies to a subcommittee for study, which he also chaired, but the proposal was rejected.[143]

The Interdepartmental Housing Committee recommended that all federal housing authority be centralized. To convince a reluctant Cabinet, Mansur, Sharp, Godsoe, and Gordon wrote a jointly signed memorandum to Ilsley and Howe on 22 November, urging this course of action. The memo suggested that housing responsibility be placed under an existing department, such as finance or reconstruction. Heeney suggested to King that a separate department of housing, with a minister who was not overburdened, would be preferable in the face of rising criticism. But this did not happen. Instead, all authority was concentrated in CMHC, including Wartime Housing and Emergency Shelter (which had been under the Wartime Prices and Trade Board). CMHC was placed under the minister of reconstruction, C.D. Howe. Mansur, Clark, Mackintosh, and Gold took four of the five seats on CMHC's executive board.[144] The act to create CMHC received royal assent in mid-December and the corporation came into existence on 1 January 1946. David Mansur became the first president and Sharp attended board meetings as Clark's representative.[145]

The creation of CMHC effectively took the control of housing policy out of Clark's hands. From this point onward Clark maintained an avid interest in the issue but kept his distance. When E. Litchfield, a general contractor from Vancouver, asked for advice in 1947, Clark's response was revealing. 'It carries me a long way back,' he wrote, 'to the days when I really had some responsibility for housing ... A lot of water has passed under the bridge since that time and in particular in the field of housing, for which the Central Mortgage and Housing Corporation is now responsible.'[146]

But the main event that Clark was forced to miss because of his illness was the 1945 Dominion-Provincial Conference on Reconstruction, originally slated for the previous year. The conference was scheduled for 6 August. It was organized to deal with the significant shifts that had occurred in Canadian federalism during the war, including the *Report of the Rowell-Sirois Commission.* In essence, however, it was designed to frame the federal–provincial relationship for the post-war era.[147] According to Dexter, Ilsley was very worried: 'He doesn't believe the dominion can strong arm the provinces. Ottawa must be patient and succeed by persuasion, aiming arguments over the head of the provincial governments at the electors of the provinces.'[148]

One of the main issues to be discussed was a comprehensive health insurance scheme. The federal government favoured provincial grants in order to place governments in a financial position to develop and administer a program worked out through progressive stages.[149] Quoting an estimate of $256 million, the dominion proposed to meet about three-fifths of the cost by grants-in-aid to the provinces. Under the heading of health grants, the dominion proposed to offer nearly $14 million, broadly on a per capita basis among the nine provinces. Loans were offered to those provinces that entered health insurance agreements.

Other proposals to be discussed at the conference included coverage of the employable unemployed who were not covered by UI, an extension of the Unemployment Insurance Scheme, an extension of Employment Services, and occupational guidance and rehabilitation on a joint dominion-provincial basis. Defects in the old age pension program were also to be corrected.[150] A two-level pension plan was proposed, even though the finance department preferred a contributory plan because it avoided the necessity of a constitutional amendment. The proposal was for a $30 per month pension for everyone over the age of seventy, which would cost about $200 million and be paid by the federal government. Extending that program to those aged sixty-five to sixty-nine would increase costs by about two-thirds, while providing a means-tested pension to those in that age group would cost $34–$40 million, with the costs split between the federal and provincial governments.[151] But the social programs were linked, as Clark wanted, to the tax and fiscal arrangements being worked out with the provinces. Without the latter, the programs would not proceed. The federal proposals also included a public investment policy designed to mitigate or offset deficiencies in export income or private investment expenditures. Provinces and municipalities would be encouraged to harmonize their public investments by having Ottawa lend technical assistance, provide factual information and cash grants covering part of the cost of planning approved projects, and pay 20 per cent of the public work costs, provided they were executed within a period designated by the federal government.

In return, federal officials proposed that the provinces should by agreement forgo the imposition of personal income taxes, corporation taxes, and succession duties, leaving to Ottawa the full and exclusive access to these revenue sources. Although the provinces would benefit from the proposals, the federal government realized they would not surrender the taxation fields unless assured of adequate alternative revenue sources. Ottawa proposed to pay each provincial government twelve dollars per capita annually, increased or decreased in proportion to the value of gross national production per capita as compared with that of 1941. This proposed annual payment would, however, be subject to an irreducible minimum equal to twelve dollars per capita of the 1941 population. The federal government wanted to avoid seeking an amendment to the BNA Act in order to introduce these tax changes but provincial governments would have the right to withdraw from the arrangement at any time. However, it was suggested that an agreement could be concluded under which the provincial governments would commit themselves not to withdraw before an initial trial period of three years.

At the time the provinces were deriving a total of $125 million from grants and subsidies from Ottawa as well as from their share of succession duties being collected by both levels of government during the war. The new proposals offered the provinces an irreducible minimum of $138 million based on the 1941 income. As a result of the rise in the national income, in 1944 the payments would have aggregated $206.8 million. The total would reach $172.3 million in 1948 if the gross national production had fallen by approximately $2 billion from the wartime peak. If the gross national production had risen to $12.5 billion, the total payments to the nine provinces would be $215.4 million. The federal government was prepared to give a little when it came to its proposed exclusive tax jurisdiction in the income and estates field. As in the case with the wartime tax agreements, the provinces could tax profits on mining and logging operations, yet retain such taxes as the equivalent of royalties, Crown dues, and similar provincial charges. These charges were seen to be associated with provincial control over natural resources.[152]

The federal government's program became known as the 'Green

Book' proposals, described by historians as containing a 'comprehensive and audacious' plan to 'restructure Canadian federalism to give the central government the financial power and the legislative authority to guide the economy through the perils of the depression, while ensuring individual Canadians against disease, old age, and extended unemployment.' The centralist bent of Canadian historians, however, is evident in the description of the provincial premiers: 'The sight that greeted King could scarcely have been encouraging. Around him sat the sleeping dogs of provincial power, yawning and stretching after five years in mothballs.' There is little doubt that Ottawa's proposals were sweeping. But there is also little doubt that they contained a strong-armed attempt to increase the powers of the federal government at provincial expense. The premiers were surprised by their sudden and far-reaching nature and it quickly became apparent that an agreement was unlikely if not impossible. Premier Drew of Ontario secured a delay in the proceedings and then departed to Toronto to study the proposals further. Duplessis of Quebec soon followed suit. The conference was aborted.[153]

With the conference a failure, the delayed budget was presented on 12 October 1945. It also had to be undertaken in Clark's absence. Ilsley introduced the document by pointing out that it was the first to follow the end of the war. As such, it reviewed the entire scope of wartime financing. The war had witnessed a pay-as-you-go approach that meant rapid increases in taxation and savings. The finance minister went over the various tax and saving initiatives introduced and detailed the wartime principles of keeping interest rates as low as possible while rejecting inflationary finance. Ilsley noted, however, that because the budget was coming down so late in the year, it was still considered 'a war budget' because war and demobilization expenditures were continuing at high levels. In addition, substantial financial requirements outside the budget were necessary because of the need to extend credits to Allied countries for reconstruction. Still, despite the large requirements, the government indicated an intention to move toward a general reduction in taxes.[154] The personal income tax was reduced by 4 per cent for 1945 and 16 per cent for 1946. The excess profits tax was retained but with reduced rates, while the war exchange tax, which had applied at 10 per cent to all imports except those under British Preferential rates (or their equivalent), was repealed. One of the most lasting changes dealt with sales tax exemptions for apparatus and machinery used in manufacturing and production. Ilsley estimated that the tax reductions would reduce anticipated revenue totals by $100 million.[155] Clark missed the budget preparations and delivery but he was now well enough to resume work. Whether he had learned his lesson from the breakdown of his health was less certain.

10

The Post-war World and New Beginnings, 1946

> Dr Clark is really the one who is responsible for members of govt not doing what I think the judgment of most of them inclines them to do. Ilsley feels helpless without him. Does not favour I know some of his views, but yields to them as he cannot himself handle things without him.
>
> – King Diaries, 27 April 1946

Early in 1946 Clifford Clark returned to work. In many ways it was a time of new beginnings. The workload and stresses of wartime had very nearly killed him. Those nearest now warned Clark that he would have to learn his lesson, slow down, and take a new, more relaxed approach to work. By the time he returned, Clark's secretary had taken advantage of his absence to 'revolutionize' his office. This process included a good cleaning, new furniture, and even new carpet, a common topic of discussion with first-time visitors to the East Wing.[1] The war was over and Clark was returning to a less hectic work environment. Or so he hoped.

But the workload and atmosphere in the finance department were anything but light. Even though the war was over, financial anxiety continued to grip the nation and there was pressure on government officials to prevent a return to the post-war recession that had taken hold after the First World War. The Canadian government had done a remarkable job at handling the war effort. National unity was intact, despite another divisive conscription crisis, but most impressive was the state of the economy. Canada had doubled its gross national product and increased its budget ten-fold in five years.[2] But there was no room for complacency. Indeed, financial officials, including Clark, were cautious and even at times pessimistic about the post-war prognosis. 'A forecaster at the close of the war would have had some warrant for taking a gloomy view of Canada's prospects during the succeeding half-dozen years,' Clark observed:

> The war had cost our nation of just over 12 million people not far from 20 billion dollars, and while Canada's war finance policy had been as intelligent and as rigorous as that of any belligerent, nevertheless the net national debt had increased from 3.2 billion dollars prewar to 13.4 billions on March 31, 1946. Our industry had been vastly expanded for war purposes and we faced a task of suddenly integrating into a peacetime economy a very large volume of war plant capacity as well as nearly 1½ million war workers and men and women demobilized from the armed services. Finally, as a country in which export trade normally accounts for 20 to 25 per cent of total production, we were forced to look with concern on the vast destruction and dislocation which war had brought to a large part of the world and particularly on the impaired strength of our traditional major customers in Western Europe and the breakdown of the multilateral system of trade and payments.[3]

The workload was still heavy, but at least Clark was surrounded by a talented, energetic, and efficient staff within the Department of Finance, a group he had recruited himself and had proven they could carry on if necessary without their chief.[4]

Clark returned to his old department but there was talk of a new boss. J.L. Ilsley, the talented but temperamental minister of finance, was spent. On 17 January he asked to see the prime minister at Laurier House. Ilsley admitted to Mackenzie King that he was finding it difficult to do any work at all: 'He could not be enthusiastic about anything. It was all a heavy burden ... had come to feel the problems could not be solved ... he had found himself quite unable to work with any zest at all. He did not want to embarrass me ... he felt that, sooner or later, he would have to give up. He went on to say that he felt he perhaps owed it to me and to the govt to stick on, through this session, no matter how hard it was going to be.'

The workload in the finance department, Ilsley explained, was quite simply too heavy. King suggested shifting some of the burden onto other departments, such as the new housing ministry. Ilsley responded positively, suggesting that Howe, who was now minister of reconstruction and supply, might also pick up some of the slack. Ilsley then reviewed the issues and concerns that lay ahead in the near future, including plans for another dominion-provincial conference, preparations for the budget, financial negotiations with the British, and a new series of trade agreements. 'He spoke about Dr Clark being in good condition now, having been away for nine months,' King recorded. 'Said that at times Clark had gotten where he could not think at all. Was quite incapable of constructive thought which I am not surprised at. Says he is a bit highly strung yet which, of course, Ilsley himself is to the degree of almost no other Minister.' The discussion turned to Ilsley moving to another portfolio, perhaps justice, and according to the prime minister, 'his face lighted up at once.' The two men agreed to discuss possible changes in the near future.[5]

Negotiations between Ottawa and the provinces continued throughout January in preparation for a resumption of the aborted conference. Throughout his long career Mackenzie King waffled on the issue of increased federal centralization. While he defended the distribution of powers as laid out by the Fathers of Confederation in the BNA Act, the Depression and Second World War demonstrated that some form of change was necessary. On the eve of the 1945 conference the prime minister seemed to support the centralization of taxation and social spending power to Ottawa: 'The Conference may well prove, with the material we have prepared, to be the instrument of completely changing the emphasis of administration and legislation on social problems from the Provinces to the Dominion.'[6] But King did not advocate moving as far in a centralist direction as the 'Ottawa Men.'

On 23 January the Cabinet reviewed the situation and it became evident that King was unsure how to proceed: 'The committee of experts, Clark, Mackintosh, Skelton, etc., have found it necessary to make an increase in the amount the Dominion should be prepared to pay – if agreement is to be reached with the provinces to increase from 12 to 15 million the amounts to be given the provinces in lieu of their surrendering some sources of taxation.' King voiced his concern 'at the method of federal proposed finances which made one Government the taxing power and the other Governments the spending power.' It was a 'double concern' because taxation was obviously unpopular: 'From the point of view of economic and public finance I do not see how the system can be defended.' King also criticized Ilsley: 'He does not decide these matters on his own judgment. Almost invariably he takes the advice given by officials, then holds tenaciously to it at all costs.'[7]

By the end of January the prime minister saw hope for a resolution of differences between Ontario and the federal government. After meetings with Premier Drew, it seemed Ontario was prepared to let Ottawa take over personal and corporation taxes while holding back on succession duties, which King thought might be left with the provinces. Clark was adamant, however, that the federal government should not back down from its 'Green Book' position. King characterized the argument as 'a line shaped out pretty much by Clark, after conference with Towers. I personally felt they were going rather too far in the way of sticking all but irrevocably to the position we had taken.'[8] A Cabinet meeting was held on 31 January to discuss strategy, with Clark and Sandy Skelton present. King now agreed with Ontario's position that there were certain sources of revenue to which the provinces should have exclusive rights, such as gasoline and electricity, with appropriate reductions in federal subsidies to the provinces. Clark objected. As a result, he was signalled out for criticism by the prime minister: 'I could see that Clark is in very poor shape, he is highly strung. He realizes the terrible extent of obligations which the Dominion has undertaken to assume and realizes that it is going to be almost impossible to meet these obligations ... It just excites him tremendously. I felt we had to be very careful with him. He is liable to break down completely at any moment. Ilsley is not far from the same position.'

The prime minister did not press the point. In meetings with the premiers, it became clear that Drew and Duplessis were not prepared to surrender taxation powers, regardless. King was again critical of the position taken by his own officials. He believed that the mandarins were so focused on their own agenda that they had lost sight of the political ramifications: 'The Finance Department, behind which is the Bank of Canada, have completely changed the generally accepted procedure which has been to keep as largely as possible the spending authority responsible for the tax-raising. I think their effort is in the direction of centralization of financial control. That may be desirable from the point of view of more effective administration, etc., from Ottawa's end, but politically it will not be possible I believe for a long time to come.'[9]

The decision was made to resume the dominion-provincial conference on 25 April. To avoid having positions harden in the meantime, an agreement was reached in Cabinet to keep the federal proposals secret until then. Clark, Towers, and Skelton wanted them made public, presumably to put pressure on the premiers. In King's opinion, Clark and the finance department had backed themselves into a corner. Their financial strategy had gone 'too far, I think, in the way of permitting expenditures to ever hope to recover the ground needed to balance budgets.'[10]

Once the date of the conference was set, Clark was able to turn his attention temporarily to two other issues. One was the bureaucracy's staffing problems. Talent attracted to Ottawa during the war was now dispersing at the same time as the role of the federal government expanded, and with it, an increased and now expected need for technical, professional, and administrative personnel. An interdepartmental committee reported to the Cabinet in late 1945 that the salary levels for these categories were inadequate if present and future needs were to be fulfilled. There were delays in hiring as well as a need for improved arrangements for promotion and transfer among departments. Clark and Robertson recommended that the top levels of administration be examined as a first step toward increasing general efficiency. To this end, Clark approached Walter Gordon and asked him to head a royal commission inquiry into administrative classifications. Clark was clear on what he wanted done but it was considered advisable that an external body be charged with making the recommendations.[11] The Civil Service Commission (already in existence and whose statutory mandate included just such work) was considered too weak and ineffective to take on the task. The Treasury Board, the other body with significant responsibility for personnel but also the organization responsible for keeping a tight rein on government spending, was also viewed as insufficient.[12] The Cabinet approved creation of a royal commission and its membership on 15 February.

Walter Gordon learned of his appointment from Clark. The deputy minister sweetened the deal by telling Gordon that it was the prime minister who wanted him to serve as chairman. 'As Mr King barely knew of my existence,' Gordon later wrote, 'I took this last remark with several grains of salt.' Gordon tried to avoid the appointment by alluding to the amount of work his law firm had undertaken after the war. He declined the offer, but Clark was insistent. In the end Gordon agreed to accept the position on the understanding that it would not be full time and that the work would be completed in a few months. The report was hastily completed by the end of June.[13]

The other problem Clark tackled was a loan to help Britain rebuild after the war and keep its markets open to Canadian goods. Clark believed that Canada had to loosen the purse strings. In providing for Britain, Canada was also attempting to maintain a counterweight to the United States.[14] But significant political changes had taken place in both nations. In July the British Labour Party assumed office with its first parliamentary majority, and after Roosevelt's death in April, Harry S Truman became president of the United States. Britain's economic situation had become critical when American support through Lend-Lease and Mutual Aid was cut off with the end of the Pacific War on 2 September 1945. That autumn the British held acrimonious negotiations with the Americans for aid to cope with reconstruction and a massive deficit in its international balance of payment position. Finally, on 16 December, it was announced that the United States had agreed to a loan of $3.75 billion – far less than Canadian officials had hoped would be provided – drawable to the end of 1951, with a schedule of repayments over fifty years at an interest rate of 2 per cent.

Despite the complexities and high-pressure stakes involved, Clark thoroughly enjoyed dealing with international trade. It was this issue that he first worked on with the finance department back in 1932 during the Imperial Conference. The topic was demanding, but it offered Clark a 'complex, intractable mixture of economics with political difficulties, of finance with history, of welfare with industrial efficiency, of defence with economic development.' In 1946 it was engaging the attention of the best economists around the world. In Clark's opinion, it was also the issue that would shape Canada's future because it represented the nation's status on the world stage vis-à-vis Britain and the United States. According to Bryce, Clark 'read omnivorously on it and discussed it at the drop of a hat.'

Clark believed that the solution to the commercial problems of Britain and other nations of the sterling area lay 'in the direction of expansion of trade, not its restriction; in competition, not discrimination; in the use of the price system, not controls; in reducing the overload on the economy, not in aid.' He realized that the prescription he advocated would be viewed as 'distasteful and risky, easier to propose than accept,' but he was convinced that it was 'practical and very much in Britain's own interest – not merely in the distant future but within a few years.' At the same time, the solution of the sterling area problem was very much in Canada's interest: 'Hence he felt it his duty to urge upon his British friends, through his many contacts with them, some solution along these lines.'[15]

On 8 February Clark spent most of the morning with King, Ilsley, St Laurent, Howe, Mackenzie, Towers, and Robertson discussing the British situation. St Laurent noted that the British wanted to keep about $2 million in Canadian securities (in the Canadian Pacific Railway and others) while continuing to receive interest of some $50 million, money that had to come from the Canadian budget. St Laurent was opposed if the costs were not to be offset against what the British already owed or against the new loan presently being sought. King agreed. He was worried that 'we are mortgaging Canada's future too much. On top of all else are these enormous loans to China and other countries, many of which I do not believe will ever be repaid.'[16] According to Dexter, the difficulties in negotiating the loan were due to St Laurent's 'Quebec anti-British sentiment' and King's support for that position.[17] The prime minister noted that 'all our officials – Clark, Towers, Mackintosh, Robertson, etc. – seemed to be in entire agreement with the British and to feel that the argument St Laurent was putting forward would not be carried out if an agreement was reached.'[18]

Negotiations with the British commenced on 11 February.[19] They were at times prickly, with both sides emphasizing the difficulties they would have getting a deal passed through their respective parliaments. The British suggested that Canada's good name would be tarnished if there was no loan or a loan on terms that were too stringent. Despite King's misgivings about another loan, he believed there were serious dangers in the present condition of Britain and Europe, especially with the growing power of the Soviet Union. He feared that a third world war threatened if Europe could not be stabilized: 'I felt that we should go ahead and work towards some agreement.'[20]

Clark met with Sir Wilfrid Eady, the chief British negotiator, on 14 February. Clark explained that as a result of the first three days of meetings between the two groups, the Canadians were not likely to press the suggestions made by St Laurent but they would find it impossible to accept the proposals put forward by the British: 'I said, therefore, that the view seemed to be that it would be desirable for himself and myself to have a frank talk to see if we could narrow the area of disagreement.' Clark offered two possibilities to Eady. The first involved wiping out the old debt as a war debt with the repatriation of securities to provide Britain's cash needs; the second involved a credit for Britain's new cash requirements on the same terms as the U.S.–U.K. loan, a negative pledge of Britain's securities against the debt, and the elimination of interest on the old debt, as long as the proceeds of sales and redemptions of British securities amounted to $100 million a year. Eady responded that neither of these proposals would be acceptable to his government. He objected to any repatriation of securities, saying 'that it would be very difficult to explain to their members of Parliament why Canada should strip them of capital assets to enable them to buy food to feed their people.' Eady also expressed the desire 'in the strongest possible terms' to have the new credit bear no interest. Britain was possibly prepared to consider an annual payment of about $40 million, of which $25 million would be for amortization and the remaining $15 million might be used as interest on the old loan. He indicated a willingness to drop the British hope that Canada would be prepared to wipe out the debt based on the air training plan. 'I expressed great surprise,' Clark noted, 'pointing out that the two sides were much further apart than even I had realized, that it would, I feared, be impossible for our side to justify no interest on the new credit or a failure to do anything at all with the securities.'[21] When King learned of the British response, he claimed to feel 'deep indignation' at Eady's proposals as well as his indication that the British did not 'wish to be haunted with obligations.' The prime minister told Clark, Ilsley, Gardiner, and Abbott, that the British 'must take us for a lot of infants and children to present a document of that kind ... we received a document which implied that we were gullible and, as I saw it, not in the nature of negotiation, but a demand for something for nothing and the equivalent of and going the length of even stating that if this were not done we would be responsible for failure in the case of the U.S. loan ... I did not use the expression but it kept coming into my mind of there being a threat of blackmail in the whole attitude.'[22]

During these talks the Canadian public learned what the RCMP and a few members of the government had known for six months – since the defection of Igor Gouzenko on 5 September – that a Soviet spy ring was operating in Canada. 'Norman Robertson, Clark and Towers came to dinner,' Eady informed Keynes, '... and Norman was quite grave on the consequences of finding that public servants could have split loyalty to their country and to C[ommunist]. P[arty].'[23] The Cold War had come to Canada.

After a meeting on 22 February, Mackenzie King again noted the difficulty in selling another British loan to the Canadian public: 'I feel that Clark and all his group and all the Finance Department and the

Bank people, the big trade interests and so forth have only one point of view and really are a world of finance – feeling a greater common interest in finance than they do any interest in common with the political world.'[24] He noted, however, that Towers was opposed to accepting a deal without interest on the loan. For Clark and Towers, part of the problem lay in the popular assumption that Canada had been 'easy' with Britain during the war. Canada provided substantial amounts of supplies via the billion-dollar gift and Mutual Aid, but these actions were taken 'for the defense of Canada rather than as a contribution to the United Kingdom.' Indeed, as a result of these policies as well as others including the development of the BCATP, 'Canada has enriched herself at the expense of the United Kingdom to the extent of approximately two billions during the war.' Over and above these arrangements, Canada had received $500 million in gold or its equivalent, as well as substantial amounts of U.S. dollars through sales of securities, payment for imports in sterling, etc.: 'In one way or another, our special war-time arrangements with the United Kingdom have probably resulted in our US dollar position being more than $600 million better than it would have otherwise have been.' To Clark and Towers, 'by and large, Canada has looked after her own interests very well.' In contrast, the British were facing a possible position of being down some $24 billion. This was an 'impossible situation' because, if left unchecked, all efforts toward the establishment of a free-trading multilateral world would fail, and the impact on Canada would be disastrous. The financial tribunes argued that Canada's response to the British dilemma would have a direct impact on any financial arrangements made with other nations, particularly in Western Europe. The decision to be reached for Towers was indeed 'a political one': 'Again speaking to Mr King, I referred to our political relationships with the United Kingdom over a long period of years. I suggested that in times past there were good reasons, political and otherwise, for an attitude which stressed Canadian independence and unwillingness to be drawn into anything which could possibly be interpreted as assistance to a strong, rich and often complacent United Kingdom. I believed that political thinking of this type was now outmoded. The U.K. was relatively weak; and Russia had grown to be a great power. Our interest lay in strengthening the U.K. and Western Europe within the limits of our power to do so.'[25]

The Cabinet discussed the British loan for over three hours on 25 February. Ilsley had been working with Clark and St Laurent over the

Sunday to come up with an agreement involving no interest payments 'but which would bring more in the way of money into our treasury over some of the years.' King believed the proposal was 'altogether too involved' and argued that 'anything which was next to impossible of explanation would do more harm than good.' Clark, Ilsley, and St Laurent agreed that the British would not accept a 2 per cent loan, with Canada holding them to their war loan with interest contracted in 1942 (interest-free up to five years and to payment of $425 million on remaining indebtedness for air training). If this was the Canadian position, negotiations would break down. Clark argued that Canada was attempting to drive a harder bargain than the United States had done with its loan 'inasmuch as the U.S. had written off an amount relatively equivalent to ours on account of certain war charges which the U.S. had against the British. We had nothing corresponding to that.' King feared that such a hard position might lead the Americans to reconsider their agreement and it would 'certainly lead to the Government being criticized in our own press – so largely British controlled.' One of the prime minister's major concerns was that 'whatever was done, it was desirable that it was made very simple.' He suggested that a loan be offered to the British at 1 per cent interest, with the money being used to purchase Canadian products over the next few years. The arrangement would be reviewed in five years. Clark and Ilsley still believed that such an offer to Britain seemed 'tougher' than the American loan.

This decision met with the general approval of Cabinet until St Laurent put up resistance on the basis that while Britain was borrowing money from Canada at 1 per cent, 'it would cost us 3% to raise it from our own people.' King suggested increasing the interest to 2 per cent, with Britain having to repay its 1942 loan of $500 million through securities but being forgiven for the amount owing on air training. It was a war expenditure and 'similar in its nature to what the Americans had themselves foregone.' King did not believe the British would ever pay this particular debt, regardless. St Laurent agreed with this approach, as did other members of the Cabinet. Clark wanted a loan without interest, but he was opposed by the majority, who felt it would be 'difficult politically.' According to King, 'Clark and Ilsley both thought the British would now accept these terms though they would not have done so a night or two ago. They had come to feel pretty much concerned lest they could not get any loan at all from Canada. While it was not what they wished, or what they had expected, they wanted the loan free of interest. They both believed they would accept it now.' Although he was exhausted after the afternoon's long session, King was confident that the best strategy had been formulated. He felt more confident because, despite Clark's opposition, the deputy minister seemed comfortable with the path being followed.[26] Clark met with Eady on March 5 to explain the Cabinet's decision and work out the details.[27]

The loan agreement between Canada and the United Kingdom was signed on 6 March. The Canadian loan of $1.25 billion paralleled the American in duration, interest rate, and terms of repayment. In addition, the Canadian government agreed to cancel the $425 million balance due from Britain for its share of the costs of the air training plan and to accept a lump sum of $150 million in gold in lieu of collecting the outstanding indebtedness for essential purchases made by Britain from the termination of Mutual Aid to the end of February 1946. Under the agreement, an earlier interest-free loan of $700 million, which had been reduced by some $161 million through the sale of Canadian securities in London, was to continue free of interest until payments of interest and principal on the new loan commenced. The loan was extended again in 1951 and 1953, on an interest-free basis, and paid off in full in 1958, largely through earnings of liquidation of Canadian securities owned by British residents. According to Plumptre, the amount of the loan was more generous than the American loan, but the terms were the same. The conditions were severe, given Britain's condition, but 'once the terms of the U.S. loan were known, it was not practicable for the Canadian government to place before Parliament a proposal in which Canada was, in effect, underwriting Britain's capacity to meet the more demanding terms exacted by the Americans.'[28]

Looking back on the negotiations, Graham Towers claimed that the loan was too generous. In a rare instance of disagreement between the two officials, Towers clearly resented Clark's role. The governor of the Bank of Canada felt his opinion had been solicited but then ignored by the finance department: 'Clifford very often asked me to join the party, so to speak, if he thought that our views were alike and I could be of some help; but there were other occasions, particularly the negotiations with the U.K. on the post-war loan, where I think he felt that I would take a very dark view; so I never got in on them at all. I could have if I had persisted, but wrongly or rightly I didn't want to insist. I think now wrongly because I think the British got away with too much, much too much. In fact some of them told me so afterwards themselves.' Towers claimed not to understand 'why Clark was feeling so generous at that time.' He noted that both King and Ilsley 'relied very heavily on Clark.'[29]

In early March 1946 Clark travelled with Ilsley to Savannah, Georgia, for the inaugural meetings of the International Monetary Fund and the International Bank for Reconstruction and Development.[30] Upon returning, Ilsley told King that the American Secretary of the Treasury Fred Vinson had asked him to become manager of the IMF.[31] Ilsley indicated that he had spoken to no one except Clark about the offer and admitted that he was not sure he had the knowledge to handle the position. When the prime minister learned of the offer, he was opposed on the basis that Ilsely was 'too high strung' and would not have men like Clark at his side. On 10 April American President Harry S Truman phoned King and requested either Ilsley or Towers as IMF manager. King met with Ilsley and warned him of the pressures he would be under, not to mention the impact on his health. Ilsley agreed and that night King phoned the White House to say neither Ilsley nor Towers was available.[32]

By spring the dominion-provincial conference was back on the agenda. Ilsley saw 'no hope' of reaching an agreement on financial matters with the provinces and had come to the conclusion that the federal government was being too generous. The prime minister was not impressed: 'He was like a man in a fog; did not know just where he was at all.'[33] On 23 April the Cabinet met in preparation for the conference. Ilsley claimed that budgets over the next few years would reach $2 billion and he did not see how they could be balanced while reducing taxation and increasing spending on social services. Doubt was expressed in Cabinet about whether a settlement was even possible at the forthcoming conference. Prime Minister King claimed that a 'great mistake has been made by taking vast sums from the federal treasury and giving them to provinces by way of subsidies.'[34] He felt 'pushed into this new method of financing,' mainly by Keynes but also by Clark: 'I personally doubt very much if a serious situation does not come within a very few years. It may be that a period of prosperity will carry the situation for a couple of years, but a high level of employment, adequate to our needs, to prevent a reduction of taxation, is not something that I believe any country can keep up.'[35]

The next day the Cabinet spent another five hours working through the dominion-provincial proposals with both Clark and Alex Skelton present. There was considerable concern about high taxes on corporations and also the unfair situation in which Ontario Hydro was not taxed, while the equivalent but privately owned power company in Quebec was taxed. Clark suggested that where the federal and provincial governments were both taxing, the sums could be lumped together and split in half, with the provinces credited with their share. After the meeting Ilsley again confessed to King that his health could not hold out. 'He would wake at 4 o'clock in the morning,' King recorded, 'and would be going over what could be done, his budget, also what would take place at the Conference – too many things coming together. He wanted to get out of the Finance Department altogether. He spoke of the possibility of Clark taking this on.' Ilsley concluded that he would have to leave the government by August, if he could last that long.[36]

The Dominion-Provincial Conference on Reconstruction recommenced on 25 April. Most of the day was taken up explaining the federal proposals to secure the full control of personal income, corporation, and succession duties for three years. The federal payments to the provinces in compensation would amount to a minimum of $181.4 million and would rise to $198.2 million, based on 1947 estimates, compared to $124.5 million under the wartime agreements.[37] Ilsley was convinced the federal government was offering too much. According to King, he was not being constructive and seemed to want the conference to fail: 'I could see he is almost ready for the breaking point. Indeed, I feel terribly sorry for him. He is just like a lamb being slaughtered.'[38] King also had serious concerns over the federal proposals and he blamed the finance department: 'I have never agreed with what was done by a group of the Cabinet working in close association with the Finance Department at a time when I was either away or not in a position to give much attention to the Dominion's financial proposals ... I think the really sound position is along lines that would reserve definite fields of taxation to the Dominion and Provincial Governments respectively, avoiding double taxation and causing the Government which has to do with the spending of public money to be obliged for the raising of the necessary revenues.'[39]

The conference adjourned for the weekend, but the Cabinet met on the Saturday. In the face of what he perceived as increasing centralization coming from within his own government and civil service, Mackenzie King reverted to traditional Liberal ground in support of provincial autonomy. He insisted that the provinces had to have exclusive fields of taxation and that the federal government was moving too fast on social legislation, particularly in giving grants to the provinces for health measures. Howe suggested the amusement tax be left with the provinces if they surrendered the health grants. The gasoline tax could be left with the provinces in exchange for something else, perhaps the provinces taking over old age pensions under seventy years of age. But it was apparent that King viewed Clark as largely responsible for the push toward centralization: 'Dr Clark is really the one who is responsible for members of govt not doing what I think the judgment of most of them inclines them to do. Ilsley feels helpless without him. Does not favour I know some of his views, but yields to them as he cannot himself handle things without him.' The prime minister warned the Cabinet that the dominion–provincial situation might cost the Liberal party the next election. Drew of Ontario was being allowed to steal 'the Liberal position' while building support among the other premiers.[40] The following day, King's mind was on his opening speech for the conference and who would be best suited to help him write it. 'Mackintosh and Clark,' he noted, 'are brilliant and able men but I am afraid have more the academic than the political mind.'[41]

The conference resumed on 29 April. King opened the meeting and then Drew put forward Ontario's position. The premier suggested an approach to tax-sharing that differed significantly in principle from the federal proposals. In return for exclusive federal jurisdiction in the personal and corporate income tax fields, Drew proposed that each province receive an annual subsidy per capita. The amount would be augmented by the ratio of gross national product per capita in each of the three years of the agreement to gross national product per capita in the base year of 1941. In addition, the federal government would vacate the succession duty field and concede the gasoline, amusement, parimutuel, security transfer, and electricity tax fields to the provinces. King admitted that it was 'a very good speech' and that he was 'more sympathetic with his point of view than I was with our own.' If not for the need to find a temporary measure in the transitional post-war period, King claimed, 'I would not try to defend our position for a moment.'[42]

After Drew's speech, Clark, St Laurent, Ilsley, Howe, and Skelton gathered in the prime minister's office. According to King, Ilsley felt that there was no hope of an agreement being reached. The prime minister suggested that the federal government 'consider trying to secure from the Provinces payment for letting them have the smaller revenue fields themselves and reducing correspondingly the payments we are making for the fields they had sold to us.' Clark immediately raised objections 'on the score that we must have all the fields to be able to meet what will be required in the way of taxes.' King repeated his criticisms: 'The truth is the Finance Department has allowed such tremendous expenditures, and made so many commitments that it finds itself in the position that it is going to be very difficult to work out. Ilsley is too worn and tired and sensitive to expect anything from him.'[43] The next day another meeting took place in King's office, this time consisting of the prime minister, Clark, Ilsley, St Laurent, Howe, and Claxton. King again argued for providing the provinces minor taxation powers, but Clark and Ilsley were again opposed: 'I feared the Finance Department's attitude was too much that of a small boy trying to take nuts out of a jar and in the end endeavouring to take them all or he will lose them all.'[44]

Ilsley provided the reply of the federal government on 1 May. King was pleasantly surprised, calling it 'an exceptionally fine speech. Indeed, I have heard him make no better speech. It is something that I think all Finance Ministers will in years to come have to take account of ... our position has been correctly placed on the record.' By the end of the day, however, after speeches by premiers Drew, Duplessis, and Manning of Alberta that attacked Ottawa's position, King was more sympathetic to the provinces. It was 'a mistake to hold on to all these little taxes ... we should have come out and tried to give the Provinces at least two or three small fields of their own.' The strong and united front of the provinces, in conjunction with Ilsley's doubts, increased King's belief that the moves toward centralization were undesirable. And again, Clark was caught in the prime minister's cross hairs: 'From the beginning I have taken the position that public feeling in all Provinces would be against centralization ... But you cannot get Clark, whose mind is wholly academic, to realize that no matter how theoretically accurate you may be or in accord with strict financial rules that what you are doing is no good unless you can get the public to understand and support it ... The truth is the Finance Department, all through the war, have allowed far too much in the way of expenditures. Indeed, the whole system of financing by vast sums contributed here and there and everywhere, meeting every request that has been made, was bound sooner or later to create a desperate situation – the chickens are now coming home to roost.'[45]

The next day, St Laurent spoke for the dominion government. He argued that the federal position was being misrepresented as the provinces surrendering large tax fields in exchange for only minor ones. Instead, the federal government was 'giving payment or rent for exclusive right in three large tax fields and the Provinces were unwilling to give any payment or rent to the Dominion for being given an exclusive right in the minor fields of gasoline, amusements, and pari-mutuels taxes.' St Laurent claimed that neither Ontario nor Quebec clarified its position on what it would regard as adequate payment for giving the dominion exclusive rights in fields of personal income, corporation, and inheritance taxes.[46] The following morning, Ilsley explained the implications of the Ontario proposal and how much more it would cost than the federal plan.[47] In criticizing the federal rigidity and the influential role of the 'brain-trust,' George Drew took shots directly at Clifford Clark. There was, he claimed, a 'small detached group of men without responsibility to anyone.' The proposals of the federal government, according to the Ontario premier, were too highly academic and impractical.[48] Maurice Duplessis indicated that he would not continue on the basis of one authority taxing and the other authority spending, and he even used quotes from past speeches by Mackenzie King, in which the prime minister had described such a process as 'vicious.' The Quebec premier never indicated whether he would accept Drew's proposals. He did indicate that he was leaving the conference, which he did after lunch. That afternoon, the conference adjourned sine die, but never met again.[49]

There was much casting of blame in the wake of the conference's collapse. Clark characterized Drew's final proposals as 'full of misstatements and half-truths.' To the deputy minister the conference demonstrated serious defects within the Canadian federal system: 'If the selfish interests of the two principal Provinces are going to hamstring the Federal Government in its efforts to provide machinery which will permit it to fulfill the functions of a central government in this modern age, then Confederation is a failure and Canada cannot be a nation.'[50] According to Bryce, 'Such was the climax of the problem that gave Clark his most persistent concern over his twenty years in office.'[51] When consensus proved unattainable, Clark advocated agreements with individual provinces 'on the wartime principle but the post-war formula.' He believed such action was required not only to strengthen the financial position of the less wealthy provinces, but also 'to make it easier for the Federal Government to follow fiscal and economic policies designed to minimize cyclical fluctuations.' According to Bryce, 'Clark regarded this plan as much superior to fiscal need subsidies on the one hand, or conditional grants for specific expenditures on the other, leaving provinces with the means and the responsibility to discharge their constitutional duties to such degree and in such manner as their governments, legislatures, and electors see fit.'[52] But as had become clear during the lead up to and during the conference itself, Clark was facing harsh criticism from the prime minister: 'Members of the civil service seemed to take most things out of the hands of the Ministers and seek to arrange them themselves. I see evidences of bureaucracy on every side, partly I think Ministers being hesitant themselves but even more the desire of individuals in the public service to shape policies and to gain a sense of power which goes therewith. I think we have been far too much controlled by Bank and financial influences all along.'[53]

At a Cabinet meeting on 6 May, the implications of and reasons for the conference's failure were reviewed. King 'reminded' his colleagues, 'I had said all along we were taking the wrong course in handing to the Provinces an excuse for an attack on us on the score of centralization and not allowing certain tax fields to the Provinces.' While he claimed that he did not want to attack Ilsley, what Premier Drew had said about the finance minister's rigidity was in fact 'the rigidity of Clark and Towers' that had, in the end, turned the provinces against Ottawa.[54] According to King, 'the main source of difficulty' was that the government was 'acting at the instance' of Clark, Towers, and their appointees. While it might make 'an admirable financial plan' to have Ottawa in complete control of provincial expenditures, 'the people would never stand for it politically.' The prime minister again harkened back to the days when the Liberal party championed provincial rights: 'It makes me really very sad to see how this whole ground has been turned out from under us ... The Liberal position which we had held for years is being now turned against us.' Ilsley reminded King that he had originally approved the federal position presented at the conference. The prime minister responded that he had 'always been opposed to centralizing aspects' and that 'the proposals were only a basis. They had been changed since and gone much further since.'[55]

The failure of the conference meant there was no arrangement over taxation powers. When the Cabinet met on 18 June to discuss preparations for the budget, a tax rental formula acceptable to the provinces still had to be formulated. King urged flexibility but the Cabinet was divided.[56] When King asked to go over the budget material, and Ilsley hesitated, the prime minister interpreted the reaction as another example of the finance minister being a pawn of his deputy. 'The truth is he does not, in his own mind, understand some of these problems and feels he must adhere rigidly to anything that Clark proposes. I suggested he have Clark bring the material and let us go over it together as to the wording.' Once again Ilsely requested being moved to another department: 'He could not stand the terror of this kind any longer. This is the explanation and describes his real condition.' When the budget plan was explained to Cabinet, Clark did most of the talking.[57]

King spent the morning of 22 June on the draft budget speech prepared by Clark. He made revisions, 'the most important of all was striking out anything which indicated that the Conference was a failure.' Instead, King wanted it made clear that the conference had educated the federal government and the provinces on each other's positions. But the tension between King and Clark continued to mount when the deputy minister took exception to the revisions. Clark was opposed to Ottawa softening its position. He believed that Drew was now feeling guilty for how the conference ended and was accepting some blame. King reminded Clark that the premiers blamed 'the rigid views taken by the Department of Finance.' Clark did stress that Ilsley did not want any further conferences, which struck the prime minister as being exceedingly short-sighted.[58]

Clark was relieved to be able to move on to other issues. Dominion–provincial relations rarely brought satisfaction and usually ended in frustration. In the realm of international finance, however, Clark was in his element. On 24 June, Canada signed a wheat deal with the United Kingdom, which provided for sales of at least 160 million bushels in each of the first two years (much more than normal British consumption of Canadian wheat) and 140 million bushels in the last two years. The price was to be set at $1.55 a bushel in the first and second years (well below U.S. and Argentine prices when the deal was being negotiated) and not less than $1.25 a bushel in the third year and $1.00 in the fourth. The prices in the third and fourth year were to be negotiated with 'regard to' any difference between prices paid under the agreement and world prices for deliveries in the first two years. In fact, the price paid in the previous two years was set at $2.00, well above the $1.80 ceiling price of a 1948 world agreement. By 1949 wheat was being purchased under the Marshall Plan and thus was basically a gift from North America. Both countries considered the deal good business, though many Canadians and certainly many farmers considered it part of Canada's generosity to post-war Britain. That generosity was tarnished somewhat by Canadian insistence that Britain pay more for the first two years under the 'have regard to' clause. The British refused and would not even contribute $65 million unspent from the 1946 loan; in the end the Canadian government contributed that amount to the Prairie wheat pool instead, although the amount had no connection to the wheat agreement.[59]

The budget speech was delivered on the evening of 27 June. According to Clark, it offered a blueprint for post-war Canada.[60] The key aspect was the announcement of the plan for tax rental agreements, which could be entered into by any individual province. In compliance with the agreements, the federal government undertook to reduce the standard corporation income tax from 40 per cent to 30 per cent, effective 1 January 1947. The budget simplified the complex structure of income tax that had developed during the war by offering higher exemptions and lower rates. Corporate taxes were increased while excess profit taxes were reduced. The rates on federal succession duties were doubled, with an allowance up to half for provincial duties on the same estate as part of federal-provincial arrangements. The creation of the Income Tax Appeal Board (later to become the Tax Court of Canada) was announced. Ilsley estimated that the tax changes would reduce the expected revenue for 1946–7 of $2,510 million by $35 million. The deficit for the year would be $300 million; it turned out to be a surplus of $374 million.[61]

If a province agreed to withdraw from the personal and corporate income tax and succession duty fields for five years, it would receive an annual per capita subsidy under the terms presented at the Dominion-Provincial Conference. Provinces that accepted these terms would be required to levy a 5 per cent tax on net corporate income within the province, to be collected by the federal government and deducted from the annual subsidy. In working out these agreements, Clark claimed, Ottawa sought to achieve three aims: to avoid the difficulties that the financially weaker provinces experienced during the Depression, to eliminate multiple and conflicting taxation, and to make it easier for the federal government to follow fiscal and economic policies designed to minimize cyclical fluctuations. The agreements would allow Ottawa to 'rent' the right to levy income taxes, corporation taxes, and succession duties from the provinces in return for annual subsidies based on population and gross national production per capita.[62]

But a new issue at the end of June threatened to jeopardize Canada's financial situation and Canadian–American relations in particular. The United States lifted its price controls and although they were partially restored several weeks later, general controls were gone by the end of October. Inflation soared as a result. Between June and December, American wholesale prices increased by 25 per cent and consumer prices rose by 15 per cent.[63] The pressure on Canada's price controls was immense. With the nation's dollar worth approximately ninety-one cents in relation to the American dollar, the cost of imports would be very high. With higher prices in the United States, Canadian-made goods required for the domestic market would be drawn south instead, creating an artificial scarcity in Canada and yet more pressure on the price ceiling.[64] To cope with this inflation, Donald Gordon, along with his price board colleagues James Coyne and Douglas Gibson, convinced Ilsley and Clark that the value of the Canadian dollar should be raised on par with the American dollar.[65]

Clark, Ilsley, Gordon, and Towers met the prime minister at Laurier House on 3 July to discuss what King called 'matters of high policy.' King agreed to move toward parity. It would, he felt, 'be helpful to the masses of the people, particularly to farming communities.' Towers was less enthusiastic, arguing that there was always objection when a rate was changed because 'matters get settled around a certain ratio.'[66] King brought the issue to Cabinet two days later, with Clark, Gordon, and Towers present. Two hours later the decision was announced publicly.[67] Along with its impact on prices, the higher Canadian dollar made imports more attractive, providing the British and Europeans a chance to sell their goods in Canada, a necessity if they were to repay Canadian reconstruction loans.[68] But the decision did have negative consequences, however successful it may have been in curbing inflation. It hampered the inflow of American investment, made Canadian exports more expensive, and encouraged Canadian debtors to pay off their American debts. All of these factors reduced Canada's supply of American dollars.[69]

In his announcement to Parliament that night, Ilsley indicated that the International Monetary Fund would be notified that the new exchange rate was to be Canada's initial rate. The IMF legal department felt Canada should have consulted with the fund before making the exchange rate change, but it did not press the point. According to Plumptre, adjusting the exchange rate to cushion price movements at home from those abroad was unusual, although not unheard of. Moreover, 'It involved a recognition of the role of the exchange rate as a link, and an adjustable link, between the Canadian economy and those of other countries, particularly the United States. In the second place it disclosed a willingness to consider the Canadian exchange rate as an instrument which could, if necessary, be brought into play in pursuit of Canadian economic objectives.' These attitudes, Plumptre later claimed, were 'quite novel at the time.'[70]

On 4 July the *Report of the Royal Commission on Administrative Classifications in the Public Service*, or the Gordon Commission, was released. The Canadian civil service had undergone a dramatic transformation in a short time. In essence, the framework for the modern civil service in Canada had been built. The release of the report, however, sparked a bitter controversy within the bureaucracy that would simmer for several years. 'With the increasing complexity of society,' the report claimed, 'there has been a steady growth in the activities and responsibilities of government which has imposed increasing demands upon the civil service and particularly upon its principal officials.'[71] The commission reported four defects in the organization of the civil service resulting from this expansion. There were not enough men of high calibre at the top levels, resulting in deputy ministers and other principal officials being unable to delegate work and becoming overburdened as a result. There was no clear assignment of responsibility for the overall management and direction of the civil service, and there was no effective machinery for adequately training, seeking out, transferring, and promoting able people in the junior and intermediate ranks. There was no machinery capable of dealing decisively and promptly with changes in organization or with the problem of redundant, unsuitable, or incompetent personnel. And lastly, there were considerable delays in making appointments and promotions at all levels of the service.[72] The commission argued that these flaws stemmed from 'overlapping of duties and responsibilities between the Civil Service Commission and Treasury Board.'[73]

To solve these problems, the report recommended reducing the functions of the Civil Service Commission primarily to recruitment and appointment. The growing number of agencies, boards, and commissions, as well as their employees, should be brought under the Civil Service Act. An establishments and personnel division was recommended for the Treasury Board to coordinate government personnel policy. It was not to come under the control of the Department of Finance (all employees of the Treasury Board up until this time were under finance). This division would be headed by a director-general, assisted by an advisory committee, who would have broad powers over organization of departments, including establishments and rates of pay, promotions, training, selection, and working conditions.[74]

The Gordon Commission also proposed higher salaries for senior officials. Its report noted that direct comparisons could not be made between public service and private sector pay levels because public sector work involved compensations including 'comparative security of tenure,' 'a relatively generous pension,' and provision for a pension for widows and 'the satisfaction of rendering public service.' Nevertheless, 'if men of outstanding ability are to be secured for and retained in the higher ranks of the civil service, they should not be asked, and cannot be expected to accept too great a differentiation between the salary scales offered in the service and what they could earn outside of it.' Therefore, the commission recommended the salary of deputy ministers be fixed at $15,000, $12,000, or $10,000, 'depending upon the nature of their responsibilities and the duties they are called upon to perform.' It also recommended that a special category carrying a salary of $17,500 be created in recognition of highly meritorious services or of particularly onerous responsibilities. Clifford Clark was recommended for this category and as a result his salary increased by almost 50 per cent.[75]

But the report was a rush job and Gordon would later boast that the work had taken only three months to complete. The research was superficial, and the terse and shallow report ended up being only twenty-eight pages long. According to J.E. Hodgetts, it 'failed to sketch out in adequate detail the concrete steps which would have to be taken to realize the substantial changes recommended.'[76] Nineteen recommendations were offered but they were largely empty of substance: 'It was too brief and facile to function as the basis for a reorganization of the civil service, and having met the hostility of the CSC, it virtually disappeared without action by the government.'[77]

By July the provinces were responding to the federal government's new tax rental proposals. Ilsley complained of terrible depression and stomach problems. He admitted that he was obsessing over every decision and that he felt like he was 'bordering on insanity.' King assumed that Ilsley was terrified at the prospect of reopening the dominion–

provincial quagmire: 'I think the thing that worried Ilsley was the thought of the different provincial premiers coming to bargain with him about further agreements. The truth is that so far as finance department with their policies is concerned, he sees no way out of meeting a situation that is greater than he is capable of meeting. I do not wonder he feels concerned. The expenditures should never have reached the proportions they have.'[78] Ilsley was particularly concerned about having to act as prime minister while King was in Paris for the upcoming peace conference. King agreed to have St Laurent act instead and Douglas Abbott would handle the budget debate. On 12 July, King proposed that Ilsley go to the UNRRA Council in Geneva.

Saskatchewan Premier Tommy Douglas requested another dominion-provincial conference. Ilsley was opposed but King said he would never allow the federal government to say it would not at least confer with the provinces. Ilsley wanted Clark brought into the discussion 'to do the talking.' In formulating a response to Douglas, 'Clark was very insistent on keeping in paragraphs to the effect that we could not hope for any settlement with the provinces and drawing attention to attitude of Ont. and Quebec.' King objected, arguing that it was 're-hashing, and reviving old grievances. What they wanted to know was for the future, not the past.' King decided to leave the issue to Abbott, who would be acting minister of finance, to work out the revised response with Clark. The prime minister made sure to provide his own paragraph for inclusion at the beginning of the statement, indicating that the federal government would meet with the provinces to discuss welfare matters. Clark reluctantly agreed with the changes.[79]

Despite Mackenzie King's mounting criticisms of Clark, the prime minister recognized his value. On 5 July King spoke with Norman Robertson of external affairs, who also claimed to be exhausted from his wartime service. King had already been warned by Pickersgill that Robertson's health was breaking and that he would be lost to the bureaucracy unless he was given a less stressful post. Robertson was expressing interest in becoming high commissioner in London. The prime minister recorded that 'he would begin perhaps to regret that he had given up the most influential post in the service of the country (excepting possibly that of the Deputy Minister of Finance).'[80] King was aware how much his government relied on Clifford Clark.

Much to his chagrin, the deputy minister of finance spent the summer of 1946 negotiating with the provinces. 'My own holidays,' Clark wrote to his sister Muriel, 'will not come before September as I have to negotiate with a lot of provincial governments. However, my present plan is that Margaret and myself will both go West for the month of September, all through to the Coast. Margaret is now beginning to get "panicky" about the trip but I think it is time that we went a long way off and took a good holiday. If we do this, we may not get down to the farm for some time. Without a car, other than a borrowed one, it is pretty difficult to arrange; but things have been so busy here that it has been completely impossible for me to move even at weekends.'[81] That September, Clifford and Margaret did take the vacation to the West Coast as planned. His vacations were so rare that the event even warranted a news story.[82] The Clarks left Ottawa by train 1 September, spent a day in Winnipeg, and arrived in Edmonton three days later. They drove to Jasper and Banff and then travelled by train to Vancouver, which they reached on 11 September.[83]

When Clark returned to Ottawa, the bitterness of dominion–provincial relations still hung in the air. By mid-October it was clear that the situation was hopeless. It was a defining moment in the history of Canadian federalism and it set Ottawa's course for the next decade. Mackenzie King might have felt that the provinces were being strong-armed by an aggressive and centralist department of finance but he could do little to stop the overall direction taken. On 10 October, Clark approved a reply from King to Drew. It ended the possibility of another conference. King intimated that 'until financial relations with the provinces are satisfactorily settled, the Government does not feel anything will be gained by resuming the Conference unless the provinces of Ontario and Quebec in their reaction to the proposed budget make it clear that they are prepared for modifications of their positions which would make it probable that a Conference would succeed.'[84] The morning of 22 October was spent preparing replies to George Drew of Ontario and Angus Macdonald of Nova Scotia, who were making last ditch efforts to seek a resumption of the conference. The prime minister called it 'a tangled skein which I am thoroughly tired of dealing with' and he now blamed both sides for the resulting mess: 'Both Drew and Duplessis have made it a game of the most demagogic type of politics. On the other hand, our Finance Department has been far too rigid in matters of negotiation ... Indeed, there is far too much Bank of Canada influence on the Finance Department and the Finance Department on Government policies. Could I see any possibility of having matters settled without a wrangle and making the last state worse than the first, I would, despite the wishes of the Finance Department, bring the provinces together anew ... I have, at the moment, neither the heart nor the head for anything of the kind.'[85]

Clifford Clark sat down for an interview with Grant Dexter in mid-October. Despite the miserable state of federalism, the *Free Press* correspondent and Ottawa insider found Clark his usual optimistic self. According to the deputy minister, government revenues were greater than anticipated and the federal treasury would find itself with a substantial surplus. While such news was obviously reason for optimism, it did create 'untoward repercussions.' For example, the country was suffering from 'a taxation psychosis' and would demand reductions. At the same time, the surplus would place Ottawa in a difficult position when dealing with the provinces. It 'would lead Drew to abuse the Dominion for "quibbling" about a score or two of millions.' Clark indicated that it would be in the public interest to 'ditch' the surplus one way or another and he was confident that the accounts when produced would not show much on the surplus side. When it came to looking into the future, Clark was confident. He saw no 'bump' along the road to prosperity, and inflation would remain under control. Clark felt that the price structure would hold steady and he was 'supremely confident that with the intelligent use of present techniques of control (Bank of Canada and taxation, etc.) we will never experience other than relatively minor economic disturbances.'[86] Dexter was impressed and did not doubt Clark's wisdom or analysis, but journalists by this point were wary of the deputy's upbeat nature. As Bruce Hutchinson once pointed out, 'I think also one must remember Clark's temperamental optimism which is legendary and against which I have been warned by many people.'[87]

From 10 October to 26 November, International Trade Organization (ITO) talks were held in London. While Clark did not attend, he viewed the need for multilateral trade organizations as essential for Canada's economy. Canada was a classic example of an 'open economy,' heavily dependent on foreign trade. Traditionally, the nation had come to rely on earning a surplus from its overseas trade to pay for a deficit in its trade with the United States. Canada was 'vitally dependent on a trading world organized so as to encourage a high level of multilateral trade and exchange convertibility.' Indeed, the creation of such an environment was 'the main driving force behind Canada's trade and exchange policies in the postwar period.'[88] But Clark did not have high expectations when it came to the ITO talks. He told Dexter that he would be satisfied if there was agreement on principle and the trade organization was created. He could not see how eighteen nations could negotiate trade agreements simultaneously; the result would be that 'the least trade-minded of the 18 would set the pace for all.' It would be preferable if two of the larger trading nations negotiated an agreement that was then open to all. This way, tariffs could be substantially reduced.[89]

In October the first annual sale of Canada Savings Bonds took place. During the period of winding up the National War Finance Committee from November 1945 to January 1946, many large corporations suggested a continuation of regular savings encouraged by the Victory Loan campaigns. Towers liked the idea but Clark was initially opposed on the grounds that he did not think a large and growing portion of the government's public debt should be on a demand basis (cashable at any time). He did, however, come around to the idea. 'The contra-inflationary aim of fiscal policy during this period,' he later claimed, 'was supplemented by intensive annual savings bond campaigns designed to encourage individuals to continue the habits of systematic saving developed during the war.'[90]

At the end of the month the Cabinet resumed discussion over the federal–provincial impasse. 'Ilsley seems in a very excited nervous condition,' King recorded. 'Spoke about the agony and pain of negotiating agreement and said Clark was also nervous.'[91] A month later Ilsley met with King after returning from Nova Scotia, where he had spoken with Premier Angus Macdonald. 'Said they had a pretty hot discussion in Nova Scotia,' King wrote, 'but he believes that, with some adjustments which he is considering ... that he may be able to work out an agreement with Macdonald. If this had been done while the Conference was on, as I had urged, he would have had agreements with all the provinces. Clark has been the stumbling block and is only just now coming around.'[92] During a further discussion several days later, Ilsley intimated to the prime minister that he hoped he had reached a successful conclusion in negotiations with Macdonald: 'He said he had undertaken to meet his wishes on the gasoline tax. Kept going back and forth as to whether this had been best or not. Clark had now come to the opinion he thought it was all right. I could not help saying that if Clark could have made this concession at the right time, with one or two other minor things, we would have had the whole business settled months ago.'[93]

Brooke Claxton telephoned the prime minister on 2 December

with an alarming description of Ilsley's condition. Ilsley's wife had been phoning Claxton and urging him to put pressure on King to shuffle portfolios. Claxton indicated that Ilsley would have a 'complete breakdown' if he did not get out of finance at once. To King, Ilsley had created the situation with his unbending position at the Dominion-Provincial Conference and through his unwillingness to stand up to Clark: 'It is Clark who does not want a conference at any cost and Ilsley is backing Clark … It is very serious and indeed well nigh tragic situation.'[94]

Later that day King met with Premier John Hart of British Columbia who was in Ottawa for talks with the Department of Finance. The BC premier was impatient for a resolution and indicated that some of the premiers who had not yet reached tax rental agreements were working together to present a united front to the government, along with a demand for another conference. Hart indicated he would join such a front unless offered better terms: 'He said he would not talk with Ilsley, that he was a sick man, and did not exercise any authority of his own, but was guided solely by Clark, who was an autocrat, telling Ilsley what to do and what not to do … He said he did not come down here to be greeted pleasantly by Ministers and then turned over to Deputies.'[95]

The long-delayed change in portfolios finally came on 10 December. Ilsley moved to justice and was replaced in finance by Douglas Abbott. Ilsley was relieved. While he was a nervous and likely neurotic individual, the portrayal that emerges from Mackenzie King's diary is one-sided and unfairly slanted against Ilsley. Other than the prime minister, Ilsley shared widespread respect from his colleagues. That said, there is little doubt that Ilsley was intensely emotional, as indicated by a Dexter interview in February 1947: 'Ilsley is some better than I found him in October but is still a broken man. He wept as he discussed Angus [Macdonald] and the consequences in Nova Scotia but he did not shout or storm. With tears running down his cheeks he told about his relationship with Angus … In the end, Ilsley had to go out and wash his face and I felt like crying too.'[96] Clark genuinely respected Ilsley. Mitchell Sharp later wrote that 'Clark treated ministers with respect, particularly Ilsley, for whom he had great admiration. When Ilsley eventually moved to become minister of justice in 1946, Clark regarded it as the end of an era.'[97] According to Bryce, however, Abbott was the more impressive minister. While 'Ilsley was very dear to our hearts because he was such a good guy and such an austere man,' it was Abbott who was 'the most skillful Minister of Finance.'[98]

Douglas Abbott immediately took up the negotiations with Premier Hart and on 11 December King was surprised to learn that an agreement had been reached. For the prime minister the result was evidence that Ilsley and Clark had formed the stumbling block to progress: 'Hart agrees with me that the concessions that are now being made had they been made when the Conference was first held, the whole business would have gone off amicably. Indeed matters could have been settled at a distinctly less cost to the Dominion. I felt and said at the time that later on the Department would pay for its rigidity. It has pretty nearly cost Ilsley and Clark their lives. Certainly in large part their health.'[99]

The deal struck between Ottawa and BC broke the united provincial front formed by Drew and Macdonald. Clark was in contact with the Ontario and Nova Scotia premiers when they learned about the BC deal. According to Clark, Drew was 'terribly taken aback and disappointed' and gave the impression that Hart had 'gone back on him.' Hart defended his actions by indicating that as far as he was concerned, 'he had never been a party to the scheme that was being planned by Drew and Macdonald to have all the Premiers come and set their own terms and demand another conference.' The Ontario premier was further annoyed that Macdonald was caving in to the pressure from Ottawa and 'was now ready to accept what was going to be proposed to him.' Hart was confident that Drew would have little choice but to return to Ottawa for more negotiations.[100] Mackenzie King was pleased: 'Getting matters into Abbott's hands is the surest guarantee that a settlement will be reached. Ilsley had got to where members of other governments would not have anything to do with either Clark or himself.'[101]

At the end of 1946 the Cabinet approved a raise in pay for senior civil servants in line with the recommendations of the Gordon Commission for a special category of pay above that of other deputy ministers. Clark received an increase to $17,500.[102] His salary was only $500 less than that of his minister (including the minister's car allowance, his sessional indemnity, and extra compensation as an MP).[103] Controversy, however, continued to follow in the wake of the commission's report. In particular, the civil service associations opposed transfer of powers to the Treasury Board: 'Their fears were partly based on a deep-seated suspicion of the Treasury Board, as opposed to the Civil Service Commission, and a fear that the weakening of the Commission would result in an increase of political patronage and personal favoritism.'[104] They argued that the *Gordon Report* 'did not pay sufficient attention to the problem of achieving equity and fairness in the treatment of individual Civil Servants, but concentrated too much on the problem of securing efficiency and speed in the handling of establishment problems.' There was also criticism that the Gordon Commission 'had not consulted fully or fairly with all the interested parties in these matters, and in particular had relied too much on consultations with Deputy Ministers rather than with other Civil Servants, their organizations and the Civil Service Commission.'[105] John Deutsch dismissed the concerns of the professional civil service organizations and the Civil Service Commission because 'both these groups inevitably are more interested in the maintenance of paper equities and rigid procedures than in securing efficiency and speed in the transaction of public business.' In an attempt to overcome 'patronage and favouritism,' they had become 'stultified.' The result, according to Deutsch, was that the Canadian civil service was not producing its own leaders from within, but had to bring them in from the outside.[106]

French-Canadian civil servants were opposed for a different reason and one that was particularly unflattering to Clark. Treasury Board recommendations were perceived as emanating largely from the Department of Finance, whose employees included few French-speaking members among its senior personnel. The staff who performed Treasury Board functions had no French-Canadian members in any position of major responsibility. The Department of Finance claimed that efforts to recruit 'qualified' French Canadians were unsuccessful.[107] As with most of the mandarinate, Clark was biased against French Canadians when it came to recruitment and hiring. He shared the belief that Quebec's education system was archaic, out of touch with the modern trends in social science education and the use of experts in government, and generally inadequate. Despite his university training and an ability to read the language, Clark did not speak French. Back in October 1940 Clark had written to V.F. Coe of the U.S. Treasury to recommend Jean Chapdelaine of the Department of External Affairs for any positions that became available. Chapdelaine had studied economics at Oxford as a Rhodes scholar and was, according to Clark, 'an example of what French Canada can produce with some finishing outside.'[108]

But despite reforms to the bureaucracy, the war was over, and for Clark this meant a reduction in personnel for his department. The bureaucracy had expanded drastically in wartime and its numbers would never go back to pre-war levels, but some shrinking was inevitable. The prime minister requested a survey of the personnel situation in the Department of Finance (and other associated agencies) at the end of October. Clark was preoccupied with provincial negotiations and thus unable to complete the survey until mid-November. The deputy minister noted that total staff in finance had already declined from the wartime peak by 4,413 or 25.6 per cent. By the end of 1946 he expected a further decrease of 635 and by 31 March 1947, a still further decrease of 1,391. This added up to a total reduction from the wartime peak of 6,439 or approximately 38 per cent.[109]

11

The Trials of Prosperity, 1947–1949

> The emergence of a great body of expert administrators in the federal civil service ... has brought about a professionalization of our public services which is surely the greatest advance in the functioning of Canadian democratic government in our generation. The net result is that our federal government is now equipped with an expert civil service which can reasonably be compared for its high standards with that paragon of public organizations, the British Civil Service ... the secret of the success of this important instrument of democratic government in our country is professionalization, the establishment in the civil service of standards similar to those which prevail in the learned professions.
>
> – Frank H. Underhill, *In Search of Canadian Liberalism*

By 1947 the government's desire to reduce expenditures (as well as the costs of living for Canadians) while delivering the social welfare agenda ran headlong into the realities of the Cold War. On 9 January the Cabinet Defence Committee met to consider the annual defence budget. Prime Minister King wanted major reductions in defence spending now that the Second World War was over, to accommodate other significant financial expenditures, including old age pensions and family allowances. In King's eyes the federal government had a choice to make: 'whether we were going in for increased military expenditures or to seek to carry out our programme of social legislation.' The aging prime minister clearly favoured the latter. He wanted the finance department to formulate the budget first and look at defence needs second. Douglas Abbott pushed for the overall preliminary estimate of \$2.3 billion to be reduced to below \$2.0 billion, which would entail reducing defence numbers from a preliminary 1947–8 estimate of $326 million to $200 million. This was a major reduction, since the defence department budget for 1946–7 was $440 million.[1]

The Cabinet discussed defence spending again at the end of January. Brooke Claxton brought forward revised numbers, but Abbott argued that the proposed budget of $255 million was still too high and he asked for another $25 million in cuts. Claxton resisted strongly, but in early February the finance minister won approval for another $12 million reduction. In the wake of these discussions Claxton concluded that a closer liaison with finance was needed. A review committee was established to coordinate production of defence estimates. The result in the future was that the estimates, which took much of the year to prepare, represented the thinking of both departments.[2]

It was rare for Clifford Clark to reveal his personal views on politically contentious issues facing the government. His position, however, could often be gleaned through advice he offered his minister or others in government. On 21 April a meeting was held of the Cabinet committee to discuss problems arising from the internment of Japanese Canadians. The committee was discussing the appointment of a commissioner to inquire into claims being made 'of persons of the Japanese race' for pecuniary loss to property sustained through their 'evacuation from the protected areas of British Columbia.' Clark was concerned that the draft recommendation prepared by the justice department listing the types of claims was 'too broad.' The government would have to be 'extremely careful in defining the types of claims to be heard by the Commission' and should consider only 'claims for loss in respect of real or personal property resulting from really bad management.' Clark's 'strict limitation' was justified on the basis that many Canadians faced losses caused by various measures and controls introduced during the war: 'I remember, for instance, that as a result of the War Exchange Conservation Act we forced a considerable number of private persons or firms completely out of business and in many other cases we caused them grievous loss and forced them to change their business completely if they were going to survive. However, no one ever thought of paying compensation for loss of business or of income in such cases.'[3]

But the major issue for the finance department in 1947 was another dollar shortage with the United States. Prime Minister King met with President Truman on 23 April in Washington. King informed Truman of Canada's shortage of American dollars and the desire to correct the problem by exporting more to the United States.[4] At a cocktail party Clark informed Julian Harrington, minister at the American Embassy in

Ottawa, that if more dollars were not made available, Canadian restrictions on trade with the United States might be necessary. According to Harrington, Clark 'frankly said that the present situation could not be allowed to continue indefinitely. Either exports to the United States must be stepped up substantially ... or some means must be found to discourage imports. He hoped that it would never be necessary to control imports since restrictions of this nature run counter to the postwar efforts of the major powers to restore a free and natural flow of goods.' Harrington believed that the Canadians were seeking a general solution akin to the Hyde Park Agreement.[5] According to Clark, however, the problem was much more specific: 'By mid-1947, we found ourselves in balance-of-payment difficulties on dollar account with our exchange reserves falling in less than two years from 1,500 million dollars to the dangerously low figure of under 500 millions. Our position was unique in a sense, because we had a significant surplus in our over-all current account during 1946 and 1947. The problem was simply this. By extending large credits abroad, we were selling part of our exports on credit at a time when buoyant levels of domestic investment and consumption greatly stimulated imports. The export of capital greatly exceeded the current account surplus, with the difference coming out of our exchange reserves. This experience brought home to Canada in an emphatic way the simple lesson that still needs to be learned in some quarters: that there is a close relationship between the balance of payments and the pressure on available resources.'[6]

The 1947 budget, delivered on 29 April, was Doug Abbott's first as finance minister. Despite concerns over a shortage of American dollars, optimism characterized the budget speech: 'Today we have just ended a year in which our accounts show a surplus – a surplus larger than the accumulated total of all the previous surpluses in our history. Today we see a Canada enjoying a degree of prosperity never exceeded in living memory.'[7] Much of the focus was on income taxes. Further reductions were announced, and a minor concession in personal income taxes offered an additional exemption for persons over the age of sixty-five. A complete redraft of the Income War Tax Act was submitted to Parliament and made public for discussion as Bill 454. The excess profits tax was repealed, wartime allowances for mining exploration were extended, and a gasoline tax that had been imposed during the war (the retention of which irritated the provinces) was repealed.

The budget also announced that tax rental agreements had been entered into with seven provinces – all except Quebec and Ontario. These agreements employed a formula that provided the provinces with compensation for continuing to suspend their personal and corporate income tax and for withdrawing their succession duties. There were two exceptions to this provision. The provinces could enact a 5 per cent corporate income tax, administered by the dominion, to maintain harmony with taxes enacted by the 'non-agreeing' provinces. The revenue would be deducted from the payment to the province. An 'agreeing' province also had the option of continuing to impose a succession duty, thereby gaining a credit to be used against the federal duty. The 'non-agreeing' provinces could levy their own taxes, but the dominion would allow a concession against its own taxes of up to 5 per cent of income on a corporation, up to 8 per cent of the tax on an individual, and up to 50 per cent duty on an estate or succession. 'This was the basis of the first postwar agreements,' Harvey Perry notes, 'which lasted from 1947 to 1951.'[8]

According to Mackenzie King, the House was 'astounded' at the size of the budget surplus. As usual, the prime minister declared the budget speech a landmark in the history of Canada: 'I did not think there had been comparable budgets in relieving burdens of taxation directly or indirectly, in the history of our country. It is a budget which has brought real relief to the people of Canada, taking a tremendous burden off the shoulders of many.'[9] The budget did, however, harbour portents of danger. The prosperity rested primarily on the large volume of exports financed in part by the loan to Britain and by export credits to other countries. Abbott noted that while Canada was a creditor to some countries, it was a debtor to the United States. Most of the imports had been 'paid for in United States dollars at a time when our receipts of United States dollars from abroad were greatly reduced by the fact that many of our customers had to obtain credit for a substantial proportion of their purchases from us.' The result was that Canada had to draw substantially upon large exchange reserves built up in the last years of the war. Canada, Abbott admitted, despite the general prosperity, had 'a United States dollar problem.'[10]

Concerns also plagued the British side of the equation. In February, Clark asked Bryce to prepare a memo opposing British import restrictions.[11] But both the United Kingdom and Canada had problems. Once again Britain was drawing on its loan from Canada more quickly than expected. By the end of 1946, Britain had used up $540 million and was expected to withdraw $40 million a month for the next nine months. After the loan was exhausted, Canadian officials feared Britain would face a serious financial situation. Clark apparently even told Dexter that in the event of collapse, Canada would have little option but to seek a customs union with the United States.[12]

A British delegation arrived in Ottawa in May to discuss the exchange situation. Among them were Sir Wilfrid Eady and Otto Clarke of the British Treasury. Bank of Canada and Department of Finance officials had for some months been watching the decline in American dollar reserves and they were conscious of the difficulties in meeting a large exchange deficit by non-discriminatory restrictions without commencing a spiralling reduction in world trade. The lack of American dollars was forcing Britain to restrict imports from dollar countries such as Canada and could soon force Canada to restrict trade with the United States, thereby threatening the multilateral trading system being negotiated at the GATT and ITO talks, as well as the post-war prosperity Canada was enjoying. Encouraged by several mandarins, including Lester Pearson, *Financial Post* reporter Ken Wilson wrote a series of educational articles on the problem. He was advised by various economists, including Bill Mackintosh, who had returned to Queen's University. But Abbott, to avoid pessimism in the business community, downplayed the seriousness of the situation.[13]

On 6 May Louis Rasminsky sent a memo to Clark outlining the threat to Canada's prosperity. 'The exchange difficulties represent a United States dollar squeeze,' Rasminsky argued, 'which arises primarily because Canada has shouldered more than her proportionate share of the burden of world reconstruction, and European reconstruction has been slower than hoped for.' Canada had already put up $2 billion in post-war credits, compared to $9 billion by the Americans: 'It was an overestimation of Canada's capacity to suppose that we could extend credit to the U.K. in the ratio of 1:3 as compared with the United States without imposing restrictions over and above those enforced at the end of the war, to protect our United States dollar position.' While Europe was adjusting slowly, the United States had converted to peacetime very rapidly, thereby increasing American exports. Canada could restrict Britain drawing on its loan, but the ultimate solution lay with Washington because the dollar shortage was global.[14] Clark told Eady that Canada's financial troubles stemmed 'in large part through the magnitude of the credit which she has extended to the U.K. and the rapid rate it has been drawn upon.' Many nations were short of American dollars and Canada would be prepared to tell U.S. officials that the situation could be helped only by making large amounts of American dollars available to countries other than the United Kingdom and Canada. The

British responded that their import restrictions were on a discriminatory basis because many currencies were inconvertible.[15]

The Canadian Parliament was informed on 26 May that Britain had already taken $680 million in advances on the $1.25 million loan since the first instalment had become available in May 1946. The loan was supposed to last five years.[16] Clark hoped a solution could be found in the close relationship that had developed during wartime between Canadian and American officials. He emphasized the importance of discussing the dollar shortage with the Americans prior to the retirement of Undersecretary of State Dean Acheson.[17] Towers, Rasminsky, and Wrong met with American officials, including Acheson, on 29 May. They tried to impress upon the Americans that the dollar shortage was a general problem that threatened a general economic collapse. The Americans responded that their problem was political. Every proposal the American officials had made to solve post-war problems – UNRRA, the loan to Britain, the IMF and World Bank – had failed.[18] Abbott believed that a solution would likely be found only by going to the president himself. Meanwhile, Clark was advancing an idea that involved building up the Canpay and War Supplies Limited claims and counterclaims into a general war claims settlement between the two nations. The deputy minister also had Abbott's ear when it came to 'doing something big in regard to uranium.' If uranium was going to be 'as vital to the future of civilization as scientists now appear to believe, and if the supplies of high-grade ore reserves are as limited as they seem to be,' then Canada was sitting on a 'virtual gold mine.' Abbott believed that Clark's ideas were 'unduly ambitious and expansive' but they were also 'difficult to argue successfully against.' The price of uranium would rise, 'having in mind that the supplies of reasonably rich uranium ores are very much more limited than the supply of gold and that on the demand side, while gold has practically no useful purpose other than for money, uranium may be the most vital and essential of all metals or commodities in the era which we have just entered.'[19]

In June Clifford Clark was involved in talks concerning Newfoundland's entry into Canada. In 1934, in order to save the deeply indebted dominion from reneging on its financial obligations and possibly damaging the credit of the empire, a commission was appointed to govern Newfoundland temporarily. Security threats during the war demonstrated the need to sort out the situation. By 1946 a financially strapped Britain wished to be freed of its Newfoundland obligations. The National Convention was established to recommend possible forms of future government to be put before the people in a referendum. The convention visited Ottawa and at a dinner on 24 June, hosted by the prime minister, government officials encouraged Newfoundland's union with Canada. Alexander Clutterbuck, who had been knighted in January 1946 and became British high commissioner to Canada (to complete the Newfoundland deal), felt 'a very good start' had been made. The Newfoundland delegates received a brief explanation on the workings of Canada's federal system and how the new province would be accommodated.

But not everyone in the federal government was enthusiastic about the entry of Newfoundland into Confederation. According to Peter Neary, the 'basic distinction' was between senior civil servants and some ministers. The mandarins, led by the Department of External Affairs, eagerly supported the project. But even within this group there was cynicism. Julian Harrington noted that Clifford Clark, the 'pro-Confederation deputy minister of finance and one of the most powerful mandarins in Ottawa, had told him that if Newfoundland did become the tenth province, Canada would have a "little Ireland" on its hands – a disgruntled people no matter what is done for them.' Clark was impressed, however, by the dominion's recent attempts to rectify its financial record. He believed that Newfoundland's per capita debt was now less than Canada's. More importantly, Clark believed 'that Quebec could be reconciled to Newfoundland's entry into Confederation without any change being made to the existing Labrador boundary.'[20]

On 15 July, Britain restored convertibility of the pound into dollars as required by the loan agreement with the United States. The result was a run on the pound and $700 million vanished. Convertibility of sterling between countries outside the sterling area was suspended on 21 August. Clark, Abbott, Towers, Gordon, Coyne, and Rasminsky were briefed by a British delegation. According to Clark, Canada was 'embarrassed' by the 'intimation' that the British wished to modify the agreed-upon arrangement for drawing on Canadian credit: 'We should make more clear our belief that the action which the U.K. was taking involved a breach of our agreement and that we should express shock at the offer to cease drawings on the U.S. credit.'

That evening, Clark, Towers, Gordon, Pearson, and Coyne hosted Cameron Cobbold (the deputy governor of the Bank of England) and Clutterbuck for dinner at the Towers residence. 'All angles' of the problem were discussed in 'very frank and vigorous terms.' The Canadians argued that their loan agreement provided the same protection as that given to the United States and that the British action constituted a 'technical breach.' While the Canadians were sympathetic to the situation, they urged the British to act in consultation with the Canadian government. According to Clark, the British delegation was 'left in no doubt as to the Canadian view as to the necessity and the generosity of this arrangement.' The British responded that they wished to take up with Canada, at an early date, the relaxation of the loan arrangement. Towers argued that there was 'very little room for discussion.' He asserted that the Canadian reserve position was 'actually worse' than the British in relation to the size of the relative annual deficits in the balance of payments: 'The whole question was just as simple as that.' The Canadian officials were further annoyed at Eady's public announcement that Canada would be hardest hit by Britain's sterling conversion. Eady claimed that he had been misquoted and he had, in fact, indicated that it would be the shortage of dollars that would affect Canada and not the sterling convertibility.[21]

Bob Bryce, who was in London, exchanged messages with Clark. The deputy minister of finance was convinced that the British were intent on renegotiating the fifty-fifty arrangement, despite continued and emphatic Canadian opposition. The British planned to open these discussions when Abbott arrived in London the following week, and Clark was concerned that Abbott would not hold the fort. 'It will be necessary,' he instructed Bryce, 'to see that the Minister is given every assistance in maintaining the continuance of the arrangement as it stands.'[22] British officials in Washington, meanwhile, claimed that Canada had taken the calculated step of weakening Britain's finances by demanding partial payment in American dollars for its exports to the United Kingdom. This angered Canadian officials who as recently as June requested that no more than half of future imports be financed from Canada's loan, with the rest coming from American dollars. By September the desperate British were even seeking concessions on that agreement.[23]

Something had to be done. In early September Abbott was in London, ostensibly to attend an IMF meeting, but in reality to resolve this latest Anglo-Canadian 'misunderstanding.' A rankled Clark again warned Bryce, 'However you may be influenced by sympathy for the British position, it is quite clear no sympathy can be wasted in that quarter. In this connection, at least, it is quite true that charity begins at home.'[24] Clark was frustrated with the British refusal to accept the Canadian position: 'There is a complete failure to understand our position and the attitude seems to be that they can't continue the arrangement and therefore we should send someone over to accept an accomplished fact.' The deputy minister was also annoyed that Eady kept making careless statements to the press, thereby damaging Canada's economic status. 'If Canada should have a crisis in the near future,' Clark told Bryce, 'it would be comparatively easy to trace it to its source.' Much of Clark's frustration came from the fact that Britain did not seem concerned about the Canadian situation. Canada could not be more generous and there was 'no question as to which country has the most serious exchange position.' As it was, Clark asserted, Canada's position resulted not from a failure to produce or export, but rather from its disproportionate share of the burden of European reconstruction. Bryce met with Eady, who attempted to relay the desperation of the British situation. For Clark, it was a typical British performance seen repeatedly during the war. But the war was over. Much of the 'Eady interview,' Clark told Bryce, 'has been a desire to take you through the gloom room but I am surprised that at this late date ... there should be a failure to grasp the realities of our position.' Eady's interpretation of the discussions in Washington about convertibility and discrimination, according to Clark, was not 'realistic.'[25]

When journalist Ken Wilson wrote an assessment of the Canadian position that emphasized Canada's generosity to Britain, he was articulating the key points Canadian officials wanted stressed. Wilson's information came largely from Clark after the two men met for lunch at the Rideau Club prior to Abbott's departure for London. According to Patrick Brennan, 'Wilson's relations with the Department of Finance were excellent. Clark disliked being pestered by reporters and found most of them dull. His well-deserved reputation for discussing every question in economic technicalities and carefully avoiding any comments that could remotely be construed as "political" ensured that all but a few gallery members avoided him. But Wilson's understanding of economics allowed him to follow most of Clark's tedious explanations, and straight politics was seldom his primary interest anyway. The two men liked each other and Clark invariably found time for the *Financial Post*'s man whenever he requested it. Wilson, for his part, did not abuse the privilege.'[26]

After many exacerbating meetings, the Canadian delegation in London was finally able to convince the British that Canada's own shortage of American dollars was serious and that no revisions to the loan agreement could be expected. In order to gain British acquiescence,

Abbott made it clear that Canada would impose import restrictions.[27] 'Our moral position is, of course, unassailable,' Abbott recorded, 'and I have no doubt they realize this.'[28] At least this was Abbott's recollection of a meeting he had with the chancellor of the exchequer, Hugh Dalton, on 11 September. Two days later, however, Abbott was informed that Dalton had a different account of the meeting. According to Dalton, he told Abbott that the British could not maintain the present loan arrangement. If, however, the Canadians insisted that it be maintained, the British would find it necessary to reduce its imports on some Canadian commodities.[29] Within days, the British acknowledged that under no circumstances would the loan be revised. But they also repeated their threat to reduce Canadian imports. Abbott believed the British would not be able to reduce the main agricultural imports and therefore, 'if import cuts have to be made, it can't be helped.'[30]

Bryce and Rasminsky met with Eady on18 September. Eady claimed that Canada's import policy raised political difficulties in the United Kingdom because Britain was paying American dollars to Canada at a time when Canada had no restrictions on American imports. Rasminsky fired back that 'most people in Canada would find it difficult to understand on what basis the United Kingdom would feel entitled to express any views regarding our import policy and that there seemed to be a fair amount of confusion regarding who was helping whom in the matter of exchange.' According in Rasminsky, Eady accepted the comments 'gracefully enough,' but the Dominions Office representatives were 'obviously embarrassed' and phoned later to apologize for Eady's assertions.[31]

To drive the message home in the United States, Clark led a delegation that met with American officials in Washington and New York from 16 to 20 September. The key meeting took place on 18 September, in which Clark and Ambassador to the United States Hume Wrong met Tyler Wood, the deputy assistant secretary of state, Paul Nitze, a leading figure in the State Department's international economic planning, along with other officials. The objective was to lay out Canada's choices as well as American actions that could aid the situation. Wrong warned that having Canada's position understood required not only a frank detailing of the facts but restrictions that would make 'a lot of people squeal both at the consuming end in Canada and at the producing end in the United States.'[32] Clark came away from the talks more pessimistic than ever that the United States would offer help from the Marshall Plan. He did not believe that the State Department officials were either influential or imaginative enough to solve the problem by constructive rather than restrictive and deflationary measures. But he was still convinced, for the same reasons Abbott had outlined, that it was too early to act.[33] Clark felt restrictions would be needed 'before the Americans will believe there is anything in our problem or that it means anything to them.'[34] More discussions between Wrong and American officials led to further scepticism that discriminatory restrictions could be avoided.[35]

In the last week of September, Canada and the United States reached an agreement in the first round of multilateral tariff reductions under the General Agreement on Tariffs and Trade (GATT). Negotiations were conducted bilaterally, product by product, with the results extended to all other contracting parties in accordance with Article I of the GATT. Article I required contracting parties to extend, immediately and unconditionally, to every member any trade advantage, favour, privilege, or immunity granted to any contracting party. In the Canada-U.S. agreement, the United States maintained the duty-free status for all important Canadian exports as per the 1938 trade treaty. A concession was obtained on almost every item of which Canada was the principal supplier. In many cases, as with lumber, shingles, wheat, and flour, Washington reduced tariffs by 50 per cent, the lowest the president was permitted to go under the Trade Agreements Act. According to Bruce Muirhead, 'By the end of the negotiations, Canadian officials estimated that concessions extended by the US would bring the general level of American import duties to the lowest point since the Underwood Tariff, which had been in force from October 1913 to May 1921. Under that tariff, exports from Canada to the United States had increased by more than 200 percent.'[36]

The GATT agreement solved the Canadian–American problem. Without an agreement between Britain and the United States, however, the entire multilateral program would be placed in jeopardy. Tough negotiations between Britain and the United States led to a 30 September meeting of St Laurent, Clark, and Deutsch to plan strategy in the event that an agreement was not reached. Norman Robertson (who was travelling on the same ship to New York as Assistant Secretary of State Will Clayton) was told to pressure the Americans to keep the negotiations going. St Laurent, Clark, and Deutsch also discussed the idea of intimating to the British that Canada would likely have to seek release from its 1937 U.K. trade agreement if talks in Geneva failed. Clark and Deutsch undertook to prepare a memorandum on that possibility.[37]

The next day, Clark devised Canada's strategy for dealing with the Americans.

At the end of October, Clark, Towers, Deutsch, and McKinnon met with American officials. The Canadians indicated that Canada had a 'drastic Plan A' and a 'less severe Plan B' to cope with its declining U.S. dollar reserve. Clark explained that Canada had an adverse balance with the United States of $1.2 billion against receipts from Britain of $300 million. The two plans were designed to make up the $900 million gap. Both plans called for rationing pleasure travel, which might save $30 to $40 million, a loan from the Export-Import Bank, import restrictions, and diversion of exports to the United States. Plan A called for a loan from the Export-Import Bank of $350 million, while Plan B called for a loan of $500 million. Plan A entailed a complete ban on importing almost every identifiable consumer item from the United States. An exception would be made for citrus fruits, prunes, cabbages, carrots, and textiles, which would be placed under quotas to reduce imports by one-third to one half. Capital goods would also be restricted. Net savings would be about $300 million. Plan B would apply import restrictions in a way that did not discriminate against the United States, and thus was in keeping with the GATT. Restrictions would be by quota, although there would be some outright bans. By selecting which items would have quotas, the restrictions would mainly hit the United States. The aim was to produce a net saving of $175 million. Finally, Plan A called for diverting exports to save a net of $50 million. Plan B suggested that diversion of exports could take place under a trade treaty with the United States that would reduce the American tariff. It also called for Canadian participation in the Marshall Plan, either through the United States buying from Canada or allowing European countries to buy from Canada using their Marshall Plan dollars. The Americans were particularly receptive to discussing a trade treaty that went beyond the tariff reductions agreed to in Geneva, although there might be difficulty with Congress. Negotiations for a loan and discussion of the Marshall Plan took two more weeks.[38] On 30 October 1947, the GATT was signed in Geneva, and an agreement was reached between Canada and Britain. The agreement had limited effect because of non-tariff barriers raised by Britain in its efforts to cope with its shortage of dollars.[39]

Deutsch and McKinnon approached American State Department officials about a possible free trade agreement on 29 October. According to the American record of the discussions, the Canadians indicated they were authorized by Cabinet to negotiate for 'a comprehensive agreement involving, wherever possible, the complete elimination of duties.' Such a perception, however, was erroneous. The idea might have been suggested during discussions of GATT or the exchange problems, but there was no Cabinet authority and no mention of any approval in King's diary.[40] In meeting with American officials, Deutsch and McKinnon made it clear that they did not want a customs union, a point Clark made later to Paul Nitze, because it would involve raising tariffs against Britain. Rasminsky also told Nitze that a customs union was not negotiable because Canada would be an unequal partner and would have to adjust her tariffs to those of the United States. What was desired, Deutsch indicated, was 'a better balance in the one-way trade associated with our branch plants.' Millions of dollars in parts went north to American branch plants, most of which served only the Canadian or the commonwealth market.[41]

On 12 November the U.S. Export-Import Bank approved giving Canada a standby credit of $300 million, to be available to the end of 1948. Three days later, American officials indicated they would likely meet Canadian expectations for offshore purchases through the Marshall Plan.[42] Why Canada did not seek a loan from the IMF is not clear. One reason may have been that the amount required equalled 100 per cent of Canada's IMF quota, which would have meant considerable negotiation. And given Canada's failure to consult with the IMF before the 5 July 1946 revaluation, Canada may not have been in the fund's good books.[43]

Canada imposed import and travel restrictions against the United States on 17 November in line with Clark's 'Plan B.'[44] These restrictions were announced immediately after Prime Minister King announced that the GATT had been signed. Abbott rejected devaluation, since Canada's difficulties were likely to be short-term. Instead he announced measures to encourage more Canadian exports as well as gold mining, which had been hard hit by the rise of the Canadian dollar in July 1946. The subsidy for gold mining would have to be negotiated by the IMF. But most of the plan focused on import restrictions, which in accordance with GATT rules would be non-discriminatory.[45] Taxes were imposed by regulation on goods from the United States, to discourage further importation, including automobiles, cameras, electric or gas appliances, firearms, bicycles, motorcycles, outboard motors, toilet articles, and musical instruments.[46] According to Clark, the objective was to adopt a comprehensive program to correct the imbalance and to restore the reserves to a more adequate level:

> The program was based partly on short-term emergency measures, including import restrictions, exchange controls, and substantially higher commodity taxes. At the same time, more fundamental steps were taken to slow down the rate of foreign lending, to expand output, and to increase dollar exports. The purpose of the direct controls was to arrest the drain on reserves and to provide time for the more basic and longer-term measures to take effect. Incidentally, the alternative possibility of lowering the Canadian exchange rate was rejected by the government at this time, partly because the problem was not one of lack of competitiveness of Canadian exports and partly because of its belief that price elasticities of the goods entering into Canada's foreign trade under the conditions then prevailing in world markets were such that a change in the par value of the Canadian dollar would have little effect.[47]

Parliament was summoned early on 5 December and Abbott rejected devaluation. According to King, the government was in for a difficult time because 'matters at home have been allowed to drift with the Americans.' He concluded that 'too much has been left on Clark's shoulders and there has been too great a readiness to accept anything he might suggest.' The prime minister blamed himself for giving in on issues because of 'fatigue and over-weariness and exhaustion.'[48]

Less than a week later, Abbott adjusted the restrictions against the United States. But King was right about the difficulties faced in the House. All three political parties criticized the fact that the measures were put into effect through Order in Council and that wide discretionary powers, judged unacceptable in peacetime, had been granted to the minister of reconstruction and supply relating to restrictions on capital goods. It was also pointed out that the restrictions, though officially non-discriminatory, were in fact aimed at the United States. Canada could ill afford to provide a precedent for discrimination, since the practice was one Canada opposed when Britain applied it. Finally, the recent decision to raise the value of the dollar was also criticized for contributing to the imbalance of trade. It took until March to pass the Emergency Exchange Conservation Act, and the debate was 'the most arduous and contentious to take place on an economic issue since before the war.'[49] Progressive Conservative MP John Diefenbaker went so far as to suggest that Clark, Towers, Rasminsky, 'and others of that group' be brought before a committee of the House and questioned about 'whether they made the recommendation to the Government on November 17 prior thereto or whether it was the Government that suggested to them the means whereby they could utilize the Foreign Exchange Control Act for the purposes they had in view.' Diefenbaker was rebuked for his suggestion by Abbott, on the basis that advice given to a government by civil servants was confidential.[50]

The restrictions were phased out beginning in late 1948 and they were gone completely by January 1951.[51] According to Clark, they were quickly dismantled for several reasons. Even though it was emphasized that the restrictions would be removed as soon as Canadian reserves improved, the incidental protection that they afforded had the effect of stimulating high-cost production of some of the goods subject to import control. As a result, 'distortions and rigidities' were introduced into the Canadian economy: 'Vested interests were being created and doubts began to be expressed concerning the merits of trying to follow liberal trading policies in a world of widespread restrictionism, discrimination, and inconvertibility. In a sense, the very basis of Canada's traditional trade policies was being questioned.' Clark went on to argue that if Canada was to continue to market her exports in the United States in large volume, it was essential to keep costs down, encourage productive efficiency, maintain competition, and retain sufficient flexibility in the economy 'to permit adjustments to the inevitable shocks of a dynamic and rapidly changing world.' In Clark's view, the government 'decided to resist the pressures towards increased bilateralism.' The emergency restrictions and discriminations were eliminated when the exchange reserves showed improvement: 'The maintenance of a flexible economy was adopted as a positive purpose, and exporters who found themselves excluded from overseas markets were encouraged to find new outlets in dollar markets.'[52] Regardless, as far as King was concerned, the onus for the whole problem rested with Clark and his staff: 'I think the Finance Department are most to blame for having gone too far.'[53]

If King felt that his finance officials had gone too far with the dollar shortage, his criticisms increased when the mandarins began discussing a free trade deal to help solve the financial mess that had overtaken Canadian–American trade relations. But the onus came not only from Canada. Abbott was approached by American officials. According to King, 'Abbott himself pointed out that this would be the answer to all our present restrictions. If we could get complete reciprocity, he felt we would no longer be dependent on uncertain markets of Europe, which are bound to be uncertain for some time and that this would give what was needed to maintain, as far as could be maintained, the prosperity of our country.' The prime minister noted that Clark, Deutsch, and Towers were all in favour of pursuing an agreement. Initially, the prime minister offered his approval as well.[54]

On 22 January, Woodbury Willoughy of the U.S. Commercial Policy Division wrote a memo welcoming Canadian support for reciprocity. Canada and Britain, he wrote, were apparently at a parting of the ways and a trade deal would not hurt the Americans: 'Taken as a whole, imports from Canada would offer little threat to American producers. Nearly three-fourths by value of our present imports from Canada are already on the free list and in most other cases the duties do not offer a serious barrier.' Canadian manufacturers would face more difficulties, he noted, since the Americans had the advantage of the size of their market. A transition period in which duties were progressively lowered would ease problems of adjustment for Canadian industries. The Canadians believed that many products could be manufactured as cheaply in Canada as in the United States, and eliminating the duties would encourage specialization and the production of some products in Canada for the whole North American market.[55] The prime minister seemed fully onside: 'Both Abbott and I agreed that the measure was of such advantages to Canada that we should not risk the chance of [not] having an agreement of the kind made. I told him he could say that he and I were agreed, that our govt would be prepared to ask Parlt to support a Treaty of the kind, should it be negotiated before midsummer.'[56]

Talks in February led to a general plan for free trade between Canada and the United States. The proposed deal called for the immediate removal of all duties by both nations, the prohibition of all quantitative restrictions on imports after five years (with exemptions given to U.S. wheat and flour and Canadian fruits and vegetables), the joint consultation on joint marketing agreements for agricultural products, and the continued free access of products, even in the event of war.[57]

Mackenzie King was enthusiastic about the plan when he met with Abbott on 6 March. Three days later, Deutsch returned to Washington after discussing the free trade proposals with Clark, Towers, Abbott, St Laurent, and King.[58] But the prime minister's enthusiasm was waning by the middle of March. Newspaper and magazine commentary was debating eventual economic and even political integration between the U.S. and Canada. The discussion unsettled King, who was becoming increasingly concerned that Canada was falling too much under American influence. The prime minister claimed to be relieved when Abbott assured him that what was being negotiated 'was not any immediate complete free trade but rather trade so arranged as to make possible the gradual integrating of our systems along lines of the Hyde Park Agreement.'[59]

If King was able to view a free trade deal as part of his role as lynchpin between the United States and Britain, or as part of Canada's contribution toward improving relations among the Western allies, he was more likely to be supportive. On 22 March he had a long discussion with Clark, Deutsch, McKinnon, St Laurent, and Howe over calls from Britain for the creation of a regional security pact. King told the assembled group that he was concerned over the secret negotiations then underway that would lead ultimately to the creation of the North Atlantic Treaty Organization (NATO). 'I said I would have to swear [the] three members of the [civil] Service present to absolute secrecy,' King recorded, 'and to tell them that, at the moment, negotiations were on at Washington for the establishment of an Atlantic Security Pact – negotiations between the United Kingdom, United States and Canada.' King viewed the free trade deal as fitting into this 'larger Atlantic Pact' by encouraging the Americans to be more generous and possibly even nudging both the United States and Britain 'in the direction of anything that would disclose a closer unity of interest between them.' Indeed, King was talking of more liberal trade among the Western allies, including France: 'All three – Clark, Deutsch and McKinnon – were strongly taken with the idea.'[60]

But doubts were plaguing King. He feared bringing a free trade deal before Parliament and being attacked, as he had throughout his career, for urging 'annexation with the States.' He admitted to feeling overwhelmed at the serious implications and 'really so depressed and weary in my head that I wanted to get away from everything. What has been suggested to me today is almost the largest proposal that, short of war, any leader of a govt has been looked to undertake. Its possibilities are so far reaching for good on the one hand, but possible disaster if project were defeated that I find it necessary to reflect a good deal before attempting a final decision.'[61]

Much of the problem was that Mackenzie King was old and tired, and he was increasingly out of step with his colleagues, particularly when it came to responding to the post-war world. He was seventy-four years old and in August the Liberal party would select a new leader. King did not believe he had the constitution to lead the government in a battle over reciprocity. He would feel unprepared to defend the agreement in the House against the Conservatives because the civil servants who most supported the deal would not be present: 'I was likely to be a liability rather than an asset ... I was really not in any shape to aid a movement of the kind in Canada. That I had not the mental power. Was feeling fatigued and exhausted ... I said I was even beginning to doubt my own judgment on many matters. I found myself much too cautious and conservative in international matters to feel that my views were shared by some of the younger men around me.'[62]

On 24 March, King indicated that he was now opposed to a free trade deal. The prime minister knew that Clark viewed the deal as 'the only way we could come to balance our accounts with the States and was pressing very strongly for something of the kind.' In fact, King argued that 'the whole proposal had come from Clark of the Finance Department but that, while it might be sound economically, I believed it would be fatal politically. Quite impossible of carrying out at this time in the limited time that was being suggested. It was the sort of thing that would require months, if not years of education.'[63] According to Arnold Heeney, there was nothing surprising about King's sudden reversal. 'It was, rather, the instinctive reaction of the old politician.' King realized that the proposed free trade deal was attractive and 'accorded well with traditional Liberal economic doctrine.' The civil servants had every reason to believe that 'they were producing precisely what Mackenzie King would want.' But the prime minister 'would have none of it. He was not going to be responsible for a second 1911 and disaster for a Liberal government.'[64]

The prime minister met with Hume Wrong at the end of March to discuss the reasons for halting the trade negotiations. His explanation revolved around fears of American domination: 'The long objective of the Americans was to control this Continent. They would want to get Canada under their aegis. If I was an American, I would have the same view specially considering Russia's position, etc.'[65] To the Americans, the sudden reversal of policy occurred for two reasons: a desire not to overload the Canadian people with two major initiatives at the same time (a security pact and a free trade deal), and a desire to broaden the free trade area beyond North America.[66]

On 3 April the Marshall Plan Law was passed by Congress. The provisions for purchases outside the United States were 'probably broader than even the most optimistic in Ottawa had dared to hope.' In the initial period from 3 April to 1 December, 34 per cent of the amounts allocated for food and agricultural commodities and 42 per cent of industrial goods could be purchased outside the United States. For

Canada that amount totalled $593.4 million. Although Canadian officials had pressed for such provision, it was not offered as a special favour or exemption for Canada. The U.S. administration argued that if all Marshall Plan purchases were made in the United States, it would create shortages of certain commodities and cause inflationary price increases. The 'off-shore' purchases were allocated not just to Canada but also to Latin America, Eastern Europe, European recipients of Marshall Plan aid, as well as other countries. Moreover, it was predicted that the money spent in other countries would eventually find its way back to the United States as recipient countries (all short of American dollars) expanded their normal purchases of American goods. It was recognized that Canada's import restrictions of 17 November were hurting U.S. manufacturers, who would benefit if Canada's supply of American dollars grew. 'Offshore purchases in Canada under the Marshall Plan were proposed, not as a handout, concession or exemption for Canada,' Plumptre claimed, 'but as an effective means of alleviating damage to U.S. interests.'[67] On 5 May, the European Co-operation Administration set up to administer the plan, authorized British use of Marshall Plan money to purchase Canadian goods. Over a ten-month period, $670 million of ECA money was spent in Canada.[68]

Despite King's decision on free trade, not all of his officials seemed certain that the issue was dead. On 21 April the prime minister met with Abbott, Howe, St Laurent, Pearson, and McKinnon. The prime minister again indicated that an agreement was not going to take place. Yet on 5 May, King was surprised to learn that while in Washington, Howe was still talking of a free trade deal. The prime minister blamed the civil servants for driving their own agenda and taking 'it into their hands to try and settle the great national policies.' To King, 'It is only too clear that Clark with McKinnon and Deutsch and Towers of the Bank of Canada have all got it into their heads that this is the only way to balance trade with the United States.'[69] According to Donald Creighton, 'In what was historically one of the most contentious and dangerous of all Canadian issues, the career men of the new specialized civil service had taken the initiative, and, urged forward by American encouragement and impatient eagerness, they devised a plan of grandiose, if not frightening, proportions ... The fact was, of course, that the new Canadian bureaucrats were, to a large extent, both ignorant of Canadian traditions and out of touch with contemporary Canadian opinion. For them the economic unity of the North American continent had all the beautiful validity of an economist's model.'[70]

But by April Clark's attentions were shifting from trade to health policy. Health Minister Paul Martin brought up the issue in Cabinet of grants to the provinces for health purposes.[71] He proposed that the grants be made to all provinces, whether or not they had signed a tax rental agreement with Ottawa, thereby circumventing the issue of linking tax arrangements and social programs that Clark and others had insisted on in the 1945 proposals. 'This,' Martin claimed, 'would prepare the way for introducing health insurance at some later date.' The proposal called for $30 million in federal grants.[72] The costs were $7.7 million in the first year (1948–9) but would rise to $27.3 million in 1952–3, for a total of almost $94 million by the end of that year.[73] Martin returned to Cabinet on 6 May to press the issue. A committee of officials from the health department, as well as from finance, was set up to study the proposal and report back within five days. The official report indicated that the proposal formed a popular and important health program apart from health insurance (although it would serve as a foundation for insurance). The distinction helped overcome opposition from Abbott and Howe, who opposed health insurance in general.[74]

By the time the report was issued, Martin had the prime minister solidly onside. The Cabinet followed by 13 May (despite Abbott's continuing objections) and the entire package was approved.[75] The following day King announced the grants in Parliament, arguing that they were for 'the development by stages of a nationwide health program, leading up to, and ultimately including, health insurance.' According to Martin, 'There was no doubt that approval of the grants was a de facto departure from the practice of federalism, emphasizing the role of the central government in confederation. The acceptance of the health program recognized that, in the post-war age, Ottawa was responsible for initiating programs that would bring about national standards, instead of leaving each province to work out its own criteria under the authority of the British North America Act.'[76]

In the Speech from the Throne, the prime minister substituted the word *nationwide* for *national* to avoid criticism that the government was advancing centralization: 'This has been the real mistake that has been made in our policies. It has been forced much too strongly by the Finance Dept, the influence of Clark and others toward centralizing as I felt all along, had been premature.'[77] A few weeks later, King and Clark were at a dinner together. The prime minister again indicated that Clark had made a mistake when dealing with the provinces in 'not yielding up the small sources of income' and in allowing the premiers 'to take from us the old doctrine of provincial autonomy.' Clark responded that Duplessis and Drew had ganged up and were determined to defeat the government, and that they would never have agreed to a settlement, regardless. King disagreed and told Clark that it was his illness that prevented him from handling the situation properly.[78]

The budget of 1948, brought down on 18 May, came and went with little commotion. 'There was little enthusiasm about the Budget,' King observed. 'There being no income tax relief was a natural disappointment. Also using large surpluses to reduce the public debt was anything but popular.'[79] The revised Income Tax Act was passed and would come into effect on 1 January 1949. Tariff revisions were offered up to implement the GATT negotiations. The last of the short-lived exchange emergency taxes were repealed and the exemption under the succession duties legislation was increased from $5,000 to $50,000.[80] Abbott was hesitant to offer significant tax cuts at a time when the Americans were making major expenditures for the European Recovery Programme (ERP). Cuts might cause the United States to hesitate about placing ERP orders in Canada, thus damaging Canadian employment. But the prime minister was also aware that it was politically advantageous to hold off making tax cuts until the following year, when an election would be called. At a caucus meeting the day after the budget was delivered, Ian Mackenzie (who was no longer in Cabinet) argued that the budget did nothing for the poor and 'was a thoroughly Tory budget.' King responded that the government was moving out of controls on prices and that a tax cut that increased inflation would not help the poor, regardless. He also pointed to the health grants aimed at aiding the less affluent.[81]

By 1948 the emphasis on reconstruction work was finally diminishing. In May the Cabinet Committee on Reconstruction was replaced by the Cabinet Committee on Economic and Industrial Development. The new body was to advise government on measures required to maintain a high level of employment and income, as well as policy related to public investment including projects for resource development. The chairman of the new committee was C.D. Howe, minister of trade and commerce, and reconstruction and supply.[82]

When Maurice Duplessis and his Union Nationale won a major victory in the Quebec provincial election on 28 July 1948, the extent of Mackenzie King's concern and paranoia about the influence of the mandarins became manifest. The prime minister blamed Duplessis' victory on the failure of the dominion-provincial conference, which was

Clark's fault. Increases in the cost of living and taxation were also responsible for discontent in Quebec, and again blame was placed at the feet of Clark: 'The Finance Department's insistence on having a so-called cyclical budget, taking vast surpluses to use to pay off the debts, and not giving any reduction in taxation at this time,' King claimed, led to the results in Quebec.[83]

But Mackenzie King was retiring. A Liberal leadership convention, the first since 1919, was held on 5–7 August 1948. To the surprise of no one, Louis St Laurent was selected as the new Liberal leader. On 15 November, King officially stepped down and St Laurent succeeded him as prime minister. As testament to the continued dominance of the 'Government Party,' as well as the smooth transition in leadership, the Cabinet under St Laurent remained almost the same as under King. The dominance of the Department of Finance also continued. In fact, with the increasingly suspicious King gone, the department's influence increased. In the new St Laurent government, Clifford Clark 'still reigned supreme.'[84]

Concern over Britain's financial position, meanwhile, continued. The American dollar shortage still plagued Britain and Canada, and both countries were worried over the aid to be received through the Marshall Plan as well as the drain on British reserves. By August concerns shifted to the fact that the United Kingdom was contemplating balancing its sterling dealings with Canada through a substantial decrease in Canadian imports. Britain was looking to obtain more goods from the United States and to divert foodstuff purchases from Canada to sterling area and non-dollar sources.[85] Henry Wilson Smith had replaced Wilfrid Eady in charge of overseas finance in the British Treasury. On 4 August he travelled to Ottawa to meet with Canadian officials. The objective of the meeting was an informal exchange of views. Clark emphasized the common purpose of speedy reconstruction of Western Europe while also restoring and expanding multilateral trade: 'We had been assured that the multilateral goal was also the objective of United Kingdom policy but recently there had been evidence that this might no longer be the case.' Clark went so far as to suggest that 'the inflexibility and delays encountered in respect of these matters have caused us to wonder whether a policy of particular toughness has been adopted towards Canada because of her present and future position in relation to dollar exchange.' The British responded that many of the developments of concern to Canada were 'of an emergency or short run character with deviated temporarily from longer run objectives.'[86] In September Chancellor of the Exchequer Stafford Cripps visited Canada before going on to Washington to attend the Board of Governor annual meetings of the IMF and the International Bank for Reconstruction and Development. Clark was heavily involved in planning the trip, as well as in all the scheduled meetings. The Canadian government expected Britain to use the opportunity to raise the possibility of an early renewal of drawings upon the Canadian loan and to explain its four-year program for achieving reconstruction and economic viability under the European Recovery Programme. As a result of Canada's own exchange difficulties, the drawings upon the British loan were suspended by the middle of April. Up to this point, a total of $1,015 million ($540 million in 1946, $423 million in 1947, and $52 million in 1948) had been drawn, leaving a balance of $235 million out of the $1,250 million originally provided.[87]

The budget of 1949, delivered on 22 March, was a prosperity budget. According to Bryce, the staff at finance called it the 'sunshine budget.'[88] Abbott noted that it was brought down 'amid conditions of sustained – one might almost say unexcelled – prosperity.' The international field was marked by 'grave uncertainties,' but 'Canadians as a whole have continued throughout the past year to enjoy higher standards of living than ever before.' The Department of Finance was now prepared to announce that 'the post-war world price inflation appears to have run its course.' The problems connected with foreign exchange seemed to have been solved as improved trade figures and the recovery of the exchange reserve indicated, mainly through increased exports to the United States.[89]

The budget offered a general round of tax reforms that included decreases in general rates and increases in exemptions under the personal income tax. The small business rate was established at 10 per cent on the first $10,000 of corporate income and 33 per cent on the excess. The dividend tax credit was inaugurated at 10 per cent in order to prevent small businesses from facing double taxation. The carryover of business losses was extended from three to five years. Wartime excise taxes still in effect were either repealed or reduced. The revenue for 1949–50 had been estimated at $2,800 million; as a result of the tax reductions, it was now anticipated to be $369 million less. A surplus was forecast of $87 million.[90]

The budget took what Clark called the first step toward 'a program designed to lessen and ultimately to eliminate the double taxation of business profits.'[91] The Department of Finance was confident that post-war inflation had subsided, at least for the time being: 'There were indications in business trends ... that it was time to shift from the anti-inflationary bias of fiscal policy.' The budget, according to Clark, was seeking to 'complete the process of tax reduction to levels that might be expected to persist in peacetime and aimed at little better than a balance in the accounts.' Reductions to income taxes were offered, but the 'main feature' was the drastic recasting of commodity taxes.[92] Despite total reductions in personal income tax that by 1949 amounted to a reduction of 60–70 per cent for most taxpayers, there were also large budget surpluses. Clark later noted that 'in each of the fiscal years 1947, 1948, and 1949, despite the substantial magnitude of the tax reductions that had been made, actual revenues exceeded actual expenditures by a substantial amount. In fact, the surpluses amounted to 14, 31, and 27 per cent, respectively, of total revenues and in the aggregate to 1,645 million dollars or 12.3 per cent of the net debt at its war-end peak. In the last two of these years when expenditures ran a little under 2,200 million dollars a year the Minister had budgeted for substantial surpluses, but even his optimistic forecasts were exceeded.'[93]

It was a good time in the life of Clifford Clark. His family was doing well and his health was holding. The previous May, Clark's youngest child, Ken, married Patricia Jowsey at Aylmer, Quebec. In the spring of 1949 both Ken and George graduated from Queen's University. George graduated with an MD and Ken with a bachelor of commerce. George moved to Calgary, while Ken joined the store-chain Simpson's. On 1 March, Clark became the longest-serving federal deputy minister then in office.[94] As well as being the most senior deputy minister, he was given the title of 'the most influential civil servant in Ottawa' in a *National Home Magazine* discussion of Ottawa's bureaucrats.[95]

By the summer, however, the British situation was again precarious. Monetary reserves of gold and dollars were low and declining. In the three previous months, gold and dollar reserves declined by 14 per cent.[96] Countries still using sterling deposited their reserves in London and, since the pound was not freely convertible into dollars, they purchased in the British market or from other sterling countries. Britain had to buy raw materials and food with dollars but was not receiving dollars in return, creating a reduction in reserves, despite high employment at home.[97] Talks were arranged in London between British officials and U.S. Treasury Secretary John Snyder. Canada was anxious to be part of the discussions and Clark was expected to be a key player. Clark would have to leave immediately by ship, because his health problems with his back supposedly prevented him from flying. Clark's fear of flying was further justified on the basis that the trip by sea (that would include Norman Robertson and Louis Rasminsky as representatives of the Bank of Canada) would provide an opportunity to discuss the approach to be taken. Abbott would then fly over a few days in advance of the meeting date.[98] There was one small problem, however. Canada had not been invited to participate.

The plan was to send the Canadian delegation to London even without an invitation.[99] This proved unnecessary when the United States accepted Canada's participation and the chancellor of the exchequer invited Canada to send a minister.[100] On 7 July, in preparation for a meeting among the three countries, Clark, Robertson, Rasminsky, and M.W. Mackenzie, deputy minister of trade and commerce, in addition to Dana Wilgress and A.E. Ritchie from Canada House, met eight British officials, including the British ambassador to Washington, Sir Oliver Franks, the high Commissioner to Ottawa, and the secretary to the Cabinet.[101] Franks informed the Canadians that Britain was being forced to adopt measures to check the drain on British reserves. On 8–9 July, Snyder met with Chancellor of the Exchequer Stafford Cripps, along with Doug Abbott. Cripps indicated that Britain had to save $500 million in the next year. This would require reducing Canadian imports to Britain, increasing access to the Canadian loan, increasing British exports to Canada (Abbott was given a list of eight things Canada could do to help), as well as other measures.[102] The Canadian officials met the British again on 11 July, under the umbrella of the Anglo-Canadian Continuing Committee on Trade and Economic Affairs. Further talks were to be held in Washington in September, and the British promised to speak with the Canadians before implementing any further restrictions. But Clark rejected a request for the British to draw more rapidly on the loan. The present rate was difficult enough, Clark argued, and an increase was not justified. Clark also 'emphasized the relationship between anything which Canada might be able to do … and the action which the U.K. might take to reduce costs [and thus increase its exports] and generally to provide evidence that there was some hope of the U.K. returning to multilateral trading.'[103] This was, after all, one of the reasons the loan had been provided in the first place.[104]

Two days later the commonwealth finance ministers met. According to Clark's account, 'Canada made it clear from the outset that she was by history and force of economic circumstances, a member of the dollar area rather than the sterling area, and that she could not therefore be considered as giving approval in any sense to the decisions of the others to restrict dollar imports.' Abbott employed more colourful metaphors to describe the situation: 'When a hemorrhage was in process it might be appropriate temporarily to apply a tourniquet to stop the flow of blood, but ... the greatest care was necessary to avoid allowing the tourniquet to become a substitute for other positive measures designed to avoid the loss of the limb.' The Canadian delegation argued that the U.S. recession was not the cause of the difficulties; the problem was the high cost level in the sterling area. According to Granatstein, the Canadians were providing an implicit call for devaluation of the pound. The meeting agreed to defer action until after the American-British-Canadian talks to be held in Washington in September. By 20 July, the Canadian party, after four sets of meetings, was ready to depart England.[105]

Throughout the summer of 1949 anticipation grew that Britain would devalue the pound. Speculation also increased, further reducing British reserves of gold and dollars. Between 30 June and 18 September the reserves fell by another 20 per cent. But despite this evidence of British need, the atmosphere for the Washington talks was negative. British criticism of the Americans had not helped. Clark informed a contact in the U.S. embassy that there would be 'no rabbit pulled out of a hat' to save the situation.[106] But regardless, there seems to have been a few magicians in attendance when the discussions resumed in Washington on 7 September. As had been publicly speculated for months, the British intended to devalue the pound. The main purpose of the Washington discussions was to ensure that Canadian and American policies would not counter the gains Britain hoped to gain from devaluation. An agreement was reached.[107] The British decision created goodwill and the meeting even produced consensus that the Marshall Plan would provide Britain with $175 million for wheat purchases from Canada, a practice that had been discontinued in March.[108]

The British presented their proposed devaluation to the IMF on 17 September and, after it was studied on the weekend and approved, the 30.5 per cent reduction (from US$4.03 to US$2.80) was announced on 19 September. This decision, according to Plumptre, signalled Britain's first significant move towards non-discrimination and multilateralism, as Canada had been urging. But with the devaluation of the pound – and more than two dozen other currencies related to or affected by the pound – Canada had a decision to make. If Canada also devalued its currency by the full amount of the British precedent, it would not help Britain export more to Canada in order to earn dollars. On the other hand, if Canada did not devalue, the economy would face strains from the improved competitiveness of the countries that had devalued, while still facing its imbalance in trade with the United States.[109] Graham Towers had previously suggested a range of options to Abbott, depending on the extent of the British devaluation. The finance minister essentially followed that advice and a decision was reached on a 9.1 per cent devaluation of the dollar.[110] The announcement was delayed for a day, however, because Howe argued that such action would push up the cost of machinery and equipment that Canadian producers were buying from the United States. Abbott hurried home from Washington for an emergency Cabinet meeting, in which his position was upheld and the devaluation was announced on 20 September.[111]

The intervention of a summer election prevented the budget of March 1949 being passed. Even though most of the changes had gone into effect, the minister of finance re-introduced his tax proposals on 20 October in Parliament. The budget speech laid out the devaluation crisis that had occurred and explained the government's policies.[112] The changes to the budget, overall, were minor. Revisions to the personal income and corporate profits taxes remained in place. The new dividend tax credit was extended to include dividends from all classes of shares (rather than limiting it to common shares). The commodity tax reductions remained, but they were of minor revenue significance. Abbott expected that his forecast surplus would be unchanged at $87 million. It turned out to be closer to $132 million.[113]

The surplus was reason for optimism. 'I believe Canada is on the brink of one of the greatest periods of productivity in her history,' Clark indicated in an interview. The recent oil discoveries in Alberta bolstered his usual optimism: 'I think it is one of the biggest things that has happened to this country for many years. I believe that within the next three to five years, Canada will reach a greater state of self-sufficiency through development of her oil. Once the oil pipe lines have been laid and the oil begins to flow eastward through them, I'm sure we will see a great number of benefits arising out of this field.' While Clark did not expect complete self-sufficiency in oil supply, he did feel that reduced imports would improve Canada's balance of payments. In addition, recent mineral discoveries also fuelled his optimism: 'We have only just begun to tap these rich areas. Canada, I believe, is without a doubt the richest nation in the world in natural resources.' The deputy minister was confident that demands on the building industry would be accelerated through construction of the planned Trans-Canada Highway (the federal government indicated it would pay half the cost), which would also boost tourism and open up new areas to development and new industries. 'It is no wonder that Doug Abbott's pictures show him as a smiling, carefree youth with few worries,' the interview noted. 'He merely reflects the infectious spirit of the boundless confidence radiated by his chief advisor, Dr Clark.'[114]

But Clark's influence behind the scenes was still cause of some public criticism. An article in the *Montreal Gazette* called the deputy minister 'one of the most controversial figures in federal financial circles during the last war ... before and after that struggle.' It went on to describe him as 'a crafty manipulator of the many economic agencies he has devised to stifle individual enterprise, discourage initiative, and extract from the taxpayer the last cent with which to promote public paternalism.' Clark was not particularly bothered by the criticisms. As long as they remained in the realm of economic and fiscal policy, his defence was reasoned, calm, and confident. But, the article observed, 'a soft-spoken man with a smile of diffidence, Dr Clark lets his voice rise to a heroic pitch only when denying charges that he likes bureaucratic power or that he might wield that power to the injury of anyone.' Such attacks on Clark's non-partisan role, or suggestions that he craved power and influence, rankled the deputy. He clung to his belief that above all he was a civil servant. 'If there is anyone less a bureaucrat than I am, I would like to know who he is,' Clark was reported as saying in the interview. 'None in the public service whom I know likes to court or provoke public controversy on a subject such as this, and as for myself, I want to do my job the best way I can. And that job, quite simply, is to make recommendations and direct steps to carry out the policies determined by the cabinet and by Parliament ... And if a deputy minister is worth his salt,' Clark added, 'he will be in a position to present to his minister alternatives from which to make a choice. It should also be said that our finance ministers have been quick to see through the intricacies of modern financial policy, and it is not true to say they have been forced to rely heavily on departmental advice.'[115] It would be difficult, if not impossible, for Clark to admit just how influential his role had actually been.

12

The End of an Era, 1950–1952

> Without a doubt, the greatest Brain Truster of them all is William Clifford Clark, Deputy Minister of Finance. He is the Super Duper of the Species, the great grand-daddy of all Brain Trusters, the very apotheosis of cerebral controls. Indeed, as much of what we live under today is *Clarkism* as Canadianism. Much more of our latter day economy may be traced back to Clark than to the Fathers of Confederation.
>
> – Austin Cross, Autumn 1951

It is often assumed that the preoccupation of the Canadian federal government in the post-war era was social security; in fact, it was defence.[1] By 1950 turf wars were again erupting between the finance and defence departments, much as they had during the Second World War. But Douglas Abbott was also having difficulty convincing the other departments to cut expenditures. The problem was compounded because the fixed expenditures were already high.[2] On 18 January Brooke Claxton asked for $425 million for defence in 1951–2, not including possible special assistance to NATO countries. This request reflected a significant increase from the $384.8 million that had been allocated for the previous year, which already amounted to 15.7 per cent of the total federal budget. Abbott pointed out that to avoid a deficit or alternatively higher taxes, $160 million would have to come from other departments. Paul Martin opposed the increase for defence until more was known about what NATO expected of Canada. It would not be possible, he noted, to continue such heavy defence expenditures while also expanding social services. Jimmy Gardiner agreed with Martin. Prime Minister Louis St Laurent, however, settled the matter: 'Any amount lower than $425 would involve ... a change in policy ... [and] would likely be interpreted as withdrawing from North Atlantic Treaty commitments.' Claxton received his $425 million, for the first time battling Abbott and winning. The sharp escalation in Cold War tensions shifted the balance in spending priorities.[3]

Clark had been 'the principal hold-out against an early Canadian contribution' to Western European defence, according to a memo from Arnold Heeney on 20 February. Since the previous June, when the U.S. administration had decided on a program for military assistance to Europe, pressure had increased for Canada to help. But the federal treasury was being depleted of funds allocated to supplement the unemployment insurance program, and Clark looked askance at any additional spending that was not directly aimed at relieving unemployment and stimulating the economy.[4]

Overall, however, Clark was pleased with the financial situation. In an interview he claimed not to subscribe to the common belief that the second half of 1950 would prove a difficult economic time for the United States and therefore Canada. Clark had expected the rapid decline in the American index of industrial activity in 1949 to reflect a paralleled decline in Canadian exports to the United States. But this did not occur. Trade improved and 'we got through the U.S. recession without a ripple in Canada.' There was also considerable uncertainty regarding British devaluation, yet the economy came through relatively unscathed. In 1950 'there were no such uncertainties.' Clark did note that Canada was in the first stages of a general price adjustment. Agricultural prices were artificially high and would come down; business would face stiff competition. A general downward readjustment of the price-wage-cost complex was unavoidable.[5]

Plans for another dominion-provincial conference were underway by the end of 1949. Clark was emphatic that the federal government be fully prepared for this gathering. In crucial instances in the past, Ottawa and the provinces had wrestled with fundamental issues in the federal relationship without being adequately prepared or establishing workable objectives. Clark believed the provinces would raise such issues as financial arrangements and taxation provisions, social security (responsibility for the unemployed, relief to distressed areas, and old age pensions), and health insurance.[6] The federal government had to be ready if it was going to continue to guide the direction of Canadian federalism. Early in March a meeting was held to plan for the upcoming conference and deal with possible topics of discussion. But the general sense at both the federal and provincial levels was that there were now few contentious topics. Regardless, this arena had been the most frustrating for Clark throughout his career and he was not going to be caught complacent.

The central issue in Canadian federalism was provincial financing. Clark wished to focus attention on the tax rental agreements, the national adjustment grants, and the need 'for an allocation of tax fields to the provinces that would be roughly equated to their responsibilities.' The latter had been 'examined repeatedly,' Clark noted, 'and it did not appear to be at all feasible to make any allocation that would be workable for all provinces.' There was no choice, however, but to revisit the matter. The *Rowell-Sirois Report* had been shelved but the spirit of the Commission continued to haunt dominion-provincial relations.[7] Clark called for an examination of government expenditures at all levels.[8] The onus would be on social security. Bryce, however, was concerned with the approach to be taken vis-à-vis new or additional conditional grants. He believed the major concern was the sharing of expenditures with the provinces in fields that were primarily or partially a provincial responsibility: 'Already we are heavily engaged in a number of these fields and there are currently developing plans in others and pending plans in still more.' Bryce was not thinking of social security in this regard; rather he was focusing on Ottawa's share of the costs for public investments, including such projects as highways, forestry, flood control, irrigation, land settlement, vocational training, and frontier development.[9]

On 28 March the budget of 1950 was brought down. Abbott announced that $4.2 billion was the expected target for national expenditures. There was thus little likelihood of further tax reductions, although tax increases were also unlikely. The budget dealt largely with technical matters, such as the treatment of undistributed income and capitalization of income, profit-sharing plans, and charitable organizations under the corporate income tax rules.[10]

In the following months, the government's focus turned to old age pensions. A joint Senate–House of Commons Committee held hearings on the issue and all but two submissions argued that the means test should be eliminated or reduced.[11] Support for a contributory pension had diminished, largely as a result of the administrative difficulties. The only other option discussed was a universal pension. The views of the departments of finance and national health and welfare clashed at the hearings. The debate took the form of a conflict between the committee's two principal advisers: George Davidson, deputy minister of welfare, and Mitchell Sharp, director of the finance department's economic policy division. Davidson believed that the contributory principle was a 'cumbersome and ineffective way of overcoming the evils of the means test.' Sharp put forward the position of finance that a contributory plan provided the only adequate control over costs. But the finance department was now prepared to include a small minimum pension (smaller than the forty dollars a month being paid under the means-test plan) which would be payable to anyone who had made any contributions. According to Ken Bryden, 'Sharp's case was bound to fail.' Most committee members wanted to get rid of the means test as soon as possible: 'Even with provision for a minimum pension, a contributory plan would not accomplish that objective completely because non-contributors would still be uncovered. In any case, a minimum of less than $40 a month was regarded as politically unacceptable.'[12] Clark favoured the replacement of the means test with a universal system, although he was concerned that universal pensions not related to individual contributions might be difficult to keep under control. The committee, however, was interested only in getting rid of the means test.[13]

The committee on pensions tabled its report amidst the activity surrounding the beginning of the Korean War in June. The report came down in favour of a universal pension at the age of seventy and a means-test pension at sixty-five, both based on the prevailing figure of forty dollars a month. No proposals were made for financing the plan. In testifying before the committee, Sharp put forward his department's position. Finance opposed an insurance plan, which would fund pensions in such a way that the worker would be paying into a collective annuity for old age. The department preferred a pay-as-you-go plan and Sharp outlined the alternatives for finding $250 million in taxes to pay for a $40 a month universal pension at age seventy, plus a means-test pension between sixty-five and seventy. An increase in the federal sales tax of 5 per cent, to a total of 13 per cent, would also raise the full amount. A third option was a payroll tax, paid by the employer and passed on to the consumer. Other ways of raising the money included a universal tax of 2.5 per cent on all personal income, an increase in income tax rates, or a reduction in personal exemptions. The Department of Justice indicated that paying for a pension out of general revenues was within the federal government's powers but a contributory plan was not. Any proposal to finance the plan with a tax specifically for the pension (which

St Laurent wanted as a second-best alternative to a contributory plan) would need a constitutional amendment.[14]

But the demands of the Korean War increased in the summer of 1950 and altered the government's fiscal plan. The Cabinet authorized another $40–50 million for the fiscal year. On 2 August, the Cabinet approved a special service force to serve in Korea, or if not needed there, to be employed as part of Canada's NATO commitment. At the same time defence spending was again increased. An extra $90 million was committed (an increase of 20 per cent in two weeks); the money came from the budgetary surplus. According to Abbott, Canada 'would probably have to go on a semi-war economy.' The finance minister was also concerned about inflation. He indicated that the government would have to either increase taxes or cut expenditures in other areas. On 9 August Abbott suggested that the Treasury Board review all departmental spending to determine which projects could be postponed.[15] On the same day, Prime Minister St Laurent informed Cabinet that defence spending for 1951–2 could be expected to reach $850 million. Pearson told Dexter that he believed the total would reach $1 billion when the military assistance to NATO was included. The total budget was only $2.6 billion. The Cabinet discussed the option of cutting spending on the projected new universal old age pension, thereby saving an estimated $324 million. Paul Martin indicated that it would prove difficult to explain to the public that the government could find the money for defence but not for old age security.[16] Parliament was recalled on 29 August and the Defence Appropriation Act, approving $709 million, was passed.[17] By September, both St Laurent and Pearson provided assurances that the government had no intention of shelving the revised pension scheme.[18]

A second budget was delivered in 1950, because of the revisions caused by the war. The expanded defence program now necessitated tax increases. But the increased defence spending also reflected the costs of the Cold War and these costs would not end with the Korean conflict. Defence remained a priority for the rest of the decade. During the 1950s, $18 billion would be spent, amounting to 40 per cent of the federal budget for five years and reaching a peak in excess of 45 per cent in 1952–3.[19] Abbott's tax program in the second budget of 1950 was intended to raise revenues by approximately 10 per cent. The principal increase was in the corporation income tax. There was, however, also a mass revival of excises on such items as liquor, candy, electrical appliances, sporting and leisure equipment, and automobiles. The increased taxes yielded impressive results. As a result of inflation, an active economy, and swelling corporate profits, the revenue for 1951 topped $3.1 billion rather than an expected $2.7 billion.[20]

By September, Canada was facing yet another dollar problem with the United States, but this dilemma was of a very different nature. American dollars were now flowing into Canada too quickly. Canada was a good place to invest, partly because of the Korean War and the Marshall Plan, and partly because there was recognition of the abundance of mineral wealth being exploited. But there was also a significant amount of short-term money flowing into the country, based on hopes for a speculative profit on a Canadian dollar perceived to be undervalued and likely to rise. According to Clark, 'During the spring and summer of 1950, as our economic situation improved, a large and increasing number of people, both inside and outside Canada, came to the conclusion that the Canadian dollar was undervalued at the chosen official rate and, therefore, on top of a large inflow of investment capital interested in the development of our oil and other natural resources, we had an avalanche of speculative capital lured by the almost "sure bet" of an upward revaluation of our dollar.'[21] Towers indicated that the influx had to be halted because it was creating a false impression that Canada was wealthy, thereby reducing the economy's bargaining power. The influx was also fuelling inflation while keeping interest rates low. The government had to borrow to carry the increased reserves.[22]

In order to defend the fixed exchange rate, and keep the value of the Canadian dollar down, Canadian authorities purchased U.S. dollars totalling $34 million from July to September. Canada held its international reserves in the Exchange Fund (a government account in the form of deposits in the banking system) rather than the Bank of Canada. The government expanded its sales of short-term securities, sold to the central bank and commercial banks, in an attempt to obtain Canadian dollars to buy American dollars (or other foreign exchanges). The commercial banks had large holdings of short-term securities and reserves at the central bank, and were in a position to expand loans and investments. Such expansion was not what the government planned in September 1950 when the economy was booming and restraint to control inflation was needed. As a result, the exchange rate had to be abandoned.[23] As Clark pointed out, 'In ten weeks in the third quarter of 1950, our exchange reserves increased by over 500 million dollars. The flood, which of course increased the already strong pressures toward inflation, seemed to acquire momentum steadily. It was clear beyond peradventure that the existing rate could not be held. It was equally clear that in the unsettled state of world conditions – and having in mind the common pool of highly mobile capital serving our two countries – no one could pick some new fixed rate "out of the air" or select it by any theoretical equation and say with any assurance that that new rate could be maintained.'[24]

Shifting to parity with the U.S. dollar was one possibility, but that could lead to a rapid fall in exchange reserves; selecting a rate below parity risked choosing the wrong rate and not solving the problem at all. The only solution, Towers and Clark concluded, was to let the value of the dollar fluctuate and float.[25] 'Forced off a fixed rate for the second time since the war's end,' Clark observed, 'we had no choice but to leave the rate free to find its own level in the market.'[26] The Canadian dollar was strong as a result of trade and investment related to the Korean War (which could end at any time) and the Marshall Plan (which would end in 1952). Meanwhile, Canada's trade balance was negative because British and European recovery had still not occurred. Fixing a new par value was difficult. But Canada's experience with a flexible exchange rate in the 1930s had been positive. Abbott accepted the recommendation and on 30 September the finance minister announced that Canada's dollar would be allowed to float.[27]

There was, however, one problem. Canada had made a commitment through the IMF to maintain a fixed exchange rate. It fell to Louis Rasminsky to make Canada's case before the other executive directors, which he did prior to the announcement. Rasminsky argued that Canada was in a unique position relative to the United States and the large and very volatile American investment in Canadian securities. The IMF staff stressed the importance of conforming to the rules and thus urged other measures to deal with Canada's problems, such as domestic anti-inflation measures or restrictions on capital imports. Rasminsky responded that the government was particularly opposed to the latter idea, which might be interpreted as being hostile to U.S. investment. The IMF executive directors gave Canada permission to experiment with a floating exchange rate 'for a short period.'[28] Rasminsky would have to defend Canada's floating exchange rate many times before the 'short period' ended.

The floating exchange rate left the Canadian dollar almost totally at the whims of the marketplace. The Exchange Fund was directed, confidentially, to buy or sell foreign exchange in such amounts as were needed to avoid extreme day-to-day fluctuations. It was not to establish any particular exchange rate and had to remain subject to limits on the amounts that could be spent to achieve this result. The decision and resulting provisions marked 'the initiation, indeed the invention, by Canada of what subsequently became known, internationally as well as nationally, as a "clean float."' Canadian policy, Clark noted, was 'to allow the rate to be determined by the normal play of economic forces, without official intervention except to ensure orderly conditions in the exchange market. No attempt is made to hold back a trend in either direction but only to smooth out excessive short-run fluctuations.'[29]

The Bank of Canada, meanwhile, was taking its own action to curb inflation. 'Anti-inflationary fiscal policy in this recent period has been supplemented by monetary and credit policies with a similar bias,' Clark observed. In October 1950 the bank raised its discount rate from 1.5 to 2.0 per cent. Because the commercial banks had not been borrowing from the central bank, 'the effect of this action was essentially psychological: it served as an indication of the central bank's appraisal of the market and a warning that its open market operations would likely be used in the direction of restraint rather than of expansion. The Bank continued to follow a policy of keeping the commercial banks in a fairly tight cash position.' The government moved to restrain the expansion of credit by the introduction of consumer credit regulations, which were sharply stiffened four months later. In February 1951, after a substantial growth in the outstanding volume of bank credit had occurred, a conference of the ten chartered banks called by the Bank of Canada resulted in a voluntary agreement under which the banks agreed to revise their lending policies.[30]

A dominion-provincial conference was scheduled for December. Prime Minister St Laurent suggested to the provinces that the gathering be limited to fiscal matters and social security.[31] In preparation, an interdepartmental committee on social security considered possible revisions to the old age pension scheme. Clark, however, was not pleased with any alterations to the old pension plan or its means test. The economy was now in a 'semi-war' condition and further social security measures would best be postponed. On the other hand, Clark admitted that if the government did not go ahead with the pension plan, organized labour would likely extract plans, regardless, from private industry. These private pension plans would be expensive and 'violently inflationary.' They would 'make any government plan of the future look pitifully stingy and thus encourage demands for a more costly government plan. In other words, the government might better get into the field economically, before private industry gets in extravagantly with hugely inflationary effects.'[32]

Abbott shared Clark's concerns and questioned whether the government should act on the pension issue at present, given its commitments to the war in Korea. The finance minister argued that an additional $20 million or more to existing financial commitments would be inflationary and a new tax for pensions could inhibit economic growth. Abbott acknowledged that the increased spending power of those receiving pensions could provide compensation, but imposing levies for old age pensions would make it more difficult to raise taxes to meet the country's defence needs. The concern was that 'taxes essential to subvent contributory pensions would provoke higher wage demands, and the government would expose itself to the charge of bumping up prices and diluting the pension's value.' Both Clark and Abbott made it clear that they were not opposed to the scheme but rather to its timing. Abbott suggested that the government postpone the pension program until its other commitments had been fulfilled and that the conference should schedule another meeting in eighteen months.[33]

But according to Martin, even if the dominion-provincial conference implemented the joint committee's report, it would still take at least nine months to pass the necessary legislation and complete the administrative arrangements. Moreover, it would now be embarrassing, after all the time, effort, studies, and publicity, 'if the government were to turn up at the conference without a plan.' In addition, Martin claimed that if the government did not move to establish a contributory scheme, 'it would soon have to earmark more funds, to supplement existing pensions by $5 or $10 a month. Federal expenditures would then grow by $40 to $50 million a year and thus make it extremely difficult to introduce universal pensions at a $40 level.' In the end, St Laurent sided with Martin and indicated that the government had little choice but to proceed with the universal pensions.[34]

The government's old age pension proposal was submitted to the Dominion-Provincial Conference that opened 4 December 1950, the first such gathering since the failed conference in 1946. By the end of the conference three days later, no province opposed the federal plan to seek a constitutional amendment to introduce universal pensions for those over the age of seventy, financed by special taxes. Quebec, Alberta, and Nova Scotia were non-committal, while the other provinces were in favour. To maintain the momentum, a draft constitutional amendment was sent to the provinces within two weeks.[35] The scheme was approved by Parliament and provided a pension of forty dollars a month to those above seventy, while a means test was demanded of those between sixty-five and seventy.[36]

But the conference was also expected to deal with the tax rental agreements. Ottawa had entered traditional fields of provincial taxation supposedly out of wartime necessity but mainly because the federal system had broken down during the Depression. The Rowell-Sirois Commission had been appointed to solve this problem but the commission's major solution to the fiscal problems – the national adjustment grant – had not been implemented. The federal government entered provincial jurisdiction without agreement and the failed conferences that followed were testament to the fact that the problems had not been solved. Since 1945 certain provinces – Nova Scotia, Saskatchewan, Manitoba, and New Brunswick – had been calling for a return to Rowell-Sirois. The Saskatchewan government, for example, protested that the tax rental agreement formula resulted in 'an unequal standard of social services for the different provinces,' the exact situation Rowell-Sirois was attempting to rectify. The present conference therefore should be used to press for action 'along the lines advocated by the Rowell-Sirois Commission.'

But federal finance officials, including Clark and Bryce, who previously supported the commission's report, were now critical. In particular they opposed the national adjustment grant. They saw three major difficulties: the measurement of the grants, the determination of comparable standards of services among provinces, and the extent of the discretionary power to be given a federal finance commission responsible for the grants. But regardless of these concerns, the main obstacle that had always plagued the Rowell-Sirois Commission remained – the opposition of the affluent provinces: 'There is thus the political problem of getting the National Adjustment Grant formula approved by all the provinces. The three prosperous provinces are asked to vacate their richest tax fields and receive no grants by way of compensation except the implied prospect of assistance in times of extreme adversity. It is true that they would be relieved of their expenditures for relief and for servicing their public debt, but these compensations which may have been sufficient in 1937, now seem to be outweighed by their loss of revenue and the potential reduction in their independence.' Despite their opposition to the national adjustment grant, the finance department took the position that the direction of Canadian federalism was actually following the course charted by Rowell-Sirois. Clark claimed that 'most of the Sirois recommendations ... have been carried out in whole or in part.' The main difference between the commission proposals and the tax rental agreements was 'one of emphasis, reflecting the environmental circumstances prevailing at the time each was conceived.' As a result, 'whatever may have been the merits of the recommendations of the Rowell-Sirois Commission in the context of 1939, they are, in many respects, no longer relevant.'[37]

The Dominion-Provincial Conference was also supposed to deal with the tax agreements because they were designed to be temporary and scheduled to expire. There was no sense of immediacy, however, because of the prosperous economic conditions facing the nation. Dominion–provincial conflict was at a minimum and Ottawa was able to 'raise adequate revenue without interfering with the existing financial independence of the provinces.' The tax agreements provided guaranteed revenues to the 'less-favoured' provinces at a level that would not have been possible without increased rates of taxation. That said, Clark was well aware that while conditions at present were 'propitious for the attainment of federal aims,' there was no guarantee they would 'remain so in the future.'[38] Regardless, it was decided not to upset the applecart. The agreements were renewed.

By the following May, provincial approval was given to a constitutional amendment to permit the proposed federal pension plan changes. The amendment did not transfer authority from the provinces to the federal government, as had occurred in 1940 with unemployment insurance. Instead, it provided jurisdiction to both levels of government. In the event of conflict, however, provincial law would prevail. The legislation was held over until the fall to permit the finance department time to work out the details of how to finance the scheme.[39]

Early in 1951 the Cabinet met to discuss another bill for increased military preparations. Claxton and Pearson offered a gloomy report to Cabinet, pointing to the entry of China into the Korean War and the serious dangers of Communist attacks elsewhere, and urging that Canada press ahead with its NATO requirements.[40] A report for the Cabinet Defence Committee estimated the total outlay for 1951–2 at $1.9 billion, not including any costs for possible expansion of NATO air training in Canada. This amount was $1.2 billion more than the original 1950–1 budget, almost 40 per cent of the entire federal budget, and according to Abbott, 10 per cent of gross national product. There would have to be tax increases and spending cuts, and possibly even commodity controls.[41]

Brooke Claxton laid out a plan for funding and rearming the military that involved a $5 billion program over three years. The Cabinet met on 21 February, and the mounting costs of defence dominated discussions. The Cabinet approved construction of the Pinetree Line, consisting of thirty-two radar stations to be constructed along the forty-ninth parallel, with two-thirds of the cost, or about $29 million, to be borne by Canada, and the rest by the United States.[42] The same Cabinet meeting authorized sending the rest of the 25th Canadian Infantry Brigade to Korea, ending any hopes that these troops would not be needed and could instead be used to meet Canada's NATO responsibilities.[43] At the meeting on 22 March, Cabinet approved creation of the new Department of Defence Production, with C.D. Howe as minister.[44]

The federal budget of 1951 was delivered on 10 April and the impact of the Korean War, as well as the Cold War, was evident. 'The Korean situation is significant of even greater dangers,' Abbott announced. 'It indicates that Russia is prepared to take steps involving the risk of a general war ... In the months that lie ahead, perhaps indeed for several years, we shall face a test of nerves, of our readiness to sacrifice immediate interests for future security. This is the background against which the budget must be viewed.'[45] In response to the increase in prices of critical materials in short supply, the government was urged to follow the U.S. lead and introduce price ceilings while also taxing excess profits. Instead, however, the government adopted selective controls and imposed heavier general taxation to combat inflation. A surtax of 20 per cent was imposed on both personal and corporate income taxes. In addition, the sales tax was increased from 8 to 10 per cent (the first change since 1936). Many of the 15 per cent excise taxes were increased to 25 per cent and new taxes were imposed on a variety of new household appliances, including stoves, refrigerators, and washing machines. As it turned out, revenue yields proved more optimistic than expected and nearly $4 billion was generated rather than the expected $3.7 billion. The result was a substantial budget surplus of $211.3 million, which was approximately 7 per cent of expenditure.[46]

The Korean War interrupted a promising period of sustained peacetime expansion. As Clark noted, 'Suddenly we had to superimpose a defense program involving expenditures rising to four or five times their previous size on an economy which was already straining its resources to meet the demands of an unprecedented capital investment program and of a public anxious to increase both its volume of consumption and its leisure.' The wartime conditions were too close in memory, causing 'a wave of abnormally heavy buying, by consumers as well as by trade and industry, in order to forestall the expected shortages and higher prices of a war period.' The result was inflation: 'There was great temptation and pressure to use the direct method and apply immediately over-all price controls.' But the imposition of price controls had succeeded during the Second World War as a result of their combination with other factors: 'The control of inflation during the war had been highly successful and the public tended to attribute this success solely to the spectacular imposition and maintenance of a general price ceiling and failed to understand how much it depended on the powerful indirect controls that were also at work – the very heavy taxation, the stiff controls over credit, and the vigor with which the campaigns to maximize and mobilize public savings were conducted – as well as on a massive application of direct controls on many other aspects of economic life and on general patriotic support which can be sustained only in a full-out war effort.'

Close analysis of the situation, according to Clark, revealed 'an entirely new set of conditions.' Canada was facing 'a hot phase of a cold war of indeterminate duration,' which would likely use '10 to 20 per cent of our national product rather than 40 to 50 per cent.' Price controls were undesirable because they could not obtain the almost universal support needed to make them administratively feasible and they might have to be maintained for a long time. As a result, 'they would tend to impair the productive efficiency of the economy and to undermine the foundations of the very freedom we were seeking to defend.' Regardless, price controls 'would do nothing to attack the root causes of the threatened inflation.' According to Clark's analysis, the federal budgets were demonstrating a reversal in Canadian fiscal policy. Faced by the prospect of soon reaching more than double the recent levels of total expenditures, the Department of Finance was seeking to produce balanced budgets through tax increases while also looking to secure certain supplementary anti-inflationary benefits by the particular distribution of these tax increases: 'Nearly half of the increased revenue yield was designed to come from increased sales and excise taxes, because the Minister believed that while such commodity taxes would, in the first instance, raise prices, it was fundamentally more anti-inflationary to restrain consumption and encourage saving by such taxes on spending than still further to increase taxes on incomes which are, in effect, taxes on producing.'[47]

For Clifford Clark it was time to re-examine the entire system of Canadian government finance. To a large extent his career had undertaken such a process, regardless. As far back as the 1930s Clark realized that the system required overhauling and reshaping in line with national growth and expansion. The war intervened, but in the post-war era the deputy minister of finance looked to revise the Consolidated Revenue Audit Act in order to place government finance on what he considered a more sound basis. The Financial Administration Act drafted by Clark consolidated all pertinent practices into a concise legal description of the structure and functions of the institutions connected with financial policy, public accounting, and auditing. Without altering basic principles of parliamentary control of finance, it modified much of the relevant machinery and drew clearer lines between the functions of the Audit Office, Treasury Board, Comptroller of the Treasury, and Cabinet. The act removed the auditor general's responsibility for auditing expenditures and enlarged the powers of the comptroller of the treasury to judge the legality of expenditures before they were made. It increased the power of the Treasury Board, transforming it into an inner Cabinet with undisputed power over financial and administrative policy, subject only to a final check by the full Cabinet. 'By its clear separation of functions,' Norman Ward notes, 'and their allocation to specific officers, the Financial Administration Act not merely made statutory a system of financial control which was unique in the Commonwealth, but also greatly facilitated parliamentary surveillance of it.' The act also brought parliamentary control over public property and stores that did not previously exist. It empowered the auditor general to determine whether adequate records were kept, and appropriate rules and procedures were followed to control stores and property. It attempted to bring Crown corporations, which had proliferated during the war, under the same kind of audit as government departments. In sum, Ward claims, it was 'a great legislative landmark.'[48]

The Financial Administration Act was introduced into the House on 25 June, and Doug Abbott perceived an opportunity to acknowledge and praise the career of Clifford Clark: 'I know, Mr Chairman, that it is not customary to call the attention of the house to the work of departmental officers in connection with the preparation of legislation, but on this occasion I feel impelled to depart from the usual practice and to mention the name of my deputy minister. In the preparation of this bill, as in so many matters of importance to this house and this country, Dr Clark's contribution cannot be over-emphasized, and I consider it fitting that I should record this fact.'[49] But the Financial Administration Act had one important critic – Auditor General Watson Sellar. Apparently, when Sellar first saw the text of the act, 'he wondered how high-ranking finance department officials could have laboured twelve months to come up with such an inadequate product.' Sellar's particular concern was with the section of the bill bringing the financial affairs of Crown corporations under parliamentary control. He even drafted a revised section. Some of the changes Sellar wanted were incorporated, but financial control over Crown corporations fell far short of his expectations. The best the auditor general would say in the end was that the final act was an improvement on the earlier draft.[50]

By the summer of 1951 Clark was having health problems again. He hoped to take Margaret 'out to Jasper for a week or so and then go down in the interior of B.C., exploring the old Caribou Trail, amongst other things.' Unfortunately, a gall bladder operation 'knocked his summer plans into a cocked hat.'[51] By autumn Clark claimed to have recovered and to be feeling well again. On 19 October he attended the ceremony at Queen's University that made W.A. Mackintosh the university's twelfth principal and the first Queen's grad or member of faculty or vice-principal to hold the position. Clark was more than a mere spectator to the event. He had been a member of the trustees' search committee to find a new principal and he had been one of the majority that strongly favoured the selection of his old friend and colleague.[52]

The federal pension plan was introduced in October, and Abbott explained the financing to Parliament. St Laurent still favoured a contributory plan and felt something of that concept could be achieved if an earmarked levy was set up that represented the actuarial cost of the $40 universal pension. To this end, the Department of Finance was instructed to come up with a formula that covered the estimated $343 million cost of the universal pension (it was accepted that the means-tested pension would be paid out of general revenue). The department was further instructed 'to ensure that the revenues to be raised would, if anything, be somewhat less than estimated expenditures in order to avoid an accumulation of surpluses which might give rise to new demands.'[53] On 8 November, the new pension plan was approved by the House.

By mid-December the foreign exchange controls were ended. Graham Towers was convinced that Canada's economic position was now the strongest it had been since the end of the Second World War. Moreover, the floating Canadian dollar provided protection against a run on reserves. Towers discussed the situation with Clark, then with Abbott, and the details of the arrangements to end the controls were worked out and announced on 14 December.[54] 'We would be better advised not to rely on exchange restrictions but rather on the general handling of our domestic economic situation to keep it in reasonable balance with the rest of the world,' the finance minister announced, 'and to maintain the Canadian dollar over the years in an appropriate relationship with foreign currencies.' Clark believed that the decision to let the dollar 'go free,' combined with the decision to abolish foreign exchange control, were 'dramatic moves' leading to increased interest by foreign investors. Considerable investment had come in during 1950 (what Clark called 'the great influx of capital in 1950, amounting to over a billion dollars') but had been largely speculative and short-term. While the capital influx was smaller in 1951 ($563 million), it was more permanent. As Clark pointed out, 'Almost 300 million dollars went into direct investment in Canadian resources and industries and most of the rest represented borrowings by Canadians, chiefly provincial and municipal governments, in the New York market.' The influx continued into 1952.

Clark was careful, however, not to attribute the strength of the Canadian dollar and the economy in general to an influx of capital. Instead that strength was due to 'our balance on current account.' The reversal in Canada's balance of trade was impressive. 'In the twelve months ended in October, 1951,' Clark observed, 'our imports exceeded our exports by 122 million dollars. In the twelve months ended in October of this year, our exports exceeded our imports by 235 million dollars. This net reversal of over 357 million, with its consequent shift in the supply of and demand for Canadian dollars, has been, I am sure, the dominant influence on our exchange rate.' The success in achieving both external and internal stability 'in a highly disjointed world' was evidenced by the strength of the dollar, the size of the exchange reserves, the record level of foreign trade, and the unprecedented expansion of the economy. But Clark was too modest to chalk up all of the economic success to sound financial management. 'In some respects, of course, Canada has been especially fortunate in comparison with other countries,' he noted. 'Our good fortune in being spared the direct ravages of war and in being blessed by Providence with rich and extensive natural resources has contributed in a significant way to the difficult postwar adjustments.' The existence of alternative markets for many of Canada's basic exports in the United States, together with the buoyancy of that market in recent years, were also 'fundamental conditions of our relatively successful adaptation to the changing pattern of world trade.'[55] A post-Christmas letter in early 1952 summarized Clark's view on the Canadian economy: 'I also have always been a bull on Canada. I am proud of the developments of the last few years and the older and wiser (?) I get, I attribute more and more of the responsibility to the character of our people. We are not very brilliant but we are rather stable and solid and industrious and, fortunately, we are increasingly unified, despite our racial and religious diversities.'[56]

The 1952 budget came and passed in April with little commotion. Minor adjustments were made to excise taxes to soften their impact. Rates were reduced and some goods were exempted, but the revenue loss was less than expected.[57] The economy was functioning well, with little signs of trouble, and Clifford Clark had reason to be pleased. He had witnessed so many crises come and go that it should have been a time for relaxation and contemplation. As a result of what he called 'a happy combination of good luck, good geography, and good people – the Canadian Government of course would add good management – postwar Canada has confounded the pessimists and has enjoyed a period of unexampled development.' The deputy minister was the first to admit that it had not 'all been plain sailing.' There had been 'some squalls to weather, some stormy seas to test our seamanship, but on the whole the log reveals a record of rapid, forward advance in all the major indices of Canadian growth.' Clark pointed to the estimates of Canada's gross national product as evidence of impressive economic stewardship: 'At the low point of the depression in 1933, that product had fallen to 3.6 billion dollars; in 1939 it had climbed to 5.7 billions and by 1945 to 11.9 billions. Today it is running at an annual rate in excess of 23 billion dollars. Since 1946, it has increased in real terms by over 24 per cent. This period of rapid expansion could be called a boom were it not that the growth has been so balanced and the traditional excesses and distortions of a boom so little in evidence.' There could be no doubt, however, that Canadian industry converted from war to peace 'with an amazing rapidity and smoothness.' But Clark was too much the economist to assume the boom would continue unabated: 'There is nothing more certain in these dynamic and uncertain times than that we shall have fresh problems to face and new adjustments to make. Of these, the continuing disequilibrium in world trade and payments … and the constant threat of inflation arising from the cold war as well as from the impatient striving of a virile people for bigger and better things plus greater security and more leisure are likely to present the most compelling challenge. But there will probably be others as well.'

The persistent imbalance of many of Canada's important overseas trade partners, for example, required a number of difficult adjustments and posed continuing problems. Markets for some minor agricultural products were closed, with few alternatives in sight. Some manufactured goods suffered sharp reductions in their sales to overseas markets. 'As long as our major overseas customers find it necessary to hedge themselves about with discriminatory trade restrictions and keep their currencies inconvertible,' Clark admitted, 'we shall have problems to solve and shall retain a measure of vulnerability because of our heavy dependence on one market, great and expanding as it is.' Much was still left to be done, the deputy minister told an American audience, for the establishment of an effective system of multilateral trade and payments over the widest possible area: 'If perhaps this record of developments in Canada since the end of the war has been tinged with some pride in Canada's recent growth and confidence in its future, I would like to warn you that we are worthy neither of the idolatrous esteem with which you sometimes seem to regard us nor yet of the low estate to which you consign us at other times in moments of disillusionment. We are just a young country trying to get along with some of the strengths and limitations of youth!'[58]

Despite Clark's modesty, he had played a highly significant role in building the modern Canadian economy and in creating the prosperity being enjoyed by the nation. Walter Gordon was planning a luncheon to be held in Toronto in honour of that contribution. Gordon went to Ottawa to discuss the matter with the modest deputy minister. Clark's reaction to the invitation reveals much about his character but also about his strong, unrelenting views as to the role of civil servant. 'As I might have expected,' Gordon wrote, 'Clark's reaction was quite automatic. He said that it had been his privilege to assist various ministers and prime ministers in the formulation and implementation of a variety of policies. He went on to say that as a civil servant he could not accept credit or other form of public recognition for his services. He thought civil servants should remain anonymous and that credit for successful policies should always be accorded the public's elected representatives.' But Gordon asked Mackintosh to pressure Clark to accept the honour. Mackintosh responded that Clark would not accept unless pressed to do so by his minister. Abbott urged Clark to attend and he agreed to come to Toronto immediately following a visit he was planning to Chicago: 'The dinner was arranged and to the best of our ability we planned a great tribute to the man who, in the opinion of many of us, had in his own way contributed more than any other to the effort Canada had put forward in the war.'[59]

An article in *Saturday Night* agreed with Gordon. It discussed the impressive state of the Canadian civil service, noting that Clark was the only deputy minister hired to his post by Bennett. At the age of sixty-three, Clark was not the oldest deputy (that distinction belonged to Arthur Macnamara in the Department of Labour, who was sixty-seven) but he was the longest serving. The article also observed that 'in some of these departments, notably Finance, the deputy has built up a first-rate staff immediately under him, and the succession is already provided for.'[60]

Life at home for Clark was now more relaxed. In August 1950 Clifford and Margaret purchased a new house in the upper-class Ottawa neighbourhood of Rockcliffe for $26,000. The Clarks now lived directly across the street from the Pickersgills. On 21 October 1952, Clark's younger brother, died. Linden had been in poor health for some time and had sold off the dairy herd from the old farm.

Clifford and Margaret spent the Christmas of 1952 in Kingston with Eleanor, David, and their two children. Peggy and her two older children joined them on Boxing Day. Clark interspersed his few leisure hours with preparation for a speech he was to give in Chicago at the Political Science Association. His health seemed to be in order. He had just visited the doctor and been given a clean bill of health. 'He was in good spirits when he was with us,' Eleanor recalled. 'He was a little annoyed because nobody else would make this speech in Chicago and he was forced [by his minister] to do it. He wanted somebody else to do it.'[61] Clifford and Margaret gave each of their four children money for Christmas and Clark was pleased to see how they were all getting along financially. He had signed the note to back a mortgage on a house for Peggy and her family and he advised his sister Muriel on how to invest her money. 'So everything,' Peggy observed, 'was right with the world.'[62]

But everything was not right. On the evening of 26 December Clark took the overnight train to Chicago with Frank Knox, an economics professor at Queen's. Clark's son-in-law, David, drove him to the train: 'I'll never forget the evening because I took him out to the station,

Boxing Day night. The train was supposed to leave Kingston at 7, I think, and it was snowing. It was pretty cold too, quite a wind, and we got out there and the train was 45 minutes late … we sat there in the car and passed the time of day … Finally the train came in ... But during the course of the conversation he got talking about his paper that he was going to give in Chicago the next day. He said: "I just don't know what I'm going to do about it, somehow I've got to cut 45 minutes out of my talk and I don't know where to cut." He was really fussing over that speech that he was going to deliver.'[63]

The train arrived at Dearborn Street station in Chicago, where Clark and Knox were met by James Bell, professor emeritus of economics at Northwestern University. Clark complained for the first time that he did not feel well. He was hurried to the nearby Conrad Hilton Hotel on Michigan Avenue – just a half kilometre south of the Straus Building where he had worked nearly thirty years earlier. He registered at the hotel but was stricken in the lobby with a massive heart attack. He was rushed to the house physician's office for treatment, but it was too late.[64] Clifford Clark was dead at the age of sixty-three.

13

Conclusion

> The part played by an able Deputy Minister is played always behind the scenes, and Dr Clark was meticulous to keep it so, but successive Ministers of Finance, Rhodes, Dunning, Ralston, Ilsley, and Abbot – able men all of them – would be the first to admit that they leaned heavily on the sagacity and experience of their right hand man.
>
> – *Montreal Star*, 29 December 1952

News of Clark's death was relayed to Ottawa by the Canadian consul-general in Chicago. Doug Abbott and others including Bob Bryce, Ken Eaton, and John Deutsch met the Chicago train carrying his body at Union Station in Toronto early Monday morning, 29 December. The minister and his officials walked slowly behind the coffin as it was conveyed along the platform and through the station concourse. Ken Taylor and George Lowe accompanied the body from Toronto to Ottawa.[1] The funeral was held on 30 December at Chalmers United Church. Bryce, Eaton, Taylor, McIntyre, Deutsch, and Lowe served as pallbearers.[2] In Clark's department, the many officials who had been recruited and fostered by the all-powerful deputy minister felt lost without their mentor. On 1 January 1953, Ken Taylor became deputy minister of finance.

In the aftermath of Clark's sudden death, his colleagues were convinced that, as with O.D. Skelton, it was the burdens of war that had played assassin. Prime Minister Louis St Laurent admitted that Clark's 'constant devotion and sheer overwork in the war years impaired his health and undoubtedly contributed to his early death.'[3] As early as 1938, even before the war had begun, Hume Wrong asked Clark a pertinent question: 'Why cannot something be done to prevent our best officials in Ottawa from being half killed by the demands made upon them?'[4] If the demands posed by the Great Depression were heavy, the demands of the Second World War were staggering. Harvey Perry agreed: 'I think the war truly killed him as much as any one at the front.'[5]

The atmosphere pervading the budget preparations in January and February of 1953 was sombre. For twenty years Clifford Clark had dominated the process. He had always taken so much of the task onto himself that those left behind were unsure how to proceed. When the budget speech was given on 19 February, it was an ideal opportunity for Parliament to pay its respects to Clark. 'The people of Canada owe him a greater measure of gratitude than they realize,' Abbott observed. The long-time deputy minister of finance, who had worked so diligently and consistently behind the scenes, and who was always uncomfortable having his name directly mentioned in the House, perhaps would have conceded the tribute in this instance. Then again, probably not. Regardless, Abbott pointed to the difficulties inherent in the position of deputy minister of finance. But, inevitably, he found himself speaking directly to how Clark had shaped the post, along with the Department of Finance, the Canadian civil service, and ultimately, the Canadian economy:

> Dr Clark for more than twenty years was a great deputy minister. He was always forthright and vigorous in his presentation of the relevant considerations and the implications of whatever matter was under discussion. He was always completely loyal in carrying out whatever decisions were reached. His capacity for work and his tireless devotion to duty were extraordinary. At the same time he was a quiet and unassuming man, who shunned all personal publicity. His personal and intellectual integrity was of the highest order, his appreciation of the public interest and his love of Canada were intense. His technical skill in matters of financial administration held the admiration of all who knew him, not least among them those in other countries who had occasion to consult or negotiate with him. His sudden and unexpected death was a great shock to me and has been a severe personal loss to his many friends in this house ... He has left a lasting imprint on the quality of the public service in Canada, and his life and work will remain an inspiration to those who follow him.[6]

In responding to the budget, Clark's colleague from Queen's and Conservative MP for Greenwood in Toronto, J.M. Macdonnell, observed that 'as regards every member of this house, regardless of where he sat, the late deputy minister of finance was only too anxious to assist so far as he could in the discharge of the duties of any and every one of us.'[7]

Journalists from across the country paid tribute to the influential civil servant. The Regina *Leader-Post* commented on Clark's approachability. When asked financial queries, the deputy minister would invite the newspapermen to join him while he provided responses in simple, concise sentences. When the 'friendly and easily approachable, Dr Clark' was asked for information or explanation, 'his eyes would twinkle and he would reply: "Now, you wouldn't want any comment from me on that. I'm just what some people call a bureaucrat civil servant working in an ivory tower."' The journalists were well aware of Clark's legendary work ethic. 'Dr Clark was a terrific worker,' the *Toronto Star* recorded, 'so much so that he had little time for recreation or social affairs.' One of the most revealing tributes was offered in a *Victoria Times* editorial:

> Few men, even prime ministers, have had a greater effect on Canada's life ... by the testimony of foreign governments there was no abler civil servant in the world. He was one of those self-effacing persons who maintain the stability of the democratic system, execute the long-range plans and guarantee the integrity of government, untouched by the temporary accidents of party politics. Dr Clark was more than a financier, economist and administrator. He was also a dreamer. With a vision of the future denied to most men he foresaw the greatness of Canada and prepared for it. The fiscal policies which have made Canada the envy of the current world were largely his work. It was on his advice and on his dream that these policies were built ... As surely as any soldier in battle he gave his life for his country. The labors which he undertook far beyond the demands of duty have removed him at the height of his powers when he could be least spared ... The history of this era in Canada will recognize him as one of its major figures.[8]

The most impressive tribute, however, came from Clark's old friend Bill Mackintosh. No brief account of the legendary 'Dr Clark,' Mackintosh claimed, could accurately or adequately convey the scope and contribution of his career. Indeed, only those who worked alongside the deputy minister could appreciate his range of powers, his patience with important details, his zest for a promising project, his critical judgment, and his moral courage. Clark was a pioneer in bringing applied economics to the art of government. Indeed, he deserved credit for so many impressive achievements including the response to the Great

Depression, the establishment of the Bank of Canada, the development of housing policy, the expansion and restructuring of the banking system both domestically and internationally, the development of intergovernmental finance, the evolution of federalism, the construction of the Canadian welfare state, the improvements in the system of tax policy and administration, the extension of consideration to venture capital, the cooperative relationship between business and government, the revolution in economic thinking, the successful handling of Canada's economy during the Second World War, and the reconstruction efforts in the post-war period.

Beyond the official record, Mackintosh could not help but remark upon Clark's 'amazing capacity for rapid, almost frantic work.' 'The desk piled high in disorder, the brief case carried home protesting at the volume of papers bundled into it, the variable hours for meals – these all indicated Clark's optimistic hope of getting more done than any human could manage to accomplish. He was behind schedule on most things but on the crucial ones he just managed to meet the deadline. Whether it was business or social contacts he always tried to crowd more into an hour than could possibly be accommodated.' But despite his modest demeanour, Clark was also a sociable person. He preferred the company of people to being alone and he loved to spend hours in conversation. The conversation, however, had to be of interest and on a topic deemed of importance. Time was not to be wasted in idle chit-chat. Mackintosh also remembered Clark's particular tact when debating a contentious issue with his colleagues: 'He rose to an argument. When he no longer argued, one knew he was tired or ill. Indeed he had a habit, which could be annoying at times, of arguing vehemently and even indignantly against a proposal, on which he was not too well briefed, only to accept it willingly in the end if it was effectively defended. Having accepted it, he embraced it. Younger men were sometimes intimidated, strangers sometimes bewildered but the method though wearing had some pedagogical soundness.'

It was Clark's 'pioneering' skills as a deputy minister, as the consummate civil servant, that most impressed Mackintosh. His devotion to his successive ministers was exemplary: 'No personal preference or social engagement kept him from being at his Minister's side if he could be of help. Often he was there when he could easily have escaped. A good civil servant is alert to keep his Minister from stubbing his toe on the public, the opposition or the press, and Clifford Clark was a good civil servant.' Mackintosh was aware that public knowledge of Clark's achievements would likely live and die with those who knew him. Thus was the fate of the civil servant. Mackintosh hoped that despite Clark's attempts to avoid the public spotlight or even the credit he was due from his nation, he would be remembered: 'I think that knowledgeable historians will record that, adding momentum to what O.D. Skelton had begun and aided by the swift rush of events, Clifford Clark was a prime mover in the remarkable transformation of the Civil Service of Canada. If, as others say, Canada is served in its public service by a team of first-rate quality, if there is talent without doctrine and integrity without timidity, we can safely impute a generous share of the credit to Clifford Clark ... As long as the public service of Canada is held in high repute, as long as university people of integrity and creative ability are attracted to it as a career, Clifford Clark will have his enduring monument.'[9]

Clark was instrumental in the creation of the modern civil service in Canada. O.D. Skelton may have commenced the process, but Clark fostered and completed it. 'When I came,' J.J. Deutsch observed, 'the main structure of the modern Canadian Civil Service was well established.' The service had been converted from a patronage-ridden organization into a career based upon a merit system. 'It had acquired a goodly number of very outstanding personalities. I am convinced that this accomplishment will remain for all time the most fundamental single advance in public administration in Canada.'[10] As Taylor Cole points out, 'Clark was at the center of a small coterie of deputy ministers and of permanent and temporary senior civil servants and officials, mostly economists, who constituted the inner spring of the governmental mechanism in Canada and largely determined its economic policies.' While Cole argues that the mandarins did not represent a cabal or even a well-organized group with fixed membership, they did dominate highly influential organizations and committees. They possessed a shared university background and an academic overtone that fitted into the tradition established by Skelton: 'The members of this group were firm believers in the need for a class of employees in Canada modeled after the administrative class in Great Britain ... In fact, it has been suggested that these Canadian officials constituted themselves the Canadian counterpart of an administrative class.' One of the main attractions of the public service was the 'excitement, the spirit of accomplishment and the satisfaction of being at the center of things.' And the mandarins enjoyed exerting their new-found influence. They were drawn to planning and to the extension of governmental controls: 'The overall price ceiling, which was originally advocated by Towers, and the family allowance system, which was later initiated by Clark, illustrate vital public policies which emanated from this source.'[11]

'Clark's boys' certainly constituted a 'team,' which, as one observer commented, 'for sheer capacity, excelled anything that I have ever known and which was perhaps the equal of any that ever was.' Clark made the ideal captain because he 'had a real love for a good mind and he seems to have been inspired and stimulated but never threatened by the fact that keen rigorous thinking was going on close about him … there is bigness in wanting to be in contact with keen able minds and smallness in being threatened by them.' Observers were also impressed by the common sense of purpose: 'One could talk at length with different members of the team and detect differences in emphasis and sometimes in general approach, but seldom could one discern any important differences in central purpose.' This derived from 'a sort of common philosophic understanding as to the proper functions of the state.'[12]

The staff of the Bank of Canada and agencies tangential to the Department of Finance, as John Porter notes, 'joined with "Clark's boys" to create the golden age of Canadian public administration.'[13] And most of the 'Ottawa Men' were 'Clark's boys.' According to Perry, 'The guiding spirit, and the person whom we came almost to worship was Clifford Clark.'[14] Jack Pickersgill expressed the same sentiment. 'I had had the good fortune to meet Clark shortly after I joined the Prime Minister's Office in 1937,' he wrote, 'and I fell under his charm at once. Clark had a remarkably open mind and the faculty of treating younger people as equals and listening seriously to what they had to say. He was full of ideas himself and absorbed ideas from others like a sponge absorbing water. It would be difficult to measure the impact of his mind on the whole range of government policy. For twenty years his office was the balance wheel of the administration and the spearhead of innovation in the art of influencing and directing the national economy in a free society.'[15]

Clark's place in history ultimately rests on his handling of the economy during the Second World War. Relative to how it handled the disasters of the Great War, the Canadian government's response to the crisis is nothing short of remarkable. That the war was 'brilliantly managed,' Granatstein claims, 'means that it ranks among the greatest government feats in Canada's history.'[16] Mackenzie King's success in leading the nation through what had become 'Canada's War' was significantly built upon the work of Clifford Clark. One of Clark's major achievements was his handling of wartime relations with the United States. Indeed, he was the lead player in this pivotal relationship.

During the discussions leading to the Hyde Park Agreement, for example, Clark was the voice of the Department of Finance. Ilsley, who had only recently taken on the minister's post, had very limited involvement. The relationship between Clifford Clark and Henry Morgenthau was testament to the influence of the deputy minister in Washington's highest financial circles. 'We should note the fact,' Bob Bryce observes, 'that Clark himself, rather than his minister or his subordinates, did most of the reporting and negotiating with Morgenthau and White, both of whom respected and trusted him. He understood more about the United States and its attitudes and institutions than he did about their British counterparts, and more than the rest of us did. This, perhaps, was because of his years of work in the US during the 1920s, though he was working in the private sector then and the times were very different. He had many American friends and read more about the United States than he did about other countries. Whatever the reason, his ability to deal effectively with the Treasury Department was of real advantage to Canada at this important time.'[17]

But for all his achievements, Clifford Clark was not without his critics. The creation of what was derisively dubbed 'The Brain Trust' was the main criticism consistently hurled at the deputy minister. 'It has been suggested,' Mackintosh admitted, 'that he usurped ministerial functions and framed policies, that government became bureaucratic rather than democratic,' that Clark was the 'centre or head of a "brain-trust."' Indeed, it was the influence wielded by this group that caused Mackenzie King to become increasingly critical and suspect of Clark, particularly towards the end of their careers. 'Slighting remarks are sometimes made about the men who work behind the scenes as "brain trusters" and "bureaucrats" with enormous power,' the *Ottawa Evening Citizen* noted. 'They have to leave it to others to answer the charges, for they can say nothing in their own behalf.'[18]

To Mackintosh, such charges reflected 'a complete misconception of the nature of the Canadian public service.' The original 'brain-trust' was a group set up by President Roosevelt outside the normal executive positions of government. This group enjoyed extraordinary access to the president. 'Nothing analogous could be set up in the Canadian service,' Mackintosh argued, 'unless such a group was gathered about the Prime Minister and derived authority from him independently of Ministers. Nothing approaching this ever existed in Ottawa.' The work of civil servants in framing policy was channelled through ministers and then through Cabinet. But the real evidence came in the often strained relationship between this group and the prime minister.[19] Within the relationship between senior civil servants and Cabinet ministers it had become 'extremely difficult to separate influence from power.' The remarkable growth of governmental operations resulted in the creation of 'a new and relatively autonomous system of power and decision-making.'[20] Critics (even the erratic Pouliot) had a valid point when they complained about the influence wielded by the behind-the-scenes bureaucrats and their lack of accountability. As Doug Owram points out, the rise of government interventionism, the power of the bureaucracy, the decline of parliamentary authority, in conjunction with the dominance of the Liberals at the polls, raised a disturbing question: 'What were the long-term implications of this relation between an assertive bureaucracy, a government with wartime powers, and an apparently complacent public?'[21]

Clark has also been criticized for being a stalwart defender of the capitalist system. The deputy minister was proud of his role in housing policy, yet in John Bacher's analysis, Clark is presented as the 'anti-hero.' According to Bacher, Clark's 'ingenious machinations' upheld the private marketplace and thwarted the development of social housing. Bacher is largely correct. Clark may have pushed the federal government into the realm of housing by leading the charge and authoring the legislation, but his primary concern was with stabilizing the economy, controlling unemployment, and encouraging private enterprise. Canada faced a severe housing crisis, and ultimately the policies of Clifford Clark have to be judged a failure. The effective reforming of Canadian housing policy would not occur until after Clark was dead.[22]

Some historians also dispute the claim that Clifford Clark deserves credit for implementing social policies, such as family allowances, health insurance, or old age pensions, or at the very least that his role in these initiatives was driven by economic rather than altruistic motives. These criticisms also hold some validity. Clark would have fit into what James Struthers calls the 'industrialism school,' associated with the work of Harold Wilensky. According to this functionalist perspective, welfare programs were viewed

> as a logical and inevitable response to the forces of industrialization, urbanization, and the expansion of a wage-earning labour force. Interested in comparative statistical indicators of development such as the gross national product, the degree of urbanization, and the percentage of workers engaged in industry rather than agriculture, functionalist theorists

> argued that the path of welfare state development was a smooth trajectory on which all industrial nations eventually converged, albeit at different rates and with somewhat different mix and blend of programs. The most important explanatory variable was industrialism itself, which severed workers and their families from earlier kin-based networks of mutual aid, created the economic vulnerabilities associated with wage dependency, and generated the societal surplus needed to finance welfare state programs of redistribution and social insurance as well as the bureaucratic structure necessary to administer them.

Such analyses flew in the face of liberal claims 'that viewed most programs as the product of enlightened and altruistic reformers.' It also 'drew attention to the critical correlations between economic and bureaucratic growth as the necessary preconditions for the financing and implementation of welfare policy' and 'stressed the functional fit between the welfare state and capitalism, structures previously assumed to exist in tension, if not opposition to each other.'[23]

Clifford Clark was not a socialist; he was not a social democrat. He was, however, a 'new' Liberal who saw a new role for the state in the economy and society. While he could embrace and help implement the spate of social security measures undertaken by the Canadian government during the 1930s and 1940s, he was always careful to ensure that all economic considerations were taken into account, and this meant protecting the capitalist system and the role of private enterprise. At the same time, however, he also fell prey to the criticism of the Canadian business community, who viewed Clark as too willing to use the role of the state to direct economic development. For Clark, the fact that he was under fire from both sides of the political spectrum was proof that he was where he wanted to be – in the middle. According to Bryce, 'Clark, my own chief, wasn't moved by a general political attitude ... He was a believer in the reform of institutions and the reform of governments in Canada which the Depression had shown were unable to cope with economic adversity ... He also had included with that some sense of social responsibility but whether that could be regarded as social reform, whether it could be regarded as a democratic mood, I find it hard to say. He was a very complex character and he had been very much influenced by the Depression which he went through and he suffered very severely from it himself.[24]

Barry Ferguson gives credit to Clark and his group for establishing a twentieth-century liberal-democratic position that was powerful and pervasive yet distinct 'from the paternalistic reform program of social gospellers and sociologists, from the limited welfare-state-capitalism of post-social gospellers, and from the doctrines of social and political inevitability that each was based upon.'[25] According to Owram, the mandarinate consciously sought to avoid political ideology by employing the language of 'technocratic pragmatism.' In viewing their profession as a science, economists in particular believed it was possible to free themselves from doctrine and dogma and instead focus on efficiency and reform. Such a belief, however, was mere fantasy: 'Shaping this perspective was the fact that, for all their denial of class in the traditional sense, these writers reflected the views of the new "managerial" middle class, especially that component of it drawn from the academic world.'[26]

The period that encompassed Clark's career witnessed not only the creation of the welfare state and the triumph of Keynesian financing, but also the centralization of the Canadian government and federal system. This development is not surprising in the wake of the Great Depression and the two world wars. These historical developments led naturally to the formation of such an influential group of civil servants. The 'Ottawa Men' shared a strong vision of the nation they were shaping, and that process was certainly much easier to control if power lay at the centre with the federal government. As J.A. Corry points out, this trend also occurred as a result of the forces of nationalism and because Ottawa had relatively easy access to tax revenues, compared with the provinces. In addition, there was a 'sharp difference' in quality between the federal and provincial public services.[27] Clark and his 'boys' in Ottawa played a critical role in helping create a more centralized federal structure. But while Canadian history has been kind (indeed too kind) to this trend toward centralization, it was another source of Mackenzie King's criticism of Clark. King held (albeit not always consistently) to the traditional tenets of Canadian federalism that called for a balancing act between the two levels of government. While the Depression made it clear that adjustments to the machine were necessary, he was not prepared for a complete overhaul. This position brought the prime minister into conflict with his civil servants. The mandarins advanced their cause without hesitation and, in the end, they got their way. The federal system that emerged out of the Second World War was the most centralized Canada has ever witnessed.

But as Owram points out, the triumph of Keynesianism has been exaggerated. The importance of Keynes's ideas to the evolution of economic theory during the Depression and Second World War is indisputable, but Owram is correct in arguing that 'there is, however, somewhat of a myth surrounding the impact of Keynesian theory.' The triumph of Keynesianism led to a flawed belief in the inevitability and even the infallibility of the theory. It led to 'later Keynesians viewing it 'as not merely good economic theory but as permanent economic law.'[28] It also led to historical revisionism. An examination of the economic thinking of such influential individuals as Clark demonstrates that these ideas affected government policy in Canada more gradually and modestly than usually assumed. There is indeed danger 'in portraying Keynesian theory as bursting upon the mid-Depression as a revelation out of nowhere.' Changing views of the ability of the marketplace to correct itself and of the role of government to ameliorate economic conditions developed throughout the first half of the twentieth century, as Clark's writings make clear. But 'in formal terms classical economic theory remained intact. The belief still held that the natural point of equilibrium was at full employment and production.' Clark clung to these economic principles.[29]

Clifford Clark's death marked the passing of a generation. It was the end of an era. The civil service founded and built by Skelton and Clark expanded dramatically in the following decades but it became much less personal and informal. It also became less influential. 'In those days,' J.V. Clyne remembered, 'governments did not operate as many departments as they do today, so that the various deputy ministers knew each other well and met frequently. The deputies, within their spheres, exerted considerable influence on government.' In particular, Clyne remembers one of his first encounters with the legendary 'Dr Clark':

> It was not long after I arrived that I was appointed a member of the External Trade Policy Committee, reporting to the cabinet … At my second committee meeting, however, a subject came up for discussion that involved a shipping matter about which I did know something. The committee was about to reach a decision when I said, 'Gentlemen, if we choose to adopt this course it will be completely contrary to present government policy,' and I briefly outlined my reasons.
>
> There was complete silence around the table for a moment, and then Cliff Clark leaned across the table and said to me, 'Jack, are you absolutely sure you are right?'
>
> I replied, 'Absolutely.'
>
> Cliff leaned back and then, looking around the table with a beatific smile, said, 'In that case, gentlemen, we must change government policy.'[30]

Clark wielded such influence because he was a skilled civil servant. 'Top public servants,' Mitchell Sharp wrote, 'are powerful persons in the machinery of government at the federal level. They wield great influence. They do so because they are, in the main, professionals who have been selected for proven administrative ability and who devote their full time to government. In many cases, they have a greater influence upon the course of events than have Ministers, particularly the weaker and less competent.'[31]

Clark's death marked the end of this golden age for the Canadian civil service. The mandarins wielded too much power and the ensuing expansion in the civil service meant that the influence of individuals was superseded by a bureaucratic class. This expansion went unchecked as a result of the continued dominance of the Liberal Party and its close relationship with the civil service. Politics was replaced by 'the purer and tidier process of administration ... the administration of things had come to replace the government of men.' According to Denis Smith, 'The separation between Cabinet ministers and their senior advisers grew indistinct as the Cabinet and the Liberal party came to depend increasingly on the mandarins for ideas and policies; and a career in the higher ranks of the federal civil service became one of the favoured paths into the federal Cabinet. The political process of general elections and parliamentary debate appeared less and less central to the real business of managing the country's affairs. Politics was a quaint and frequently tiresome ritual to be fulfilled, providing diversion for some members of the government who had it in their blood; but power and authority were to be acquired elsewhere.'[32]

The speech that Clifford Clark was to deliver that fateful day in Chicago was published posthumously in the *American Economic Review*. He opened it with what could only have been a tongue-in-cheek comment about his *lack* of influence: 'I must resist the temptation to debate the merits of alternative public policies and confine myself primarily to the simple task of a reporter, sketching the general economic background and outlining the policies the government of Canada devised to meet the changing economic problem.'[33] The comment was as modest as the man himself.

Notes

Preface

1 Austin Cross, *Ottawa Evening Citizen*, 30 December 1952.
2 Granatstein, *Ottawa Men*, xi; see also McCall-Newman, *Grits.*
3 Bryce, 'William Clifford Clark,' 416.
4 Gordon, *Memoir*, 33.
5 Owram, *Government Generation.*
6 Ferguson, *Remaking Liberalism*, xi–xiii.
7 Cross, 'Watchdog.'
8 Cross, 'Meet Eight Key Men,' 37.
9 Granatstein, *Man of Influence*, vii.
10 Sharp, 'The Bureaucratic Elite and Policy Formation' in *Bureaucracy in Canadian Government: Selected Readings,* ed. W.D.K. Kernaghan (Toronto: Methuen, 1969), 69.

Chapter 1

1 Dumbrille, *Up and Down*, 1.
2 W.C. Clark to John Urquhart, 9 June 1941, personal collection, W.C. Clark Papers (hereafter CP).
3 McLean, *People of Glengarry*, 4.
4 R.C.M. Grant, *Story of Martintown* , 42–3.
5 MacGillivray and Ross, *History of Glengarry*, 355–7; R.C.M Grant, *Story of Martintown,* 26–7.
6 MacGillivray and Ross, *History of Glengarry*, 358.
7 R.C.M. Grant, *Horse and Buggy Days,* 3.
8 Editorial, *Winnipeg Free Press*, 29 December 1952.

9 R.C.M. Grant, *Horse and Buggy Days*, 3, 21.
10 Ibid., 21, 73; R.C.M. Grant, *Story of Martintown*, 104, 128–9; MacGillivray and Ross, *History of Glengarry*, 431–42.
11 It may have been 1894. Clark was no longer certain by the time he set down some biographical notes.
12 Clark's biographical notes, CP.
13 Clark's biographical notes, CP; Clark's 1939 autobiographical sketch.
14 MacGillivray and Ross, *History of Glengarry*, 246–7.
15 W.C. Clark to Charles Dunning, n.d., CP; Mackintosh, 'Skelton,' 74.
16 MacGillivray and Ross, *History of Glengarry*, 254.
17 Clark's biographical notes, CP; R.C.M. Grant, *Horse and Buggy Days*, 18, 19.
18 Clark's biographical notes, CP.
19 Ibid.
20 Macdonald reference letter, n.d., CP.
21 Osborne and Swainson. The 1901 population of Kingston was 17,961 and the 1911 population was over 20,000. The population of all of Glengarry had peaked in 1891 at 22,447.
22 The quotation is from Clark's 1935 speech given on the occasion of receiving his honorary doctorate from Queen's.
23 Queen's College had been founded in 1841, primarily to train Presbyterian ministers. When the break was completed in 1912, the renamed Queen's University was non-denominational and thus entitled to much more generous provincial support. Gibson, *To Serve*, 2:4; Neatby, *To Strive*, 1:265, 277, 284, 334.
24 W.A. Mackintosh could not 'resist speculating on what impact Clifford Clark with his optimism, his incorrigible love of projects, his persuasive enthusiasm would have had on the mining industry.' Mackintosh, 'William Clifford Clark: Memoir,' 2.
25 Clark's biographical notes, CP.
26 Mackintosh, 'William Clifford Clark: Memoir.'
27 Calvin Scholarship in Latin, 1908; Professor's Prize in English History and Professor's Prize in Preliminary Honours Latin, 1909; Prize for Latin Prose Composition, 1910; the Medal in Latin, 1910; the Medal in French, 1910.
28 Mackintosh, 'William Clifford Clark: Memoir,' 2–3.
29 W.C. Clark, 'University Training,' 13–14.
30 Mackintosh, 'William Clifford Clark: Memoir,' 2–3.
31 Clark's biographical notes, CP.
32 In 1908 he was licensed by the Department of Education in Saskatchewan to teach in Cambridge School District No. 342 (near present-day Rocanville, approximately two hundred kilometres east of Regina); Mackintosh, 'William Clifford Clark: Memoir,' 2–3.

33 Creighton, *Harold Adams Innis*, 27.
34 Winnifred Clark, interview, 24 November 1996.
35 Ibid.
36 None of Clark's children had any real idea as to what caused the break. They were aware that it was a subject that was not to be broached; and none of them ever did.
37 Cox, '"Cliff" Clark.'
38 Gibson, *To Serve*, 2:23–4.
39 W.C. Clark, 'Oscar Douglas Skelton,' 143.
40 Mackintosh, 'William Clifford Clark: Memoir,' 2–3.
41 W.C. Good, farm activist and later member of Parliament, wrote, 'I met Clark first in 1912 in the house of Dr O.D. Skelton, then head of the Economics Department of Queen's University, Kingston. He had recently graduated as one of Skelton's distinguished students.' Good, *Farmer Citizen*, 138.
42 Crowley, *Marriage of Minds*, 118.
43 K.W. Taylor, 'Economic Scholarship in Canada,' 7, 8; W.J. Ashley was one of the only other economists, appointed in 1888 as chair of political economy and constitutional history at the University of Toronto. Harris, *History of Higher Education*, 142–3.
44 K.W. Taylor, 'Economic Scholarship in Canada,' 7–8.
45 Owram, *Government Generation*, 346–7; George Britnell completed his doctorate at the University of Toronto.
46 Galbraith, *A Life in Our Times*, 44–5.
47 Mackintosh, 'William Clifford Clark: Memoir,' 3.
48 Galbraith, *A Life in Our Times*, 44–5.
49 Mason, 'Frank W. Taussig.'
50 Owram, *Government Generation*, 195.
51 The Clark and Henery Construction Company was a general contracting firm that specialized in bridge, wharf, sewer, and concrete construction and asphalt paving.
52 Arthur W. Clark to George Ellis Clark, 16 November 1912, CP; Arthur W. Clark to Clifford Clark, 2 December 1912.
53 Reports of the President and the Treasurer of Harvard College, Harvard University Archives.
54 Harvard University Catalogue, 1914–15, Harvard University Archives.
55 Clark's 1939 biographical sketch, CP.
56 O.D. Skelton to W.C. Clark, 7 April 1913, CP.
57 The first meeting was held in Ottawa in 1913; although a second meeting was scheduled for September 1914, the outbreak of war put plans on hold. The association was not reconvened until 1929. Owram, *Government Genera-*

tion, 64; K.W. Taylor, 'Foundation of the Canadian Political Science Association,' 582.

58 J.L. Morison to W.C. Clark, 5 January 1913, CP.

59 O.D. Skelton to W.C. Clark, 18 June 1913, CP.

60 Clark's 1939 biographical sketch, CP.

61 O.D. Skelton to W.C. Clark, n.d., CP.

62 Ibid.

63 Clark's handwritten notes, CP.

64 Smails, 'Story of Commerce,' 1–3.

65 Mackintosh, 'William Clifford Clark: Memoir,' 3–4.

66 Smails, 'Story of Commerce,' 1–3.

67 Faculty members who volunteered were paid half their regular salary while on active duty.

68 Gibson, *To Serve*, 11–12.

69 Neatby, *To Strive*, 299; Gibson, *To Serve*, 12.

70 Neatby, *To Strive*, 258–9.

71 Ibid., 267; Gibson, *To Serve*, 8.

72 Queen's University was embroiled in debates over Canada's attachment to the British Empire. The debate was so divisive that when the university was seeking a new principal in 1917, Adam Shortt was ruled out because of his stand as leader of a liberal nationalist group that included Skelton. Gibson, *To Serve*, 13.

73 Swanson was a Queen's grad with a University of Chicago PhD while Mitchell was from England and been trained at Oxford and Heidelburg. See Ferguson, *Remaking Liberalism*, 25–6, 31.

74 Ferguson, *Remaking Liberalism*, 25–31.

75 Smails, 'Story of Commerce,' 1.

76 Ibid., 1–2.

77 W.C. Clark, 'Financing the War,' 2.

78 W.C. Clark, 'Country Elevator,' 1, 6, 11, 22.

79 Morton and Wright, *Winning the Second Battle*, 14–15.

80 O.D. Skelton to W.C. Clark, 8 July 1916, CP.

81 Ibid., 6 August 1916.

82 Ibid., 7 September 1916.

83 George Chown to W.C. Clark, 2 September 1916, CP.

84 O.D. Skelton to W.C. Clark, 9 August 1916, CP.

85 Ibid., 26 August 1916, CP.

86 George Clark, interview, 19 March 1995.

87 Granatstein, *Ottawa Men*, 46.

88 W.C. Clark, 'Inflation and Prices'; W.C. Clark, 'Should Maximum Prices Be Fixed?' 432–61.

89 Bryce, 'William Clifford Clark, 1889–1952,' 414.

90 R.H. Coats, 'Memorandum for the Civil Service Commission,' 29 April 1918, vol. 47, RG32, Library and Archives Canada (LAC); R.H. Coats to W.C. Clark, 30 April 1918; Clark to Coats, 30 April 1918; Coats to Clark, 2 May 1918; Clark to Coats, 4 May 1918; Coats to Clark, 14 May 1918; Clark to Coats, 20 May 1918.

91 R.H. Coats to W.C. Clark, 31 October 1918, vol. 47, RG32, LAC.

92 Struthers, *No Fault*, 17–20.

93 Ibid.

94 As quoted in Sautter, 'Measuring Unemployment,' 481–2.

95 W.C. Clark to R.H. Coats, 7 June 1920, vol. 47, RG32, LAC.

96 No record survives of Clark's particular speech for the conference but it is likely that it was the same speech given in September 1920 in Buffalo to the International Association of Public Employment Services under a similar title: 'Regularization,' 16–17.

97 W.C. Clark to R.H. Coats, 7 June 1920, vol. 47, RG32, LAC.

98 Struthers, *No Fault*, 21.

99 Ibid., 38–40.

100 Stevenson, *Canada's Greatest*, 13.

101 Gibson, *To Serve*, 24, 36.

102 Smails, 'Story of Commerce,' 2; see also Shortt, *Search for an Ideal.*

103 Harris, *History of Higher Education*, 242–5.

104 Several years later Clark would publish several articles in the journal. The statistician in charge of preparing the index of business conditions was Warren M. Persons, who in 1924 would edit a book on business forecasting that included an article by Clark.

105 W.C. Clark, 'Business Research,' 206, 216.

106 Gibson, *To Serve*, 37.

107 Ibid., 39.

108 Walker produced what became the standard text on accounting. Smails eventually became director of the School of Commerce. Smails, 'Story of Commerce,' 7.

109 Gibson, *To Serve*, 39.

110 Smails, 'Story of Commerce,' 13.

111 W.C. Clark, 'Current Events,' 301–4.

112 Ibid., 296–301.

113 W.C. Clark, 'Business Cycles.' Part of this article was reprinted as 'The Pattern of a Postwar Depression: Here's What Happened after World War I as Seen from the Viewpoint of 20 Years Ago,' *Financial Post*, 11 January 1947.

114 W.C. Clark, 'Business Cycles,' 1–24.

115 Owram, *Government Generation*, 121.
116 Mackintosh, 'William Clifford Clark: Memoir,' 5.
117 *Queen's Journal*, 9 March 1923.
118 George Clark, interview, 29–30 April 1998.
119 Obituary for George Clark, *Cornwall Standard*, 23 March 1922.
120 MacDonnell, 'Decline of the Arts Faculty.'
121 W.C. Clark, 'University Training.'

Chapter 2

1 *New York Times*, 8 September 1930.
2 H.N. Gottlieb to W.C. Clark, 27 October 1922, CP.
3 There is another story of how Clark first came to the attention of the Straus Company. According to Wellington Jeffers of the *Globe and Mail*, 29 December 1952, in 1922 Clark gave advice to *Saturday Night* magazine: 'Straus issued bonds against buildings all over the continent and one issue was recommended in Canada for the branches of the former Home Bank. Dr Clark, then professor of economics for Queen's University, was asked to give an opinion. His opinion was adverse, but the bonds were nevertheless issued. Dr Clark was right and his stock went very high with the corporation which offered him its chief post.' The seventy branches of the Home Bank locked their doors in Canada's most celebrated bank failure in August 1923.
4 H.N. Gottlieb to W.C. Clark, 27 October 1922, CP.
5 Barry Ferguson argues that both Skelton and Clark by this time were becoming increasingly discontented with the administration at Queen's. The commerce courses were not proceeding as Clark had hoped and were 'only loosely related to the general arts curriculum, and the wider areas of public policy and social services were ignored. In fact, the new programs comprised exactly the narrow and technical courses the political economists disdained, and the university's limited adoption of reform represented a rejection of the essence of Skelton's aims.' Ferguson, *Remaking Liberalism*, 34–5.
6 W.C. Clark to H.N. Gottlieb, 1 November 1922, CP.
7 Ferguson, *Remaking Liberalism*, 35; Gibson, *To Serve*, 51–7.
8 Bryce, 'William Clifford Clark,' 414.
9 W.C. Clark to H.N. Gottlieb, 17 November 1922, CP.
10 Ibid., 4 December 1922, CP.
11 H.N. Gottlieb to W.C. Clark, 22 December 1922, CP.
12 As quoted in Crowley, *Marriage of Minds*, 130–1.

13 *Cornwall Standard*, 3 August 1923.
14 W.C. Clark, 'Forecasting Building Construction,' 113–29.
15 Bryce, 'William Clifford Clark,' 414.
16 Rediscounting is the practice of a central bank or authority lending money to private banks. The rediscount or discount rate is the interest rate charged for such loans, and is usually described as the bank rate. Adjusting that rate was one of the recognized methods for checking inflation and deflation and of stabilizing price levels and the purchasing power of money. Raising the rate discourages commercial banks from borrowing from the central bank or raises the cost of doing so, and thus discourages them from making loans of their own or even encourages them to call in loans. Thus the expansion of the supply of money is constrained, tending to check inflation. *House of Commons Debates* (2 July 1924), p. 3950 (Mr Good, MP).
17 Good complained that the deputy minister of finance admitted in 1924 that he had never thought of or discussed altering the bank rate, which is why Good felt the need for guidance of the experts that Clark's memorandum had proposed. Ibid.
18 Ibid., p. 3949. Years later, in his autobiography, Good revealed that 'the gentleman who sent me the memorandum on control of credit and banking in Canada, whose qualifications I mentioned in the House in 1924, was W.C. Clark … It is sad to reflect on the critical years of 1924–1934, during which practically nothing was done to head off the oncoming depression. No one would dream of asserting that the lack of adequate monetary controls was the sole cause of what happened; but I am quite confident that if Clark had come to Ottawa about 1925 remedial action might and would have probably been taken to mitigate some of the miseries which overtook all of us.' Good, *Farmer Citizen*, 137–8.
19 Watts, *Bank of Canada*, 8.
20 Owram, *Government Generation*, 212.
21 George Clark, interview, 19 March 1995.
22 Peggy Johnson, interview, 20 August 1995.
23 The building is described in detail in Condit, *Chicago*, 101–2, 108; Sheridan and Clark, 'Straus Building.'
24 W.C. Clark, 'Some Considerations.'
25 W.C. Clark to Charles Bullock, 26 May 1926, CP.
26 Tauranac, *Empire State Building*, 69–70.
27 George Clark, interview, 29–30 April 1998.
28 Nicholas Roberts to Clifford Clark, 22 December 1926, CP.
29 Ibid.

30 Grant, *Money of the Mind*, 165–6.
31 Ibid., 165.
32 Ibid., 167–9.
33 Ibid., 167.
34 Tauranac, *Empire State Building*, 79.
35 Ibid., 81.
36 Ibid.
37 Ibid., 79–84.
38 Granatstein, *Ottawa Men*, 46.
39 Clark's biographical sketch, CP.
40 W.C. Clark, 'Federal Reserve System.'
41 Gibson, *To Serve*, 62.
42 Ibid., 86.
43 England, *Living Learning Remembering*, 46.
44 W.C. Clark, 'Construction Industry: 1930,' 26–7.
45 W.C. Clark, 'Construction Industry 1932.'
46 W.C. Clark and Kingston, *Skyscraper*, 146–50.
47 Bryce, 'William Clifford Clark,' 415.
48 Clark and Kingston, *Skyscraper*, 144.
49 Bacher, 'Keeping to the Private Market,' 149–50.
50 Myers and Newton, *Hoover Administration*; Hayes, *Activities*, 113–14.
51 W.C. Clark to G.C. Monture, 7 November 1931, CP.
52 W.C. Clark to J.U. MacEwan, 18 February 1931, CP.
53 *Newark Evening News*, 17 March 1931.
54 Granatstein, *Ottawa Men*, 47; Mackintosh, 'William Clifford Clark: Memoir,' 6.
55 State of New York Banking Department to Clark, 14 July 1931, CP.
56 H.R. Amott to W.C. Clark, 23 September 1931, CP.
57 W.C. Clark to Charles Dunning, 29 May 1939, CP.
58 Principal Fyfe to W.C. Clark, 25 April 1931, CP.
59 W.A. Mackintosh to W.C. Clark, 17 April 1931, CP.
60 Ibid., 29 April 1931, CP.
61 Joseph Willits to W.C. Clark, 19 June 1931, CP; Charles Bullock to W.C. Clark, 28 May 1931.
62 O.D. Skelton to W.C. Clark, 29 May 1931, CP.
63 F.W. Taussig to W.C. Clark, 1 June 1931, CP.
64 W.C. Clark to O.D. Skelton, 10 September 1932, CP.
65 W.C. Clark to H.G. Stapells, 30 September 1931, CP.
66 W.A. Mackintosh to W.C. Clark, 13 July 1931, CP.

67 W.C. Clark to D.M. Allan, 12 November 1931, CP.
68 W.A. Mackintosh, 'William Clifford Clark: Memoir,' 6.
69 Gibson, *To Serve*, 96–8.
70 Harry Herwitz to W.C. Clark, 28 September 1931, CP.
71 Bryce, 'William Clifford Clark, 1889–1952,' 416.
72 W.C. Clark to H.R. Amott, 28 September 1931, CP.
73 W.C. Clark, 'Flight.'
74 Ibid.
75 Ibid.
76 Ibid.
77 W.C. Clark to L.D. Edie, 27 October 1931, CP.
78 Chisholm, 'Canadian Monetary Policy,' 242–3; Bryce, *Maturing in Hard Times*, 127.
79 Watts, *Bank of Canada*, 8–9; Fullerton, *Graham Towers*, 41; Bryce, *Maturing in Hard Times*, 127.
80 Chisholm, 242–3.
81 Owram, *Government Generation*, 212.
82 Chisholm, 'Canadian Monetary Policy,' 227; Bryce, *Maturing in Hard Times*, 127.
83 Chisholm, 'Canadian Monetary Policy,' 226–8, Bryce, *Maturing in Hard Times*, 126–8.
84 John Courtney had been hired in 1869 as chief clerk for the newly created Treasury Board and was trained by the first deputy minister of finance, John Langton, whom he succeeded in 1878. Courtney held the post from 1878 to 1906. Bryce, *Maturing in Hard Times*, 4, 9, 236.
85 As quoted in Bryce, *Maturing in Hard Times*, 37.
86 Ibid., 67.
87 R.B. Bennett to F. Martin Turnbull, 23 April 1931, 203501, M1045, Bennett Papers, LAC; Chisholm, 'Canadian Monetary Policy,' 245.
88 Richard Wilbur, *Bennett Administration*, 7.
89 W.C. Clark, 'Flight,' 761–3.
90 Meredith B. Givens to W.C. Clark, 17 June 1931, CP; Givens to Clark, 8 July 1931; Givens to Clark, 5 October 1931; Clark to Givens, 13 October 1931.
91 W.C. Clark, 'Construction Industry,' Harvard; W.C. Clark, 'Limitations of Financial Statistics'; Charles Bulloch to W.C. Clark, 27 October 1931, CP. The association's board had approved creating a Committee on Real Estate Statistics, with Clark as one of its four members. John R. Riggleman to W.C. Clark, 13 August 1931, CP.

92 Harry Herwitz to W.C. Clark, 2 September 1931, CP.
93 National Bureau of Economic Research, *Report,* 12–14.
94 W.C. Clark to Simon Kuznets, 23 September 1931, CP; W.C. Clark to Meredith B. Givens, 13 October 1931.
95 W.C. Clark to L.D. Edie, 27 October 1931, CP.
96 W.C. Clark to Frederick C. Mills, 7 November 1931, CP.
97 W.C. Clark, 'Economic Changes, 1929–1931,' CP; W.C. Clark to Frederick C. Mills, 7 November 1931.
98 W.C. Clark to Lionel Edie, 27 October 1931, CP.
99 Roy Amott to W.C. Clark, 25 September 1931, CP.
100 Ibid., 9 November 1931; W.C. Clark to Roy Amott, 16 November 1931; Kenneth Clark to Nicholas Roberts, 6 November 1931; Amott to Kenneth Clark, 9 November 1931; *New York Times,* 17 November 1931.
101 James Rosenwals to W.C. Clark, 17 February 1932, CP; Roy Amott to W.C. Clark, 7 March 1932.
102 W.C. Clark, 'Construction Industry 1932,' 74–5.
103 Ibid., 78–9.
104 Swettenham and Kealy, *Serving the State,* 194, 199.
105 W.C. Clark, 'What's Wrong with Us?' 3, speech made in Ottawa to the Professional Institute of the Civil Service of Canada. A similar speech, 'The Current Business Situation,' was given December 1931 to the Empire Club in Toronto.
106 W.C. Clark, 'What's Wrong with Us?' 10.
107 Ibid., 7.
108 Ibid., 9–10.
109 *Financial Post,* 19 December 1931.
110 Kindleberger, *World Depression,* 154; A.J.P. Taylor, *English History,* 287.
111 W.C. Clark to James Rosenwald, 14 December 1931, CP.
112 D.I. McLeod to W.C. Clark, 4 January 1932, CP; Clark to McLeod, 12 January 1932.
113 W.C. Clark to W.M. Houston, 15 January 1932, CP.
114 J.C. Macfarlane to W.C. Clark, 8 February 1932, CP; W.S. Campbell to J.E. Walsh, 4 February 1932; J.E. Walsh to W.S. Campbell, 6 February 1932.
115 As quoted in Drummond, *Floating Pound,* 65–6.
116 McIvor, *Canadian Monetary,* 129–30.
117 W.C. Clark, 'Current Economic Problems.' This was an updated version of a speech given 19 February 1932 to the annual dinner of the Ontario Institute of Chartered Accountants.
118 W.C. Clark to Robert B. Warren, 13 April 1932, CP.

Chapter 3

1 Hilliker, *Canada's Department of External Affairs,* 1:143.
2 Chisholm, 'Canadian Monetary Policy,' 247.
3 Bryce, *Maturing in Hard Times,* 80; Chisholm, 'Canadian Monetary Policy,' 247–8; W.C. Clark to O.D. Skelton, 30 August 1932, CP.
4 W.C. Clark to Harry Herwitz, 9 May 1932, CP.
5 Ibid.; W.C. Clark to Lionel D. Edie, 17 May 1932, CP.
6 Keynes, 'World's Economic Outlook,' 521–6; Thompson and Seager, *Canada 1922–1939,* 217.
7 As quoted in Granatstein, *Ottawa Men,* 47; W.C. Clark to O.D. Skelton, 12 May 1932, file 621, vol. 8111, External Affairs Records, LAC.
8 Chisholm, 'Canadian Monetary Policy,' 247–8.
9 Memorandum on Monetary Reconstruction, RG19, vol. 4666, LAC; Chisholm, 'Canadian Monetary Policy,' 248.
10 Granatstein, *Ottawa Men,* 47.
11 Memorandum on Monetary Reconstruction, RG19, vol. 4666, LAC; Chisholm, 'Canadian Monetary Policy,' 249.
12 Memorandum on Monetary Reconstruction, RG19, vol. 4666, LAC.
13 Owram, *Government Generation,* 213.
14 Chisholm, 'Canadian Monetary Policy,' 250–1.
15 H. Mitchell to W.C. Clark, 16 July 1932, CP; Ferguson, *Remaking Liberalism,* 31.
16 Norman Robertson to W.C. Clark, 16 July 1932, CP.
17 Bryce, *Maturing in Hard Times,* 80, 67.
18 C.A. Curtis to W.C. Clark, 18 April 1932, CP.
19 Berton, *Great Depression,* 161, 181.
20 Bryce, *Maturing in Hard Times,* 81.
21 'Minutes of the Imperial Economic Conference: Monetary Sub-Committee,' 2 August 1932, vol. 3440, RG19, LAC.
22 H. Blair Neatby, *William Lyon Mackenzie King,* 19; Neatby mistakenly refers to Clark as the deputy minister of finance, a position to which he was not yet appointed.
23 Bryce, *Maturing in Hard Times,* 81.
24 Ibid., 93–4.
25 'A History of Monetary Policy in Canada,' n.d., vol. 3970, RG19, LAC.
26 O.D. Skelton to W.C. Clark, 30 August 1932, CP.
27 Chisholm, 'Canadian Monetary Policy,' 253–4; W.C. Clark to R.N. Kershaw, 28 October 1932, CP.

28 W.C. Clark to L.D. Edie, 13 September 1932, CP.
29 *New York Times*, 24 August 1932.
30 Ibid., 24 September 1932.
31 *New York Times*, 8 October 1932; James Grant, *Money of the Mind*, 171–2.
32 Roy Amott to W.C. Clark, 4 November 1932, CP.
33 *New York Times*, 3 March 1933.
34 Ibid., 30 August 1933.
35 Ibid., 8 October 1933.
36 Nicholas Roberts to W.C. Clark, 8 January 1934, CP.
37 As quoted in Granatstein, *Ottawa Men*, 48.
38 Mackintosh, 'O.D. Skelton,' 74.
39 W.C. Clark to O.D. Skelton, 10 September 1932, CP; R.S. Stevens to W.C. Clark, 4 October 1932.
40 Ernest M. Fisher to W.C. Clark, 13 September 1932, CP; W.C. Clark to Ernest M. Fisher, 4 October 1932; Ernest M. Fisher to W.C. Clark, 11 October 1932.
41 W.C. Clark to R.B. Bennett, 15 October 1932, CP.
42 Ibid., 22 October 1932, CP.
43 *Canadian Press*, 24 October 1932, CP.
44 Granatstein, *Ottawa Men*, 48. Granatstein heard the story from David Mansur. There is nothing in the Bennett papers to indicate that the prime minister consulted Rhodes on the appointment.
45 Bryce claimed he heard this information on 'good authority.' He was referring to interviews he had with Douglas Abbott, Clark's last minister, and with Bank of Canada official, George Watts, who heard the story from the bank's first governor, Graham Towers. Bryce, *Maturing in Hard Times*, 82.
46 Principal Fyfe to Clark, 21 April 1933, CP.
47 S.A. Cudmore to W.C. Clark, 26 October 1932, CP.
48 W.C. Clark to R.A. Mackay, 2 November 1932, CP.
49 W.C. Clark to Henry T. Ross, 25 October 1932, CP; W.C. Clark to Watson Sellar, 25 October 1932.
50 W.C. Clark to W.C. Good, 18 November 1932, CP.
51 Rutherford Williamson to W.C. Clark, 27 October 1932, CP.
52 Mac MacEwan to W.C. Clark, 18 November 1932, CP.
53 Chisholm, 'Canadian Monetary Policy,' 261.
54 W.C. Clark to R.S. Stevens, 31 October 1932, CP.
55 George Clark, interview, 29–30 April 1998. George rebelled and insisted on attending public school.
56 Glassford, *Reaction and Reform*, 133.

57 Bryce, *Maturing in Hard Times*, 21, 74, 151, 154, 248.
58 Ibid., 76.
59 Ibid., 27, 93.
60 Owram, *Government Generation*, 131.
61 Bryce, *Maturing in Hard Times*, 84.
62 Bryce, 'William Clifford Clark,' 416.
63 Mackintosh, 'William Clifford Clark: Memoir,' 7.
64 Glassford, *Reaction and Reform*, 76–8.
65 Ibid., 112–16.
66 Ibid., 111–17.
67 Ibid., 118–19.
68 Ibid., 260–1.
69 As quoted in Black, 'Finance and Insurance,' 324–5; Chisholm, 'Canadian Monetary Policy,' 260–1.
70 As quoted in Chisholm, 261–2.
71 W.C. Clark to Bryce Stewart, 12 December 1932, CP.
72 Struthers, *No Fault of Their Own*, 85–6.
73 W.C. Clark to Bryce Stewart, 2 December 1932, CP.
74 Bryce Stewart to W.C. Clark, 16 January 1932, CP; W.C. Clark to Bryce Stewart, 12 December 1932.
75 W.C. Clark to R.B. Bennett, 18 January 1933, 501802, M1459, Bennett Papers, LAC.
76 Mackintosh, 'William Clifford Clark: Memoir,' 7.
77 Armstrong, *Politics of Federalism*, 149.
78 Bryce, *Maturing in Hard Times*, 175–6.
79 Armstrong, *Politics of Federalism*, 149.
80 Bryce, *Maturing in Hard Times*, 175; Struthers, *No Fault of Their Own*, 90.
81 Struthers, *No Fault of Their Own*, 87.
82 Armstrong, *Politics of Federalism*, 150.
83 Ibid.
84 Struthers, *No Fault of Their Own*, 91.
85 Glassford, *Reaction and Reform*, 125.
86 As quoted in Struthers, *No Fault of Their Own*, 87; Bryce, *Maturing in Hard Times*, 176.
87 As quoted in Pal, *State, Class and Bureaucracy*, 105.
88 Armstrong, *Politics of Federalism*, 150.
89 W.C. Clark to R.B. Bennett, 17 January 1933, 347183, Bennett Papers, LAC.
90 Bryce, *Maturing in Hard Times*, 199–200.
91 Ibid., 200–1; Armstrong, *Politics of Federalism*, 150.

92 Bryce, *Maturing in Hard Times*, 200–1.
93 As quoted in Granatstein, *Ottawa Men*, 50.
94 Clark found sympathy for a central bank at the Canadian Political Science Association meeting in May 1933. Owram, *Government Generation*, 214; Granatstein, *Ottawa Men*, 290.
95 King Diaries, 8 February 1933.
96 Struthers, *No Fault of Their Own*, 91.
97 Ibid., 92–3.
98 Bryce, *Maturing in Hard Times*, 108.
99 Perry, *Taxes, Tariffs, and Subsidies*, 256.
100 Bryce, *Maturing in Hard Times*, 108.
101 Perry, *Taxes, Tariffs, and Subsidies*, 268.
102 Bryce, *Maturing in Hard Times*, 135.
103 Chester Crossman to R.B. Bennett, 12 February 1933, 350310–11, M1281, Bennett Papers, LAC.
104 Edgar Rhodes to E.A. McPherson, 18 February 1933, 350312, M1281, Bennett Papers, LAC.
105 John Bracken to R.B. Bennett, 18 March 1933, 350318–23, M1281, Bennett Papers, LAC.
106 R.B. Bennett to Chester Crossman, 31 May 1933, 350309, M1281, Bennett Papers, LAC.
107 Wilgress, *Dana Wilgress*, 97; Chalmers, *Both Sides of the Street*, 94.
108 A.J.P. Taylor, *English History*, 335.
109 The agreement on silver was intended to have the major producers and users mitigate fluctuations in price. Clark participated for Canada in negotiations that produced an agreement on 24 July, which limited the sale of silver by three countries with large silver holdings and required five silver-producing countries, including Canada, to buy stated amounts of the silver produced in the mines for currency purposes. The agreement resulted in the rise in the price and production of silver in Canada. Bryce, *Maturing in Hard Times*, 134.
110 Mackintosh, 'William Clifford Clark: Memoir,' 8.
111 McIvor, *Canadian Monetary*, 144.
112 Bryce, *Maturing in Hard Times*, 136; Granatstein, *Ottawa Men*, 49; Fullerton, *Graham Towers*, 44.
113 Bryce, *Maturing in Hard Times*, 136.
114 Owram, *Government Generation*, 215.
115 Material for speech introducing Central Bank of Canada, n.d., vol. 2673, RG19, LAC.
116 Fullerton, *Graham Towers*, 46.

117 Bryce, *Maturing in Hard Times,* 137.
118 As quoted in Granatstein, *Ottawa Men,* 51.
119 Stokes, *Bank of Canada,* 170–2.
120 Ibid., 172.
121 Bryce, *Maturing in Hard Times,* 138–9.
122 As quoted in Stokes, *Bank of Canada,* 213–15.
123 Waite, *The Loner,* 83–4.
124 Stokes, *Bank of Canada,* 207–8.
125 Ibid., 208.
126 Bryce, *Maturing in Hard Times,* 147.
127 Ferguson, *Remaking Liberalism,* 186.
128 As quoted in Ferguson, *Remaking Liberalism,* 194–5.
129 W.C. Clark to R.B. Bennett, 2 January 1934, 346788–9, M1279, Bennett Papers, LAC; Clark to Bennett, 2 December 1933, 346791, M1279, Bennett Papers, LAC.
130 Waite, *The Loner,* 84.
131 Farm Credit Corporation, *Development of Farm Credit,* 26–7.
132 Bryce, *Maturing in Hard Times,* 111.
133 Ibid., 111; Perry, *Taxes, Tariffs, and Subsidies,* 266, 277.
134 W.C. Clark to R.K. Finlayson, 27 June 1934, R.B. Bennett Papers, LAC; as quoted in Glassford, *Reaction and Reform,* 144.
135 As quoted in Fullerton, *Graham Towers,* 52–3.
136 W.C. Clark to R.B. Bennett, 27 June 1934, Bennett Papers, LAC; as quoted in Granatstein, *Ottawa Men,* 51; Chisholm, 'Canadian Monetary Policy,' 279.
137 As quoted in Owram, *Government Generation,* 215.
138 Watts, *Bank of Canada,* 23.
139 Fullerton, *Graham Towers,* 31.
140 Bryce, *Maturing in Hard Times,* 143.
141 Fullerton, *Graham Towers,* 38, 45; Granatstein, *Ottawa Men,* 52.
142 Fullerton, *Graham Towers,* 55.
143 Stokes, *Bank of Canada,* 204.
144 Plumptre, 'Constitution of the Bank of Canada,' 248.
145 *Financial Post,* 15 September 1934.
146 Bryce, 'William Clifford Clark,' 417; Mackintosh, 'William Clifford Clark: Memoir,' 8–9; Slater, *War Finance,* 24; Fullerton, *Graham Towers,* 60–2.
147 Cross, 'Oligarchs at Ottawa.'
148 Dexter Memorandum, 16 January 1948, box 5, Dexter Papers.
149 Gordon, *Political Memoir,* 35.

Chapter 4

1 King Diaries, 2 August 1934.
2 J.R.H. Wilbur, *Bennett New Deal,* 80–90.
3 W.C. Clark to R.K. Finlayson, 3 January 1935, vol. 3986, RG19, LAC; Bryce, *Maturing in Hard Times,* 182.
4 W.C. Clark to R.K. Finlayson, 5 January 1935, vol. 3986, RG19, LAC.
5 *House of Commons Debates* (24 January 1935), pp. 153–62 (Rt Hon. R.B. Bennett, PM).
6 Oberlander and Fallick, *Housing a Nation,* 12.
7 Ibid.
8 Bacher, *Keeping to the Marketplace,* 66–70.
9 As quoted in Glassford, *Reaction and Reform,* 164.
10 *House of Commons Debates* (24 January 1935), pp. 170–1 (Rt Hon. R.B. Bennett, PM).
11 As quoted in Glassford, *Reaction and Reform,* 165.
12 Oberlander and Fallick, *Housing a Nation,* 14.
13 Bacher, *Keeping to the Marketplace,* 37.
14 Glassford, *Reaction and Reform,* 160–2.
15 As quoted in Glassford, *Reaction and Reform,* 162.
16 Perry, *Taxes, Tariffs, and Subsidies,* 269–70; Bryce, *Maturing in Hard Times,* 112–13.
17 Struthers, *Limits of Affluence,* 71.
18 *Report of the Special Committee on Housing,* House of Commons, 16 April 1935, 8, 16.
19 Oberlander and Fallick, *Housing a Nation,* 16.
20 Chartered banks would not be allowed to lend for mortgages until 1954.
21 Hulchanski, '1935 Dominion Housing Act,' 25.
22 As quoted in Oblerlander and Fallick, *Housing a Nation,* 15–16.
23 Hulchanski, '1935 Dominion Housing Act,' 24.
24 Bacher, *Keeping to the Marketplace,* 83.
25 As quoted in Bacher, 'Keeping to the Private Market,' 152.
26 *Report of the Special Committee on Housing,* 21–2.
27 Bacher, *Keeping to the Marketplace,* 83–4.
28 Convocation Speech, Queen's University, 8 May 1935, CP.
29 Glassford, *Reaction and Reform,* 169.
30 As quoted in Bacher, *Keeping to the Marketplace,* 86. Mackintosh argues that 'the Housing Act was peculiarly Clifford Clark's own invention,' but this is an exaggeration made long after the fact. Bacher points out Leonard's critical role, calling him the 'virtual author.' The letters between Clark and

Leonard certainly show that the act was closer to Leonard's views that those Clark had put forward before the parliamentary committee, although not inconsistent with Clark's views. Mackintosh, 'William Clifford Clark: Memoir,' 9.

31 *House of Commons Debates* (18 June 1935), pp. 3771–7 (Mr Wilfrid Hanbury, MP).

32 Bryce, 'William Clifford Clark, 1889–1952,' 417–18.

33 Bacher, *Keeping to the Marketplace*, 87–8.

34 Leonard, 'Dominion Housing Act,' 300.

35 *House of Commons Debates* (24 June 1935), p. 3930 (Mr Arthur Ganong, MP).

36 Hulchansky, '1935 Dominion Housing Act,' 28.

37 Ibid., 30.

38 *House of Commons Debates* (18 June 1935), p. 3775 (Mr William Lyon Mackenzie King).

39 W.C. Clark, 'Housing.' This is an extended text of an address given before the 32nd annual convention of the Union of Nova Scotia Municipalities at Sydney, Nova Scotia, 24–26 August 1937. Part of it appeared as 'The Housing Act and Low Cost Housing,' *Social Welfare* 17, nos. 2 and 3 (June–September 1937): 18–20.

40 Bryce, 'William Clifford Clark, 1889–1952,' 418.

41 W.C. Clark to J. Clark Reilly, 4 July 1935, vol. 3979, RG19, LAC.

42 W.C. Clark to Percy E. Nobbs, 30 January 1936, vol. 3979, RG19, LAC.

43 The act was amended once, to include provision for the government to make arrangements not only through lending institutions but also with a 'local authority.' This changed little, however, since the act was really aimed at lending institutions. No loans were ever made to municipalities, which would have had to find 80 per cent of the funds needed for a housing project in the market, since the federal share was limited to 20 per cent. Hulchansky, '1935 Dominion Housing Act,' 30.

44 Bryce, 'William Clifford Clark, 1889–1952,' 418.

45 Hulchansky, '1935 Dominion Housing Act,' 30–1.

46 As quoted in ibid., 32.

47 Speech for the Conference on Canada–America Relations, St Lawrence University, 18 June 1935 CP.

48 Glassford, *Reaction and Reform*, 123.

49 Wilgress, *Dana Wilgress*, 100–1.

50 George Clark, interview, 29–30 April 1998.

51 W.A. Mackintosh, 'William Clifford Clark: Memoir,' 13–16.

52 'Treasury Department and Central Bank Work Well Handling Federal Finance,' *Financial Times*, 6 September 1935.

53 Keenleyside, *Memoirs,* 1:443.
54 Neatby, *William Lyon Mackenzie King,* 153–5.
55 Ibid., 129–30.
56 King Diaries, 22 October 1935. Rod Finlayson provides a slightly altered account of the conversation but the intent is basically the same. As quoted in Bryce, *Maturing in Hard Times,* 229–30.
57 Bryce, *Maturing in Hard Times,* 96–7.
58 *Canadian Annual Review,* 1935–6, 650–1.
59 Saywell, *'Just Call Me Mitch,'* 248.
60 W.C. Clark to C. Cockroft, 14 March 1936, vol. 3985, RG19, LAC.
61 Memorandum on Dominion Provincial Discussions re Loan Councils, 18 April 1936, file 15, Towers Papers.
62 Fisher, *Duff Pattullo,* 285–6.
63 Bryce, *Maturing in Hard Times,* 182, 207–8.
64 Granatstein, *Ottawa Men,* 57–8; Neatby, *William Lyon Mackenzie King,* 150–7.
65 Saywell, 'Just Call Me Mitch,' 248.
66 Harvey Perry, interview, September 1995.
67 W.C. Clark to D.M. Allan, 20 January 1936, vol. 3979, RG19, LAC.
68 This reluctance of the lending institutions to loan money in western Canada was due to the provincial debt adjustment legislation as well as the past experience of the companies in connection with western loans. The interest rate was also a problem. The housing act loans were to be made at 5 per cent, which was lower than the prevailing rate in much of the region. W.C. Clark to R.B. MacInnes, 11 May 1936, vol. 3979, RG19, LAC.
69 *House of Commons Debates* (24 February 1936), pp. 436–7; (27 February 1936), pp. 577–8; (3 April 1936), p. 1765 (Mr Mackenzie King, MP); 'The Ill-Fated Economic Council,' *Canadian Congress Journal* 15, no. 3 (March 1936): 8; 'Dominion Housing Act,' *Canadian Congress Journal* 14, no. 9 (September 1935): 12; Leonard, 'Dominion Housing Act,' 299.
70 The Dominion Housing Act, n.d., vol. 2734, RG19, LAC.
71 W.C. Clark, 'The Housing Act.'
72 Neatby, *William Lyon Mackenzie King,* 157.
73 W.C. Clark to C. Cockroft, 14 March 1936, vol. 3985, RG19, LAC.
74 W.C. Clark to Charles Dunning, 17 March 1936, vol. 3985, RG19, LAC.
75 Ibid., 25 March 1936, vol. 3985, RG19, LAC.
76 W.C. Clark to Charles Dunning, 4 April 1936, vol. 3986, RG19, LAC.
77 Duff Pattullo to Mackenzie King, 6 May 1936, vol. 3986, RG19, LAC.
78 Neatby, 'The Liberal Way,' 268.
79 Memorandum in Regard to Loan Councils and Certain Alternatives to Present Problems, 18 April 1936, file 14, Towers Papers.

80 W.C. Clark to Charles Dunning, 18 May 1936, vol. 3985, RG19, LAC.
81 Alberta's Proposal, 19 May 1936, vol. 3985, RG19, LAC.
82 W.C. Clark to Charles Dunning, 18 May 1936, vol. 3985, RG19, LAC.
83 Charles Dunning to Bill Aberhart, 27 May 1936, vol. 3985, RG19, LAC.
84 Ibid., 25 June 1936, vol. 3985, RG19, LAC.
85 As quoted in Bryce, *Maturing in Hard Times*, 60.
86 Perry, *Taxes, Tariffs, and Subsidies*, 268.
87 Ibid., 278.
88 Bryce, *Maturing in Hard Times*, 210–11.
89 Ibid., 98.
90 W.C. Clark to Charles Dunning, 19 November 1936, vol. 3427, RG19, LAC.
91 King Diaries, 19 August 1936.
92 W.C. Clark to W.L.M. King, 30 November 1936, 185139–43, J1, MG26, William Lyon Mackenzie King Papers, LAC.
93 Bryce, *Maturing in Hard Times*, 209–10.
94 R.M. Burns, *Acceptable Mean*, 10.
95 According to Fullerton, it was Sandy Skelton and Graham Towers who came up with the idea. Fullerton, *Graham Towers*, 79–81.
96 W.C. Clark, Confidential Memorandum: 'Royal Commission on Economic Basis of Confederation,' 7 December 1936, vol. 22, RG19, LAC.
97 Dunning to Aberhart, 25 June 1936, vol. 3985, RG19, LAC.
98 Aberhart to King, 26 August 1937, vol. 3985, RG19, LAC.
99 King Diaries, 21 January 1937.
100 King to Aberhart, 31 August 1937, vol. 3985, RG19, LAC.
101 Bryce, *Maturing in Hard Times*, 212–13.
102 Ibid., 60.
103 Ibid., 114; Neatby, *William Lyon Mackenzie King*, 187–91.
104 King Diaries, 25 February 1937.
105 Ibid., 21 July 1937.
106 Bryce, *Maturing in Hard Times*, 114; Swettenham and Kealy, *Serving the State*, 37.
107 Bryce, *Maturing in Hard Times*, 196, 182.
108 Ibid., 156.
109 W.C. Clark to O.D. Skelton, 9 April 1938, vol. 2741, RG19, LAC.
110 Walters, *History of the League of Nations*, 177–8.
111 Minutes of meeting of EAC, 2 February 1943, vol. 3448, RG19, LAC; E. Ritchie Clark, *The IDB*, 11–12, 399.
112 Bryce, *Maturing in Hard Times*, 185–7.
113 King Diaries, 25 January 1938.

114 Margaret Clark to Narragansett Mortgage Company, 16 May 1931, CP; Margaret Clark to Narragansett Mortgage Company, 17 June 1938; US B&M Liquidation Corporation to W.C. Clark, 24 February 1938; McIlraith and McIlraith to W.C. Clark, 10 June 1938; New York Life Insurance Company to Margaret Clark, 21 April 1938; F.D. Higson to W.C. Clark, 11 May 1938; F.D. Higson to W.C. Clark, 28 May 1938; F.D. Higson to W.C. Clark, 9 December 1938; F.D. Higson to W.C. Clark, 8 May 1939.
115 W.C. Clark to F.P. Varcoe, 30 May 1938, vol. 3985, RG19, LAC.
116 Neatby, *William Lyon Mackenzie King*, 350.
117 'The National Housing Act,' vol. 2734, RG19, LAC.
118 *House of Commons Debates* (16 June 1938), Budget Speech (Mr Charles Dunning, MP).
119 Perry, *Taxes, Tariffs, and Subsidies*, 283.
120 Memorandum to Rowell Commission on Deficit Spending, 13 March 1939, Towers Papers.
121 King Diaries, 16 June 1938.
122 Fullerton, *Graham Towers*, 69.
123 King Diaries, 22 June 1938.
124 Ibid., 6 July 1938.
125 Clark tried to convince Rasminsky to return from Geneva and take a job in the Department of Finance dealing with taxation matters. He added the inducement that the job would likely serve as a 'jumping-off place for the new central bank.' Clark to Louis Rasminsky, 5 November 1933, CP; Clark to Rasminsky, 8 January 1934; see Muirhead, *Against the Odds*, 19–21.
126 W.C. Clark to Louis Rasminsky, 29 August 1938, CP.
127 Bryce, *Maturing in Hard Times*, 227.
128 Newman, *Canadian Establishment*, 1:333.
129 Bryce, *Maturing in Hard Times*, 228.
130 W.C. Clark to R.B. Bryce, 30 September 1939, vol. 3983, RG19, LAC.
131 Bryce, *Maturing in Hard Times*, 228.
132 James Gibson, interview, 6 August 1994.
133 'The Case for Federal Administration of Unemployment Relief,' 1 November 1938, vol. 3991, RG19, LAC; Struthers, *No Fault of Their Own*, 194–6.
134 W.C. Clark to J.W. Pickersgill, 1 November 1938, vol. 3991, RG19, LAC; Struthers, *No Fault of Their Own*, 196.
135 Schull, *The Great Scot*, 34.
136 Fullerton, *Graham Towers*, 96–8.
137 Slater, *War Finance*, 16.

138 Bryce, *Maturing in Hard Times*, 228.
139 Bryce, *Canada and the Cost of World War II*, 87–8.
140 Bacher, *Keeping to the Marketplace*, 108–9.
141 W.C. Clark to Charles Dunning, 6 February 1939, vol. 3980, RG19, LAC.
142 W.C. Clark to Humphrey Carver, 9 February 1939, vol. 3980, RG19, LAC.
143 W.C. Clark, 'Loans for Low Rental Housing Projects under Part II of the National Housing Act,' address delivered to the National Conference on Housing, 20 February 1939, Toronto, vol. 2734, RG19, LAC.
144 Carver, *Compassionate Landscape*, 55–7.
145 Bacher, *Keeping to the Marketplace*, 109.
146 Carver, *Compassionate Landscape*, 55–7.
147 As quoted in Stacey, *Canada and the Age of Conflict*, 2:241.
148 Graham Towers to Charles Dunning, 14 April 1939, vol. 3986, RG19, LAC.
149 As quoted in Perry, *Taxes, Tariffs, and Subsidies*, 257.
150 Bryce, *Maturing in Hard Times*, 119–21; Newman, *Canadian Establishment*, 1:333–4.
151 Simon Reisman, interview, 31 July 1995.
152 King Diaries, 25 April 1939.
153 Ibid., 27 April 1939.
154 Bryce, *Maturing in Hard Times*, 101. See also Drummond and Hillmer, *Negotiating Freer Trade*.
155 Stacey, *Arms, Men and Governments*, 3–4.
156 W.C. Clark, 'Memorandum on Central Mortgage Bank Bill,' 3 May 1939, vol. 3975, RG19, LAC.
157 Graham Towers to W.C. Clark, 12 April 1939, vol. 3975, RG19, LAC.
158 W.C. Clark to *Monetary Times*, 27 May 1939, vol. 3975, RG19, LAC.
159 R.B. Bryce, 'Memorandum on Wartime Activities of the Finance Department and Related Agencies,' 5 February 1940, vol. 3537, RG19, LAC.
160 Fullerton, *Graham Towers*, 82–4.
161 Bryce, *Maturing in Hard Times*, 168–71.
162 Bain, 'Wordiest MP,' 17, 94; J.E. Hodgetts et al., *Biography of an Institution*, 155.
163 Bain, 'Wordiest MP' 94.
164 R. MacGregor Dawson commented on 'the bizarre character of its proceedings, which have probably never been duplicated in Canadian history. For this the Chairman must shoulder the chief responsibility, for many members repeatedly protested against his eccentric behaviour and the way in which the investigation was being conducted.' As quoted in Hodgetts et al., *Biography of an Institution*, 156; Bain, 'Wordiest MP,' 94.

165 Hodgetts et al., 156–7.
166 Bain, 'Wordiest MP,' 94.
167 *House of Commons Debates* (14 March 1939), p. 1864 (Mr Jean Francois Pouliot, MP).
168 *House of Commons Debates* (26 May 1939), pp. 4596–7 (Mr Jean Francois Pouliot, MP).
169 Ibid., p. 4599.
170 *House of Commons Debates* (2 June 1939), pp. 4893–4; (3 June 1939), pp. 4895–9 (Mr Jean Francois Pouliot, MP).
171 Peggy Johnston, interview, 20 August 1995; George Clark, interview, 19 March 1995.
172 W.C. Clark to Charles Dunning, 29 May 1939, CP.
173 Ibid.
174 Duff Pattullo to W.L.M. King, 26 April 1939, vol. 3986, RG19, LAC.
175 W.C. Clark to Charles Dunning, 8 May 1939, vol. 3986, RG19, LAC.
176 Fullerton, *Graham Towers*, 307.
177 In 1937 Clark had commenced the search in earnest. He wrote to Onesime Gagnon, the provincial minister of mines, game, and fisheries in Quebec City, about possible sites in the Gatineau region. Granatstein, *Ottawa Men*, 15.
178 W.C. Clark to Fred Davey, 14 February 1940, CP.
179 Mackintosh, 'William Clifford Clark: Memoir,' 15.
180 Granatstein, *Ottawa Men*, 15.
181 Ibid., 15–16.
182 W.C. Clark to W.A. Mackintosh, 14 August 1939, CP.
183 W.C. Clark to Bryce Stewart, 17 August 1939, CP.
184 *Ottawa Journal*, 29 December 1952.
185 Stacey, *Canada and the Age of Conflict*, 259.
186 Stacey, *Six Years of War*, 1.
187 A.F.W. Plumptre, *Mobilizing Canada's Resources*, 8–9.
188 Mackintosh, 'William Clifford Clark: Memoir,' 9–10.
189 Hutchison, *Incredible Canadian*, 265–6.
190 W.C. Clark to Bryce Stewart, 23 August 1939, CP.
191 Bryce Stewart to W.C. Clark, 13 June 1945, CP.
192 Mackintosh, 'William Clifford Clark: Memoir,' 15.

Chapter 5

1 Pickersgill, *Seeing Canada Whole*, 172–3. See also Heeney, *Things That Are Caesar's*.

2 Stacey, *Canada and the Age of Conflict*, 260.
3 Pickersgill, *Seeing Canada Whole*, 173–4.
4 Granatstein, *Canada's War*, 174.
5 Schull, *Great Scot*, 51; K.W. Taylor, 'War-Time Control,' 52.
6 Text of presidential address never delivered but scheduled for the 1941 meeting of the Canadian Political Science Association, CP.
7 W.C. Clark, 'Should Maximum Prices Be Fixed?' 432–61.
8 Davis, *FDR*, 489–90.
9 W.C. Clark, 'Canadian–American Relations,' 259–62.
10 W.C. Clark, 'The International Exchange Situation,' 72–9.
11 Granatstein, *Canada's War*, 60–1.
12 Schull, *Great Scot*, 35–6.
13 Neatby, *William Lyon Mackenzie King*, 322.
14 Dexter Memorandum, 23 June 1939, box 2, Dexter Papers.
15 King Diaries, 16 April 1937.
16 Slater, *War Finance*, 35.
17 Granatstein, *Canada's War*, 10.
18 W.C. Clark to J.L. Ilsley, 5 September 1939, vol. 3426, RG19, LAC.
19 Gibson and Robertson, *Ottawa at War*, 39.
20 King Diaries, 5 September 1939.
21 Pickersgill, *Mackenzie King Record*, 1:28.
22 Bryce, *Canada and the Cost of World War II*, 4.
23 Granatstein, *Canada's War*, 19.
24 'Funeral on Tuesday for Dr W.C. Clark,' *Ottawa Journal*, 29 December 1952. Mackintosh also noted that the budget 'was of necessity a hastily drawn financial plan.' Mackintosh, 'Canadian War Financing,' 481.
25 *House of Commons Debates* (12 September 1939), Budget Speech (Mr John Ilsley, MP).
26 Fullerton, *Graham Towers*, 137.
27 W.C. Clark, 'Is Our Taxation Policy Sound?' From a speech Clark made to the 15th annual meeting of the Canadian Chamber of Commerce, Seigniory Club, Montebello, QC, 30 September–1 October 1942.
28 Perry, *Fiscal History of Canada*, 333–4.
29 *House of Commons Debates* (11 September 1939), p. 139 (Mr John Ilsley, MP).
30 W.C. Clark to A.W. Neill, 26 June 1942, vol. 3385, RG19, LAC.
31 W.C. Clark, 'Is Our Taxation Policy Sound?' 55.
32 W.C. Clark, 'Should Maximum Prices Be Fixed?'
33 *House of Commons Debates* (11 September 1939), 140 (Mr John Ilsley, MP).
34 Ibid.

35 W.C. Clark, 'Is Our Taxation Policy Sound?'
36 Stacey, *Arms, Men and Governments*, 11.
37 *House of Commons Debates* (11 September 1939), pp. 137, 141 (Mr John Ilsley, MP).
38 That increase did not actually come into the government's coffers until the next spring (income taxes were paid once a year, not deducted by employers) and it affected relatively few people. Only 200,000–250,000 people, or perhaps 5 per cent of the working population, paid income tax and most taxpayers were well off; more than four-fifths of the total revenue came from incomes above $5,000. Perry, *Fiscal History of Canada*, 360. Most federal revenue still came from customs and excise taxes. In the 1937–8 fiscal year, for example, income taxes, both individual and corporate, produced only 23 cents of every dollar of revenue that year. *Canadian Annual Review*, 1937/8, 64–5.
39 Perry, *Fiscal History of Canada*, 607; *House of Commons Debates* (11 September), pp. 142–3 (Mr John Ilsley, MP).
40 Perry, *Fiscal History of Canada*, 242.
41 W.C. Clark, 'Should Maximum Prices Be Fixed?'
42 *House of Commons Debates* (11 September 1939), p. 143 (Mr John Ilsley, MP).
43 As quoted in Newman, *Canadian Establishment*, 1:333–4.
44 R.B. Bryce, 'Memorandum on Wartime Activities of the Finance Department and Related Agencies,' 5 February 1940, vol. 3537, RG19, LAC.
45 Granatstein, *Canada's War*, 10.
46 Granatstein, *Ottawa Men*, 159; W.C. Clark to Norman Robertson, 21 November 1939, vol. 3538, RG19, LAC; Memorandum on Advisory Committee on Economic Policy, 20 January 1940, vol. 4660.
47 King Diaries, 12 September 1939.
48 Memorandum on EAC, 31 August 1943, vol. 4660, RG19, LAC; Granatstein, *Man of Influence*, 92–3.
49 Carter, 'Organization and Work,' 362.
50 Memorandum on the EAC, 31 August 1943, vol. 4660, RG19, LAC.
51 Bryce, *Canada and the Cost of World War II*, 32.
52 Granatstein, *Man of Influence*, 93.
53 King Diaries, 27 September 1939.
54 Carter, 'Organization and Work,' 363.
55 Slater, *War Finance*, 98.
56 Fullerton, *Graham Towers*, 123–4.
57 Bryce, 'William Clifford Clark, 1889–1952,' 419–20.

58 Interim Report to the PMO on the Work of the EAC, 29 April 1940, vol. 4660, RG19, LAC.
59 Memorandum on the EAC, 31 August 1943, vol. 4660, RG19, LAC.
60 W.C. Clark to J.L. Ralston, 9 September 1939, vol. 2687, RG19, LAC; W.C. Clark to J.L. Ralston, 13 September 1939.
61 Granatstein, *Canada's War*, 26; Plumptre, *Mobilizing Canada's Resources*, 21.
62 Granatstein, *Ottawa Men*, 137; Schull, *Great Scot*, 37.
63 Schull, *Great Scot*, 37–9; Rasminsky, 'Foreign Exchange Control' 89.
64 W.C. Clark, 'Canadian–American Relations,' 264.
65 King Diaries, 13 September 1939.
66 Granatstein, *Man of Influence*, 91.
67 Schull, *Great Scot*, 37.
68 Gordon, *Political Memoir*, 27–30.
69 Granatstein, *Ottawa Men*, 138.
70 David Mansur, interview, 11 June 1986.
71 W.C. Clark, 'Canadian–American Relations,' 263.
72 Granatstein, *Canada's War*, 24.
73 King Diaries, 18 September, 1939.
74 Ibid., 18 September 1939.
75 Stacey, *Arms, Men and Governments*, 12.
76 Bacher, *Keeping to the Marketplace*, 121.
77 Graham Towers to J.L. Ralston, 11 September 1939, vol. 3976, RG19, LAC.
78 As quoted in Bacher, 'Keeping to the Private Market,' 274.
79 W.C. Clark to J.L. Ralston, 25 October 1939, vol. 2679, RG19, LAC.
80 Granatstein, *Canada's War*, 45.
81 Ibid., 47.
82 As quoted in Granatstein, *Canada's War*, 61–2.
83 Ibid., 62.
84 Stacey, *Arms, Men and Governments*, 30.
85 Granatstein, *Canada's War*, 62–3.
86 Bryce memorandum, October 1939, vol. 3440, RG19, LAC; Granatstein, *Canada's War*, 63.
87 Fullerton, *Graham Towers*, 126–7.
88 Barnett, *Keynesian Arithmetic*, 11.
89 Fullerton argues that this percentage was based on the argument that even Germany had found it difficult to allocate more than half its national output for war purposes. Fullerton, *Graham Towers*, 127. David Slater argues that these were 'primitive, uncertain and incomplete numbers' and too much weight was given to them, regardless. Slater, *War Finance*, 33–5.

90 Stacey, *Arms, Men and Governments*, 11; Granatstein, *Canada's War*, 52; Fullerton, *Graham Towers*, 127.
91 Heeney, *Things That Are Caesar's*, 61.
92 Stacey, *Arms, Men and Governments*, 21.
93 As quoted in Granatstein, *Canada's War*, 48.
94 Stacey, *Arms, Men and Governments*, 21.
95 Power, *Party Politician*, 199–200.
96 King Diaries, 31 October 1939.
97 Stacey, *Arms, Men and Governments*, 21; Granatstein, *Canada's War*, 52.
98 Stacey, *Arms, Men and Governments*, 21–2.
99 As quoted in Stacey, *Arms, Men and Governments*, 22.
100 Britain at that time was buying wheat on the world market at the going rate, which was well below the Canadian price. Crerar wanted a price that would provide a fair return to farmers who had suffered from the decade of the Depression; Britain insisted on as low a price as possible to keep down the price of bread and avoid increases in the cost of living, which would take away from a maximum war effort. Crerar suggested a price of 93.5 cents a bushel for twelve months; the British suggested 70 cents. Granatstein, *Canada's War*, 63–4; Slater, *War Finance*, 127–9.
101 Fullerton, *Graham Towers*, 127.
102 Gibson and Robertson, *Ottawa at War*, 18.
103 Stacey, *Canada and the Age of Conflict*, 307.
104 W.C. Clark, 'Canadian–American Relations in Defence,' 259–60.
105 Granatstein, *Canada's War*, 53.
106 Ibid., 53; King Diaries, 14 November 1939.
107 Granatstein, *Canada's War*, 54.
108 Stacey, *Arms, Men and Governments*, 26; Stacey, *Canada and the Age of Conflict*, 296.
109 Roberts, *Canada's War in the Air*, 17.
110 James Gibson, interview, 6 August 1994
111 As quoted in Granatstein, *Canada's War*, 65.
112 W.C. Clark to J.L. Ralston, 12 December 1939, vol. 2685, RG19, LAC.
113 Granatstein, *Canada's War*, 64; Fullerton, *Graham Towers*, 129.
114 *House of Commons Debates* (24 June 1940), p. 1012 (Mr T.A. Crerar, MP).
115 Fullerton, *Graham Towers*, 129.
116 As quoted in Gibson, *To Serve and Yet Be Free*, 300.
117 Granatstein, *Ottawa Men*, 159–60.
118 Mackintosh, 'William Clifford Clark: Memoir,' 13–16.
119 George Clark, interview, 19 March 1995.
120 Peggy Johnston, interview, 20 August 1995.
121 Granatstein, *Canada's War*, 254.

122 Stacey, *Arms, Men and Governments*, 30.
123 King Diaries, 7 December 1939.
124 Ibid., 8 December 1939; Slater, *War Finance*, 102–3.
125 King Diaries, 8 December 1939.
126 R.B. Bryce, Memorandum on Wartime Activities of the Finance Department and Related Agencies, 5 February 1940, vol. 3537, RG19, LAC.
127 Fullerton, *Graham Towers*, 157–8.
128 King Diaries, 5 January 1940.
129 Struthers, *No Fault of Their Own*, 198.
130 King Diaries, 16 January 1940.
131 As quoted in Struthers, *No Fault of Their Own*, 200.
132 W.C. Clark to J. Fred Davey, 14 February 1940, CP.
133 W.C. Clark to Percy Nobbs, 20 February 1940, CP.
134 Granatstein, *Ottawa Men*, 15–16.
135 Mackintosh, 'William Clifford Clark: Memoir,' 15.
136 Granatstein, *Ottawa Men*, 15–17.
137 Minutes of EAC Meeting, 12 March 1940, vol. 4660, RG19, LAC.
138 Minutes of EAC Meeting, 1 May 1940, vol. 4660, RG19, LAC.
139 Perry, *Fiscal History of Canada*, 307.
140 Bryce, *Maturing in Hard Times*, 218.
141 Report of the Royal Commission on Dominion–Provincial Relations, Book II (Ottawa: King's Printer, 1940), 23–4.
142 Granatstein, *Canada's War*, 91.
143 Wright, 'Mackenzie King,' 288–9.
144 Jack Pickersgill, 25 May 1989, Interview 5, 'Ottawa Decides, 1945–1971,' Institute for Research on Public Policy Collection, LAC.

Chapter 6

1 Bothwell and Kilbourn, *C.D. Howe*, 128–9.
2 Rasminsky, 'Foreign Exchange Control,' 115–16.
3 Pickersgill, *Seeing Canada Whole*, 195.
4 Stacey, *Arms, Men and Governments*, 32.
5 Carter, 'Political Developments in Canada,' 294.
6 Gibson and Robertson, *Ottawa at War*, 67.
7 King Diaries, 23 May 1940.
8 King Diaries, 23 May 1940; 27 May 1940.
9 Ker and Goodman, *Press Promotion*, 31.
10 *House of Commons Debates* (24 June 1940), p. 1013 (Mr J.L. Ralston, MP); Slater, *War Finance*, 83.
11 Wellington Jeffers, *Globe and Mail*, 29 December 1952.

12 Fullerton, *Graham Towers,* 159; Slater, *War Finance,* 83–7.
13 Gibson and Robertson, *Ottawa at* War, 66.
14 King Diaries, 5 June 1940.
15 Granatstein, *Canada's War,* 98.
16 Fullerton, *Graham Towers,* 130.
17 W.C. Clark to E.W. Willard, 19 September 1940, vol. 3444, RG19, LAC.
18 King Diaries, 10 June 1940.
19 W.C. Clark to Bryce Stewart, 15 June 1940, CP.
20 W.C. Clark, 'Canadian–American Relations in Defence,' 265.
21 Slater, *War Finance,* 106.
22 Report of the Chairman of the Sub-Committee on Wartime Economic Organization, 10 July 1941, vol. 3976, RG19, LAC.
23 Pickersgill, *Seeing Canada Whole,* 197.
24 Fullerton, *Graham Towers,* 130; Gordon, *Political Memoir,* 30.
25 Gordon, *Political Memoir,* 30–1; Granatstein, *Canada's War,* 125–6.
26 Clark, 'Canadian-American Relations in Defence,' 265.
27 See Bothwell and Kilbourn, *C.D. Howe,* 135.
28 Clark, 'Canadian–American Relations in Defence,' 267.
29 Granatstein, *Man of Influence,* 94.
30 *House of Commons Debates* (24 June 1940), p. 1011 (Mr J.L. Ralston, MP); Slater, *War Finance,* 35.
31 *House of Commons Debates* (24 June 1940), p. 1015 (Mr J.L. Ralston, MP).
32 Ibid., pp. 1013–18.
33 Economic Survey of the First Year of War, 16 September 1940, vol. 4661, RG19, LAC.
34 *House of Commons Debates* (24 June 1940), pp. 1020–2 (Mr J.L. Ralston, MP).
35 Ibid., 1022.
36 Rasminsky, 'Foreign Exchange Control,' 123.
37 Clark, 'Canadian–American Relations in Defence,' 269.
38 *House of Commons Debates* (24 June 1940), p. 1022 (Mr J.L. Ralston, MP); Slater, *War Finance,* 41–5.
39 King Diaries, 26 June 1940.
40 Pickersgill, *Seeing Canada Whole,* 196.
41 Bothwell and Kilbourn, *C.D. Howe,* 140.
42 *House of Commons Debates* (30 July 1940), p. 2128 (Mr J.L. Ralston, MP).
43 Fullerton, 151–2.
44 Armstrong, *Politics of Federalism,* 223.
45 Fullerton, *Graham Towers,* 152.
46 Granatstein, *Canada's War,* 162–3.

47 As quoted in Armstrong, *Politics of Federalism*, 223.
48 Armstrong, *Politics of Federalism*, 223.
49 As quoted in Granatstein, *Canada's War*, 163.
50 Granatstein, *Canada's War*, 164
51 Granatstein puts the date at 20 September, *Canada's War*, 164; Armstrong, *Politics of Federalism*, 224.
52 Armstrong, *Politics of Federalism*, 224.
53 Gibson and Robertson, *Ottawa at War*, 78.
54 Ibid.
55 Ibid., 76.
56 *House of Commons Debates* (2 August 1940), p. 2321 (Mr J.L. Ilsley, MP).
57 Cuff and Granatstein, *Ties That Bind*, 71.
58 Bacher, 'Keeping to the Private Market,' 289–90.
59 As quoted in Bacher, 'Keeping to the Private Market,' 289.
60 Bacher, *Keeping to the Marketplace*, 121–2, quoting minutes of a meeting of the Economic Advisory Committee, 2, 15 October 1940, vol. 3890, RG19, LAC.
61 As quoted in Bacher, *Keeping to the Marketplace*, 121–2, memorandum for Dr Clark, 19 August 1940, and memorandum for the Economic Advisory Committee of wartime housing policy, both vol. 3890, RG19, LAC.
62 Bacher, *Keeping to the Marketplace*, 122, quoting W.C. Clark, Report of the Economic Advisory Committee on Housing Policy, 4–5, vol. 3890, RG19, LAC.
63 Bacher, *Keeping to the Marketplace*, 123, quoting W.C. Clark to Angus L. MacDonald, 30 December 1940, vol. 3890, RG19, LAC; also minutes of a meeting of the EAC, vol. 3890, RG19.
64 Bacher, *Keeping to the Marketplace*, 123. Bacher's reference here is odd: Memorandum for the Economic Advisory Committee on Housing Policy, 4. Previously, that reference seemed to be to a Nicoll's memo. And the previous Clark reference was to his report of the EAC to Cabinet, 13 November.
65 Bacher, *Keeping to the Marketplace*, 125; summary of government housing programs, file 203-1A, vol. 706, RG19.
66 Firestone, *Residential Real Estate*, 486.
67 Stacey, *Arms, Men and Governments*, 50.
68 King Diaries, 24 October 1940.
69 Ibid., 21 November 1940.
70 Ibid., 26 November 1940.
71 Granatstein, *Canada's War*, 165.
72 Ibid., 166.

73 W.C. Clark to Joseph Sirois, 15 November 1940, vol. 4447, RG19, LAC.
74 Gibson and Robertson, *Ottawa at War*, 89.
75 Granatstein, *Man of Influence*, 96–7.
76 King Diaries, 28 November 1940.
77 Gibson and Robertson, *Ottawa at War*, 94, 73.
78 Bothwell and Kilbourn, *C.D. Howe*, 140–1.
79 Ibid., 144; Report of the Economic Advisory Committee on the establishment of a Board of Committee for Wartime Planning, 31 October 1940, vol. 3984, RG19, LAC.
80 Drushka, *HR*, 210.
81 Bothwell and Kilbourn, *C.D. Howe*, 141–3.
82 Gibson and Robertson, *Ottawa at War*, 124.
83 Bothwell and Kilbourn, *C.D. Howe*, 144–5; Gibson and Robertson, *Ottawa at War*, 124.
84 Bothwell and Kilbourn, *C.D. Howe*, 145–7.
85 Ibid., 145–6; Gibson and Robertson, *Ottawa at War*, 125–6.
86 Gibson and Robertson, *Ottawa at War*, 127.
87 Rasminsky, 'Foreign Exchange Control,' 125. See also Granatstein, *Canada's War*, 135, 175. Imposition of this act corresponded to the end of the flow of gold from Britain.
88 Gordon, *Political Memoir*, 33.
89 *House of Commons Debates* (5 December 1940) (Mr J.L. Ilsley, MP).
90 *House of Commons Debates* (2 June 1941) (Mr Jean-Francois Pouliot, MP).
91 *House of Commons Debates* (4 June 1942) (Mr J.L. Ralston, MP).
92 Bryce, *Canada and the Cost of World War II*, 99–100.
93 King Diaries, 5 December 1940.
94 Bryce, *Canada and the Cost of World War II*, 100.
95 Gordon, *Political Memoir*, 36.
96 King Diaries, 19 December 1940.
97 Ibid., 14 January 1941.
98 Granatstein, *Canada's War*, 168–9.
99 King Diaries, 13 December 1940.
100 As quoted in Eggleston, *Road to Nationhood*, 170–2.
101 See Wardaugh and Ferguson, '"Impossible Conditions of Inequality,"' 551–84; Fisher, *Duff Pattullo*, 317–39.
102 King Diaries, 15 January 1941.
103 Gordon, *Political Memoir*, 38–9.
104 Gibson and Robertson, *Ottawa at War*, 78.
105 Bryce, 'William Clifford Clark, 1889–1952,' 421.
106 Slater, *War Finance*, 48–9.

107 Ibid., 49.
108 As quoted in Fisher, *Duff Pattullo*, 357–8.
109 King Diaries, 14 January 1941.
110 As it turned out, net national income for 1940 turned out to be $5.112 billion; for 1941 it was $6.514 billion, and for 1942, it was $8.277 billion.
111 Stacey, *Arms, Men and Governments*, 50.
112 Granatstein, *Man of Influence*, 102.
113 W.C. Clark, 'Oscar Douglas Skelton,' 141–7.
114 Ibid.
115 Ibid.
116 King Diaries, 26 February 1941; Granatstein, *Canada's War*, 137–8; Bothwell and Kilbourn, *C.D. Howe*, 150–1.
117 Gibson and Robertson, *Ottawa at War*, 129–30.
118 Granatstein, *Canada's War*, 137.
119 W.C. Clark to A.F.W. Plumptre, 4 June 1942, vol. 3991, RG19, LAC.
120 King Diaries, 13 March 1941.
121 Granatstein, *Canada's War*, 135, 138–9.
122 Ibid., 140; Cuff and Granatstein, *Ties That Bind*, 80.
123 King Diaries, 13 March 1941.
124 Granatstein, *Canada's War*, 137–8, 141.
125 Report on Visit to Washington March 17–21, 21 March 1941, vol. 3991, RG19, LAC; Bryce, *Canada and the Cost of World War II*, 102.
126 Granatstein, *Canada's War*, 173.
127 King Diaries, 26 March 1941.
128 Slater, *War Finance*, 180.

Chapter 7

1 James McCook, 'Dr Clark Vital Part in Shaping War Financing,' *Ottawa Journal*, 29 December 1952.
2 25 May 1989, Interview 5, 'Ottawa Decides, 1945–1971,' Institute for Research on Public Policy Collection, LAC.
3 Memorandum on the Joint Economic Committees of Canada and the United States, 2 September 1943, vol. 3977, RG19, LAC.
4 As quoted in Granatstein, *Canada's War*, 140.
5 The Canadian 'legation' in Washington became an 'embassy' in 1943.
6 Report on Visit to Washington March 17–21, 21 March 1941, vol. 3991, RG19, LAC.
7 Ibid.; Granatstein, *Canada's War*, 141.
8 Bothwell and Kilbourn, *C.D. Howe*, 151–2.

9 As quoted in Stacey, *Canada and the Age of Conflict*, 316; Bryce, *Canada and the Cost of World War II*, 104.
10 King Diaries, 16 April 1941.
11 J.E. Coyne, Memorandum of Meeting with Morgenthau, 18 April 1941, vol. 3971, RG19, LAC; as quoted in Stacey, *Canada and the Age of Conflict*, 316.
12 As quoted in Stacey, *Canada and the Age of Conflict*, 316–17; Granatstein, *Canada's War*, 142.
13 Rohmer, *E.P. Taylor*, 104.
14 Ibid., 104–5.
15 Ibid.
16 King Diary, 20 April 1941.
17 Granatstein, *Canada's War*, 143; Granatstein, *Man of Influence*, 115.
18 J.E. Coyne, Memorandum of Meeting with Morgenthau, 22 April 1941, vol. 3971, RG19, LAC.
19 King Diaries, 20 April 1941.
20 Ibid.
21 Gibson and Robertson, *Ottawa at War*, 153–4.
22 As quoted in Cuff and Granatstein, *Ties That Bind*, 191.
23 Granatstein, *How Britain's Weakness Forced Canada*, 36; Stacey, *Canada and the Age of Conflict*, 317.
24 As quoted in Stacey, *Canada and the Age of Conflict*, 317.
25 J.E. Coyne, Memorandum of Meeting with Morgenthau, 22 April 1941, vol. 3971, RG19, LAC.
26 J.E. Coyne to W.C. Clark, 9 June 1941, vol. 3991, RG19, LAC.
27 W.C. Clark to James Coyne, 29 April 1941, vol. 3991, RG19, LAC.
28 J.E. Coyne, Memorandum on 'Defence Articles Obtained by the U.K. under the Lend-Lease Act for Delivery in Canada,' 27 June 1941, vol. 3446, RG19, LAC.
29 'Canada's Adverse Balance with the United States as Affected by the Hyde Park Agreement,' Memorandum Prepared by Joint Economic Committees of Canada and the United States, Sub-Committee on Hyde Park Agreement, 4 August 1941, vol. 3971, RG19, LAC.
30 Memorandum on 'Some Problems in Connection with the Hyde Park Agreement,' n.d., vol. 3971, RG19, LAC.
31 Bryce, *Canada and the Cost of World War II*, 130–1.
32 W.C. Clark to James Coyne, 28 July 1941, vol. 3991, RG19, LAC.
33 Memorandum on the Joint Economic Committees of Canada and the United States, 7 October 1943, vol. 3569, RG19, LAC.
34 Memorandum on the Joint Economic Committees of Canada and the

United States, 2 September 1943, vol. 3977, RG19, LAC; W.A. Mackintosh to Carl Goldenberg, 28 September 1943, vol. 3569.
35 Mackintosh to H.L. Keenleyside, 2 February 1943, vol. 3572, RG19, LAC.
36 Alex Skelton, Memorandum on the Role of the Joint Economic Committees, 3 February 1943, vol. 3572, RG19, LAC. For a full discussion, see Bryce, *Canada and the Cost of World War II*, 113–16.
37 W.C. Clark, 'Is Our Taxation Policy Sound?' 54–7.
38 Slater, *War Finance*, 49.
39 Ibid., 51.
40 Ibid., 51–3.
41 Gillespie, *Tax, Borrow and Spend*, 81.
42 W.C. Clark, 'Is Our Taxation Policy Sound?' 54–7.
43 King Diaries, 29 April 1941.
44 W.C. Clark, 'Canada's Wartime Economy,' draft of presidential address to be given at the annual meeting of the Canadian Political Science Association, 24 May 1941, CP. The paper, however, was never presented.
45 W.C. Clark, 'Canadian-American Relations in Defence,' 274.
46 Granatstein, *Canada's War*, 176–7.
47 Slater, *War Finance*, 130.
48 Ibid.
49 Gibson and Robertson, *Ottawa at War*, 201–2.
50 Slater, *War Finance*, 130.
51 As quoted in Fullerton, *Graham Towers*, 148.
52 Ibid., 149.
53 Slater, *War Finance*, 130; King Diaries, 13 August 1941.
54 Gibson and Robertson, *Ottawa at War*, 201–2.
55 Slater, *War Finance*, 131, 132, 139.
56 Ibid., 132–3, 139, 162.
57 Gibson and Robertson, *Ottawa at War*, 203.
58 As quoted in Granatstein, *Canada's War*, 177–8.
59 Slater, *War Finance*, 134.
60 Gibson and Robertson, *Ottawa at War*, 207.
61 W.C. Clark to John Urquhart, 13 October 1941, CP.
62 Slater, *War Finance*, 158–9.
63 Ibid., 127–37, 157–8.
64 King Diaries, 31 October 1941.
65 W.L.M. King to W.C. Clark, 21 October 1941, 255824, J1, King Papers.
66 Pickersgill, *Seeing Canada Whole*, 212.
67 Gibson and Robertson, *Ottawa at War*, 204.

68 Ibid., 204; Fullerton, *Graham Towers*, 150.
69 Fullerton, *Graham Towers*, 150.
70 King Diaries, 7 November 1941; Granatstein, *Canada's War*, 179.
71 Slater, *War Finance*, 135.
72 Gibson and Robertson, *Ottawa at War*, 224.
73 Slater, *War Finance*, 136, 152.
74 Bryce, 'William Clifford Clark, 1889–1952,' 420.
75 As quoted in Bothwell, 'Health of the Common People,' 199–200.
76 As quoted in Struthers, *Limits of Affluence*, 74–5.
77 W.C. Clark to G.K. Sheils, 11 December 1941, vol. 3446, RG19, LAC.
78 George Clark, interview, 19 March 1995.
79 W.C. Clark to Lorie Tarshis, 12 May 1941, vol. 3444, RG19, LAC.
80 Sharp, *Which Reminds Me*, 15–25.
81 Mitchell Sharp, interview, 3 August 1995.
82 Sharp, *Which Reminds Me*, 19–24.
83 Ibid., 25–7.
84 R.B. Bryce to W.C. Clark, 7 March 1942, vol. 445, RG19, LAC; Barnett, *Keynesian Arithmetic*, 27–8.
85 W.C. Clark to J.L. Ilsley, 13 April 1942, vol. 3440, RG19, LAC.
86 Graham Towers to W.C. Clark, 17 June 1941, vol. 3440, RG19, LAC.
87 Ibid., 6 January 1942.
88 J.J. Deutsch, Memorandum on National Income Statistics, 17 June 1941, vol. 3440, RG19, LAC.
89 R.B. Bryce, Notes on Meeting on National Income Statistics, 9 April 1942, vol. 3440, RG19, LAC.
90 W.C. Clark to J.L. Ilsley, 13 April 1942, vol. 3440, RG19, LAC; L.D. Wilgress to W.C. Clark, 22 April 1942; W.C. Clark to Graham Towers, 25 April 1942; L.D. Wilgress to W.C. Clark, 18 September 1942; L.D. Wilgress to Donald Gordon, 18 September 1942; W.C. Clark to Donald Gordon, 23 September 1942.
91 J.J. Deutsch, Memorandum on National Income Statistics, 17 June 1941, vol. 3440, RG19, LAC.
92 W.C. Clark to Norman Robertson, 29 October 1942, vol. 3440, RG19, LAC.
93 Report of the Canadian Representatives at the 'Post-War Economic Talks' Held in London, 9 November 1942, vol. 3440, RG19, LAC.
94 Barnett, *Keynesian Arithmetic*, 49.
95 J.E. Coyne to W.C. Clark, 29 April 1941, vol. 3449, RG19, LAC.
96 Memorandum, 6 August 1941, Graham Towers Papers.
97 Granatstein, *Canada's War*, 194.
98 J.M. Keynes to Robert Bryce, 11 April 1942, vol. 3444, RG19, LAC.

99 Charles Towers to W.C. Clark, 11 March 1942, vol. 3971, RG19, LAC.
100 W.C. Clark to A.F.W. Plumptre, 14 March 1942, vol. 3971, RG19, LAC.
101 R.B. Bryce to W.C. Clark, 20 March 1942, vol. 3971, RG19, LAC.
102 R.B. Bryce, Notes on Conversation with Sir Frederick Phillips and Mr Munro, 24 March 1942, vol. 3437, RG19, LAC; R.B. Bryce, Notes on Canada's U.S. Dollar Exchange Situation, 14 April 1942, vol. 3971; R.B. Bryce, Note on Canadian U.S. Dollar Position in First Quarter of 1942 in Comparison with Latest Forecast, 2 May 1942.
103 Memorandum on 'A Suggested Plan for Solving Canada's U.S. Dollar Deficit Under Joint Arrangements for Pooling War Production,' 6 May 1942, vol. 3971, RG19, LAC; W.C. Clark, 'Canada's Dollar Exchange Problem,' 8 May 1942.
104 W.C. Clark to A.F.W. Plumptre, 16 November 1942, vol. 3437, RG19, LAC; A.F.W. Plumptre to W.C. Clark, 20 November 1942; W.C. Clark to A.F.W. Plumptre, 24 November 1942.
105 Slater, *War Finance*, 62.
106 Sharp, *Which Reminds Me*, 18.
107 Slater, *War Finance*, 62.
108 Gillespie, *Tax, Borrow and Spend*, 97.
109 Slater, *War Finance*, 62–9.
110 As quoted in Gillespie, *Tax, Borrow and Spend*, 90.
111 Slater, *War Finance*, 157, 160.
112 *Canadian Business*, November 1942, 56.
113 King Diaries, 16 July 1942.
114 Slater, *War Finance*, 89.
115 Memorandum on the Financing and the Conscription of Capital, 1 April 1942, vol. 3978, RG19, LAC.
116 Floyd Chalmers to Grant Dexter, 4 April 1941, box 2, Dexter Papers.
117 *Canadian Business*, March 1942, 22.
118 W.C. Clark to J.L. Ilsley, 1 May 1942, vol. 3986, RG19, LAC.
119 As quoted in Stacey, *Canada and the Age of Conflict*, 331–2.
120 W.C. Clark to J.L. Ilsley, 13 August 1942, vol. 3437, RG19, LAC.
121 As quoted in Granatstein, *Canada's War*, 307–8.
122 Ibid.
123 Stacey, *Canada and the Age of Conflict*, 332.
124 W.C. Clark to Norman Robertson, 25 August 1942, vol. 3992, RG19, LAC.
125 Bryce, *Canada and the Cost of World War II*, 124–5.
126 W.C. Clark, 'Is Our Taxation Policy Sound?' 54–7, 100.
127 Ibid., 56–7.
128 'Taxes Will Come Down in Canada,' *Vancouver Sun*, 24 October 1942. See

also *House of Commons Debates* (10 March 1947), p. 1220 (Mr Victor Quelch, MP).

129 Ibid., 57, 100.

130 'Dr Clark's Work Highly Praised,' *Glengarry News*, 23 October 1942.

Chapter 8

1 Heeney, *Things That Are Caesar's*, 60.

2 Young, 'Reining in James,' 603.

3 Memorandum for Clark from R.B. Bryce, 22 October 1942, vol. 4660, RG19, LAC.

4 Granatstein, *Ottawa Men*, 161–2.

5 As quoted in Granatstein, *Ottawa Men*, 161–2; Minutes of EAC meeting, 10 November 1942, vol. 4660, RG19, LAC.

6 Minutes of EAC meeting, 10 November 1942, vol. 4660, RG19, LAC.

7 Ibid.

8 Arnold Heeney to W.C. Clark, 26 December 1942, vol. 4660, RG19, LAC.

9 As quoted in Granatstein, *Canada's War*, 162–3.

10 F. Cyril James to W.A. Mackintosh, 28 December 1942, vol. 4660, RG19, LAC; Minutes of EAC meeting, 7 January 1943.

11 As quoted in Young, 'Reining in James,' 605.

12 R.B. Bryce to W.C. Clark, 31 December 1942, vol. 4660, RG19, LAC.

13 Granatstein, *Ottawa Men*, 5.

14 As quoted in Bacher, *Keeping to the Marketplace*, 137–8.

15 Ibid., 139.

16 Its members included Pigott; Nicolls; real property controller Russel Smart; construction controller C. Blake Jackson; Assistant Deputy Minister of Labour Arthur Macnamara; and Henry Borden, coordinator of controls for Munitions and Supply and chairman of the committee. Bacher, *Keeping to the Marketplace*, 140; W.C. Clark to Donald Gordon, 9 November 1942, vol. 3980, RG19, LAC.

17 Bacher, *Keeping to the Marketplace*, 140.

18 Granatstein, *Canada's War*, 309.

19 The term *United Nations* was used generally to refer to the Allies.

20 R.B. Bryce, 'Figures Mentioned by Sir Frederick Phillips,' 11 December 1942, vol. 3449, RG19, LAC.

21 Granatstein, *Canada's War*, 309.

22 As quoted in Granatstein, *Canada's War*, 310–11.

23 Ibid.

24 Ibid.

25 W.C. Clark to Blanche Clark, 2 January 1943, CP.

26 Ibid.

27 W.C. Clark to Alexander Loveday, 14 August 1942, vol. 3981, RG19, LAC.

28 W.C. Clark to A.F.W. Plumptre, 5 October 1942, vol. 3991, RG19, LAC.

29 Slater, 177–8.

30 Order in Council establishing an Advisory Committee on Economic Policy, 23 January 1943, vol. 3448, RG19, LAC; Owram, *Government Generation*, 286.

31 Bercuson, *True Patriot*, 114–15.

32 W.C. Clark, 'Canada's Postwar Finance,' 6.

33 Owram, *Government Generation*, 293–5.

34 Ibid., 297.

35 Sharp, *Which Reminds Me*, 20–1.

36 W.C. Clark, 'Postwar International Monetary Stabilization.'

37 Ibid., 209–10.

38 Frederick Phillips to W.C. Clark, 4 September 1942, vol. 3981, RG19, LAC.

39 W.C. Clark, Memorandum on Suggestions as to a Reasonable Reserve of U.S. Dollar Exchange to be Maintained by Canada, 8 January 1943, vol. 3972, RG19, LAC.

40 W.C. Clark, Memorandum on Discussions with the United States Treasury, 11 January 1943, vol. 3971, RG19, LAC.

41 A.F.W. Plumptre to W.C. Clark, 20 January 1943, vol. 3972, RG19, LAC.

42 CANSHIP referred to identifiable Lend-Lease components obtained by Britain from the United States and sent to Canadian manufacturers. CANEX referred to components for cash but with British compensation by having Canada transfer other defence articles of an equivalent value that Canada otherwise would have had to purchase in the United States. CANPAY referred to items that Canada purchased and paid for to get the benefit of U.S. service priorities and prices. Bryce, *Canada and the Cost of World War II*, 107.

43 War Supplies Limited was a Canadian corporation created in early May 1941 out of the Hyde Park Agreement discussions to negotiate contracts with the U.S. government and sublet to Canadian suppliers.

44 A.F.W. Plumptre to W.C. Clark, 31 March 1943, vol. 3972, RG19, LAC; A.F.W. Plumptre to W.C. Clark, 1 April 1943; W.C. Clark, Memorandum re Trip to Washington, 9 April 1943; R.B. Bryce, Memorandum on Exchange Situation, 3 December 1943.

45 A.F.W. Plumptre to W.C. Clark, 16 January 1943, vol. 3447, RG19, LAC.

46 Granatstein, *Ottawa Men*, 144–6.

47 J.M. Keynes to Hume Wrong, 19 May 1943, vol. 3981, RG19, LAC.

48 W.C. Clark to Norman Robertson, 6 March 1943, vol. 3981, RG19, LAC.
49 W.C. Clark to J.L. Ilsley, 9 April 1943, vol. 3981, RG19, LAC.
50 J.L. Ilsley to H. Morgenthau, 8 April 1943, vol. 3980, RG19, LAC.
51 Malcolm Taylor, *Health Insurance and Canadian Public Policy*, 19.
52 Bothwell, 'Health of the Common People' 201–2.
53 Granatstein, *Ottawa Men*, 163–4.
54 Minutes of Meeting of the Economic Advisory Committee, 16 January 1943, vol. 4660, RG19, LAC; Owram, *Government Generation*, 298–9.
55 Bothwell, 'Health of the Common People,' 210–11.
56 Report of the Economic Advisory Committee on the Proposal to Establish a National System of Health Insurance, 20 January 1943, vol. 4662, RG19, LAC; Malcolm Taylor, *Health Insurance and Canadian Public Policy*, 19.
57 As quoted in Granatstein, *Ottawa Men*, 164.
58 Bothwell, 'Health of the Common People,' 204.
59 As quoted in Malcolm Taylor, *Health Insurance and Canadian Public Policy*, 19–20.
60 King Diaries, 22 January 1943.
61 Malcolm Taylor, *Health Insurance and Canadian Public Policy*, 20.
62 Granatstein, *Ottawa Men*, 164.
63 R.B. Bryce, 27 January 1989, Interview 1, 'Ottawa Decides, 1945–1971,' Institute for Research on Public Policy Collection, LAC.
64 King Diaries, 22 January 1943.
65 Granatstein, *Canada's War*, 312–14.
66 As quoted in Granatstein, *Canada's War*, 312.
67 Stacey, *Arms, Men and Governments*, 51.
68 Slater, *War Finance*, 165–6.
69 W.C. Clark to G.K. Sheils, 27 March 1943, vol. 497, RG19, LAC.
70 W.C. Clark to A. MacNamara, 14 July 1943, vol. 497, RG19, LAC.
71 Donald Gordon to W.C. Clark, 17 July 1943, vol. 497, RG19, LAC; Clark to Gordon, 19 July 1943.
72 R.B. Bryce, Memorandum for Dr Clark re: Discussion on Wages Order Changes, 22 February 1944, vol. 497, RG19, LAC.
73 King Diaries, 5 February 1943.
74 *House of Commons Debates* (2 March 1943), Budget Speech (Mr J.L. Ilsley, MP).
75 Slater, *War Finance*, 57.
76 Ibid., 68, 70–1.
77 Ilsley told King that he had 'never known a time when everyone seemed so bitter against everyone else.' The prime minister observed that 'the

hardest thing to defend will be the billion dollar expenditure for materials for United Nations where there is not enough money to provide for our own forces first.' He felt, however, that 'between demand now for men as well as for money, we have reached a ceiling that pretty well settles the question of any attempt at any further conscripting of men for overseas service. That issue has been silenced by holding the fort for a year.' King Diaries, 19 February, 24 February, 1943.

78 Slater, *War Finance*, 65.

79 Clark to Robertson, 5 March 1943, 290855, J1, King Papers; as quoted in Hilliker, *Canada's Department of External Affairs*, 1:783–4.

80 English, *Shadow of Heaven*, 1:282–3.

81 Plumptre, *Three Decades*, 70–1; Bercuson, *True Patriot*, 120.

82 Plumptre, *Three Decades*, 71.

83 Malcolm Taylor, *Health Insurance and Canadian Public Policy*, 21.

84 Bothwell, 'Health of the Common People,' 206.

85 Gibson and Robertson, *Ottawa at War*, 406.

86 The levy would be 3 per cent of income over $660 to a maximum of $30 for an individual, and 5 per cent of income over $1,200 with a maximum of $50 for a married person. The levy was to be collected by Ottawa along with income tax.

87 Malcolm Taylor, *Health Insurance and Canadian Public Policy*, 36.

88 As quoted in Bothwell, 'Health of the Common People,' 210–11.

89 Minutes of a meeting of the Advisory Committee on Economic Policy, 22 April 1943, vol. 4660, RG19, LAC.

90 Memorandum on Post-War Policy, 19 April 1943, vol. 3446, RG19, LAC.

91 Memorandum on Constitutional Problems of Dominion Post-War Policy, 27 April 1943, vol. 4660, RG19, LAC.

92 Report of the EAC on the Report of the Advisory Committee on Reconstruction, 20 November 1943, vol. 4663, RG19, LAC.

93 J.W. Dafoe, 'The Canadian Federal System under Review' (draft), vol. 2701, RG19, LAC, later published in *Foreign Affairs.*

94 Kitchen, 'Introduction of Family Allowances,' 40–1.

95 Blake, 'Mackenzie King,' 326.

96 Christie, *Engendering the State*, 4.

97 Minutes of meeting of the Advisory Committee on Economic Policy, 7 July 1943, vol. 4660, RG19, LAC.

98 Blake, 'Mackenzie King,' 327.

99 'Meeting with Sir William Beveridge with Advisory Committee on Economic Policy and Advisory Committee on Reconstruction,' 31 May 1943, vol. 3977, RG19, LAC.

100 Malcolm Taylor, *Health Insurance and Canadian Public Policy*, 34.
101 Struthers, *Limits of Affluence*, 75.
102 W.C. Clark to A.D.P. Heeney, 15 April 1943, vol. 3985, RG19, LAC.
103 Slater, *War Finance*, 169–70.
104 Gibson and Robertson, *Ottawa at War*, 423–4.
105 Ibid., 426–7.
106 Slater, *War Finance*, 171.
107 King Diaries, 30 September 1943.
108 Ibid., 1 October 1943. King's wording has surely mixed up the argument Finance was making. It must be lower *income* that is exempt from taxation.
109 Ibid., 7 October 1943.
110 Dexter Memorandum, 21 October 1943, Dexter Papers.
111 Louis Rasminsky to John H. Williams, 15 July 1943, vol. 3982, RG19, LAC.
112 King Diaries, 2 June 1943.
113 Granatstein, *Ottawa Men*, 150.
114 W.C. Clark to Norman Robertson, 2 August 1943, vol. 3989, RG19, LAC.
115 W.C. Clark to Frederick Phillips, 5 July 1943, vol. 3981, RG19, LAC; W.C. Clark to H.D. White, 29 July 1943; H.D. White to W.C. Clark, 1 September 1943; W.C. Clark to A.F.W. Plumptre, 10 June 1943, vol. 3982, RG19, LAC; W.C. Clark to H.D. White, 12 August 1943, vol. 3447, RG19, LAC.
116 A.F.W. Plumptre to Norman Robertson, 4 October 1943, vol. 3447, RG19, LAC.
117 H. Morgenthau to J.L. Ilsley, 14 September 1943, vol. 3980, RG19, LAC.
118 W.C. Clark, 'Canadian Plan'; 'General Observations of Canadian Experts on Plans for Post-War Monetary Organization,' 9 June 1943, vol. 3448, RG19, LAC.
119 W.C. Clark, 'The Problem of Monetary Stabilization,' 15 December 1943, 211–13, no. 11, series II, New York University Institute on Postwar Reconstruction.
120 The Liberal members were A.G. Slaght and Gerald McGeer. King Diaries, 25 September 1943.
121 Ibid., 23 December 1943.
122 Ibid., 1 November 1943.
123 C.D. Howe to W.C. Clark, 27 September 1943, vol. 3972, RG19, LAC.
124 H.D. White to W.C. Clark, 17 November 1943, vol. 3972, RG19, LAC; W.C. Clark to H.D. White, 23 November 1943.
125 R.B. Bryce, Memorandum for Dr Clark re: US Exchange Problem, 29 November 1943, vol. 3972, RG19, LAC.

126 R.B. Bryce, Memorandum on Exchange Situation, 3 December 1943, vol. 3972, RG19, LAC; W.C. Clark, Memorandum re Visit to Washington, 7–8 December 1943.

Chapter 9

1 Mackintosh, 'William Clifford Clark: Memoir,' 11.
2 Bryce, 'William Clifford Clark, 1889–1952,' 420.
3 Bothwell, 'Health of the Common People,' 210–11; Fullerton, *Graham Towers*, 182; Slater, *War Finance*, 197–8.
4 King Diaries, 6 January 1944.
5 Ibid., 11 January 1944.
6 W.C. Clark to J.D. Ilsley, 10 January 1944, vol. 304, RG19, LAC.
7 Granatstein, *Canada's War*, 282.
8 As quoted in ibid., 281.
9 As quoted in Slater, *War Finance*, 199.
10 King Diaries, 13 January 1944.
11 Ibid., 13 January 1944.
12 Eaton, *Essays in Taxation*, 134.
13 Ibid., 136.
14 Bryce, 'William Clifford Clark, 1889–1952,' 421.
15 Christie, *Engendering the State*, 251, 268.
16 Porter, *Vertical Mosaic*, 427.
17 R.B. Bryce, 27 January 1989, Interview 1, 'Ottawa Decides, 1945–1971,' Institute for Research on Public Policy Collection, LAC.
18 King Diaries, 24 January 1944.
19 Bothwell, 'Health of the Common People,' 211; King Diaries, 24 January 1944.
20 Bothwell, 'Health of the Common People,' 211; King Diaries, 25 January 1944.
21 Bothwell, 'Health of the Common People,' 212.
22 Slater, *War Finance*, 202.
23 Malcolm Taylor, *Health Insurance and Canadian Public Policy*, 40; Granatstein, *Canada's War*, 276; Bothwell, 'Health of the Common People,' 212.
24 Malcolm Taylor, *Health Insurance and Canadian Public Policy*, 37–8; Bothwell, 'Health of the Common People,' 212–14.
25 English, 'Dominion–Provincial Relations,' 8–9.
26 D.K. MacTavish to W.C. Clark, 15 January 1944, vol. 3985, RG19, LAC;

Minutes of the Fifth Meeting of the Advisory Committee on Post Hostilities Problems, 20 December 1944.

27 W.C. Clark to D.K. MacTavish, 20 May 1944, vol. 3985, RG19, LAC.

28 Memorandum on Post-War Defence of Newfoundland and Labrador: Canadian Position, 28 December 1944, vol. 3985, RG19, LAC.

29 King Diaries, 24 February 1944.

30 Ibid., 8 March 1944.

31 Ibid., 20 April 1944.

32 W.C. Clark, 'Canada's Postwar Finance,' 6.

33 Minutes of meeting of EAC, 2 February 1944, vol. 3448, RG19, LAC.

34 Slater, *War Finance*, 204.

35 King Diaries, 20 April 1944.

36 Norman Robertson to W.C. Clark, 10 March 1944, vol. 3989, RG19, LAC.

37 W.C. Clark to Norman Robertson, 11 March 1944, vol. 3989, RG19, LAC.

38 Mackenzie, 'Path to Temptation,' 196.

39 Plumptre, *Three Decades of Decision*, 66–7.

40 A.F.W. Plumptre to W.C. Clark, 8 May 1944, vol. 3972, RG19, LAC.

41 Granatstein, *Canada's War*, 315.

42 Ibid., 286.

43 Ibid., 283.

44 King Diaries, 13 June 1944; Slater, *War Finance*, 216.

45 King Diaries, 22 June 1944.

46 Ibid.

47 Thomas, *Making of a Socialist*, 170; McLeod and McLeod, *Tommy Douglas*, 135.

48 Thomas, *Making of a Socialist*, 170.

49 As quoted in ibid., 170.

50 McLeod and McLeod, *Tommy Douglas*, 135.

51 Sharp, *Which Reminds Me*, 30.

52 Shackleton, *Tommy Douglas*, 165.

53 Ibid.; McLeod and McLeod, *Tommy Douglas*, 136.

54 As quoted in Thomas, *Making of a Socialist*, 171. One source on Douglas claims that the crucial Cabinet meeting Douglas referred to took place in September 1945. McLeod and McLeod, *Tommy Douglas*, 136. Yet that was during the period that Clark was away from work, recovering from his collapse at the end of the war.

55 Sharp, *Which Reminds Me*, 30–1.

56 Dexter Memorandum, n.d., box 4, Dexter Papers.

57 Keynes, *Collected Writings*, 26:60.

58 The fact that no MPs from other parties were included and there were no

experts from outside government was criticized in the House two days later. Soward, *Canada in World Affairs*, 174; *House of Commons Debates* (3 July 1944), pp. 4429–30 (Mr J.L. Ilsley, MP).

59 Horsefield, *International Monetary Fund*, 1:91–2.
60 Bryce, 'William Clifford Clark, 1889–1952,' 420–1.
61 Granatstein, *Man of Influence*, 134.
62 Keynes, *Collected Writings*, 26:80.
63 Granatstein, *Man of Influence*, 134.
64 King Diaries, 14 August 1944.
65 A.F.W. Plumptre to W.C. Clark, 17 April 1944, vol. 3597, RG19, LAC; W.C. Clark to A.F.W. Plumptre, 18 April 1944.
66 Granatstein, *Canada's War*, 314.
67 Slater, *War Finance*, 73.
68 Bothwell, Drummond, and English, *Canada: 1900–1945*, 392–3; *House of Commons Debates* (26 June 1944), Budget Speech (Mr J.L. Ilsley, MP).
69 King Diaries, 18 July 1944.
70 Slater, *War Finance*, 211–12.
71 Mackintosh, 'William Clifford Clark: A Personal Memoir,' 12.
72 Bryce, 'William Clifford Clark, 1889–1952,' 420.
73 W.C. Clark, 'Canada's Postwar Finance,' 6.
74 Mackintosh, 'William Clifford Clark: Memoir,' 12.
75 Bacher, 'Keeping to the Private Market,' 377–87.
76 Mackintosh, 'William Clifford Clark: Memoir,' 12.
77 Bacher, 'Keeping to the Private Market,' 400–10.
78 Slater, *War Finance*, 206–7.
79 Ibid., 208.
80 Bacher, 'Keeping to the Private Market,' 412–13.
81 Bacher, *Keeping to the Marketplace*, 164.
82 Bryce, 'William Clifford Clark, 1889–1952,' 421.
83 Sharp, *Which Reminds Me*, 42.
84 Slater, *War Finance*, 213–14.
85 Ibid., 214–15.
86 Ibid., 215.
87 Stacey, *Arms, Men and Governments*, 64.
88 Bothwell, Drummond, and English, *Canada since 1945*, 99.
89 Power, *Party Politician*, 403.
90 King Diaries, 22 September 1944.
91 Keynes, *Collected Writings*, 24:80.
92 Ibid., 24:98.
93 Ibid., 24:99–101.

94 Ibid., 24:106–7; Granatstein, *Man of Influence*, 134.
95 Ibid., 24:143–49, 85; R.B. Bryce, 'Notes on Discussion of Air Force Matters with United Kingdom Treasury Delegation,' 2 December 1944, vol. 3672, RG19, LAC.
96 English, 'Dominion–Provincial Relations,' 11.
97 Ibid., 11–12.
98 Bryce, 'William Clifford Clark, 1889–1952,' 421.
99 W.C. Clark to Donald Gordon, 2 October 1944, vol. 3993, RG19, LAC; Donald Gordon to W.C. Clark, 7 October 1944; W.C. Clark to Donald Gordon, 16 October 1944.
100 Gordon, *Political Memoir*, 43–4.
101 J.M. Keynes to W.C. Clark, 16 January 1945, vol. 3992, RG19, LAC; Keynes, *Collected Writings*, 24:233.
102 R.B. Bryce, Notes on Meeting to Discuss Immediate Post-War Commercial Policy Outlook, 20 January 1945, vol. 3437, RG19, LAC; Granatstein, *Man of Influence*, 135; Fullerton, *Graham Towers*, 206–9.
103 As quoted in Granatstein, *Canada's War*, 315.
104 Granatstein, *Man of Influence*, 135, 210–11.
105 Keynes, *Collected Writings*, 24:297–8.
106 Gibson and Robertson, *Ottawa at War*, 500.
107 W.C. Clark to L. Rasminsky, 14 May 1945, vol. 3981, RG19, LAC.
108 L. Rasminsky to W.C. Clark, 20 June 1945, Bank of Canada Papers.
109 Dexter Memorandum, 1 March 1945, Dexter Papers.
110 W.C. Clark to H.J. Chater, 27 March 1945, vol. 3392, RG19, LAC.
111 Dexter Memorandum, 1 March 1945, Dexter Papers.
112 Bothwell, Drummond, and English, *Canada since 1945*, 71.
113 Gratton O'Leary, 'The Man behind Ilsley,' *Maclean's Magazine*, 1 May 1945.
114 Bacher, 'Keeping to the Private Market,' 446.
115 As quoted in Bacher, 'Keeping to the Private Market,' 447.
116 Bacher, 'Keeping to the Private Market,' 450.
117 Ibid., 450–1.
118 Ibid., 451.
119 Ibid., 451–4.
120 R.B. Bryce, interview, 1 March 1987.
121 As quoted in Fullerton, *Graham Towers*, 213.
122 Dexter Memorandum, 14 June 1945, box 4, Grant Dexter Papers.
123 Mackintosh, 'William Clifford Clark: Memoir,' 12.
124 King Diaries, 15 June 1945.

125 Arthur W. Rogers to W.C. Clark, 25 June 1945, CP.
126 Dexter Memorandum, 21 June 1945, box 4, Grant Dexter Papers.
127 J.L. Ralston to Margaret Clark, 23 July 1945, CP.
128 Bryce Stewart to W.C. Clark, 13 July 1945, CP.
129 As quoted in *Winnipeg Free Press*, 29 December 1952.
130 Mackintosh, 'William Clifford Clark: Memoir,' 12.
131 Bryce Stewart to W.C. Clark, 24 July 1945, CP.
132 Stanley McLean to W.C. Clark, 24 August 1945, CP.
133 'Deputy Minister of Finance Lands Big Lunge,' *Cornwall Freeholder-Standard*, 10 September 1945.
134 W.C. Clark to S.H. Falkner, 9 November 1945, CP.
135 J.H. Gundy to W.C. Clark, 21 December 1945, CP.
136 Keynes, *Collected Writings*, 24:392; Fullerton *Graham Towers*, 211.
137 Mackenzie, 'Path to Temptation,' 202; Granatstein, *Man of Influence* 136; Fullerton, *Graham Towers*, 211.
138 Bacher, 'Keeping to the Private Market,' 458–9.
139 Ibid., 460.
140 Ibid., 462–3.
141 Sharp, *Which Reminds Me*, 45.
142 Bacher, 'Keeping to the Private Market,' 465–70.
143 Ibid., 473–5.
144 Ibid., 475–7.
145 Sharp, *Which Reminds Me*, 45.
146 W.C. Clark to E. Litchfield, 23 June 1947, vol. 3405, RG19, LAC.
147 Burns, *Acceptable Mean*, 39.
148 Dexter Memorandum, 21 June 1945, box 4, Grant Dexter Papers.
149 In the first stage the services would embrace general practitioner service, hospital care, and visiting nursing service. In later stages these would be extended to include consultant, specialist, and surgical services, other nursing services (including private duty), dental care, pharmaceutical services, and laboratory services.
150 Bryden, *Old Age Pensions*, 115.
151 Ibid., 116.
152 Eggleston, *Road to Nationhood*, 215–23.
153 Most Canadian historians hold a strong centralist and federalist bias when discussing dominion–provincial relations. The provinces, regardless of the merit in their positions, are portrayed as clinging to 'petty provincialism and jurisdictional rivalries.' Bothwell, Drummond, and English, *Canada since 1945*, 91–6.

154 *House of Commons Debates* (12 October 194), Budget Speech (Mr J.L. Isley, MP).

155 Perry, *Fiscal History of Canada*, 40.

Chapter 10

1 W.C. Clark to G.R. Cottrelle, 21 December 1945, CP. Clark's office carpet contained a notorious tear that went years without repair and was often commented upon by visitors.

2 Granatstein, *Canada's War*, vii.

3 W.C. Clark, 'Canada's Postwar Finance,' 1.

4 Mackintosh, 'William Clifford Clark: Memoir,' 12.

5 King Diaries, 17 January 1946.

6 Ibid., 5 August 1945.

7 Ibid., 23 January 1946.

8 Ibid., 28–30 January 1946.

9 Ibid., 31 January 1946.

10 Ibid.

11 Hodgetts et al., *Biography of an Institution*, 209.

12 Ibid., 210, 188, 201.

13 Gordon, *Political Memoir*, 44–5; Azzi, *Walter Gordon*, 22–4.

14 Bothwell, Drummond, and English, *Canada since 1945*, 81–2.

15 Bryce, 'William Clifford Clark, 1889–1952,' 422.

16 King Diaries, 8 February 1946.

17 Dexter Memorandum, 6 March 1946, box 4, Dexter Papers.

18 King Diaries, 11 February 1946.

19 See Mackenzie, 'Path to Temptation,' 212–19.

20 King Diaries, 11–13 February 1946.

21 W.C. Clark to J.L. Ilsley, 14 February 1946, vol. 763, RG19, LAC.

22 King Diaries, 18 February 1946.

23 As quoted in Granatstein, *Man of Influence*, 177.

24 King Diaries, 22 February 1946.

25 Memorandum on Canada-UK Loan Discussions, 22 February 1946, file 502, Towers Papers.

26 King Diaries, 25 February 1946.

27 W. Eady to W.C. Clark, 5 March 1946, vol. 763, RG19, LAC; W.C. Clark to W. Eady, 5 March 1946.

28 Plumptre, *Three Decades of Decision*, 77–9.

29 Fullerton, *Graham Towers*, 221.

30 Horsefield, *International Monetary Fund*, 121.

31 Fullerton, *Graham Towers*, 196; King Diaries, 21 March 1946.
32 King Diaries, 21 March 1946; 11 April 1946.
33 Ibid., 12 April 1946.
34 Ibid., 23 April 1946.
35 Ibid.
36 Ibid., 24 April 1946.
37 Burns, *Acceptable Mean*, 63.
38 King Diaries, 27 April 1946.
39 Ibid., 25 April 1946.
40 Ibid., 27 April 1946.
41 Ibid., 28 April 1946.
42 Ibid., 29 April 1946.
43 Ibid.
44 Ibid., 30 April 1946.
45 Ibid., 1 May 1946.
46 Ibid., 2 May 1946.
47 Ibid., 3 May 1946.
48 As quoted in the *Ottawa Evening Citizen*, 4 October 1948.
49 Burns, *Acceptable Mean*, 71.
50 As quoted in Bothwell, Drummond, and English, *Canada since 1945*, 96.
51 Bryce, 'William Clifford Clark, 1889–1952,' 421.
52 Ibid., 421–2.
53 King Diaries, 4 May 1946.
54 Ibid., 3 May 1946.
55 Ibid., 6 May 1946.
56 Ibid., 18 June 1946.
57 Ibid.
58 Ibid., 22 June 1946.
59 Plumptre, *Three Decades of Decision*, 79–81.
60 W.C. Clark, 'Canada's Postwar Finance,' 6–7.
61 Perry, *Fiscal History of Canada*, 40; *House of Commons Debates* (27 June 1946), Budget Speech (Mr J.L. Isley, MP).
62 W.C. Clark, 'Canada's Postwar Finance,' 8.
63 Fullerton, *Graham Towers*, 225–6.
64 Schull, *Great Scot*, 105.
65 R.D. Cuff, *American Dollars*, 27; Fullerton, *Graham Towers*, 225–6.
66 King Diaries, 3 July 1946.
67 Ibid., 5 July 1946.
68 Cuff and Granatstein, *American Dollars*, 27.
69 Ibid.

70 Plumptre, *Three Decades of Decision*, 96.
71 As quoted in Hodgetts et al., *Biography of an Institution*, 211.
72 As quoted in Cole, *Canadian Bureaucracy*, 53.
73 As quoted in Hodgetts et al., *Biography of an Institution*, 211.
74 Cole, *Canadian Bureaucracy*, 54; Hodgetts et al., *Biography of an Institution*, 211–12.
75 Azzi, *Walter Gordon*, 24; Hodgetts et al., *Biography of an Institution*, 211–13.
76 Hodgetts et al., *Biography of an Institution*, 213.
77 Azzi, *Walter Gordon*, 24.
78 King Diaries, 5 July 1946.
79 Ibid.
80 Ibid., 5 July 1946; Granatstein, *Man of Influence*, 197–9.
81 W.C. Clark to Muriel Clark, 29 July 1946, CP.
82 'Dr W. Clark, Deputy Finance Minister, Passes through City,' *Winnipeg Free Press*, 5 September 1946.
83 W.C. Clark to A. Lowery, 19 August 1946, CP.
84 King Diaries, 10 October 1946.
85 Ibid., 22 October 1946.
86 Dexter Memorandum, 16 October 1946, box 4, Dexter Papers.
87 Dexter Memorandum, 2 February 1950, box 5, Dexter Papers.
88 W.C. Clark, 'Canada's Postwar Finance,' 13.
89 Dexter Memorandum, 16 October 1946, box 4, Dexter Papers.
90 W.C. Clark, 'Canada's Postwar Finance,' 8–9.
91 King Diaries, 29 October 1946.
92 Ibid., 26 November 1946.
93 Ibid., 30 November 1946.
94 Ibid., 2 December 1946.
95 Ibid.
96 Dexter Memorandum, 6 February 1947, box 5, Dexter Papers.
97 Sharp, *Which Reminds Me*, 21.
98 R.B. Bryce Interview, 31 March 1989, Interview 3, 'Ottawa Decides, 1945–1971,' Institute for Research on Public Policy Collection, LAC.
99 King Diaries, 11 December, 1946.
100 Ibid.
101 Ibid.
102 *House of Commons Debates* (10 February 1947), pp. 242–3 (Mr Douglas Abbott, MP).
103 Buck, *Financing Canadian Government*, 37.
104 Cole, *Canadian Bureaucracy*, 56.
105 R.B. Bryce to J.J. Deutsch, 19 July 1947, vol. 3431, RG19, LAC.

106 J.J. Deutsch to Bryce, 6 August 1947, vol. 3431, RG19, LAC.
107 Cole, *Canadian Bureaucracy*, 56–7.
108 W.C. Clark to V.F. Coe, 15 October 1940, vol. 3444, RG19, LAC.
109 W.C. Clark to A.D.P. Heeney, 13 November 1946, vol. 3975, RG19, LAC.

Chapter 11

1 Bercuson, *True Patriot*, 166–7; King Diaries, 3 January 1947.
2 Bercuson, *True Patriot*, 168–70.
3 W.C. Clark to D. Abbott, 19 April 1947, vol. 3986, RG19, LAC.
4 Cuff, *American Dollars*, 34.
5 As quoted in ibid., 35.
6 W.C. Clark, 'Canada's Postwar Finance,' 13–14.
7 *House of Commons Debates* (29 April 1947), p. 2543 (Mr Douglas Abbott, MP).
8 Perry, *Fiscal History of Canada*, 41.
9 King Diaries, 29 April 1947.
10 *House of Commons Debates* (29 April 1947), p. 2543 (Mr Douglas Abbott, MP).
11 Muirhead, *Development of Postwar Canadian Trade Policy*, 50.
12 Cuff, *American Dollars*, 32.
13 W.C. Clark to Norman Robertson, 13 May 1947, vol. 3437, RG19, LAC; Brennan, *Reporting the Nation's Business*, 85.
14 As quoted in Cuff, *American Dollars*, 35–6.
15 W.C. Clark to Norman Robertson, 13 May 1947, vol. 3437, RG19, LAC; Granatstein, *Man of Influence*, 217–18.
16 Plumptre, *Three Decades of Decision*, 98; *House of Commons Debates* (26 May 1947), p. 3420 (Mr Douglas Abbott, MP).
17 Cuff, *American Dollars*, 37.
18 Ibid., 37–8.
19 D. Abbott to C.D. Howe, 30 June 1947, vol. 3438, RG19, LAC.
20 Neary, *Newfoundland*, 303–4.
21 W.C. Clark, 'Memorandum re Discussions with British re Limitations on Convertibility of Sterling,' 21 August 1947, vol. 3437, RG19, LAC; Muirhead, *Development of Postwar Canadian Trade Policy*, 20.
22 W.C. Clark to R.B. Bryce, 25 August 1947, vol. 3437, RG19, LAC; R.B. Bryce to W.C. Clark, 28 August 1947.
23 W.C. Clark to R.B. Bryce, 26 August 1947, vol. 3992, RG19, LAC; Brennan, *Reporting the Nation's Business*, 87–8.
24 W.C. Clark to R.B. Bryce, 3 September 1947, vol. 3992, RG19, LAC.

25 W.C. Clark to R.B. Bryce, 3 September 1947, vol. 3437, RG19, LAC.
26 Brennan, *Reporting the Nation's Business*, 88.
27 Ibid.
28 Memorandum of Discussions with Chancellor of Exchequer, 11 September 1947, vol. 3992, RG19, LAC.
29 D.V. Le Pan to Abbott, 13 September 1947, vol. 3992, RG19, LAC.
30 D. Abbott to W.C. Clark, 18 September 1947, vol. 3992, RG19, LAC.
31 L. Rasminsky to W.C. Clark, 18 September 1947, vol. 3437, RG19, LAC.
32 As quoted in Brennan, *Reporting the Nation's Business*, 89.
33 Clark Memorandum, 16–20 September 1947, vol. 3438, RG19, LAC.
34 W.C. Clark to Hume Wrong, 24 September 1947, vol. 3438, RG19, LAC.
35 Hume Wrong to W.C. Clark, 1 October 1947, vol. 3438, RG19, LAC.
36 Muirhead, *Development of Postwar Canadian Trade Policy*, 51–2.
37 Ibid., 54–5; Minutes of Meeting, 30 September 1947, vol. 3610, RG19, LAC.
38 Cuff, *American Dollars*, 55–8.
39 Muirhead, *Development of Postwar Canadian Trade Policy*, 52–3.
40 Stacey, *Canada and the Age of Conflict*, 419.
41 Cuff, *American Dollars*, 65–6, 59.
42 Ibid., 58–9.
43 Plumptre, *Three Decades of Decision*, 99.
44 Muirhead, *Development of Postwar Canadian Trade Policy*, 54.
45 Plumptre, *Three Decades of Decision*, 99–100.
46 Perry, *Fiscal History of Canada*, 41.
47 W.C. Clark, 'Canada's Postwar Finance,' 14.
48 King Diaries, 6 December 1947.
49 Plumptre, *Three Decades of Decision*, 99–102.
50 Fleming, *So Very Near*, 1:132–3.
51 Plumptre, *Three Decades of Decision*, 103.
52 W.C. Clark, 'Canada's Postwar Finance,' 14–15.
53 King Diaries, 9 December 1947.
54 Ibid., 13 January 1948.
55 As quoted in Granatstein, 'Free Trade between Canada and the United States,' 41.
56 King Diaries, 13 February 1948.
57 Cuff, *American Dollars*, 73–4.
58 Ibid., 77, 75.
59 King Diaries, 16 March 1948.
60 Ibid., 22 March 1948.
61 Ibid.

62 Ibid.
63 Ibid., 24–25 March 1948.
64 Heeney, *Things That are Caesar's*, 92–3.
65 King Diaries, 30 March 1948.
66 Cuff, *American Dollars*, 79–80.
67 Plumptre, *Three Decades of Decision*, 85, 114.
68 Muirhead, *Development of Postwar Canadian Trade Policy*, 27.
69 King Diaries, 21 April 1948, 27 April 1948; Stacey, *Canada and the Age of Conflict*, 424.
70 Creighton, *Forked Road*, 154–5.
71 King Diaries, 21 April 1948.
72 Paul Martin, *Very Public Life*, 2:46–8.
73 Perry, *Fiscal History of Canada*, 563.
74 Martin, *Very Public Life*, 2:49–50.
75 Martin, *Very Public Life*, 2:51–2; King Diaries, 13 May 1948.
76 Martin, *Very Public Life*, 2:53.
77 King Diaries, 13 May 1948.
78 Ibid., 27 May 1948. King repeats this claim even more emphatically in his diary on 28 July 1948.
79 Ibid., 18 May 1948.
80 Perry, *Fiscal History of Canada*, 41–2; *House of Commons Debates* (18 May 1948), Budget Speech (Mr Douglas Abbott, MP).
81 King Diaries, 19 May 1948.
82 Cabinet Directive on Cabinet Committee on Economic and Industrial Development, 7 May 1948, vol. 3434, RG19, LAC.
83 King Diaries, 28 July 1948.
84 Bothwell, Drummond, and English, *Canada since 1945*, 132.
85 W.C. Clark to Lester Pearson, 12 August 1948, vol. 3436, RG19, LAC.
86 Memorandum on Informal Discussions with Sir Henry Wilson Smith of the United Kingdom Treasury, 2–4 August 1948, vol. 3436, RG19, LAC.
87 Memorandum on the Visit of Sir Stafford Cripps, United Kingdom Chancellor of the Exchequer, September 1948, vol. 343, RG19, LAC.
88 R.B. Bryce Interview, 31 March 1989, Interview 3, 'Ottawa Decides, 1945–1971,' Institute for Research on Public Policy Collection, LAC.
89 *House of Commons Debates* (22 March 1949), Budget Speech (Mr Douglas Abbott, MP).
90 Perry, *Fiscal History of Canada*, 42.
91 W.C. Clark, 'Canada's Postwar Finance,' 8.
92 Ibid., 7–8.
93 Ibid., 8.

94 G.S.H. Barton was replaced as deputy minister of agriculture by J.G. Taggart. Barton had been hired just sixteen days earlier than Clark and he remained in the department as special assistant to the minister until 1952. Two others who held a rank roughly equivalent to deputy minister had longer service: Arthur Beauchesne, clerk of the House of Commons, appointed 7 January 1925, and Jules Castonguay, chief electoral officer, appointed July 1927.
95 Roberts, 'Are We Governed by Bureaucrats?' 9.
96 De Vries and Horsefield, *International Monetary Fund 1945–1965*, 97.
97 Plumptre, *Three Decades of Decision*, 103–4.
98 Mackenzie, *Documents on Canadian External Relations*, 15:956–7.
99 Ibid., 958.
100 Ibid., 959.
101 Granatstein, *Man of Influence*, 262–3; Muirhead, *Development of Postwar Canadian Trade Policy*, 37.
102 Granatstein, *Man of Influence*, 263; Muirhead, *Development of Postwar Canadian Trade Policy*, 36.
103 As quoted in Granatstein, *Man of Influence*, 264.
104 Muirhead, *Development of Postwar Canadian Trade Policy*, 37.
105 Granatstein, *Man of Influence*, 264.
106 Muirhead, *Development of Postwar Canadian Trade Policy*, 40.
107 Plumptre, *Three Decades of Decision*, 104–5.
108 Muirhead, *Development of Postwar Canadian Trade Policy*, 40.
109 Plumptre, *Three Decades of Decision*, 106–8, 124.
110 Fullerton, *Graham Towers*, 241.
111 Plumptre, *Three Decades of Decision*, 108–9.
112 *House of Commons Debates* (20 October 1949), Budget Speech (Mr Douglas Abbott, MP).
113 Perry, *Fiscal History of Canada*, 42.
114 Inglis, '"No Depression Ahead,"' 21, 28; Inglis, 'Deputy Minister of Finance,' 27–8.
115 Mears, 'People on Parliament Hill.'

Chapter 12

1 Bothwell, Drummond, and English, *Canada since 1945*, 135.
2 Dexter Memorandum, 31 January 1950, box 5, Dexter Papers.
3 Bercuson, *True Patriot*, 205–6.
4 Eayrs, *In Defence of Canada*, 196.
5 Dexter Memorandum, 2 February 1950, box 5, Dexter Papers.

6 Norman Robertson to Stuart Garson, 4 November 1949, vol. 3440, RG19, LAC.
7 For a nuanced discussion of the impact of Rowell-Sirois, see Henderson, *Angus L. Macdonald.*
8 Memorandum on Dominion–Provincial Conference of 1950, vol. 3440, RG19, LAC.
9 R.B. Bryce to W.C. Clark, 18 May 1950, vol. 3440, RG19, LAC.
10 Perry, *Fiscal History of Canada,* 42, 439; *House of Commons Debates* (28 March 1950), Budget Speech (Mr Douglas Abbott, MP).
11 One from a Catholic agricultural group in Quebec and the other from Charlotte Whitton.
12 Bryden, *Old Age Pensions,* 121–2.
13 Sharp, *Which Reminds Me,* 42.
14 Bryden, *Old Age Pensions,* 122–3; Martin, *Very Public Life,* 2:90–1.
15 Bercuson, *True Patriot,* 209–14.
16 Ibid., 214–15.
17 Eayrs, *In Defence of Canada,* 203.
18 Martin, *Very Public Life,* 2:95.
19 Perry, *Fiscal History of Canada,* 43.
20 Ibid.
21 W.C. Clark, 'Canada's Postwar Finance,' 15–16.
22 Fullerton, *Graham Towers,* 242.
23 Plumptre, *Three Decades of Decision,* 143–5.
24 W.C. Clark, 'Canada's Postwar Finance,' 15–16.
25 Fullerton, *Graham Towers,* 242–3.
26 W.C. Clark, 'Canada's Postwar Finance,' 15–16.
27 Plumptre, *Three Decades of Decision,* 142–7.
28 Fullerton, *Graham Towers,* 243; Horsefield, *International Monetary Fund,* 2:159–60; Plumptre, *Three Decades of Decision,* 194.
29 W.C. Clark, 'Canada's Postwar Finance,' 15–16.
30 The revisions included avoiding any further increase in the aggregate volume of bank loans and investments and restricting certain categories of loans, including loans on securities and for instalment financing. Ibid., 11–12.
31 R.G. Robertson to Douglas Abbott, 25 October 1950, vol. 3440, RG19, LAC.
32 Dexter Memorandum, 17 October 1950, box 5, Dexter Papers.
33 Martin, *Very Public Life,* 2:96–7.
34 Ibid., 97–8.
35 Ibid., 101.

36 Granatstein, *Man of Influence*, 255; Pickersgill, *My Years with Louis St Laurent*, 134; Thomson, *Louis St Laurent*, 302–3; Burns, *Acceptable Mean*, 94.
37 Memorandum on Federal–Provincial Financial Relations, 4 August 1950, vol. 3440, RG19, LAC.
38 Review of Dominion–Provincial Financial Arrangements, 4 August 1950, vol. 3440, RG19, LAC; Memorandum on Federal–Provincial Financial Relations, 4 August 1950.
39 Martin, *Very Public Life*, 2:101; Perry, *Fiscal History of Canada*, 565.
40 Bercuson, *True Patriot*, 222.
41 Ibid., 223.
42 Ibid.
43 Ibid., 225–6.
44 Ibid., 228.
45 *House of Commons Debates* (10 April 1951), Budget Speech (Mr Douglas Abbott, MP).
46 Perry, *Fiscal History of Canada*, 43–4.
47 W.C. Clark, 'Canada's Postwar Finance,' 9–11.
48 Ward, *Public Purse*, 211–16.
49 *House of Commons Debates* (25 June 1951), p. 4625 (Mr Douglas Abbott, MP).
50 Sinclair, *Cordial But Not Cosy*, 54–5.
51 W.C. Clark to Robert A. Uihlein, 4 January 1952, CP; W.C. Clark to Frank A. Sherman, 2 January 1952, CP.
52 Gibson, *To Serve and Yet Be Free*, 303–6, 472–3.
53 Departmental officers calculated that an annual contribution of $60 over forty years would purchase a monthly annuity of approximately $40 for a male at age seventy. A 2 per cent income tax with a $60 ceiling would raise the required amount from all those whose taxable income was $3,000 a year or more, while imposing a proportionately smaller but still identifiable burden on those with lower incomes who were subject to income tax. Bryden, *Old Age Pensions*, 123.
54 Fullerton, *Graham Towers*, 244–5.
55 W.C. Clark, 'Canada's Postwar Finance,' 16–17.
56 W.C. Clark to Robert A. Uihlein, 4 January 1952, CP.
57 Perry, *Fiscal History of Canada*, 44.
58 W.C. Clark, 'Canada's Postwar Finance,' 1–18.
59 Gordon, *Political Memoir*, 33–4.
60 Barkway, 'No Civil Service Ivory Tower.'
61 Eleanor McGinnis, interview, 23 August 1996.

62 Peggy Johnstone, interview, 20 August 1995.
63 David McGinnis, interview, 23 August 1996.
64 'Burial of Dr William Clark to Be in Catanaqui Cemetery,' *Kingston Whig-Standard*, 29 December 1952; 'Canadian Expert on Finance, Dr W.C. Clark, 63, Dies,' *Edmonton Journal*, 29 December 1952; 'Funeral on Tuesday for W.C. Clark,' *Ottawa Journal*, 29 December 1952.

Chapter 13

1 'Funeral of Tuesday for Dr W.C. Clark,' *Ottawa Journal*, 29 December 1952.
2 Ibid.
3 Ibid.
4 Hume Wrong to W.C. Clark, 21 December 1938, vol. 3981, RG19, LAC.
5 As quoted in Slater, *War Finance*, 74.
6 *House of Commons Debates* (19 February 1953), p. 2116 (Mr Douglas Abbott, MP).
7 *House of Commons Debates Debates* (24 February 1953), p. 2334 (Mr Douglas Abbott, MP).
8 *Regina Leader-Post*, 29 December 1952; *Montreal Gazette*, 29 December 1952; *Globe and Mail*, 29 December 1952; 'A Great Canadian,' *Victoria Times*, 30 December 1952; *Toronto Star*, 29 December 1952.
9 W.A. Mackintosh, 'William Clifford Clark: Memoir,' 13–16.
10 Deutsch, 'Some Thoughts on the Public Service,' 183.
11 Cole, *Canadian Bureaucracy*, 268–71.
12 D.M. Stephens to Ken Taylor, 31 December 1952, box 1, Ken Taylor Papers, QUA.
13 Porter, *Vertical Mosaic*, 426.
14 As quoted in Slater, *War Finance*, 74.
15 Pickersgill, *My Years with Louis St Laurent*, 180.
16 J.L. Granatstein, 'Afterword,' in Bryce, *Canada and the Cost of World War II*, 325.
17 Bryce, *Canada and the Cost of World War II*, 145.
18 Austin Cross, *Evening Citizen*, 30 December 1952.
19 W.A. Mackintosh, 'William Clifford Clark and Canadian Economic Policy,' 411.
20 Porter, *Vertical Mosaic*, 427, 418.
21 Owram, *Government Generation*, 263.
22 Bacher, *Keeping to the Marketplace*, viii–ix.
23 Struthers, *The Limits of Affluence*, 5–6.

24 R.B. Bryce Interview, 27 January 1989, Interview 1, 'Ottawa Decides, 1945–1971,' Institute for Research on Public Policy Collection, LAC.
25 Ferguson, *Remaking Liberalism*, xv.
26 Owram, *Government Generation*, 262–3.
27 Corry, *Memoirs of J.A. Corry*, 111.
28 Owram, 'Economic Thought in the 1930s,' 179.
29 Ibid., 180, 183.
30 Clyne, *Jack of All Trades*, 133.
31 Sharp, 'Cabinet and Public Service,' 179.
32 Smith, *Gentle Patriot*, 10–12.
33 Clark, 'Canada's Postwar Finance,' 1.

Bibliography

Primary Sources

Douglas Abbott Papers, Library and Archives Canada (LAC), Ottawa
Richard Bedford Bennett Papers, LAC
Robert Bryce Papers, LAC
Floyd Chalmers Papers, LAC
W.C. Clark Papers, private collection
W.C. Clark Papers, QUA
J.A. Corry Papers, Queen's University Archives (QUA), Kingston
Thomas Alexander Crerar Papers, QUA
C.A. Curtis Papers, QUA
Department of Finance, RG19, LAC
John J. Deutsch Papers, QUA
Grant Dexter Papers, QUA
Charles A. Dunning Papers, QUA
Donald Gordon Papers, QUA
Walter Gordon Papers, LAC
James Ilsley Papers, LAC
F.A. Knox Papers, QUA
William Lyon Mackenzie King Papers, LAC
William A. Mackintosh Papers, QUA
James Ralston Papers, LAC
Louis Rasminsky Paper, LAC
Edgar Rhodes Papers, LAC
Norman Rogers Papers, QUA
Louis St Laurent Papers, LAC
Isabel Skelton Papers, QUA

Oscar Douglas Skelton Papers, LAC
Kenneth W. Taylor Papers, QUA
Graham Towers Papers, Bank of Canada Archives, Ottawa
Graham Towers Papers, LAC

Newspapers

Cornwall Standard
Evening Citizen (Ottawa)
Financial Post
Montreal Star
New York Times
New York Sun
Northern Minor
Ottawa Journal
Regina Leader-Post
Saturday Night
Scarsdale Inquirer
Times (London UK)
Toronto Daily Star
Vancouver Province
Victoria Times
Winnipeg Free Press

Magazines

Canadian Business
National Home Monthly
Western Business & Industry

Interviews

Douglas Abbott
Frances Bryce
Robert Bryce
George Clifford Clark
Stephanie Deutsch
James Gibson
Peggy Johnston
Walter Koerner

John MacEwan
David Mansur
Eleanor McGinnis
Jack Pickersgill
Simeon Reisman
Mitchell Sharp
David Slater
Kenneth Skelton Clark

Secondary Sources

Anderson, George. 'Housing Policy in Canada: Lecture Series.' Vancouver: Canada Mortgage and Housing Corporation, 1992.

Anderson, J.E. 'Pressure Groups and the Canadian Bureaucracy.' In *Public Administration in Canada: Selected Readings*, edited by W.D.K. Kernaghan and A.M. Williams. Toronto: Methuen, 1968.

Armstrong, Christopher. *The Politics of Federalism: Ontario's Relations with the Federal Government 1967–1942.* Toronto: University of Toronto Press, 1981.

Azzi, Stephen. *Walter Gordon and the Rise of Canadian Nationalism.* Montreal and Kingston: McGill-Queen's University Press, 1999.

Babad, Michael, and Catherine Mulroney. *Where the Buck Stops: The Dollar, Democracy, and the Bank of Canada.* Toronto: Stoddart, 1995.

Bacher, John C. 'Canadian Housing "Policy" in Perspective.' *Urban History Review* 15, no. 1 (1986): 3–18.

– *Keeping to the Marketplace: The Evolution of Canadian Housing Policy.* Montreal and Kingston: McGill-Queen's University Press, 1993.

– 'Keeping to the Private Market: The Evolution of Canadian Housing Policy: 1900–1949.' PhD diss., McMaster University, 1985.

– 'W.C. Clark and the Politics of Canadian Housing Policy, 1935–1952.' *Urban History Review* 17, no. 1 (1988): 5–11.

Bain, George. 'The Wordiest MP in Ottawa.' *Maclean's Magazine*, 15 September 1954.

Balls, Herbert R. 'The Public Accounts, Their Purposes and Factors Affecting Their Form: An Administrative View.' *Canadian Public Administration* 7 (1964): 422–41.

Barkway, Michael. 'No Civil Service Ivory Tower.' *Saturday Night*, 11 October 1952, 4–6.

Barnett, Enid. *Keynes's 'How to Pay for the War' in Canada: The Story of Compulsory Savings, 1939–1944.* Kingston, ON: Harbinger House, 2000.

– *The Keynesian Arithmetic in War-Time Canada: Development of the National Accounts, 1939–1945*. Kingston: Harbinger House, 2000.

– *The War Budget of September 1939: Keynes Comes to Canada*. Kingston, ON: Harbinger House, 2000.

Bercuson, David J. *True Patriot: The Life of Brooke Claxton, 1898–1960*. Toronto: University of Toronto Press, 1993.

Berton, Pierre. *The Great Depression 1929–1939*. Toronto: McClelland and Stewart, 1990.

Black, Harvey. 'Finance and Insurance.' In *Canadian Annual Review of Public Affairs*, 360–402. Toronto: Canadian Review, 1934.

Blake, Raymond. 'Mackenzie King and the Genesis of Family Allowances in Canada 1939–1944.' In *Social Welfare Policy in Canada: Historical Readings*, edited by Raymond Blake and Jeffrey Keshen, 203–20. Toronto: Copp Clark, 1995.

Bordo, Michael D., and Angela Redish. 'Why Did the Bank of Canada Emerge in 1935?' In *Perspectives on Canadian Economic History*, edited by Douglas McCalla and Michael Huberman, 263–76. Toronto: Copp Clark, 1994.

Bothwell, Robert. 'The Health of the Common People.' In *Mackenzie King: Widening the Debate*, edited by John English and J.O. Stubbs, 191–220. Toronto: Macmillan Canada, 1977.

Bothwell, Robert, Ian Drummond, and John English. *Canada since 1945: Power, Politics, and Provincialism*. Toronto: University of Toronto Press, 1981.

– *Canada: 1900–1945*. Toronto: University of Toronto Press, 1987.

Bothwell, Robert, and John English. 'Canadian Trade Policy in the Age of American Dominance and British Decline, 1943–1947.' *Canadian Review of American Studies* 8 (1977): 52–65.

Bothwell, Robert, and William Kilbourn. *C.D. Howe: A Biography*. Toronto: McClelland and Stewart, 1979.

Brecher, Irving. *Monetary and Fiscal Thought and Policy in Canada 1919–1939*. Toronto: University of Toronto Press, 1957.

Brennan, Patrick. *Reporting the Nation's Business: Press–Government Relations during the Liberal Years, 1935–1957*. Toronto: University of Toronto Press, 1994.

Broad, Graham. 'Shopping for Victory.' *Beaver*, April/May 2005, 40–45.

– 'A Small Price to Pay: Consumerism on the Canadian Home Front, 1939–1945.' PhD diss., University of Western Ontario, 2009.

Bryce, Robert B. *Canada and the Cost of World War II: The International Operations of Canada's Department of Finance, 1939–1947*. Montreal and Kingston: McGill-Queen's University Press, 2005.

– *Maturing in Hard Times: Canada's Department of Finance through the Great Depression.* Montreal and Kingston: McGill-Queen's University Press, 1986.
– 'Public Servants as Economic Advisers.' In *Economic Policy Advising in Canada: Essays in Honour of John Deutsch*, edited by David C. Smith, 51–68. Montreal: C.D. Howe Institute, 1981.
– 'William Clifford Clark, 1889–1952.' *Canadian Journal of Economics and Political Science* 19, no. 3 (1953): 413–23.
Bryden, Kenneth. *Old Age Pensions and Policy-Making in Canada.* Montreal and Kingston: McGill-Queen's University Press, 1974.
Buck, A.E. *Financing Canadian Government.* Chicago: Lakeside, 1949.
Burns, Dan. *Housing Policy.* Waterloo, ON: Wilfrid Laurier University Press, 1978.
Burns, R.M. *The Acceptable Mean: The Tax Rental Agreements 1941–1962.* Toronto: Canadian Tax Foundation, 1980.
Campbell, Robert. *Grand Illusions: The Politics of the Keynesian Experience in Canada, 1945–1975.* Peterborough: Broadview, 1987.
Carter, Gwendolen M. 'The Organization and Work of the Canadian War Administration.' In *The British Commonwealth at War*, edited by William Yandell Elliott and H. Duncan Hall, 329–64. New York: Knopf, 1943.
– 'Political Developments in Canada.' In *The British Commonwealth at War*, edited by William Yandell Elliott and H. Duncan Hall. New York: Knopf, 1943.
Carver, Humphrey. *Compassionate Landscape: Places and People in a Man's Life.* Toronto: University of Toronto Press, 1975.
Chalmers, Floyd S. *Both Sides of the Street: One Man's Life in Business and the Arts in Canada.* Toronto: Macmillan Canada, 1983.
Chapnick, Adam. *The Middle Power Project: Canada and the Founding of the United Nations.* Vancouver: University of British Columbia Press, 2005.
Chisholm, Derek. 'Canadian Monetary Policy 1914–1934: The Enduring Glitter of the Gold Standard.' PhD diss., Cambridge University, 1979.
– 'The International Monetary System: In Retrospect and Prospect.' Conference Board of Canada, Ottawa, 1983.
Christie, Nancy. *Engendering the State: Family, Work, and Welfare in Canada.* Toronto: University of Toronto Press, 2000.
Clark, E.R. *The IDB: A History of Canada's Industrial Development Bank.* Toronto: University of Toronto Press, 1985.
Clark, W.C. 'The Bank of Canada.' *Canadian Chartered Accountant* 25, no. 5 (1934): 330–42.
– Book Review: 'Business Cycles and Unemployment: Report by National

Bureau of Economic Research for a Committee of the President's Conference on Unemployment Economists. New York: McGraw-Hill Book Company. 1923.' *Journal of the American Statistical Association* 18 (1923): 105–8.

– 'The Building Industry.' *Straus Investors Magazine*, February 1925, 13–15.

– 'The Business and Investment Outlook.' *Straus Investors Magazine*, February 1924, 19–21.

– 'Business Cycles and the Depression of 1920–21.' *Bulletins of the Department of History and Political and Economic Science in Queen's University, Kingston, Ontario, Canada* 40 (August 1921): 1–24.

– 'Business Research and Business Statistics.' *Journal of the Canadian Bankers' Association* 28, no. 2 (1921): 206–16.

– 'Canada's Postwar Finance.' *American Economic Review* 43, no. 2 (1953): 1–18. Also published in *Canadian Banker* 60, no. 2 (Spring 1953): 5–23 and *Canadian Tax Journal* 1, no. 1 (January–February 1953), 6–12, 100–11.

– 'Canadian-American Relations in Defence: Economics from the Canadian Point of View.' In *The Road to Ogdensburg: The Queen's / St Laurence Conference on Canadian-American Affairs, 1935–1941*, edited by Frederick W. Gibson and Jonathan G. Rossie, 257–75. East Lansing: Michigan State University Press, 1993.

– 'The Canadian Plan for Post-War International Monetary Stabilization.' In Robert Norris Associates, *Monthly Bulletin of Robert Morris Associates,* 18–32. New York, 1943.

– 'The Construction Industry.' Harvard Economic Conference, 14 November 1931.

– 'The Construction Industry.' In *Representative Industries in the United States,* edited by H.T. Warshow, 182–223. New York: Holt, 1928.

– 'The Construction Industry in 1932.' *Review of Economic Statistics* 14, no. 2 (1932): 74–9.

– 'The Construction Industry: Outlook for 1930.' *Review of Economic Statistics* 12, no. 1 (1930): 23–9.

– 'The Country Elevator in the Canadian West.' *Bulletins of the Department of History and Political and Economic Sciences in Queen's University, Kingston, Ontario, Canada* (1916): 46–68.

– 'Current Economic Problems.' *Canadian Chartered Accountant* 22, no. 1 (1932): 2–9.

– 'Current Events: Dominion By-elections; Political Currents; the Tariff Commission; the Board of Commerce.' *Queen's Quarterly* 28, no. 3 (1921): 296–308.

– 'The Federal Reserve System.' *The Federal Reserve System* (March 1927): 27–9.
– 'Financial Administration of the Government of Canada.' *Canadian Journal of Economics and Political Science* 4, no. 3 (1938): 391–419.
– 'Financing the War.' *Queen's University Economics Bulletin* (1916): 1–64.
– 'Flight from the Gold Standard.' *Queen's Quarterly* 38, no. 4 (1931): 751–63.
– 'Forecasting Building Construction.' Paper presented at the 85th annual meeting of the American Statistical Association, Boston, 1924.
– '"Glossary of Monetary Terms": Memorandum and Tables Respecting the Bank of Canada.' *Canadian Banker* 46, no. 4 (1939): 480–93.
– 'Housing.' *Dalhousie University Bulletin on Public Affairs* (1938): 1–28.
– 'The Housing Act and Low Cost Housing.' *Social Welfare* 17, nos. 2 and 3 (1937): 36–7.
– 'Inflation and Prices.' *Journal of the Canadian Bankers' Association* 25 (1917–18): 126–33.
– 'The International Exchange Situation.' *Journal of the Canadian Bankers Association* 27, no. 1 (1919): 72–9.
– 'Is Our Taxation Policy Sound?' *Canadian Business* 15, no. 11 (November 1942): 54–7.
– 'Limitations of Financial Statistics Relating to Building Activity.' *Proceedings of the American Statistical Association* (March 1932), 133–43.
– 'A Month of Earthquakes: Despite Disturbances, the Business and Investment Outlook Continues Favorable.' *Straus Investors Magazine*, October 1923, 21–3.
– 'Oscar Douglas Skelton 1878–1941.' Paper presented at the Minutes of Proceedings of the Royal Society of Canada, Ottawa, May 1941.
– 'The Outlook for Business.' *Straus Investors Magazine*, April 1925, 28–30.
– 'Postwar Currencies.' *Public Affairs*, 7 March 1944, 88–93.
– 'Postwar International Monetary Stabilisation.' *New York University Institute on Postwar Reconstruction Series*, 208–42. New York: New York University Institute on Postwar Reconstruction, 1943. An abbreviated version was published in 'Post-War Currencies,' *Public Affairs* 7, no. 2 (Winter 1944): 88–93.
– 'Real Estate and the Construction Industry.' *National Monthly Building Survey* (December 1925).
– 'Regularization of National Demand for Labour by Government Employment.' Paper presented at the Proceedings of the Eight Annual Meeting, International Association of Public Employment Services, Ottawa, 20–22 September 1920.
– 'Retrospect and Prospect.' *Straus Investors Magazine*, January 1925, 28–30.

– 'Should Maximum Prices Be Fixed?' *Bulletins of the Department of History and Political and Economic Sciences in Queen's University, Kingston, Ontario, Canada* (1918): 432–61.

– 'Some Considerations Affecting the Long-Run Trend of the Building Industry.' *Review of Economic Statistics* 8, no. 1 (1926): 47–52.

– 'University Training for Business: A Reply.' *Bulletins of the Department of History and Political and Economic Science in Queen's University, Kingston, Ontario, Canada* (1923): 10–25.

– 'What's Wrong with Us? Diagnosis of World Economic Situation and Suggestions for Remedy.' *Journal of Professional Institute of the Civil Service of Canada* 10, no. 10 (1931): 1–11.

Clark, W.C., and J.L. Kingston. *The Skyscraper: A Study in the Economic Height of Modern Office Buildings.* New York: American Institute of Steel Construction, 1930.

Clark, W.C., and L.J. Sheridan. 'The Straus Building, Chicago.' *Architectural Forum* 42 (1925): 225–8.

Clyne, C.V. *Jack of All Trades: Memories of a Busy Life.* Toronto: McClelland and Stewart, 1985.

Cole, Taylor. *The Canadian Bureaucracy: A Study of Canadian Civil Servants and Other Public Employees 1939–1947.* Durham, NC: Duke University Press, 1949.

Condit, C.W. *Chicago 1910–1929: Building, Planning and Urban Technology.* Chicago: University of Chicago Press, 1973.

Corry, J.A. *Memoirs of J.A. Corry: My Life and Work, a Happy Partnership.* Montreal and Kingston: McGill-Queen's University Press, 1981.

– 'Public Affairs: Some Aspects of Canada's War Effort.' *Queen's Quarterly* 47, no. 3 (1940): 356–68.

Cox, Carolyn. '"Cliff" Clark Has an Old Carpet.' *Saturday Night,* 1 May 1943, 20–1.

Creighton, Donald. *The Forked Road: Canada 1939–1957.* Toronto: McClelland and Stewart, 1976.

– *Harold Adams Innis: Portrait of a Scholar.* Toronto: University of Toronto Press, 1978.

– 'The Ogdensburg Agreement and F.H. Underhill.' In *The West and the Nation: Essays in Honour of W.L. Morton,* edited by Carl Berger and Ramsay Cook, 300–20. Toronto: McClelland and Stewart, 1976.

Cross, Austin. 'Meet Eight Key Men Who Help Run Canada.' *Western Business & Industry,* July 1946, 37.

– 'Oligarchs at Ottawa.' *Public Affairs* (Autumn 1951): 16–24.

– 'Watchdog of Our Treasury.' *Canadian Business,* March 1942, 20.

Crow, John. *Making Money: An Insider's Perspective on Finance, Politics, and Canada's Central Bank.* Toronto: Wiley, 2002.

Crowley, Terry. *Marriage of Minds: Isabel and Oscar Skelton Reinventing Canada.* Toronto: University of Toronto Press, 2003.

Cuff, R.D. *American Dollars, Canadian Prosperity: Canadian–American Economic Relations 1945–1950.* Toronto: Samuel Stevens, 1978.

Cuff, R.D., and J.L. Granatstein. *Ties That Bind: Canadian–American Relations in Wartime from the Great War to the Cold War.* 2nd ed. Toronto: Samuel Stevens Hakkert, 1977.

Dafoe, J.W. 'The Canadian Federal System Under Review.' *Foreign Affairs* 18, no. 4 (1940): 653–8.

Davis, Ken. *FDR: Into the Storm, 1937–1940.* New York: Random House, 1993.

De Vries, M.G., and J. Keith Horsefield. *The International Monetary Fund 1945–1965: Twenty Years of International Monetary Co-operation.* Vol. 2. Washington: IMF, 1969.

Deutsch, J.J. 'Some Thoughts on the Public Service.' *Canadian Journal of Economics and Political Science* 23 (1957): 83–9.

Drummond, Ian. *The Floating Pound and the Sterling Area, 1931–1939.* Cambridge: Cambridge University Press, 1981.

– *Imperial Economic Policy, 1917–39.* London: Allen & Unwin, 1974.

Drummond, Ian, and Norman Hillmer. *Negotiating Freer Trade: The United Kingdom, the United States, Canada, and the Trade Agreements of 1938.* Waterloo, ON: Wilfrid Laurier University Press, 1989.

Drushka, Ken. *HR: A Biography of H.R. Macmillan.* Madeira Park, BC: Harbour, 1995.

Dumbrille, Dorothy. *Up and Down the Glens: The Story of Glengarry.* Toronto: Ryerson, 1954.

Eaton, A.K. *Essays in Taxation.* Toronto: Canadian Tax Foundation, 1966.

Eayrs, James. *In Defence of Canada: Appeasement and Rearmament.* Toronto: University of Toronto Press, 1965.

– *In Defence of Canada: From the Great War to the Great Depression.* Toronto: University of Toronto Press, 1964.

– *In Defence of Canada: Growing Up Allied.* Toronto: University of Toronto Press, 1965.

Eggleston, Wilfrid. *The Road to Nationhood: A Chronicle of Dominion–Provincial Relations.* Toronto: University of Toronto Press, 1946.

England, Robert. *Living Learning Remembering: Memoirs of Robert England.* Vancouver: Centre for Continuing Education, University of British Columbia, 1980.

English, John. 'Dominion–Provincial Relations and Reconstruction Planning, 1943–1946.' In *Proceedings of the First Conference of the Canadian Committee for the History of the Second World War.* Ottawa: Department of National Defence, 1977.

– *Shadow of Heaven: The Life of Lester Pearson, 1897–1948.* Vol. 1, *1897–1948.* Toronto: Lester & Orpen Dennys, 1989.

– *The Worldly Years: The Life of Lester Pearson.* Vol. 2, *1949–1972.* Toronto: Knopf Canada, 1992.

Farm Credit Corporation. *The Development of Farm Credit in Canada.* Ottawa: Farm Credit Corporation, 1980.

Ferguson, Barry. *Remaking Liberalism: The Intellectual Legacy of Adam Shortt, O.D. Skelton, W.C. Clark, and W.A. Mackintosh, 1890–1925.* Montreal and Kingston: McGill-Queen's University Press, 1993.

Firestone, O.J. *Residential Real Estate in Canada.* Toronto: University of Toronto Press, 1951.

Fisher, Robin. *Duff Pattullo of British Columbia.* Toronto: University of Toronto Press, 1991.

Fleming, Donald. *So Very Near: The Political Memoirs of the Honourable Donald M. Fleming.* Vol. 1, *The Rising Years.* Toronto: McClelland and Stewart, 1985.

Frost, S.B. *The Man in the Ivory Tower: F. Cyril James of McGill.* Montreal and Kingston: McGill-Queen's University Press, 1991.

Fullerton, Douglas H. *Graham Towers and His Times: A Biography.* Toronto: McClelland and Stewart, 1986.

Galbraith, John Kenneth. *A Life in Our Times: Memoirs.* Boston: Houghton Mifflin, 1981.

Gibson, Frederick W. *To Serve and Yet Be Free: Queen's University.* Vol. 2, *1917–1961.* Montreal and Kingston: McGill-Queen's University Press, 1983.

Gibson, Frederick W., and Barbara Robertson, eds. *Ottawa at War: The Grant Dexter Memoranda, 1939–1945.* Winnipeg: Manitoba Record Society, 1994.

Gibson, Frederick W., and Jonathan Rossie, eds. *The Road to Ogdensburg: The Queen's / St Lawrence Conferences on Canadian American Affairs, 1935–1941.* East Lansing: Michigan State University Press, 1993.

Gillespie, W. Irwin. *Tax, Borrow and Spend: Financing Federal Spending in Canada, 1867–1990.* Ottawa: Carleton University Press, 1991.

Glassford, Larry A. *Reaction and Reform: The Politics of the Conservative Party under R.B. Bennett, 1927–1938.* Toronto: University of Toronto Press, 1992.

Good, W.C. *Farmer Citizen: My Fifty Years in the Canadian Farmers' Movement.* Toronto: Ryerson, 1958.

Gordon, Walter. *A Political Memoir.* Toronto: McClelland and Stewart, 1977.

Granatstein, J.L. *Canada 1957–1967: The Years of Uncertainty and Innovation.* Toronto: McClelland and Stewart, 1986.

– *Canada's War: The Politics of the Mackenzie King Government, 1939–1945.* Toronto: Oxford University Press, 1975.

– 'Free Trade between Canada and the United States: The Issue That Will Not Go Away.' In *The Politics of Canada's Economic Relationship with the United States,* edited by Dennis Stairs and Gilbert R. Whitman, 11–54. Toronto: University of Toronto Press, 1985.

– *How Britain's Weakness Forced Canada into the Arms of the United States: The 1988 Joanne Goodman Lectures.* Toronto: University of Toronto Press, 1989.

– *A Man of Influence: Norman A. Robertson and Canadian Statecraft, 1929–1968.* Toronto: Deneau, 1981.

– *The Ottawa Men: The Civil Service Mandarins, 1935–1957.* Toronto: Oxford University Press, 1982.

– 'Queen's Mandarin Corps.' *Queen's Alumni Review* (November–December 1987): 6–11.

– 'Settling the Accounts: Anglo-Canadian War Finance, 1943–1945.' *Queen's Quarterly* 83 (1976): 234–49.

– 'Staring into the Abyss.' In *An Introduction to Canadian History,* edited by A.I. Silver, 694–710. Toronto: Canadian Scholars' Press, 1991.

Granatstein, J.L., and Irving M. Abella, David J. Bercuson, R. Craig Brown, and H. Blair Neatby. *Twentieth Century Canada.* Toronto: McGraw-Hill Ryerson, 1983.

Granatstein, J.L., and Robert D. Cuff. *Canadian–American Relations in Wartime.* Toronto: University of Toronto Press, 1975.

– 'The Hyde Park Declaration, 1941: Origins and Significance.' *Canadian Historical Association* 55, no. 1 (March 1974): 59–80.

Granatstein, J.L., and Norman Hillmer. *For Better or for Worse: Canada and the United States in the 1990s.* Toronto: Copp Clark Pitman, 1991.

Granatstein, J.L., and Desmond Morton. *A Nation Forged in Fire: Canadians and the Second World War 1939–1945.* Toronto: Lester & Orpen Dennys, 1989.

Granatstein, J.L., and Peter Neary, ed. *The Good Fight: Canadians and World War II.* Toronto: Copp Clark, 1995.

Grant, James. *Money of the Mind: Borrowing and Lending in America from the Civil War to Michael Milken.* New York: Noonday, 1992.

Grant, R.C.M. *Horse and Buggy Days in Martintown, 1900–1940.* Gardenvale, QC: Harpell's, 1976.

– *The Story of Martintown.* Gardenvale, QC: Harpell's, 1974.

Grayson, Linda. 'The Formation of the Bank of Canada, 1913–38.' PhD diss., University of Toronto, 1974.

Harkness, John Graham. *Stormont, Dundas and Glengary: A History 1784–1945.* Oshawa: Mundy-Goodfellow, 1946.

Harris, Robin S. *A History of Higher Education in Canada 1663–1960.* Toronto: University of Toronto Press, 1976.

Hayes, E.P. *Activities of the President's Emergency Committee for Employment, October 17, 1930–August 19, 1931.* Concord, 1936.

Heeney, Arnold. *The Things That Are Caesar's: The Memoirs of a Canadian Public Servant.* Toronto: University of Toronto Press, 1972.

Henderson, Stephen T. *Angus L. Macdonald: A Provincial Liberal.* Toronto: University of Toronto Press, 2007.

Hilliker, John F., ed. *Canada's Department of External Affairs.* Vol. 1, *The Early Years, 1909–1946.* Montreal and Kingston: McGill-Queen's University Press, 1990.

Hockin, Thomas A., ed. *Apex of Power: The Prime Minister and Political Leadership in Canada.* Scarborough, ON: Prentice-Hall, 1977.

Hodgetts, J.E. *The Canadian Public Service: A Physiology of Government, 1867–1970.* Toronto: University of Toronto Press, 1973.

Hodgetts, J.E., and D.C. Corbett, eds. *Canadian Public Administration.* Toronto: Macmillan Canada, 1960.

Hodgetts, J.E., William McCloskey, Reginald Whitaker, and V. Seymour Wilson. *The Biography of an Institution: The Civil Service Commission of Canada 1908–1967.* Montreal and Kingston: McGill-Queen's University Press, 1972.

Holmes, John. *The Shaping of Peace.* Vol. 1, *Canada and the Search for World Order, 1943–1957.* Toronto: University of Toronto Press, 1979.

Horn, M., ed. *The Depression in Canada: Response to Economic Crisis.* Toronto: Copp Clark, 1988.

Horsefield, J.K. *The International Monetary Fund 1945–1965: Twenty Years of International Monetary Co-operation.* Washington: International Monetary Fund, 1969.

Hulchanski, J. David. 'The 1935 Dominion Housing Act: Setting the Stage for a Permanent Federal Presence in Canada's Housing Sector.' *Urban History Review* 15, no. 1 (1986): 1–2.

Hutchison, F. *The Incredible Canadian.* London: Longmans, Green, 1952.

Inglis, Fred R. 'The Deputy Minister of Finance Looks for an Expanding Canada.' *Western Business and Industry* (January 1950): 27–8.

– '"No Depression Ahead" Says Dr Clark: On the Brink of One of Her Greatest Periods of Productivity, Canada's Future Looks Rosy.' *Heating and Sanitary Age* (October 1949): 21, 28.

Keenleyside, Hugh. *Memoirs of Hugh L. Keenleyside.* Toronto: McClelland and Stewart, 1982.

Kendle, John. *John Bracken: A Political Biography.* Toronto: University of Toronto Press, 1979.

Ker, F.I., and Wilfred H. Goodman. *Press Promotion of War Finance.* Toronto: Southam, 1946.

Keshen, Jeffrey. *Saints, Sinners, and Soldiers: Canada's Second World War.* Vancouver: University of British Columbia Press, 2004.

Keynes, John Maynard. *The Collected Writings of John Maynard Keynes,* Vol. 24, *Activities 1944–1946: The Transition to Peace,* edited by Donald Moggridge. Cambridge: Cambridge University Press, 1979.

– *The Collected Writings of John Maynard Keynes.* Vol. 26, *Activities 1941–1946: Shaping the Post-War World: Breton Woods and Reparations,* edited by Donald Moggridge. Cambridge: Cambridge University Press, 1979.

– 'The World's Economic Outlook.' *Atlantic Monthly* 149 (1932): 521–6.

Kindleberger, C.P. *The World Depression, 1929–1939.* Berkeley: University of California Press, 1986.

Kitchen, B. 'The Introduction of Family Allowances in Canada.' In *The 'Benevolent' State: The Growth of Welfare in Canada,* edited by Allan Moscovitch and Jim Albert, 222–41. Toronto: Garamond, 1987.

Knox, F.A. 'William Clifford Clark 1889–1952.' Paper presented at the Proceedings and Transactions of the Royal Society of Canada, Ottawa, June 1953.

Leonard, T. D'Arcy. 'The Dominion Housing Act (1935).' *Journal of the Canadian Bankers Association* 43, no. 3 (1936): 297–303.

Macdonell, J.M. 'The Decline of the Arts Faculty.' In *Bulletins of the Department of History and Political and Economic Science in Queen's University, Kingston, Ontario, Canada* (1923): 1–9.

MacGillivray, Royce, and Ewan Ross. *A History of Glengarry.* Belleville, ON: Mika, 1979.

Mackenzie, Hector, ed. *Documents on Canadian External Relations.* Vol. 15, *1949.* Ottawa: Minister of Supply and Services Canada for the Department of Foreign Affairs and International Trade, 1995.

– 'The Path to Temptation: The Negotiation of Canada's Reconstruction Loan to Britain in 1946.' *Historical Papers / Communications historiques* 17, no. 1 (1982): 196–220.

Mackintosh, W.A. 'Canadian War Financing.' *Journal of Political Economy* 50, no. 4 (August 1942): 481–500.

– 'Economic Coordination of the War Effort.' In *Canadian War Economics,* edited by J.F. Parkinson, 180–6. Toronto: University of Toronto Press, 1941.

– 'O.D. Skelton.' In *Canada's Past and Present, a Dialogue: Our Living Tradition*, edited by Robert L. McDougall, 59–77. Toronto: University of Toronto Press, 1965.

– 'William Clifford Clark and Canadian Economic Policy.' *Canadian Journal of Economics and Political Science* 19, no. 3 (1953): 411–13.

– 'William Clifford Clark: A Personal Memoir.' *Queen's Quarterly* 60, no. 1 (1953): 1–16.

Martin, Paul. *A Very Public Life*. Vol. 1, *Far from Home*. Ottawa: Deneau, 1983.

– *A Very Public Life*. Vol. 2, *So Many Worlds*. Ottawa: Deneau, 1985.

Mason, Edward S. 'Frank W. Taussig.' *The Dictionary of American Biography*, 650–2. New York: Charles Scribner's Sons, 1958.

McCall-Newman, Christina. *Grits: An Intimate Portrait of the Liberal Party*. Toronto: Macmillan Canada, 1982.

McIvor, R. Craig. *Canadian Monetary, Banking and Fiscal Development*. Toronto: Macmillan Canada, 1961.

McKenzie, Francine. *Redefining the Bonds of Commonwealth, 1939–1948: The Politics of Preference*. New York: Palgrave Macmillan, 2002.

McLean, Marianne. *The People of Glengarry: Highlanders in Transition, 1745–1820*. Montreal and Kingston: McGill-Queen's University Press, 1993.

McLeod, T.H., and Ian McLeod. *Tommy Douglas: The Road to Jerusalem*. Edmonton: Hurtig, 1987.

Mears, F.C. 'People on Parliament Hill: Controversial Figure.' *Montreal Gazette*, 15 October 1949.

Moggridge, Donald. *Maynard Keynes: An Economist's Biography*. New York: Routledge, 1992.

Morton, Desmond, and Glen Wright. *Winning the Second Battle: Canadian Veterans and the Return to Civilian Life, 1915–1930*. Toronto: University of Toronto Press, 1987.

Muirhead, Bruce W. *Against the Odds: The Public Life and Times of Louis Rasminsky*. Toronto: University of Toronto Press, 1999.

– *The Development of Postwar Canadian Trade Policy: The Failure of the Anglo-European Option*. Montreal and Kingston: McGill-Queen's University Press, 1992.

Myers, William Starr, and Walter H. Newton. *The Hoover Administration: A Documented Narrative*. New York: Scribner's, 1936.

National Bureau of Economic Research Inc. *Report of the President and Report of the Directors of Research for the Year 1930*. New York: National Bureau of Economic Research, 1931.

Neary, Peter. *Newfoundland in the North Atlantic World, 1929–1949*. Montreal and Kingston: McGill-Queen's University Press, 1988.

Neatby, H. Blair. 'The Liberal Way: Fiscal and Monetary Policy in the 1930s.'

In *The Depression in Canada: Response to Economic Crisis,* edited by Michiel Horn, 257–73. Toronto: Copp Clark Pitman, 1988.

– *William Lyon Mackenzie King: The Prism of Unity, 1932–1939.* Toronto: University of Toronto Press, 1976.

Neatby, Hilda. *To Strive, to Seek, to Find and Not to Yield: Queen's University.* Vol. 1, *1841–1917,* edited by Frederick W. Gibson and Roger Graham. Montreal and Kingston: McGill-Queen's University Press, 1978.

Neufeld, E.P. *Bank of Canada Operations and Policy.* Toronto: University of Toronto Press, 1958.

– ed. *Money and Banking in Canada: Historical Documents and Commentary.* Toronto: McClelland and Stewart, 1964.

Newman, P.C. *The Canadian Establishment.* Toronto: McClelland and Stewart, 1975.

Oberlander, H. Peter, and Arthur L. Fallis. *Housing a Nation: The Evolution of Canadian Housing Policy.* Vancouver: Centre for Human Settlements, University of British Columbia for Canada Mortgage and Housing Corporation, 1992.

Osborne, B.S., and Donald Swainson, eds. *Kingston: Building on the Past.* Westport, CT: Butternut, 1988.

Owram, Doug. 'Economic Thought in the 1930s: The Prelude to Keynesianism.' *Canadian Historical Review* 66, no. 3 (1985): 344–77.

– *The Government Generation: Canadian Intellectuals and the State 1900–1945.* Toronto: University of Toronto Press, 1986.

Pal, L.A. *State, Class and Bureaucracy: Canadian Unemployment Insurance and Public Policy.* Montreal and Kingston: McGill-Queen's University Press, 1988.

Parkinson, J.F. 'Some Problems of War Finance.' *Canadian Journal of Economics and Political Science* 6, no. 3 (1940): 403–23.

Pearson, L.B. *Mike: The Memoirs of the Right Honourable Lester B. Pearson.* Edited by John A. Munro and Alex. I. Inglis. Vol. 1, *1897–1948.* Toronto: University of Toronto Press, 1972.

– *Mike: The Memoirs of the Right Honourable Lester B. Pearson.* Vol. 2, *1948–1957.* Edited by John A. Munro and Alex I. Inglis. Toronto: University of Toronto Press, 1972.

Perry, J. Harvey. *A Fiscal History of Canada: The Postwar Years.* Toronto: The Canadian Tax Foundation, 1989.

– *Taxes, Tariffs, and Subsidies: A History of Canadian Fiscal Development.* Toronto: University of Toronto Press, 1955.

Pickersgill, Jack. *The Mackenzie King Record.* Vol. 1, *1939–1944.* Toronto: University of Toronto Press, 1960.

– 'Mackenzie King's Political Attitudes and Public Policies: A Personal Impression.' In *Mackenzie King: Widening the Debate*, edited by John English and J.O. Stubbs, 15–29. Toronto: Macmillan of Canada, 1977.

– *My Years with Louis St Laurent: A Political Memoir.* Toronto: University of Toronto Press, 1975.

– *Seeing Canada Whole: A Memoir.* Toronto: Fitzhenry & Whiteside, 1994.

Plumptre, A.F.W. 'Constitution of the Bank of Canada.' In *Money and Banking in Canada: Historical Documents and Commentary*, edited by E.P. Neufeld, 247–52. Toronto: McClelland and Stewart, 1964.

– *Mobilizing Canada's Resources for War.* Toronto: Macmillan Canada, 1941.

– *Three Decades of Decision: Canada and the World Monetary System, 1944–75.* Toronto: McClelland and Stewart, 1972.

Porter, John. *The Vertical Mosaic: An Analysis of Social Class and Power in Canada.* Toronto: University of Toronto Press, 1965.

Power, Chubby. *A Party Politician: The Memoirs of Chubby Power.* Edited by N. Ward. Toronto: Macmillan Canada, 1966.

Rasminsky, L. 'Foreign Exchange Control: Purposes and Methods.' In *Canadian War Economics*, edited by J.F. Parkinson, 89–127. Toronto: University of Toronto Press, 1941.

Rasmussen, K.B. 'Canada and the Reconstruction of the International Economy, 1941–1947.' Toronto: University of Toronto Press, 2001.

Rea, J.E. *T.A. Crerar: A Political Life.* Montreal and Kingston: McGill-Queen's University Press, 1997.

Reid, Escott. *Radical Mandarin: The Memoirs of Escott Reid.* Toronto: University of Toronto Press, 1989.

– *Advisory Committee on Reconstruction, Final Report 4: Housing and Community Planning.* Ottawa: King's Printer, 1944.

– *Report of the Royal Commission on Dominion–Provincial Relations, Book 2.* Ottawa King's Printer, 1940.

Roberts, Leslie. 'Are We Governed by Bureaucrats?' *National Home Magazine*, March 1949, 9.

– *Canada's War in the Air.* Montreal: Beatty, 1943.

– *C.D.: The Life and Times of Clarence Decatur Howe.* Toronto: Clarke, Irwin, 1957.

Robertson, Gordon. *Memoirs of a Very Civil Servant: Mackenzie King to Pierre Trudeau.* Toronto: University of Toronto Press, 2000.

Rohmer, Richard. *E.P. Taylor: The Biography of Edward Plunket Taylor.* Toronto: McClelland and Stewart, 1978.

Safarian, A.E. *The Canadian Economy in the Great Depression.* Toronto: McClelland and Stewart, 1970.

Sautter, Udo. 'Measuring Unemployment in Canada: Federal Efforts before World War II.' *Social History / Histoire Sociale* 15, no. 30 (1982): 475–88.

Saywell, John. *'Just Call Me Mitch': The Life of Mitchell F. Hepburn*. Toronto: University of Toronto Press, 1991.

Schull, Joseph. *The Great Scot: A Biography of Donald Gordon*. Montreal and Kingston: McGill-Queen's University Press, 1979.

Shackleton, Doris. *Tommy Douglas*. Regina: Goodread Biography, 1983.

Sharp, Mitchell. 'The Bureaucratic Elite and Policy Formation.' In *Bureaucracy in Canadian Government: Selected Readings*, edited by W.D.K. Kernaghan, 82–7. Toronto: Methuen, 1969.

– 'The Cabinet and the Public Service: Reflections of Mitchell Sharp, J. Chretien, Et Al.' In *Apex of Power: The Prime Minister and Political Leadership in Canada*, edited by Thomas Hockin, 170–95. Toronto: Prentice-Hall Canada, 1977.

– 'Decision-making in the Federal Cabinet,' *Canadian Public Administration* 19 (1976): 1–8.

– 'The Role of Economic Advice in Political Decisions.' In *Economic Policy Advising in Canada: Essays in Honour of John Deutsch*, edited by David C. Smith, 213–25. Toronto: C.D. Howe Institute, 1981.

– *Which Reminds Me: A Memoir*. Toronto: University of Toronto Press, 1993.

Sheridan, Leo J., and W.C. Clark. 'The Straus Building, Chicago.' *Architectural Forum* 42 (April 1925): 225–8.

Shortt, S.E.D. *The Search for an Ideal: Six Canadian Intellectuals and Their Convictions in an Age of Transition, 1890–1930*. Toronto: University of Toronto Press, 1976.

Sinclair, Sonja. *Cordial But Not Cosy: A History of the Office of the Auditor General*. Toronto: McClelland and Stewart, 1979.

Slater, David. *War Finance and Reconstruction: The Role of Canada's Department of Finance 1939–1946*. Ottawa: Slater, 1995.

Smails, R.G.H. 'The Story of Commerce at Queen's.' In *30th Anniversary of Commerce at Queen's*. Kingston, ON, 1949.

Smith, Denis. *Gentle Patriot: A Political Biography of Walter Gordon*. Edmonton: Hurtig, 1973.

Soward, F.H. *Canada in World Affairs: From Normandy to Paris, 1944–1946*. Oxford: Oxford University Press, 1950.

Stacey, C.P. *Arms, Men and Governments: The War Policies of Canada 1939–1945*. Ottawa: Queen's Printer, 1970.

– *Canada and the Age of Conflict: A History of Canadian External Policies*. Vol. 2, *1921–1948, The Mackenzie King Era*. Toronto: University of Toronto Press, 1981.

– *Six Years of War: The Army in Canada, Britain and the Pacific.* Ottawa: Queen's Printer, 1955.

Stevenson, Michael D. *Canada's Greatest Wartime Muddle: National Selective Service and the Mobilization of Human Resources during World War II.* Montreal and Kingston: McGill-Queen's University Press, 2001.

Stewart, Bryce. 'War-Time Labour Problems.' In *Canadian War Economics,* edited by J.F. Parkinso, 72–88. Toronto: University of Toronto Press, 1941.

Stokes, Milton. *The Bank of Canada: The Development and Present Position of Central Banking in Canada.* Toronto: Macmillan, 1939.

Struthers, James. *The Limits of Affluence: Welfare in Ontario, 1920–1970.* Toronto: University of Toronto Press, 1994.

– *No Fault of Their Own: Unemployment and the Canadian Welfare State 1914–1941.* Toronto: University of Toronto Press, 1983.

– 'Shadows from the Thirties: The Federal Government and Unemployment Assistance, 1941–1956.' In *The Canadian Welfare State: Evolution and Transition,* edited by J.S. Ismael, 3–32. Edmonton: University of Alberta Press, 1987.

Swettenham, John, and David Kealy. *Serving the State: A History of the Professional Institute of the Public Service of Canada 1920–1970.* Ottawa: Le Droit–Ottawa, 1970.

Tauranac, John. *The Empire State Building: The Making of a Landmark.* New York: Scribner, 1995.

Taylor, A.J.P. *English History, 1914–1945.* London: Oxford University Press, 1967.

Taylor, K.W. 'Economic Scholarship in Canada.' *Canadian Journal of Economics and Political Science* 26, no. 1 (1960): 6–18.

– 'The Foundation of the Canadian Political Science Association.' *Canadian Journal of Economics and Political Science* 33, no. 4 (1967): 581–5.

– 'The War-Time Control of Prices.' In *Canadian War Economics,* edited by J.F. Parkinson, 47–71. Toronto: University of Toronto Press, 1941.

Taylor, Malcolm. *Health Insurance and Canadian Public Policy: The Seven Decisions That Created the Health Insurance System.* Montreal and Kingston: McGill-Queen's University Press, 1978.

Thomas, Lewis, ed. *The Making of a Socialist: The Recollections of T.C. Douglas.* Edmonton: University of Alberta Press, 1982.

Thompson, John Herd, and Allen Seager. *Canada 1922–1939: Decades of Discord.* Toronto: McClelland and Stewart, 1985.

Thomson, Dale C. *Louis St Laurent: Canadian.* Toronto: Macmillan Canada, 1967.

Trotter, Reginald G., and Albert B. Corey, eds. *Conference on Canadian–American Affairs.* Toronto: Ginn, 1941.

Underhill, Frank. *In Search of Canadian Liberalism.* Toronto: Macmillan Canada, 1961.

Ursel, Jane. *Private Lives, Public Policy: 100 Years of State Intervention in the Family.* Toronto: Women's Press, 1992.

Waddell, C.R. 'The Wartime Prices and Trade Board: Price Control in Canada in World War II.' PhD diss., York University, 1981.

Wade, C.J. 'Wartime Housing Ltd., 1941–1947: Canadian Housing Policy at the Crossroads.' PhD diss., University of British Columbia, 1984.

Waite, P.B. *The Loner: Three Sketches of the Personal Life and Ideas of R.B. Bennett, 1870–1947.* Toronto: University of Toronto Press, 1992.

Walters, F.P. *A History of the League of Nations.* London: Oxford University Press, 1952.

Ward, Norman, ed. *The Memoirs of Chubby Power: A Party Politician.* Toronto: Macmillan Canada, 1966.

– *The Public Purse: A Study in Canadian Democracy.* Toronto: University of Toronto Press, 1962.

Ward, Norman, and David E. Smith. *Jimmy Gardiner: Relentless Liberal.* Toronto: University of Toronto Press, 1990.

Wardhaugh, Robert. 'From Behind the Scenes: W.C. Clark, the Department of Finance, and Canada in the 1940s.' In *Engaging the Enemy: Canada in the 1940s,* edited by Andrew Hiscock and Muriel Chamberlain, 191–208. Llandybie, Carmarthenshire: Dinefwr, 2006.

– *Mackenzie King and the Prairie West.* Toronto: University of Toronto Press, 2000.

Wardhaugh, Robert, and Barry Ferguson. '"Impossible Conditions of Inequality": John W. Dafoe, the Rowell-Sirois Royal Commission, and the Interpretation of Canadian Federalism.' *Canadian Historical Review* 84, no. 4 (2003): 551–84.

Watts, George S. *The Bank of Canada: Origins and Early History.* Edited by Thomas K. Rymes. Ottawa: Carleton University Press, 1993.

Whitaker, Reginald. *The Government Party: Organization and Financing the Liberal Party of Canada 1930–58.* Toronto: University of Toronto Press, 1977.

Wilbur, J.R.H., ed. *The Bennett New Deal: Fraud or Portent?* Toronto: Copp Clark, 1968.

Wilbur, Richard. *The Bennett Administration, 1930–35.* Ottawa: Canadian Historical Association, 1969.

Wilgress, Dana. *Dana Wilgress: Memoirs.* Toronto: Ryerson, 1967.

Wilson, C.F. *A Century of Canadian Grain: Government Policy to 1951.* Saskatoon: Western Producer Prairie Books, 1978.

Wolfe, David A. 'The Rise and Demise of the Keynesian Era in Canada: Economic Policy, 1932–1982.' In *Modern Canada: 1930–1980s*, edited by Michael Gross and Gregory Kealey, 46–78. Toronto: McClelland and Stewart, 1992.

Worton, David A. *The Dominion Bureau of Statistics: A History of Canada's Central Statistical Office and Its Antecedents, 1841–1972.* Montreal and Kingston: McGill-Queen's University Press, 1998.

Wright, Gerald C.V. 'Mackenzie King: Power over the Political Executive.' In *Apex of Power: The Prime Minister and Political Leadership in Canada*, edited by Thomas A. Hockin, 200–8. Scarborough, ON: Prentice-Hall Canada, 1971.

Young, R.A. 'Reining in James: The Limits of the Task Force.' *Canadian Public Administration* 24, no. 4 (1981): 596–611.

Young, W.R. 'Making the Truth Graphic: The Canadian Government's Home Front Information Structure and Programmes during World War II.' PhD diss., University of British Columbia, 1978.

Zimmerman, Erich, and W.C. Clark. 'Foreign Trade and Shipping.' New York: Alexander Hamilton Institute, 1917.

Index

The Institute of Public Administration of Canada Series in Public Management and Governance

Networks of Knowledge: Collaborative Innovation in International Learning, Janice Stein, Richard Stren, Joy Fitzgibbon, and Melissa Maclean

The National Research Council in the Innovative Policy Era: Changing Hierarchies, Networks, and Markets, G. Bruce Doern and Richard Levesque

Beyond Service: State Workers, Public Policy, and the Prospects for Democratic Administration, Greg McElligott

A Law unto Itself: How the Ontario Municipal Board Has Developed and Applied Land Use Planning Policy, John G. Chipman

Health Care, Entitlement, and Citizenship, Candace Redden

Between Colliding Worlds: The Ambiguous Existence of Government Agencies for Aboriginal and Women's Policy, Jonathan Malloy

The Politics of Public Management: The HRDC Audit of Grants and Contributions, David A. Good

Dream No Little Dreams: A Biography of the Douglas Government of Saskatchewan, 1944–1961, Albert W. Johnson

Governing Education, Ben Levin

Executive Styles in Canada: Cabinet Structures and Leadership Practices in Canadian Government, edited by Luc Bernier, Keith Brownsey, and Michael Howlett

The Roles of Public Opinion Research in Canadian Government, Christopher Page

The Politics of CANDU Exports, Duane Bratt

Policy Analysis in Canada: The State of the Art, edited by Laurent Dobuzinskis, Michael Howlett, and David Laycock

Digital State at the Leading Edge: Lessons from Canada, Sanford Borins, Kenneth Kernaghan, David Brown, Nick Bontis, Perri 6, and Fred Thompson

The Politics of Public Money: Spenders, Guardians, Priority Setters, and Financial Watchdogs inside the Canadian Government, David A. Good

Court Government and the Collapse of Accountability in Canada and the U.K., Donald Savoie

Professionalism and Public Service: Essays in Honour of Kenneth Kernaghan, edited by David Siegel and Ken Rasmussen

Searching for Leadership: Secretaries to Cabinet in Canada, edited by Patrice Dutil

Foundations of Governance: Municipal Government in Canada's Provinces, edited by Andrew Sancton and Robert Young

Provincial and Territorial Ombudsman Offices in Canada, edited by Stewart Hyson

Local Government in a Global World: Australia and Canada in Comparative Perspective, edited by Emmanuel Brunet-Jailly and John F. Martin

Behind the Scenes: The Life and Work of William Clifford Clark, Robert A.Wardhaugh